"**大学堂**"开放给所有向往知识、崇尚科学，对宇宙和人生有所追问的人。

"**大学堂**"中展开一本本书，阐明各种传统和新兴的学科，导向真理和智慧。既有接引之台阶，又具深化之门径。无论何时，无论何地，请你把它翻开……

后浪
大学堂067

MODERN
SOCIOLOGICAL
THEORY, 7E

现代社会学理论

［美］乔治·瑞泽尔　著

（双语第7版）

GEORGE RITZER

北京联合出版公司
Beijing United Publishing Co.,Ltd.

To Jeremy, with love

出版前言

美国马里兰大学乔治·瑞泽尔教授对于中国读者尤其是社会学界早已不再陌生。《社会的麦当劳化》是作者最早被引入国内的著作之一，对人类正在走向以麦当劳化为代表的"理性牢笼"提出质疑。作为美国社会学会理论社会学分会主席（1989），瑞泽尔教授不但在后现代社会和应用性理论阐释以及元理论的基础研究等方面皆有杰出贡献，更撰写了一系列自面世以来即享有极佳口碑的社会学理论教材，它们先后被译成10多种语言，在世界各地广泛流传。

瑞泽尔社会学理论系列教材最大的特色在于内容全面、脉络清晰，且将许多艰深晦涩的理论概念解释得深入浅出，易于理解。相比于一些充斥着冗长注释和艰涩概念的学术著作，它们更能有效地引导初学者一窥社会学的全貌，使其寻门径而入，尤其适合作为高校社会学专业的参考书和向一般读者普及社会学知识的读物。理论阐发与思想史论述两条线索相结合的方式，外加简约准确的行文，令读者以点带面地建立对知识点的系统理解和记忆。上述特色在我们于2014年先后推出《古典社会学理论（第6版）》的影印版及中文版已得到充分体现，近年来读者也给予了大量积极反馈，认为这两本书在奠定学科基础的阶段确是不可多得的参考读物。

《现代社会学理论（第7版）》是瑞泽尔社会学理论系列教材中的又一本佳作。从它的框架设计，我们不难看到这一系列教材素来为读者称道的权威性与全面性。瑞泽尔将这本书划分为四个部分，第一部分概要性地介绍了社会学理论的历史，将其划分为以古典社会学为代表的早期阶段和以现代、当代社会学为代表的后期阶段；第二部分即"现代社会学理论之主要流派"占据了全书大约二分之一的篇幅，是本书的主体部分，着重介绍了自第一次世界大战之后社会学研究中心由欧洲转向美国以来直至20世纪80年代涌现出的结构功能主义、新马克思主义、系统理论、符号互动论等核心理论。瑞泽尔一直重视古典社会学思想对现代理论发展的滋养，因此，他在第一部分概要地介绍了社会学理论历史，将其划分为以古典社会学为代表的早期阶段和以现代、当代社会学为代表的后期阶段。在第三及第四部分，瑞泽尔侧重强调自进入后工业社会以来社会学界整合宏观研究与微观研究分歧的努力、对现代性思潮的批判以及对全球化现象的关注，等等。

瑞泽尔在每次教材增订之际必然会补入新的内容，以便与时俱进地反映社会学理论的新发展。为方便读者阅读，我们在英文章节标题处增加了相应的中文，以帮助读者更快速地了解全书架构。

除了本次推出的《现代社会学理论》及《当代社会学理论》的影印版，我们还将很快推出这两本著作的中文版，希望这一系列社会学理论著作的出版，有助于读者更全面地掌握社会学理论的精髓，进一步形成综合性概览。

服务热线：133-6631-2326　　188-1142-1266
服务邮箱：reader@hinabook.com

后浪出版公司
2018年2月

About the Author
关于作者

George Ritzer is Distinguished University Professor at the University of Maryland, where he has also been a Distinguished Scholar-Teacher and received a Teaching Excellence Award. In 2000, he received the Distinguished Contributions to Teaching Award of the American Sociological Association, and in 2004, he received an honorary doctorate from LaTrobe University in Melbourne, Australia.

Dr. Ritzer served as Chair of the American Sociological Association's Sections on Theoretical Sociology and Organizations and Occupations. He held the UNESCO Chair in Social Theory at the Russian Academy of Sciences and a Fulbright-Hays Chair at York University in Canada, and he received a Fulbright-Hays award to the Netherlands. He was Scholar-in-Residence at the Netherlands Institute for Advanced Study and at the Swedish Collegium for Advanced Study in the Social Sciences.

Professor Ritzer's main theoretical interests lie in metatheory and in applied social theory. In metatheory, his contributions include *Sociology: A Multiple Paradigm Science* (1975, 1980), *Toward an Integrated Sociological Paradigm* (1981), and *Metatheorizing in Sociology* (1991). George Ritzer is perhaps best known, however, for *The McDonaldization of Society* (4th ed., 2004), translated into more than a dozen languages, and for several related books (also with a number of translations), including *Expressing America: A Critique of the Global Credit Card Society* (1995), *Enchanting a Disenchanted World: Revolutionizing the Means of Consumption* (2nd ed., 2005), *The Globalization of Nothing 2* (2nd ed., 2007), and the forthcoming (with Craig Lair) *Outsourcing: Globalization and Beyond*. He edited the two-volume *Encyclopedia of Social Theory* (2005), the eleven-volume *Encyclopedia of Sociology* (2007), and *The Blackwell Companion to Globalization* (2007), and he is the founding editor of the *Journal of Consumer Culture*.

In 2006, McGraw-Hill published the second edition of Professor Ritzer's *Contemporary Sociological Theory and Its Classic Roots: The Basics*. In 2008, McGraw-Hill will publish the seventh edition of *Sociological Theory* and the fifth edition of *Classical Sociological Theory*. The latter two texts, as well as this one, have been translated into a number of languages.

Biographical and
Autobiographical Sketches
社会学家生平传略

Preface
前言

This new edition of *Modern Sociological Theory,* like its six predecessors, offers a comprehensive overview of contemporary theories and theorists. As in earlier editions, in-depth discussions of theories (often enlivened with examples) are accompanied by informative and—I believe—engaging biographical sketches of many of the most important thinkers in contemporary theory. Once again, two introductory chapters survey the early history of the field (Chapter 1) and recent developments (Chapter 2). These chapters provide an overview that allows students to put the work of each theorist in its historical, social, and political context.

In one convenient volume, this book offers students a handy overview of much of what they need to know about contemporary sociological theory and the context in which it arose. The social world is a complex and difficult subject, and so are many of the theories about it. I have striven to make theory interesting, relevant, and as clear and accessible as possible.

Changes in the Seventh Edition

As is always the case, I faced some difficult decisions about what to add and what to cut. There are some important additions to this edition, but I took care to be sure that the text did not grow long and cumbersome. Among the major changes/additions are the following:

- Two chapters were added: Chapter 12, "Globalization Theory," covers the major economic, political, and cultural theories of globalization. Chapter 14, "Cutting-Edge Developments in Contemporary Theory," covers queer theory, critical theories of race and racism, actor-network theory, and practice theory.
- What previously were separate chapters on micro-macro integration and agency-structure integration were combined into a single streamlined chapter (Chapter 10).
- Two new sections were added: to Chapter 1, a discussion of Alexis de Tocqueville; to Chapter 4, on neo-Marxian theory, later developments in cultural critique.
- A biographical sketch of Alexis de Tocqueville was added to Chapter 1.

For this edition, I drew heavily on my recent work as editor of the two-volume *Encyclopedia of Social Theory* (Sage, 2005) and the eleven-volume *Encyclopedia of*

Sociology (Blackwell, 2007). Throughout this edition, I reference entries from those encyclopedias so that readers will have handy and up-to-date resources should they want to read further on a particular topic.

Cuts were made in various places, but no major theories or theorists were eliminated. Thus, the text is much as it always has been but is renewed once again. The wonderful things about theory are its continuity and its ever-changing character. I have tried to communicate those and other joys of sociological theory to readers in the early stages of their exposure to it.

Acknowledgments

Once again, I want to thank Patricia Lengermann and Gillian Niebrugge for revising Chapter 9, their pathbreaking chapter on contemporary feminist theory. Their chapter not only has made this book much stronger but also has had a strong influence on theorizing independent of the book. I also thank Matthias Junge for his contribution to the section on Niklas Luhmann (in Chapter 5) and Mike Ryan for his contribution on queer theory (in Chapter 14). Thanks also to Mike Yaksich for his assistance in the preparation of this edition. Unfortunately, Doug Goodman, coauthor of the previous edition, was unable to participate in this new edition. However, many of his contributions continue to be found in this text.

Thanks also go to a panel of reviewers whose comments and suggestions helped to make this a better book:

David Boyns, *California State University, Northridge*
Margaret Stephanie Crowdes, *California State University, San Marcos*
Gregory Hooks, *Washington State University*
Kinko Ito, *University of Arkansas, Little Rock*
William A. (Bill) Reese II, *Augusta State University*
Allen Scarboro, *Augusta State University*
Susan Tiano, *University of New Mexico*

George Ritzer

Contents
目录

第一部分 社会学理论入门
Introduction to Sociological Theory

C H A P T E R **1**

A Historical Sketch of Sociological Theory: The Early Years

第一章 社会学理论历史概要：早期阶段

Chapter Outline

Introduction
Social Forces in the Development of Sociological Theory
Intellectual Forces and the Rise of Sociological Theory
The Development of French Sociology
The Development of German Sociology
The Origins of British Sociology
The Key Figure in Early Italian Sociology
Turn-of-the-Century Developments in European Marxism

A useful way to begin a book designed to introduce modern sociological theory is with several one-line summaries of various theories:

- The modern world is an iron cage of rational systems from which there is no escape.
- Capitalism tends to sow the seeds of its own destruction.
- The modern world has less moral cohesion than earlier societies had.
- The city spawns a particular type of personality.
- In their social lives, people tend to put on a variety of theatrical performances.
- The social world is defined by principles of reciprocity in give-and-take relationships.
- People create the social worlds that ultimately come to enslave them.
- People always retain the capacity to change the social worlds that constrain them.

- Society is an integrated system of social structures and functions.
- Society is a "juggernaut" with the ever-present possibility of running amok.
- While it appears that the Western world has undergone a process of liberalization, in fact it has grown increasingly oppressive.
- The world has entered a new postmodern era increasingly defined by the inauthentic, the fake, and simulations of reality.
- Paradoxically, globalization is associated with the world wide spread of "nothing."
- Nonhuman objects are increasingly seen as key actors in the social world.

This book is devoted to helping the reader better understand these and many other theoretical ideas, as well as the larger theories from which they are drawn.

Introduction 导言

Presenting a history of sociological theory is an important task (S. Turner, 1998), but because I devote only two chapters (1 and 2) to it, what I offer is a highly selective historical sketch (Giddens, 1995). The idea is to provide the reader with a scaffolding that should help put the later detailed discussions of theorists and theories in a larger context. As the reader proceeds through the later chapters, it will prove useful to return to these two overview chapters to place the discussions in their context. (It will be especially useful to glance back occasionally to Figures 1.1 and 2.1, which are schematic representations of the histories covered in those chapters.)

The theories treated in the body of this book have a *wide range* of application, deal with *centrally important social issues,* and have *stood the test of time.* These criteria constitute our definition of *sociological theory.*[1] The focus is on the important theoretical work of sociologists or the work done by individuals in other fields that has come to be defined as important in sociology. To put it succinctly, this is a book about the "big ideas" in sociology that have stood the test of time (or promise to)—idea systems that deal with major social issues and that are far-reaching in scope.

We cannot establish the precise date when sociological theory began. People have been thinking about, and developing theories of, social life since early in history. But we will not go back to the early historic times of the Greeks or Romans or even to the Middle Ages. We will not even go back to the seventeenth century, although Olson (1993) has traced the sociological tradition to the mid-1600s and the work of James Harrington on the relationship between the economy and the

---

[1] These three criteria constitute my definition of sociological theory. Such a definition stands in contrast to the formal, "scientific" definitions (Jasso, 2001) that often are used in theory texts of this type. A scientific definition might be that a theory is a set of interrelated propositions that allows for the systematization of knowledge, explanation, and prediction of social life and the generation of new research hypotheses (Faia, 1986). Although such a definition has a number of attractions, it simply does not fit many of the idea systems that are discussed in this book. In other words, most classical (and contemporary) theories fall short on one or more of the formal components of theory, but they are nonetheless considered theories by most sociologists.

SOCIAL FORCES	**France**						
	Enlightenment Montesquieu (1689–1755) Rousseau (1712–1778)	*Conservative Reaction* de Bonald (1754–1840) de Maistre (1753–1821)	Saint-Simon (1760–1825)	Comte (1798–1857)	Tocqueville (1805–1859)		Durkheim (1858–1917)
Political revolutions	**Germany**						
Industrial Revolution and the rise of capitalism			Kant (1724–1804)		Hegel (1720–1831)	*Young Hegelians* Feuerbach (1804–1872)	Marx (1818–1883)
							Economic Determinists Kautsky (1854–1938)
							German Historicism Dilthey (1833–1911)
Rise of socialism							*Hegelian Marxists* Lukács (1885–1971)
						Nietzsche (1844–1900)	Max Weber (1864–1920) Marianne Weber (1870–1954)
Feminism							Simmel (1858–1918)
Urbanization	**Italy**					Pareto (1848–1923)	Mosca (1858–1941)
Religious change	**Great Britain**						
Growth of science		*Political Economy* Smith (1723–1790)	Ricardo (1772–1823)	Martineau (1802–1876) *Evolutionary Theory* Spencer (1820–1903)			

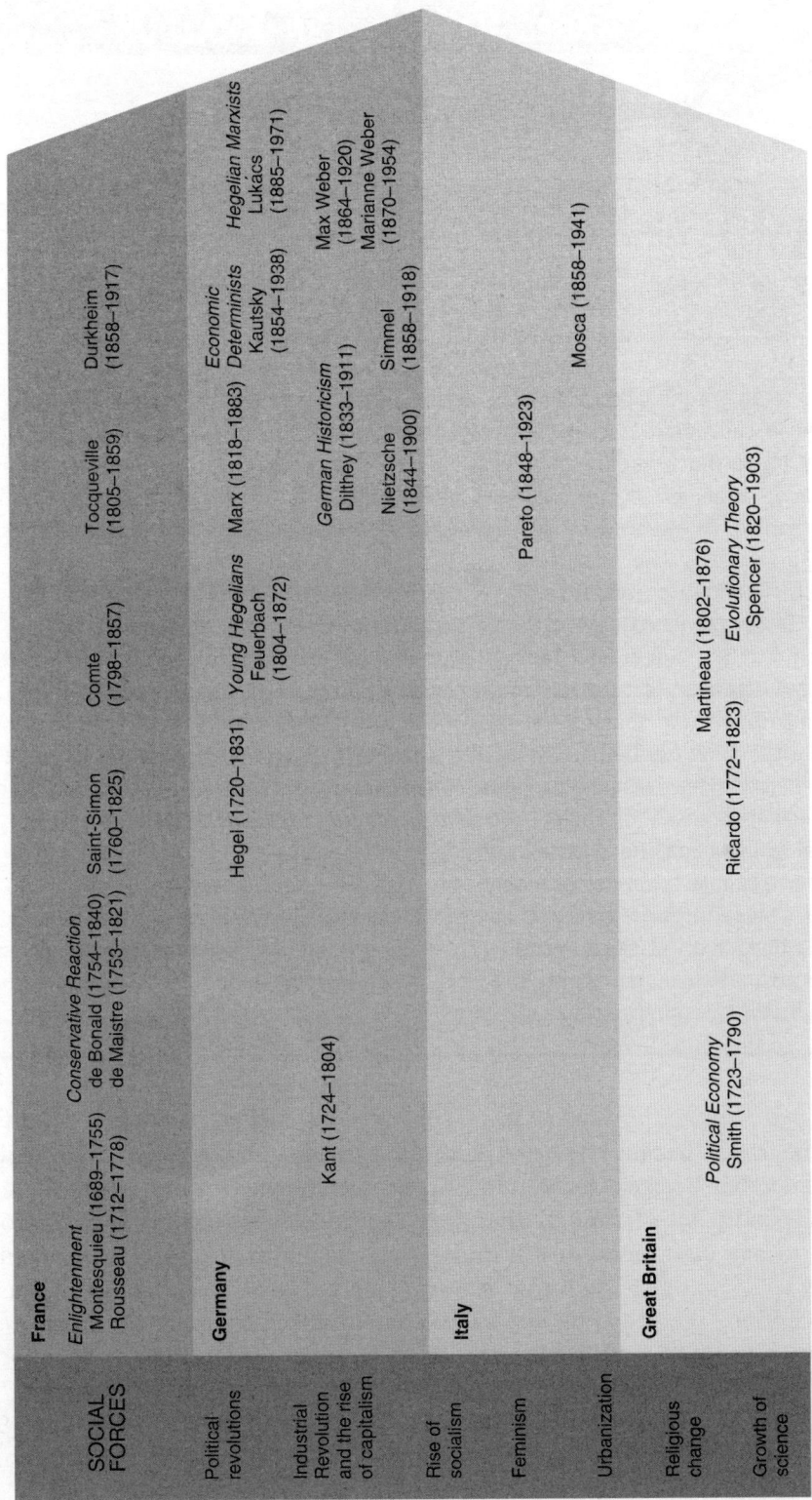

FIGURE 1.1 *Sociological Theory: The Early Years*

ABDEL RAHMAN IBN-KHALDUN

A Biographical Sketch

There is a tendency to think of sociology as exclusively a comparatively modern, Western phenomenon. In fact, however, scholars were developing sociological ideas and theories long ago and in other parts of the world. One example is Abdel Rahman Ibn-Khaldun.

Ibn-Khaldun was born in Tunis, North Africa, on May 27, 1332 (Faghirzadeh, 1982). Born to an educated family, Ibn-Khaldun was schooled in the Koran (the Muslim holy book), mathematics, and history. In his lifetime, he served a variety of sultans in Tunis, Morocco, Spain, and Algeria as ambassador, chamberlain, and member of the scholars' council. He also spent two years in prison in Morocco for his belief that state rulers were not divine leaders. After approximately two decades of political activity, Ibn-Khaldun returned to North Africa, where he undertook an intensive five-year period of study and writing. Works produced during this period increased his fame and led to a lectureship at the center of Islamic study, Al-Azhar Mosque University in Cairo. In his well-attended lectures on society and sociology, Ibn-Khaldun stressed the importance of linking sociological thought and historical observation.

By the time he died in 1406, Ibn-Khaldun had produced a corpus of work that had many ideas in common with contemporary sociology. He was committed to the scientific study of society, empirical research, and the search for causes of social phenomena. He devoted considerable attention to various social institutions (for example, politics, economy) and their interrelationships. He was interested in comparing primitive and modern societies. Ibn-Khaldun did not have a dramatic impact on classical sociology, but as scholars in general, and Islamic scholars in particular, rediscover his work, he may come to be seen as being of greater historical significance.

polity. This is not because people in those epochs did not have sociologically relevant ideas, but because the return on our investment in time would be small; we would spend a lot of time getting very few ideas that are relevant to modern sociology. In any case, none of the thinkers associated with those eras thought of themselves as sociologists, and few are now thought of as such. (For a discussion of one exception, see the biographical sketch of Ibn-Khaldun.) It is only in the 1800s that we begin to find thinkers who can be clearly identified as sociologists. These are the classical sociological thinkers we are interested in (Camic, 1997; for a debate about what makes theory classical, see Connell, 1997; R. Collins, 1997), and we begin by examining the main social and intellectual forces that shaped their ideas.

Social Forces in the Development of Sociological Theory 推动社会学理论发展的社会力量

All intellectual fields are profoundly shaped by their social settings. This is particularly true of sociology, which not only is derived from that setting but takes the social setting as its basic subject matter. We will focus briefly on a few of the most important social conditions of the nineteenth and early twentieth centuries, conditions that were of the utmost significance in the development of sociology.

Political Revolutions 政治革命

The long series of political revolutions that were ushered in by the French Revolution in 1789 and carried over through the nineteenth century was the most immediate factor in the rise of sociological theorizing. The impact of these revolutions on many societies was enormous, and many positive changes resulted. However, what attracted the attention of many early theorists was not the positive consequences, but the negative effects of such changes. These writers were particularly disturbed by the resulting chaos and disorder, especially in France. They were united in a desire to restore order to society. Some of the more extreme thinkers of this period literally wanted a return to the peaceful and relatively orderly days of the Middle Ages. The more sophisticated thinkers recognized that social change had made such a return impossible. Thus they sought instead to find new bases of order in societies that had been overturned by the political revolutions of the eighteenth and nineteenth centuries. This interest in the issue of social order was one of the major concerns of classical sociological theorists, especially Comte and Durkheim.

工业革命和资本主义兴起
The Industrial Revolution and the Rise of Capitalism

At least as important as political revolution in the shaping of sociological theory was the Industrial Revolution, which swept through many Western societies, mainly in the nineteenth and early twentieth centuries. The Industrial Revolution was not a single event but many interrelated developments that culminated in the transformation of the Western world from a largely agricultural to an overwhelmingly industrial system. Large numbers of people left farms and agricultural work for the industrial occupations offered in the burgeoning factories. The factories themselves were transformed by a long series of technological improvements. Large economic bureaucracies arose to provide the many services needed by industry and the emerging capitalist economic system. In this economy, the ideal was a free marketplace where the many products of an industrial system could be exchanged. Within this system, a few profited greatly while the majority worked long hours for low wages. A reaction against the industrial system and against capitalism in general followed and led to the labor movement as well as to various radical movements aimed at overthrowing the capitalist system.

The Industrial Revolution, capitalism, and the reaction against them all involved an enormous upheaval in Western society, an upheaval that affected sociologists greatly. Four major figures in the early history of sociological theory—Karl Marx,

Max Weber, Emile Durkheim, and Georg Simmel—were preoccupied, as were many lesser thinkers, with these changes and the problems they created for society as a whole. They spent their lives studying these problems, and in many cases, they endeavored to develop programs that would help solve them.

The Rise of Socialism 社会主义的兴起

One set of changes aimed at coping with the excesses of the industrial system and capitalism can be combined under the heading "socialism" (Beilharz, 2005g). Although some sociologists favored socialism as a solution to industrial problems, most were personally and intellectually opposed to it. On one side, Karl Marx actively supported overthrowing the capitalist system and replacing it with a socialist system. Although Marx did not develop a theory of socialism per se, he spent a great deal of time criticizing various aspects of capitalist society. In addition, he engaged in a variety of political activities that he hoped would help bring about the rise of socialist societies.

However, Marx was atypical in the early years of sociological theory. Most of the early theorists, such as Weber and Durkheim, were opposed to socialism (at least as it was envisioned by Marx). Although they recognized the problems within capitalist society, they sought social reform within capitalism rather than the social revolution argued for by Marx. They feared socialism more than they did capitalism. This fear played a far greater role in shaping sociological theory than did Marx's support of the socialist alternative to capitalism. In fact, as we will see, in many cases, sociological theory developed as a reaction *against* Marxian and, more generally, against socialist theory.

Feminism 女权运动

In one sense there has always been a feminist perspective. Wherever women are subordinated—and they have been subordinated almost always and everywhere—they seem to have recognized and protested that situation in some form (Lerner, 1993). While precursors can be traced to the 1630s, high points of feminist activity and writing occurred in the liberationist moments of modern Western history. A first flurry of productivity occurred in the 1780s and 1790s with the debates surrounding the American and French revolutions; a far more organized, focused effort in the 1850s as part of the mobilization against slavery and for political rights for the middle class; and the massive mobilization for women's suffrage and for industrial and civic reform legislation in the early twentieth century, especially the Progressive Era in the United States.

All of this had an impact on the development of sociology, in particular on the work of a number of women in or associated with the field, such as Harriet Martineau, Charlotte Perkins Gilman, Jane Addams, Florence Kelley, Anna Julia Cooper, Ida Wells-Barnett, Marianne Weber, and Beatrice Potter Webb. But their creations were, over time, pushed to the periphery of the profession, annexed, discounted, or written out of sociology's public record by the men who were organizing sociology as a professional power base. Feminist concerns filtered into sociology only on the margins, in the work of marginal male theorists or of the increasingly marginalized female theorists. The men who assumed centrality in the profession—from Spencer, through Weber and Durkheim—made basically conservative responses to the feminist arguments going on around them, making issues of gender an inconsequential topic to which they responded conventionally rather than critically in what they identified and publicly promoted as sociology. They responded in this way even as women were writing a significant body of sociological theory. The history of gender politics in the profession, which is also part of the history of male response to feminist claims, is only now being written (for example, see Deegan, 1988; Fitzpatrick, 1990; L. Gordon, 1994; Lengermann and Niebrugge-Brantley, 1998; Rosenberg, 1982).

Urbanization 城市化

Partly as a result of the Industrial Revolution, large numbers of people in the nineteenth and twentieth centuries were uprooted from their rural homes and moved to urban settings. This massive migration was caused, in large part, by the jobs created by the industrial system in the urban areas. But it presented many difficulties for those people who had to adjust to urban life. In addition, the expansion of the cities produced a seemingly endless list of urban problems, including overcrowding, pollution, noise, and traffic. The nature of urban life and its problems attracted the attention of many early sociologists, especially Max Weber and Georg Simmel. In fact, the first major school of American sociology, the Chicago school, was in large part defined by its concern for the city and its interest in using Chicago as a laboratory in which to study urbanization and its problems.

Religious Change 宗教改革

Social changes brought on by political revolutions, the Industrial Revolution, and urbanization had a profound effect on religiosity. Many early sociologists came from religious backgrounds and were actively, and in some cases professionally, involved in religion (Hinkle and Hinkle, 1954). They brought to sociology the same objectives as they had in their religious lives. They wished to improve people's lives (Vidich and Lyman, 1985). For some (such as Comte), sociology was transformed into a religion. For others, their sociological theories bore an unmistakable religious imprint. Durkheim wrote one of his major works on religion. Morality played a key role not only in Durkheim's sociology but also in the work of Talcott Parsons. A large portion of Weber's work also was devoted to the religions of the world. Marx, too, had an interest in religiosity, but his orientation was far more critical.

The Growth of Science 科学发展

As sociological theory was being developed, there was an increasing emphasis on science, not only in colleges and universities but also in society as a whole. The technological products of science were permeating every sector of life, and science was acquiring enormous prestige. Those associated with the most successful sciences (physics, biology, and chemistry) were accorded honored places in society. Sociologists (especially Comte, Durkheim, Spencer, Mead, and Schutz) from the beginning were preoccupied with science, and many wanted to model sociology after the successful physical and biological sciences. However, a debate soon developed between those who wholeheartedly accepted the scientific model and those (such as Weber) who thought that distinctive characteristics of social life made a wholesale adoption of a scientific model difficult and unwise (Lepenies, 1988). The issue of the relationship between sociology and science is debated to this day, although even a glance at the major journals in the field, at least in the United States, indicates the predominance of those who favor sociology as a science.

Intellectual Forces and the Rise of Sociological Theory 知识界的力量和社会学理论的兴起

Although social factors are important, the primary focus of this chapter is the intellectual forces that played a central role in shaping sociological theory. In the real world, of course, intellectual factors cannot be separated from social forces. For example, in the discussion of the Enlightenment that follows, we will find that that movement was intimately related to, and in many cases provided the intellectual basis for, the social changes discussed above.

The many intellectual forces that shaped the development of social theories are discussed within the national context where their influence was primarily felt (Levine, 1995; Rundell, 2001). We begin with the Enlightenment and its influences on the development of sociological theory in France.

The Enlightenment 启蒙运动

It is the view of many observers that the Enlightenment constitutes a critical development in terms of the later evolution of sociology (Hawthorn, 1976; Hughes, Martin, and Sharrock, 1995; Nisbet, 1967; Zeitlin, 1996). The Enlightenment was a period of remarkable intellectual development and change in philosophical thought.[2] A number of long-standing ideas and beliefs, many of which related to social life, were overthrown and replaced during the Enlightenment. The most prominent thinkers associated with the Enlightenment were the French philosophers Charles Montesquieu (1689–1755) and Jean Jacques Rousseau (1712–1778) (B. C. J. Singer, 2005a, 2005b). The influence of the Enlightenment on sociological theory, however, was more indirect and negative than it was direct and positive. As Irving Zeitlin puts it, "Early sociology developed as a reaction to the Enlightenment" (1996:10).

The thinkers associated with the Enlightenment were influenced, above all, by two intellectual currents—seventeenth-century philosophy and science.

---

[2] This section is based on the work of Irving Zeitlin (1996). Although Zeitlin's analysis is presented here for its coherence, it has a number of limitations: (a) there are better analyses of the Enlightenment, (b) there are many other factors involved in shaping the development of sociology, and (c) Zeitlin tends to overstate his case in places (for example, on the impact of Marx). But on the whole, Zeitlin provides us with a useful starting point, given our objectives in this chapter.

Seventeenth-century philosophy was associated with the work of thinkers such as René Descartes, Thomas Hobbes, and John Locke. The emphasis was on producing grand, general, and very abstract systems of ideas that made rational sense. The later thinkers associated with the Enlightenment did not reject the idea that systems of ideas should be general and should make rational sense, but they did make greater efforts to derive their ideas from the real world and to test them there. In other words, they wanted to combine empirical research with reason (Seidman, 1983:36–37). The model for this was science, especially Newtonian physics. At this point, we see the emergence of the application of the scientific method to social issues. Not only did Enlightenment thinkers want their ideas to be, at least in part, derived from the real world, they also wanted them to be useful to the social world, especially in the critical analysis of that world.

Overall, the Enlightenment was characterized by the belief that people could comprehend and control the universe by means of reason and empirical research. The view was that because the physical world was dominated by natural laws, it was likely that the social world was, too. Thus it was up to the philosopher, using reason and research, to discover these social laws. Once they understood how the social world worked, the Enlightenment thinkers had a practical goal—the creation of a "better," more rational world.

With an emphasis on reason, the Enlightenment philosophers were inclined to reject beliefs in traditional authority. When these thinkers examined traditional values and institutions, they often found them to be irrational—that is, contrary to human nature and inhibitive of human growth and development. The mission of the practical and change-oriented philosophers of the Enlightenment was to overcome these irrational systems. The theorists who were most directly and positively influenced by Enlightenment thinking were Alexis de Tocqueville and Karl Marx, although the latter formed his early theoretical ideas in Germany.

针对启蒙运动的保守反应
The Conservative Reaction to the Enlightenment

On the surface, we might think that French classical sociological theory, like Marx's theory, was directly and positively influenced by the Enlightenment. French sociology became rational, empirical, scientific, and change-oriented, but not before it was also shaped by a set of ideas that developed in reaction to the Enlightenment. In Seidman's view, "The ideology of the counter-Enlightenment represented a virtual inversion of Enlightenment liberalism. In place of modernist premises, we can detect in the Enlightenment critics a strong anti-modernist sentiment" (1983:51). As we will see, sociology in general, and French sociology in particular, have from the beginning been an uncomfortable mix of Enlightenment and counter-Enlightenment ideas.

The most extreme form of opposition to Enlightenment ideas was French Catholic counterrevolutionary philosophy, as represented by the ideas of Louis de Bonald (1754–1840) and Joseph de Maistre (1753–1821) (Bradley, 2005a, 2005b; Reedy, 1994). These men were reacting against not only the Enlightenment but also the French Revolution, which they saw partly as a product of the kind of thinking characteristic of the Enlightenment. Bonald, for example, was disturbed by the revolutionary changes and yearned for a return to the peace and harmony of the Middle Ages. In this view, God was the source of society; therefore, reason, which was so important to the Enlightenment philosophers, was seen as inferior to traditional religious beliefs. Furthermore, it was believed that because God had created society, people should not tamper with it and should not try to change a holy creation. By extension, Bonald opposed anything that undermined such traditional institutions as patriarchy, the monogamous family, the monarchy, and the Catholic Church.

Although Bonald represented a rather extreme form of the conservative reaction, his work constitutes a useful introduction to its general premises. The conservatives turned away from what they considered the "naive" rationalism of the Enlightenment. They not only recognized the irrational aspects of social life but also assigned them positive value. Thus they regarded such phenomena as tradition, imagination, emotionalism, and religion as useful and necessary components of social life. In that they disliked upheaval and sought to retain the existing order, they deplored developments such as the French Revolution and the Industrial Revolution, which they saw as disruptive forces. The conservatives tended to emphasize social order, an emphasis that became one of the central themes of the work of several sociological theorists.

Zeitlin (1996) outlined ten major propositions that he sees as emerging from the conservative reaction and providing the basis for the development of classical French sociological theory.

1. Whereas Enlightenment thinkers tended to emphasize the individual, the conservative reaction led to a major sociological interest in, and emphasis on, society and other large-scale phenomena. Society was viewed as something more than simply an aggregate of individuals. Society was seen as having an existence of its own with its own laws of development and deep roots in the past.
2. Society was the most important unit of analysis; it was seen as more important than the individual. It was society that produced the individual, primarily through the process of socialization.
3. The individual was not even seen as the most basic element within society. A society consisted of such component parts as roles, positions, relationships, structures, and institutions. Individuals were seen as doing little more than filling these units within society.
4. The parts of society were seen as interrelated and interdependent. Indeed, these interrelationships were a major basis of society. This view led to a conservative political orientation. That is, because the parts were held to be interrelated, it followed that tampering with one part could lead to the undermining of other parts and, ultimately, of the system as a whole. This meant that changes in the social system should be made with extreme care.
5. Change was seen as a threat not only to society and its components but also to the individuals in society. The various components of society were seen as satisfying people's needs. When institutions were disrupted, people were likely to suffer, and their suffering was likely to lead to social disorder.
6. The general tendency was to see the various large-scale components of society as useful for both society and the individuals in it. As a result, there

was little desire to look for the negative effects of existing social structures and social institutions.

7. Small units, such as the family, the neighborhood, and religious and occupational groups, also were seen as essential to individuals and society. They provided the intimate, face-to-face environments that people needed to survive in modern societies.

8. There was a tendency to see various modern social changes, such as industrialization, urbanization, and bureaucratization, as having disorganizing effects. These changes were viewed with fear and anxiety, and there was an emphasis on developing ways of dealing with their disruptive effects.

9. While most of these feared changes were leading to a more rational society, the conservative reaction led to an emphasis on the importance of nonrational factors (ritual, ceremony, and worship, for example) in social life.

10. Finally, the conservatives supported the existence of a hierarchical system in society. It was seen as important to society that there be a differential system of status and reward.

These ten propositions, derived from the conservative reaction to the Enlightenment, should be seen as the immediate intellectual basis of the development of sociological theory in France. Many of these ideas made their way into early sociological thought, although some of the Enlightenment ideas (empiricism, for example) were also influential.[3]

The Development of French Sociology 法国社会学的发展

We turn now to the actual founding of sociology as a distinctive discipline—specifically, to the work of four French thinkers, Alexis de Tocqueville, Claude Saint-Simon, Auguste Comte, and especially Emile Durkheim.

亚历克西斯·德·托克维尔（1805—1859）
Alexis de Tocqueville (1805–1859)

We begin with Alexis de Tocqueville even though he was born after both Saint-Simon and Comte. We do so because he and his work were such pure products of the Enlightenment (he was strongly and directly influenced by Montesquieu [B. C. J. Singer, 2005b]), especially his *The Spirit of the Laws* [1748]) and because his work was not part of the clear line of development in French social theory from Saint-Simon and Comte to the crucially important Durkheim. Tocqueville has long been seen as a political scientist, not a sociologist, and furthermore many have not perceived the existence of a social theory in his work (e.g., Seidman, 1983:306). However, not only is there a social theory in his work, but it is one that deserves a much more significant place in the history of social theory not only in France but in the rest of the world.

---

[3] Although we have emphasized the discontinuities between the Enlightenment and the counter-Enlightenment, Seidman makes the point that there also are continuities and linkages. First, the counter-Enlightenment carried on the scientific tradition developed in the Enlightenment. Second, it picked up the Enlightenment emphasis on collectivities (as opposed to individuals) and greatly extended it. Third, both had an interest in the problems of the modern world, especially its negative effects on individuals.

ALEXIS DE TOCQUEVILLE

A Biographical Sketch

Alexis de Tocqueville was born on July 29, 1805, in Paris. He came from a prominent though not wealthy aristocratic family. The family had suffered during the French Revolution. Tocqueville's parents had been arrested but managed to avoid the guillotine. Tocqueville was well educated, became a lawyer and judge (although he was not very successful at either), and became well and widely read especially in the Enlightenment philosophy (Rousseau and Montesquieu) that played such a central role in much classical social theory.

The turning point in Tocqueville's life began on April 2, 1831, when he and a friend (Gustave de Beaumont) journeyed to the United States ostensibly to study the American penitentiary system. He saw America as a laboratory in which he could study, in their nascent state, such key phenomena to him as democracy, equality, and freedom. He traveled widely throughout much of the then-developed (and some undeveloped) parts of the United States (and a bit of Canada), getting as far west as Green Bay (Wisconsin) and Memphis (Tennessee) and New Orleans (Louisiana), traveling through large parts of the northeastern, middle Atlantic, and southern states, as well as some midwestern states east of the Mississippi River. He talked to all sorts of people along the way, asked systematic questions, took copious notes, and allowed his interest to evolve on the basis of what he found along the way. Tocqueville (and Beaumont) returned to France on February 20, 1832, having spent less than a year studying the vast physical and social landscape of the United States as it existed then.

It took Tocqueville some time to get started on the first volume of *Democracy in America,* but he began in earnest in late 1833 and the book was published by 1835. It was a great success and made him famous. The irony here is that one of the classic works on democracy in general, and American democracy in particular, was written by a French aristocrat. He launched a political career while putting the finishing touches on volume two of *Democracy,* which appeared in 1840. This volume was more sociological (Aron, 1965) than the first, which was clearly about politics, particularly the American political system and how it compared to other political systems, especially the French system.

Tocqueville is best known for the legendary and highly influential *Democracy in America* (1835/1840/1969), especially the first volume, which deals, in a very laudatory way, with the early American democratic system and came to be seen as an early contribution to the development of "political science." However, in the later volumes of that work, as well as in later works, Tocqueville clearly develops a broad social theory that deserves a place in the canon of social theory.

(In general, Tocqueville was very favorably disposed to the American system, although he had reservations about democracy more generally.) Volume two was not well received, perhaps because of this shift in orientation, as well as the book's more abstract nature.

Tocqueville continued in politics and, even though he was an aristocrat, was comparatively liberal in many of his views. Of this, he said:

> People ascribe to me alternatively aristocratic and democratic prejudices. If I had been born in another period, or in another country, I might have had either one or the other. But my birth, as it happened, made it easy for me to guard against both. I came into the world at the end of a long revolution, which, after destroying ancient institutions, created none that could last. When I entered life, aristocracy was dead and democracy was yet unborn. My instinct, therefore, could not lead me blindly either to the one or the other.
>
> (Tocqueville, cited in Nisbet, 1976–1977:61)

It is because of this ambivalence that Nisbet (1976–1977:65) argues that unlike the development of Marxism flowing from Marx's intellectual certainty, "at no time has there been, or is there likely to be, anything called Tocquevilleism."

Tocqueville lived through the Revolution of 1848 and the abdication of the king. However, he opposed the military coup staged by Louis Napoleon, spent a few days in jail, and saw, as a result, the end of his political career (he had become minister of foreign affairs but was fired by Louis Napoleon). He never accepted the dictatorship of Napoleon III and grew increasingly critical of the political direction taken by France. As a way of critiquing the France of his day Tocqueville decided to write about the French Revolution of 1789 (although he believed it continued through the first half of the nineteenth century and to his day) in his other well-known book, *The Old Regime and the Revolution,* which was published in 1856. The book focused on French despotism but continued the concerns of *Democracy in America* with the relationship between freedom, equality, and democracy. Unlike the second volume of *Democracy in America, Old Regime* was well received and quite successful. It made Tocqueville the "grand old man" of the liberal movement of the day in France.

Tocqueville died at age 53 on April 16, 1859 (Mancini, 1994; Zunz and Kahan, 2002). One can gain a great deal of insight into the man and his thinking through *The Recollections of Alexis de Tocqueville* (Tocqueville, 1893/1959), his posthumously published memoirs of the Revolution of 1848 and his role in it.

Three interrelated issues lie at the heart of Tocqueville's theory. As a product of the Enlightenment, he is first and foremost a great supporter of, and advocate for, *freedom.* However, he is much more critical of *equality,* which he sees as tending to produce mediocrity in comparison to the superiority produced by the aristocrats (he himself was an aristocrat) of a prior, more inegalitarian, era. More importantly, equality and mediocrity are also linked to what most concerns him, and that is the growth of *centralization,* especially in the government, and the threat centralized government poses to freedom. In his view, it was the inequality of the prior age, the power of the aristocrats, that acted to keep government centralization in check. However, with the demise of aristocrats, and the rise of greater equality, there are no groups capable of countering the ever-present tendency toward centralization. The mass of largely equal people are too "servile" to oppose this trend. Furthermore, Tocqueville links equality to "individualism" (an important concept that he claimed to "invent" and for which he is credited), and the resulting individualists are far less interested in the well-being of the larger "community" than were the aristocrats who preceded them.

It is for this reason that Tocqueville is critical of democracy and especially socialism. Democracy's commitment to freedom was ultimately threatened by its parallel commitment to equality and its tendency toward centralized government. Of course, from Tocqueville's point of view the situation would be far worse in socialism because its far greater commitment to equality, and the much greater likelihood of government centralization, posed a far greater threat to freedom. The latter view is quite prescient given what transpired in the Soviet Union and other societies that operated, at least in name, under the banner of socialism.

Thus the strength of Tocqueville's theory lies in the interrelated ideas of freedom, equality, and especially centralization. His "grand narrative" on the increasing control of central governments anticipates other theories including Weber's work on bureaucracy and especially the more contemporary work of Michel Foucault on "governmentality" and its gradual spread, increasing subtlety, and propensity to invade even the "soul" of the people controlled by it. There is a very profound social theory in Tocqueville's work, but it had no influence on the theories and theorists to be discussed in the remainder of this section on French social theory. Its influence was largely restricted to the development of political science and to work on American democracy and the French Revolution (Tocqueville, 1856/1983). There are certainly sociologists (and other social scientists) who recognized his importance, especially those interested in the relationship between individualism and community (Riesman, 1950; Nisbet, 1953; Bellah et al., 1985; Putnam, 2001), but to this day Tocqueville's theories have not been accorded the place they deserve in social theory in general, and even in French social theory (Gane, 2003).

克劳德・亨利・圣西门（1760—1825）

Claude Henri Saint-Simon (1760–1825)

Saint-Simon was older than Auguste Comte, and in fact, Comte, in his early years, served as Saint-Simon's secretary and disciple (see below). There is a very strong similarity between the ideas of these two thinkers, yet a bitter debate developed between them that led to their eventual split (Pickering, 1993; K. Thompson, 1975).

The most interesting aspect of Saint-Simon was his significance to the development of *both* conservative (like Comte's) and radical Marxian theory. On the conservative side, Saint-Simon wanted to preserve society as it was, but he did not seek a return to life as it had been in the Middle Ages, as did Bonald and Maistre. In addition, he was a *positivist* (Durkheim, 1928/1962:142), which meant that he believed that the study of social phenomena should employ the same scientific techniques that were used in the natural sciences. On the radical side, Saint-Simon saw the need for socialist reforms, especially the centralized planning of the economic system. But Saint-Simon did not go nearly as far as Marx did later. Although he, like Marx, saw the capitalists superseding the feudal nobility, he felt it inconceivable that the working class would come to replace the capitalists. Many of Saint-Simon's ideas are found in Comte's work, but Comte developed them in a more systematic fashion (Pickering, 1997).

Auguste Comte (1798–1857) 奥古斯特・孔德（1798—1857）

Comte was the first to use the term *sociology* (Pickering, 2000; J. H. Turner, 2001a).[4] He had an enormous influence on later sociological theorists (especially Herbert Spencer and Emile Durkheim). And he believed that the study of sociology should be scientific, just as many classical theorists did and most contemporary sociologists do (Lenzer, 1975).

Comte was greatly disturbed by the anarchy that pervaded French society and was critical of those thinkers who had spawned both the Enlightenment and the French Revolution. He developed his scientific view, "positivism," or "positive philosophy," to combat what he considered to be the negative and destructive philosophy of the Enlightenment. Comte was in line with, and influenced by, the French counterrevolutionary Catholics (especially Bonald and Maistre). However, his work can be set apart from theirs on at least two grounds. First, he did not think it possible to return to the Middle Ages; advances in science and industry made that impossible. Second, he developed a much more sophisticated theoretical system than his predecessors, one that was adequate to shape a good portion of early sociology.

Comte developed *social physics,* or what in 1839 he called *sociology* (Pickering, 2000). The use of the term *social physics* made it clear that Comte sought to model sociology after the "hard sciences." This new science, which in his view would ultimately become *the* dominant science, was to be concerned with both social statics (existing social structures) and social dynamics (social change). Although both involved the search for laws of social life, he felt that social dynamics was more important than social statics. This focus on change reflected his interest in social reform, particularly reform of the ills created by the French Revolution and the Enlightenment. Comte did not urge revolutionary change, because he felt the natural evolution of society would make things better. Reforms were needed only to assist the process a bit.

This leads us to the cornerstone of Comte's approach—his evolutionary theory, or the *law of the three stages.* The theory proposes that the world has gone through three intellectual stages. According to Comte, not only does the world go through this process, but groups, societies, sciences, individuals, and even minds go through the same three stages. First is the *theological* stage, which characterized the world prior

---

[4] While he recognizes that Comte created the label "sociology," Eriksson (1993) has challenged the idea that Comte is the progenitor of modern, scientific sociology. Rather, Eriksson sees people like Adam Smith and more generally the Scottish Moralists as the true source of modern sociology. See also L. Hill (1996) on the importance of Adam Ferguson, Ullmann-Margalit (1997) on Ferguson and Adam Smith, and Rundell (2001).

AUGUSTE COMTE

A Biographical Sketch

Auguste Comte was born in Montpelier, France, on January 19, 1798 (Orenstein, 2007; Wernick, 2005; Pickering, 1993:7). His parents were middle class, and his father eventually rose to the position of official local agent for the tax collector. Although a precocious student, Comte never received a college-level degree. He and his whole class were dismissed from the Ecole Polytechnique for their rebelliousness and their political ideas. This expulsion had an adverse effect on Comte's academic career. In 1817 he became secretary (and "adopted son" [Manuel, 1962:251]) to Claude Henri Saint-Simon, a philosopher forty years Comte's senior. They worked closely together for several years, and Comte acknowledged his great debt to Saint-Simon: "I certainly owe a great deal intellectually to Saint-Simon . . . he contributed powerfully to launching me in the philosophic direction that I clearly created for myself today and which I will follow without hesitation all my life" (Durkheim, 1928/1962:144). But in 1824 they had a falling-out because Comte believed that Saint-Simon wanted to omit Comte's name from one of his contributions. Comte later wrote of his relationship with Saint-Simon as "catastrophic" (Pickering, 1993:238) and described him as a "depraved juggler" (Durkheim, 1928/1962:144). In 1852, Comte said of Saint-Simon, "I owed nothing to this personage" (Pickering, 1993:240).

Heilbron (1995) describes Comte as short (perhaps 5 feet, 2 inches), a bit cross-eyed, and very insecure in social situations, especially ones involving women. He was also alienated from society as a whole. These facts may help account for the fact that Comte married Caroline Massin (the marriage lasted from 1825 to 1842). She was an illegitimate child whom Comte later called a "prostitute," although that label has been questioned recently (Pickering, 1997:37). Comte's personal insecurities stood in contrast to his great security about his own intellectual capacities, and it appears that his self-esteem was well founded:

to 1300. During this period, the major idea system emphasized the belief that supernatural powers and religious figures, modeled after humankind, are at the root of everything. In particular, the social and physical world is seen as produced by God. The second stage is the *metaphysical* stage, which occurred roughly between 1300 and 1800. This era was characterized by the belief that abstract forces like "nature," rather than personalized gods, explain virtually everything. Finally, in 1800 the world entered the *positivistic* stage, characterized by a belief in science. People now tended to give up the search for absolute causes (God or nature) and concentrated

> Comte's prodigious memory is famous. Endowed with a photographic memory he could recite backwards the words of any page he had read but once. His powers of concentration were such that he could sketch out an entire book without putting pen to paper. His lectures were all delivered without notes. When he sat down to write out his books he wrote everything from memory.
>
> (Schweber, 1991:134)
>
> In 1826, Comte concocted a scheme by which he would present a series of seventy-two public lectures (to be held in his apartment) on his philosophy. The course drew a distinguished audience, but it was halted after three lectures when Comte suffered a nervous breakdown. He continued to suffer from mental problems, and once in 1827, he tried (unsuccessfully) to commit suicide by throwing himself into the Seine River.
>
> Although he could not get a regular position at the Ecole Polytechnique, Comte did get a minor position as a teaching assistant there in 1832. In 1837, Comte was given the additional post of admissions examiner, and this, for the first time, gave him an adequate income (he had often been economically dependent on his family until this time). During this period, Comte worked on the six-volume work for which he is best known, *Cours de Philosophie Positive*, which was finally published in its entirety in 1842 (the first volume had been published in 1830). In that work Comte outlined his view that sociology was the ultimate science. He also attacked the Ecole Polytechnique, and the result was that in 1844 his assistantship there was not renewed. By 1851 he had completed the four-volume *Systeme de Politique Positive*, which had a more practical intent, offering a grand plan for the reorganization of society.
>
> Heilbron argues that a major break took place in Comte's life in 1838, and it was then that he lost hope that anyone would take his work on science in general, and sociology in particular, seriously. It was also at that point that he embarked on his life of "cerebral hygiene"; that is, Comte began to avoid reading the work of other people, with the result that he became hopelessly out of touch with recent intellectual developments. It was after 1838 that he began developing his bizarre ideas about reforming society that found expression in *Systeme de Politique Positive*. Comte came to fancy himself as the high priest of a new religion of humanity; he believed in a world that eventually would be led by sociologist-priests. (Comte had been strongly influenced by his Catholic background.) Interestingly, in spite of such outrageous ideas, Comte eventually developed a considerable following in France, as well as in a number of other countries.
>
> Auguste Comte died on September 5, 1857.

instead on observing the social and physical world in search of the laws governing them.

It is clear that in his theory of the world, Comte focused on intellectual factors. Indeed, he argued that intellectual disorder is the cause of social disorder. The disorder stemmed from earlier idea systems (theological and metaphysical) that continued to exist in the positivistic (scientific) age. Only when positivism gained total control would social upheavals cease. Because this was an evolutionary process, there was no need to foment social upheaval and revolution. Positivism would come, although perhaps not as quickly as some would like. Here Comte's social reformism and his sociology coincide. Sociology could expedite the arrival of positivism and hence bring order to the social world. Above all, Comte did not want to seem to be espousing revolution. There was, in his view, enough disorder in the world. In any case, from Comte's point of view, it was intellectual change that was needed, and so there was little reason for social and political revolution.

We have already encountered several of Comte's positions that were to be of great significance to the development of classical sociology—his basic conservatism, reformism, and scientism and his evolutionary view of the world. Several other aspects of his work deserve mention because they also were to play a major role in the development of sociological theory. For example, his sociology does not focus on the individual but rather takes as its basic unit of analysis larger entities such as the family. He also urged that we look at both social structure and social change. Of great importance to later sociological theory, especially the work of Spencer and Parsons, is Comte's stress on the systematic character of society—the links among and between the various components of society. He also accorded great importance to the role of consensus in society. He saw little merit in the idea that society is characterized by inevitable conflict between workers and capitalists. In addition, Comte emphasized the need to engage in abstract theorizing and to go out and do sociological research. He urged that sociologists use observation, experimentation, and comparative historical analysis. Finally, Comte believed that sociology ultimately would become the dominant scientific force in the world because of its distinctive ability to interpret social laws and to develop reforms aimed at patching up problems within the system.

Comte was in the forefront of the development of positivistic sociology (Bryant, 1985; Halfpenny, 1982). To Jonathan Turner, Comte's positivism emphasized that "the social universe is amenable to the development of abstract laws that can be tested through the careful collection of data," and "these abstract laws will denote the basic and generic properties of the social universe and they will specify their 'natural relations'" (1985:24). As we will see, a number of classical theorists (especially Spencer and Durkheim) shared Comte's interest in the discovery of the laws of social life. While positivism remains important in contemporary sociology, it has come under attack from a number of quarters (Morrow, 1994).

Even though Comte lacked a solid academic base on which to build a school of Comtian sociological theory, he nevertheless laid a basis for the development of a significant stream of sociological theory. But his long-term significance is dwarfed by that of his successor in French sociology and the inheritor of a number of its ideas, Emile Durkheim. (For a debate over the canonization of Durkheim, as well as other classical theorists discussed in this chapter, see D. Parker, 1997; Mouzelis, 1997.)

Emile Durkheim (1858–1917) 埃米尔·涂尔干（1858—1917）

Durkheim's relation to the Enlightenment was much more ambiguous than Comte's. Durkheim has been seen as an inheritor of the Enlightenment tradition because of his emphasis on science and social reformism. However, he also has been seen as the inheritor of the conservative tradition, especially as it was manifested in Comte's work. But whereas Comte had remained outside of academia (as had Tocqueville), Durkheim developed an increasingly solid academic base as his career progressed. Durkheim legitimized sociology in France, and his work ultimately became a dominant force in the development of sociology in general and of sociological theory in particular (Rawls, 2007; R. A. Jones, 2000).

Durkheim was politically liberal, but he took a more conservative position intellectually. Like Comte and the Catholic counterrevolutionaries, Durkheim feared and hated social disorder. His work was informed by the disorders produced by the general social changes discussed earlier in this chapter, as well as by others (such as industrial strikes, disruption of the ruling class, church–state discord, the rise of political anti-Semitism) more specific to the France of Durkheim's time (Karady, 1983). In fact, most of his work was devoted to the study of social order. His view was that social disorders are not a necessary part of the modern world and could be reduced by social reforms. Whereas Marx saw the problems of the modern world as inherent in society, Durkheim (along with most other classical theorists) did not. As a result, Marx's ideas on the need for social revolution stood in sharp contrast to the reformism of Durkheim and the others. As classical sociological theory developed, it was the Durkheimian interest in order and reform that came to dominate, while the Marxian position was eclipsed.

Social Facts   社会事实

Durkheim developed a distinctive conception of the subject matter of sociology and then tested it in an empirical study. In *The Rules of Sociological Method* (1895/1982), Durkheim argued that it is the special task of sociology to study what he called *social facts* (Nielsen, 2005a, 2007a). He conceived of social facts as forces (Takla and Pope, 1985) and structures that are external to, and coercive of, the individual. The study of these large-scale structures and forces—for example, institutionalized law and shared moral beliefs—and their impact on people became the concern of many later sociological theorists (Parsons, for example). In *Suicide* (1897/1951), Durkheim reasoned that if he could link such an individual behavior as suicide to social causes (social facts), he would have made a persuasive case for the importance of the discipline of sociology. But Durkheim did not examine why individual A or B committed suicide; rather, he was interested in the causes of differences in suicide rates among groups, regions, countries, and different categories of people (for example, married and single). His basic argument was that it was the nature of, and changes in, social facts that led to differences in suicide rates. For example, a war or an economic depression would create a collective mood of depression that would in turn lead to increases in suicide rates. There is much more to be said on this subject, but the key point is that Durkheim developed a distinctive view of sociology and sought to demonstrate its usefulness in a scientific study of suicide.

In *The Rules of Sociological Method* (1895/1982), Durkheim differentiated between two types of social facts—material and nonmaterial. Although he dealt with both in the course of his work, his main focus was on *nonmaterial social facts* (for example, culture, social institutions) rather than *material social facts* (for example,

EMILE DURKHEIM

A Biographical Sketch

Emile Durkheim was born on April 15, 1858, in Epinal, France. He was descended from a long line of rabbis and studied to be a rabbi, but by the time he was in his teens, he had largely disavowed his heritage (Strenski, 1997:4). From that time on, his lifelong interest in religion was more academic than theological (Mestrovic, 1988). He was dissatisfied not only with his religious training but also with his general education and its emphasis on literary and esthetic matters. He longed for schooling in scientific methods and in the moral principles needed to guide social life. He rejected a traditional academic career in philosophy and sought instead to acquire the scientific training needed to contribute to the moral guidance of society. Although he was interested in scientific sociology, there was no field of sociology at that time. So between 1882 and 1887, he taught philosophy in a number of provincial schools in the Paris area.

His appetite for science was whetted further by a trip to Germany, where he was exposed to the scientific psychology being pioneered by Wilhelm Wundt (Durkheim, 1887/1993). In the years immediately after his visit to Germany, Durkheim published a good deal, basing his work, in part, on his experiences there (R. A. Jones, 1994). These publications helped him gain a position in the department of philosophy at the University of Bordeaux in 1887 (Pearce, 2005). There Durkheim offered the first course in social science in a French university. This was a particularly impressive accomplishment, because only a decade earlier, a furor had erupted in a French university by the mention of Auguste Comte in a student dissertation. Durkheim's main responsibility, however, was teaching courses in education to schoolteachers, and his most important course was in the area of moral education. His goal was to communicate a moral system to the educators, who he hoped would then pass the system on to young people in an effort to help reverse the moral degeneration he saw around him in French society.

The years that followed were characterized by a series of personal successes for Durkheim. In 1893 he published his French doctoral thesis, *The Division of Labor in Society*, as well as his Latin thesis on Montesquieu (Durkheim, 1892/1997; W. Miller, 1993). His major methodological statement, *The Rules of Sociological Method*, appeared in 1895, followed (in 1897) by his empirical application of those methods in the study *Suicide*. By 1896 he had become a full professor at Bordeaux. In 1902 he was summoned to the famous French university the Sorbonne, and in 1906 he was named professor of the science of education, a title that was changed in 1913 to professor of the science of education and sociology. The other of his most famous works, *The Elementary Forms of Religious Life*, was published in 1912.

Durkheim is most often thought of today as a political conservative, and his influence within sociology certainly has been a conservative one. But in his time, he was considered a liberal, and this was exemplified by the active public role he played in the defense of Alfred Dreyfus, the Jewish army captain whose court-martial for treason was felt by many to be anti-Semitic (Farrell, 1997).

Durkheim was deeply offended by the Dreyfus affair, particularly its anti-Semitism. But Durkheim did not attribute this anti-Semitism to racism among the French people. Characteristically, he saw it as a symptom of the moral sickness confronting French society as a whole (Birnbaum and Todd, 1995). He said:

> When society undergoes suffering, it feels the need to find someone whom it can hold responsible for its sickness, on whom it can avenge its misfortunes: and those against whom public opinion already discriminates are naturally designated for this role. These are the pariahs who serve as expiatory victims. What confirms me in this interpretation is the way in which the result of Dreyfus's trial was greeted in 1894. There was a surge of joy in the boulevards. People celebrated as a triumph what should have been a cause for public mourning. At least they knew whom to blame for the economic troubles and moral distress in which they lived. The trouble came from the Jews. The charge had been officially proved. By this very fact alone, things already seemed to be getting better and people felt consoled.
>
> (Lukes, 1972:345)

Thus, Durkheim's interest in the Dreyfus affair stemmed from his deep and lifelong interest in morality and the moral crisis confronting modern society.

To Durkheim, the answer to the Dreyfus affair and crises like it lay in ending the moral disorder in society. Because that could not be done quickly or easily, Durkheim suggested more specific actions such as severe repression of those who incited hatred of others and government efforts to show the public how it was being misled. He urged people to "have the courage to proclaim aloud what they think, and to unite together in order to achieve victory in the struggle against public madness" (Lukes, 1972:347).

Durkheim's (1928/1962) interest in socialism is also taken as evidence against the idea that he was a conservative, but his kind of socialism was very different from the kind that interested Marx and his followers. In fact, Durkheim labeled Marxism as a set of "disputable and out-of-date hypotheses" (Lukes, 1972:323). To Durkheim, socialism represented a movement aimed at the moral regeneration of society through scientific morality, and he was not interested in short-term political methods or the economic aspects of socialism. He did not see the proletariat as the salvation of society, and he was greatly opposed to agitation or violence. Socialism for Durkheim was very different from what we usually think of as socialism; it simply represented a system in which the moral principles discovered by scientific sociology were to be applied.

Durkheim, as we will see throughout this book, had a profound influence on the development of sociology, but his influence was not restricted to it (Halls, 1996). Much of his impact on other fields came through the journal *L'année sociologique*, which he founded in 1898. An intellectual circle arose around the journal with Durkheim at its center. Through it, he and his ideas influenced such fields as anthropology, history (especially the "Annales school" [Nielsen, 2005b]), linguistics, and—somewhat ironically, considering his early attacks on the field—psychology.

Durkheim died on November 15, 1917, a celebrated figure in French intellectual circles. But it was not until over twenty years later, with the publication of Talcott Parsons's *The Structure of Social Action* (1937), that Durkheim's work became a significant influence on American sociology.

bureaucracy, law). This concern for nonmaterial social facts was already clear in his earliest major work, *The Division of Labor in Society* (1893/1964). His focus there was a comparative analysis of what held society together in the primitive and modern cases. He concluded that earlier societies were held together primarily by nonmaterial social facts, specifically, a strongly held common morality, or what he called a strong *collective conscience.* However, because of the complexities of modern society, there had been a decline in the strength of the collective conscience. The primary bond in the modern world was an intricate division of labor, which tied people to others in dependency relationships. However, Durkheim felt that the modern division of labor brought with it several "pathologies"; it was, in other words, an inadequate method of holding society together. Given his conservative sociology, Durkheim did not feel that revolution was needed to solve these problems. Rather, he suggested a variety of reforms that could "patch up" the modern system and keep it functioning. Although he recognized that there was no going back to the age when a powerful collective conscience predominated, he did feel that the common morality could be strengthened in modern society and that people thereby could cope better with the pathologies that they were experiencing.

Religion 宗教

In his later work, nonmaterial social facts occupied an even more central position. In fact, he came to focus on perhaps the ultimate form of a nonmaterial social fact—religion—in his last major work, *The Elementary Forms of Religious Life* (1912/1965). Durkheim examined primitive society to find the roots of religion. He believed that he would be better able to find those roots in the comparative simplicity of primitive society than in the complexity of the modern world. What he found, he felt, was that the source of religion was society itself. Society comes to define certain things as religious and others as profane. Specifically, in the case he studied, the clan was the source of a primitive kind of religion, *totemism,* in which things like plants and animals are deified. Totemism, in turn, was seen as a specific type of nonmaterial social fact, a form of the collective conscience. In the end, Durkheim came to argue that society and religion (or, more generally, the collective conscience) were one and the same. Religion was the way society expressed itself in the form of a nonmaterial social fact. In a sense, then, Durkheim came to deify society and its major products. Clearly, in deifying society, Durkheim took a highly conservative stance: one would not want to overturn a deity *or* its societal source. Because he identified society with God, Durkheim was not inclined to urge social revolution. Instead, he was a social reformer seeking ways of improving the functioning of society. In these and other ways, Durkheim was clearly in line with French conservative sociology. The fact that he avoided many of its excesses helped make him the most significant figure in French sociology.

Durkheim's books and other important works helped carve out a distinctive domain for sociology in the academic world of turn-of-the-century France, and they earned him the leading position in that growing field. In 1898, Durkheim set up a scholarly journal devoted to sociology, *L'année sociologique* (Besnard, 1983). It became a powerful force in the development and spread of sociological ideas. Durkheim was intent on fostering the growth of sociology, and he used his journal as a focal point for the development of a group of disciples. They later would extend his ideas and carry them to many other locales and into the study of other aspects of the social world (for example, sociology of law and sociology of the city). By 1910, Durkheim had established a strong center of sociology in France, and the academic institutionalization of sociology was well under way in that nation (Heilbron, 1995).

The Development of German Sociology 德国社会学的发展

Whereas the early history of French sociology is a fairly coherent story of the progression from the Enlightenment and the French Revolution to the conservative reaction and to the increasingly important sociological ideas of Tocqueville, Saint-Simon, Comte, and Durkheim, German sociology was fragmented from the beginning. A split developed between Marx and his supporters, who remained on the edge of sociology, and the early giants of mainstream German sociology, Max Weber and Georg Simmel.[5] However, although Marxian theory itself was deemed unacceptable, its ideas found their way in a variety of positive and negative ways into mainstream German sociology.

The Roots and Nature of the Theories of Karl Marx (1818–1883) 卡尔·马克思理论的渊源和本质

The dominant intellectual influence on Karl Marx was the German philosopher G. W. F. Hegel (1770–1831).

Hegel 黑格尔

According to Terence Ball, "it is difficult for us to appreciate the degree to which Hegel dominated German thought in the second quarter of the nineteenth century. It was largely within the framework of his philosophy that educated Germans—including the young Marx—discussed history, politics and culture" (1991:25). Marx's education at the University of Berlin was shaped by Hegel's ideas as well as by the split that developed among Hegel's followers after his death. The "Old Hegelians" continued to subscribe to the master's ideas, while the "Young Hegelians," although still working in the Hegelian tradition, were critical of many facets of his philosophical system.

Two concepts represent the essence of Hegel's philosophy—the dialectic and idealism (Hegel, 1807/1967, 1821/1967; Beamish, 2007a). The *dialectic* is both a way of thinking and an image of the world. It is a way of thinking that stresses the importance of processes, relations, dynamics, conflicts, and contradictions—a dynamic rather than a static way of thinking about the world. On the other hand, it is a view

---

[5] For an argument against this and the view of continuity between Marxian and mainstream sociology, see Seidman (1983).

KARL MARX

A Biographical Sketch

Karl Marx was born in Trier, Prussia, on May 5, 1818 (Beilharz, 2005e). His father, a lawyer, provided the family with a fairly typical middle-class existence. Both parents were from rabbinical families, but for business reasons, the father had converted to Lutheranism when Karl was very young. In 1841 Marx received his doctorate in philosophy from the University of Berlin, a school heavily influenced by Hegel and the Young Hegelians, who were supportive, yet critical, of their master. Marx's doctorate was a dry philosophical treatise, but it did anticipate many of his later ideas. After graduation he became a writer for a liberal-radical newspaper and within ten months had become its editor in chief. However, because of its political positions, the paper was closed shortly thereafter by the government. The early essays published in this period began to reflect a number of the positions that would guide Marx throughout his life. They were sprinkled liberally with democratic principles, humanism, and youthful idealism. He rejected the abstractness of Hegelian philosophy, the naive dreaming of utopian communists, and those activists who were urging what he considered to be premature political action. In rejecting these activists, Marx laid the groundwork for his own life's work:

> Practical attempts, even by the masses, can be answered with a cannon as soon as they become dangerous, but ideas that have overcome our intellect and conquered our conviction, ideas to which reason has riveted our conscience, are chains from which one cannot break loose without breaking one's heart; they are demons that one can only overcome by submitting to them.
>
> (Marx, 1842/1977:20)

Marx married in 1843 and soon thereafter was forced to leave Germany for the more liberal atmosphere of Paris. There he continued to grapple with the ideas of Hegel and his supporters, but he also encountered two new sets of ideas—French socialism and English political economy. It was the unique way in which he combined Hegelianism, socialism, and political economy that shaped his intellectual orientation. Also of great importance at this point was his meeting the man who was to become his lifelong friend, benefactor, and collaborator—Friedrich Engels (Carver, 1983). The son of a textile manufacturer, Engels had become a socialist critical of the conditions facing the working class. Much of Marx's compassion for the misery of the working class came from his exposure to Engels and his ideas. In 1844 Engels and Marx had a lengthy conversation in a famous café in Paris and laid the groundwork for a lifelong association. Of that conversation Engels said, "Our complete agreement in all theoretical fields became obvious . . . and our joint work dates from that time" (McLellan, 1973:131). In the following year, Engels published a notable work, *The Condition of the Working Class in England*. During this period Marx wrote a number of abstruse works (many unpublished in his lifetime), including *The Holy Family* (1845/1956) and *The German Ideology* (1845–1846/1970) (both coauthored with Engels), but he also produced *The Economic and Philosophic Manuscripts of 1844* (1932/1964), which better foreshadowed his increasing preoccupation with the economic domain.

While Marx and Engels shared a theoretical orientation, there were many differences between the two men. Marx tended to be theoretical, a disorderly intellectual, and very oriented to his family. Engels was a practical thinker, a neat and tidy businessman, and a person who did not believe in the institution of the family. In spite of their differences, Marx and Engels forged a close union in which they collaborated on books and articles and worked together in radical organizations. Engels even helped support Marx throughout the rest of his life so that Marx could devote himself to his intellectual and political endeavors.

In spite of the close association of the names of Marx and Engels, Engels made it clear that he was the junior partner:

> Marx could very well have done without me. What Marx accomplished I would not have achieved. Marx stood higher, saw farther, and took a wider and quicker view than the rest of us. Marx was a genius.
>
> (Engels, cited in McLellan, 1973:131–132)

In fact, many believe that Engels failed to understand many of the subtleties of Marx's work (C. Smith, 1997). After Marx's death, Engels became the leading spokesperson for Marxian theory and in various ways distorted and oversimplified it, although he remained faithful to the political perspective he had forged with Marx.

Because some of his writings had upset the Prussian government, the French government (at the request of the Prussians) expelled Marx in 1845, and he moved to Brussels. His radicalism was growing, and he had become an active member of the international revolutionary movement. He also associated with the Communist League and was asked to write a document (with Engels) expounding its aims and beliefs. The result was the *Communist Manifesto* of 1848 (1848/1948), a work that was characterized by ringing political slogans (for example, "Working men of all countries, unite!").

In 1849 Marx moved to London, and, in light of the failure of the political revolutions of 1848, he began to withdraw from active revolutionary activity and to move into more serious and detailed research on the workings of the capitalist system. In 1852, he began his famous studies in the British Museum of the working conditions in capitalism. These studies ultimately resulted in the three volumes of *Capital*, the first of which was published in 1867; the other two were published posthumously. He lived in poverty during these years, barely managing to survive on a small income from his writings and the support of Engels. In 1864 Marx became reinvolved in political activity by joining the International, an international movement of workers. He soon gained preeminence within the movement and devoted a number of years to it. He began to gain fame both as leader of the International and as the author of *Capital*. But the disintegration of the International by 1876, the failure of various revolutionary movements, and personal illness took their toll on Marx. His wife died in 1881, a daughter in 1882, and Marx himself on March 14, 1883.

that the world is made up not of static structures but of processes, relationships, dynamics, conflicts, and contradictions. Although the dialectic generally is associated with Hegel, it certainly predates him in philosophy. Marx, trained in the Hegelian tradition, accepted the significance of the dialectic. However, he was critical of some aspects of the way Hegel used it. For example, Hegel tended to apply the dialectic only to ideas, whereas Marx felt that it applied to more material aspects of life as well, for example, the economy.

Hegel is also associated with the philosophy of *idealism,* which emphasizes the importance of the mind and mental products rather than the material world. It is the social definition of the physical and material worlds that matters most, not those worlds themselves. In its extreme form, idealism asserts that *only* the mind and psychological constructs exist. Some idealists believed that their mental processes would remain the same even if the physical and social worlds no longer existed. Idealists emphasize not only mental processes but also the ideas produced by these processes. Hegel paid a great deal of attention to the development of such ideas, especially to what he referred to as the "spirit" of society.

In fact, Hegel offered a kind of evolutionary theory of the world in idealistic terms. At first, people were endowed only with the ability to acquire a sensory understanding of the world around them. They could understand things like the sight, smell, and feel of the social and physical world. Later, people developed the ability to be conscious of and to understand themselves. With self-knowledge and self-understanding, people began to understand that they could become more than they were. In terms of Hegel's dialectical approach, a contradiction developed between what people were and what they felt they could be. The resolution of this contradiction lay in the development of an individual's awareness of his or her place in the larger spirit of society. Individuals come to realize that their ultimate fulfillment lies in the development and the expansion of the spirit of society as a whole. Thus, individuals in Hegel's scheme evolve from an understanding of things to an understanding of self to an understanding of their place in the larger scheme of things.

Hegel, then, offered a general theory of the evolution of the world. It is a subjective theory in which change is held to occur at the level of consciousness. However, that change occurs largely beyond the control of actors. Actors are reduced to little more than vessels swept along by the inevitable evolution of consciousness.

Feuerbach 费尔巴哈

Ludwig Feuerbach (1804–1872) was an important bridge between Hegel and Marx (Staples, 2007a). As a Young Hegelian, Feuerbach was critical of Hegel for, among other things, his excessive emphasis on consciousness and the spirit of society. Feuerbach's adoption of a materialist philosophy led him to argue that what was needed was to move from Hegel's subjective idealism to a focus not on ideas but on the material reality of real human beings. In his critique of Hegel, Feuerbach focused on religion. To Feuerbach, God is simply a projection by people of their human essence onto an impersonal force. People set God over and above themselves and become alienated from God because they project a series of positive characteristics onto God (that he is perfect, almighty, and holy), while they reduce themselves to being imperfect, powerless, and sinful. Feuerbach argued that this kind of religion must be overcome and that its defeat could be aided by a materialist philosophy in which people (not religion) became their own highest object—ends in themselves. Real people, not abstract ideas like religion, are deified by a materialist philosophy.

Marx, Hegel, and Feuerbach 马克思、黑格尔和费尔巴哈

Marx was simultaneously influenced by, and critical of, *both* Hegel and Feuerbach. Marx, following Feuerbach, was critical of Hegel's adherence to an idealist philosophy. Marx took this position not only because of his adoption of a materialist orientation but also because of his interest in practical activities. Social facts like wealth and the state are treated by Hegel as ideas rather than as real, material entities. Even when he examined a seemingly material process like labor, Hegel was looking only at abstract mental labor. This is very different from Marx's interest in the labor of real, sentient people. Thus Hegel was looking at the wrong issues as far as Marx was concerned. In addition, Marx felt that Hegel's idealism led to a very conservative political orientation. To Hegel, the process of evolution was occurring beyond the control of people and their activities. In any case, because people seemed to be moving toward greater consciousness of the world as it could be, there seemed no need for any revolutionary change; the process was already moving in the "desired" direction. Whatever problems did exist lay in consciousness, and the answer, therefore, seemed to lie in changing thinking.

Marx took a very different position, arguing that the problems of modern life can be traced to real, material sources (for example, the structures of capitalism), and that the solutions, therefore, can be found only in the overturning of those structures by the collective action of large numbers of people (Marx and Engels, 1845/1956:254). Whereas Hegel "stood the world on its head" by focusing on consciousness, not the real material world, Marx firmly embedded his dialectic in a material base.

Marx applauded Feuerbach's critique of Hegel on a number of counts (for example, its materialism and its rejection of the abstractness of Hegel's theory), but he was far from fully satisfied with Feuerbach's position (Thomson, 1994). For one thing, Feuerbach focused on the religious world, whereas Marx believed that it was the entire social world, and the economy in particular, that had to be analyzed. Although Marx accepted Feuerbach's materialism, he felt that Feuerbach had gone too far in focusing onesidedly, nondialectically, on the material world. Feuerbach failed to include the most important of Hegel's contributions, the dialectic, in his materialist orientation, particularly the relationship between people and the material world. Finally, Marx argued that Feuerbach, like most philosophers, failed to emphasize *praxis*—practical activity—in particular, revolutionary activity (Wortmann 2007). As Marx put it, "The philosophers have only *interpreted* the world, in various ways; the point, however, is to *change it*" (cited in Tucker, 1970:109).

Marx extracted what he considered to be the two most important elements from these two thinkers—Hegel's dialectic and Feuerbach's materialism—and fused them into his own distinctive orientation, *dialectical materialism,*[6] which focuses on dialectical relationships within the material world.

Political Economy 政治经济学

Marx's materialism and his consequent focus on the economic sector led him rather naturally to the work of a group of *political economists* (for example, Adam Smith and David Ricardo) (Howard and King, 2005). Marx was very attracted to a number of their positions. He lauded their basic premise that labor was the source of all wealth. This ultimately led Marx to his *labor theory of value,* in which he argued that the profit of the capitalist was based on the exploitation of the laborer. Capitalists performed the rather simple trick of paying the workers less than they deserved, because they received less pay than the value of what they actually produced in a work period. This *surplus value,* which was retained and reinvested by the capitalist, was the basis of the entire capitalist system. The capitalist system grew by continually increasing the level of exploitation of the workers (and therefore the amount of surplus value) and investing the profits for the expansion of the system.

Marx also was affected by the political economists' depiction of the horrors of the capitalist system and the exploitation of the workers. However, whereas they depicted the evils of capitalism, Marx criticized the political economists for seeing these evils as inevitable components of capitalism. Marx deplored their general acceptance of capitalism and the way they urged people to work for economic success within it. He also was critical of the political economists for failing to see the inherent conflict between capitalists and laborers and for denying the need for a radical change in the economic order. Such conservative economics was hard for Marx to accept, given his commitment to a radical change from capitalism to socialism.

Marx and Sociology 马克思和社会学

Marx was not a sociologist and did not consider himself one. Although his work is too broad to be encompassed by the term *sociology,* there is a sociological theory to be found in Marx's work. From the beginning, there were those who were heavily influenced by Marx, and there has been a continuous strand of Marxian sociology, primarily in Europe. But for the majority of early sociologists, his work was a negative force, something against which to shape their sociology. Until very recently, sociological theory, especially in America, has been characterized by either hostility to or ignorance of Marxian theory. This has, as we will see in Chapter 2, changed dramatically, but the negative reaction to Marx's work was a major force in the shaping of much of sociological theory (Gurney, 1981).

The basic reason for this rejection of Marx was ideological. Many of the early sociological theorists were inheritors of the conservative reaction to the disruptions of the Enlightenment and the French Revolution. Marx's radical ideas and the radical

---

[6] First used by Joseph Dietzgen in 1887, the term was made central by Georgi Plekhanov in 1891 (Beamish, 2007a). Although Marx certainly operated from the perspective of dialectical materialism, he never used the concept.

social changes he foretold and sought to bring to life were clearly feared and hated by such thinkers. Marx was dismissed as an ideologist. It was argued that he was not a serious sociological theorist. However, ideology per se could not have been the real reason for the rejection of Marx, because the work of Comte, Durkheim, and other conservative thinkers also was heavily ideological. It was the nature of the ideology, not the existence of ideology as such, that put off many sociological theorists. They were ready and eager to buy conservative ideology wrapped in a cloak of sociological theory, but not the radical ideology offered by Marx and his followers.

There were, of course, other reasons why Marx was not accepted by many early theorists. He seemed to be more an economist than a sociologist. Although the early sociologists would certainly admit the importance of the economy, they would also argue that it was only one of a number of components of social life.

Another reason for the early rejection of Marx was the nature of his interests. Whereas the early sociologists were reacting to the disorder created by the Enlightenment, the French Revolution, and later the Industrial Revolution, Marx was not upset by these disorders—or by disorder in general. Rather, what interested and concerned Marx most was the oppressiveness of the capitalist system that was emerging out of the Industrial Revolution. Marx wanted to develop a theory that explained this oppressiveness and that would help overthrow that system. Marx's interest was in revolution, which stood in contrast to the conservative concern for reform and orderly change.

Another difference worth noting is the difference in philosophical roots between Marxian and conservative sociological theory. Most of the conservative theorists were heavily influenced by the philosophy of Immanuel Kant. Among other things, this led them to think in linear, cause-and-effect terms. That is, they tended to argue that a change in A (say, the change in ideas during the Enlightenment) leads to a change in B (say, the political changes of the French Revolution). In contrast, Marx was most heavily influenced, as we have seen, by Hegel, who thought in dialectical rather than cause-and-effect terms. Among other things, the dialectic attunes us to the ongoing reciprocal effects of social forces. Thus, a dialectician would reconceptualize the example discussed above as a continual, ongoing interplay of ideas and politics.

Marx's Theory 马克思的理论

To oversimplify enormously, Marx offered a theory of capitalist society based on his image of the basic nature of human beings. Marx believed that people are basically productive; that is, to survive, people need to work in, and with, nature. In so doing, they produce the food, clothing, tools, shelter, and other necessities that permit them to live. Their productivity is a perfectly natural way by which they express basic creative impulses. Furthermore, these impulses are expressed in concert with other people; in other words, people are inherently social. They need to work together to produce what they need to survive.

Throughout history this natural process has been subverted, at first by the mean conditions of primitive society and later by a variety of structural arrangements erected by societies in the course of history. In various ways, these structures interfered with the natural productive process. However, it is in capitalist society that this breakdown is most acute; the breakdown in the natural productive process reaches its culmination in capitalism.

Basically capitalism is a structure (or, more accurately, a series of structures) that erects barriers between an individual and the production process, the products of that process, and other people; ultimately, it even divides the individual himself or herself. This is the basic meaning of the concept of *alienation*. It is the breakdown of the natural interconnection among people and what they produce. Alienation occurs because capitalism has evolved into a two-class system in which a few capitalists own the production process, the products, and the labor time of those who work for them. Instead of naturally producing for themselves, people produce unnaturally in capitalist society for a small group of capitalists. Intellectually, Marx was very concerned with the structures of capitalism and their oppressive impact on actors. Politically, he was led to an interest in emancipating people from the oppressive structures of capitalism.

Marx actually spent very little time dreaming about what a utopian socialist state would look like (Lovell, 1992). He was more concerned with helping to bring about the demise of capitalism. He believed that the contradictions and conflicts within capitalism would lead dialectically to its ultimate collapse, but he did not think that the process was inevitable. People had to act at the appropriate times and in the appropriate ways for socialism to come into being. The capitalists had great resources at their disposal to forestall the coming of socialism, but they could be overcome by the concerted action of a class-conscious proletariat. What would the proletariat create in the process? What is socialism? Most basically, it is a society in which, for the first time, people could approach Marx's ideal image of productivity. With the aid of modern technology, people could interact harmoniously with nature and other people to create what they needed to survive. To put it another way, in socialist society, people would no longer be alienated.

马克斯·韦伯（1864—1920）与格奥尔格·齐美尔（1858—1918）
理论的根源和本质

The Roots and Nature of the Theories of Max Weber (1864–1920) and Georg Simmel (1858–1918)

Although Marx and his followers in the late nineteenth and early twentieth centuries remained outside mainstream German sociology, to a considerable extent early German sociology can be seen as developing in opposition to Marxian theory.

Weber and Marx 韦伯和马克思

Albert Salomon, for example, claimed that a large part of the theory of the early giant of German sociology, Max Weber, developed "in a long and intense debate with the ghost of Marx" (1945:596). This is probably an exaggeration, but in many ways Marxian theory did play a negative role in Weberian theory. In other ways, however, Weber was working within the Marxian tradition, trying to "round out" Marx's theory. Also, there were many inputs into Weberian theory other than Marxian theory (Burger, 1976). We can clarify a good deal about the sources of German sociology by outlining each of these views of the relationship between Marx and Weber (Antonio and Glassman, 1985; Schroeter, 1985). It should be borne in mind that Weber was not intimately familiar with Marx's work (much of it was not published until after Weber's death) and that Weber was reacting more to the work of the Marxists than to Marx's work itself (Antonio, 1985:29; B. S. Turner, 1981:19–20).

Weber *did* tend to view Marx and the Marxists of his day as economic determinists who offered single-cause theories of social life. That is, Marxian theory was seen as tracing all historical developments to economic bases and viewing all contemporaneous structures as erected on an economic base. Although this is not true of Marx's own theory, it was the position of many later Marxists.

One of the examples of economic determinism that seemed to rankle Weber most was the view that ideas are simply the reflections of material (especially economic) interests and that material interests determine ideology. From this point of view, Weber was supposed to have "turned Marx on his head" (much as Marx had inverted Hegel). Instead of focusing on economic factors and their effect on ideas, Weber devoted much of his attention to ideas and their effect on the economy. Rather than seeing ideas as simple reflections of economic factors, Weber saw them as fairly autonomous forces capable of profoundly affecting the economic world. Weber certainly devoted a lot of attention to ideas, particularly systems of religious ideas, and he was especially concerned with the impact of religious ideas on the economy. In *The Protestant Ethic and the Spirit of Capitalism* (1904–1905/1958), he was concerned with Protestantism, mainly as a system of ideas, and its impact on the rise of another system of ideas, the "spirit of capitalism," and ultimately on a capitalist economic system. Weber had a similar interest in other world religions, looking at how their nature might have obstructed the development of capitalism in their respective societies. On the basis of this kind of work, some scholars came to the conclusion that Weber developed his ideas in opposition to those of Marx.

A second view of Weber's relationship to Marx, as mentioned earlier, is that he did not so much oppose Marx as try to round out Marx's theoretical perspective. Here Weber is seen as working more within the Marxian tradition than in opposition to it. His work on religion, interpreted from this point of view, was simply an effort to show that not only do material factors affect ideas but also ideas themselves affect material structures.

A good example of the view that Weber was engaged in a process of rounding out Marxian theory is in the area of stratification theory. In this work on stratification, Marx focused on social *class,* the economic dimension of stratification. Although Weber accepted the importance of this factor, he argued that other dimensions of stratification were also important. He argued that the notion of social stratification should be extended to include stratification on the basis of prestige (*status*) and *power.* The inclusion of these other dimensions does not constitute a refutation of Marx but is simply an extension of his ideas.

Both of the views outlined above accept the importance of Marxian theory for Weber. There are elements of truth in both positions; at some points Weber was working in opposition to Marx, while at other points he was extending Marx's ideas. However, a third view of this issue may best characterize the relationship between Marx and Weber. In this view, Marx is simply seen as only one of many influences on Weber's thought.

MAX WEBER

A Biographical Sketch

Max Weber was born in Erfurt, Germany, on April 21, 1864, into a decidedly middle-class family. Important differences between his parents had a profound effect upon both his intellectual orientation and his psychological development. His father was a bureaucrat who rose to a relatively important political position. He was clearly a part of the political establishment and, as a result, eschewed any activity or idealism that would require personal sacrifice or threaten his position within the system. In addition, the senior Weber was a man who enjoyed earthly pleasures, and in this and many other ways he stood in sharp contrast to his wife. Max Weber's mother was a devout Calvinist, a woman who sought to lead an ascetic life largely devoid of the pleasures craved by her husband. Her concerns were more otherworldly; she was disturbed by the imperfections that were signs that she was not destined for salvation. These deep differences between the parents led to marital tension, and both the differences and the tension had an immense impact on Weber.

Because it was impossible to emulate both parents, Weber was presented with a clear choice as a child (Marianne Weber, 1975:62). He first seemed to opt for his father's orientation to life, but later he drew closer to his mother's approach. Whatever the choice, the tension produced by the need to choose between such polar opposites negatively affected Max Weber's psyche.

At age 18, Max Weber left home for a short time to attend the University of Heidelberg. Weber had already demonstrated intellectual precocity, but on a social level he entered Heidelberg shy and underdeveloped. However, that quickly changed after he gravitated toward his father's way of life and joined his father's old dueling fraternity. There he developed socially, at least in part because of the huge quantities of beer he consumed with his peers. In addition, he proudly displayed the dueling scars that were the trademarks of such fraternities. Weber not only manifested his identity with his father's way of life in these ways but also chose, at least for the time being, his father's career—the law.

After three terms, Weber left Heidelberg for military service, and in 1884 he returned to Berlin and to his parents' home to take courses at the University of Berlin. He remained there for most of the next eight years as he completed his studies, earned his Ph.D., became a lawyer (see Turner and Factor, 1994, for a discussion of the impact of legal thinking on Weber's theorizing), and started teaching at the University of Berlin. In the process, his interests shifted more toward his lifelong concerns—economics, history, and sociology. During his eight years in Berlin, Weber was financially dependent on his father, a circumstance he progressively grew to dislike. At the same time, he moved closer to his mother's values, and his antipathy to his father increased. He adopted an ascetic life and plunged deeply into his work. For example, during one semester as a student, his work habits were described as follows: "He continues the rigid work discipline, regulates his life by the clock, divides the daily routine into exact sections for the various subjects, saves in his way, by feeding himself evenings in his room with a pound of raw chopped beef and four fried eggs" (Mitzman, 1969/1971:48; Marianne Weber, 1975:105). Thus Weber, following his mother, had become ascetic and diligent, a compulsive worker—in contemporary terms a "workaholic."

This compulsion for work led in 1896 to a position as professor of economics at Heidelberg. But in 1897, when Weber's academic career was blossoming, his father died following a violent argument between them. Shortly thereafter Weber began to manifest symptoms that were to culminate in a nervous breakdown. Often unable to sleep or to work, Weber spent the next six or seven years in near-total collapse. After a long hiatus, some of his powers began to return in 1903, but it was not until 1904, when he delivered (in the United States) his first lecture in six and a half years, that Weber was able to begin to return to active academic life. In 1904 and 1905, he published one of his best-known works, *The Protestant Ethic and the Spirit of Capitalism*. In this work, Weber announced the ascendance of his mother's religion on an academic level. Weber devoted much of his time to the study of religion, though he was not personally religious.

Although he continued to be plagued by psychological problems, after 1904 Weber was able to function, indeed to produce some of his most important work. In these years, Weber published his studies of the world's religions in world-historical perspective (for example, China, India, and ancient Judaism). At the time of his death (June 14, 1920), he was working on his most important work, *Economy and Society* (1921/1968). Although this book was published, and subsequently translated into many languages, it was unfinished.

In addition to producing voluminous writings in this period, Weber undertook a number of other activities. He helped found the German Sociological Society in 1910. His home became a center for a wide range of intellectuals, including sociologists such as Georg Simmel, Robert Michels and his brother Alfred, as well as the philosopher and literary critic Georg Lukács (Scaff, 1989:186–222). In addition, Weber was active politically and wrote essays on the issues of the day.

There was a tension in Weber's life and, more important, in his work, between the bureaucratic mind, as represented by his father, and his mother's religiosity. This unresolved tension permeates Weber's work as it permeated his personal life.

Other Influences on Weber 其他人对韦伯的影响

We can identify a number of sources of Weberian theory, including German historians, philosophers, economists, and political theorists. Among those who influenced Weber, the philosopher Immanuel Kant (1724–1804) stands out above all the others. But we must not overlook the impact of Friedrich Nietzsche (1844–1900) (Antonio, 2001), especially his emphasis on the hero, on Weber's work on the need for individuals to stand up to the impact of bureaucracies and other structures of modern society.

The influence of Immanuel Kant on Weber and on German sociology generally shows that German sociology and Marxism grew from different philosophical roots. As we have seen, it was Hegel, not Kant, who was the important philosophical influence on Marxian theory. Whereas Hegel's philosophy led Marx and the Marxists to look for relations, conflicts, and contradictions, Kantian philosophy led at least some German sociologists to take a more static perspective. To Kant the world was a buzzing confusion of events that could never be known directly. The world could be known only through thought processes that filter, select, and categorize these events. The content of the real world was differentiated by Kant from the forms through which that content can be comprehended. The emphasis on these forms gave the work of those sociologists within the Kantian tradition a more static quality than that of the Marxists within the Hegelian tradition.

Weber's Theory 韦伯的理论

Whereas Karl Marx offered basically a theory of capitalism, Weber's work was fundamentally a theory of the process of rationalization (Brubaker, 1984; Kalberg, 1980, 1990, 1994). Weber was interested in the general issue of why institutions in the Western world had grown progressively more rational while powerful barriers seemed to prevent a similar development in the rest of the world.

Although rationality is used in many different ways in Weber's work, what interests us here is a process involving one of four types identified by Kalberg (1980, 1990, 1994; see also Brubaker, 1984; D. Levine, 1981a), *formal rationality*. Formal rationality involves, as was usually the case with Weber, a concern for the individual making choices of means and ends. However, in this case, that choice is made in reference to universally applied rules, regulations, and laws. These, in turn, are derived from various large-scale structures, especially bureaucracies and the economy. Weber developed his theories in the context of a large number of comparative historical studies of the West, China, India, and many other regions of the world. In those studies, he sought to delineate the factors that helped bring about or impede the development of rationalization.

Weber saw the bureaucracy (and the historical process of bureaucratization) as the classic example of rationalization, but rationalization is perhaps best illustrated today by the fast-food restaurant (Ritzer, 2004a). The fast-food restaurant is a formally rational system in which people (both workers and customers) are led to seek the most rational means to ends. The drive-through window, for example, is a rational means by which workers can dispense, and customers can obtain, food quickly and efficiently. Speed and efficiency are dictated by the fast-food restaurants and the rules and regulations by which they operate.

Weber embedded his discussion of the process of bureaucratization in a broader discussion of the political institution. He differentiated among three types of authority systems—traditional, charismatic, and rational-legal. Only in the modern Western world can a rational-legal authority system develop, and only within that system does one find the full-scale development of the modern bureaucracy. The rest of the world remains dominated by traditional or charismatic authority systems, which generally impede the development of a rational-legal authority system and modern bureaucracies. Briefly, *traditional* authority stems from a long-lasting system of beliefs. An example would be a leader who comes to power because his or her family or clan has always provided the group's leadership. A *charismatic* leader derives his or her authority from extraordinary abilities or characteristics, or more likely, simply from the followers' belief that the leader has such traits. Although these two types of authority are of historical importance, Weber believed that the trend in the West, and ultimately in the rest of the world, is toward systems of *rational-legal* authority (Bunzel, 2007). In such systems, authority is derived from rules legally and rationally enacted. Thus, the president of the United States derives his authority ultimately from the laws of society. The evolution of rational-legal authority, with its accompanying bureaucracies, is only one part of Weber's general argument on the rationalization of the Western world.

Weber also did detailed and sophisticated analyses of the rationalization of such phenomena as religion, law, the city, and even music. But we can illustrate Weber's mode of thinking with one other example—the rationalization of the economic institution. This discussion is couched in Weber's broader analysis of the relationship between religion and capitalism. In a wide-ranging historical study, Weber sought to understand why a rational economic system (capitalism) had developed in the West and why it had failed to develop in the rest of the world. Weber accorded a central role to religion in this process. At one level, he was engaged in a dialogue with the Marxists in an effort to show that, contrary to what many Marxists of the day believed, religion was not merely an epiphenomenon. Instead, it had played a key role in the rise of capitalism in the West and in its failure to develop elsewhere in the world. Weber argued that it was a distinctively rational religious system (Calvinism) that played the central role in the rise of capitalism in the West. In contrast, in the other parts of the world that he studied, Weber found more irrational religious systems (for example, Confucianism, Taoism, Hinduism), which helped inhibit the development of a rational economic system. However, in the end, these religions may have provided only temporary barriers, for the economic systems—indeed, the entire social structure—of these societies ultimately would become rationalized.

Although rationalization lies at the heart of Weberian theory, it is far from all there is to the theory. A key issue in the development of sociological theory is this: Why did Weber's theory prove more attractive to later sociological theorists than Marxian theory?

The Acceptance of Weber's Theory 对韦伯理论的认可

One reason is that Weber proved to be more acceptable politically. Instead of espousing Marxian radicalism, Weber was more of a liberal on some issues and a conservative on others (for example, the role of the state). Although he was a severe critic of many aspects of modern capitalist society and came to many of the same critical conclusions as did Marx, he was not one to propose radical solutions to problems (Heins, 1993). In fact, he felt that the radical reforms offered by many Marxists and other socialists would do more harm than good.

Later sociological theorists, especially Americans, saw their society under attack by Marxian theory. Largely conservative in orientation, they cast about for theoretical alternatives to Marxism. One of those who proved attractive was Max Weber. (Durkheim and Vilfredo Pareto were others.) After all, rationalization affected not only capitalist but also socialist societies. Indeed, from Weber's point of view, rationalization constituted an even greater problem in socialist societies than in capitalist societies.

Also in Weber's favor was the form in which he presented his judgments. He spent most of his life doing detailed historical studies, and his political conclusions were often made within the context of his research. Thus they usually sounded very scientific and academic. Marx, although he did much serious research, also wrote a good deal of explicitly polemical material. Even his more academic work is laced with acid political judgments. For example, in *Capital* (1867/1967), he described capitalists as "vampires" and "werewolves." Weber's more academic style helped make him more acceptable to later sociologists.

Another reason for Weber's greater acceptance was that he operated in a philosophical tradition that also helped shape the work of later sociologists. That is, Weber operated in the Kantian tradition, which meant that he tended to think in cause-and-effect terms. This kind of thinking was more acceptable to later sociologists, who were largely unfamiliar and uncomfortable with the dialectical logic that informed Marx's work.

Finally, Weber appeared to offer a much more rounded approach to the social world than did Marx. Whereas Marx appeared to be almost totally preoccupied with the economy, Weber was interested in a wide range of social phenomena. This diverse focus seemed to give later sociologists more to work with than the apparently more single-minded concerns of Marx.

Weber produced most of his major works in the late 1800s and early 1900s. Early in his career, Weber was identified more as a historian who was concerned with sociological issues, but in the early 1900s, his focus grew more sociological. Indeed, he became the dominant sociologist of his time in Germany. In 1910, he founded (with, among others, Georg Simmel, whom we discuss below) the German Sociological Society (Glatzer, 1998). His home in Heidelberg was an intellectual center not only for sociologists but also for scholars from many fields. Although his work was broadly influential in Germany, it was to become even more influential in the United States, especially after Talcott Parsons introduced Weber's ideas (and those of other European theorists, especially Durkheim) to a large American audience. Although Marx's ideas did not have a significant positive effect on American sociological theorists until the 1960s, Weber was already highly influential by the late 1930s.

Simmel's Theory 齐美尔的理论

Georg Simmel was Weber's contemporary and a cofounder of the German Socio-logical Society. Simmel was a somewhat atypical sociological theorist (Frisby, 1981; D. Levine, Carter, and Gorman, 1976a, 1976b). For one thing, he had an immediate and profound effect on the development of American sociological theory, whereas Marx and Weber were largely ignored for a number of years. Simmel's work helped shape the development of one of the early centers of American sociology—the University of Chicago—and its major theory, symbolic interactionism (Jaworski, 1995; 1997). The Chicago school and symbolic interactionism came, as we will see, to dominate American sociology in the 1920s and early 1930s (Bulmer, 1984). Simmel's ideas were influential at Chicago mainly because the dominant figures in the early years of Chicago, Albion Small and Robert Park, had been exposed to Simmel's theories in Berlin in the late 1800s. Park attended Simmel's lectures in 1899 and 1900, and Small carried on an extensive correspondence with Simmel during the 1890s. They were instrumental in bringing Simmel's ideas to students and faculty at Chicago, in translating some of his work, and in bringing it to the attention of a large-scale American audience (Frisby, 1984:29).

Another atypical aspect of Simmel's work is his level of analysis, or at least that level for which he became best known in America. Whereas Weber and Marx were preoccupied with large-scale issues like the rationalization of society and a capitalist economy, Simmel was best known for his work on smaller-scale issues, especially individual action and interaction. He became famous early for his thinking, derived from Kantian philosophy, on *forms* of interaction (for example, conflict) and *types* of interactants (for example, the stranger). Basically, Simmel saw that under-standing interaction among people was one of the major tasks of sociology. However, it was impossible to study the massive number of interactions in social life without some conceptual tools. This is where forms of interaction and types of interactants came in. Simmel felt that he could isolate a limited number of forms of interaction that could be found in a large number of social settings. Thus equipped, he could analyze and understand these different interaction settings. The development of a limited number of types of interactants could be similarly useful in explaining interaction settings. This work had a profound effect on symbolic interactionism, which, as the name suggests, was focally concerned with interaction. One of the ironies, how-ever, is that Simmel also was concerned with large-scale issues similar to those that obsessed Marx and Weber. However, this work was much less influential than his work on interaction, although there are contemporary signs of a growing interest in the large-scale aspects of Simmel's sociology.

It was partly Simmel's style in his work on interaction that made him accessible to early American sociological theorists. Although he wrote heavy tomes like those of Weber and Marx, he also wrote a set of deceptively simple essays on such interesting topics as poverty, the prostitute, the miser and the spendthrift, and the stranger. The brev-ity of such essays and the high interest level of the material made the dissemination of Simmel's ideas much easier. Unfortunately, the essays had the negative effect of obscur-ing Simmel's more massive works (for example, *Philosophy of Money,* translated in 1978;

GEORG SIMMEL

A Biographical Sketch

Georg Simmel was born in the heart of Berlin on March 1, 1858. He studied a wide range of subjects at the University of Berlin. However, his first effort to produce a dissertation was rejected, and one of his professors remarked, "We would do him a great service if we do not encourage him further in this direction" (Frisby, 1984:23). Despite this, Simmel persevered and received his doctorate in philosophy in 1881. He remained at the university in a teaching capacity until 1914, although he occupied a relatively unimportant position as privatdozent from 1885 to 1900. In the latter position, Simmel served as an unpaid lecturer whose livelihood was dependent on student fees. Despite his marginality, Simmel did rather well in this position, largely because he was an excellent lecturer and attracted large numbers of (paying) students (Frisby, 1981:17; Salomon, 1963/1997). His style was so popular that even cultured members of Berlin society were drawn to his lectures, which became public events.

Simmel's marginality is paralleled by the fact that he was a somewhat contradictory and therefore bewildering person:

> If we put together the testimonials left by relatives, friends, students, contemporaries, we find a number of sometimes contradictory indications concerning Georg Simmel. He is depicted by some as being tall and slender, by others as being short and as bearing a forlorn expression. His appearance is reported to be unattractive, typically Jewish, but also intensely intellectual and noble. He is reported to be hard-working, but also humorous and overarticulate as a lecturer. Finally we hear that he was intellectually brilliant [Lukács, 1991:145], friendly, well-disposed—but also that inside he was irrational, opaque, and wild.
>
> (Schnabel, cited in Poggi, 1993:55)

Simmel wrote innumerable articles ("The Metropolis and Mental Life" [1903/1971]) and books (*The Philosophy of Money* [1907/1978]). He was well known in German academic circles and even had an international following, especially in the United States, where his work was of great significance in the

see Poggi, 1993), which were potentially as significant to sociology. Nevertheless, it was partly through the short and clever essays that Simmel had a much more significant effect on early American sociological theory than either Marx or Weber did.

We should not leave Simmel without saying something about *Philosophy of Money*, (1907/1978), because its English translation made Simmel's work attractive to a whole new set of theorists interested in culture and society. Although a macro orientation is birth of sociology. Finally, in 1900, Simmel received official recognition, a purely honorary title at the University of Berlin, which did not give him full academic status. Simmel tried to obtain many academic positions, but he failed in spite of the support of such scholars as Max Weber.

One of the reasons for Simmel's failure was that he was a Jew in a nineteenth-century Germany rife with anti-Semitism (Kasler, 1985). Thus, in a report on Simmel written to a minister of education, Simmel was described as "an Israelite through and through, in his external appearance, in his bearing and in his mode of thought" (Frisby, 1981:25). Another reason was the kind of work that he did. Many of his articles appeared in newspapers and magazines; they were written for an audience more general than simply academic sociologists (Ramm stedt, 1991). In addition, because he did not hold a regular academic appointment, he was forced to earn his living through public lectures. Simmel's audience, both for his writings and his lectures, was more the intellectual public than professional sociologists, and this tended to lead to derisive judgments from fellow professionals. For example, one of his contemporaries damned him because "his influence remained . . . upon the general atmosphere and affected, above all, the higher levels of journalism" (Troeltsch, cited in Frisby, 1981:13). Simmel's personal failures can also be linked to the low esteem that German academicians of the day had for sociology.

In 1914 Simmel finally obtained a regular academic appointment at a minor university (Strasbourg), but he once again felt estranged. On the one hand, he regretted leaving his audience of Berlin intellectuals. Thus his wife wrote to Max Weber's wife: "Georg has taken leave of the auditorium very badly. . . . The students were very affectionate and sympathetic. . . . It was a departure at the full height of life" (Frisby, 1981:29). On the other hand, Simmel did not feel a part of the life of his new university. Thus, he wrote to Mrs. Weber: "There is hardly anything to report from us. We live . . . a cloistered, closed-off, indifferent, desolate external existence. Academic activity is 0, the people . . . alien and inwardly hostile" (Frisby, 1981:32).

World War I started soon after Simmel's appointment at Strasbourg; lecture halls were turned into military hospitals, and students went off to war. Thus, Simmel remained a marginal figure in German academia until his death in 1918. He never did have a normal academic career. Nevertheless, Simmel attracted a large academic following in his day, and his fame as a scholar has, if anything, grown over the years.

clearer in *Philosophy of Money*, it always existed in Simmel's work. For example, it is clear in his famous work on the dyad and the triad. Simmel thought that some crucial sociological developments take place when a two-person group (or *dyad*) is transformed into a *triad* by the addition of a third party. Social possibilities emerge that simply could not exist in a dyad. For example, in a triad, one of the members can become an arbitrator or mediator of the differences between the other two. More important, two of the

SIGMUND FREUD

A Biographical Sketch

Another leading figure in German social science in the late 1800s and early 1900s was Sigmund Freud. Although he was not a sociologist, Freud influenced the work of many sociologists (for example, Talcott Parsons and Norbert Elias) and continues to be of relevance to social theorists (Chodorow, 1990; A. Elliott, 1992; Kaye, 1991, 2003; Kurzweil, 1995; Leledaki, 2005; Prager, 2005; Movahedi, 2007).

Sigmund Freud was born in the Austro-Hungarian city of Freiberg on May 6, 1856. In 1859, his family moved to Vienna, and in 1873, Freud entered the medical school at the University of Vienna. Freud was more interested in science than in medicine and took a position in a physiology laboratory. He completed his degree in medicine, and after leaving the laboratory in 1882, he worked in a hospital and then set up a private medical practice with a specialty in nervous diseases.

Freud at first used hypnosis in an effort to deal with a type of neurosis known as hysteria. He had learned the technique in Paris from Jean Martin Charcot in 1885. Later he adopted a technique, pioneered by a fellow Viennese physician, Joseph Breuer, in which hysterical symptoms disappeared when the patient talked through the circumstances in which the symptoms first arose. By 1895, Freud had published a book with Breuer with a series of revolutionary implications: that the causes of neuroses like hysteria were psychological (not physiological, as had been believed) and that the therapy involved talking through the original causes. Thus was born the practical and theoretical field of psychoanalysis. Freud began to part company with Breuer as he came to see sexual factors, or more generally the libido, at the root of neuroses. Over the next several years, Freud refined his therapeutic techniques and wrote a great deal about his new ideas.

By 1902, Freud began to gather a number of disciples around him, and they met weekly at his house. By 1903 or 1904, others (like Carl Jung) began to use Freud's ideas in their psychiatric practices. In 1908, the first Psychoanalytic Congress was held, and the next year a periodical for disseminating psychoanalytic knowledge was formed. As quickly as it had formed, the new field of psychoanalysis became splintered as Freud broke with people like Jung and they went off to develop their own ideas and found their own groups. World War I slowed the development of psychoanalysis, but psychoanalysis expanded and developed greatly in the 1920s. With the rise of Nazism, the center of psychoanalysis shifted to the United States, where it remains to this day. But Freud remained in Vienna until the Nazis took over in 1938, despite the fact that he was Jewish and the Nazis had burned his books as early as 1933. On June 4, 1938, only after a ransom had been paid and President Roosevelt had interceded, Sigmund Freud left Vienna. Freud had suffered from cancer of the jaw since 1923, and he died in London on September 23, 1939.

members can band together and dominate the other member. This represents, on a small scale, what can happen with the emergence of large-scale structures that become separate from individuals and begin to dominate them.

This theme lies at the base of *Philosophy of Money*. Simmel was concerned primarily with the emergence in the modern world of a monetary economy that becomes separate from the individual and predominant. This theme, in turn, is part of an even broader and more pervasive one in Simmel's work—the domination of the culture as a whole over the individual. As Simmel saw it, in the modern world, the larger culture and all its various components (including the monetary economy) expand, and as they expand, the importance of the individual decreases. Thus, for example, as the industrial technology associated with a modern economy expands and grows more sophisticated, the skills and abilities of the individual worker grow progressively less important. In the end, the worker is confronted with an industrial machine over which he or she can exert little, if any, control. More generally, Simmel thought that in the modern world, the expansion of the larger culture leads to the growing insignificance of the individual.

Although sociologists have become increasingly attuned to the broader implications of Simmel's work, his early influence was primarily through his studies of small-scale social phenomena, such as the forms of interaction and types of interactants.

The Origins of British Sociology 英国社会学的起源

We have been examining the development of sociology in France (Comte, Durkheim) and Germany (Marx, Weber, and Simmel). We turn now to the parallel development of sociology in England. As we will see, continental European ideas had their impact on early British sociology, but native influences were more important.

政治经济学、改良主义以及社会进化
Political Economy, Ameliorism, and Social Evolution

Philip Abrams (1968) contended that British sociology was shaped in the nineteenth century by three often conflicting sources—political economy, ameliorism, and social evolution.[7] Thus when the Sociological Society of London was founded in 1903, there were strong differences over the definition of *sociology*. However, there were few who doubted the view that sociology could be a science. It was the differences that gave British sociology its distinctive character, and we will look at each of them briefly.

Political Economy 政治经济学

We have already touched on political economy, which was a theory of industrial and capitalist society traceable in part to the work of Adam Smith (1723–1790).[8] As we saw, political economy had a profound effect on Karl Marx. Marx studied political

---

[7] For later developments in British sociology, see Abrams et al. (1981).
[8] Smith is usually included as a leading member of the Scottish Enlightenment (Strydom, 2005; Chitnis, 1976) and as one of the Scottish Moralists (L. Schneider, 1967:xi), who were establishing a basis for sociology.

economy closely, and he was critical of it. But that was not the direction taken by British economists and sociologists. They tended to accept Smith's idea that there was an "invisible hand" that shaped the market for labor and goods. The market was seen as an independent reality that stood above individuals and controlled their behavior. The British sociologists, like the political economists and unlike Marx, saw the market as a positive force, as a source of order, harmony, and integration in society. Because they saw the market, and more generally society, in a positive light, the task of the sociologist was not to criticize society but simply to gather data on the laws by which it operated. The goal was to provide the government with the facts it needed to understand the way the system worked and to direct its workings wisely.

The emphasis was on facts, but which facts? Whereas Marx, Weber, Durkheim, and Comte looked to the structures of society for their basic facts, the British thinkers tended to focus on the individuals who made up those structures. In dealing with large-scale structures, they tended to collect individual-level data and then combine them to form a collective portrait. In the mid-1800s it was the statisticians who dominated British social science, and this kind of data collection was deemed to be the major task of sociology. The objective was the accumulation of "pure" facts without theorizing or philosophizing. These empirical sociologists were detached from the concerns of social theorists. Instead of general theorizing, the "emphasis settled on the business of producing more exact indicators, better methods of classification and data collection, improved life tables, higher levels of comparability between discrete bodies of data, and the like" (Abrams, 1968:18).

It was almost in spite of themselves that these statistically oriented sociologists came to see some limitations in their approach. A few began to feel the need for broader theorizing. To them, a problem such as poverty pointed to failings in the market system as well as in the society as a whole. But most, focused as they were on individuals, did not question the larger system; they turned instead to more detailed field studies and to the development of more complicated and more exact statistical techniques. To them, the source of the problem had to lie in inadequate research methods, not in the system as a whole. As Philip Abrams noted, "Focusing persistently on the distribution of individual circumstances, the statisticians found it hard to break through to a perception of poverty as a product of social structure. . . . They did not and probably could not achieve the concept of structural victimization" (1968:27). In addition to their theoretical and methodological commitments to the study of individuals, the statisticians worked too closely with government policy makers to arrive at the conclusion that the larger political and economic system was the problem.

Ameliorism 改良主义

Related to, but separable from, political economy was the second defining characteristic of British sociology—*ameliorism,* or a desire to solve social problems by reforming individuals. Although British scholars began to recognize that there were problems in society (for example, poverty), they still believed in that society and wanted to preserve it. They desired to forestall violence and revolution and to reform the system so that it could continue essentially as it was. Above all, they wanted to prevent the coming of a socialist society. Thus, like French sociology and some branches of German sociology, British sociology was conservatively oriented.

Because the British sociologists could not, or would not, trace the source of problems such as poverty to the society as a whole, the source had to lie within the individuals themselves. This was an early form of what William Ryan (1971) later called "blaming the victim." Much attention was devoted to a long series of individual problems—"ignorance, spiritual destitution, impurity, bad sanitation, pauperism, crime, and intemperance—above all intemperance" (Abrams, 1968:39). Clearly, there was a tendency to look for a simple cause for all social ills, and the one that suggested itself before all others was alcoholism. What made this perfect to the ameliorist was that this was an individual pathology, not a social pathology. The ameliorists lacked a theory of social structure, a theory of the social causes of such individual problems.

Social Evolution 社会进化论

But a stronger sense of social structure was lurking below the surface of British sociology, and it burst through in the latter part of the nineteenth century with the growth of interest in social evolution (Maryanski, 2005; Sanderson, 2001). One important influence was the work of Auguste Comte, part of which had been translated into English in the 1850s by Harriet Martineau (Hoecker-Drysdale, 2000). Although Comte's work did not inspire immediate interest, by the last quarter of the century, a number of thinkers had been attracted to it and to its concern for the larger structures of society, its scientific (positivistic) orientation, its comparative orientation, and its evolutionary theory. However, a number of British thinkers sharpened their own conception of the world in opposition to some of the excesses of Comtian theory (for example, the tendency to elevate sociology to the status of a religion).

In Abrams's view, the real importance of Comte lay in his providing one of the bases on which opposition could be mounted against the "oppressive genius of Herbert Spencer" (Abrams, 1968:58). In both a positive and a negative sense, Spencer was a dominant figure in British sociological theory, especially evolutionary theory (J. H. Turner, 2000, 2007a).

Herbert Spencer (1820–1903) 斯宾塞（1820—1903）

In attempting to understand Spencer's ideas (J. H. Turner, 2005; Haines, 2005), it is useful to compare and contrast them with Comtian theory.

Spencer and Comte 斯宾塞和孔德

Spencer is often categorized with Comte in terms of their influence on the development of sociological theory (J. H. Turner, 2001a), but there are some important differences between them. For example, it is more difficult to categorize Spencer as a conservative. In fact, in his early years, Spencer is better seen as a political liberal,

HERBERT SPENCER

A Biographical Sketch

Herbert Spencer was born in Derby, England, on April 27, 1820. He was not schooled in the arts and humanities, but rather in technical and utilitarian matters. In 1837 he began work as a civil engineer for a railway, an occupation he held until 1846. During this period, Spencer continued to study on his own and began to publish scientific and political works.

In 1848 Spencer was appointed an editor of *The Economist*, and his intellectual ideas began to solidify. By 1850, he had completed his first major work, *Social Statics*. During the writing of this work, Spencer first began to experience insomnia, and over the years, his mental and physical problems mounted. He was to suffer a series of nervous breakdowns throughout the rest of his life.

In 1853 Spencer received an inheritance that allowed him to quit his job and live for the rest of his life as a gentleman scholar. He never earned a university degree or held an academic position. As he grew more isolated, and physical and mental illness mounted, Spencer's productivity as a scholar increased. Eventually, Spencer began to achieve not only fame within England but also an international reputation. As Richard Hofstadter put it: "In the three decades after the Civil War it was impossible to be active in any field of intellectual work without mastering Spencer" (1959:33). Among his supporters was the important industrialist Andrew Carnegie, who wrote the following to Spencer during the latter's fatal illness of 1903:

> Dear Master Teacher . . . you come to me every day in thought, and the everlasting "why" intrudes—Why lies he? Why must he go? . . . The world jogs on unconscious of its greatest mind. . . . But it will wake some day to its teachings and decree Spencer's place is with the greatest.
>
> (Carnegie, cited in Peel, 1971:2)

and he retained elements of liberalism throughout his life. However, it is also true that Spencer grew more conservative during the course of his life and that his basic influence, as was true of Comte, was conservative.

One of his liberal views, which coexisted rather uncomfortably with his conservatism, was his acceptance of a laissez-faire doctrine. He felt that the state should not intervene in individual affairs except in the rather passive function of protecting people. This meant that Spencer, unlike Comte, was not interested in social reforms; he wanted social life to evolve free of external control.

This difference points to Spencer as a *Social Darwinist* (Weiler, 2007a; G. Jones, 1980). As such, he held the evolutionary view that the world was growing progressively

But that was not to be Spencer's fate.

One of Spencer's most interesting characteristics, one that was ultimately to be the cause of his intellectual undoing, was his unwillingness to read the work of other people. In this, he resembled another early giant of sociology, Auguste Comte, who practiced "cerebral hygiene." Of the need to read the works of others, Spencer said: "All my life I have been a thinker and not a reader, being able to say with Hobbes that 'if I had read as much as other men I would have known as little'" (Wiltshire, 1978:67). A friend asked Spencer's opinion of a book, and "his reply was that on looking into the book he saw that its fundamental assumption was erroneous, and therefore did not care to read it" (Wiltshire, 1978:67). One author wrote of Spencer's "incomprehensible way of absorbing knowledge through the powers of his skin . . . he never seemed to read books" (Wiltshire, 1978:67).

If he didn't read the work of other scholars, where, then, did Spencer's ideas and insights come from? According to Spencer, they emerged involuntarily and intuitively from his mind. He said that his ideas emerged "little by little, in unobtrusive ways, without conscious intention or appreciable effort" (Wiltshire, 1978:66). Such intuition was deemed by Spencer to be far more effective than careful study and thought: "A solution reached in the way described is more likely to be true than one reached in the pursuance of a determined effort [which] causes perversion of thought" (Wiltshire, 1978:66).

Spencer suffered because of his unwillingness to read seriously the works of other people. In fact, if he read other work, it was often only to find confirmation for his own, independently created ideas. He ignored those ideas that did not agree with his. Thus, his contemporary, Charles Darwin, said of Spencer: "If he had trained himself to observe more, even at the expense of . . . some loss of thinking power, he would have been a wonderful man" (Wiltshire, 1978:70). Spencer's disregard for the rules of scholarship led him to a series of outrageous ideas and unsubstantiated assertions about the evolution of the world. For these reasons, sociologists in the twentieth century came to reject Spencer's work and to substitute for it careful scholarship and empirical research.

Spencer died on December 8, 1903.

better. Therefore, it should be left alone; outside interference could only worsen the situation. He adopted the view that social institutions, like plants and animals, adapted progressively and positively to their social environment. He also accepted the Darwinian view that a process of natural selection, "survival of the fittest," occurred in the social world. That is, if unimpeded by external intervention, people who were "fit" would survive and proliferate whereas the "unfit" eventually would die out. (Interestingly, it was Spencer who coined the phrase "survival of the fittest" several years before Charles Darwin's work on natural selection.) Another difference was that Spencer emphasized the individual, whereas Comte focused on larger units such as the family.

Comte and Spencer shared with Durkheim and others a commitment to a science of sociology (Haines, 1992), which was a very attractive perspective to early theorists. Another influence of Spencer's work, shared with both Comte and Durkheim, was his tendency to see society as an *organism*. In this, Spencer borrowed his perspective and concepts from biology. He was concerned with the overall structure of society, the interrelationship of the *parts* of society, and the *functions* of the parts for each other as well as for the system as a whole.

Most important, Spencer, like Comte, had an evolutionary conception of historical development (Maryanski, 2005). However, Spencer was critical of Comte's evolutionary theory on several grounds. Specifically, he rejected Comte's law of the three stages. He argued that Comte was content to deal with evolution in the realm of ideas, in terms of intellectual development. Spencer, however, sought to develop an evolutionary theory in the real, material world.

Evolutionary Theory 进化论

It is possible to identify at least two major evolutionary perspectives in Spencer's work (Haines, 1988; Perrin, 1976).

The first of these theories relates primarily to the increasing size of society. Society grows through both the multiplication of individuals and the union of groups (compounding). The increasing size of society brings with it larger and more differentiated social structures, as well as the increasing differentiation of the functions they perform. In addition to their growth in size, societies evolve through compounding, that is, by unifying more and more adjoining groups. Thus, Spencer talks of the evolutionary movement from simple to compound, doubly-compound, and trebly-compound societies.

Spencer also offers a theory of evolution from *militant* to *industrial* societies. Earlier, militant societies are defined by being structured for offensive and defensive warfare. While Spencer was critical of warfare, he felt that in an earlier stage it was functional in bringing societies together (for example, through military conquest) and in creating the larger aggregates of people necessary for the development of industrial society. However, with the emergence of industrial society, warfare ceases to be functional and serves to impede further evolution. Industrial society is based on friendship, altruism, elaborate specialization, recognition for achievements rather than the characteristics one is born with, and voluntary cooperation among highly disciplined individuals. Such a society is held together by voluntary contractual relations and, more important, by a strong common morality. The government's role is restricted and focuses only on what people ought not to do. Obviously, modern industrial societies are less warlike than their militant predecessors. Although Spencer sees a general evolution in the direction of industrial societies, he also recognizes that it is possible that there will be periodic regressions to warfare and more militant societies.

In his ethical and political writings, Spencer offered other ideas on the evolution of society. For one thing, he saw society as progressing toward an ideal, or perfect, moral state. For another, he argued that the fittest societies survive and that unfit societies should be permitted to die off. The result of this process is adaptive upgrading for the world as a whole.

Thus Spencer offered a rich and complicated set of ideas on social evolution. His ideas first enjoyed great success, then were rejected for many years, and more recently have been revived with the rise of neoevolutionary sociological theories (Buttel, 1990).

The Reaction against Spencer in Britain 英国国内对斯宾塞的抵制

Despite his emphasis on the individual, Spencer was best known for his large-scale theory of social evolution. In this, he stood in stark contrast to the sociology that preceded him in Britain. However, the reaction against Spencer was based more on the threat that his idea of survival of the fittest posed to the ameliorism so dear to most early British sociologists. Although Spencer later repudiated some of his more outrageous ideas, he did argue for a survival-of-the-fittest philosophy and against government intervention and social reform:

> Fostering the good-for-nothing at the expense of the good, is an extreme cruelty. It is a deliberate stirring-up of miseries for future generations. There is no greater curse to posterity than that of bequeathing to them an increasing population of imbeciles and idlers and criminals. . . . The whole effort of nature is to get rid of such, to clear the world of them, and make room for better. . . . If they are not sufficiently complete to live, they die, and it is best they should die.
>
> (Spencer, cited in Abrams, 1968:74)

Such sentiments were clearly at odds with the ameliorative orientation of the British reformer-sociologists.

意大利早期社会学的重要人物

The Key Figure in Early Italian Sociology

We close this sketch of early, primarily conservative, European sociological theory with a brief mention of one Italian sociologist, Vilfredo Pareto (1848–1923). Pareto was influential in his time, but his contemporary relevance is minimal (for one exception, see Powers, 1986). There was a brief outburst of interest in Pareto's (1935) work in the 1930s, when the major American theorist, Talcott Parsons, devoted as much attention to him as he gave to Weber and Durkheim. However, in recent years, except for a few of his major concepts, Pareto also has receded in importance and contemporary relevance (Femia, 1995).

Zeitlin argued that Pareto developed his "major ideas as a refutation of Marx" (1996:171). In fact, Pareto was rejecting not only Marx but also a good portion of Enlightenment philosophy. For example, whereas the Enlightenment philosophers emphasized rationality, Pareto emphasized the role of nonrational factors such as human instincts (Mozetič and Weiler, 2007). This emphasis also was tied to his rejection of Marxian theory. That is, because nonrational, instinctual factors were so important and so unchanging, it was unrealistic to hope to achieve dramatic social changes with an economic revolution.

Pareto also developed a theory of social change that stood in stark contrast to Marxian theory. Whereas Marx's theory focused on the role of the masses, Pareto offered an elite theory of social change, which held that society inevitably is dominated by a small elite that operates on the basis of enlightened self-interest (Adams, 2005). It rules over the masses of people, who are dominated by nonrational forces. Because they lack rational capacities, the masses, in Pareto's system, are unlikely to be a revolutionary force. Social change occurs when the elite begins to degenerate and is replaced by a new elite derived from the nongoverning elite or higher elements of the masses. Once the new elite is in power, the process begins anew. Thus we have a cyclical theory of social change instead of the directional theories offered by Marx, Comte, Spencer, and others. In addition, Pareto's theory of change largely ignores the plight of the masses. Elites come and go, but the lot of the masses remains the same.

This theory, however, was not Pareto's lasting contribution to sociology. That lay in his scientific conception of sociology and the social world: "My wish is to construct a system of sociology on the model of celestial mechanics [astronomy], physics, chemistry" (cited in Hook, 1965:57). Briefly, Pareto conceived of society as a system in equilibrium, a whole consisting of interdependent parts. A change in one part was seen as leading to changes in other parts of the system. Pareto's systemic conception of society was the most important reason Parsons devoted so much attention to Pareto's work in his 1937 book, *The Structure of Social Action*, and it was Pareto's most important influence on Parsons's thinking. Fused with similar views held by those who had an organic image of society (Comte, Durkheim, and Spencer, for example), Pareto's theory played a central role in the development of Parsons's theory and, more generally, in structural functionalism.

Although few modern sociologists now read Pareto's work, it can be seen as a rejection of the Enlightenment and of Marxism and as offering an elite theory of social change that stands in opposition to the Marxian perspective.

Turn-of-the-Century Developments in European Marxism 世纪之交马克思主义在欧洲的发展

While many nineteenth-century sociologists were developing their theories in opposition to Marx, there was a simultaneous effort by a number of Marxists to clarify and extend Marxian theory (Beilharz, 2005f; Steinmetz, 2007). Between roughly 1875 and 1925, there was little overlap between Marxism and sociology. (Weber is an exception to this.) The two schools of thought were developing in parallel fashion with little or no interchange between them.

After the death of Marx, Marxian theory was first dominated by those who saw in his theory scientific and economic determinism (Bakker, 2007a). Wallerstein calls this the era of "orthodox Marxism" (1986:1301). Friedrich Engels, Marx's benefactor and collaborator, lived on after Marx's death and can be seen as the first exponent of such a perspective. Basically, this view was that Marx's scientific theory had uncovered the economic laws that ruled the capitalist world. Such laws pointed to the inevitable collapse of the capitalist system. Early Marxian thinkers, like Karl Kautsky, sought to gain a better understanding of the operation of these laws. There were several problems with this perspective. For one thing, it seemed to rule out political action, a cornerstone of Marx's position. That is, there seemed no need for individuals, especially workers, to do anything. In that the system was inevitably crumbling, all they had to do was sit back and wait for its demise. On a theoretical level, deterministic Marxism seemed to rule out the dialectical relationship between individuals and larger social structures.

These problems led to a reaction among Marxian theorists and to the development of *"Hegelian Marxism"* in the early 1900s. The Hegelian Marxists refused to reduce Marxism to a scientific theory that ignored individual thought and action. They are labeled Hegelian Marxists because they sought to combine Hegel's interest in consciousness (which some, including the author of this text, view Marx as sharing) with the determinists' interest in the economic structures of society. The Hegelian theorists were significant for both theoretical and practical reasons. Theoretically, they reinstated the importance of the individual, consciousness, and the relationship between thought and action. Practically, they emphasized the importance of individual action in bringing about a social revolution.

The major exponent of this point of view was Georg Lukács (Markus, 2005; Fischer, 1984). According to Martin Jay, Lukács was "the founding father of Western Marxism" and his work *History and Class Consciousness* (1922/1968) is "generally acknowledged as the charter document of Hegelian Marxism" (1984:84). Lukács had begun in the early 1900s to integrate Marxism with sociology (in particular, Weberian and Simmelian theory). This integration was soon to accelerate with the development of critical theory in the 1920s and 1930s.

Summary 总结

This chapter sketches the early history of sociological theory. The first section deals with the various social forces involved in the development of sociological theory. Although there were many such influences, we focus on how political revolution, the Industrial Revolution, and the rise of capitalism, socialism, feminism, urbanization, religious change, and the growth of science affected sociological theory. The second part of the chapter examines the influence of intellectual forces on the rise of sociological theory in various countries. We begin with France and the role played by the Enlightenment, stressing the conservative and romantic reaction to it. It is out of this interplay that French sociological theory developed. In this context, we examine the major figures in the early years of French sociology—Alexis de Tocqueville, Claude Henri Saint-Simon, Auguste Comte, and Emile Durkheim.

Next we turn to Germany and the role played by Karl Marx in the development of sociology in that country. We discuss the parallel development of Marxian theory and sociological theory and the ways in which Marxian theory influenced sociology, both positively and negatively. We begin with the roots of Marxian theory in Hegelianism, materialism, and political economy. Marx's theory itself is touched upon briefly. The discussion then shifts to the roots of German sociology. Max Weber's work is examined to show the diverse sources of German sociology. Also discussed are some of the reasons why Weber's theory proved more acceptable to later sociologists than did Marx's ideas. This section closes with a brief discussion of Georg Simmel's work.

The rise of sociological theory in Britain is considered next. The major sources of British sociology were political economy, ameliorism, and social evolution. In this context, we touch on the work of Herbert Spencer as well as on some of the controversy that surrounded it.

This chapter closes with a brief discussion of Italian sociological theory, in particular the work of Vilfredo Pareto, and the turn-of-the-century developments in European Marxian theory, primarily economic determinism and Hegelian Marxism.

A Historical Sketch of Sociological Theory: The Later Years
第2章 社会学理论的历史概要：后期阶段

Chapter Outline

Early American Sociological Theory

Women in Early Sociology

W. E. B. Du Bois and Race Theory

Sociological Theory to Midcentury

Sociological Theory from Midcentury

Late-Twentieth-Century Developments in Sociological Theory

Theories of Modernity and Postmodernity

Theories to Watch in the Early Twenty-first Century

It is difficult to give a precise date for the founding of sociology in the United States. A course in social problems was taught at Oberlin as early as 1858, Comte's term *sociology* was used by George Fitzhugh in 1854, and William Graham Sumner taught social science courses at Yale beginning in 1873. During the 1880s, courses specifically bearing the title "Sociology" began to appear. The first department with *sociology* in its name was founded at the University of Kansas in 1889. In 1892, Albion Small moved to the University of Chicago and set up the new department of sociology. The Chicago department became the first important center of American sociology in general and of sociological theory in particular (F. H. Matthews, 1977).

Early American Sociological Theory 美国早期社会学理论

Politics 政治

Schwendinger and Schwendinger (1974) argue that the early American sociologists are best described as political liberals and not, as was true of most early European theorists, as conservatives. The liberalism characteristic of early American sociology had basically two elements. First, it operated with a belief in the freedom and welfare of the individual. In this belief, it was influenced far more by Spencer's orientation than by Comte's more collective position. Second, many sociologists associated with this orientation adopted an evolutionary view of social progress (W. F. Fine, 1979). However, they were split over how best to bring about this progress. Some argued that steps should be taken by the government to aid social reform, whereas others pushed a laissez-faire doctrine, arguing that the various components of society should be left to solve their own problems.

Liberalism, taken to its extreme, comes very close to conservatism. The belief in social progress—in reform or a laissez-faire doctrine—and the belief in the importance of the individual both lead to positions supportive of the system as a whole. The overriding belief is that the social system works or can be reformed to work. There is little criticism of the system as a whole; in the American case this means, in particular, that there is little questioning of capitalism. Instead of imminent class struggle, the early sociologists saw a future of class harmony and class cooperation. Ultimately this meant that early American sociological theory helped rationalize exploitation, domestic and international imperialism, and social inequality (Schwendinger and Schwendinger, 1974). In the end, the political liberalism of the early sociologists had enormously conservative implications.

社会变迁和知识趋势
Social Change and Intellectual Currents

In their analyses of the founding of American sociological theory, Roscoe Hinkle (1980) and Ellsworth Fuhrman (1980) outline several basic contexts from which that body of theory emerged. Of utmost importance are the social changes that occurred in American society after the Civil War (Bramson, 1961). In Chapter 1, we discussed an array of factors involved in the development of European sociological theory; several of these factors (such as industrialization and urbanization) were also intimately involved in the development of theory in America. In Fuhrman's view, the early American sociologists saw the positive possibilities of industrialization, but they also were well aware of its dangers. Although these early sociologists were attracted to the ideas generated by the labor movement and socialist groups about dealing with the dangers of industrialization, they were not in favor of radically overhauling society.

Arthur Vidich and Stanford Lyman (1985) make a strong case for the influence of Christianity, especially Protestantism, on the founding of American sociology. American sociologists retained the Protestant interest in saving the world and merely substituted one language (science) for another (religion). "From 1854, when the first works in sociology appeared in the United States, until the outbreak of World War I, sociology was a moral and intellectual response to the problems of American life and thought, institutions, and creeds" (Vidich and Lyman, 1985:1). Sociologists sought to define, study, and help solve these social problems. While the clergyman worked within religion to help improve it and people's lot within it, the sociologist did the same thing within society. Given their religious roots and the religious parallels, the vast majority of sociologists did not challenge the basic legitimacy of society.

Another major factor in the founding of American sociology discussed by both Hinkle and Fuhrman is the simultaneous emergence in America, in the late 1800s, of academic professions (including sociology) and the modern university system. In Europe, in contrast, the university system was already well established *before* the emergence of sociology. Although sociology had a difficult time becoming established in Europe, it had easier going in the more fluid setting of the new American university system.

Another characteristic of early American sociology (as well as other social science disciplines) was its turn away from a historical perspective and in the direction of a positivistic, or "scientistic," orientation. As Dorothy Ross puts it, "The desire to achieve universalistic abstraction and quantitative methods turned American social scientists away from interpretive models available in history and cultural anthropology, and from the generalizing and interpretive model offered by Max Weber" (1991:473). Instead of interpreting long-term historical changes, sociology had turned in the direction of scientifically studying short-term processes.

Still another factor was the impact of established European theory on American sociological theory. European theorists largely created sociological theory, and the Americans were able to rely on this groundwork. The Europeans most important to the Americans were Spencer and Comte. Simmel was of some importance in the early years, but the influence of Durkheim, Weber, and Marx was not to have a dramatic effect for a number of years. The history of Herbert Spencer's ideas provides an interesting and informative illustration of the impact of early European theory on American sociology.

斯宾塞对社会学的影响
Herbert Spencer's Influence on Sociology

Why were Spencer's ideas so much more influential in the early years of American sociology than those of Comte, Durkheim, Marx, and Weber? Hofstadter (1959) offered several explanations. To take the easiest first, Spencer wrote in English, whereas the others did not. In addition, Spencer wrote in nontechnical terms, making his work broadly accessible. Indeed, some have argued that the lack of technicality is traceable to Spencer's *not* being a very sophisticated scholar. But there are other, more important reasons for Spencer's broad appeal. He offered a scientific orientation that was attractive to an audience that was becoming enamored of science and its technological products. He offered a comprehensive theory that seemed to deal with the entire sweep of human history. The breadth of his ideas, as well as the voluminous work he produced, allowed his theory to be many different things to many different people. Finally, and perhaps most important, his theory was soothing and reassuring to a society undergoing the wrenching process of industrialization—society was, according to Spencer, steadily moving in the direction of greater and greater progress.

Spencer's most famous American disciple was William Graham Sumner, who accepted and expanded upon many of Spencer's Social Darwinist ideas. Spencer also influenced other early American sociologists, among them Lester Ward, Charles Horton Cooley, E. A. Ross, and Robert Park.

Spencer
(1820–1903)

Lévi-Strauss
(1908–   )

Social Darwinism
Sumner
(1840–1910)
Ward
(1841–1913)

Durkheim
(1858–1917)

Du Bois
(1868–1963)

Skinner
(1904–1990)

Sorokin
(1889–1968)

Parsons
(1902–1979)

Weber
(1864–1920)

Mannheim
(1893–1947)

Marx
(1818–1883)

Freud
(1858–1939)

Veblen
(1857–1929)

Critical School
Horkheimer
(1895–1973)

*Economic
Determinism*
Kautsky
(1854–1938)

*Hegelian
Marxism*
Lukács
(1885–1971)

Adorno
(1903–1969)

Husserl
(1859–1938)

Schutz
(1899–1959)

Simmel
(1858–1918)

Small
(1854–1926)
Park
(1864–1944)

Sartre
(1905–1980)

*Symbolic
Interactionism*
Blumer
(1900–1987)
M. Kuhn
(1911–1963)

Mead
(1863–1931)
Cooley
(1864–1929)

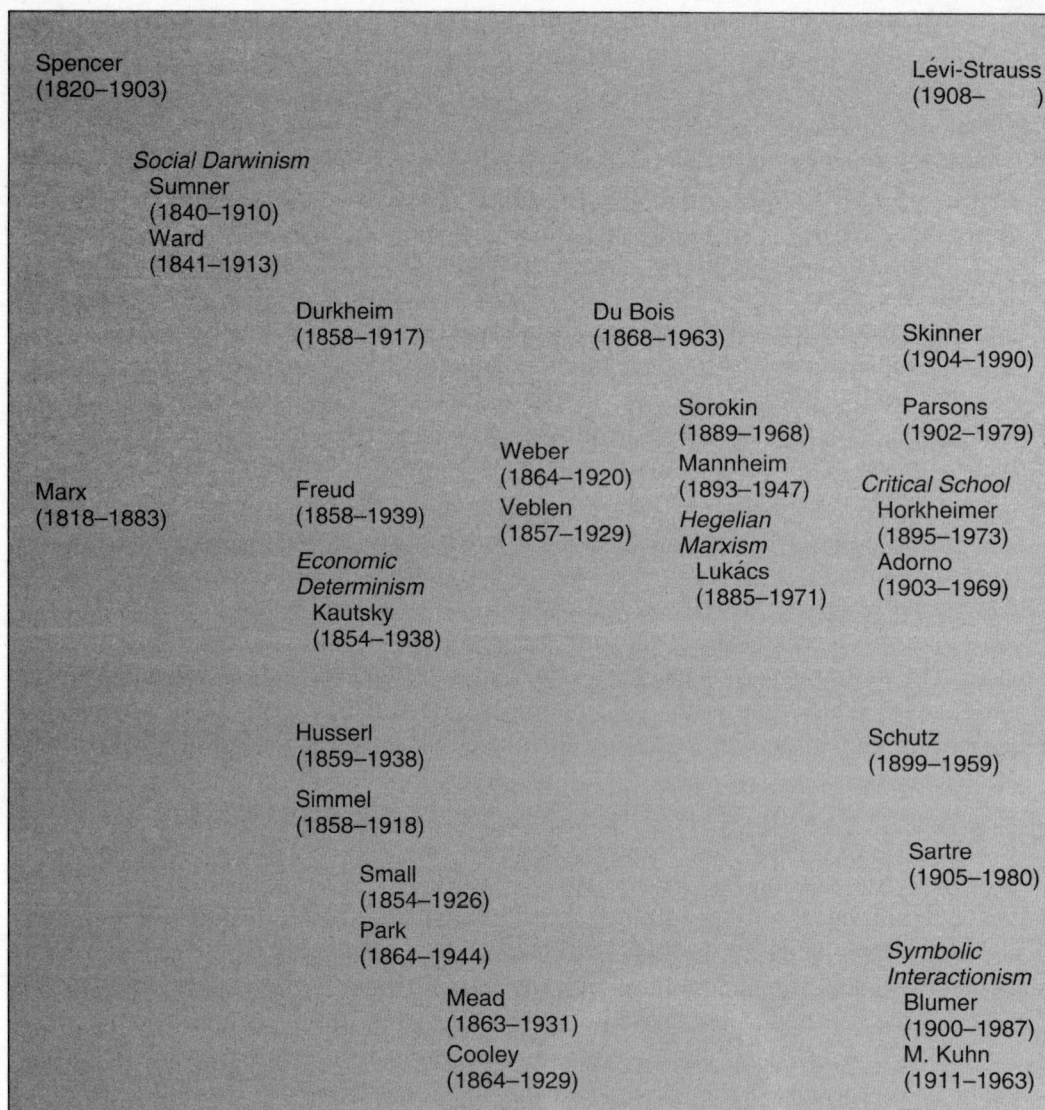

FIGURE 2.1   *Sociological Theory: The Later Years*

By the 1930s, however, Spencer was in eclipse in the intellectual world in general, as well as in sociology. His Social Darwinist, laissez-faire ideas seemed ridiculous in the light of massive social problems, a world war, and a major economic depression. In 1937, Talcott Parsons announced Spencer's intellectual death for sociology when he echoed historian Crane Brinton's words of a few years earlier, "Who now reads Spencer?" Today Spencer is of little more than historical interest, but his ideas *were* important in shaping early American sociological theory. Let us look briefly at the work of two American theorists who were influenced, at least in part, by Spencer's work.

Structuralism

Poststructuralism
Foucault (1926–1984)

Actor-Network
Theory
Latour
(1947–   )

Network Theory

Exchange Theory
Blau
(1918–2002)
Emerson
(1925–1982)

Rational Choice Theory
Coleman
(1926–1995)

Homans
(1910–1989)

Postmodern
Social Theory
Baudrillard
(1929–2007)

Structural Functionalism
Merton
(1910–2003)

Neofunctionalism
Alexander
(1947–   )

Systems Theory
Luhmann
(1927–1998)

Post-Postmodern
Social Theory

Radical Sociology
Mills
(1916–1962)

Conflict Theory
Dahrendorf
(1929–   )

Spatial Marxism

Structural Marxism
Althusser
(1918–1990)

Micro-Macro and
Agency Structure
Integration Theory

Feminist
Sociological Theory

Economic Marxism
Sweezy
(1910–   )
Braverman
(1920–1976)

Habermas
(1929–   )

Synthetic
Theory

Theories of
Consumption

Multiculturalism

Historical Marxism
Wallerstein
(1930–   )

Phenomenological
Sociology
Berger
(1929–   )
Luckmann
(1927–   )

Theories of
Modernity
Giddens
(1938–   )

Ethnomethodology
Garfinkel
(1929–   )

Existential Sociology
Goffman
(1922–1982)

Globalization
Theory
Robertson
(1938–   )

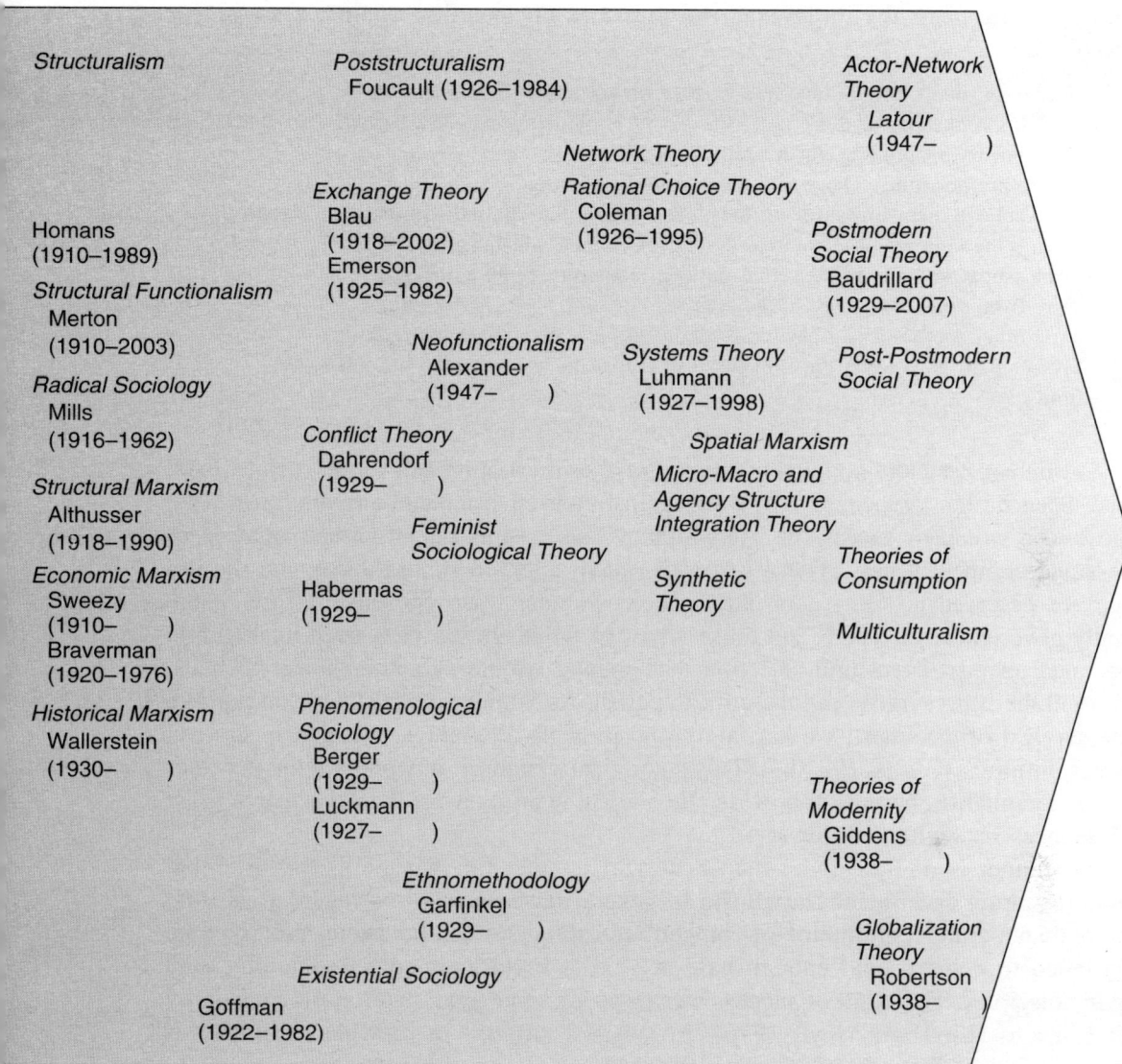

FIGURE 2.1   *continued*

William Graham Sumner (1840–1910)   William Graham Sumner was the person who taught the first course in the United States that could be called sociology (Delaney, 2007b). Sumner contended that he had begun teaching sociology "years before any such attempt was made at any other university in the world" (Curtis, 1981:63).

Sumner was the major exponent of Social Darwinism in the United States, although he appeared to change his view late in life (N. E. Smith, 1979). The following exchange between Sumner and one of his students illustrates his "liberal" views on the need for individual freedom and his position against government interference:

> "Professor, don't you believe in any government aid to industries?"
> "No! It's root, hog, or die."
> "Yes, but hasn't the hog got a right to root?"
> "There are no rights. The world owes nobody a living."
> "You believe then, Professor, in only one system, the contract-competitive system?"
> "That's the only sound economic system. All others are fallacies."
> "Well, suppose some professor of political economy came along and took your job. away from you. Wouldn't you be sore?"
> "Any other professor is welcome to try. If he gets my job; it is my fault.
> My business is to teach the subject so well that no one can take the job away
> from me."
>
> (Phelps, cited in Hofstadter, 1959:54)

Sumner basically adopted a survival-of-the-fittest approach to the social world. Like Spencer, he saw people struggling against their environment, and the fittest were those who would be successful. Thus Sumner was a supporter of human aggressiveness and competitiveness. Those who succeeded deserved it, and those who did not succeed deserved to fail. Again like Spencer, Sumner was opposed to efforts, especially government efforts, to aid those who had failed. In his view such intervention operated against the natural selection that, among people as among lower animals, allowed the fit to survive and the unfit to perish. As Sumner put it, "If we do not like the survival of the fittest, we have only one possible alternative, and that is survival of the unfittest" (Curtis, 1981:84). This theoretical system fit in well with the development of capitalism because it provided theoretical legitimacy for the existence of great differences in wealth and power.

Sumner is of little more than historical interest for two main reasons. First, his orientation and Social Darwinism in general have come to be regarded as little more than a crude legitimation of competitive capitalism and the status quo. Second, he failed to build a solid enough base at Yale to build a school of sociology with many disciples. That kind of success was to occur some years later at the University of Chicago (Heyl and Heyl, 1976). In spite of success in his time, "Sumner is remembered by few today" (Curtis, 1981:146).

Lester F. Ward (1841–1913)   Lester Ward had an unusual career in that he spent most of it as a paleontologist working for the federal government. During that time, Ward read Spencer and Comte and developed a strong interest in sociology. He published a number of works in the late 1800s and early 1900s in which he expounded his sociological theory. As a result of the fame that this work achieved, in 1906 Ward was elected the first president of the American Sociological Society. It was only then that he took his first academic position, at Brown University, a position that he held until his death (M. R. Hill, 2007).

Ward, like Sumner, accepted the idea that people had evolved from lower forms to their present status. He believed that early society was characterized by its simplicity and its moral poverty, whereas modern society was more complex, happier, and offered greater freedom. One task of sociology, *pure sociology,* was to study the basic laws of social change and social structure. But Ward was not content simply to have sociology study social life. He believed that sociology should have a practical side; there should also be an *applied sociology.* This applied sociology involved the conscious use of scientific knowledge to attain a better society. Thus, Ward was not an extreme Social Darwinist; he believed in the need for and importance of social reform.

Although of historical importance, Sumner and Ward have not been of long-term significance to sociological theory. However, now we turn briefly to a theorist of the time, Thorstein Veblen, who has been of long-term significance and whose influence today in sociology is increasing. Then we will look at a group of theorists, especially Mead, and a school, the Chicago school, that came to dominate sociology in America. The Chicago school was unusual in the history of sociology in that it was one of the few (the Durkheimian school in Paris was another) "collective intellectual enterprises of an integrated kind" in the history of sociology (Bulmer, 1984:1). The tradition begun at the University of Chicago is of continuing importance to sociology and its theoretical (and empirical) status.

Thorstein Veblen (1857–1929) 索尔斯坦·凡勃伦（1857—1929）

Veblen, who was not a sociologist but mainly held positions in economics departments, and even in economics was a marginal figure, nonetheless produced a body of social theory that is of enduring significance to those in a number of disciplines, including sociology (Powers, 2005b). The central problem for Veblen was the clash between business and industry. By *business,* Veblen meant the owners, leaders, and "captains" of industry who focused on the profits of their own companies but, to keep prices and profits high, often engaged in efforts to limit production. In so doing, they obstructed the operation of the industrial system and adversely affected society as a whole (through higher rates of unemployment, for example), which is best served by the unimpeded operation of industry. Thus, business leaders were the source of many problems within society, which, Veblen felt, should be led by people (e.g., engineers) who understood the industrial system and its operation and were interested in the general welfare.

Most of Veblen's importance today is traceable to his book *The Theory of the Leisure Class* (1899/1994; Varul, 2007). Veblen is critical of the leisure class (which is closely tied to business) for its role in fostering wasteful consumption. To impress the rest of society, the leisure class engaged in both *conspicuous leisure* (the nonproductive use of time) and *conspicuous consumption* (spending more money on goods than they are worth). People in all other social classes are influenced by this example and seek, directly and indirectly, to emulate the leisure class. The result is a society characterized by the waste of time and money. What is of utmost importance about this work is that unlike most other sociological works of the time (as well as most of Veblen's other works), *The Theory of the Leisure Class* focuses on consumption rather than production. Thus, it anticipated the current shift in social theory away from a focus on production and toward a focus on consumption (Slater, 1997; Ritzer, 2005a;

THORSTEIN VEBLEN

A Biographical Sketch

Thorstein Veblen was born in rural Wisconsin on July 30, 1857. His parents were poor farmers of Norwegian origin (Dorfman, 1966). Thorstein was the sixth of twelve children. He was able to escape the farm and at the age of 17 began studying at Carleton College in Northfield, Minnesota. Early in his schooling he demonstrated both the bitterness and the sense of humor that were to characterize his later work. He met his future first wife, niece of the president of Carleton College, at the school (they eventually married in 1888). Veblen graduated in 1880 and obtained a teaching position, but the school soon closed and he went east to study philosophy at Johns Hopkins University. However, he failed to obtain a scholarship and moved on to Yale in the hopes of finding economic support for his studies. He managed to get by economically and obtained his Ph.D. from Yale in 1884 (one of his teachers was an early giant of sociology, William Graham Sumner). However, in spite of strong letters of recommendation, he was unable to obtain a university position because, at least in part, of his agnosticism, his lack (at the time) of a professional reputation, and the fact that he was perceived as an immigrant lacking the polish needed to hold a university post. He was idle for the next few years (he attributed this idleness to ill health), but by 1891 he returned to his studies, this time focusing more on the social sciences at Cornell University. With the help of one of his professors of economics (A. Laurence Laughlin) who was moving to the University of Chicago, Veblen was able to become a fellow at that university in 1892. He did much of the editorial work associated with *The Journal of Political Economy,* one of the many new academic journals created during this period at Chicago. Veblen was a marginal figure at Chicago, but he did teach some courses and, more importantly, used the *Journal of Political Economy* as an outlet for his writings. His work also began to appear in other outlets, including *The American Journal of Sociology,* another of the University of Chicago's new journals.

In 1899 he published his first and what became his best-known book, *The Theory of the Leisure Class,* but his position at Chicago remained tenuous. In fact, when he asked for a customary raise of a few hundred dollars, the university president made it clear that he would not be displeased if Veblen left the university. However, the book received a great deal of attention, and Veblen was eventually promoted to the position of assistant professor. Although some students found his teaching inspiring, most found it abysmal. One of his Chicago students said that he was "'an exceedingly queer fish . . . Very commonly with his cheek in hand, or in some such position, he talked in a low, placid monotone, in itself a most uninteresting delivery and manner of conducting the class'" (Dorfman, 1966:248–249). It was not unusual for him to begin a course with a large number of students who had heard of his growing fame, but for the class to dwindle to a few diehards by the end of the semester.

Veblen's days at Chicago were numbered for various reasons, including the fact that his marriage was crumbling and he offended Victorian sentiments with affairs with other women. In 1906 Veblen took an associate professorship at

Stanford University. Unlike the situation at Chicago, he taught mainly undergraduates at Stanford, and many of them were put off by his appearance (one said he looked like a "tramp") and his boring teaching style. What did Veblen in once again was his womanizing, which forced him to resign from Stanford in 1909 under circumstances that made it difficult for him to find another academic position. But with help of a colleague and friend who was the head of the department of economics at the University of Missouri, Veblen was able to obtain a position there in 1911. He also obtained a divorce in that year, and in 1914 married a divorcee and former student.

Veblen's appointment at Missouri was at a lower rank (lecturer) and paid less than the position at Stanford. In addition, he hated the then-small town, Columbia, Missouri, that was the home of the university (he reportedly called it a "woodpecker hole of a town" and the state a "rotten stump" [Dorfman, 1966:306]). However, it was during his stay at Missouri that another of his best-known books, *The Instinct of Workmanship and the State of the Industrial Arts* appeared (1914).

Veblen's stormy academic career took another turn in 1917 when he moved to Washington, D.C., to work with a group commissioned by President Woodrow Wilson to analyze possible peace settlements for World War I. After working for the U.S. Food Administration for a short time, Veblen moved to New York City as one of the editors of a magazine, *The Dial*. The magazine shifted its orientation, and within a year Veblen lost his editorial position. However, in the interim he had become connected with the New School for Social Research. His pay there was comparatively high (a good portion of it contributed by one of his former students at Chicago), and because he lived frugally, the great critic of American business began investing his money, at first in raisin vineyards in California and later in the stock market.

Veblen returned to California in 1926, and by the next year he was living in a town shack in northern California. His economic situation became a disaster as he lost the money he had invested in the raisin industry and his stocks became worthless. He continued to earn $500 to $600 a year from royalties, and his former Chicago student continued to send him $500 a year.

Veblen was, to put it mildly, an unusual man. For example, he often could sit for hours and contribute little or nothing to a conversation going on around him. His friends and admirers made it possible for him to become president of the American Economic Association, but he declined the offer. The following vignette offered by a bookseller gives a bit more sense of this complex man:

> a man used to appear every six or eight weeks quite regularly, an ascetic, mysterious person . . . with a gentle air. He wore his hair long . . . I used to try to interest him in economics . . . I even once tried to get him to begin with *The Theory of the Leisure Class*. I explained to him what a brilliant port of entry it is to social consciousness . . . He listened attentively to all I said and melted like a snow drop through the door. One day he ordered a volume of Latin hymns. "I shall have to take your name because we will order this expressly for you," I told him. "We shall not have an audience for such a book as this again in a long time, I am afraid." "My name is Thorstein Veblen," he breathed rather than said.
>
> (cited in Tilman, 1992:9–10)

Thorstein Veblen died on August 3, 1929, just before the Great Depression, which many felt his work anticipated (Powers, 2005b).

Ritzer, Goodman and Wiedenhoft, 2001; also a journal—*Journal of Consumer Culture*—began publication in 2001).

The Chicago School[1] 芝加哥学派

The department of sociology at the University of Chicago was founded in 1892 by Albion Small (J. Williams, 2007). Small's intellectual work is of less contemporary significance than is the key role he played in the institutionalization of sociology in the United States (Faris, 1970; Matthews, 1977). He was instrumental in creating a department at Chicago that was to become the center of the discipline in the United States for many years. Small collaborated on the first sociology textbook in 1894. In 1895 he founded the *American Journal of Sociology,* a journal that, to this day, is a dominant force in the discipline. In 1905, Small cofounded the American Sociological Society, *the* major professional association of American sociologists to this date (Rhoades, 1981). The embarrassment caused by the initials of the American Sociological Society (ASS) led to the name being changed in 1959 to the American Sociological Association (ASA).

Early Chicago Sociology 早期芝加哥学派

The early Chicago department had several distinctive characteristics. For one thing, it had a strong connection with religion. Some members were ministers themselves, and others were sons of ministers. Small, for example, believed that "the ultimate goal of sociology must be essentially Christian" (Matthews, 1977:95). This opinion led to a view that sociology must be interested in social reform, and this view was combined with a belief that sociology should be scientific.[2] Scientific sociology with an objective of social amelioration was to be practiced in the burgeoning city of Chicago, which was beset by the positive *and* negative effects of urbanization and industrialization.

W. I. Thomas (1863–1947)   In 1895, W. I. Thomas became a fellow at the Chicago department, where he wrote his dissertation in 1896 (T. McCarthy, 2005). Thomas's lasting significance was in his emphasis on the need to do scientific research on sociological issues (Lodge, 1986). Although he championed this position for many years, its major statement came in 1918 with the publication of *The Polish Peasant in Europe and America,* which Thomas coauthored with Florian Znaniecki (Stebbins, 2007a, 2007b; Halas, 2005). Martin Bulmer sees it as a landmark study because it moved sociology away from "abstract theory and library research and toward the study of the empirical world utilizing a theoretical framework" (1984:45). Norbert Wiley

---

[1] See Bulmer (1985) for a discussion of what defines a school and why we can speak of the "Chicago school." Tiryakian (1979, 1986) also deals with schools in general, and the Chicago school in particular, and emphasizes the role played by charismatic leaders as well as methodological innovations. For a discussion of this school within the broader context of developments in American sociological theory, see Hinkle (1994).

[2] As we will see, however, the Chicago school's conception of science was to become too "soft," at least in the eyes of the positivists who later came to dominate sociology.

sees *The Polish Peasant* as crucial to the founding of sociology in the sense of "clarifying the unique intellectual space into which this discipline alone could see and explore" (1986:20). The book was the product of eight years of research in both Europe and the United States and was primarily a study of social disorganization among Polish migrants. The data were of little lasting importance. However, the methodology was significant. It involved a variety of data sources, including autobiographical material, paid writings, family letters, newspaper files, public documents, and institutional letters.

Although *The Polish Peasant* was primarily a macrosociological study of social institutions, over the course of his career, Thomas gravitated toward a microscopic, social-psychological orientation. He is best known for the following social-psychological statement (made in a book coauthored by Dorothy Thomas): "If men define situations as real, they are real in their consequences" (Thomas and Thomas, 1928:572). The emphasis was on the importance of what people think and how this affects what they do. This microscopic, social-psychological focus stood in contrast to the macroscopic, social-structural and social-cultural perspectives of such European scholars as Marx, Weber, and Durkheim. It was to become one of the defining characteristics of Chicago's theoretical product—symbolic interactionism (Rock, 1979:5).

Robert Park (1864–1944)   Another figure of significance at Chicago was Robert Park (Shils, 1996). Park had come to Chicago as a part-time instructor in 1914 and quickly worked his way into a central role in the department. Park's importance in the development of sociology lay in several areas. First, he became the dominant figure in the Chicago department, which, in turn, dominated sociology into the 1930s. Second, Park had studied in Europe and was instrumental in bringing continental European thinkers to the attention of Chicago sociologists. Park had taken courses with Simmel, and Simmel's ideas, particularly his focus on action and interaction, were instrumental in the development of the Chicago school's theoretical orientation (Rock, 1979:36–48). Third, prior to becoming a sociologist, Park had been a reporter, and that experience gave him a sense of the importance of urban problems and the need to go out into the field to collect data through personal observation (Lindner, 1996; Strauss, 1996). Out of this emerged the Chicago school's substantive interest in urban ecology (Gaziano, 1996; Maines, Bridger and Ulmer, 1996; Perry, Abbott, and Hutter, 1997). Fourth, Park played a key role in guiding graduate students and helping develop "a cumulative program of graduate research" (Bulmer, 1984:13). Finally, in 1921, Park and Ernest W. Burgess published the first truly important sociology textbook, *An Introduction to the Science of Sociology*. It was to be an influential book for many years and was particularly notable for its commitments to science, research, and the study of a wide range of social phenomena.

Beginning in the late 1920s and early 1930s, Park began to spend less time in Chicago. Finally, his lifelong interest in race relations (he had been secretary to Booker T. Washington before becoming a sociologist) led him to take a position at Fisk University (a black university) in 1934. Although the decline of the Chicago

ROBERT PARK

A Biographical Sketch

Robert Park did not follow the typical career route of an academic sociologist—college, graduate school, professorship. Instead, he had a varied career before he became a sociologist late in life. Despite his late start, Park had a profound effect on sociology in general and on theory in particular. Park's varied experiences gave him an unusual orientation to life, and this view helped shape the Chicago school, symbolic interactionism, and, ultimately, a good portion of sociology.

Park was born in Harveyville, Pennsylvania, on February 14, 1864 (Matthews, 1977). As a student at the University of Michigan, he was exposed to a number of great thinkers, such as John Dewey. Although he was excited by ideas, Park felt a strong need to work in the real world. As Park said, "I made up my mind to go in for experience for its own sake, to gather into my soul . . . 'all the joys and sorrows of the world'" (1927/1973:253). Upon graduation, he began a career as a journalist, which gave him this real-world opportunity. He particularly liked to explore ("hunting down gambling houses and opium dens" [Park, 1927/1973:254]). He wrote about city life in vivid detail. He would go into the field, observe and analyze, and then write up his observations. In fact, he was already doing essentially the kind of research ("scientific reporting") that came to be one of the hallmarks of Chicago sociology—that is, urban ethnology using participant observation techniques (Lindner, 1996).

Although the accurate description of social life remained one of his passions, Park grew dissatisfied with newspaper work because it did not fulfill his familial or, more important, his intellectual needs. Furthermore, it did not seem to contribute to the improvement of the world, and Park had a deep interest in social reform. In 1898, at age 34, Park left newspaper work and enrolled in the

department was not caused solely or even chiefly by Park's departure, its status began to wane in the 1930s. But before we discuss the decline of Chicago sociology and the rise of other departments and theories, we need to return to the early days of the school and the two figures whose work was of the most lasting theoretical significance—Charles Horton Cooley and, most important, George Herbert Mead.[3]

Charles Horton Cooley (1864–1929)   The association of Cooley with the Chicago school is interesting in that he spent his career at the University of Michigan. But

---

[3] There were many other significant figures associated with the Chicago school, including Everett Hughes (Chapoulie, 1996; Strauss, 1996).

philosophy department at Harvard. He remained there for a year but then decided to move to Germany, which at that time was the heart of the world's intellectual life. In Berlin he encountered Georg Simmel, whose work was to have a profound influence on Park's sociology. In fact, Simmel's lectures were the *only* formal sociological training that Park received. As Park said, "I got most of my knowledge about society and human nature from my own observations" (1927/1973:257). In 1904, Park completed his doctoral dissertation at the University of Heidelberg. Characteristically, he was dissatisfied with his dissertation: "All I had to show was that little book and I was ashamed of it" (Matthews, 1977:57). He refused a summer teaching job at the University of Chicago and turned away from academe as he had earlier turned away from newspaper work.

His need to contribute to social betterment led him to become secretary and chief publicity officer for the Congo Reform Association, which was set up to help alleviate the brutality and exploitation then taking place in the Belgian Congo. During this period, he met Booker T. Washington, and he was attracted to the cause of improving the lot of black Americans. He became Washington's secretary and played a key role in the activities of the Tuskegee Institute. In 1912 he met W. I. Thomas, the Chicago sociologist, who was lecturing at Tuskegee. Thomas invited him to give a course on "the Negro in America" to a small group of graduate students at Chicago, and Park did so in 1914. The course was successful, and he gave it again the next year to an audience twice as large. At this time he joined the American Sociological Society, and only a decade later, he became its president. Park gradually worked his way into a full-time appointment at Chicago, although he did not get a full professorship until 1923, when he was 59 years old. Over the approximately two decades that he was affiliated with the University of Chicago, he played a key role in shaping the intellectual orientation of the sociology department.

Park remained peripatetic even after his retirement from Chicago in the early 1930s. He taught courses and oversaw research at Fisk University until he was nearly 80 years old. He traveled extensively. He died on February 7, 1944, one week before his 80th birthday.

Cooley's theoretical perspective was in line with the theory of symbolic interactionism that was to become Chicago's most important product. (Sandstrom and Kleinman, 2005; Schubert, 2007).

Cooley received his Ph.D. from the University of Michigan in 1894. He had developed a strong interest in sociology, but there was as yet no department of sociology at Michigan. As a result, the questions for his Ph.D. examination came from Columbia University, where sociology had been taught since 1889 under the leadership of Franklin Giddings. Cooley began his teaching career at Michigan in 1892 before completion of his doctorate.

Although Cooley theorized about large-scale phenomena such as social classes, social structures, and social institutions, he is remembered today mainly for his insights into the social-psychological aspects of social life (Schubert, 2005,

2007). His work in this area is in line with that of George Herbert Mead, although Mead was to have a deeper and more lasting effect on sociology than Cooley had. Cooley had an interest in consciousness, but he refused (as did Mead) to separate consciousness from the social context. This is best exemplified by a concept of his that survives to this day—the *looking-glass self.* By this concept, Cooley understood that people possess consciousness and that it is shaped in continuing social interaction.

A second basic concept that illustrates Cooley's social-psychological interests, and is also of continuing interest and importance, is that of the primary group. *Primary groups* are intimate, face-to-face groups that play a key role in linking the individual to the larger society. Especially crucial are the primary groups of the young—mainly the family and the peer group. Within these groups, the individual grows into a social being. It is basically within the primary group that the looking-glass self emerges and that the ego-centered child learns to take others into account and, thereby, to become a contributing member of society.

Both Cooley (Winterer, 1994) and Mead rejected a *behavioristic* view of human beings, the view that people blindly and unconsciously respond to external stimuli. They believed that people had consciousness, a self, and that it was the responsibility of the sociologist to study this aspect of social reality. Cooley urged sociologists to try to put themselves in the place of the individuals they were studying, to use the method of *sympathetic introspection,* to analyze consciousness. By analyzing what they as individuals might do in various circumstances, sociologists could understand the meanings and motives that are at the base of social behavior. The method of sympathetic introspection seemed to many to be very unscientific. In this area, among others, Mead's work represents an advance over Cooley's. Nevertheless, there is a great deal of similarity in the interests of the two men, not the least of which is their shared view that sociology should focus on such social-psychological phenomena as consciousness, action, and interaction.

George Herbert Mead (1863–1931)   The most important thinker associated with the Chicago school and symbolic interactionism was not a sociologist but a philosopher, George Herbert Mead.[4] Mead started teaching philosophy at the University of Chicago in 1894, and he taught there until his death in 1931 (Chriss, 2005b; G. Cook, 1993). He is something of a paradox, given his central importance in the history of sociological theory, both because he taught philosophy, not sociology, and because he published comparatively little during his lifetime. The paradox is, in part, resolved by two facts. First, Mead taught courses in social psychology in the philosophy department, and they were taken by many graduate students in sociology. His ideas had a profound effect on a number of them. These students combined Mead's ideas with those they were getting in the sociology department from people such as Park and Thomas. Although at the time there was no theory known as symbolic interactionism, it was created by students out of these various inputs. Thus Mead had a deep, personal impact on the people who were later to develop symbolic

---

[4] For a dissenting view, see J. D. Lewis and Smith (1980).

interactionism. Second, these students put together their notes on Mead's courses and published a posthumous volume under his name. The work, *Mind, Self and Society* (Mead, 1934/1962), moved his ideas from the realm of oral to that of written tradition. Widely read to this day, this volume forms the main intellectual pillar of symbolic interactionism.

We deal with Mead's ideas in Chapter 6, but it is necessary at this point to underscore a few points to situate him historically. Mead's ideas need to be seen in the context of psychological behaviorism. Mead was quite impressed with this orientation and accepted many of its tenets. He adopted its focus on the individual and his or her behavior. He regarded as sensible the behaviorists' concern with the rewards and costs involved in the behaviors of the individuals. What troubled Mead was that behaviorism did not seem to go far enough. That is, it excluded consciousness from serious consideration, arguing that it was not amenable to scientific study. Mead vehemently disagreed and sought to extend the principles of behaviorism to an analysis of the mind. In so doing, Mead enunciated a focus similar to that of Cooley. But whereas Cooley's position seemed unscientific, Mead promised a more scientific conception of consciousness by extending the highly scientific principles and methods of psychological behaviorism.

Mead offered American sociology a social-psychological theory that stood in stark contrast to the primarily societal theories offered by most of the major European theorists (Shalin, 2000). The most important exception was Simmel. Thus symbolic interactionism was developed, in large part, out of Simmel's interest in action and interaction and Mead's interest in consciousness. However, such a focus led to a weakness in both Mead's work and in symbolic interactionism in general at the societal and cultural levels.

The Waning of Chicago Sociology Chicago sociology reached its peak in the 1920s, but by the 1930s, with the death of Mead and the departure of Park, the department had begun to lose its position of central importance in American sociology (Cortese, 1995). Fred Matthews (1977; see also Bulmer, 1984) pinpoints several reasons for the decline of Chicago sociology, two of which seem of utmost importance.

First, the discipline had grown increasingly preoccupied with being scientific—that is, using sophisticated methods and employing statistical analysis. However, the Chicago school was viewed as emphasizing descriptive, ethnographic studies (Prus, 1996), often focusing on their subjects' personal orientations (in Thomas's terms, their "definitions of the situation"). Park progressively came to despise statistics (he called it "parlor magic") because it seemed to prohibit the analysis of subjectivity, of the idiosyncratic, and of the peculiar. The fact that important work in quantitative methods was done at Chicago (Bulmer, 1984:151–189) tended to be ignored in the face of its overwhelming association with qualitative methods.

Second, more and more individuals outside Chicago grew increasingly resentful of Chicago's dominance of both the American Sociological Society and the *American Journal of Sociology*. The Eastern Sociological Society was founded in 1930, and eastern sociologists became more vocal about the dominance of the

Midwest in general and Chicago in particular (Wiley, 1979:63). By 1935, the revolt against Chicago had led to a non-Chicago secretary of the association and the establishment of a new official journal, the *American Sociological Review* (Lengermann, 1979). According to Wiley, "the Chicago school had fallen like a mighty oak" (1979:63). This signaled the growth of other power centers, most notably Harvard and the Ivy League in general. Symbolic interactionism was largely an indeterminate, oral tradition and as such eventually lost ground to more explicit and codified theoretical systems like the structural functionalism associated with the Ivy League (Rock, 1979:12).

Women in Early Sociology 早期社会学中的女性学者

Simultaneously with the developments at the University of Chicago described in the previous section, even sometimes in concert with them, and at the same time that Durkheim, Weber, and Simmel were creating a European sociology, and sometimes in concert with them as well, a group of women who formed a broad and surprisingly connected network of social reformers were also developing pioneering sociological theories. These women included Jane Addams (1860–1935), Charlotte Perkins Gilman (1860–1935), Anna Julia Cooper (1858–1964), Ida Wells-Barnett (1862–1931), Marianne Weber (1870–1954), and Beatrice Potter Webb (1858–1943). With the possible exception of Cooper, they can all be connected through their relationship to Jane Addams. That they are not today known or recognized in conventional histories of the discipline as sociologists or sociological theorists is a chilling testimony to the power of gender politics within the discipline of sociology and to sociology's essentially unreflective and uncritical interpretation of its own practices. Although the sociological theory of each of these women is a product of individual theoretical effort, when they are read collectively, they represent a coherent and complementary statement of early feminist sociological theory.

The chief hallmarks of their theories, hallmarks which may in part account for their being passed over in the development of professional sociology, include (1) an emphasis on women's experience and women's lives and works being equal in importance to men's; (2) an awareness that they spoke from a situated and embodied standpoint and therefore, for the most part, not with the tone of imperious objectivity that male sociological theory would come to associate with authoritative theory making (Lemert, 2000); (3) the idea that the purpose of sociology and sociological theory is social reform—that is, the end is to improve people's lives through knowledge; and (4) the claim that the chief problem for amelioration in their time was inequality. What distinguishes these early women most from each other is the nature of and the remedy for the inequality on which they focused—gender, race, or class, or the intersection of these factors. But all these women translated their views into social and political activism that helped shape and change the North Atlantic societies in which they lived, and this activism was as much a part of their sense of practicing sociology as creating theory was. They believed in social science research as part of both their theoretical and activist enactments of sociology and were highly creative innovators of social science method.

As the developing discipline of sociology marginalized these women as sociologists and sociological theorists, it often incorporated their research methods into its own practices, while using their activism as an excuse to define these women as "not sociologists." Thus they are remembered as social activists and social workers rather than sociologists. Their heritage is a sociological theory that is a call to action as well as to thought.

W. E. B. Du Bois and Race Theory[5] 杜波伊斯与种族理论

Although W. E. B. Du Bois (1868–1963) taught in a sociology department (Atlanta University) for a considerable amount of time, he usually is not thought of as a sociologist, let alone as a theorist. He is far better known as a public intellectual and for his founding and leadership roles in various civil rights organizations, including the National Association for the Advancement of Colored People (NAACP). However, there is powerful sociology in many of his writings, and there are a number of abstract ideas that can be seen as theory, even though Du Bois (like Marx) was loath to distinguish between theory and practice. That is, he was uninterested in theory in itself, but rather developed abstract ideas in the service of advancing the cause of civil rights, primarily for African Americans.

Within sociology, Du Bois's reputation has been based to a large degree on his empirical study, *The Philadelphia Negro* (1899/1996). This study of the seventh ward in Philadelphia was conducted single-handedly by Du Bois, and although he employed a multitude of methods, it is best known as a pioneering ethnography. Over his long career, Du Bois wrote an unbelievable number of books, articles, and editorials, but few would be immediately obvious as "theory." However, there is theory in his work, especially in his several unique autobiographical efforts (the best-known of which is *The Souls of Black Folk* [Du Bois, 1903/1996]) that allowed him to develop interesting theoretical ideas in the context of reflections on his own life. Overarching all was his interest in the "race idea," which he considered the "the central thought of all history" (Du Bois, 1897/1995:21), and the "color line," which he saw as drawn across not only the United States but also much of the world. One of his best-known theoretical ideas is the *veil,* which creates a clear separation, or barrier, between African Americans and whites. The imagery is *not* of a wall but rather of a thin, porous material through which each race can see the other, but which nonetheless serves to separate the races. Another key theoretical idea is *double-consciousness,* a sense of "two-ness," or a feeling among African Americans of seeing and measuring themselves through others' eyes. There is not a full-fledged theory of society in Du Bois's work, but there is a series of theoretical ideas about race and race relations in the United States and the world. With the rise of multicultural (and feminist) theories in recent years, Du Bois's focus on race and his view of the world from the African American perspective have attracted a large number of new admirers and, more important, thinkers who are building on his pioneering ideas, perspectives, and commitments.

---

[5] We will discuss a more specific and contemporary version of race theory—critical theories of race and racism—at the close of this chapter and in Chapter 14.

W. E. B. Du Bois

A Biographical Sketch

William Edward Burghardt Du Bois was born on February 23, 1868, in Great Barrington, Massachusetts (D. L. Lewis, 1993). Compared to the vast majority of blacks of his day, Du Bois had a comparatively advantaged upbringing that led to college at Fisk University and later to a Ph.D. from Harvard University with a stop along the way at the University of Berlin. At Harvard and in Germany, Du Bois came into contact with some of the great thinkers of his day, including philosophers William James and Josiah Royce, as well as the great social theorist Max Weber.

Du Bois took his first job teaching Greek and Latin at a black college (Wilberforce). He notes that "the institution would have no sociology, even though I offered to teach it on my own time" (Du Bois, 1968:189). Du Bois moved on in the fall of 1896 when he was offered a position as assistant instructor at the University of Pennsylvania to do research on blacks in Philadelphia. That research led to the publication of one of the classic works of early sociology, *The Philadelphia Negro* (1899/1996). When that project was completed, Du Bois moved (he never had a regular faculty position at Pennsylvania, and that, like many other things in his lifetime, rankled him) to Atlanta University, where he taught sociology from 1897 to 1910 and was responsible for a number of research reports on various aspects of Negro life in America. It was also in this period that he authored the first and most important of his autobiographical memoirs, *The Souls of Black Folk* (1903/1996). This was a highly literary and deeply personal work that also made a series of general theoretical points and contributed greatly to the understanding of black Americans and of race relations. Du Bois published a number of such autobiographical works during the course of his life, including *Darkwater: Voices from within the Veil* (1920/1999), *Dusk of Dawn: An Essay toward an Autobiography of a Race Concept* (1940/1968), and *The Autobiography of W. E. B. Du Bois: A Soliloquy on Viewing My Life from the Last Decade of Its First Century* (1968). Of *Dusk of Dawn*, Du Bois (1968:2) says, "I have written then what is meant to be not so much my autobiography as the autobiography of a concept of race, elucidated, magnified and doubtless distorted in the thoughts and deeds that were mine." (Du Bois was not lacking in self-esteem and has often been criticized for his outsized ego.)

While at Atlanta University, Du Bois became more publicly and politically engaged. In 1905 he called for and attended a meeting near Buffalo, New York, that led to the formation of the Niagara Movement, an interracial civil rights organization interested in such things as the "abolition of all caste distinctions based simply on race and color" (Du Bois, 1968:249). This formed the basis of the similarly interracial National Association for the Advancement of Colored People (NAACP), which came into existence in 1910 with Du Bois as its director of publications and research. He founded the NAACP's magazine, *The Crisis,* and in its pages authored many essays on a wide range of issues relating to the state of the Negro in America. Du Bois took this new position because it offered him a platform for the widespread dissemination of his ideas (he was solely responsible for the editorial opinions of *The Crisis*). In addition, his position at Atlanta University had become untenable because of his conflict with the then very popular and powerful Booker T. Washington, who was regarded by most white leaders and politicians as the spokesman for black America. Du Bois came to view Washington as far too conservative and much too willing to subordinate Negroes to whites in general and specifically within the white-dominated economy, where they were to be trained for, and satisfied with, manual work.

For the next half century, Du Bois was a tireless writer and activist on behalf of Negro and other racial causes (D. L. Lewis, 2000). He attended and participated in meetings throughout the United States and much of the world on Negroes in particular, and all "colored" races in general. He took positions on many of the pressing issues of the day, almost always from the vantage point of Negroes and other minorities. For example, he had views on which presidential candidates Negroes should support, whether the United States should enter World Wars I and II, and whether Negroes should support those wars and participate in them.

By the early 1930s the Great Depression had begun to wreak havoc on the circulation of *The Crisis,* and Du Bois lost control to young dissidents within the NAACP. He returned to Atlanta University and scholarly work and, among other things, authored *Black Reconstruction in America, 1860–1880* (1935/1998). His tenure lasted a little more than a decade, and in 1944, Du Bois (then seventy-six) was forcibly retired by the university. Under pressure, the NAACP invited him back as an ornamental figure, but Du Bois refused to play that role or to act his age and was dismissed in 1948. His ideas and work grew increasingly radical over the ensuing nearly two decades of his life. He joined and participated in various peace organizations and eventually was indicted by a grand jury in 1951 for failing to register as an agent of a foreign power in the peace movement.

Early in his life, Du Bois had hope in America in general and, more specifically, believed that it could solve its racial problems peacefully within the context of a capitalist society. Over the years, he lost faith in capitalists and capitalism and grew more supportive of socialism. Eventually, he grew more radical in his views and drifted toward communism. He was quite impressed with the advances communism brought to the Soviet Union and China. In the end, he joined the Communist Party. Toward the very end of his long life, Du Bois seemed to give up hope in the United States and moved to the African nation of Ghana. Du Bois became a citizen of Ghana and died there on August 27, 1963, the day before Martin Luther King Jr. delivered his "I have a dream" speech on the Mall in Washington, D.C. Du Bois was 95.

While wide-scale recognition of Du Bois as an important theorist may be relatively recent, he has long been influential within the black community. For example, on becoming chairman of the board of the NAACP, Julian Bond said: "I think for people of my age and generation, this [a picture in his home of a young Bond holding Du Bois's hand] was a normal experience—not to have Du Bois in your home, but to have his name in your home, to know about him in your home. . . . This was table conversation for us" (cited in Lemert, 2000:346).

发展至世纪中叶的社会学理论

Sociological Theory to Midcentury

The Rise of Harvard, the Ivy League, and Structural Functionalism 哈佛、常春藤盟校以及结构功能主义的崛起

We can trace the rise of sociology at Harvard from the arrival of Pitirim Sorokin in 1930 (Jeffries, 2005; Johnston, 1995). When Sorokin arrived at Harvard, there was no sociology department, but by the end of his first year, one had been organized, and he had been appointed its head. Although Sorokin was a sociological theorist and continued to publish into the 1960s, his work is surprisingly little cited today. Although some disagree (e.g., Tiryakian, 2007b), the dominant view is that his theorizing has not stood the test of time very well. Sorokin's long-term significance may well have been the creation of the Harvard sociology department and the hiring of Talcott Parsons (who had been an instructor of economics at Harvard) for the position of instructor in sociology. Parsons became *the* dominant figure in American sociology for introducing European theorists to an American audience, for his own sociological theories, and for his many students who themselves became major sociological theorists.

Talcott Parsons (1902–1979) 塔尔科特·帕森斯（1902—1979）

Although Parsons published some early essays, his major contribution in the early years was his influence on graduate students, many of whom became notable sociological theorists themselves. The most famous was Robert Merton, who received his Ph.D. in 1936 and soon became a major theorist and the heart of Parsonsian-style theorizing at Columbia University. In the same year (1936), Kingsley Davis received his Ph.D., and he, along with Wilbert Moore (who received his Harvard degree in 1940), wrote one of the central works in structural-functional theory, the theory that was to become the major product of Parsons and the Parsonsians. But Parsons's influence was not restricted to the 1930s. Remarkably, he produced graduate students of great influence well into the 1960s.

The pivotal year for Parsons and for American sociological theory was 1937, the year in which he published *The Structure of Social Action*. This book was of significance to sociological theory in America for four main reasons. First, it served to introduce grand European theorizing to a large American audience. The bulk of the book was devoted to Durkheim, Weber, and Pareto. His interpretations of these theorists shaped their images in American sociology for many years.

Second, Parsons devoted almost no attention to Marx or to Simmel (D. Levine, 1991a), although he emphasized the work of Durkheim, Weber, and even Pareto. As a result, Marxian theory continued to be largely excluded from legitimate sociology.

Third, *The Structure of Social Action* made the case for sociological theorizing as a legitimate and significant sociological activity. The theorizing that has taken place in the United States since then owes a deep debt to Parsons's work (Lidz, 2000).

Finally, Parsons argued for specific sociological theories that were to have a profound influence on sociology. At first, Parsons was thought of, and thought of himself, as an action theorist (Joas, 1996). He seemed to focus on actors and their thoughts and actions. But by the close of his 1937 work and increasingly in his later work, Parsons sounded more like a structural-functional theorist focusing on large-scale social and cultural systems. Although Parsons argued that there was no contradiction between these theories, he became best known as a structural functionalist, and he was the primary exponent of this theory, which gained dominance within sociology and maintained that position until the 1960s. Parsons's theoretical strength, and that of structural functionalism, lay in delineating the relationships among large-scale social structures and institutions (see Chapter 3).

Parsons's major statements on his structural-functional theory came in the early 1950s in several works, most notably *The Social System* (1951) (Barber, 1994). In that work and others, Parsons tended to concentrate on the structures of society and their relationship to each other. These structures were seen as mutually supportive and tending toward a dynamic equilibrium. The emphasis was on how order was maintained among the various elements of society (Wrong, 1994). Change was seen as an orderly process, and Parsons (1966, 1971) ultimately came to adopt a neoevolutionary view of social change. Parsons was concerned not only with the social system per se but also with its relationship to the other *action systems,* especially the cultural and personality systems. But his basic view on intersystemic relations was essentially the same as his view of intrasystemic relations; that is, that they were defined by cohesion, consensus, and order. In other words, the various *social structures* performed a variety of positive *functions* for each other.

It is clear, then, why Parsons came to be defined primarily as a *structural functionalist.* As his fame grew, so did the strength of structural-functional theory in the United States. His work lay at the core of this theory, but his students and disciples also concentrated on extending both the theory and its dominance in the United States.

Although Parsons played a number of important and positive roles in the history of sociological theory in the United States, his work also had negative consequences (Holton, 2001). First, he offered interpretations of European theorists that seemed to reflect his own theoretical orientation more than theirs. Many American sociologists were initially exposed to erroneous interpretations of the European masters. Second, as already pointed out, early in his career Parsons largely ignored Marx, which resulted in Marx's ideas being on the periphery of sociology for many years. Third, his own theory, as it developed over the years, had a number of serious weaknesses. However, Parsons's preeminence in American sociology served for many years to mute or overwhelm the critics. Not until much later did the weaknesses of Parsons's theory, and of structural functionalism in general, receive a full airing.

But returning to the early 1930s and other developments at Harvard, we can gain a good deal of insight into the development of the Harvard department by looking at it through an account of its other major figure, George Homans.

George Homans (1910–1989) 乔治·霍曼斯（1910—1989）

A wealthy Bostonian, George Homans received his bachelor's degree from Harvard in 1932 (Homans, 1962, 1984; see also Bell, 1992). As a result of the Great Depression, he was unemployed but certainly not penniless. In the fall of 1932, L. J. Henderson, a physiologist, was offering a course in the theories of Vilfredo Pareto, and Homans was invited to attend; he accepted. (Parsons also attended the Pareto seminars.) Homans's description of why he was drawn to and taken with Pareto says much about why American sociological theory was so highly conservative, so anti-Marxist:

> I took to Pareto because he made clear to me what I was already prepared to believe. . . . Someone has said that much modern sociology is an effort to answer the arguments of the revolutionaries. As a Republican Bostonian who had not rejected his comparatively wealthy family, I felt during the thirties that I was under personal attack, above all from the Marxists. I was ready to believe Pareto because he provided me with a defense.
>
> (Homans, 1962:4)

Homans's exposure to Pareto led to a book, *An Introduction to Pareto* (coauthored with Charles Curtis), published in 1934. The publication of this book made Homans a sociologist even though Pareto's work was virtually the only sociology he had read up to that point.

In 1934, Homans was named a junior fellow at Harvard, a program started to avoid the problems associated with the Ph.D. program. In fact, Homans never did earn a Ph.D., even though he became one of the major sociological figures of his day. Homans was a junior fellow until 1939, and in those years, he absorbed more and more sociology. In 1939, Homans was affiliated with the sociology department, but the connection was broken by the war.

By the time Homans had returned from the war, the department of social relations had been founded by Parsons at Harvard, and Homans joined it. Although Homans respected some aspects of Parsons's work, he was highly critical of Parsons's style of theorizing. A long-running exchange began between the two men that later manifested itself publicly in the pages of many books and journals. Basically, Homans argued that Parsons's theory was not a theory at all but rather a vast system of intellectual categories into which most aspects of the social world fit. Further, Homans believed that theory should be built from the ground up on the basis of careful observations of the social world. Parsons's theory, however, started on the general theoretical level and worked its way down to the empirical level.

In his own work, Homans amassed a large number of empirical observations over the years, but it was only in the 1950s that he hit upon a satisfactory theoretical approach with which to analyze those data. That theory was psychological behaviorism, as it was best expressed in the ideas of his colleague at Harvard, the psychologist B. F. Skinner. On the basis of this perspective, Homans developed his exchange theory. We will pick up the story of this theoretical development later in this chapter. The crucial point here is that Harvard and its major theoretical product, structural functionalism, became preeminent in sociology in the late 1930s, replacing the Chicago school and symbolic interactionism.

The Chicago School in Decline 芝加哥学派的衰落

We left the Chicago department in the mid-1930s on the wane with the death of Mead, the departure of Park, the revolt of eastern sociologists, and the founding of the *American Sociological Review.* But the Chicago school did not disappear. Into the early 1950s it continued to be an important force in sociology.

The central figure in the Chicago department in this era was Herbert Blumer (1900–1987) (Maines, 2005; Blumer, 1969a). He was a major exponent of the theoretical approach developed at Chicago out of the work of Mead, Cooley, Simmel, Park, Thomas, and others. In fact, it was Blumer who coined the phrase *symbolic interactionism* in 1937. Blumer played a key role in keeping this tradition alive through his teaching at Chicago. He wrote a number of essays that were instrumental in keeping symbolic interactionism vital into the 1950s. Despite this flurry of activity, the Chicago school was in decline, especially given the movement of Blumer in 1952 from Chicago to the University of California at Berkeley. Whatever the state of the Chicago school, the Chicago tradition has remained alive to this day with major exponents dispersed throughout the country and the world (Sandstrom, Martin, and Fine, 2001).

Developments in Marxian Theory 马克思理论的发展

From the early 1900s to the 1930s, Marxian theory continued to develop largely independently of mainstream sociological theory. The exception to this, at least partially, was the emergence of the critical, or Frankfurt, school out of the earlier Hegelian Marxism.

The idea of a school for the development of Marxian theory was the product of Felix J. Weil. The Institute of Social Research was officially founded in Frankfurt, Germany, on February 3, 1923 (Jay, 1973; Wiggershaus, 1994). Over the years, a number of the most famous thinkers in Marxian theory were associated with the critical school—Max Horkheimer (Schulz, 2007a), Theodor Adorno (Schulz, 2007b), Erich Fromm (N. McLaughlin, 2007), Herbert Marcuse (Dandaneau, 2007a), and, more recently, Jurgen Habermas.

The Institute functioned in Germany until 1934, but by then things were growing increasingly uncomfortable under the Nazi regime. The Nazis had little use for the Marxian ideas that dominated the Institute, and their hostility was heightened because many of those associated with it were Jewish. In 1934 Horkheimer, as head of the Institute, came to New York to discuss its status with the president of Columbia University. Much to Horkheimer's surprise, he was invited to affiliate the Institute with the university, and he was even offered a building on campus. And so *a* center of Marxian theory moved to *the* center of the capitalist world. The Institute stayed there until the end of the war, but after the war, pressure mounted to return it to Germany. In 1949, Horkheimer did return to Germany, and he brought the Institute with him. Although the Institute itself moved to Germany, many of the figures associated with it took independent career directions.

It is important to underscore a few of the most significant aspects of critical theory (Calhoun and Karaganis, 2001). In its early years, those associated with the Institute tended to be fairly traditional Marxists, devoting a good portion of their attention to the economic domain. But around 1930, a major change took place as this group of thinkers began to shift its attention from the economy to the cultural system, which it came to see as the major force in modern capitalist society. This was consistent with, but an extension of, the position taken earlier by Hegelian Marxists such as Georg Lukács. To help them understand the cultural domain, the critical theorists were attracted to the work of Max Weber. The effort to combine Marx and Weber and thereby create "Weberian Marxism"[6] (Dahms, 1997; Lowy, 1996) gave the critical school some of its distinctive orientations and served in later years to make it more legitimate to sociologists who began to grow interested in Marxian theory.

A second major step taken by at least some members of the critical school was to employ the rigorous social-scientific techniques developed by American sociologists to research issues of interest to Marxists. This, like the adoption of Weberian theory, made the critical school more acceptable to mainstream sociologists.

Third, critical theorists made an effort to integrate individually oriented Freudian theory with the societal- and cultural-level insights of Marx and Weber. This seemed to many sociologists to represent a more inclusive theory than that offered by either Marx or Weber alone. If nothing else, the effort to combine such disparate theories proved stimulating to sociologists and many other intellectuals.

The critical school has done much useful work since the 1920s, and a significant amount of it is of relevance to sociologists. However, the critical school had to await the late 1960s before it was "discovered" by large numbers of American theorists.

卡尔·曼海姆和知识社会学
Karl Mannheim and the Sociology of Knowledge

At this point, the work of Karl Mannheim (1893–1947) should be mentioned briefly (Ruef, 2007; Kettler and Meja, 1995). Born in Hungary, Mannheim was forced to move first to Germany and later to England. Influenced by the ideologies of Marx, Weber, Simmel, and the neo-Marxist Georg Lukács, Mannheim is best known for his work on systems of knowledge (for example, conservatism). In fact, he is almost single-handedly responsible for the creation of the contemporary field known as the sociology of knowledge. Also of significance is his thinking on rationality, which tends to pick up themes developed in Weber's work on this topic but deals with them in a far more concise and a much clearer manner (Ritzer, 1998).

From a base in England starting in the 1930s, Karl Mannheim was busy creating a set of theoretical ideas that provided the foundation for an area of sociology—the sociology of knowledge—that continues to be important to this day (E. D. McCarthy, 2007, 1996; Stehr, 2001). Mannheim, of course, built on the work of many predecessors, most notably Karl Marx, although Mannheim was far from being a Marxist. Basically, the sociology of knowledge involves the systematic study of knowledge, ideas, or intellectual phenomena in general. To Mannheim, knowledge is determined by social existence. For example, Mannheim seeks to relate the ideas of a group to that group's position in the social structure. Marx did this by relating ideas to social classes, but Mannheim extends this perspective by linking ideas to a variety of different positions within society (for example, differences between generations).

In addition to playing a major role in creating the sociology of knowledge, Mannheim is perhaps best known for his distinction between two idea systems—*ideology*

---

[6] This label fits some critical theorists better than others, and it also applies to a wide range of other thinkers (Agger, 1998).

and *utopia* (B. S. Turner, 1995). An ideology is an idea system that seeks to conceal and conserve the present by interpreting it from the point of view of the past. A utopia, in contrast, is a system of ideas that seeks to transcend the present by focusing on the future. Conflict between ideologies and utopias is an ever-present reality in society (Mannheim, 1931/1936).

20 世纪中叶以来的社会学
Sociological Theory from Midcentury

结构功能主义：鼎盛和衰落
Structural Functionalism: Peak and Decline

The 1940s and 1950s were paradoxically the years of greatest dominance and the beginnings of the decline of structural functionalism. In those years, Parsons produced his major statements that clearly reflected his shift from action theory to structural functionalism. Parsons's students had fanned out across the country and occupied dominant positions in many of the major sociology departments (for example, Columbia and Cornell). These students were producing works of their own that were widely recognized contributions to structural-functional theory.

However, just as it was gaining theoretical hegemony, structural functionalism came under attack, and the attacks mounted until they reached a climax in the 1960s and 1970s. There was an attack by C. Wright Mills on Parsons in 1959, and other major criticisms were mounted by David Lockwood (1956), Alvin Gouldner (1959/1967, 1970; Chriss, 2005a), and Irving Horowitz (1962/1967). In the 1950s, these attacks were seen as little more than "guerrilla raids," but as sociology moved into the 1960s, the dominance of structural functionalism was clearly in jeopardy.

George Huaco (1986) linked the rise and decline of structural functionalism to the position of American society in the world order. As America rose to world dominance after 1945, structural functionalism achieved hegemony within sociology. Structural functionalism supported America's dominant position in the world in two ways. First, the structural-functional view that "every pattern has consequences which contribute to the preservation and survival of the larger system" was "nothing less than a celebration of the United States and its world hegemony" (Huaco, 1986:52). Second, the structural-functional emphasis on equilibrium (the best social change is no change) meshed well with the interests of the United States, then "the wealthiest and most powerful empire in the world." The decline of U.S. world dominance in the 1970s coincided with structural functionalism's loss of its preeminent position in sociological theory.

美国的激进社会学：C·赖特·米尔斯
Radical Sociology in America: C. Wright Mills

As we have seen, although Marxian theory was largely ignored or reviled by mainstream American sociologists, there were exceptions, the most notable of which is C. Wright Mills (1916–1962). Mills is noteworthy for his almost single-handed effort to keep a Marxian tradition alive in sociological theory. Modern Marxian sociologists have far outstripped Mills in theoretical sophistication, but they owe him a deep debt nonetheless for the personal and professional activities that helped set the stage for their own work

C. WRIGHT MILLS

A Biographical Sketch

C. Wright Mills was born on August 28, 1916, in Waco, Texas (Dandaneau, 2007b; Domhoff, 2005). He came from a conventional middle-class background: his father was an insurance broker, and his mother was a housewife. He attended the University of Texas and by 1939 had obtained both a bachelor's degree and a master's degree. He was quite an unusual student who, by the time he left Texas, already had published articles in the two major sociology journals. Mills did his doctoral work at, and received a Ph.D. from, the University of Wisconsin (Scimecca, 1977). He took his first job at the University of Maryland but spent the bulk of his career, from 1945 until his death, at Columbia University.

Mills was a man in a hurry (Horowitz, 1983). By the time he died at 45 from his fourth heart attack, Mills had made a number of important contributions to sociology.

One of the most striking things about C. Wright Mills was his combativeness; he seemed to be constantly at war. He had a tumultuous personal life, characterized by many affairs, three marriages, and a child from each marriage. He had an equally tumultuous professional life. He seemed to have fought with and against everyone and everything. As a graduate student at Wisconsin, he took on a number of his professors. Later, in one of his early essays, he engaged in a thinly disguised

(Alt, 1985–1986). Mills was not a Marxist, and he did not read Marx until the mid-1950s. Even then he was restricted to the few available English translations because he could not read German. Because Mills had published most of his major works by then, his work was not informed by a very sophisticated Marxian theory.

Mills published two major works that reflected his radical politics as well as his weaknesses in Marxian theory. The first was *White Collar* (1951), an acid critique of the status of a growing occupational category, white-collar workers. The second was *The Power Elite* (1956), a book that sought to show how America was dominated by a small group of businessmen, politicians, and military leaders. Sandwiched in between was his most theoretically sophisticated work, *Character and Social Structure* (Gerth and Mills, 1953), coauthored with Hans Gerth (N. Gerth, 1993).

Mills's radicalism put him on the periphery of American sociology. He was the object of much criticism, and he, in turn, became a severe critic of sociology. The critical attitude culminated in *The Sociological Imagination* (1959). Of particular note is Mills's severe criticism of Talcott Parsons and his practice of grand theory.

Mills died in 1962, an outcast in sociology. However, before the decade was out, both radical sociology and Marxian theory would begin to make important inroads into the discipline.

critique of the ex-chairman of the Wisconsin department. He called the senior theorist at Wisconsin, Howard Becker, a "real fool" (Horowitz, 1983). He eventually came into conflict with his coauthor, Hans Gerth, who called Mills "an excellent operator, whippersnapper, promising young man on the make, and Texas cowboy á la ride and shoot" (Horowitz, 1983:72). As a professor at Columbia, Mills was isolated and estranged from his colleagues. Said one of his Columbia colleagues:

> There was no estrangement between Wright and me. We began estranged. Indeed, at the memorial services or meeting that was organized at Columbia University at his death, I seemed to be the only person who could not say: 'I used to be his friend, but we became somewhat distant.' It was rather the reverse.
>
> (cited in Horowitz, 1983:83)

Mills was an outsider, and he knew it: "I am an outlander, not only regionally, but down deep and for good" (Horowitz, 1983:84). In *The Sociological Imagination* (1959), Mills challenged not only the dominant theorist of his day, Talcott Parsons, but also the dominant methodologist, Paul Lazarsfeld, who also happened to be a colleague at Columbia.

Mills, of course, was at odds not only with people; he was also at odds with American society and challenged it on a variety of fronts. But perhaps most telling is the fact that when Mills visited the Soviet Union and was honored as a major critic of American society, he took the occasion to attack censorship in the Soviet Union with a toast to an early Soviet leader who had been purged and murdered by the Stalinists: "To the day when the complete works of Leon Trotsky are published in the Soviet Union!" (Tilman, 1984:8).

C. Wright Mills died in Nyack, New York, on March 20, 1962.

The Development of Conflict Theory 冲突理论的发展

Another precursor to a true union of Marxism and sociological theory was the development of a conflict-theory alternative to structural functionalism. As we have just seen, structural functionalism had no sooner gained leadership in sociological theory than it came under increasing attack. The attack was multifaceted: structural functionalism was accused of such things as being politically conservative, unable to deal with social change because of its focus on static structures, and incapable of adequately analyzing social conflict.

One of the results of this criticism was an effort on the part of a number of sociologists to overcome the problems of structural functionalism by integrating a concern for structure with an interest in conflict. This work constituted the development of *conflict theory* as an alternative to structural-functional theory. Unfortunately, it often seemed little more than a mirror image of structural functionalism with little intellectual integrity of its own.

The first effort of note was Lewis Coser's (1956) book on the functions of social conflict (Delaney, 2005a; Jaworski, 1991). This work clearly tried to deal with social conflict from within the framework of a structural-functional view of the world.

Although it is useful to look at the functions of conflict, there is much more to the study of conflict than an analysis of its positive functions.

The biggest problem with most of conflict theory was that it lacked what it needed most—a sound basis in Marxian theory. After all, Marxian theory was well developed outside of sociology and should have provided a base on which to develop a sophisticated sociological theory of conflict. The one exception here is the work of Ralf Dahrendorf (born 1929).

Dahrendorf is a European scholar who is well versed in Marxian theory. He sought to embed his conflict theory in the Marxian tradition. However, in the end, his conflict theory looked more like a mirror image of structural functionalism than like a Marxian theory of conflict. Dahrendorf's major work, *Class and Class Conflict in Industrial Society* (1959), was the most influential piece in conflict theory, but that was largely because it sounded so much like structural functionalism that it was palatable to mainstream sociologists. That is, Dahrendorf operated at the same level of analysis as the structural functionalists (structures and institutions) and looked at many of the same issues. In other words, structural functionalism and conflict theory are part of the same paradigm (see the Appendix). Dahrendorf recognized that although aspects of the social system could fit together rather neatly, there also could be considerable conflict and tension among them.

In the end, conflict theory should be seen as little more than a transitional development in the history of sociological theory. It failed because it did not go far enough in the direction of Marxian theory. It was still too early in the 1950s and 1960s for American sociology to accept a full-fledged Marxian approach. But conflict theory was helpful in setting the stage for the beginning of that acceptance by the late 1960s.

The Birth of Exchange Theory 交换理论的兴起

Another important theoretical development in the 1950s was the rise of exchange theory (Molm, 2001). The major figure in this development is George Homans, a sociologist whom we left earlier, just as he was being drawn to B. F. Skinner's psychological behaviorism. Skinner's behaviorism is a major source of Homans's, and sociology's, exchange theory.

At first, Homans did not see how Skinner's propositions, developed to help explain the behavior of pigeons, might be useful for understanding human social behavior. But as Homans looked further at data from sociological studies of small groups and anthropological studies of primitive societies, he began to see that Skinner's behaviorism was applicable and that it provided a theoretical alternative to Parsonian-style structural functionalism. This realization led in 1961 to Homans's book *Social Behavior: Its Elementary Forms*. This work represented the birth of exchange theory as an important perspective in sociology.

Homans's basic view was that the heart of sociology lies in the study of individual behavior and interaction. He was little interested in consciousness or in the various kinds of large-scale structures and institutions that were of concern to most sociologists. Rather his main interest was in the reinforcement patterns, the history of rewards and costs, that lead people to do what they do. Basically, Homans argued that people continue to do what they have found to be rewarding in the past. Conversely, they cease doing what has proved to be costly in the past. To understand behavior, we need to understand an individual's history of rewards and costs. Thus, the focus of sociology should be not on consciousness or on social structures and institutions but rather on patterns of reinforcement.

As its name suggests, exchange theory is concerned not only with individual behavior but also with interaction between people involving an exchange of rewards and costs. The premise is that interactions are likely to continue when there is an exchange of rewards. Conversely, interactions that are costly to one or both parties are much less likely to continue.

Another major statement in exchange theory is Peter Blau's *Exchange and Power in Social Life,* published in 1964. Blau basically adopted Homans's perspective, but there was an important difference. Whereas Homans was content to deal mainly with elementary forms of social behavior, Blau wanted to integrate this with exchange at the structural and cultural levels, beginning with exchanges among actors but quickly moving on to the larger structures that emerge out of this exchange. He ended by dealing with exchanges among large-scale structures.

Although he was eclipsed for many years by Homans and Blau, Richard Emerson (1981) has emerged as a central figure in exchange theory (Cook and Whitmeyer, 2000). He is noted particularly for his effort to develop a more integrated micro-macro approach to exchange theory. Exchange theory has now developed into a significant strand of sociological theory, and it continues to attract new adherents and to take new directions (Cook, O'Brien, and Kollock, 1990; Szmatka and Mazur, 1996).

拟剧论：戈夫曼的研究
Dramaturgical Analysis: The Work of Erving Goffman

Erving Goffman (1922–1982) is often thought of as the last major thinker associated with the original Chicago school (Travers, 1992; Tseelon, 1992); Fine and Manning (2000) see him as arguably the most influential twentieth-century American sociologist. Between the 1950s and the 1970s, Goffman published a series of books and essays that gave birth to dramaturgical analysis as a variant of symbolic interactionism. Although Goffman shifted his attention in his later years, he remained best known for his *dramaturgical theory.* (P. Manning, 2005a, 2007).

Goffman's best-known statement of dramaturgical theory, *Presentation of Self in Everyday Life,* was published in 1959. To put it simply, Goffman saw much in common between theatrical performances and the kinds of "acts" we all put on in our day-to-day actions and interactions. Interaction is seen as very fragile, maintained by social performances. Poor performances or disruptions are seen as great threats to social interaction just as they are to theatrical performances.

Goffman went quite far in his analogy between the stage and social interaction. In all social interaction there is a *front region,* which is the parallel of the stage front in a theatrical performance. Actors both on the stage and in social life are seen as being interested in appearances, wearing costumes, and using props. Furthermore, in both there is a *back region,* a place to which the actors can retire to prepare themselves for their performance. Backstage or offstage, in theater terms, the actors can shed their roles and be themselves.

Dramaturgical analysis is clearly consistent with its symbolic-interactionist roots. It has a focus on actors, action, and interaction. Working in the same arena as traditional symbolic interactionism, Goffman found a brilliant metaphor in the theater to shed new light on small-scale social processes (P. Manning, 1991, 1992).

日常生活社会学的发展
The Development of Sociologies of Everyday Life

The 1960s and 1970s witnessed a boom (Ritzer, 1975a, 1975b) in several theoretical perspectives that can be lumped together under the heading of sociologies of everyday life (Schutte, 2007; Fontana, 2005; J. Douglas, 1980; Weigert, 1981).

现象学社会学和阿尔弗雷德·舒茨（1899—1959）的研究
Phenomenological Sociology and the Work of Alfred Schutz (1899–1959)

The philosophy of phenomenology (Srubar, 2005), with its focus on consciousness, has a long history, but the effort to develop a sociological variant of phenomenology (Ferguson, 2001) can be traced to the publication of Alfred Schutz's *The Phenomenology of the Social World* in Germany in 1932 (Hall, 2007; Prendergast, 2005a; Rogers, 2000). Schutz was focally concerned with the way in which people grasp the consciousness of others while they live within their own stream of consciousness. Schutz also used intersubjectivity in a larger sense to mean a concern with the social world, especially the social nature of knowledge.

Much of Schutz's work focuses on an aspect of the social world called the *life-world,* or the world of everyday life. This is an intersubjective world in which people both create social reality and are constrained by the preexisting social and cultural structures created by their predecessors. Although much of the life-world is shared, there are also private (biographically articulated) aspects of that world. Within the life-world, Schutz differentiated between intimate face-to-face relationships ("we-relations") and distant and impersonal relationships ("they-relations"). While face-to-face relations are of great importance in the life-world, it is far easier for the sociologist to study more impersonal relations scientifically. Although Schutz turned away from consciousness and to the intersubjective life-world, he did offer insights into consciousness, especially in his thoughts on meaning and people's motives.

Overall, Schutz was concerned with the dialectical relationship between the way people construct social reality and the obdurate social and cultural reality that they inherit from those who preceded them in the social world.

Ethnomethodology 民族方法学

Although there are important differences between them, ethnomethodology and phenomenology are often seen as closely aligned (Langsdorf, 1995). One of the major reasons for this association is that the creator of this theoretical perspective, Harold Garfinkel, was a student of Alfred Schutz at the New School. Interestingly, Garfinkel previously had studied under Talcott Parsons, and it was the fusion of Parsonsian and Schutzian ideas that helped give ethnomethodology its distinctive orientation.

Basically, *ethnomethodology* is the study of "the body of common-sense knowledge and the range of procedures and considerations [the methods] by means of which the ordinary members of society make sense of, find their way about in, and act on the circumstances in which they find themselves" (Heritage, 1984:4). Writers in this tradition are heavily tilted in the direction of the study of everyday life (Sharrock, 2001). Whereas phenomenological sociologists tend to focus on what people think, ethnomethodologists are more concerned with what people actually do. Thus, ethnomethodologists devote a lot of attention to the detailed study of conversations. Such mundane concerns stand in stark contrast to the interest of many mainstream sociologists in such abstractions as bureaucracies, capitalism, the division of labor, and the social system. Ethnomethodologists might be interested in the way a sense of these structures is created in everyday life; they are not interested in such structures as phenomena in themselves.

In the last few pages, we have dealt with several micro theories—exchange theory, phenomenological sociology, and ethnomethodology. Although the last two theories share a sense of a thoughtful and creative actor, such a view is not held by exchange theorists. Nevertheless, all three theories have a primarily micro orientation to actors and their actions and behavior. In the 1970s, such theories grew in strength in sociology and threatened to replace more macro-oriented theories (such as structural functionalism, conflict theory, neo-Marxian theories) as the dominant theories in sociology (Knorr-Cetina, 1981; Ritzer, 1985).

马克思主义理论的兴起与衰落（？）
The Rise and Fall (?) of Marxian Sociology

In the late 1960s, Marxian theory finally began to make significant inroads into American sociological theory (Cerullo, 1994). An increasing number of sociologists turned to Marx's original work, as well as to that of many Marxists, for insights that would be useful in the development of a Marxian sociology. At first this simply meant that American theorists were finally reading Marx seriously, but later there emerged many significant pieces of Marxian scholarship by American sociologists.

American theorists were particularly attracted to the work of the critical school, especially because of its fusion of Marxian and Weberian theory (Calhoun and Karaganis, 2001). Many of the works have been translated into English, and a number of scholars have written books about the critical school (for example, Jay, 1973; Kellner, 1993).

Along with an increase in interest came institutional support for such an orientation. Several journals devoted considerable attention to Marxian sociological theory, including *Theory and Society, Telos,* and *Marxist Studies.* A section on Marxist sociology was created in the American Sociological Association in 1977. Not only did the first generation of critical theorists become well known in America, but second-generation thinkers, especially Jurgen Habermas, received wide recognition.

Of considerable importance was the development of significant pieces of American sociology practiced from a Marxian point of view. One very significant strand is a group of sociologists practicing historical sociology from a Marxian perspective (for example, Skocpol, 1979; Wallerstein, 1974, 1980, 1989). Another is a group analyzing the economic realm from a sociological perspective (e.g., Baran and Sweezy, 1966; Braverman, 1974; Burawoy, 1979). Still others are doing fairly traditional empirical sociology, but work that is informed by a strong sense of Marxian theory (e.g., Kohn, 1976). A relatively recent and promising development is spatial Marxism. A number of important social thinkers (D. Harvey, 2000; Lefebvre, 1974/1991; Soja, 1989) have been examining social geography from a Marxian perspective.

However, with the disintegration of the Soviet Union and the fall of Marxist regimes around the world, Marxian theory fell on hard times in the 1990s. Some people remain unreconstructed Marxists; others have been forced to develop modified versions of Marxian theory (see the discussion below of the post-Marxists; there is also a journal entitled *Rethinking Marxism*). Still others have come to the conclusion that Marxian theory must be abandoned. Representative of the latter position is Ronald Aronson's book *After Marxism* (1995). The very first line of the book tells the story: "Marxism is over, and we are on our own" (Aronson, 1995:1). This from an avowed Marxist! Although Aronson recognizes that some will continue to work with Marxian theory, he cautions that they must recognize it is no longer part of the larger Marxian project of social transformation. That is, Marxian theory is no longer related, as Marx intended, to a program aimed at changing the basis of society; it is theory without practice. One-time Marxists are on their own in the sense that they can no longer rely on the Marxian project, but rather must grapple with modern society with their "own powers and energies" (Aronson, 1995:4).

Aronson is among the more extreme critics of Marxism from within the Marxian camp. Others recognize the difficulties, but seek in various ways to adapt some variety of Marxian theory to contemporary realities (Brugger, 1995; Kellner, 1995). Nevertheless, larger social changes have posed a grave challenge for Marxian theorists, who are desperately seeking to adapt to these changes in a variety of ways. Whatever else can be said, the "glory days" of Marxian social theory appear to be over. Marxian social theorists of various types will survive, but they are not likely to approach the status and power of their predecessors in the recent history of sociology.

While neo-Marxian theory will never achieve the status it once had, it is undergoing a mini-renaissance (e.g., Hardt and Negri, 2000) in light of globalization, perceptions that the rich nations are growing richer and the poor are growing poorer (Stiglitz, 2002), and the resulting worldwide protests against these disparities and other abuses. There are many who believe that globalization has served to open the entire world, perhaps for the first time, to unbridled capitalism and the excesses that Marxists believe inevitably accompany it (Ritzer, 2004b). If that is the case, and if the excesses continue and even accelerate, we will see a resurgence of interest in Marxian theory, this time applied to a truly global capitalist economy.

The Challenge of Feminist Theory 女性主义理论的挑战

Beginning in the late 1970s, precisely at the moment when Marxian sociology gained significant acceptance from American sociologists, a new theoretical outsider issued a challenge to established sociological theories—and even to Marxian sociology itself. This latest brand of radical social thought is contemporary feminist theory (Rogers, 2001).

In Western societies, one can trace the record of critical feminist writings back almost 500 years, and there has been an organized political movement by and for women for more than 150 years. In America in 1920, the movement finally won the right for women to vote; fifty-five years after that right had been constitutionally extended to all men. Exhausted and to a degree satiated by victory, the American women's movement over the next thirty years weakened in both size and vigor, only to spring back to life, fully reawakened, in the 1960s. Three factors helped create this new wave of feminist activism: (1) the general climate of critical thinking that characterized the period; (2) the anger of women activists who flocked to the antiwar, civil rights, and student movements only to encounter the sexist attitudes of the liberal and radical men in those movements (Densimore, 1973; Evans, 1980; Morgan, 1970; Shreve, 1989); and (3) women's experience of prejudice and discrimination as they moved in ever-larger numbers into wage work and higher education (Bookman and Morgen, 1988; Garland, 1988). For these reasons, particularly the last one, the women's movement continued into the twenty-first century, even though the activism of many other 1960s movements has faded. Moreover, during these years, activism by and for women became an international phenomenon, drawing in women from many societies. Feminist writing has now entered its "third wave" in the writings of women who will spend most of their adult lives in the twenty-first century (C. Bailey, 1997; Orr, 1997). The most significant recent change in the women's movement has been the emergence among activist women of both a feminist and an anti-feminist movement (Fraser, 1989).

A major feature of this international women's movement has been an explosively growing new literature on women that makes visible all aspects of women's previously unconsidered lives and experiences. This literature, which is popularly referred to as *women's studies,* is the work of an international and interdisciplinary community of writers, located both within and outside universities and writing for both the general public and specialized academic audiences. Feminist scholars have launched a probing, multifaceted critique that makes visible the complexity of the system that subordinates women.

Feminist theory is the theoretical strand running through this literature: sometimes implicit in writings on such substantive issues as work or rape or popular culture; sometimes centrally and explicitly presented, as in the analyses of motherhood; and increasingly the sole, systematic project of a piece of writing. Of this recent spate of wholly theoretical writing, certain statements have been particularly salient to sociology because they are directed to sociologists by people well versed in sociological theory. Journals such as *Signs, Feminist Studies, Sociological Inquiry,* and *Gender & Society* bring feminist theory to the attention of sociologists; however, there is hardly a sociological journal that could not be called pro-feminist.

Feminist theory looks at the world from the vantage points of women, with an eye to discovering the significant but unacknowledged ways in which the activities of women—subordinated by gender and variously affected by other stratificational practices such as class, race, age, enforced heterosexuality, and geosocial inequality—help create our world. This viewpoint dramatically reworks our understanding of social life. From this base, feminist theorists have begun to challenge sociological theory, especially its classical statements and early research.

Feminist writings now assume a critical mass in sociology. They offer an exciting paradigm for the study of social life. And those whose experiences and perceptions make them a receptive audience for this theory—women in general and both women and men affected by feminism in particular—may now constitute a numerical majority in the sociological community. For all these reasons, implications of feminist theory are moving increasingly into the mainstream of the discipline; engaging all its subspecialties; influencing many of its long-established theories, both macro and micro; and interacting with the new poststructuralist and postmodernist developments described below.

Structuralism and Poststructuralism 结构主义和后结构主义

One development that we have said little about up to this point is the increase in interest in *structuralism* (Lemert, 1990). We can get a preliminary feeling for structuralism by delineating the basic differences that exist among those who support a structuralist perspective. There are those who focus on what they call the "deep structures of the mind." It is their view that these unconscious structures lead people to think and act as they do. The work of the psychoanalyst Sigmund Freud might be seen as an example of this orientation. Then there are structuralists who focus on the invisible larger structures of society and see them as determinants of the actions of people as well as of society in general. Marx is sometimes thought of as someone who practiced such a brand of structuralism, with his focus on the unseen economic structure of capitalist society. Still another group sees structures as the models they construct of the social world. Finally, a number of structuralists are concerned with the dialectical relationship between individuals and social structures. They see a link between the structures of the mind and the structures of society. The anthropologist Claude Lévi-Strauss is most often associated with this view.

As structuralism grew within sociology, outside sociology a movement called *poststructuralism* was developing beyond the early premises of structuralism (McCormick 2007; Lemert, 1990). The major representative of poststructuralism is Michel Foucault (Dean, 2001; J. Miller, 1993). In his early work, Foucault focused on structures, but he later moved beyond structures to focus on power and the linkage between knowledge and power. More generally, poststructuralists accept the importance of structure but go beyond it to encompass a wide range of other concerns.

Poststructuralism is important not only in itself, but also because it is often seen as a precursor to postmodern social theory (to be discussed later in this chapter). In fact, it is difficult, if not impossible, to draw a clear line between poststructuralism and postmodern social theory. Thus Foucault, a poststructuralist, is often seen as a postmodernist, whereas Jean Baudrillard (1972/1981), who is usually labeled a postmodernist, certainly did work that is poststructuralist in character.

Late-Twentieth-Century Developments in Sociological Theory 20 世纪末社会学理论的发展

While many of the developments discussed in the preceding pages continued to be important in the late twentieth century, in this section we will deal with three broad movements—micro-macro integration, agency-structure integration, and theoretical syntheses—that were of utmost importance in that era and are to this day.

Micro-Macro Integration 微观—宏观的整合

A good deal of recent work in American sociological theory has been concerned with the linkage between micro and macro theories and levels of analysis (Berk, 2006; J. M. Ryan, 2005a; Barnes, 2001). In fact, Ritzer (1990a) argued that micro-macro linkage emerged as the central problem in American sociological theory in the 1980s, and it continued to be of focal concern in the 1990s. The contribution of European sociologist Norbert Elias (1939/1994) is an important precursor to contemporary American work on the micro-macro linkage and aids our understanding of the relationship between micro-level manners and the macro-level state (Kilminster and Mennell, 2000; Van Krieken, 2001).

There are a number of examples of efforts to link micro-macro levels of analysis and/or theories. I sought to develop a sociological paradigm that integrates micro and macro levels in both their objective and their subjective forms (Ritzer, 1979, 1981a). Thus, there are four major levels of social analysis that must be dealt with in an integrated manner: macro subjectivity, macro objectivity, micro subjectivity, and micro objectivity. Jeffrey Alexander (1982–1983) created a "multidimensional sociology" that deals, at least in part, with a model of levels of analysis that closely resembles my model. James Coleman (1986) concentrated on the micro-to-macro problem, while Allen Liska (1990) extended Coleman's approach to deal with the macro-to-micro problem as well. Coleman (1990) extended his micro-to-macro model and has developed a much more elaborate theory of the micro-macro relationship based on a rational choice approach derived from economics (see the following section on agency-structure integration).

Agency-Structure Integration 能动—结构的整合

Paralleling the growth in interest in the United States in micro-macro integration has been a concern in Europe for agency-structure integration (J. M. Ryan, 2005b; Sztompka, 1994). Just as I saw the micro-macro issue as the central problem in American theory, Margaret Archer (1988) saw the agency-structure topic as the basic concern in European social theory. Although there are many similarities between the micro-macro and agency-structure literatures (Ritzer and Gindoff, 1992, 1994), there are also substantial differences. For example, while agents are usually micro-level actors, collectivities such as labor unions can also be agents. And while structures are usually macro-level phenomena, we also find structures at the micro level. Thus, we must be careful in equating these two bodies of work and must take much care when trying to interrelate them.

There are several major efforts in contemporary European social theory that can be included under the heading of agency-structure integration. The first is Anthony Giddens's (1984) structuration theory. Giddens's approach sees agency and structure as a "duality." That is, they cannot be separated from one another: agency is implicated in structure, and structure is involved in agency. Giddens refuses to see structure as simply constraining (as, for example, does Durkheim), but instead sees structure as both constraining *and* enabling. Margaret Archer (1982) rejects the idea that agency and structure can be viewed as a duality, but rather sees them as a dualism. That is, agency and structure can and should be separated. In distinguishing them, we become better able to analyze their relationship to one another. Archer (1988) is also noted for extending the agency-structure literature to a concern for the relationship between culture and agency and for developing a more general agency-structure theory (Archer, 1995).

While both Giddens and Archer are British, another major contemporary figure involved in the agency-structure literature is Pierre Bourdieu from France (Bourdieu, 1977; Bourdieu and Wacquant, 1992; Swartz, 1997). In Bourdieu's work, the agency-structure issue translates into a concern for the relationship between habitus and field (Eisenberg, 2007). *Habitus* is an internalized mental, or cognitive, structure through which people deal with the social world. The habitus both produces, and is produced by, the society. The *field* is a network of relations among objective positions. The structure of the field serves to constrain agents, whether they are individuals or collectivities. Overall, Bourdieu is concerned with the relationship between habitus and field. The field conditions the habitus, and the habitus constitutes the field. Thus, there is a dialectical relationship between habitus and field.

The final major theorist of the agency-structure linkage is the German social thinker Jurgen Habermas. I have already mentioned Habermas as a significant contemporary contributor to critical theory. Habermas (1987a) has also dealt with the agency-structure issue under the heading of "the colonization of the life-world." The life-world is a micro world where people interact and communicate. The system has its roots in the life-world, but it ultimately comes to develop its own structural characteristics. As these structures grow in independence and power, they come to exert more and more control over the life-world. In the modern world, the system has come to "colonize" the life-world—that is, to exert control over it.

The theorists discussed in this section are not only the leading theorists on the agency-structure issue, they are arguably (especially Bourdieu, Giddens, and Habermas) the leading theorists in the world today. After a long period of dominance by American theorists (Mead, Parsons, Merton, Homans, and others), the center of social theory seems to be returning to its birthplace—Europe. Furthermore, Nedelmann and Sztompka argued that with the end of the Cold War and the fall of communism, we were about to "witness another Golden Era of European Sociology" (1993:1). This seems to be supported by the fact that today the works that catch the attention of large numbers of the world's theorists are European.

Theoretical Syntheses 理论走向综合

The movements toward micro-macro and agency-structure integration began in the 1980s, and both continued to be strong in the 1990s. They set the stage for the broader movement toward theoretical syntheses, which began at about the beginning of the 1990s. Reba Lewis (1991) has suggested that sociology's problem (assuming it has a problem) may be the result of excessive fragmentation, and that the movement toward greater integration may enhance the status of the discipline. What is involved here is a wide-ranging effort to synthesize two or more theories (for example, structural functionalism and symbolic interactionism). Such efforts have occurred throughout the history of sociological theory (Holmwood and Stewart, 1994). However, there are two distinctive aspects of the recent synthetic work in sociological theory. First, it is very widespread and not restricted to isolated attempts at synthesis. Second, the goal is generally a relatively narrow synthesis of theoretical ideas, and not the development of a grand synthetic theory that encompasses all of sociological theory. These synthetic works are occurring within and among many of the theories discussed in this chapter.

Then there are efforts to bring perspectives from outside sociology into sociological theory. There have been works oriented to bring biological ideas into sociology in an effort to create sociobiology (Crippen, 1994; Maryanski and Turner, 1992). Rational choice theory is based in economics, but it has made inroads into a number of fields including sociology (Heckathorn, 2005; Coleman, 1990). Systems theory has its roots in the hard sciences, but in the late twentieth century, Niklas Luhmann (1984/1995) made a powerful effort to develop a system theory that could be applied to the social world.

现代性和后现代性理论

Theories of Modernity and Postmodernity

Over the last several decades, social theorists[7] have become increasingly preoccupied with whether society (as well as theories about it) has undergone a dramatic transformation. On one side is a group of theorists (for example, Jurgen Habermas and Anthony Giddens) who believe that we continue to live in a society that still can best be described as modern and about which we can theorize in much the same way that social thinkers have long contemplated society. On the other side is a group of thinkers (for example, Jean Baudrillard, Jean-François Lyotard, and Fredric Jameson) who contend that society has changed so dramatically that we now live in a qualitatively different, postmodern society. Furthermore, they argue that this new society needs to be thought about in new and different ways.

The Defenders of Modernity 现代性的捍卫者

All the great classical sociological theorists (Marx, Weber, Durkheim, and Simmel) were concerned, in one way or another, with the modern world and its advantages and disadvantages (Sica, 2005). Of course, the last of these (Weber) died in 1920, and the world has changed dramatically since then. Although all contemporary theorists recognize these dramatic changes, there are some who believe that there is more continuity than discontinuity between the world today and the world that existed around the last *fin de siècle*.

Mestrovic (1998:2) has labeled Anthony Giddens "the high priest of modernity." Giddens (1990, 1991, 1992) uses terms such as "radical," "high," or "late" modernity to describe society today and to indicate that while it is not the same society as the one described by the classical theorists, it is continuous with that society. Giddens sees modernity today as a "juggernaut" that is, at least to some degree, out of control. Ulrich Beck (2005a, 1992) contends that whereas the classical stage of modernity was associated with

---

[7] The term *social* theorist rather than *sociological* theorist is used here to reflect the fact that many contributors to the recent literature are not sociologists, although they are theorizing about the social world.

industrial society, the emerging new modernity is best described as a "risk society." Whereas the central dilemma in classical modernity was wealth and how it ought to be distributed, the central problem in new modernity is the prevention, minimization, and channeling of risk (from, for example, a nuclear accident). Jurgen Habermas (1981, 1987b) sees modernity as an "unfinished project." That is, the central issue in the modern world continues, as it was in Weber's day, to be rationality. The utopian goal is still the maximization of the rationality of both the "system" and the "life-world." I also see rationality as the key process in the world today (Ritzer, 2004a). However, I pick up on Weber's focus on the problem of increasing formal rationality and the danger of an "iron cage" of rationality. Weber focused on the bureaucracy. Today I see the paradigm of this process as the fast-food restaurant, and I describe the increase in formal rationality as the McDonaldization of society.

The Proponents of Postmodernity 后现代性的支持者

Postmodernism was hot (Crook, 2001; Kellner, 1989a; Ritzer, 1997; Ritzer and Goodman, 2001). Indeed it was so hot and was discussed so endlessly in many fields in the late twentieth century, including sociology, that it seems already in the process of burning out (Lemert, 1994). We need to differentiate, at least initially, between postmodernity and postmodern social theory (Best and Kellner, 1991). *Postmodernity* is a historical epoch that is supposed to have succeeded the modern era, or modernity. *Postmodern social theory* is a way of thinking about postmodernity; the world is so different that it requires entirely new ways of thinking. Postmodernists would tend to reject the theoretical perspectives outlined in the previous section, as well as the ways in which the thinkers involved created their theories.

There are probably as many portrayals of postmodernity as there are postmodern social theorists. To simplify things, I will summarize some of the key elements of a depiction offered by one of the most prominent postmodernists, Fredric Jameson (1984, 1991). First, postmodernity is a depthless, superficial world; it is a world of simulation (for example, a jungle cruise at Disneyland rather than the real thing). Second, it is a world that is lacking in affect and emotion. Third, there is a loss of a sense of one's place in history; it is hard to distinguish past, present, and future. Fourth, instead of the explosive, expanding, productive technologies of modernity (for example, automobile assembly lines), postmodern society is dominated by implosive, flattening, reproductive technologies (television, for example). In these and other ways, postmodern society is very different from modern society.

Such a different world requires a different way of thinking. Rosenau (1992; Ritzer, 1997) defines the postmodern mode of thought in terms of the things that it opposes, largely characteristics of the modern way of thinking. First, postmodernists reject the kind of grand narratives that characterize much of classical sociological theory. Instead, postmodernists prefer more limited explanations, or even no explanations at all. Second, there is a rejection of the tendency to put boundaries between disciplines—to engage in something called sociological (or social) theory that is distinct from, say, philosophical thinking or even novelistic storytelling. Third, postmodernists are often more interested in shocking or startling the reader than they are in engaging in careful, reasoned academic discourse. Finally, instead of looking for the core of society (say, rationality or capitalistic exploitation), postmodernists are more inclined to focus on more peripheral aspects of society.

Although postmodern theory seems to have reached its peak and now is in decline, it continues to exert a powerful impact on theory. On the one hand, new contributions to the theory continue to appear (for example, Powell and Owen, forthcoming). On the other, it is very difficult to theorize these days without talking into account postmodern theory, especially its critiques of modern theorizing and its analyses of the contemporary world. Thus, Zygmunt Bauman (2007, 2006, 2005, 2003, 2000), to take one example, is producing a series of basically modern analyses of what he calls the "liquid" world, but it is a perspective strongly influenced by postmodern social theory including his own contributions to that theory.

21 世纪初的社会学理论展望

Theories to Watch in the Early Twenty-first Century

多元文化社会理论、酷儿理论以及对种族和种族主义的批判

Multicultural Social Theory, Queer Theory, and Critical Theories of Race and Racism

A recent development, closely tied to postmodernism—especially its emphasis on the periphery and its tendency to level the intellectual playing field—is the rise of multicultural social theory (Lemert, 2001; Rogers, 1996). This rise of multicultural theory was foreshadowed by the emergence of feminist sociological theory in the 1970s. The feminists complained that sociological theory had been largely closed to women's voices, and in the ensuing years, many minority groups echoed the feminists' complaints. In fact, minority women (for example, African Americans and Latinas) began to complain that feminist theory was restricted to white, middle-class females and had to be more receptive to many other voices. Today, feminist theory has become far more diverse, as has sociological theory.

Multicultural theory has taken a series of diverse forms. Examples include Afrocentric theory (Asante, 1996), Appalachian studies (Banks, Billings, and Tice, 1996), Native American theory (Buffalohead, 1996), and even theories of masculinity (Connell, 1996; Kimmel, 1996). Among the things that characterize multicultural theory are the following:

- Multicultural theories reject universalistic theories that tend to support those in power; multicultural theories seek to empower those who lack clout.
- Multicultural theory seeks to be inclusive, to offer theory on the behalf of many disempowered groups.
- Multicultural theorists are not value-free; they often theorize on behalf of those without power and work in the social world to change social structure, culture, and the prospects for individuals.
- Multicultural theorists seek to disrupt not only the social world but also the intellectual world; they seek to make it far more open and diverse.
- There is no effort to draw a clear line between theory and other types of narratives.

- There is ordinarily a critical edge to multicultural theory; it is both self-critical and critical of other theories and, most important, of the social world.
- Multicultural theorists recognize that their work is limited by the particular historical, social, and cultural context in which they happen to live (Rogers, 1996:11–16).

Two of the most important of today's multicultural theories are *queer theory* and *critical theories of race and racism (CTRR)*.

Queer theory grew out of a series of key publications, academic conferences, political organizations, and published texts largely during the early 1990s. Its theoretical roots lie in a number of fields including feminist studies, literary criticism, and, most notably, social constructionism and poststructuralism. Queer theory also has political sources, notably in the larger project of queer politics and groups such as ACT UP and Queer Nation. Academically, queer theory has strong early roots in the works of Michel Foucault, Judith Butler, Eve Kosofsky Sedgwick, and Teresa de Lauretis.

Queer theory involves a range of intellectual ideas rooted in the contention that identities are not fixed and stable and do not determine who we are. Rather, identities are seen as historically and socially constructed processes that are both fluid and contested. Further, these identities need not be gay or lesbian. In fact, queer theory does not seek to explain homosexual or heterosexual identities by themselves, but rather approaches the homosexual/heterosexual divide as a figure of knowledge and power that orders desires, behaviors, social institutions, and social relations. Thus, although queer theory does take sexuality as one of its central concerns, it is a much broader intellectual project than gay and lesbian, or even sexuality, studies. Queer theory is therefore both more than and less than a theory of queers.

Sociologists and other social scientists have been making significant contributions to theories of racism at least since W. E. B. Du Bois's work early in the twentieth-century. Such theorizing received an important impetus in recent years from the development of "critical race theory" largely in the field of law (Delgado and Stefancic, 2001). That theory was a result of the growing recognition that the momentum of the civil rights movement of the 1960s had been lost and what was needed was not only a revival of social activism but also new ways of theorizing race. Among the ideas of critical race theory are the following:

- Racism is endemic to American life and therefore difficult to deal with.
- There is little incentive to whites to deal with racism.
- Race is a social construction and therefore subject to manipulation, and this leads to skepticism about the law, which can be similarly manipulated.
- Different minority groups have been racialized at different times.
- Racial identity is not unidimensional or fixed.
- The experiences and communities of origin of racial minorities are of great importance and serve to give racial minorities unique expertise.
- Critical race theory is oriented to the elimination of racial oppression.

Critical theories of race and racism (CTRR) are rooted much more in the social sciences, including sociology, than is critical race theory. Thus, CTRR deal with such cutting-edge issues in theory as the relationship between race and racism and agency-structure, political economy, and globalization (including how race and racism relate to nation-states, nationalism, colonialism, neocolonialism, decolonization, imperialism, and empire). CTRR have a much broader, even global, focus than critical race theory. CTRR are also open to a much wider array of classical and contemporary theories as they apply to race, and they adopt a much broader macrostructural and macrocultural approach, especially one that focuses on power. A general conclusion to be derived from CTRR is that "race matters" and continues to matter not only in the legal system but throughout the structures and institutions of society (West, 1994). For example, Bonilla-Silva (2003) is critical of the view that racism today is of little more than historical interest. Rather, he sees color blindness as a smoke screen that allows white Americans to continue to perpetuate racial discrimination. Also in tune with CTRR is Bonilla-Silva's proposal for a variety of practical steps to deal with this new form of racism. Another distinctive characteristic of CTRR is their effort to show that race also matters globally (Winant, 2001).

Overall, there is as yet no "theory," critical or otherwise, of race and racism. However, there is a historical body of theory to draw on, and there are many available theoretical ideas and perspectives of great relevance, as well as a series of ideas developed already from within CTRR (e.g., intersectionality). This heritage, as well as ongoing work, will provide the base for the continuing development of CTRR.

后现代和后现代社会理论
Postmodern and Post-Postmodern Social Theories

Although postmodern social theories are no longer as hot as they once were, it is safe to assume that they will continue to influence sociology and many other fields. At the same time, there is already well established, primarily in France (the center of theoretical movements such as postmodernism), a body of work that is best thought of as post-postmodernism. For example, postmodern social theory is associated with a critique of a liberal, humanistic perspective and a shift away from a concern with the human subject. However, Ferry and Renaut (1985/1990) seek to rescue humanism and subjectivity, and Lilla (1994:20) offers a defense of human rights. Manent (1994/1998) self-consciously analyzes modernity and the human subject. Lipovetsky (1987/1994) attacks the tendency of postmodern social theorists to be hypercritical of the contemporary world by defending the importance of fashion. He argues, for example, that fashion enhances rather than detracts from individuality.

Theories of Consumption 消费理论

Coming of age during the Industrial Revolution, and animated by its problems and prospects, sociological theory has long had a "productivist bias." That is, theories have tended to focus on industry, industrial organizations, work, and workers. This bias is most obvious in Marxian and neo-Marxian theory, but it is found in many other theories, such as Durkheim's thinking on the division of labor, Weber's work on the rise of capitalism in the West and the failure to develop it in other parts of the world, Simmel's analysis of the tragedy of culture produced by the proliferation of human products, the interest of the Chicago school in work, and the concern in conflict theory with relations between employers and employees, leaders and followers, and so on. Much less attention has been devoted to consumption and the consumer. There are exceptions such as Thorstein Veblen's (1899/1994) famous work on "conspicuous consumption" and Simmel's thinking on money and fashion, but for the most part, social theorists have had far less to say about consumption than about production.

Postmodern social theory has tended to define postmodern society as a consumer society, with the result that consumption plays a central role in that theory (Venkatesh, 2007). Most notable is Jean Baudrillard's (1970/1998) *The Consumer Society.* Lipovetsky's post-postmodern work on fashion is reflective of the growing interest in and out of postmodern social theory in consumption. Since consumption is likely to continue to grow in importance, especially in the West, and production is likely to decline, it is safe to assume that we will see a dramatic increase in theoretical (and empirical) work on consumption (Ritzer, Goodman, and Wiedenhoft, 2001; for an overview of extant theories of consumption, see Slater, 1997, 2005). To take one example, we are witnessing something of an outpouring of theoretically based work on the settings in which we consume, such as *Consuming Places* (Urry, 1995), *Enchanting a Disenchanted World: Revolutionizing the Means of Consumption* (Ritzer, 2005a), and *Shelf Life: Supermarkets and the Changing Cultures of Consumption* (Humphery, 1998). We are likely to see much more work on such settings, as well as on consumers, consumer goods, and the process of consumption.

Theories of Globalization 全球化理论

Although there have been other important developments in theory in the early twenty-first century (see below), it seems clear that *the* most important developments are in theories of globalization (W. Robinson, 2007). Theorizing globalization is nothing new. In fact, it could be argued that although classical theorists such as Marx and Weber lacked the term, they devoted much attention to theorizing globalization. Similarly, many theories (e.g., modernization, dependency, and world-system theory) and theorists (e.g., Alex Inkeles, Andre Gunder Frank, and Immanuel Wallerstein) were theorizing about globalization in different terms and under other theoretical rubrics. Precursors to theorizing about globalization go back to the 1980s (and even before; see Moore, 1966; Nettl and Robertson, 1968) and began to gain momentum in the 1990s (Albrow and King, 1990; Albrow, 1996; Appadurai, 1996; Bauman, 1998; Garcia Canclini, 1995; Meyer, Boli, and Ramirez, 1997; Robertson, 1992). Such theorizing has really taken off in the twenty-first century (Beck, 2000, 2005b; Giddens, 2000; Hardt and Negri, 2000, 2004; Ritzer, 2004b, 2007c; Rosenau, 2003). Theorizing globalization has become so important that an entire chapter (Chapter 12) is devoted to it in this edition.

Theories of globalization can be categorized under three main headings—economic, political, and cultural theories. Economic theories, undoubtedly the best known, can be broadly divided into two categories: theories that celebrate the neoliberal global economic market (e.g., T. Friedman, 2000, 2005; see Antonio, 2007a, for a critique of

Friedman's celebration of the neoliberal market) and theories, often from a Marxian perspective (Hardt and Negri, 2000, 2004; W. Robinson, 2004; Sklair, 1992), that are critical of it.

In political theory, one position is represented by the liberal approach (derived from the classical work of John Locke, Adam Smith, and others) (MacPherson, 1962), especially in the form of neoliberal thinking (J. Campbell and Pederson, 2001) (often called the "Washington consensus" [Williamson, 1990, 1997]), which favors political systems that support and defend the free market. On the other side are thinkers more on the left (e.g., Hardt and Negri, 2000, 2004; D. Harvey, 2005) who are critical of this view.

A central issue in political theory is the continued viability of international relations. On the one side are those who see the nation-state as dead or dying in an era of globalization. This is naturally accompanied by the death of international relations and therefore of the global study of the relations among and between nation-states. On the other side of this issue are the defenders of the continued importance of the nation-state. At least one of them (J. Rosenberg, 2005) has gone so far as to argue that globalization theory has already come and gone as a result of the continued existence, even reassertion, of the nation-state (e.g., France and the Netherlands vetoing the EU constitution in 2005). As a result, it is argued that the field of international relations is, as it was before, at the center of global studies.

Although economic and political issues are of great importance, it is cultural issues and cultural theories that have attracted the most attention in sociology. We can divide cultural theories into three broad approaches (Pieterse, 2004). The first is *cultural differentialism,* in which the argument in made that among cultures there are deep and largely impervious differences that are unaffected or are affected only superficially by globalization (Huntington, 1996). Second, the proponents of *cultural convergence* argue that although important differences remain among cultures, there is also convergence, increasing homogeneity, across cultures (Boli and Lechner, 2005; Meyer et al., 1997; DiMaggio and Powell, 1983; Ritzer, 2004a, 2004b, 2007). Third, there is *cultural hybridization*, in which it is contended that the global and the local interpenetrate to create unique indigenous realities that can seen as "glocalization" (Robertson, 1992, 2001), "hybridization" (Canclini, 1995), and "creolization" (Hannerz, 1987). Much of the sociological thinking on globalization has been concerned with the issue, implied above, of the degree to which globalization is leading to homogenization or to heterogeneization.

It seems clear that the various theories of globalization, as well as later variants of it that will come to the fore in the coming years, will continue to dominate new developments in sociological theory. However, other developments are worth watching.

Actor-Network Theory 行动者—网络理论

Actor-network theory receives more attention in this edition because it seems to be growing increasingly important and expanding its influence into a variety of specific domains in sociology (e.g., in the study of consumption; see Warde, 2005), On the one hand it is part of the broad and increasing interest in networks of various kinds (e.g., Castells, 1996; Mizruchi, 2005). But on the other hand it has a variety of unique orientations, not the least of which is its notion of the *actant,* which involves a number of obvious inclusions such as human agents but also includes a wide variety of nonhuman actors such as the Internet, ATMs, and telephone answering machines. This is in line with the move in the social world toward, and increasing scholarly interest in, the *posthuman* (Franklin, 2007) and the *postsocial* (Knorr Cetina, 2001, 2005, 2007). That is, we are increasingly involved in networks that encompass both human and nonhuman components, and in their relationships with the latter, humans are clearly in a posthuman and postsocial world.

Practice Theory 实践理论

Another emerging theory, so new that it was not discussed in previous editions of this book, is practice theory. Actually, the work of some of the major contributors to this theory (such as Garfinkel, Bourdieu, Giddens, and Foucault) has been dealt with previously, but practice theory now shows signs of cohering into a distinctive theory that unites these and many other inputs. The focus is on practice, or human conduct, especially the impact of taken-for-granted assumptions on it. These assumptions are "pre-theoretical" in the sense that actors do not fully understand the nature of these assumptions and the degree of their impact on their practice (Biernacki, 2007). Practice is a routinized way of acting in which taken-for-granted assumptions affect how we act, especially how we manage our bodies, handle objects, treat subjects, describe things, and understand the world.

Take bodies, for example. In most other theories, the body is seen as being controlled by rational choices, larger structures, or normative systems. But to practice theory, practices are, at least in part, bodily performances that have been routinized. Practices come about as a result of training the body in a given way. Thus, for example, taking tennis lessons results in the ability of the body to hit a backhand or an overhead smash. This idea also extends to training the body so that talking, reading, and writing are made possible.

We are now at the close of the chapter reviewing developments in contemporary theory, but we certainly have not reached the end of theory development. Some of the theories discussed in this chapter will increase in importance (CTRR) while others (neo-functionalism) will experience a decline. One thing seems sure—the landscape of social theory is likely to be dotted with more theories, none of them is likely to gain hegemony in the field. Postmodernists have criticized the idea of "totalizations," or overarching theoretical frameworks. It seems unlikely that social theory will come to be dominated by a single totalization. Rather, we are likely to see a field with a proliferating number of perspectives that have some supporters and that help us understand part of the social world. Sociological theory will not be a simple world to understand and to use, but it will be an exciting world that offers a plethora of old and new ideas.

Summary 总结

This chapter picks up where Chapter 1 left off and deals with the history of sociological theory since the beginning of the twentieth century. We begin with the early history of American sociological theory, which was characterized by its liberalism, by its interest in Social Darwinism, and consequently by the influence of Herbert Spencer. In this context, the work of the two early sociological theorists, Sumner and Ward, is discussed. However, they did not leave a lasting imprint on American sociological theory. In contrast, the Chicago school, as embodied in the work of people such as Small, Park, Thomas, Cooley, and especially Mead, did leave a strong mark on sociological theory, especially on symbolic interactionism.

While the Chicago school was still predominant, a different form of sociological theory began to develop at Harvard. Pitirim Sorokin played a key role in the founding of sociology at Harvard, but it was Talcott Parsons who was to lead Harvard to a position of preeminence in American theory, replacing Chicago's symbolic interactionism. Parsons was important not only for legitimizing "grand theory" in the United States and for introducing European theorists to an American audience, but also for his role in the development of action theory and, more important, structural functionalism. In the 1940s and 1950s, structural functionalism was furthered by the disintegration of the Chicago school that began in the 1930s and was largely complete by the 1950s.

The major development in Marxian theory in the early years of the twentieth century was the creation of the Frankfurt, or critical, school. This Hegelianized form of Marxism also showed the influence of sociologists like Weber and of the psychoanalyst Sigmund Freud. Marxism did not gain a widespread following among sociologists in the early part of the century.

Structural functionalism's dominance within American theory in midcentury was rather short-lived. Although traceable to a much earlier date, phenomenological sociology, especially the work of Alfred Schutz, began to attract significant attention in the 1960s. Marxian theory was still largely excluded from American theory, but C. Wright Mills kept a radical tradition alive in America in the 1940s and 1950s. Mills also was one of the leaders of the attacks on structural functionalism, attacks that mounted in intensity in the 1950s and 1960s. In light of some of these attacks, a conflict-theory alternative to structural functionalism emerged in that period. Although influenced by Marxian theory, conflict theory suffered from an inadequate integration of Marxism. Still another alternative born in the 1950s was exchange theory, which continues to attract a small but steady number of followers. Although symbolic interactionism lost some of its steam, the work of Erving Goffman on dramaturgical analysis in this period gained a following.

Important developments took place in other sociologies of everyday life (symbolic interactionism can be included under this heading) in the 1960s and 1970s, including some increase in interest in phenomenological sociology and, more important, an outburst of work in ethnomethodology. During this period, Marxian theories of various types came into their own in sociology, although those theories were seriously compromised by the fall of the Soviet Union and other communist regimes in the late 1980s and early 1990s. Also of note during this period was the growing importance of structuralism and then poststructuralism, especially in the work of Michel Foucault. Of overwhelming significance was the explosion of interest in feminist theory, an outpouring of work that continues apace as we move through the 21st century.

In addition to those just mentioned, three other notable developments occurred in the 1980s and continued into the 1990s. First was the rise in interest in the United States in the micro-macro link. Second was the parallel increase in attention in Europe to the relationship between agency and structure. Third was the growth, especially in the 1990s, of a wide range of synthetic efforts: Finally, there was considerable interest in a series of theories of modernity and postmodernity in the latter part of the twentieth and early in the twenty-first century.

The chapter concludes with a discussion of some theories to watch as we move through the first decade of the twenty-first century. Multicultural theories, especially those associated with race (CTRR) and queer theory, are likely to flourish. Postmodern theories will not go away, but more attention may well be devoted to post-postmodern theories—theories that use postmodern ideas and that go beyond them. We can also expect increasing interest in consumption and in theorizing about it. This relates to postmodern theory (consumer society is closely associated with postmodern society), reflects changes in society from an emphasis on production to consumption, as well as a reaction against the productivist bias that has dominated sociological theory since its inception. Perhaps the most dramatic growth is taking place, and is likely to continue to take place, in theories of globalization. Other theories to watch are actor-network and practice theory.

PART II

第二部分　现代社会学理论：主要流派
Modern Sociological Theory: The Major Schools

CHAPTER 3

Structural Functionalism, Neofunctionalism, and Conflict Theory
第3章　结构功能主义、新功能主义和冲突理论

Chapter Outline
Structural Functionalism
Neofunctionalism
Conflict Theory

Structural functionalism, especially in the work of Talcott Parsons, Robert Merton, and their students and followers, was for many years *the* dominant sociological theory. However, in the last three decades it has declined dramatically in importance (Chriss, 1995) and, in at least some senses, has receded into the recent history of sociological theory. This decline is reflected in Colomy's (1990a) description of structural functionalism as a theoretical "tradition." Structural functionalism is now mainly of historical significance, although it is also notable for the role it played in the emergence of neofunctionalism in the 1980s (Nielsen, 2007b). After offering an overview of structural functionalism, we will discuss neofunctionalism as a possible successor to it as well as an example of the recent movement toward synthesis within sociological theory (Abrahamson, 2001). However, the future of neofunctionalism itself has been cast into doubt by the fact that its founder, Jeffrey Alexander (personal communication, October 17, 1994), has arrived at the conclusion that neofunctionalism "is no longer satisfactory to me." He states, "I am now separating myself from the movement I started."

For many years, the major alternative to structural functionalism was conflict theory. We will discuss Ralf Dahrendorf's traditional version of conflict theory, as well as a more recent integrative and synthetic effort by Randall Collins.

Before turning to the specifics of structural functionalism and conflict theory, we need, following Thomas Bernard (1983), to place these theories in the broader context of the debate between consensus theories (one of which is structural functionalism) and conflict theories (one of which is the sociological conflict theory that will be discussed in this chapter). *Consensus theories* see shared norms and values as fundamental to society, focus on social order based on tacit agreements, and view social change as occurring in a slow and orderly fashion. In contrast, *conflict theories* emphasize the dominance of some social groups by others, see social order as based on manipulation and control by dominant groups, and view social change as occurring rapidly and in a disorderly fashion as subordinate groups overthrow dominant groups.

Although these criteria broadly define the essential differences between the sociological theories of structural functionalism and conflict theory, Bernard's view is that the disagreement is far broader and has "been a recurring debate that has taken a variety of different forms throughout the history of Western thought" (1983:6). Bernard traced the debate back to ancient Greece (and the differences between Plato [consensus] and Aristotle [conflict]) and through the history of philosophy. Later, in sociology, the debate was joined by (the conflict theorist is listed first) Marx and Comte, Simmel and Durkheim, and Dahrendorf and Parsons. We already have examined briefly the ideas of the first two pairs of sociologists (although, as we have seen, their work is far broader than is implied by the label "conflict" or "consensus" theorist); in this chapter we examine Dahrendorf's conflict theory and Parsons's consensus theory, among others.

Although we emphasize the differences between structural functionalism and conflict theory, we should not forget that they have important similarities. In fact, Bernard argues that "the areas of agreement among them are more extensive than the areas of disagreement" (1983:214). For example, they are both macro-level theories focally concerned with large-scale social structures and social institutions. As a result, in my terms, both theories exist within the same sociological ("social facts") paradigm (see the Appendix) (Ritzer, 1980).

Structural Functionalism 结构功能主义

Robert Nisbet argued that structural functionalism was "without any doubt, the single most significant body of theory in the social sciences in the present [20th] century" (cited in J. H. Turner and Maryanski, 1979:xi). Kingsley Davis (1959) took the position that structural functionalism was, for all intents and purposes, synonymous with sociology. Alvin Gouldner (1970) implicitly took a similar position when he attacked Western sociology largely through a critical analysis of the structural-functional theories of Talcott Parsons.

Despite its undoubted hegemony in the two decades after World War II, structural functionalism has declined in importance as a sociological theory. Even Wilbert

Moore, a man who was intimately associated with this theory, argued that it had "become an embarrassment in contemporary theoretical sociology" (1978:321). Two observers even stated: "Thus, functionalism as an explanatory theory is, we feel, 'dead' and continued efforts to use functionalism as a theoretical explanation should be abandoned in favor of more promising theoretical perspectives" (J. H. Turner and Maryanski, 1979:141).[1] Nicholas Demerath and Richard Peterson (1967) took a more positive view, arguing that structural functionalism is not a passing fad. However, they admitted that it is likely to evolve into another sociological theory, just as this theory itself evolved out of the earlier organicism. The rise of neofunctionalism (which we will discuss later in this chapter) seems to support Demerath and Peterson's position rather than the more negative perspective of Turner and Maryanski.

In structural functionalism, the terms *structural* and *functional* need not be used in conjunction, although they typically are conjoined. We could study the structures of society without being concerned with their functions (or consequences) for other structures. Similarly, we could examine the functions of a variety of social processes that may not take a structural form. Still, the concern for both elements characterizes structural functionalism. Although structural functionalism takes various forms (Abrahamson, 1978), *societal functionalism* is the dominant approach among sociological structural functionalists (Sztompka, 1974) and as such will be the focus of this chapter. The primary concern of societal functionalism is the large-scale social structures and institutions of society, their interrelationships, and their constraining effects on actors.

阶层化的功能理论及其批评
The Functional Theory of Stratification and Its Critics

The functional theory of stratification as articulated by Kingsley Davis and Wilbert Moore (1945) is perhaps the best-known single piece of work in structural-functional theory. Davis and Moore made it clear that they regarded social stratification as both universal and necessary. They argued that no society is ever unstratified, or totally classless. Stratification is, in their view, a *functional* necessity. All societies need such a system, and this need brings into existence a system of stratification.[2] They also viewed a stratification system as a structure, pointing out that stratification refers not to the individuals in the stratification system but rather to a system of *positions*. They focused on how certain positions come to carry with them different degrees of prestige, not on how individuals come to occupy certain positions.

Given this focus, the major functional issue is how a society motivates and places people in their "proper" positions in the stratification system. This is reducible to two problems. First, how does a society instill in the "proper" individuals the desire to fill certain positions? Second, once people are in the right positions, how does society then instill in them the desire to fulfill the requirements of those positions?

---

[1] Despite this statement, Jonathan Turner and Alexandra Maryanski (1979) are willing to argue that functionalism can continue to be useful as a method.

[2] This is an example of a teleological argument. We will have occasion to discuss this issue later in the chapter, but for now we can define a *teleological argument* as one that sees the social world as having purposes, or goals, which bring needed structures or events into being. In this case society "needs" stratification, and so it brings such a system into existence.

Proper social placement in society is a problem for three basic reasons. First, some positions are more pleasant to occupy than others. Second, some positions are more important to the survival of society than others. Third, different social positions require different abilities and talents.

Although these issues apply to all social positions, Davis and Moore were concerned with the functionally more important positions in society. The positions that rank high within the stratification system are presumed to be those that are *less* pleasant to occupy but *more* important to the survival of society and that require the greatest ability and talent. In addition, society must attach sufficient rewards to these positions so that enough people will seek to occupy them and the individuals who do come to occupy them will work diligently. The converse was implied by Davis and Moore but was not discussed. That is, low-ranking positions in the stratification system are presumed to be *more* pleasant and *less* important and to require less ability and talent. Also, society has less need to be sure that individuals occupy these positions and perform their duties with diligence.

Davis and Moore did not argue that a society consciously develops a stratification system in order to be sure that the high-level positions are filled, and filled adequately. Rather, they made it clear that stratification is an "unconsciously evolved device." However, it is a device that every society does, and *must,* develop if it is to survive.

To be sure that people occupy the higher-ranking positions, society must, in Davis and Moore's view, provide these individuals with various rewards, including great prestige, a high salary, and sufficient leisure. For example, to ensure enough doctors for our society, we need to offer them these and other rewards. Davis and Moore implied that we could not expect people to undertake the "burdensome" and "expensive" process of medical education if we did not offer such rewards. The implication seems to be that people at the top must receive the rewards that they do. If they did not, those positions would remain understaffed or unfilled and society would crumble.

The structural-functional theory of stratification has been subject to much criticism since its publication in 1945 (see Tumin, 1953, for the first important criticism; Huaco, 1966, for a good summary of the main criticisms to that date; and P. McLaughlin, 2001, for a philosophical overview).

One basic criticism is that the functional theory of stratification simply perpetuates the privileged position of those people who already have power, prestige, and money. It does this by arguing that such people deserve their rewards; indeed, they need to be offered such rewards for the good of society.

The functional theory also can be criticized for assuming that simply because a stratified social structure existed in the past, it must continue to exist in the future. It is possible that future societies will be organized in other, nonstratified ways.

In addition, it has been argued that the idea of functional positions varying in their importance to society is difficult to support. Are garbage collectors really any less important to the survival of society than advertising executives? Despite the lower pay and prestige of the garbage collectors, they actually may be *more* important to the survival of the society. Even in cases where it could be said that one position serves a more important function for society, the greater rewards do not necessarily accrue to the more important position. Nurses may be much more important to society than movie stars are, but nurses have far less power, prestige, and income than movie stars have.

Is there really a scarcity of people capable of filling high-level positions? In fact, many people are prevented from obtaining the training they need to achieve prestigious positions even though they have the ability. In the medical profession, for example, there is a persistent effort to limit the number of practicing doctors. In general, many able people never get a chance to show that they can handle high-ranking positions even though there is a clear need for them and their contributions. Those in high-ranking positions have a vested interest in keeping their own numbers small and their power and income high.

Finally, it can be argued that we do not have to offer people power, prestige, and income to get them to want to occupy high-level positions. People can be equally motivated by the satisfaction of doing a job well or by the opportunity to be of service to others.

帕森斯的结构功能论
Talcott Parsons's Structural Functionalism

Over the course of his life, Talcott Parsons did a great deal of theoretical work (Münch, 2005; Holmwood, 1996; Lidz, 2000). There are important differences between his early work and his later work. In this section we deal with his later, structural-functional theorizing. We begin this discussion of Parsons's structural functionalism with the four functional imperatives for all "action" systems, his famous AGIL scheme. After this discussion of the four functions, we will turn to an analysis of Parsons's ideas on structures and systems.

AGIL AGIL

A *function* is "a complex of activities directed towards meeting a need or needs of the system" (R. Stryker, 2007; Rocher, 1975:40). Using this definition, Parsons believes that there are four functional imperatives that are necessary for (characteristic of) all systems—adaptation (A), goal attainment (G), integration (I), and latency (L), or pattern maintenance. Together, these four functional imperatives are known as the AGIL scheme. In order to survive, a system must perform these four functions:

1. *Adaptation:* A system must cope with external situational exigencies. It must adapt to its environment and adapt the environment to its needs.
2. *Goal attainment:* A system must define and achieve its primary goals.
3. *Integration:* A system must regulate the interrelationship of its component parts. It also must manage the relationship among the other three functional imperatives (A, G, L).
4. *Latency (pattern maintenance):* A system must furnish, maintain, and renew both the motivation of individuals and the cultural patterns that create and sustain that motivation.

FIGURE 3.1   *Structure of the General Action System*

Parsons designed the AGIL scheme to be used at *all* levels in his theoretical system (for one example, see Paulsen and Feldman, 1995). In the discussion below on the four action systems, we will illustrate how Parsons uses AGIL.

The *behavioral organism* is the action system that handles the adaptation function by adjusting to and transforming the external world. The *personality system* performs the goal-attainment function by defining system goals and mobilizing resources to attain them. The *social system* copes with the integration function by controlling its component parts. Finally, the *cultural system* performs the latency function by providing actors with the norms and values that motivate them for action. Figure 3.1 summarizes the structure of the action system in terms of the AGIL schema.

The Action System 行为体系

We are now ready to discuss the overall shape of Parsons's action system. Figure 3.2 is an outline of Parsons's schema.

It is obvious that Parsons had a clear notion of "levels" of social analysis as well as their interrelationship. The hierarchical arrangement is clear, and the levels are integrated in Parsons's system in two ways. First, each of the lower levels provides the conditions, the energy, needed for the higher levels. Second, the higher levels control those below them in the hierarchy.

In terms of the environments of the action system, the lowest level, the physical and organic environment, involves the nonsymbolic aspects of the human body, its anatomy and physiology. The highest level, ultimate reality, has, as Jackson Toby suggests "a metaphysical flavor," but Toby also argues that Parsons "is not referring to the supernatural so much as to the universal tendency for societies to address symbolically the uncertainties, concerns, and tragedies of human existence that challenge the meaningfulness of social organization" (1977:3).

The heart of Parsons's work is found in his four action systems. In the assumptions that Parsons made regarding his action systems we encounter the problem of order that was his overwhelming concern and that has become a major source of criticism of his work (Schwanenberg, 1971). The Hobbesian problem of order—what prevents a social war of all against all—was not answered to Parsons's (1937) satisfaction by the earlier philosophers. Parsons found his answer to the problem of order

High information
(controls)

⇧

Hierarchy of
conditioning
factors

⇧

High energy
(conditions)

1. Environment of action:
   ultimate reality
2. Cultural system
3. Social system
4. Personality system
5. Behavioral organism
6. Environment of action:
   physical-organic environment

High information
(controls)

⇩

Hierarchy of
conditioning
factors

⇩

High energy
(conditions)

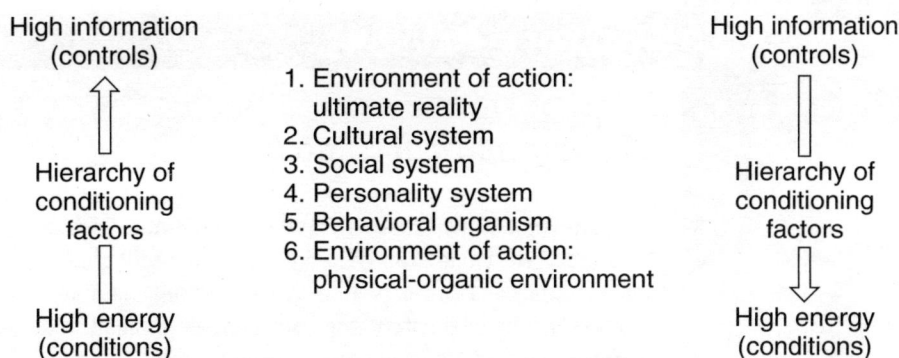

FIGURE 3.2   *Parsons's Action Schema*

in structural functionalism, which operates in his view with the following set of
assumptions:

1. Systems have the property of order and interdependence of parts.
2. Systems tend toward self-maintaining order, or equilibrium.[3]
3. The system may be static or involved in an ordered process of change.
4. The nature of one part of the system has an impact on the form that the other
    parts can take.
5. Systems maintain boundaries with their environments.
6. Allocation and integration are two fundamental processes necessary for a
    given state of equilibrium of a system.
7. Systems tend toward self-maintenance involving the maintenance of
    boundaries and of the relationships of parts to the whole, control of
    environmental variations, and control of tendencies to change the system
    from within.

These assumptions led Parsons to make the analysis of the *ordered* structure of
society his first priority. In so doing, he did little with the issue of social change, at
least until later in his career:

> We feel that it is uneconomical to describe changes in systems of variables before
> the variables themselves have been isolated and described; therefore, we have
> chosen to begin by studying particular combinations of variables and to move
> toward description of how these combinations change only when a firm foundation
> for such has been laid.

(Parsons and Shils, 1951:6)

Parsons was so heavily criticized for his static orientation that he devoted more
and more attention to change; in fact, as we will see, he eventually focused on the
evolution of societies. However, in the view of most observers, even his work on social
change tended to be highly static and structured.

---

[3] Most often, to Parsons, the problem of order related to the issue of why action was nonrandom or patterned. The
issue of equilibrium was a more empirical question to Parsons. Nonetheless, Parsons himself often conflated the issues
of order and equilibrium.

TALCOTT PARSONS

A Biographical Sketch

Talcott Parsons was born in 1902 in Colorado Springs, Colorado. He came from a religious and intellectual background; his father was a Congregational minister, a professor, and ultimately the president of a small college. Parsons got an undergraduate degree from Amherst College in 1924 and set out to do graduate work at the London School of Economics. In the next year, he moved on to Heidelberg, Germany. Max Weber had spent a large portion of his career at Heidelberg, and although he had died five years before Parsons arrived, Weber's influence survived and his widow continued to hold meetings in her home, meetings that Parsons attended. Parsons was greatly affected by Weber's work and ultimately wrote his doctoral thesis at Heidelberg, dealing, in part, with Weber's work (Lidz, 2007).

Parsons became an instructor at Harvard in 1927, and although he switched departments several times, Parsons remained at Harvard until his death in 1979. His career progress was not rapid; he did not obtain a tenured position until 1939. Two years previously, he had published *The Structure of Social Action*, a book that not only introduced major sociological theorists such as Weber to large numbers of sociologists but also laid the groundwork for Parsons's own developing theory.

After that, Parsons made rapid academic progress. He was made chairman of the Harvard sociology department in 1944 and two years later set up and chaired the innovative department of social relations, which included not only sociologists but a variety of other social scientists. By 1949 he had been elected president of the American Sociological Association. In the 1950s and into the 1960s, with the publication of such books as *The Social System* (1951), Parsons became the dominant figure in American sociology.

However, in the late 1960s, Parsons came under attack from the emerging radical wing of American sociology. Parsons was seen as a political conservative, and his theory was considered highly conservative and little more than an elaborate categorization scheme. But in the 1980s, there was a resurgence in interest in Parsonian theory not only in the United States but around the world (Alexander, 1982–1983; Buxton, 1985; Camic, 1990; Holton and Turner, 1986; Sciulli and Gerstein, 1985). Holton and Turner have perhaps gone the farthest, arguing that

In reading about the four action systems, the reader should keep in mind that they do not exist in the real world but are, rather, analytical tools for analyzing the real world.

"Parsons' work . . . represents a more powerful contribution to sociological theory than that of Marx, Weber, Durkheim or any of their contemporary followers"
(1986:13). Furthermore, Parsons's ideas influenced not only conservative thinkers
but neo-Marxian theorists as well, especially Jurgen Habermas.

Upon Parsons's death, a number of his former students, themselves sociologists of considerable note, reflected on his theory, as well as on the man behind
the theory (for a more recent, and highly personal, reminiscence, see Fox, 1997).
In their musings, these sociologists offered some interesting insights into
Parsons and his work. The few glimpses of Parsons reproduced here do not add
up to a coherent picture, but they offer some provocative glimpses of the man
and his work.

Robert Merton was one of his students when Parsons was just beginning
his teaching career at Harvard. Merton, who became a noted theorist in his own
right, makes it clear that graduate students came to Harvard in those years to
study not with Parsons but rather with Pitirim Sorokin, the senior member of the
department, who was to become Parsons's archenemy (Zafirovski, 2001):

> Of the very first generation of graduate students coming to Harvard . . . precisely
> none came to study with Talcott. They could scarcely have done so for the
> simplest of reasons: in 1931, he had no public identity whatever as a sociologist.
>   Although we students came to study with the renowned Sorokin, a
> subset of us stayed to work with the unknown Parsons.
>
> (Merton, 1980:69)

Merton's reflections on Parsons's first course in theory are interesting too,
especially because the material provided the basis for one of the most influential
theory books in the history of sociology:

> Long before Talcott Parsons became one of the Grand Old Men of world
> sociology, he was for an early few of us its Grand Young Man. This began with
> his first course in theory. . . . [It] would provide him with the core of his
> masterwork, *The Structure of Social Action* which . . . did not appear in print
> until five years after its first oral publication.
>
> (Merton, 1980:69–70)

Although all would not share Merton's positive evaluation of Parsons, they
would acknowledge the following:

> The death of Talcott Parsons marks the end of an era in sociology. When
> [a new era] does begin . . . it will surely be fortified by the great tradition of
> sociological thought which he has left to us.
>
> (Merton, 1980:71)

Social System   Parsons's conception of the social system begins at the micro level
with interaction between ego and alter ego, defined as the most elementary form of
the social system. He spent little time analyzing this level, although he did argue that

features of this interaction system are present in the more complex forms taken by the social system. Parsons defined a *social system* thus:

> A social system consists in a plurality of individual actors *interacting* with each other in a situation which has at least a physical or environmental aspect, actors who are motivated in terms of a tendency to the "optimization of gratification" and whose relation to their situations, including each other, is defined and mediated in terms of a system of culturally structured and shared symbols.
>
> (Parsons, 1951:5–6)

This definition seeks to define a social system in terms of many of the key concepts in Parsons's work—actors, interaction, environment, optimization of gratification, and culture.

Despite his commitment to viewing the social system as a system of interaction, Parsons did not take interaction as his fundamental unit in the study of the social system. Rather, he used the *status-role* complex as the basic unit of the system. This is neither an aspect of actors nor an aspect of interaction but rather a *structural* component of the social system. *Status* refers to a structural position within the social system, and *role* is what the actor does in such a position, seen in the context of its functional significance for the larger system. The actor is viewed not in terms of thoughts and actions but instead (at least in terms of position in the social system) as nothing more than a bundle of statuses and roles.

In his analysis of the social system, Parsons was interested primarily in its structural components. In addition to a concern with the status-role, Parsons (1966:11) was interested in such large-scale components of social systems as collectivities, norms, and values. In his analysis of the social system, however, Parsons was not simply a structuralist but also a functionalist. He thus delineated a number of the functional prerequisites of a social system. First, social systems must be structured so that they operate compatibly with other systems. Second, to survive, the social system must have the requisite support from other systems. Third, the system must meet a significant proportion of the needs of its actors. Fourth, the system must elicit adequate participation from its members. Fifth, it must have at least a minimum of control over potentially disruptive behavior. Sixth, if conflict becomes sufficiently disruptive, it must be controlled. Finally, a social system requires a language in order to survive.

It is clear in Parsons's discussion of the functional prerequisites of the social system that his focus was large-scale systems and their relationship to one another (societal functionalism). Even when he talked about actors, it was from the point of view of the system. Also, the discussion reflects Parsons's concern with the maintenance of order within the social system.

Actors and the Social System   However, Parsons did not completely ignore the issue of the relationship between actors and social structures in his discussion of the social system. In fact, he called the integration of value patterns and need-dispositions "the fundamental dynamic theorem of sociology" (Parsons, 1951:42). Given his central concern with the social system, of key importance in this integration are the processes of internalization and socialization. That is, Parsons was interested in the ways in which the norms and values of a system are transferred to the actors within the system. In a successful socialization process these norms and values are internalized; that is, they become part of the actors' "consciences." As a result, in pursuing their own interests, the actors are in fact serving the interests of the system as a whole. As Parsons put it, "The combination of value-orientation patterns which is acquired [by the actor in socialization] *must in a very important degree be a function of the fundamental role structure and dominant values of the social system*" (1951:227).

In general, Parsons assumed that actors usually are passive recipients in the socialization process.[4] Children learn not only how to act but also the norms and values, the morality, of society. Socialization is conceptualized as a conservative process in which need-dispositions (which are themselves largely molded by society) bind children to the social system, and it provides the means by which the need-dispositions can be satisfied. There is little or no room for creativity; the need for gratification ties children to the system as it exists. Parsons sees socialization as a lifelong experience. Because the norms and values inculcated in childhood tend to be very general, they do not prepare children for the various specific situations they encounter in adulthood. Thus socialization must be supplemented throughout the life cycle with a series of more specific socializing experiences. Despite this need later in life, the norms and values learned in childhood tend to be stable and, with a little gentle reinforcement, tend to remain in force throughout life.

Despite the conformity induced by lifelong socialization, there is a wide range of individual variation in the system. The question is: Why is this normally not a major problem for the social system, given its need for order? For one thing, a number of social control mechanisms can be employed to induce conformity. However, as far as Parsons was concerned, social control is strictly a second line of defense. A system runs best when social control is used only sparingly. For another thing, the system must be able to tolerate some variation, some deviance. A flexible social system is stronger than a brittle one that accepts no deviation. Finally, the social system should provide a wide range of role opportunities that allow different personalities to express themselves without threatening the integrity of the system.

Socialization and social control are the main mechanisms that allow the social system to maintain its equilibrium. Modest amounts of individuality and deviance are accommodated, but more extreme forms must be met by reequilibrating mechanisms. Thus, social order is built into the structure of Parsons's social system:

> Without deliberate planning on anyone's part there have developed in our type of social system, and correspondingly in others, mechanisms which, within limits, are capable of forestalling and reversing the deep-lying tendencies for deviance to get into the vicious circle phase which puts it beyond the control of ordinary approval-disapproval and reward-punishment sanctions.
>
> (Parsons, 1951:319)

---

[4] This is a controversial interpretation of Parsons's work with which many disagree. François Bourricaud, for example, talks of "the dialectics of socialization" (1981:108) in Parsons's work and not of passive recipients of socialization.

```
L                                    I


        ┌─────────────┬─────────────┐
        │  Fiduciary  │   Societal  │
        │   System    │  Community  │
        ├─────────────┼─────────────┤
        │             │             │
        │   Economy   │    Polity   │
        └─────────────┴─────────────┘

A                                    G
```

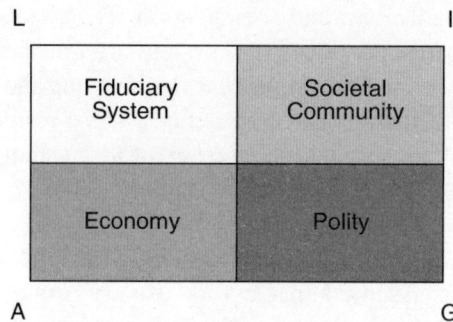

Figure 3.3   *Society, Its Subsystems, and the Functional Imperatives*

Again, Parsons's main interest was the system as a whole rather than the actor in the system—how the system controls the actor, not how the actor creates and maintains the system. This reflects Parsons's commitment on this issue to a structural-functional orientation.

Society   Although the idea of a social system encompasses all types of collectivities, one specific and particularly important social system is *society*, "a relatively self-sufficient collectivity the members of which are able to satisfy all their individual and collective needs and to live entirely within its framework" (Rocher, 1975:60).[5] As a structural functionalist, Parsons distinguished among four structures, or subsystems, in society in terms of the functions (AGIL) they perform (see Figure 3.3). The *economy* is the subsystem that performs the function for society of adapting to the environment through labor, production, and allocation. Through such work, the economy adapts the environment to society's needs, and it helps society adapt to these external realities. The *polity* (or political system) performs the function of goal attainment by pursuing societal objectives and mobilizing actors and resources to that end. The *fiduciary system* (for example, in the schools, the family) handles the latency function by transmitting culture (norms and values) to actors and allowing it to be internalized by them. Finally, the integration function is performed by the *societal community* (for example, the law), which coordinates the various components of society (Parsons and Platt, 1973).

As important as the structures of the social system were to Parsons, the cultural system was more important. In fact, as we saw earlier, the cultural system stood at the top of Parsons's action system, and Parsons (1966) labeled himself a "cultural determinist."[6]

Cultural System   Parsons conceived of culture as the major force binding the various elements of the social world, or, in his terms, the action system. Culture mediates

---

[5] Bernard Barber (1993, 1994) argues that while there is considerable terminological confusion in Parsons's work, the idea of a social system should be restricted to inclusive, total systems like societies.
[6] Interestingly Alexander and Smith (2001:139) describe Parsons as "insufficiently cultural," lacking a "thick description" of culture.

interaction among actors and integrates the personality and the social systems. Culture has the peculiar capacity to become, at least in part, a component of the other systems. Thus, in the social system culture is embodied in norms and values, and in the personality system it is internalized by the actor. But the cultural system is not simply a part of other systems; it also has a separate existence in the form of the social stock of knowledge, symbols, and ideas. These aspects of the cultural system are available to the social and personality systems, but they do not become part of them (Morse, 1961:105; Parsons and Shils, 1951:6).

Parsons defined the cultural system, as he did his other systems, in terms of its relationship to the other action systems. Thus *culture* is seen as a patterned, ordered system of symbols that are objects of orientation to actors, internalized aspects of the personality system, and institutionalized patterns (Parsons, 1990) in the social system. Because it is largely symbolic and subjective, culture is transmitted readily from one system to another. Culture can move from one social system to another through diffusion and from one personality system to another through learning and socialization. However, the symbolic (subjective) character of culture also gives it another characteristic, the ability to control Parsons's other action systems. This is one of the reasons Parsons came to view himself as a cultural determinist.

However, if the cultural system is preeminent in Parsonsian theory, we must question whether he offers a genuinely integrative theory. As pointed out in the Appendix, a truly integrative theory gives rough equivalency to all major levels of analysis. Cultural determinism, indeed any kind of determinism, is highly suspect from the point of view of an integrated sociology. (For a more integrated conception of Parsons's work, see Camic, 1990.) This problem is exacerbated when we look at the personality system and see how weakly it is developed in Parsons's work.

Personality System The personality system is controlled not only by the cultural system but also by the social system. That is not to say that Parsons did not accord some independence to the personality system:

> My view will be that, while the main content of the structure of the personality is
> derived from social systems and culture through socialization, the personality
> becomes an independent system through its relations to its own organism and
> through the uniqueness of its own life experience; it is not a mere epiphenomenon.
> (Parsons, 1970:82)

We get the feeling here that Parsons is protesting too much. If the personality system is not an epiphenomenon, it is certainly reduced to a secondary or dependent status in his theoretical system.

The *personality* is defined as the organized system of orientation and motivation of action of the individual actor. The basic component of the personality is the "need-disposition." Parsons and Shils defined *need-dispositions* as the "most significant units of motivation of action" (1951:113). They differentiated need-dispositions from drives, which are innate tendencies—"physiological energy that makes action possible" (Parsons and Shils, 1951:111). In other words, drives are better seen as part of the biological organism. Need-dispositions are then defined as "these same tendencies when they are not innate but acquired through the process of action itself" (Parsons and Shils, 1951:111). In other words, need-dispositions are drives that are shaped by the social setting.

Need-dispositions impel actors to accept or reject objects presented in the environment or to seek out new objects if the ones that are available do not adequately satisfy need-dispositions. Parsons differentiated among three basic types of need-dispositions. The first type impels actors to seek love, approval, and so forth, from their social relationships. The second type includes internalized values that lead actors to observe various cultural standards. Finally, there are the role expectations that lead actors to give and get appropriate responses.

This presents a very passive image of actors. They seem to be impelled by drives, dominated by the culture, or, more usually, shaped by a combination of drives and culture (that is, by need-dispositions). A passive personality system is clearly a weak link in an integrated theory, and Parsons seemed to be aware of that. On various occasions, he tried to endow the personality with some creativity. For example, he said: "We do not mean . . . to imply that a person's values are entirely 'internalized culture' or mere adherence to rules and laws. The person makes creative modifications as he internalizes culture; but the novel aspect is not the culture aspect" (Parsons and Shils, 1951:72). Despite claims such as these, the dominant impression that emerges from Parsons's work is one of a passive personality system.

Parsons's emphasis on need-dispositions creates other problems. Because it leaves out so many other important aspects of personality, his system becomes a largely impoverished one. Alfred Baldwin, a psychologist, makes precisely this point:

> It seems fair to say that Parsons fails in his theory to provide the personality with a reasonable set of properties or mechanisms aside from need-dispositions, and gets himself into trouble by not endowing the personality with enough characteristics and enough different kinds of mechanisms for it to be able to function.
>
> (A. Baldwin, 1961:186)

Baldwin makes another telling point about Parsons's personality system, arguing that even when Parsons analyzed the personality system, he was really not focally interested in it: "Even when he is writing chapters on personality structure, Parsons spends many more pages talking about social systems than he does about personality" (1961:180). This is reflected in the various ways Parsons linked the personality to the social system. First, actors must learn to see themselves in a way that fits with the place they occupy in society (Parsons and Shils, 1951:147). Second, role expectations are attached to each of the roles occupied by individual actors. Then there is the learning of self-discipline, internalization of value orientations, identification, and so forth. All these forces point toward the integration of the personality system with the social system, which Parsons emphasized. However, he also pointed out the possible malintegration, which is a problem for the system that needs to be overcome.

Another aspect of Parsons's work—his interest in internalization as the personality system's side of the socialization process—reflects the passivity of the personality system. Parsons (1970:2) derived this interest from Durkheim's work on internalization, as well as from Freud's work, primarily that on the superego. In emphasizing internalization and the superego, Parsons once again manifested his conception of the personality system as passive and externally controlled.

Although Parsons was willing to talk about the subjective aspects of personality in his early work, he progressively abandoned that perspective. In so doing, he limited his possible insights into the personality system. Parsons at one point stated clearly that he was shifting his attention away from the internal meanings that the actions of people may have: "The organization of observational data in terms of the theory of action is quite possible and fruitful in modified behavioristic terms, and such formulation avoids many of the difficult questions of introspection or empathy" (Parsons and Shils, 1951:64).

Behavioral Organism Though he included the behavioral organism as one of the four action systems, Parsons had very little to say about it. It is included because it is the source of energy for the rest of the systems. Although it is based on genetic constitution, its organization is affected by the processes of conditioning and learning that occur during the individual's life.[7] The behavioral organism is clearly a residual system in Parsons's work, but at the minimum Parsons is to be lauded for including it as a part of his sociology, if for no other reason than that he anticipated the interest in sociobiology and the sociology of the body (B. S. Turner, 1985) by some sociologists.

Change and Dynamism in Parsonsian Theory 帕森斯理论的变革和动力学

Parsons's work with conceptual tools such as the four action systems and the functional imperatives led to the accusation that he offered a structural theory that was unable to deal with social change. Parsons had long been sensitive to this charge, arguing that although a study of change was necessary, it must be preceded by a study of structure. But by the 1960s he could resist the attacks no longer and made a major shift in his work to the study of social change,[8] particularly the study of social evolution (Parsons, 1977:50).

Evolutionary Theory Parsons's (1966) general orientation to the study of social change was shaped by biology. To deal with this process, Parsons developed what he called "a paradigm of evolutionary change."

The first component of that paradigm is the process of *differentiation*. Parsons assumed that any society is composed of a series of subsystems that differ in both their *structure* and their *functional* significance for the larger society. As society evolves, new subsystems are differentiated. This is not enough, however; they also must be more adaptive than earlier subsystems. Thus, the essential aspect of Parsons's evolutionary paradigm was the idea of *adaptive upgrading*. Parsons described this process:

---

[7] Because of this social element, in his later work Parsons dropped the word *organism* and labeled this the "behavioral system" (1975:104).

[8] To be fair, we must report that Parsons had done some earlier work on social change (see Parsons, 1942, 1947; see also Alexander, 1981; Baum and Lechner, 1981).

> If differentiation is to yield a balanced, more evolved system, each newly
> differentiated substructure . . . must have increased adaptive capacity for
> performing its *primary* function, as compared to the performance of *that* function
> in the previous, more diffuse structure. . . . We may call this process the *adaptive
> upgrading* aspect of the evolutionary change cycle.
>
> (Parsons, 1966:22)

This is a highly positive model of social change (although Parsons certainly had a sense of its darker side). It assumes that as society evolves, it grows generally better able to cope with its problems. In contrast, in Marxian theory social change leads to the eventual destruction of capitalist society. For this reason, among others, Parsons often is thought of as a very conservative sociological theorist. In addition, while he did deal with change, he tended to focus on the positive aspects of social change in the modern world rather than on its negative side.

Next, Parsons argued that the process of differentiation leads to a new set of problems of *integration* for society. As subsystems proliferate, the society is confronted with new problems in coordinating the operations of these units.

A society undergoing evolution must move from a system of ascription to one of achievement. A wider array of skills and abilities is needed to handle the more diffuse subsystems. The generalized abilities of people must be freed from their ascriptive bonds so that they can be utilized by society. Most generally, this means that groups formerly excluded from contributing to the system must be freed for inclusion as full members of the society.

Finally, the *value* system of the society as a whole must undergo change as social structures and functions grow increasingly differentiated. However, since the new system is more diverse, it is harder for the value system to encompass it. Thus a more differentiated society requires a value system that is "couched at a higher level of generality in order to legitimize the wider variety of goals and functions of its subunits" (Parsons, 1966:23). However, this process of generalization of values often does not proceed smoothly as it meets resistance from groups committed to their own narrow value systems.

Evolution proceeds through a variety of cycles, but no general process affects all societies equally. Some societies may foster evolution, whereas others may "be so beset with internal conflicts or other handicaps" that they impede the process of evolution, or they may even "deteriorate" (Parsons, 1966:23). What most interested Parsons were those societies in which developmental "breakthroughs" occur, since he believed that once they occurred, the process of evolution would follow his general evolutionary model.

Although Parsons conceived of evolution as occurring in stages, he was careful to avoid a unilinear evolutionary theory: "We do not conceive societal evolution to be either a continuous or a simple linear process, but we can distinguish between broad levels of advancement without overlooking the considerable variability found in each" (1966:26). Making it clear that he was simplifying matters, Parsons distinguished three broad evolutionary stages—primitive, intermediate, and modern. Characteristically, he differentiated among these stages primarily on the basis of cultural dimensions. The crucial development in the transition from primitive to intermediate is the development of language, primarily written language. The key development in the shift from intermediate to modern is "the institutionalized codes of normative order," or law (Parsons, 1966:26).

Parsons next proceeded to analyze a series of specific societies in the context of the evolution from primitive to modern society. One particular point is worth underscoring here: Parsons turned to evolutionary theory, at least in part, because he was accused of being unable to deal with social change. However, his analysis of evolution is *not* in terms of process; rather, it is an attempt to "order structural types and relate them sequentially" (Parsons, 1966:111). This is comparative *structural* analysis, not really a study of the processes of social change. Thus, even when he was supposed to be looking at change, Parsons remained committed to the study of structures and functions.

Generalized Media of Interchange   One of the ways in which Parsons introduces some dynamism, some fluidity (Alexander, 1983:115), into his theoretical system is through his ideas on the generalized media of interchange within and among the four action systems (especially within the social system) discussed above (Treviño, 2005). The model for the generalized media of interchange is money, which operates as such a medium within the economy. But instead of focusing on material phenomena such as money, Parsons focuses on *symbolic* media of exchange. Even when Parsons does discuss money as a medium of interchange within the social system, he focuses on its symbolic rather than its material qualities. In addition to money, and more clearly symbolic, are other generalized media of interchange—political power, influence, and value commitments. Parsons makes it quite clear why he is focusing on symbolic media of interchange: "The introduction of a theory of media into the kind of structural perspective I have in mind goes far, it seems to me, to refute the frequent allegations that this type of structural analysis is inherently plagued with a static bias, which makes it impossible to do justice to dynamic problems" (1975:98–99).

Symbolic media of interchange have the capacity, like money, to be created and to circulate in the larger society. Thus, within the social system, those in the political system are able to create political power. More importantly, they can expend that power, thereby allowing it to circulate freely in, and have influence over, the social system. Through such an expenditure of power, leaders presumably strengthen the political system as well as the society as a whole. More generally, it is the generalized media that circulate between the four action systems and within the structures of each of those systems. It is their existence and movement that give dynamism to Parsons's largely structural analyses.

As Alexander (1983:115) points out, generalized media of interchange lend dynamism to Parsons's theory in another sense. They allow for the existence of "media entrepreneurs" (for example, politicians) who do not simply accept the system of exchange as it is. That is, they can be creative and resourceful and in this way alter not only the quantity of the generalized media but also the manner and direction in which the media flow.

罗伯特·默顿的结构功能主义

Robert Merton's Structural Functionalism

While Talcott Parsons is the most important structural-functional theorist, his student Robert Merton authored some of the most important statements on structural functionalism in sociology (Sztompka, 2000; Tiryakian, 1991). Merton criticized some of the more extreme and indefensible aspects of structural functionalism. But equally important, his new conceptual insights helped give structural functionalism a continuing usefulness (Jasso, 2000).

Although both Merton and Parsons are associated with structural functionalism, there are important differences between them. For one thing, while Parsons advocated the creation of grand, overarching theories, Merton favored more limited, middle-range theories. For another, Merton was more favorable toward Marxian theories than Parsons was. In fact, Merton and some of his students (especially Alvin Gouldner) can be seen as having pushed structural functionalism more to the left politically.

A Structural-Functional Model　结构—功能模型

Merton criticized what he saw as the three basic postulates of functional analysis as it was developed by anthropologists such as Malinowski and Radcliffe-Brown. The first is the postulate of the functional unity of society. This postulate holds that all standardized social and cultural beliefs and practices are functional for society as a whole as well as for individuals in society. This view implies that the various parts of a social system must show a high level of integration. However, Merton maintained that although it may be true of small, primitive societies, this generalization cannot be extended to larger, more complex societies.

Universal functionalism is the second postulate. That is, it is argued that *all* standardized social and cultural forms and structures have positive functions. Merton argued that this contradicts what we find in the real world. It is clear that not every structure, custom, idea, belief, and so forth, has positive functions. For example, rabid nationalism can be highly dysfunctional in a world of proliferating nuclear arms.

Third is the postulate of indispensability. The argument here is that all standardized aspects of society not only have positive functions but also represent indispensable parts of the working whole. This postulate leads to the idea that all structures and functions are functionally necessary for society. No other structures and functions could work quite as well as those that are currently found within society. Merton's criticism, following Parsons, was that we must at least be willing to admit that there are various structural and functional alternatives to be found within society.

Merton's position was that all these functional postulates rely on nonempirical assertions based on abstract, theoretical systems. At a minimum, it is the responsibility of the sociologist to examine each empirically. Merton's belief that empirical tests, not theoretical assertions, are crucial to functional analysis led him to develop his "paradigm" of functional analysis as a guide to the integration of theory and research.

Merton made it clear from the outset that structural-functional analysis focuses on groups, organizations, societies, and cultures. He stated that any object that can be subjected to structural-functional analysis must "represent a standardized (that is, patterned and repetitive) item" (Merton, 1949/1968:104). He had in mind such things as "social roles, institutional patterns, social processes, cultural patterns, culturally patterned emotions, social norms, group organization, social structure, devices for social control, etc." (Merton, 1949/1968:104).

Early structural functionalists tended to focus almost entirely on the *functions* of one social structure or institution for another. However, in Merton's view, early analysts tended to confuse the subjective motives of individuals with the functions of structures or institutions. The focus of the structural functionalist should be on social functions rather than on individual motives. *Functions,* according to Merton, are defined as "those observed consequences which make for the adaptation or adjustment of a given system" (1949/1968:105). However, there is a clear ideological bias when one focuses only on adaptation or adjustment, for they are always positive consequences. It is important to note that one social fact can have negative consequences for another social fact. To rectify this serious omission in early structural functionalism, Merton developed the idea of a *dysfunction.* Just as structures or institutions could contribute to the maintenance of other parts of the social system, they also could have negative consequences for them. Slavery in the southern United States, for example, clearly had positive consequences for white southerners, such as supplying cheap labor, support for the cotton economy, and social status. It also had dysfunctions, such as making southerners overly dependent on an agrarian economy and therefore unprepared for industrialization. The lingering disparity between the North and the South in industrialization can be traced, at least in part, to the dysfunctions of the institution of slavery in the South.

Merton also posited the idea of *nonfunctions,* which he defined as consequences that are simply irrelevant to the system under consideration. Included here might be social forms that are "survivals" from earlier historical times. Although they may have had positive or negative consequences in the past, they have no significant effect on contemporary society. One example, although a few might disagree, is the Women's Christian Temperance Movement.

To help answer the question of whether positive functions outweigh dysfunctions, or vice versa, Merton developed the concept of *net balance.* However, we never can simply add up positive functions and dysfunctions and objectively determine which outweighs the other, because the issues are so complex and are based on so much subjective judgment that they cannot be calculated and weighed easily. The usefulness of Merton's concept comes from the way it orients the sociologist to the question of relative significance. To return to the example of slavery, the question becomes whether, on balance, slavery was more functional or dysfunctional to the South. Still, this question is too broad and obscures a number of issues (for example, that slavery was functional for groups such as white slaveholders).

To cope with problems like these, Merton added the idea that there must be *levels of functional analysis.* Functionalists had generally restricted themselves to analysis of the society as a whole, but Merton made it clear that analysis also could be done on an organization, institution, or group. Returning to the issue of the functions of slavery for the South, it would be necessary to differentiate several levels of analysis and ask about the functions and dysfunctions of slavery for black families, white families, black political organizations, white political organizations, and so forth. In

ROBERT K. MERTON

*An Autobiographical Sketch**

It is easy enough to identify the principal teachers, both close at hand and at a distance, who taught me most. During my graduate studies, they were: P. A. Sorokin, who oriented me more widely to European social thought and with whom, unlike some other students of the time, I never broke although I could not follow him in the directions of inquiry he began to pursue in the late 1930s; the then quite young Talcott Parsons, engaged in thinking through the ideas which first culminated in his magisterial *Structure of Social Action;* the biochemist and sometime sociologist L. J. Henderson, who taught me something about the disciplined investigation of what is first entertained as an interesting idea; the economic historian E. F. Gay, who taught me about the workings of economic development as reconstructible from archival sources; and, quite consequentially, the then dean of the history of science, George Sarton, who allowed me to work under his guidance for several years in his famed (not to say, hallowed) workshop in the Widener Library of Harvard. Beyond these teachers with whom I studied directly, I learned most from two sociologists: Emile Durkheim, above all others, and Georg Simmel, who could teach me only through the powerful works they left behind, and from that sociologically sensitive humanist, Gilbert Murray. During the latter period of my life, I learned most from my colleague, Paul F. Lazarsfeld, who probably had no idea of how much he taught me during our uncountable conversations and collaborations during more than a third of a century.

Looking back over my work through the years, I find more of a pattern in it than I had supposed was there. For almost from the beginning of my own work, after those apprenticeship years as a graduate student, I was determined to follow my intellectual interests as they evolved rather than pursue a predetermined life-long plan. I chose to adopt the practice of my master-at-a-distance, Durkheim, rather than the practice of my master-at-close-range, Sarton. Durkheim repeatedly changed the subjects he chose to investigate. Starting with his study of the social division of labor, he examined methods of sociological inquiry and then turned successively to the seemingly unrelated subjects of suicide, religion, moral education, and socialism, all the while developing a theoretical orientation which, to his mind, could be effectively developed by attending to such varied aspects of life in society. Sarton had proceeded quite the other way: in his earliest years as a scholar, he had worked out a program of research in the history of science that was to culminate in his monumental five-volume *Introduction* [sic] *to the History of Science* (which carried the story through to the close of the fourteenth century!).

The first of these patterns seemed more suitable for me. I wanted and still want to advance sociological theories of social structure and cultural change that will help us understand how social institutions and the character of life in society come to be as they are. That concern with theoretical sociology has led me to avoid the kind of subject specialization that has become (and, in my opinion, has for the most part rightly become) the order of the day in sociology, as in other evolving disciplines. For my purposes, study of a variety of sociological subjects was essential.

In that variety, only one special field—the sociology of science—has persistently engaged my interest. During the 1930s, I devoted myself almost entirely to the social contexts of science and technology, especially in seventeenth-century England, and focused on the unanticipated consequences of purposive social action. As my theoretical interests broadened, I turned, during the 1940s and afterward, to studies of the social sources of nonconforming and deviant behavior, of the workings of bureaucracy, mass persuasion, and communication in modern complex society, and to the role of the intellectual, both within bureaucracies and outside them. In the 1950s, I centered on developing a sociological theory of basic units of social structure: the role-set and status-set and the role models people select not only for emulation but also as a source of values adopted as a basis for self-appraisal (this latter being "the theory of reference groups"). I also undertook, with George Reader and Patricia Kendall, the first large-scale sociological study of medical education, aiming to find out how, all apart from explicit plan, different kinds of physicians are socialized in the same schools of medicine, this being linked with the distinctive character of professions as a type of occupational activity. In the 1960s and 1970s, I returned to an intensive study of the social structure of science and its interaction with cognitive structure, these two decades being the time in which the sociology of science finally came of age, with what's past being only prologue. Throughout these studies, my primary orientation was toward the connections between sociological theory, methods of inquiry, and substantive empirical research.

I group these developing interests by decades only for convenience. Of course, they did not neatly come and go in accord with such conventional divisions of the calendar. Nor did all of them go, after the first period of intensive work on them. I am at work on a volume centered on the unanticipated consequences of purposive social action, thus following up a paper first published almost half a century ago and intermittently developed since. Another volume in the stocks, entitled *The Self-Fulfilling Prophecy*, follows out in a half-dozen spheres of social life the workings of this pattern as first noted in my paper by the same title, a mere third of a century ago. And should time, patience, and capacity allow, there remains the summation of work on the analysis of social structure, with special reference to status-sets, role-sets, and structural contexts on the structural side, and manifest and latent functions, dysfunctions, functional alternatives, and social mechanisms on the functional side.

Mortality being the rule and painfully slow composition being my practice, there seems small point in looking beyond this series of works in progress.

[For more on Merton, see Johnston, 2007; Sztompka, 2005; Schultz, 1995. Robert Merton died on February 23, 2003.]

terms of net balance, slavery was probably more functional for certain social units and more dysfunctional for other social units. Addressing the issue at these more specific levels helps in analyzing the functionality of slavery for the South as a whole.

Merton also introduced the concepts of *manifest* and *latent* functions. These two terms have also been important additions to functional analysis.[9] In simple terms, *manifest functions* are those that are intended, whereas *latent functions* are unintended. The manifest function of slavery, for example, was to increase the economic productivity of the South, but it had the latent function of providing a vast underclass that served to increase the social status of southern whites, both rich and poor. This idea is related to another of Merton's concepts—*unanticipated consequences.* Actions have both intended and unintended consequences. Although everyone is aware of the intended consequences, sociological analysis is required to uncover the unintended consequences; indeed, to some this is the very essence of sociology. Peter Berger (1963) has called this "debunking," or looking beyond stated intentions to real effects.

Merton made it clear that unanticipated consequences and latent functions are not the same. A latent function is one type of unanticipated consequence, one that is functional for the designated system. But there are two other types of unanticipated consequences: "those that are dysfunctional for a designated system, and these comprise the latent dysfunctions," and "those which are irrelevant to the system which they affect neither functionally or dysfunctionally . . . non-functional consequences" (Merton, 1949/1968:105).

As further clarification of functional theory, Merton pointed out that a structure may be dysfunctional for the system as a whole yet may continue to exist. One might make a good case that discrimination against blacks, females, and other minority groups is dysfunctional for American society, yet it continues to exist because it is functional for a part of the social system; for example, discrimination against females is generally functional for males. However, these forms of discrimination are not without some dysfunctions, even for the group for which they are functional. Males do suffer from their discrimination against females; similarly, whites are hurt by their discriminatory behavior toward blacks. One could argue that these forms of discrimination adversely affect those who discriminate by keeping vast numbers of people underproductive and by increasing the likelihood of social conflict.

Merton contended that not all structures are indispensable to the workings of the social system. Some parts of our social system *can* be eliminated. This helps functional theory overcome another of its conservative biases. By recognizing that some structures are expendable, functionalism opens the way for meaningful social change. Our society, for example, could continue to exist (and even be improved) by the elimination of discrimination against various minority groups.

---

[9] Colin Campbell (1982) has criticized Merton's distinction between manifest and latent functions. Among other things, he points out that Merton is vague about these terms and uses them in various ways (for example, as intended versus actual consequences and as surface meanings versus underlying realities). More important, he feels that Merton (like Parsons) never adequately integrated action theory and structural functionalism. The result is that we have an uncomfortable mixture of the intentionality ("manifest") of action theory and the structural consequences ("functions") of structural functionalism. Because of these and other confusions, Campbell believes, Merton's distinction between manifest and latent functions is little used in contemporary sociology.

Merton's clarifications are of great utility to sociologists (for example, Gans, 1972, 1994) who wish to perform structural-functional analyses.

Social Structure and Anomie 社会结构和失范

Before leaving this section, we must devote some attention to one of the best-known contributions to structural functionalism, indeed to all of sociology (Adler and Laufer, 1995; Merton, 1995; Menard, 1995)—Merton's (1968) analysis of the relationship between culture, structure, and anomie. Merton defines *culture* as "that organized set of *normative values* governing behavior which is common to members of a designated society or group" and *social structure* as "that organized set of *social relationships* in which members of the society or group are variously implicated" (1968:216; italics added). Anomie occurs "when there is an acute disjunction between the cultural norms and goals and the socially structured capacities of members of the group to act in accord with them" (Merton, 1968:216). That is, because of their position in the social structure of society, some people are unable to act in accord with normative values. The culture calls for some type of behavior that the social structure prevents from occurring.

For example, in American society, the culture places great emphasis on material success. However, by their position within the social structure, many people are prevented from achieving such success. If one is born into the lower socioeconomic classes and as a result is able to acquire, at best, only a high school degree, one's chances of achieving economic success in the generally accepted way (for example, through succeeding in the conventional work world) are slim or nonexistent. Under such circumstances (and they are widespread in contemporary American society) anomie can be said to exist, and as a result, there is a tendency toward deviant behavior. In this context, deviance often takes the form of alternative, unacceptable, and sometimes illegal means of achieving economic success. Thus, becoming a drug dealer or a prostitute in order to achieve economic success is an example of deviance generated by the disjunction between cultural values and social-structural means of attaining those values. This is one way in which the structural functionalist would seek to explain crime and deviance.

Thus, in this example of structural functionalism, Merton is looking at social (and cultural) structures, but he is not focally concerned with the functions of those structures. Rather, consistent with his functional paradigm, he is mainly concerned with dysfunctions, in this case anomie. More specifically, as we have seen, Merton links anomie with deviance and thereby is arguing that disjunctions between culture and structure have the dysfunctional consequence of leading to deviance within society.

It is worth noting that implied in Merton's work on anomie is a critical attitude toward social stratification (for example, for blocking the means of some to socially desirable goals). Thus, while Davis and Moore wrote approvingly of a stratified society, Merton's work indicates that structural functionalists can be critical of social stratification.

The Major Criticisms 主要的批评

No single sociological theory in the history of the discipline has been the focus of as much interest as structural functionalism. By the 1960s, however, criticisms of the theory had increased dramatically, and ultimately they became more prevalent than praise. Mark Abrahamson depicted this situation quite vividly: "Thus, metaphorically, functionalism has ambled along like a giant elephant, ignoring the stings of gnats, even as the swarm of attackers takes its toll" (1978:37).

Substantive Criticisms 实质性的批评

One major criticism is that structural functionalism does not deal adequately with history—that it is inherently ahistorical. In fact, structural functionalism was developed, at least in part, in reaction to the historical evolutionary approach of certain anthropologists. In its early years in particular, structural functionalism went too far in its criticism of evolutionary theory and came to focus on either contemporary or abstract societies. However, structural functionalism need not be ahistorical (J. H. Turner and Maryanski, 1979). In fact, Parsons's (1966, 1971) work on social change, as we have seen, reflects the ability of structural functionalists to deal with change if they so wish.

Structural functionalists also are attacked for being unable to deal effectively with the *process* of social change (Abrahamson, 1978; P. Cohen, 1968; Mills, 1959; J. H. Turner and Maryanski, 1979).[10] Whereas the preceding criticism deals with the seeming inability of structural functionalism to deal with the past, this one is concerned with the parallel incapacity of the approach to deal with the contemporary process of social change. Percy Cohen (1968) sees the problem as lying in structural-functional theory, in which all the elements of a society are seen as reinforcing one another as well as the system as a whole. This makes it difficult to see how these elements can also contribute to change. While Cohen sees the problem as inherent in the theory, Turner and Maryanski believe, again, that the problem lies with the practitioners and not with the theory.

Perhaps the most often voiced criticism of structural functionalism is that it is unable to deal effectively with conflict (Abrahamson, 1978; P. Cohen, 1968; Gouldner, 1970; Horowitz, 1962/1967; Mills, 1959; J. H. Turner and Maryanski, 1979).[11] This criticism takes a variety of forms. Alvin Gouldner argues that Parsons, as the main representative of structural functionalism, tended to overemphasize harmonious relationships. Irving Louis Horowitz contends that structural functionalists tend to see conflict as necessarily destructive and as occurring outside the framework of society. The issue once again is whether this is inherent in the theory or in the way practitioners have interpreted and used it (P. Cohen, 1968; J. H. Turner and Maryanski, 1979).

The overall criticisms that structural functionalism is unable to deal with history, change, and conflict have led many (for example, P. Cohen, 1968; Gouldner, 1970) to argue that structural functionalism has a conservative bias. It may indeed be true that there is a conservative bias in structural functionalism that is attributable not only to what it ignores (change, history, conflict) but also to what it chooses to

---

[10] However, there are some important works on social change by structural functionalists (C. Johnson, 1966; Smelser, 1959, 1962).

[11] Again, there are important exceptions—see Coser (1956, 1967), Goode (1960), and Merton (1975).

focus on. For one thing, structural functionalists have tended to focus on culture, norms, and values (P. Cohen, 1968; Mills, 1959; Lockwood, 1956). People are seen as constrained by cultural and social forces. As Gouldner says, to emphasize his criticism of structural functionalism, "Human beings are as much engaged in using social systems as in being used by them" (1970:220).

Related to their cultural focus is the tendency of structural functionalists to mistake the legitimizations employed by elites in society for social reality (Gouldner, 1970; Harré, 2002; Horowitz, 1962/1967; Mills, 1959). The normative system is interpreted as reflective of the society as a whole, when it may in fact be better viewed as an ideological system promulgated by, and existing for, the elite members of the society.

These substantive criticisms point in two basic directions. First, it seems clear that structural functionalism has a rather narrow focus that prevents it from addressing a number of important issues and aspects of the social world. Second, its focus tends to give it a very conservative flavor; structural functionalism has operated in support of the status quo and the dominant elites (Huaco, 1986).

Methodological and Logical Criticisms 方法论和逻辑上的批评

One of the often expressed criticisms (see, for example, Abrahamson, 1978; Mills, 1959) is that structural functionalism is basically vague, unclear, and ambiguous. Part of the ambiguity is traceable to the fact that structural functionalists choose to deal with abstract social systems instead of real societies.

A related criticism is that although no single grand scheme ever can be used to analyze all societies throughout history (Mills, 1959), structural functionalists have been motivated by the belief that there is a single theory or at least a set of conceptual categories that could be used to do this. Many critics regard this grand theory as an illusion, believing that the best sociology can hope for is more historically specific, "middle-range" (Merton, 1968) theories.

Among the other specific methodological criticisms is the issue of whether there are adequate methods to study the questions of concern to structural functionalists. Percy Cohen (1968), for instance, wonders what tools can be used to study the contribution of one part of a system to the system as a whole. Another methodological criticism is that structural functionalism makes comparative analysis difficult. If the assumption is that a part of a system makes sense only in the context of the social system in which it exists, how can we compare it with a similar part in another system? Cohen asks, for example: If the English family makes sense only in the context of English society, how can we compare it to the French family?

Teleology and Tautology   Percy Cohen (1968) and J. H. Turner and Maryanski (1979) see teleology and tautology as the two most important logical problems confronting structural functionalism. Some tend to see teleology as an inherent problem (Abrahamson, 1978; P. Cohen, 1968), but I believe that Turner and Maryanski (1979) are correct when they argue that the problem with structural functionalism is not teleology per se, but *illegitimate* teleology. In this context, *teleology* is defined as the view that society (or other social structures) has purposes or goals. In order to achieve these goals, society creates, or causes to be created, specific social structures and social institutions. Turner and Maryanski do not see this view as necessarily illegitimate; in fact, they argue that social theory *should* take into account the teleological relationship between society and its component parts.

The problem, according to Turner and Maryanski, is the extension of teleology to unacceptable lengths. An illegitimate teleology is one that implies "that purpose or end states guide human affairs when such is not the case" (J. H. Turner and Maryanski, 1979:118). For example, it is illegitimate to assume that because society needs procreation and socialization it will create the family institution. A variety of alternative structures could meet these needs; society does not "need" to create the family. The structural functionalist must define and document the various ways in which the goals do, in fact, lead to the creation of specific substructures. It also would be useful to be able to show why other substructures could not meet the same needs. A legitimate teleology would be able to define and demonstrate *empirically* and *theoretically* the links between society's goals and the various substructures that exist within society. An illegitimate teleology would be satisfied with a blind assertion that a link between a societal end and a specific substructure must exist.

The other major criticism of the logic of structural functionalism is that it is tautological. A *tautological* argument is one in which the conclusion merely makes explicit what is implicit in the premise or is simply a restatement of the premise. In structural functionalism, this circular reasoning often takes the form of defining the whole in terms of its parts and then defining the parts in terms of the whole. Thus, it would be argued that a social system is defined by the relationship among its component parts and that the component parts of the system are defined by their place in the larger social system. Because each is defined in terms of the other, neither the social system nor its parts are in fact defined at all. We really learn nothing about either the system or its parts.

Neofunctionalism 新功能主义

Under the barrage of criticisms, structural functionalism declined in significance from the mid-1960s to the present day. However, by the mid-1980s, a major effort was undertaken to revive the theory under the heading "neofunctionalism." The term *neofunctionalism* was used to indicate continuity with structural functionalism but also to demonstrate that an effort was being made to extend structural functionalism and overcome its major difficulties. Jeffrey Alexander and Paul Colomy define *neofunctionalism* as "a self-critical strand of functional theory that seeks to broaden functionalism's intellectual scope while retaining its theoretical core" (1985:11). Thus, it seems clear that Alexander and Colomy see structural functionalism as overly narrow and that their goal is the creation of a more synthetic theory, which they prefer to label "neofunctionalism."[12]

---

[12] J. H. Turner and Maryanski (1988) have challenged neofunctionalism by arguing that it is not really functional in its orientation, since it has abandoned many of the basic tenets of structural functionalism.

It should be noted that while structural functionalism in general, and Talcott Parsons's theories in particular, did become extremist, there was a strong synthetic core in the theory from its beginnings. On the one hand, throughout his intellectual life Parsons sought to integrate a wide range of theoretical inputs. On the other hand, he was interested in the interrelationship of the major domains of the social world, most notably the cultural, social, and personality systems. However, in the end, Parsons adopted a narrow structural-functionalist orientation and came to see the cultural system as determining the other systems. Thus, Parsons abandoned his synthetic orientation, and neofunctionalism can be viewed as an effort to recapture such an orientation.

Alexander (1985a:10) has enumerated the problems associated with structural functionalism that neofunctionalism needs to surmount, including "anti-individual-ism," "antagonism to change," "conservatism," "idealism," and an "antiempirical bias." Efforts were made to overcome these problems programmatically (Alexander, 1985b) and at more specific theoretical levels, for example Colomy's (1986; Alexander and Colomy, 1990b; Colomy and Rhoades, 1994) attempt to refine differentiation theory. Despite his enthusiasm for neofunctionalism, in the mid-1980s Alexander was forced to conclude that "neofunctionalism is a tendency rather than a developed theory" (1985b:16).

Although neofunctionalism may not be a developed theory, Alexander (1985a; see also Colomy, 1990b) has outlined some of its basic orientations. First, neofunc-tionalism operates with a descriptive model of society that sees society as composed of elements which, in interaction with one another, form a pattern. This pattern allows the system to be differentiated from its environment. Parts of the system are "sym-biotically connected," and their interaction is not determined by some overarching force. Thus, neofunctionalism rejects any monocausal determinism and is open-ended and pluralistic.

Second, Alexander argues that neofunctionalism devotes roughly equal atten-tion to action and order. It thus avoids the tendency of structural functionalism to focus almost exclusively on the macro-level sources of order in social structures and culture and to give little attention to more micro-level action patterns (Schwinn, 1998). Neofunctionalism also purports to have a broad sense of action, including not only rational but also expressive action.

Third, neofunctionalism retains the structural-functional interest in integration, *not* as an accomplished fact but rather as a social *possibility*! It recognizes that devi-ance and social control are realities within social systems. There is concern for equilibrium within neofunctionalism, but it is broader than the structural-functional concern, encompassing both moving and partial equilibrium. There is a disinclination to see social systems as characterized by static equilibrium. *Equilibrium,* broadly defined, is seen as a reference point for functional analysis but not as descriptive of the lives of individuals in actual social systems.

Fourth, neofunctionalism accepts the traditional Parsonsian emphasis on person-ality, culture, and social system. In addition to being vital to social structure, the interpenetration of these systems also produces tension that is an ongoing source of both change and control.

JEFFREY C. ALEXANDER

*An Autobiographical Sketch**

Since my earliest days as an intellectual I have been preoccupied with the problems of social action and social order and with the possibilities of developing approaches to these problems that avoid the extremes of one-dimensional thought. I have always been convinced that tense dichotomies, while vital as ideological currents in a democratic society, can be overcome in the theoretical realm.

My theoretical concerns first took form during the late 1960s and early 1970s, when I participated in the student protest movements as an undergraduate at Harvard College and as a graduate student at the University of California, Berkeley. New Left Marxism represented a sophisticated effort to overcome the economism of vulgar Marxism, as it tried to reinsert the actor into history. Because it described how material structures are interpenetrated with culture, personality, and everyday life, New Left Marxism—which for better or worse we largely taught ourselves—provided my first important training in the path to theoretical synthesis, which has marked my intellectual career.

In the early 1970s, I became dissatisfied with New Left Marxism, in part for political and empirical reasons. The New Left's turn toward sectarianism and violence frightened and depressed me, whereas the Watergate crisis demonstrated America's capacity for self-criticism. I decided that capitalist democratic societies provided opportunities for inclusion, pluralism, and reform that could not be envisioned even within the New Left version of Marxian thought.

Yet there were also more abstract theoretical reasons for leaving the Marxian approach to synthesis behind. As I more fully engaged classical and contemporary theory, I realized that this synthesis was achieved more by hyphenating—psychoanalytic-Marxism, cultural-Marxism, phenomenological-Marxism—than by opening up the central categories of action and order. In fact, the neo-Marxist categories of consciousness, action, community, and culture were black boxes. This recognition led me to the traditions which supplied the theoretical resources upon which New Left Marxism had drawn. I was fortunate in this graduate student effort to be guided by Robert Bellah and Neil Smelser, whose ideas about culture, social structure, and sociological theory made an indelible impression upon me and continue to be intellectual resources today.

In *Theoretical Logic in Sociology* (1982–1983), I published the results of this effort. The idea for this multivolume work began germinating in 1972, after an extraordinary encounter with Talcott Parsons's masterpiece, *The Structure of Social Action,* allowed me to see my problems with Marxism in a new way. Later, under the supervision of Bellah, Smelser, and Leo Lowenthal, I worked through classical and contemporary theory with this new framework in mind.

My ambition in *Theoretical Logic* was to show that Durkheim and Weber supplied extensive theories of the culture that Marx had neglected and that Weber actually developed the first real sociological synthesis. I concluded, however, that Durkheim ultimately moved in an idealistic direction and that Weber developed a mechanistic view of modern society. I suggested that Parsons's work should be seen as a masterly modern effort at synthesis rather than as theory in the functionalist mode. Yet Parsons, too, failed to pursue synthesis in a truly determined way, allowing his theory to become overly formal and normatively based.

In my work over the last decade I have tried to re-create the framework for synthesis which I take to be the unfulfilled promise of earlier work. In *Twenty Lectures: Sociological Theory since World War II* (1987b), I argued that the divisions in post-Parsonsian sociology—between conflict and order theories, micro and macro approaches, structural and cultural views—were not fruitful. These groupings obscured basic social processes, like the continuing play of order and conflict and the dichotomized dimensions of society, that are always intertwined.

My response to this dead end has been to return to the original concerns of Parsons (Alexander, 1985b; Alexander and Colomy, 1990a) and to the earlier classics.

Yet, in trying to push theory into a new, "post-Parsonsian" phase, I have also tried to go beyond classical and modern theory. My encounters with the powerful group of phenomenologists in my home department at UCLA, particularly those with Harold Garfinkel, were an important stimulus. In "Action and Its Environments" (1987a), which I still regard as my most important piece of theoretical work, I laid out the framework for a new articulation of the micro-macro link.

I have also concentrated on developing a new cultural theory. An early reading of Clifford Geertz convinced me that traditional social-science approaches to culture are too limited. Since that time, my approach has been powerfully affected by semiotics, hermeneutics, and poststructuralist thought. Incorporating theories from outside of sociology, I have tried to theorize the manifold ways in which social structure is permeated by symbolic codes and meanings.

I believe this movement toward theoretical synthesis is being pushed forward by events in the world at large. In the postcommunist world, it seems important to develop models that help us understand our complex and inclusive, yet very fragile, democracies. I am presently at work on a theory of democracy that emphasizes the communal dimension which I call "civil society." I am also publishing a collection of essays which I have written criticizing the growing relativism in the human studies. I would like to believe, despite a great deal of evidence to the contrary, that progress is possible not only in society but in sociology as well. It is only through a multidimensional and synthetic view of society that such progress can be achieved.

[For more on Alexander, see Colomy, 2005.]

Fifth, neofunctionalism focuses on social change in the processes of differentiation within the social, cultural, and personality systems. Thus, change is not productive of conformity and harmony but rather "individuation and institutional strains" (Alexander, 1985b:10).

Finally, Alexander argues that neofunctionalism "implies the commitment to the independence of conceptualization and theorizing from other levels of sociological analysis" (1985b:10).

Alexander and Colomy (1990a) staked out a very ambitious claim for neofunctionalism. They did not see neofunctionalism as, in their terms, a mere modest "elaboration," or "revision," of structural functionalism but rather as a much more dramatic "reconstruction" of it in which differences with the founder (Parsons) are clearly acknowledged and explicit openings are made to other theorists and theories.[13] Efforts were made to integrate into neofunctionalism insights from the masters, such as Marx's work on material structures and Durkheim's on symbolism. In an attempt to overcome the idealist bias of Parsonsian structural functionalism, especially its emphasis on macro-subjective phenomena such as culture, more materialist approaches were encouraged. The structural-functional tendency to emphasize order was countered by a call for rapprochement with theories of social change. Most important, to compensate for the macro-level biases of traditional structural functionalism, efforts were made to integrate ideas from exchange theory, symbolic interactionism, pragmatism, phenomenology, and so on. In other words, Alexander and Colomy endeavored to synthesize structural functionalism with a number of other theoretical traditions. Such a reconstruction was supposed to both revive structural functionalism and provide the base for the development of a new theoretical tradition.

Alexander and Colomy recognized an important difference between neofunctionalism and structural functionalism:

> Earlier functional research was guided by . . . envisioning a single, all embracing conceptual scheme that tied areas of specialized research into a tightly wrought package. What neofunctionalist empirical work points to, by contrast, is a loosely organized package, one organized around a general logic and possessing a number of rather autonomous "proliferations" and "variations" at different levels and in different empirical domains.
>
> (Alexander and Colomy, 1990a:52)

The thoughts of Alexander and Colomy indicate movement away from the Parsonsian tendency to see structural functionalism as a grand overarching theory. Instead, they offer a more limited, a more synthetic, but still a holistic theory.

However, as pointed out in the beginning of this chapter, the future of neofunctionalism has been cast into doubt by the fact that its founder and leading exponent, Jeffrey Alexander, has made it clear that he has outgrown a neofunctionalist orientation. This shift in thinking is apparent in the title of his book *Neofunctionalism and After* (Alexander, 1998). Alexander argues in this work that one of his major goals was the (re)establishment of the legitimacy and importance of Parsonsian theory. To

---

[13] This view seems to be in accord, at least partially, with J. H. Turner and Maryanski's (1988) claim that neofunctionalism has little in common with structural functionalism.

the degree that neofunctionalism has succeeded in this effort, Alexander regards the neofunctionalist project as completed. Thus, he is ready to move beyond Parsons, beyond neofunctionalism, although he makes it plain that his future theoretical directions will be deeply indebted to both. Neofunctionalism has grown too confining for Alexander, and he now sees it, as well as his own work, as part of what he has called "the new theoretical movement" (see Seidman and Alexander, 2001). As he puts it, "I am pointing to a new wave of theory creation that goes beyond the important achievements of neofunctionalism" (Alexander, 1998:228). Such a theoretical perspective would be even more synthetic than neofunctionalism, and more eclectic, drawing on a wide range of theoretical resources, and it would use those synthetic and eclectic resources in more opportunistic ways. Specifically, Alexander is seeking to do much more with developments in microsociological and cultural theory.

Conflict Theory 冲突理论

Conflict theory can be seen as a development that took place, at least in part, in reaction to structural functionalism and as a result of many of the criticisms discussed earlier. However, it should be noted that conflict theory has various other roots, such as Marxian and Weberian theory and Simmel's work on social conflict (Sanderson, 2007; J. H. Turner, 2005). In the 1950s and 1960s, conflict theory provided an alternative to structural functionalism, but it was superseded by a variety of neo-Marxian theories (see Chapter 4). Indeed, one of the major contributions of conflict theory was the way it laid the groundwork for theories more faithful to Marx's work, theories that came to attract a wide audience in sociology. The basic problem with conflict theory is that it never succeeded in divorcing itself sufficiently from its structural-functional roots. It was more a kind of structural functionalism turned on its head than a truly critical theory of society.

The Work of Ralf Dahrendorf 达伦多夫的理论

Like functionalists, conflict theorists are oriented toward the study of social structures and institutions. In the main, this theory is little more than a series of contentions that are often the direct opposites of functionalist positions. This antithesis is best exemplified by the work of Ralf Dahrendorf (1958, 1959; see also, Strasser and Nollman, 2005), in which the tenets of conflict and functional theory are juxtaposed. To the functionalists, society is static or, at best, in a state of moving equilibrium, but to Dahrendorf and the conflict theorists, every society at every point is subject to processes of change. Where functionalists emphasize the orderliness of society, conflict theorists see dissension and conflict at every point in the social system. Functionalists (or at least early functionalists) argue that every element in society contributes to stability; the exponents of conflict theory see many societal elements as contributing to disintegration and change.

Functionalists tend to see society as being held together informally by norms, values, and a common morality. Conflict theorists see whatever order there is in society as stemming from the coercion of some members by those at the top. Where functionalists focus on the cohesion created by shared societal values, conflict theorists emphasize the role of power in maintaining order in society.

Dahrendorf (1959, 1968) is the major exponent of the position that society has two faces (conflict and consensus) and that sociological theory therefore should be divided into two parts, conflict theory and consensus theory. Consensus theorists should examine value integration in society, and conflict theorists should examine conflicts of interest and the coercion that holds society together in the face of these stresses. Dahrendorf recognized that society could not exist without both conflict and consensus, which are prerequisites for each other. Thus, we cannot have conflict unless there is some prior consensus. For example, French housewives are highly unlikely to conflict with Chilean chess players because there is no contact between them, no prior integration to serve as a basis for a conflict. Conversely, conflict can lead to consensus and integration. An example is the alliance between the United States and Japan that developed after World War II.

Despite the interrelationship between consensus and conflict, Dahrendorf was not optimistic about developing a single sociological theory encompassing both processes: "It seems at least conceivable that unification of theory is not feasible at a point which has puzzled thinkers ever since the beginning of Western philosophy" (1959:164). Eschewing a singular theory, Dahrendorf set out to construct a conflict theory of society.[14]

Dahrendorf began with, and was heavily influenced by, structural functionalism. He noted that to the functionalist, the social system is held together by voluntary cooperation or general consensus or both. However, to the conflict (or coercion) theorist, society is held together by "enforced constraint"; thus, some positions in society are delegated power and authority over others. This fact of social life led Dahrendorf to his central thesis that the differential distribution of authority "invariably becomes the determining factor of systematic social conflicts" (1959:165).

Authority 权威

Dahrendorf concentrated on larger social structures.[15] Central to his thesis is the idea that various positions within society have different amounts of authority. Authority does not reside in individuals but in positions. Dahrendorf was interested not only in the structure of these positions but also in the conflict among them: "The *structural* origin of such conflicts must be sought in the arrangement of social roles endowed with expectations of domination or subjection" (1959:165; italics added). The first task of conflict analysis, to Dahrendorf, was to identify various authority roles within society. In addition to making the case for the study of large-scale structures such as authority roles, Dahrendorf was opposed to those who focus on the individual level. For example, he was critical of those who focus on the psychological or behavioral characteristics of the individuals who occupy such positions. He went so far as to say that those who adopted such an approach were not sociologists.

---

[14] Dahrendorf called conflict and coercion "the ugly face of society" (1959:164). We can ponder whether a person who regards them as "ugly" can develop an adequate theory of conflict and coercion.

[15] In his other work, Dahrendorf (1968) continued to focus on social facts (for example, positions and roles), but he also manifested a concern for the dangers of reification endemic to such an approach.

The authority attached to positions is the key element in Dahrendorf's analysis. Authority always implies both superordination and subordination. Those who occupy positions of authority are expected to control subordinates; that is, they dominate because of the expectations of those who surround them, not because of their own psychological characteristics. Like authority, these expectations are attached to positions, not people. Authority is not a generalized social phenomenon; those who are subject to control, as well as permissible spheres of control, are specified in society. Finally, because authority is legitimate, sanctions can be brought to bear against those who do not comply.

Authority is not a constant as far as Dahrendorf was concerned, because authority resides in positions, not in persons. Thus, a person of authority in one setting does not necessarily hold a position of authority in another setting. Similarly, a person in a subordinate position in one group may be in a superordinate position in another. This follows from Dahrendorf's argument that society is composed of a number of units that he called *imperatively coordinated associations.* These may be seen as associations of people controlled by a hierarchy of authority positions. Since society contains many such associations, an individual can occupy a position of authority in one and a subordinate position in another.

Authority within each association is dichotomous; thus two, and only two, conflict groups can be formed within any association. Those in positions of authority and those in positions of subordination hold certain interests that are "contradictory in substance and direction." Here we encounter another key term in Dahrendorf's theory of conflict—*interests.* Groups on top and at the bottom are defined by common interests. Dahrendorf continued to be firm in his thinking that even these interests, which sound so psychological, are basically large-scale phenomena:

> For purposes of the sociological analysis of conflict groups and group conflicts, it is necessary to assume certain *structurally generated* orientations of the actions of incumbents of defined *positions.* By analogy to conscious ("subjective") orientations of action, it appears justifiable to describe these as interests. . . . The assumption of "objective" interests associated with social positions has *no psychological implications* or ramifications; it belongs to the level of sociological analysis proper.
>
> (Dahrendorf, 1959:175; italics added)

Within every association, those in dominant positions seek to maintain the status quo while those in subordinate positions seek change. A conflict of interest within any association is at least latent at all times, which means that the legitimacy of authority is *always* precarious. This conflict of interest need not be conscious in order for superordinates or subordinates to act. The interests of superordinates and subordinates are objective in the sense that they are reflected in the expectations (roles) attached to positions. Individuals do not have to internalize these expectations or even be conscious of them in order to act in accord with them. If they occupy given positions, they will behave in the expected manner. Individuals are "adjusted" or "adapted" to their roles when they contribute to conflict between superordinates and subordinates. Dahrendorf called these unconscious role expectations *latent interests. Manifest interests* are latent interests that have become conscious. Dahrendorf saw the analysis of the connection between latent and manifest interests as a major task of conflict theory. Nevertheless, actors need not be conscious of their interests in order to act in accord with them.

Groups, Conflict, and Change 群体、冲突和变革

Next, Dahrendorf distinguished three broad types of groups. The first is the *quasi group,* or "aggregates of incumbents of positions with identical role interests" (Dahrendorf, 1959:180). These are the recruiting grounds for the second type of group—the *interest group.* Dahrendorf described the two groups:

> Common modes of behavior are characteristic of interest groups recruited from larger quasi-groups. Interest groups are groups in the strict sense of the sociological term; and they are the real agents of group conflict. They have a structure, a form of organization, a program or goal, and a personnel of members.
>
> (Dahrendorf, 1959:180)

Out of all the many interest groups emerge *conflict groups,* or those that actually engage in group conflict.

Dahrendorf felt that the concepts of latent and manifest interests, of quasi groups, interest groups, and conflict groups, were basic to an explanation of social conflict. Under *ideal* conditions no other variables would be needed. However, because conditions are never ideal, many different factors do intervene in the process. Dahrendorf mentioned technical conditions such as adequate personnel, political conditions such as the overall political climate, and social conditions such as the existence of communication links. The way people are recruited into the quasi group was another social condition important to Dahrendorf. He felt that if the recruitment is random and is determined by chance, an interest group, and ultimately a conflict group, is unlikely to emerge. In contrast to Marx, Dahrendorf did not feel that the *lumpenproletariat*[16] would ultimately form a conflict group, because people are recruited to it by chance. However, when recruitment to quasi groups is structurally determined, these groups provide fertile recruiting grounds for interest groups and, in some cases, conflict groups.

The final aspect of Dahrendorf's conflict theory is the relationship of conflict to change. Here Dahrendorf recognized the importance of Lewis Coser's work (see the next section), which focused on the functions of conflict in maintaining the status quo. Dahrendorf felt, however, that the conservative function of conflict is only one part of social reality; conflict also leads to change and development.

Briefly, Dahrendorf argued that once conflict groups emerge, they engage in actions that lead to changes in social structure. When the conflict is intense, the changes that occur are radical. When it is accompanied by violence, structural change will be sudden. Whatever the nature of conflict, sociologists must be attuned to the relationship between conflict and change as well as that between conflict and the status quo.

---

[16] This is Marx's term for the mass of people at the bottom of the economic system, those who stand below even the proletariat.

主要的批评与回应
The Major Criticisms and Efforts to Deal with Them

Conflict theory has been criticized on a variety of grounds. For example, it has been attacked for ignoring order and stability, whereas structural functionalism has been criticized for ignoring conflict and change. Conflict theory has also been criticized for being ideologically radical, whereas functionalism was criticized for its conservative ideology. In comparison to structural functionalism, conflict theory is rather underdeveloped. It is not nearly as sophisticated as functionalism, perhaps because it is a more derivative theory.

Dahrendorf's conflict theory has been subjected to a number of critical analyses (for example, Hazelrigg, 1972; J. H. Turner, 1973; Weingart, 1969), including some critical reflections by Dahrendorf (1968) himself. First, Dahrendorf's model is not as clear a reflection of Marxian ideas as he claimed. Second, as has been noted, conflict theory has more in common with structural functionalism than with Marxian theory. Dahrendorf's emphasis on such things as systems (imperatively coordinated associations), positions, and roles links him directly to structural functionalism. As a result, his theory suffers from many of the same inadequacies as structural functionalism. For example, conflict seems to emerge mysteriously from legitimate systems (just as it does in structural functionalism). Further, conflict theory seems to suffer from many of the same conceptual and logical problems (for example, vague concepts, tautologies) as structural functionalism (J. H. Turner, 1975, 1982). Finally, like structural functionalism, conflict theory is almost wholly macroscopic and as a result has little to offer to our understanding of individual thought and action.

Both functionalism and Dahrendorf's conflict theory are inadequate, because each is itself useful for explaining only a *portion* of social life. Sociology must be able to explain order as well as conflict, structure as well as change. This has motivated several efforts to reconcile conflict and functional theory. Although none has been totally satisfactory, these efforts suggest at least some agreement among sociologists that what is needed is a theory explaining *both* consensus and dissension. Still, not all theorists seek to reconcile these conflicting perspectives. Dahrendorf, for example, saw them as alternative perspectives to be used situationally. According to Dahrendorf, when we are interested in conflict, we should use conflict theory; when we wish to examine order, we should take a functional perspective. This position seems unsatisfactory, because there is a strong need for a theoretical perspective that enables us to deal with conflict and order *simultaneously.*

The criticisms of conflict theory and structural functionalism, as well as the inherent limitations in each, led to many efforts to cope with the problems by reconciling or integrating the two theories (K. D. Bailey, 1997; Chapin, 1994; van den Berghe, 1963; Himes, 1966). The assumption was that some combination of the two theories would be more powerful than either one alone. The best known of these works was Lewis Coser's *The Functions of Social Conflict* (1956).

The early seminal work on the functions of social conflict was done by Georg Simmel, but it has been expanded by Coser (Delaney, 2005a; Jaworski, 1991), who argued that conflict may serve to solidify a loosely structured group. In a society that seems to be disintegrating, conflict with another society may restore the integrative core. The cohesiveness of Israeli Jews might be attributed, at least in part, to the long-standing conflict with the Arab nations in the Middle East. The possible end of the conflict might well exacerbate underlying strains in Israeli society. Conflict as an agent for solidifying a society is an idea that has long been recognized by propagandists, who may construct an enemy where none exists or seek to fan antagonisms toward an inactive opponent.

Conflict with one group may serve to produce cohesion by leading to a series of alliances with other groups. For example, conflict with the Arabs has led to an alliance between the United States and Israel. Lessening of the Israeli-Arab conflict might weaken the bonds between Israel and the United States.

Within a society, conflict can bring some ordinarily isolated individuals into an active role. The protests over the Vietnam War motivated many young people to take vigorous roles in American political life for the first time. With the end of that conflict, a more apathetic spirit emerged again among American youth.

Conflict also serves a communication function. Prior to conflict, groups may be unsure of their adversary's position, but as a result of conflict, positions and boundaries between groups often become clarified. Individuals therefore are better able to decide on a proper course of action in relation to their adversary. Conflict also allows the parties to get a better idea of their relative strengths and may well increase the possibility of rapprochement, or peaceful accommodation.

From a theoretical perspective, it is possible to wed functionalism and conflict theory by looking at the functions of social conflict. Still, it must be recognized that conflict also has dysfunctions.

While a number of theorists sought to integrate conflict theory with structural functionalism, others wanted no part of conflict theory (or structural functionalism). For example, the Marxist André Gunder Frank (1966/1974) rejected conflict theory because it represented an inadequate form of Marxian theory. Although conflict theory has some Marxian elements, it is not the true heir of Marx's original theory. In the next chapter we will examine an array of theories that are more legitimate heirs. Before we do, however, we must deal with a more successfully integrative type of conflict theory.

A More Integrative Conflict Theory 更具综合性的冲突理论

Randall Collins's *Conflict Sociology* (1975; Rossel and Collins, 2001) moved in a much more micro-oriented direction than the macro conflict theory of Dahrendorf and others. Collins says of his early work, "My own main contribution to conflict theory . . . was to add a micro level to these macro-level theories. I especially tried to show that stratification and organization are grounded in the interactions of everyday life" (1990:72).[17]

Collins made it clear that his focus on conflict would not be ideological; that is, he did not begin with the political view that conflict is either good or bad. Rather, he claimed, he chose conflict as a focus on the realistic ground that conflict is a—perhaps *the*—central process in social life.

---

[17] Collins also stresses that conflict theory, more than other sociological theories, has been open to the integration of the findings of empirical research.

Unlike others who started, and stayed, at the societal level, Collins approached conflict from an individual point of view, because his theoretical roots lie in phenomenology and ethnomethodology. Despite his preference for individual-level and small-scale theories, Collins was aware that "sociology cannot be successful on the microlevel alone" (1975:11); conflict theory cannot do without the societal level of analysis. However, whereas most conflict theorists believed that social structures are external to, and coercive of, the actor, Collins saw social structures as inseparable from the actors who construct them and whose interaction patterns are their essence. Collins was inclined to see social structures as interaction patterns rather than as external and coercive entities. In addition, whereas most conflict theorists saw the actor as constrained by external forces, Collins viewed the actor as constantly creating and re-creating social organization.

Collins saw Marxian theory as the "starting point" for conflict theory, but it is, in his view, laden with problems. For one thing, he saw it (like structural functionalism) as heavily ideological, a characteristic he wanted to avoid. For another, he tended to see Marx's orientation as reducible to an analysis of the economic domain, although this is an unwarranted criticism of Marx's theory. Actually, although Collins invoked Marx frequently, his conflict theory shows relatively little Marxian influence. It is far more influenced by Weber, Durkheim, and above all phenomenology and ethnomethodology.

Social Stratification 社会分层

Collins chose to focus on social stratification because it is an institution that touches so many features of life, including "wealth, politics, careers, families, clubs, communities, lifestyles" (1975:49). In Collins's view, the great theories of stratification are "failures." He criticized Marxian theory as "a monocausal explanation for a multicausal world" (R. Collins, 1975:49). He viewed Weber's theory as little more than an "antisystem" with which to view the features of the two great theories. Weber's work was of some use to Collins, but "the efforts of phenomenological sociology to ground all concepts in the observables of every life" (R. Collins, 1975:53) were the most important to him because his major focus in the study of social stratification was small-scale, not large-scale. In his view, social stratification, like all other social structures, is reducible to people in everyday life encountering each other in patterned ways.

Despite his ultimate commitment to a microsociology of stratification, Collins began (even though he had some reservations about them) with the large-scale theories of Marx and Weber as underpinnings for his work. He started with Marxian principles, arguing that they, "with certain modifications, provide the basis for a conflict theory of stratification" (R. Collins, 1975:58).

First, Collins contended that it was Marx's view that the material conditions involved in earning a living in modern society are the major determinants of a person's lifestyle. The basis of earning a living for Marx is a person's relationship to private property. Those who own or control property are able to earn their livings in a much more satisfactory way than are those who do not and who must sell their labor time to gain access to the means of production.

Second, from a Marxian perspective, material conditions affect not only how individuals earn a living but also the nature of social groups in the different social classes. The dominant social class is better able to develop more coherent social groups, tied together by intricate communication networks, than is the subordinate social class.

Finally, Collins argued that Marx also pointed out the vast differences among the social classes in their access to, and control over, the cultural system. That is, the upper social classes are able to develop highly articulated symbol and ideological systems, systems that they often are able to impose on the lower social classes. The lower social classes have less-developed symbol systems, many of which are likely to have been imposed on them by those in power.

Collins viewed Weber as working within and developing further Marx's theory of stratification. For one thing, Weber was said to have recognized the existence of different forms of conflict that lead to a multifaceted stratification system (for example, class, status, and power). For another, Weber developed the theory of organizations to a high degree, which Collins saw as still another arena of conflict of interest. Weber was also important to Collins for his emphasis on the state as the agency that controls the means of violence, which shifted attention from conflict over the economy (means of production) to conflict over the state. Finally, Weber was recognized by Collins for his understanding of the social arena of emotional products, particularly religion. Conflict clearly can occur in this arena, and these emotional products, like other products, can be used as weapons in social conflict.

A Conflict Theory of Stratification   With this background, Collins turned to his own conflict approach to stratification, which has more in common with phenomenological and ethnomethodological theories than with Marxian or Weberian theory. Collins opened with several assumptions. People are seen as inherently sociable but also as particularly conflict-prone in their social relations. Conflict is likely to occur in social relations because "violent coercion" can always be used by one person or many people in an interaction setting. Collins believed that people seek to maximize their "subjective status" and that their ability to do this depends on their resources as well as the resources of those with whom they are dealing. He saw people as self-interested; thus, clashes are possible because sets of interests may be inherently antagonistic.

This conflict approach to stratification can be reduced to three basic principles. First, Collins believed that people live in self-constructed subjective worlds. Second, other people may have the power to affect, or even control, an individual's subjective experience. Third, other people frequently try to control the individual, who opposes them. The result is likely to be interpersonal conflict.

On the basis of this approach, Collins developed five principles of conflict analysis that he applied to social stratification, although he believed that they could be applied to any area of social life. First, Collins believed that conflict theory must focus on real life rather than on abstract formulations. This belief seems to reflect a preference for a Marxian-style material analysis over the abstraction of structural functionalism. Collins urged us to think of people as animals whose actions, motivated by self-interest, can be seen as maneuvers to obtain various advantages so that they can achieve satisfaction and avoid dissatisfaction. However, unlike exchange and rational choice theorists, Collins did not see people as wholly rational. He recognized that they are vulnerable to emotional appeals in their efforts to find satisfaction.

Second, Collins believed that a conflict theory of stratification must examine the material arrangements that affect interaction. Although the actors are likely to be affected by material factors such as "the physical places, the modes of communication, the supply of weapons, devices for staging one's public impression, tools, goods" (R. Collins, 1975:60), not all actors are affected in the same way. A major variable is the resources that the different actors possess. Actors with considerable material resources can resist or even modify these material constraints, whereas those with fewer resources are more likely to have their thoughts and actions determined by their material setting.

Third, Collins argued that in a situation of inequality, those groups that control resources are likely to try to exploit those that lack resources. He was careful to point out that such exploitation need not involve conscious calculation on the part of those who gain from the situation; rather, the exploiters are merely pursuing what they perceive to be their best interests. In the process they may be taking advantage of those who lack resources.

Fourth, Collins wanted the conflict theorist to look at such cultural phenomena as beliefs and ideals from the point of view of interests, resources, and power. It is likely that those groups with resources and, therefore, power can impose their idea systems on the entire society; those without resources have an idea system imposed on them.

Finally, Collins made a firm commitment to the scientific study of stratification and every other aspect of the social world. Thus, he prescribed several things: Sociologists should not simply theorize about stratification but should study it empirically, if possible, in a comparative way. Hypotheses should be formulated and tested empirically through comparative studies. Last, the sociologist should look for the causes of social phenomena, particularly the multiple causes of any form of social behavior.

This kind of scientific commitment led Collins to develop a wide array of propositions about the relationship between conflict and various specific aspects of social life. We can present only a few here, but they should allow readers to get a feel for Collins's type of conflict sociology.

> **1.0** Experiences of giving and taking orders are the main determinants of individual outlooks and behaviors.
> **1.1** The more one gives orders, the more he is proud, self-assured, formal, and identifies with organizational ideals in whose names he justifies the orders.
> **1.2** The more one takes orders, the more he is subservient, fatalistic, alienated from organizational ideals, externally conforming, distrustful of others, concerned with extrinsic rewards, and amoral.
>
> (R. Collins, 1975:73–74)

Among other things, these propositions all reflect Collins's commitment to the *scientific study* of the small-scale social manifestations of social conflicts.

Other Social Domains 其他社会领域

Collins was not content to deal with conflict within the stratification system but sought to extend it to various other social domains. For example, he extended his analysis of stratification to relationships between the sexes as well as among age groups. He took the view that the family is an arena of sexual conflict, in which males have been the victors, with the result that women are dominated by men and are subject to various kinds of unequal treatment. Similarly, he saw the relationship between age groups—in particular, between young and old—as one of conflict. This idea contrasts with the view of structural functionalists, who saw harmonious socialization and internalization in this relationship. Collins looked at the resources possessed by the various age groups. Adults have a variety of resources, including experience, size, strength, and the ability to satisfy the physical needs of the young. In contrast, one of the few resources young children have is physical attractiveness. This means that young children are likely to be dominated by adults. However, as children mature, they acquire more resources and are better able to resist, with the result of increasing social conflict between the generations.

Collins also looked at formal organizations from a conflict perspective. He saw them as networks of interpersonal influences and as the arenas in which conflicting interests are played out. In short, "Organizations are arenas for struggle" (R. Collins, 1975:295). Collins again couched his argument in propositional form. For example, he argued that "coercion leads to strong efforts to avoid being coerced" (R. Collins, 1975:298). In contrast, he felt that the offering of rewards is a preferable strategy: "Control by material rewards leads to compliance to the extent that rewards are directly linked to the desired behavior" (R. Collins, 1975:299). These propositions and others all point to Collins's commitment to a scientific, largely micro-oriented study of conflict.

In sum, Collins is, like Dahrendorf, not a true exponent of Marxian conflict theory, although for different reasons. Although Collins used Marx as a starting point, Weber, Durkheim, and particularly ethnomethodology were much more important influences on his work. Collins's small-scale orientation is a helpful beginning toward the development of a more integrated conflict theory. However, despite his stated intentions of integrating large- and small-scale theory, he did not accomplish that task fully.

Summary 总结

Not too many years ago, structural functionalism was *the* dominant theory in sociology. Conflict theory was its major challenger and was the likely alternative to replace it in that position. However, dramatic changes have taken place in recent years. Both theories have been the subject of intense criticism, whereas a series of alternative theories (to be discussed throughout the rest of this book) have developed that have attracted ever greater interest and ever larger followings.

Although several varieties of structural functionalism exist, our focus here is on societal functionalism and its large-scale focus, its concern with interrelationships at the societal level and with the constraining effects of social structures and institutions on actors. Structural functionalists developed a series of large-scale concerns in social systems, subsystems, relationships among subsystems and systems, equilibrium, and orderly change.

We examine three bodies of work by structural functionalists (Davis and Moore, Parsons, and Merton). Davis and Moore, in one of the best-known and most criticized pieces in the history of sociology, examined social stratification as a social system and the various positive functions it performs. We also discuss in some detail Talcott Parsons's structural-functional theory and his ideas on the four functional imperatives of all action systems—adaptation, goal attainment, integration, and latency (AGIL). We also analyze his structural-functional approach to the four action systems—the social system, cultural system, personality system, and behavioral organism. Finally, we deal with his structural-functional approach to dynamism and social change—his evolutionary theory and his ideas on the generalized media of interchange.

Merton's effort to develop a "paradigm" for functional analysis is the most important single piece in modern structural functionalism. Merton began by criticizing some of the more naive positions of structural functionalism. He then sought to develop a more adequate model of structural-functional analysis. On one point Merton agreed with his predecessors—the need to focus on large-scale social phenomena. But, Merton argued, in addition to focusing on positive functions, structural functionalism should be concerned with dysfunctions and even nonfunctions. Given these additions, Merton urged that analysts concern themselves with the net balance of functions and dysfunctions. Further, he argued, in performing structural-functional analysis, we must move away from global analyses and specify the *levels* on which we are working. Merton also added the idea that structural functionalists should be concerned not only with manifest (intended) but also with latent (unintended) functions. This section concludes with a discussion of Merton's application of his functional paradigm to the issue of the relationship of social structure and culture to anomie and deviance.

Next, we discuss the numerous criticisms of structural functionalism that have succeeded in damaging its credibility and popularity. We discuss the criticisms that structural functionalism is ahistorical, unable to deal with conflict and change, highly conservative, preoccupied with societal constraints on actors, accepting of elite legitimations, teleological, and tautological.

The criticisms of structural functionalism led to an effort to respond to them—the development of an orientation known as neofunctionalism. Neofunctionalism sought to buttress structural functionalism by synthesizing it with a wide array of other theoretical perspectives. A fair amount of work was done under the rubric of neofunctionalism in the late 1980s and early 1990s, and it attracted considerable attention. However, its future is questionable, especially since its founder, Jeffrey Alexander, has moved beyond it theoretically.

The last part of this chapter is devoted to the major alternative to structural functionalism in the 1950s and 1960s—conflict theory. The best-known work in this tradition is by Ralf Dahrendorf, who, although he consciously tried to follow the Marxian tradition, is best seen as having inverted structural functionalism. Dahrendorf looked at change rather than equilibrium, conflict rather than order, how the parts of society contribute to change rather than to stability, and conflict and coercion rather than normative constraint. Dahrendorf offered a large-scale theory of conflict that parallels the structural functionalist's large-scale theory of order. His focus on authority, positions, imperatively coordinated associations, interests, quasi groups, interest groups, and conflict groups reflects this orientation. Dahrendorf's theory suffers from some of the same problems as structural functionalism; in addition, it represents a rather impoverished effort to incorporate Marxian theory. Dahrendorf also can be criticized for being satisfied with alternative theories of order and conflict rather than seeking a theoretical integration of the two.

The chapter concludes with a discussion of Randall Collins's effort to develop a more integrative conflict theory, especially one that integrates micro and macro concerns.

Varieties of Neo-Marxian Theory
第4章 新马克思主义理论

Chapter Outline

Economic Determinism

Hegelian Marxism

Critical Theory

Neo-Marxian Economic Sociology

Historically Oriented Marxism

Neo-Marxian Spatial Analysis

Post-Marxist Theory

In this chapter we deal with a variety of theories that are better reflections of Marx's ideas than are the conflict theories discussed at the close of the preceding chapter. Although each of the theories discussed here is derived from Marx's theory, there are many important differences among them.

Economic Determinism 经济决定论

Marx often sounded like an economic determinist; that is, he seemed to consider the economic system of paramount importance and to argue that it determined all other sectors of society—politics, religion, idea systems, and so forth. Although Marx did see the economic sector as preeminent, at least in capitalist society, as a dialectician he could not have taken a deterministic position, because the dialectic is characterized by the notion that there is continual feedback and mutual interaction among the various sectors of society. Politics, religion, and so on, cannot be reduced to epiphenomena determined by the economy, because they affect the economy just as they are affected by it. Despite the nature of the dialectic, Marx still is interpreted as an economic determinist. Although some aspects of Marx's work would lead to this conclusion, adopting it means ignoring the overall dialectical thrust of his theory.

Agger (1978) argued that economic determinism reached its peak as an interpretation of Marxian theory during the period of the Second Communist International, between 1889 and 1914. This historical period often is seen as the apex of early market capitalism, and its booms and busts led to many predictions about its imminent demise. Those Marxists who believed in economic determinism saw the breakdown of capitalism as inevitable. In their view, Marxism was capable of producing a scientific theory of this breakdown (as well as other aspects of capitalist society) with the predictive reliability of the physical and natural sciences. All an analyst had to do was examine the structures of capitalism, especially the economic structures. Built into those structures was a series of processes that inevitably would bring down capitalism, and so it was up to the economic determinist to discover how these processes worked.

Friedrich Engels, Marx's collaborator and benefactor, led the way in this interpretation of Marxian theory, as did Karl Kautsky and Eduard Bernstein. Kautsky, for example, discussed the inevitable decline of capitalism as

> unavoidable in the sense that the inventors improve technic and the capitalists in their desire for profit revolutionize the whole economic life, as it is also inevitable that the workers aim for shorter hours of labor and higher wages, that they organize themselves, that they fight the capitalist class and its state, as it is inevitable that they aim for the conquest of political power and the overthrow of capitalist rule. Socialism is inevitable because the class struggle and the victory of the proletariat is inevitable.
>
> (Kautsky, cited in Agger, 1978:94)

The imagery here is of actors impelled by the structures of capitalism into taking a series of actions.

It was this imagery that led to the major criticism of scientifically oriented economic determinism—that it was untrue to the dialectical thrust of Marx's theory. Specifically, the theory seemed to short-circuit the dialectic by making individual thought and action insignificant. The economic structures of capitalism that determined individual thought and action were the crucial element. This interpretation also led to political quietism and therefore was inconsistent with Marx's thinking (Guilhot, 2002). Why should individuals act if the capitalist system was going to crumble under its own structural contradictions? Clearly, given Marx's desire to integrate theory and practice, a perspective that omits action and even reduces it to insignificance would not be in the tradition of his thinking.

Hegelian Marxism 黑格尔式马克思主义

As a result of the criticisms just discussed, economic determinism began to fade in importance, and a number of theorists developed other varieties of Marxian theory. One group of Marxists returned to the Hegelian roots of Marx's theory in search of a subjective orientation to complement the strength of the early Marxists at the objective, material level. The early Hegelian Marxists sought to restore the dialectic between the subjective and the objective aspects of social life. Their interest in subjective factors laid the basis for the later development of critical theory, which came to focus almost exclusively on subjective factors. A number of thinkers (for example, Karl Korsch) could be taken as illustrative of Hegelian Marxism, but we will focus on the work of one who has gained great prominence, Georg Lukács

(Aronowitz, 2001; Markus, 2005), especially his book *History and Class Consciousness* (1922/1968). We also pay brief attention to the ideas of Antonio Gramsci.

Georg Lukács 卢卡奇

The attention of Marxian scholars of the early twentieth century was limited mainly to Marx's later, largely economic works, such as *Capital* (1867/1967). The early work, especially *The Economic and Philosophic Manuscripts of 1844* (1932/1964), which was more heavily influenced by Hegelian subjectivism, was largely unknown to Marxian thinkers. The rediscovery of the *Manuscripts* and their publication in 1932 was a major turning point. However, by the 1920s Lukács already had written his major work, in which he emphasized the subjective side of Marxian theory. As Martin Jay puts it, "*History and Class Consciousness* anticipated in several fundamental ways the philosophical implications of Marx's *1844 Manuscripts,* whose publication it antedated by almost a decade" (1984:102). Lukács's major contribution to Marxian theory lies in his work on two major ideas—reification (Dahms, 1998) and class consciousness.

Reification 物化

Lukács made it clear from the beginning that he was not totally rejecting the work of the economic Marxists on reification, but simply seeking to broaden and extend their ideas. Lukács commenced with the Marxian concept of commodities, which he characterized as "the central, structural problem of capitalist society" (1922/1968:83). A *commodity* is at base a relation among people that, they come to believe, takes on the character of a thing and develops an objective form. People in their interaction with nature in capitalist society produce various products, or commodities (for example, bread, automobiles, motion pictures). However, people tend to lose sight of the fact that they produce these commodities and give them their value. Value comes to be seen as being produced by a market that is independent of the actors. The *fetishism of commodities* is the process by which commodities and the market for them are granted independent objective existence by the actors in capitalist society. Marx's concept of the fetishism of commodities was the basis for Lukács's concept of reification.

The crucial difference between the fetishism of commodities and reification lies in the extensiveness of the two concepts. Whereas the former is restricted to the economic institution, the latter is applied by Lukács to all of society—the state, the law, *and* the economic sector. The same dynamic applies in all sectors of capitalist society: people come to believe that social structures have a life of their own, and as a result those structures do come to have an objective character. Lukács delineated this process:

> Man in capitalist society confronts a reality "made" by himself (as a class) which appears to him to be a natural phenomenon alien to himself; he is wholly at the mercy of its "laws"; his activity is confined to the exploitation of the inexorable fulfillment of certain individual laws for his own (egoistic) interests. But even while "acting" he remains, in the nature of the case, the object and not the subject of events.
>
> (Lukács, 1922/1968:135)

In developing his ideas on reification, Lukács integrated insights from Weber and Simmel. However, because reification was embedded in Marxian theory, it was seen as a problem limited to capitalism and not, as it was to Weber and Simmel, the inevitable fate of humankind.

Class and False Consciousness 阶级意识和虚假意识

Class consciousness refers to the belief systems shared by those who occupy the same class position within society. Lukács made it clear that class consciousness is neither the sum nor the average of individual consciousnesses; rather, it is a property of a group of people who share a similar place in the productive system. This view leads to a focus on the class consciousness of the bourgeoisie and especially of the proletariat. In Lukács's work, there is a clear link between objective economic position, class consciousness, and the "real, psychological thoughts of men about their lives" (1922/1968:51).

The concept of class consciousness necessarily implies, at least in capitalism, the prior state of *false consciousness*. That is, classes in capitalism generally do not have a clear sense of their true class interests. For example, until the revolutionary stage, members of the proletariat do not fully realize the nature and extent of their exploitation in capitalism. The falsity of class consciousness is derived from the class's position within the economic structure of society: "Class consciousness implies a class-conditioned *unconsciousness* of one's own socio-historical and economic condition. . . . The 'falseness,' the illusion implicit in this situation, is in no sense arbitrary" (Lukács, 1922/1968:52; Starks and Junisbai, 2007). Most social classes throughout history have been unable to overcome false consciousness and thereby achieve class consciousness. The structural position of the proletariat within capitalism, however, gives it the unique ability to achieve class consciousness.

The ability to achieve class consciousness is peculiar to capitalist societies. In precapitalist societies, a variety of factors prevented the development of class consciousness. For one thing, the state, independent of the economy, affected social strata; for another, status (prestige) consciousness tended to mask class (economic) consciousness. As a result, Lukács concluded, "There is therefore no possible position within such a society from which the economic basis of all social relations could be made conscious" (1922/1968:57). In contrast, the economic base of capitalism is clearer and simpler. People may not be conscious of its effects, but they are at least unconsciously aware of them. As a result, "class consciousness arrived at the point where *it could become conscious*" (Lukács, 1922/1968:59). At this stage, society turns into an ideological battleground in which those who seek to conceal the class character of society are pitted against those who seek to expose it.

Lukács compared the various classes in capitalism on the issue of class consciousness. He argued that the petty bourgeoisie and the peasants cannot develop class consciousness because of the ambiguity of their structural position within capitalism. Because these two classes represent vestiges of society in the feudal era, they are not able to develop a clear sense of the nature of capitalism. The bourgeoisie can develop class consciousness, but at best it understands the development of capitalism as something external, subject to objective laws, that it can experience only passively.

The proletariat has the capacity to develop true class consciousness, and as it does, the bourgeoisie is thrown on the defensive. Lukács refused to see the proletariat as simply driven by external forces but viewed it instead as an active creator of its own fate. In the confrontation between the bourgeoisie and the proletariat, the former class has all the intellectual and organizational weapons, whereas all the latter has, at least at first, is the ability to see society for what it is. As the battle proceeds, the proletariat moves from being a "class in itself," that is, a structurally created entity, to a "class for itself," a class conscious of its position and mission (Bottero, 2007). In other words, "the class struggle must be raised from the level of economic necessity to the level of conscious aim and effective class consciousness" (Lukács, 1922/1968:76). When the struggle reaches this point, the proletariat is capable of the action that can overthrow the capitalist system.

Lukács had a rich sociological theory, although it is embedded in Marxian terms. He was concerned with the dialectical relationship among the structures (primarily economic) of capitalism, the idea systems (especially class consciousness), individual thought, and, ultimately, individual action. His theoretical perspective provides an important bridge between the economic determinists and more modern Marxists.

Antonio Gramsci 葛兰西

The Italian Marxist Antonio Gramsci also played a key role in the transition from economic determinism to more modern Marxian positions (Davidson, 2007; Beilharz, 2005b; Salamini, 1981). Gramsci was critical of Marxists who are "deterministic, fatalistic and mechanistic" (1971:336). In fact, he wrote an essay entitled "The Revolution against *'Capital'*" (Gramsci, 1917/1977) in which he celebrated "the resurrection of political will against the economic determinism of those who reduced Marxism to the historical laws of Marx's best-known work [*Capital*]" (Jay, 1984:155). Although he recognized that there were historical regularities, he rejected the idea of automatic or inevitable historical developments. Thus, the masses had to act in order to bring about a social revolution. But to act, the masses had to become conscious of their situation and the nature of the system in which they lived. Thus, although Gramsci recognized the importance of structural factors, especially the economy, he did not believe that these structural factors led the masses to revolt. The masses needed to develop a revolutionary ideology, but they could not do that on their own. Gramsci operated with a rather elitist conception in which ideas were generated by intellectuals and then extended to the masses and put into practice by them. The masses could not generate such ideas, and they could experience them, once in existence, only on faith. The masses could not become self-conscious on their own; they needed the help of social elites. However, once the masses had been influenced by these ideas, they would take the actions that lead to social revolution. Gramsci, like Lukács, focused on collective ideas rather than on social structures like the economy, and both operated within traditional Marxian theory.

Gramsci's central concept, one that reflects his Hegelianism, is hegemony (for a contemporary use of the concept of hegemony, see the discussion of the work of Laclau and Mouffe later in this chapter; Abrahamsen, 1997). According to Gramsci, "the essential ingredient of the most modern philosophy of praxis [the linking of thought and action] is the historical-philosophical concept of 'hegemony'" (1932/1975:235). *Hegemony* is defined by Gramsci as cultural leadership exercised by the ruling class. He contrasts hegemony to coercion that is "exercised by legislative or executive powers, or expressed through police intervention" (Gramsci, 1932/1975:235). Whereas economic Marxists tended to emphasize the economy and the coercive aspects of state domination, Gramsci emphasized "'hegemony' and cultural leadership" (1932/1975:235). In an analysis of capitalism, Gramsci wanted to know how some intellectuals, working on behalf of the capitalists, achieved cultural leadership and the assent of the masses.

Not only does the concept of hegemony help us understand domination within capitalism, but it also serves to orient Gramsci's thoughts on revolution. That is, through revolution, it is not enough to gain control of the economy and the state apparatus; it is also necessary to gain cultural leadership over the rest of society. It is here that Gramsci sees a key role for communist intellectuals and a communist party.

We turn now to critical theory, which grew out of the work of Hegelian Marxists such as Lukács and Gramsci and has moved even farther from the traditional Marxian roots of economic determinism.

Critical Theory 批判理论

Critical theory is the product of a group of German neo-Marxists who were dissatisfied with the state of Marxian theory (J. M. Bernstein, 1995; Kellner, 2005a, 1993; for a broader view of critical theory, see Agger, 1998), particularly its tendency toward economic determinism. The organization associated with critical theory, the Institute of Social Research, was officially founded in Frankfurt, Germany, on February 23, 1923 (Wiggershaus, 1994). Critical theory has spread beyond the confines of the Frankfurt school (Langman, 2007; Kellner, 2005c; Calhoun and Karaganis, 2001; *Telos,* 1989–1990). Critical theory was and is largely a European orientation, although its influence in American sociology has grown (Marcus, 1999; van den Berg, 1980).

针对社会生活和精神生活的主要批判
The Major Critiques of Social and Intellectual Life

Critical theory is composed largely of criticisms of various aspects of social and intellectual life, but its ultimate goal is to reveal more accurately the nature of society (Bleich, 1977).

Criticisms of Marxian Theory 对马克思主义理论的批判
Critical theory takes as its starting point a critique of Marxian theories. The critical theorists are most disturbed by the economic determinists—the mechanistic, or

mechanical, Marxists (Antonio, 1981; Schroyer, 1973; Sewart, 1978). Some (for example, Habermas, 1971) criticize the determinism implicit in parts of Marx's original work, but most focus their criticisms on the neo-Marxists, primarily because they had interpreted Marx's work too mechanistically. The critical theorists do not say that economic determinists were wrong in focusing on the economic realm but that they should have been concerned with other aspects of social life as well. As we will see, the critical school seeks to rectify this imbalance by focusing its attention on the cultural realm (Fuery, 2000; Schroyer, 1973:33). In addition to attacking other Marxian theories, the critical school critiqued societies, such as the former Soviet Union, built ostensibly on Marxian theory (Marcuse, 1958).

Criticisms of Positivism 对实证主义的批判

Critical theorists also focus on the philosophical underpinnings of scientific inquiry, especially positivism (Fuller, 2007a; Bottomore, 1984; Halfpenny, 2005; 2001; Morrow, 1994). The criticism of positivism is related, at least in part, to the criticism of economic determinism, because some of those who were determinists accepted part or all of the positivistic theory of knowledge. Positivism is depicted as accepting the idea that a single scientific method is applicable to all fields of study. It takes the physical sciences as the standard of certainty and exactness for all disciplines. Positivists believe that knowledge is inherently neutral. They feel that they can keep human values out of their work. This belief, in turn, leads to the view that science is not in the position of advocating any specific form of social action. (See Chapter 1 for more discussion of positivism.)

Positivism is opposed by the critical school on various grounds (Sewart, 1978). For one thing, positivism tends to reify the social world and see it as a natural process. The critical theorists prefer to focus on human activity as well as on the ways in which such activity affects larger social structures. In short, positivism loses sight of the actors (Habermas, 1971), reducing them to passive entities determined by "natural forces." Given their belief in the distinctiveness of the actor, the critical theorists would not accept the idea that the general laws of science can be applied without question to human action. Positivism is assailed for being content to judge the adequacy of means toward given ends and for not making a similar judgment about ends. This critique leads to the view that positivism is inherently conservative, incapable of challenging the existing system. As Martin Jay says of positivism, "The result was the absolutizing of 'facts' and the reification of the existing order" (1973:62). Positivism leads the actor and the social scientist to passivity. Few Marxists of any type would support a perspective that does not relate theory and practice. Despite these criticisms of positivism, some Marxists (for example, some structuralists, analytic Marxists) espouse positivism, and Marx himself was often guilty of being overly positivistic (Habermas, 1971).

Criticisms of Sociology 对社会学的批判

Sociology is attacked for its "scientism," that is, for making the scientific method an end in itself. In addition, sociology is accused of accepting the status quo. The critical school maintains that sociology does not seriously criticize society or seek to transcend the contemporary social structure. Sociology, the critical school contends, has surrendered its obligation to help people oppressed by contemporary society.

Members of this school are critical of sociologists' focus on society as a whole rather than on individuals in society; sociologists are accused of ignoring the interaction of the individual and society. Although most sociological perspectives are *not* guilty of ignoring this interaction, this view is a cornerstone of the critical school's attacks on sociologists. Because they ignore the individual, sociologists are seen as being unable to say anything meaningful about political changes that could lead to a "just and humane society" (Frankfurt Institute for Social Research, 1973:46). As Zoltan Tar put it, sociology becomes "an integral part of the existing society instead of being a means of critique and a ferment of renewal" (1977:x).

Critique of Modern Society 对现代社会的批判

Most of the critical school's work is aimed at a critique of modern society and a variety of its components. Whereas much of early Marxian theory aimed specifically at the economy, the critical school shifted its orientation to the cultural level in light of what it considers the realities of modern capitalist society. That is, the locus of domination in the modern world shifted from the economy to the cultural realm. Still, the critical school retains its interest in domination,[1] although in the modern world it is likely to be domination by cultural rather than economic elements. The critical school thus seeks to focus on the cultural repression of the individual in modern society.

The critical thinkers have been shaped not only by Marxian theory but also by Weberian theory, as reflected in their focus on rationality as the dominant development in the modern world. In fact, supporters of this approach often are labeled "Weberian Marxists" (Dahms, 1997; Lowy, 1996). As Trent Schroyer (1970) made clear, the view of the critical school is that in modern society the repression produced by rationality has replaced economic exploitation as the dominant social problem. The critical school clearly has adopted Weber's differentiation between *formal rationality* and *substantive rationality,* or what the critical theorists think of as *reason.* To the critical theorists, formal rationality is concerned unreflectively with the question of the most effective means for achieving any given purpose (Tar, 1977). This is viewed as "technocratic thinking," in which the objective is to serve the forces of domination, not to emancipate people from domination. The goal is simply to find the most efficient means to whatever ends are defined as important by those in power. Technocratic thinking is contrasted to reason, which is, in the minds of critical theorists, the hope for society. Reason involves the assessment of means in terms of the ultimate human values of justice, peace, and happiness. Critical theorists identified Nazism in general, and its concentration camps more specifically, as examples of formal rationality in mortal combat with reason. Thus, as George Friedman puts it,

---

[1] This is made abundantly clear by Trent Schroyer (1973), who entitled his book on the critical school *The Critique of Domination.*

"Auschwitz was a rational place, but it was not a reasonable one" (1981:15; see also Chapter 11 and the discussion of Bauman, 1989).

Despite the seeming rationality of modern life, the critical school views the modern world as rife with irrationality (Crook, 1995). This idea can be labeled the "irrationality of rationality" or, more specifically, the irrationality of formal rationality. In Herbert Marcuse's view, although it appears to be the embodiment of rationality, "this society is irrational as a whole" (1964:ix; see also Farganis, 1975). It is irrational that the rational world is destructive of individuals and their needs and abilities, that peace is maintained through a constant threat of war, and that despite the existence of sufficient means, people remain impoverished, repressed, exploited, and unable to fulfill themselves.

The critical school focuses primarily on one form of formal rationality—modern technology (Feenberg, 1996). Marcuse (1964), for example, was a severe critic of modern technology, at least as it is employed in capitalism. He saw technology in modern capitalist society as leading to totalitarianism. In fact, he viewed it as leading to new, more effective, and even more "pleasant" methods of external control over individuals. The prime example is the use of television to socialize and pacify the population (other examples are mass sports and pervasive exploitation of sex). Marcuse rejected the idea that technology is neutral in the modern world and saw it instead as a means to dominate people. It is effective because it is made to seem neutral when it is in fact enslaving. It serves to suppress individuality. The actor's inner freedom has been "invaded and whittled down" by modern technology. The result is what Marcuse called "one-dimensional society," in which individuals lose the ability to think critically and negatively about society. Marcuse did not see technology per se as the enemy, but rather technology as it is employed in modern capitalist society: "Technology, no matter how 'pure,' sustains and streamlines the continuum of domination. This fatal link can be cut only by a revolution which makes technology and technique subservient to the needs and goals of free men" (1969:56). Marcuse retained Marx's original view that technology is not inherently a problem and that it can be used to develop a "better" society.

Critique of Culture 文化批判

The critical theorists level significant criticisms at what they call the "culture industry" (Kellner and Lewis, 2007), the rationalized, bureaucratized structures (for example, the television networks) that control modern culture. Interest in the culture industry reflects their concern with the Marxian concept of "superstructure" rather than with the economic base (Beamish, 2007e). The *culture industry,* producing what is conventionally called "mass culture," is defined as the "administered . . . nonspontaneous, reified, phony culture rather than the real thing" (Jay, 1973:216).[2] Two things worry the critical thinkers most about this industry. First, they are concerned about its falseness. They think of it as a prepackaged set of ideas mass-produced and disseminated to the masses by the media. Second, the critical theorists are disturbed by its pacifying,

---

[2] In recent work (Garnham, 2007), this has been broadened to the idea of "culture industries" to include various "industries" (entertainment, knowledge, etc.) as well as the fact that there are differences among them.

repressive, and stupefying effect on people (D. Cook, 1996; G. Friedman, 1981; Tar, 1977:83; Zipes, 1994).

Douglas Kellner (1990) has self-consciously offered a critical theory of television. While he embeds his work in the cultural concerns of the Frankfurt school, Kellner draws on other Marxian traditions to present a more rounded conception of the television industry. He critiques the critical school because it "neglects detailed analysis of the political economy of the media, conceptualizing mass culture merely as an instrument of capitalist ideology" (Kellner, 1990:14). Thus, in addition to looking at television as part of the culture industry, Kellner connects it to both corporate capitalism and the political system. Furthermore, Kellner does not see television as monolithic or as controlled by coherent corporate forces but rather as a "highly conflictual mass medium in which competing economic, political, social and cultural forces intersect" (1990:14). Thus, while working within the tradition of critical theory, Kellner rejects the view that capitalism is a totally administered world. Nevertheless, Kellner sees television as a threat to democracy, individuality, and freedom and offers suggestions (for example, more democratic accountability, greater citizen access and participation, greater diversity on television) to deal with the threat. Thus, Kellner goes beyond a mere critique to offer proposals for dealing with the dangers posed by television.

The critical school is also interested in and critical of what it calls the "knowledge industry," which refers to entities concerned with knowledge production (for example, universities and research institutes) that have become autonomous structures in our society. Their autonomy has allowed them to extend themselves beyond their original mandate (Schroyer, 1970). They have become oppressive structures interested in expanding their influence throughout society.

Marx's critical analysis of capitalism led him to have hope for the future, but many critical theorists have come to a position of despair and hopelessness. They see the problems of the modern world not as specific to capitalism but as endemic to a rationalized world. They see the future, in Weberian terms, as an "iron cage" of increasingly rational structures from which hope for escape lessens all the time.

Much of critical theory (like the bulk of Marx's original formulation) is in the form of critical analyses. Even though the critical theorists also have a number of positive interests, one of the basic criticisms made of critical theory is that it offers more criticisms than it does positive contributions. This incessant negativity galls many scholars, and for this reason they feel that critical theory has little to offer to sociological theory.

The Major Contributions 主要的贡献

Subjectivity 主体性

The great contribution of the critical school has been its effort to reorient Marxian theory in a subjective direction. Although this constitutes a critique of Marx's materialism and his dogged focus on economic structures, it also represents a strong contribution to our understanding of the subjective elements of social life at both the individual and the cultural levels.

The Hegelian roots of Marxian theory are the major source of interest in subjectivity. Many of the critical thinkers see themselves as returning to those roots, as expressed in Marx's early works. In doing so, they are following up on the work of the early-twentieth-century Marxian revisionists, such as Georg Lukács, who sought not to focus on subjectivity but simply to integrate such an interest with the traditional Marxian concern with objective structures (Agger, 1978). Lukács did not seek a fundamental restructuring of Marxian theory, although the later critical theorists do have this broader and more ambitious objective.

We begin with the critical school's interest in culture. As pointed out above, the critical school has shifted to a concern with the cultural "superstructure" rather than with the economic "base." One factor motivating this shift is that the critical school feels that Marxists have overemphasized economic structures and that this emphasis has served to overwhelm their interest in the other aspects of social reality, especially the culture. In addition to this factor, a series of external changes in society point to such a shift (Agger, 1978). In particular, the prosperity of the post–World War II period in America *seems* to have led to a disappearance of internal economic contradictions in general and class conflict in particular. False consciousness *seems* to be nearly universal: all social classes, including the working class, appear to be beneficiaries and ardent supporters of the capitalist system. In addition, the former Soviet Union, despite its socialist economy, was at least as oppressive as capitalist society. Because the two societies had different economies, the critical thinkers had to look elsewhere for the major source of oppression. What they looked toward initially was culture.

To the previously discussed aspects of the Frankfurt school's concerns—rationality, the culture industry, and the knowledge industry—can be added another set of concerns, the most notable of which is an interest in ideology. By *ideology* the critical theorists mean the idea systems, often false and obfuscating, produced by societal elites. All these specific aspects of the superstructure and the critical school's orientation to them can be subsumed under the heading "critique of domination" (Agger, 1978; Schroyer, 1973). This interest in domination was at first stimulated by fascism in the 1930s and 1940s, but it has shifted to a concern with domination in capitalist society. The modern world has reached a stage of unsurpassed domination of individuals. In fact, the control is so complete that it no longer requires deliberate actions on the part of the leaders. The control pervades all aspects of the cultural world and, more important, is internalized in the actor. In effect, actors have come to dominate themselves in the name of the larger social structure. Domination has reached a complete stage where it no longer appears to be domination at all. Because domination is no longer perceived as personally damaging and alienating, it often seems as if the world is the way it is supposed to be. It is no longer clear to actors what the world *ought* to be like. Thus, the pessimism of the critical thinkers is buttressed, because they no longer can see how rational analysis can help alter the situation.

One of the critical school's concerns at the cultural level is with what Habermas (1975) called *legitimations*. These can be defined as systems of ideas generated by the political system, and theoretically by any other system, to support the existence of the system. They are designed to "mystify" the political system, to make it unclear exactly what is happening.

In addition to such cultural interests, the critical school is concerned with actors and their consciousness and what happens to them in the modern world. The consciousness of the masses came to be controlled by external forces (such as the culture industry). As a result, the masses failed to develop a revolutionary consciousness. Unfortunately, the critical theorists, like most Marxists and most sociologists, often fail to differentiate clearly between individual consciousness and culture or specify the many links between them. In much of their work, they move freely back and forth between consciousness and culture with little or no sense that they are changing levels.

Of great importance here is the effort by critical theorists, most notably Marcuse (1969), to integrate Freud's insights at the level of consciousness (and unconsciousness) into the critical theorists' interpretation of the culture. Critical theorists derive three things from Freud's work: (1) a psychological structure to work with in developing their theories, (2) a sense of psychopathology that allows them to understand both the negative impact of modern society and the failure to develop revolutionary consciousness, and (3) the possibilities of psychic liberation (G. Friedman, 1981). One of the benefits of this interest in individual consciousness is that it offers a useful corrective to the pessimism of the critical school and its focus on cultural constraints. Although people are controlled, imbued with false needs, and anesthetized, in Freudian terms they also are endowed with a libido (broadly conceived as sexual energy), which provides the basic source of energy for creative action oriented toward the overthrow of the major forms of domination.

Dialectics 辩证法

The second main positive focus of critical theory is an interest in dialectics (this idea is critiqued from the viewpoint of analytical Marxism later in this chapter). At the most general level, a dialectical approach means a focus on the social *totality*.[3] "No partial aspect of social life and no isolated phenomenon may be comprehended unless it is related to the historical whole, to the social structure conceived as a global entity" (Connerton, 1976:12). This approach involves rejection of a focus on any *specific* aspect of social life, especially the economic system, outside of its broader context. This approach also entails a concern with the interrelation of the various levels of social reality—most important, individual consciousness, the cultural superstructure, and the economic structure. Dialectics also carries with it a methodological prescription: One component of social life cannot be studied in isolation from the rest.

This idea has both diachronic and synchronic components. A *synchronic* view leads us to be concerned with the interrelationship of components of society within a contemporary totality. A *diachronic* view carries with it a concern for the historical roots of today's society as well as for where it might be going in the future (Bauman, 1976). The domination of people by social and cultural structures—the "one-dimensional" society, to use Marcuse's phrase—is the result of a specific

---

[3] Jay (1984) sees "totality" as the heart of Marxian theory in general, not just of critical theory. However, this idea is rejected by postmodern Marxists (see the discussion later in this chapter).

historical development and is not a universal characteristic of humankind. This historical perspective counteracts the common-sense view that emerges in capitalism that the system is a natural and inevitable phenomenon. In the view of the critical theorists (and other Marxists), people have come to see society as "second nature"; it is "perceived by common-sensical wisdom as an alien, uncompromising, demanding and high-handed power—exactly like non-human nature. To abide by the rules of reason, to behave rationally, to achieve success, to be free, man now had to accommodate himself to the 'second nature'" (Bauman, 1976:6).

The critical theorists also are oriented to thinking about the future, but following Marx's lead, they refuse to be utopian; rather, they focus on criticizing and changing contemporary society (Alway, 1995). However, instead of directing their attention to society's economic structure as Marx had done, they concentrate on its cultural superstructure. Their dialectical approach commits them to work in the real world. They are not satisfied with seeking truth in scientific laboratories. The ultimate test of their ideas is the degree to which they are accepted and used in practice. This process they call *authentication,* which occurs when the people who have been the victims of distorted communication take up the ideas of critical theory and use them to free themselves from that system (Bauman, 1976:104). Thus we arrive at another aspect of the concerns of the critical thinkers—the *liberation* of humankind (Marcuse, 1964:222).

In more abstract terms, critical thinkers can be said to be preoccupied with the interplay and relationship between theory and practice. The view of the Frankfurt school was that the two have been severed in capitalist society (Schroyer, 1973:28). That is, theorizing is done by one group, which is delegated, or more likely takes, that right, whereas practice is relegated to another, less powerful group. In many cases, the theorist's work is uninformed by what went on in the real world, leading to an impoverished and largely irrelevant body of Marxian and sociological theory. The point is to unify theory and practice so as to restore the relationship between them. Theory thus would be informed by practice, whereas practice would be shaped by theory. In the process, both theory and practice would be enriched.

Despite this avowed goal, most of critical theory has failed abysmally to integrate theory and practice. In fact, one of the most often voiced criticisms of critical theory is that it usually is written in such a way that it is totally inaccessible to the mass of people. Furthermore, in its commitment to studying culture and superstructure, critical theory addresses a number of very esoteric topics and has little to say about the pragmatic, day-to-day concerns of most people.

Knowledge and Human Interests   One of the best-known dialectical concerns of the critical school is Jurgen Habermas's (1970, 1971) interest in the relationship between knowledge and human interests—an example of a broader dialectical concern with the relationship between subjective and objective factors. But Habermas has been careful to point out that subjective and objective factors cannot be dealt with in isolation from one another. To him, knowledge systems exist at the objective level whereas human interests are more subjective phenomena.

Habermas differentiated among three knowledge systems and their corresponding interests. The interests that lie behind and guide each system of knowledge are generally unknown to laypeople, and it is the task of the critical theorists to uncover them. The first type of knowledge is *analytic science,* or *classical positivistic scientific systems.* In Habermas's view, the underlying interest of such a knowledge system is technical prediction and control, which can be applied to the environment, other societies, or people within society. In Habermas's view, analytic science lends itself quite easily to enhancing oppressive control. The second type of knowledge system is *humanistic knowledge,* and its interest lies in *understanding* the world. It operates from the general view that understanding our past generally helps us understand what is transpiring today. It has a practical interest in mutual and self-understanding. It is neither oppressive nor liberating. The third type is *critical knowledge,* which Habermas, and the Frankfurt school in general, espoused. The interest attached to this type of knowledge is *human emancipation.* It was hoped that the critical knowledge generated by Habermas and others would raise the self-consciousness of the masses (through mechanisms articulated by the Freudians) and lead to a social movement that would result in the hoped-for emancipation.

Criticisms of Critical Theory 对批判理论的批判

A number of criticisms have been leveled at critical theory (Bottomore, 1984). First, critical theory has been accused of being largely ahistorical, of examining a variety of events without paying much attention to their historical and comparative contexts (for example, Nazism in the 1930s, anti-Semitism in the 1940s, student revolts in the 1960s). This is a damning criticism of any Marxian theory, which should be inherently historical and comparative. Second, the critical school, as we have seen already, generally has ignored the economy. Finally, and relatedly, critical theorists have tended to argue that the working class has disappeared as a revolutionary force, a position decidedly in opposition to traditional Marxian analysis.

Criticisms such as these led traditional Marxists such as Bottomore to conclude, "The Frankfurt School, in its original form, and as a school of Marxism or sociology, is dead" (1984:76). Similar sentiments have been expressed by Greisman, who labels critical theory "the paradigm that failed" (1986:273). If it is dead as a distinctive school, that is because many of its basic ideas have found their way into Marxism, neo-Marxian sociology, and even mainstream sociology. Thus, as Bottomore himself concludes in the case of Habermas, the critical school has undergone a rapprochement with Marxism and sociology, and "at the same time some of the distinctive ideas of the Frankfurt School are conserved and developed" (1984:76).

The Ideas of Jurgen Habermas 哈贝马斯的理论

Although critical theory *may* be on the decline, Jurgen Habermas[4] and his theories are very much alive (J. M. Bernstein, 1995; R. H. Brown and Goodman, 2001; Outhwaite, 1994). We touched on a few of his ideas earlier in this chapter, but we close this

---

[4] Habermas began as Theodor Adorno's research assistant in 1955 (Wiggershaus, 1994:537).

section on critical theory with a more detailed look at his theory (still other aspects of his thinking will be covered in Chapters 10 and 11).

Differences with Marx 与马克思的差异

Habermas contends that his goal has been "to develop a theoretical program that I understand as a reconstruction of historical materialism" (1979:95). Habermas takes Marx's starting point (human potential, species-being, "sensuous human activity") as his own. However, Habermas (1971) argues that Marx failed to distinguish between two analytically distinct components of species-being—work (or labor, purposive-rational action) and social (or symbolic) interaction (or communicative action). In Habermas's view, Marx tended to ignore the latter and to reduce it to work. As Habermas put it, the problem in Marx's work is the "*reduction of the self-generative act of the human species to labor*" (1971:42). Thus, Habermas says: "I take as my starting point the fundamental distinction between *work* and *interaction*" (1970:91). Throughout his writings, Habermas's work is informed by this distinction, although he is most prone to use the terms *purposive-rational action* (work) and *communicative action* (interaction).

Under the heading "purposive-rational action," Habermas distinguishes between instrumental action and strategic action. Both involve the calculated pursuit of self-interest. *Instrumental action* involves a single actor rationally calculating the best means to a given goal. *Strategic action* involves two or more individuals coordinating purposive-rational action in the pursuit of a goal. The objective of *both* instrumental and strategic action is instrumental mastery.

Habermas is most interested in *communicative action,* in which

> the actions of the agents involved are coordinated not through egocentric calculations of success but through acts of *reaching understanding.* In communicative action participants are not primarily oriented to their own successes; they pursue their individual goals under the condition that they can *harmonize* their plans of action on the basis of *common situation definitions.*
>
> (Habermas, 1984:286; italics added)

Whereas the end of purposive-rational action is to achieve a goal, the objective of communicative action is to achieve communicative understanding (Sean Stryker, 1998).

Clearly, there is an important speech component in communicative action. However, such action is broader than that encompassing "speech acts or equivalent nonverbal expressions" (Habermas, 1984:278).

Habermas's key point of departure from Marx is to argue that communicative action, *not* purposive-rational action (work), is the most distinctive and most pervasive human phenomenon. It (not work) is the foundation of all sociocultural life as well as all the human sciences. Whereas Marx was led to focus on work, Habermas is led to focus on communication.

Not only did Marx focus on work, he took free and creative work (species-being) as his baseline for critically analyzing work in various historical epochs, especially capitalism. Habermas, too, adopts a baseline, but in the realm of communicative rather than in that of purposive-rational action. Habermas's baseline is undistorted communication, communication without compulsion. With this baseline, Habermas is able to critically analyze distorted communication. Habermas is concerned with those social structures that distort communication, just as Marx examined the structural sources of the distortion of work. Although they have different baselines, both Habermas and Marx *have* baselines, and these permit them to escape relativism and render judgments about various historical phenomena. Habermas is critical of those theorists, especially Weber and previous critical theorists, for their lack of such a baseline and their lapse into relativism.

There is still another parallel between Marx and Habermas and their baselines. For both, these baselines represent not only their analytical starting points but also their political objectives. That is, whereas for Marx the goal was a communist society in which undistorted work (species-being) would exist for the first time, for Habermas the political goal is a society of undistorted communication (communicative action). In terms of immediate goals, Marx seeks the elimination of (capitalist) barriers to undistorted work and Habermas is interested in the elimination of barriers to free communication.

Here Habermas (1973; see also Habermas, 1994:101), like other critical theorists, draws on Freud and sees many parallels between what psychoanalysts do at the individual level and what he thinks needs to be done at the societal level. Habermas sees psychoanalysis as a theory of distorted communication and as being preoccupied with allowing individuals to communicate in an undistorted way. The psychoanalyst seeks to find the sources of distortions in individual communication, that is, repressed blocks to communication. Through reflection, the psychoanalyst attempts to help the individual overcome these blocks. Similarly, through *therapeutic critique,* "a form of argumentation that serves to clarify systematic self-deception" (Habermas, 1984:21), the critical theorist attempts to aid people in general to overcome social barriers to undistorted communication. There is, then, an analogy (many critics think an illegitimate analogy) between psychoanalysis and critical theory. The psychoanalyst aids the patient in much the same way that the social critic helps those unable to communicate adequately to become "undisabled" (Habermas, 1994:112).

As for Marx, the basis of Habermas's ideal future society exists in the contemporary world. That is, for Marx elements of species-being are found in work in capitalist society. For Habermas, elements of undistorted communication are found in every act of contemporary communication.

Rationalization 理性化

This brings us to the central issue of rationalization in Habermas's work. Here Habermas is influenced not only by Marx's work but by Weber's as well. Most prior work, in Habermas's view, has focused on the rationalization of purposive-rational action, which has led to a growth of productive forces and an increase in technological control over life (Habermas, 1970). This form of rationalization, as it was to Weber and Marx, is a major, perhaps *the* major, problem in the modern world. However, the problem is rationalization of purposive-rational action, *not* rationalization in general. In fact, for Habermas, the antidote to the problem of the rationalization of purposive-rational action lies in the rationalization of communicative action. The rationalization of communicative action leads to communication free from domination, free and open communication. Rationalization here involves emancipation, "*removing restrictions on communication*" (Habermas, 1970:118; see also Habermas, 1979). This is where Habermas's previously mentioned work on *legitimations* and, more generally, *ideology* fits in. That is, these are two of the main causes of distorted communication, causes that must be eliminated if we are to have free and open communication.

At the level of social norms, such rationalization would involve decreases in normative repressiveness and rigidity leading to increases in individual flexibility and reflectivity. The development of this new, less-restrictive or nonrestrictive normative system lies at the heart of Habermas's theory of social evolution. Instead of a new productive system, rationalization for Habermas (1979) leads to a new, less-distorting normative system. Although he regards it as a misunderstanding of his position, many have accused Habermas of cutting his Marxian roots in this shift from the material level to the normative level.

The end point of this evolution for Habermas is a rational society (Delanty, 1997). *Rationality* here means removal of the barriers that distort communication, but more generally it means a communication system in which ideas are openly presented and defended against criticism; unconstrained agreement develops during argumentation. To understand this better, we need more details of Habermas's communication theory.

Communication 沟通

Habermas distinguishes between the previously discussed communicative action and discourse. Whereas communicative action occurs in everyday life, *discourse* is

> that form of communication that is removed from contexts of experience and action and whose structure assures us: that the bracketed validity claims of assertions, recommendations, or warnings are the exclusive object of discussion; that participants, themes, and contributions are not restricted except with reference to the goal of testing the validity claims in questions; that no force except that of the better argument is exercised; and that all motives except that of the cooperative search for truth are excluded.
>
> (Habermas, 1975:107–108)

In the theoretical world of discourse, but also hidden and underlying the world of communicative actions, is the "ideal speech situation," in which force or power does not determine which arguments win out; instead the better argument emerges victorious. The weight of evidence and argumentation determine what is considered valid or true. The arguments that emerge from such a discourse (and that the participants agree on) are true (Hesse, 1995). Thus Habermas adopts a consensus theory of truth (rather than a copy [or "reality"] theory of truth [Outhwaite, 1994:41]). This truth is part of all communication, and its full expression is the goal of Habermas's evolutionary theory. As Thomas McCarthy says, "The idea of truth points ultimately to a form of interaction that is free from all distorting influences. The 'good and true life' that is the goal of critical theory is inherent in the notion of truth; it is anticipated in every act of speech" (1982:308).

Consensus arises theoretically in discourse (and pretheoretically in communicative action) when four types of validity claims are raised and recognized by interactants.

First, the speaker's utterances are seen as understandable, comprehensible. Second, the propositions offered by the speaker are true; that is, the speaker is offering reliable knowledge. Third, the speaker is being truthful (veracious) and sincere in offering the propositions; the speaker is reliable. Fourth, it is right and proper for the speaker to utter such propositions; he or she has the normative basis to do so. Consensus arises when all these validity claims are raised and accepted; it breaks down when one or more are questioned. Returning to an earlier point, there are forces in the modern world that distort this process, prevent the emergence of a consensus, and would have to be overcome for Habermas's ideal society to come about (Morris, 2001).

Critical Theory Today 当代批判理论

While Habermas is the most prominent of today's social thinkers, he is not alone in struggling to develop a critical theory that is better adapted to contemporary realities (see, for example, the various essays in Wexler, 1991; Antonio and Kellner, 1994). Castells (1996) has made the case for the need for a critical theory of the new "information society." To illustrate these continuing efforts, a brief discussion follows of Kellner's (1989c) effort to develop a critical theory of what he labels "techno-capitalism."

Techno-Capitalism 技术资本主义

Kellner's theory is based on the premise that we have not moved into a postmodern, or postindustrial, age, but rather that capitalism continues to reign supreme, as it did in the heyday of critical theory. Thus, he feels that the basic concepts developed to analyze capitalism (for example, reification, alienation) continue to be relevant in the analysis of techno-capitalism. Kellner defines techno-capitalism as

> a configuration of capitalist society in which technical and scientific knowledge, automation, computers and advanced technology play a role in the process of production parallel to the role of human labor power, mechanization and machines in earlier eras of capitalism, while producing as well new modes of societal organization and forms of culture and everyday life.

> (Kellner, 1989c:178)

In technical Marxian terms, in techno-capitalism "constant capital progressively comes to replace variable capital, as the ratio between technology and labor increases at the expense of the input of human labor power" (Kellner, 1989c:179). Yet we should not lose sight of the fact that techno-capitalism remains a form of capitalism, albeit one in which technology is of far greater importance than ever before.

Kellner has learned from the failures of other Marxists. Thus, for example, he resists the idea that technology determines the "superstructure" of society. The state and culture are seen as at least partially autonomous in techno-capitalism. He also refuses to see techno-capitalism as a new stage in history, but views it as a new configuration, or constellation, within capitalism. Kellner does not simply focus on the problems caused by techno-capitalism, but also sees in it new possibilities for social progress and the emancipation of society. In fact, a key role for critical theory, in Kellner's view, is not just to criticize it, but to "attempt to analyze the emancipatory possibilities unleashed by techno-capitalism" (1989c:215). Kellner also refuses to return to the old class politics, but sees great potential in the various social movements (women, the environment) that have arisen in the last few decades.

Kellner does not endeavor to develop a full-scale theory of techno-capitalism. His main point is that although it has changed dramatically, capitalism remains predominant in the contemporary world. Thus, the tools provided by the critical school, and Marxian theory more generally, continue to be relevant in today's world. We close this section with Kellner's description of "techno-culture," since a concern with culture was so central to critical theory in its prime:

> Techno-culture represents a configuration of mass culture and the consumer society in which consumer goods, film, television, mass images and computerized information become a dominant form of culture throughout the developed world [and] which increasingly penetrate developing countries as well. In this techno-culture, image, spectacle, and aestheticized commodification, or "commodity aesthetics," come to constitute new forms of culture which colonize everyday life and transform politics, economics and social relations. In all these domains, *technology* plays an increasingly fundamental role.
>
> (Kellner, 1989c:181)

There is much here to be explored by future critical theorists, such as the nature of techno-culture itself, its commodification, its colonization of the life-world, and its dialectical impact on the economy and other sectors of society. There is much that is new here, but there is also much that is based on the fundamental ideas of critical theory.

Later Developments in Cultural Critique 文化批判晚近的发展

Kellner and Lewis (2007) see the Frankfurt school as part of a tradition of work that involves "cultural critique," which, in turn, is part of the "cultural turn" and cultural studies (McGuigan, 2005; Storey, 2007). At the center of this tradition lies the Frankfurt school, but is it predated by work by Kant, Nietzsche, Marx, and Freud (among others) and is succeeded by later work, especially that associated with the "Birmingham school."

As the name suggests, the Birmingham school, or the Centre for Contemporary Cultural Studies, was associated with the University of Birmingham in the United Kingdom (Barker, 2007). Founded in 1964, it remained in existence until 1988. Created by Richard Hoggart, the center gained its greatest fame and coherence as a center of cultural studies under the leadership of Stuart Hall (Rojek, 2003, 2005). In contrast to the literary tradition in England, which privileged and valued high art and the elite classes, the Birmingham school valued and focused on popular culture, its products, and the lower classes with which they are associated. Furthermore, popular culture was seen as the arena in which hegemonic ideas operated as mechanisms of social control, were consented to, and, most important from a Marxian perspective, were resisted by the lower classes. Concepts like hegemonic ideas, consent, and resistance clearly aligned the Birminghan school with Marxian theory, especially the theories of Antonio Gramsci (although structuralism and semiotics influenced at least some of its work). An ideological struggle was in existence, and as "organic intellectuals" (thinkers who were, at least theoretically, part of the working class) it was the responsibility (if not always fulfilled) of the Birmingham scholars to be part of popular culture and help those associated with it wage a counter-hegemonic ideological battle against those in power. They also saw as their role the debunking and demystification of dominant texts with their abundant ideologies and myths that served the interests of elites. They were not disinterested social scientists but rather "populists" who sided with the "people" against the power elite (McGuigan, 2002, 2005). Thus, like the critical theories, those associated with the Birmingham school moved away from economic determinism and a base-superstructure perspective and toward an emphasis on the superstructure, especially culture (as well as the nation-state), which was seen as relatively autonomous of the economic base.

At that level of culture, the focus was on ideology and hegemony and on the ways that power and control manifested itself and was resisted. This meant a concern, on the one hand, with how the media expressed ideologies of the dominant groups and how working-class youth reproduced their subordinate position and, on the other hand, with how working-class youth resisted that position and the ideology of the dominant groups through such things as dress and style (e.g., the "skinheads"). Relatedly, the Birmingham school was interested in analyzing a variety of texts (reflecting the influence of structuralism and semiotics; see Chapter 13)—films, advertisements, soap operas, news broadcasts—in order to show how they were hegemonic products and how their meanings were not fixed but rather were produced in various, sometimes antithetical or oppositional, ways by the audience. Again, this was a reflection of the school's dual concern with hegemony and resistance.

The power of the lower classes to redefine culture in antithetical and oppositional ways was related to a major difference between the Birmingham school and the Frankfurt school. The latter saw culture as debased by the culture industry; the former saw that as an elitist perspective. The Birmingham school had a much more positive view of culture, especially as it was interpreted and produced by the lower classes.

Neo-Marxian Economic Sociology 新马克思主义经济社会学

Many neo-Marxists (for example, critical theorists) have made relatively few comments on the economic institution, at least in part as a reaction against the excesses of the economic determinists. However, these reactions have set in motion a series of counterreactions. In this section we will deal with the work of some of the Marxists who have returned to a focus on the economic realm. Their work constitutes an effort to adapt Marxian theory to the realities of modern capitalist society (Lash and Urry, 1987; Mészáros, 1995).

We will deal with two bodies of work in this section. The first focuses on the broad issue of capital and labor. The second comprises the narrower, and more contemporary, work on the transition from Fordism to post-Fordism.

Capital and Labor 资本和劳动力

Marx's original insights into economic structures and processes were based on his analysis of the capitalism of his time—what we can think of as competitive capitalism. Capitalist industries were comparatively small, with the result that no single industry, or small group of industries, could gain complete and uncontested control over a market. Much of Marx's economic work was based on the premise, accurate for his time, that capitalism is a competitive system. To be sure, Marx foresaw the possibility of future monopolies, but he commented only briefly on them. Many later Marxian theorists continued to operate as if capitalism remained much as it had been in Marx's time.

Monopoly Capital 垄断资本

It is in this context that we must examine the work of Paul Baran and Paul Sweezy (1966; Toscano, 2007b). They began with a criticism of Marxian social science for repeating familiar formulations and failing to explain important recent developments in capitalistic society. They accused Marxian theory of stagnating because it continued to rest on the assumption of a competitive economy. A modern Marxian theory must, in their view, recognize that competitive capitalism largely has been replaced by monopoly capitalism.

In *monopoly capitalism* one or a few capitalists control a given sector of the economy. Clearly, there is far less competition in monopoly capitalism than in competitive capitalism. In competitive capitalism, organizations competed on a price basis; that is, capitalists tried to sell more goods by offering lower prices. In monopoly capitalism, firms no longer have to compete in this way because one or a few firms control a market; competition shifts to the sales domain. Advertising, packaging, and other methods of appealing to potential consumers are the main areas of competition.

The movement from price to sales competition is part of another process characteristic of monopoly capitalism—*progressive rationalization*. Price competition comes to be seen as highly irrational. That is, from the monopoly capitalist's point of view, offering lower and lower prices can lead only to chaos in the marketplace, to say nothing of lower profits and perhaps even bankruptcy. Sales competition, in contrast, is not a cutthroat system; in fact, it even provides work for the advertising industry. Furthermore, prices can be kept high, with the costs of the sales and promotion simply added to the price. Thus sales competition is also far less risky than price competition.

Another crucial aspect of monopoly capitalism is the rise of the giant corporation, with a few large corporations controlling most sectors of the economy. In competitive capitalism, the organization was controlled almost single-handedly by an entrepreneur. The modern corporation is owned by a large number of stockholders, but a few large stockholders own most of the stock. Although stockholders "own" the corporation, managers exercise the actual day-to-day control. The managers are crucial in monopoly capitalism, whereas the entrepreneurs were central in competitive capitalism. Managers have considerable power, which they seek to maintain.

They even seek financial independence for their firms by trying, as much as possible, to generate whatever funds they need internally rather than relying on external sources of funding.

Baran and Sweezy commented extensively on the central position of the corporate manager in modern capitalist society. Managers are viewed as a highly rational group oriented to maximizing the profits of the organization. Therefore, they are not inclined to take the risks that were characteristic of the early entrepreneurs. They have a longer time perspective than the entrepreneurs did. Whereas the early capitalist was interested in maximizing profits in the short run, modern managers are aware that such efforts may well lead to chaotic price competition that might adversely affect the long-term profitability of the firm. The manager will thus forgo *some* profits in the short run to maximize long-term profitability.

Baran and Sweezy have been criticized on various grounds. For example, they overemphasize the rationality of managers. Herbert Simon (1957), for example, would argue that managers are more interested in finding (and are only able to find) minimally satisfactory solutions than they are in finding the most rational and most profitable solutions. Another issue is whether managers are, in fact, the pivotal figures in modern capitalism. Many would argue that it is the large stockholders who really control the capitalistic system.

Labor and Monopoly Capital 劳动力和垄断资本主义

Harry Braverman (1974) considered the labor process and the exploitation of the worker the heart of Marxian theory. He intended not only to update Marx's interest in manual workers but also to examine what has happened to white-collar and service workers.

Toward the goal of extending Marx's analysis, Braverman argued that the concept "working class" does not describe a specific group of people or occupations but is rather an expression of a process of buying and selling labor power. In modern capitalism, virtually no one owns the means of production; therefore, the many, including most white-collar and service workers, are forced to sell their labor power to the few who do. In his view, capitalist control and exploitation, as well as the derivative processes of mechanization and rationalization, are being extended to white-collar and service occupations.

Managerial Control   Braverman recognized economic exploitation, which was Marx's focus, but concentrated on the issue of *control*. He asked the question: How do the capitalists control the labor power they employ? One answer is that they exercise such control through managers. In fact, Braverman defined *management* as "*a labor process conducted for the purpose of control within the corporation*" (1974:267).

Braverman concentrated on the more impersonal means employed by managers to control workers. One of his central concerns was the utilization of specialization to control workers. Here he carefully differentiated between the division of labor in society as a whole and specialization of work within the organization. All known societies have had a division of labor (for example, between men and women, farmers and artisans, and so forth), but the specialization of work within the organization is a special development of capitalism. Braverman believed that the division of labor at the societal level may enhance the individual, whereas specialization in the workplace has the disastrous effect of subdividing human capabilities: "The subdivision of the individual, when carried on without regard to human capabilities and needs, is a crime against the person and against humanity" (1974:73).

Specialization in the workplace involves the continual division and subdivision of tasks or operations into minute and highly specialized activities, each of which is then likely to be assigned to a *different* worker. This process constitutes the creation of what Braverman calls "detail workers." Out of the range of abilities any individual possesses, capitalists select a small number that the worker is to use on the job. As Braverman put it, the capitalist first breaks down the work process and then "dismembers the worker as well" (1974:78) by requiring the worker to use only a small proportion of his or her skills and abilities. In Braverman's terms, the worker "never voluntarily converts himself into a lifelong detail worker. This is the contribution of the capitalist" (1974:78).

Why does the capitalist do this? First, it increases the control of management. It is easier to control a worker doing a specified task than it is to control one employing a wide range of skills. Second, it increases productivity. That is, a group of workers performing highly specialized tasks can produce more than can the same number of craftspeople, each of whom has all the skills and performs all the production activities. For instance, workers on an automobile assembly line produce more cars than would a corresponding number of skilled craftspeople, each of whom produces his or her own car. Third, specialization allows the capitalist to pay the least for the labor power needed. Instead of highly paid, skilled craftspeople, the capitalist can employ lower-paid, unskilled workers. Following the logic of capitalism, employers seek to progressively cheapen the labor of workers, and this results in a virtually undifferentiated mass of what Braverman called "simple labor."

Specialization is not a sufficient means of control for capitalists and the managers in their employ. Another important means is scientific technique, including such efforts as scientific management, which is an attempt to apply science to the control of labor on the behalf of management. To Braverman, scientific management is the science of "how best to control alienated labor" (1974:90). Scientific management is found in a series of stages aimed at the control of labor—gathering many workers in one workshop, dictating the length of the workday, supervising workers directly to ensure diligence, enforcing rules against distractions (for example, talking), and setting minimum acceptable production levels. Overall scientific management contributed to control through "*the dictation to the worker of the precise manner in which work is to be performed*" (Braverman, 1974:90). For example, Braverman discussed F. W. Taylor's (Kanigel, 1997) early work on the shoveling of coal, which led him to develop rules about the kind of shovel to use, the way to stand, the angle at which the shovel should enter the coal pile, and how much coal to pick up in each motion. In other words, Taylor developed methods that ensured almost total control over the labor process. Workers were to be left with as few independent decisions as possible;

thus, a separation of the mental and the manual was accomplished. Management used its monopoly over work-related knowledge to control each step of the labor process. In the end, the work itself was left without any meaningful skill, content, or knowledge. Craftsmanship was utterly destroyed.

Braverman also saw machinery as a means of control over workers. Modern machinery comes into existence "when the tool and/or the work are given a fixed motion path by the structure of the machine itself" (Braverman, 1974:188). The skill is built into the machine rather than being left for the worker to acquire. Instead of controlling the work process, workers come to be controlled by the machine. Furthermore, it is far easier for management to control machines than to control workers.

Braverman argued that through mechanisms such as the specialization of work, scientific management, and machines, management has been able to extend its control over its manual workers. Although this is a useful insight, especially the emphasis on control, Braverman's distinctive contribution has been his effort to extend this kind of analysis to sectors of the labor force that were not included in Marx's original analysis of the labor process. Braverman argued that white-collar and service workers are now being subjected to the same processes of control that were used on manual workers in the nineteenth century (Schmutz, 1996).

One of Braverman's examples is white-collar clerical workers. At one time such workers were considered to be a group distinguished from manual workers by such things as their dress, skills, training, and career prospects (Lockwood, 1956). However, today both groups are being subjected to the same means of control. Thus it has become more difficult to differentiate between the factory and the modern factorylike office, as the workers in the latter are progressively proletarianized. For one thing, the work of the clerical worker has grown more and more specialized. This means, among other things, that the mental and manual aspects of office work have been separated. Office managers, engineers, and technicians now perform the mental work, whereas the "line" clerical workers do little more than manual tasks such as keypunching. As a result, the level of skills needed for these jobs has been lowered, and the jobs require little or no special training.

Scientific management also is seen as invading the office. Clerical tasks have been scientifically studied and, as a result of that research, have been simplified, routinized, and standardized. Finally, mechanization has made significant inroads into the office, primarily through the computer and computer-related equipment.

By applying these mechanisms to clerical work, managers find it much easier to control such workers. It is unlikely that such control mechanisms are as strong and effective in the office as they are in the factory; still, the trend is toward the development of the white-collar "factory."[5]

Several obvious criticisms can be leveled at Braverman. For one thing, he probably has overestimated the degree of similarity between manual work and clerical work. For another, his preoccupation with control has led him to devote relatively

---

[5] It is important to note that Braverman's book was written before the boom in computer technology in the office, especially the widespread use of the word processor. It may be that such technology, requiring greater skill and training than do older office technologies, will increase worker autonomy (Zuboff, 1988).

little attention to the dynamics of economic exploitation in capitalism. Nonetheless, he has enriched our understanding of the labor process in modern capitalist society (Foster, 1994; Meiksins, 1994).

Other Work on Labor and Capital 劳动力和资本研究的其他成果

The issue of control is even more central to Richard Edwards (1979). To Edwards, control lies at the heart of the twentieth-century transformation of the workplace. Following Marx, Edwards sees the workplace, both past and present, as an arena of class conflict, in his terms a "contested terrain." Within this arena, dramatic changes have taken place in the way in which those at the top control those at the bottom. In nineteenth-century competitive capitalism, "simple" control was used, in which "bosses exercised power personally, intervening in the labor process often to exhort workers, bully and threaten them, reward good performance, hire and fire on the spot, favor loyal employees, and generally act as despots, benevolent or otherwise" (Edwards, 1979:19). Although this system of control continues in many small businesses, it has proved too crude for modern, large-scale organizations. In such organizations, simple control has tended to be replaced by impersonal and more sophisticated technical and bureaucratic control. Modern workers can be controlled by the technologies with which they work. The classic example of this is the automobile assembly line, in which the workers' actions are determined by the incessant demands of the line. Another example is the modern computer, which can keep careful track of how much work an employee does and how many mistakes he or she makes. Modern workers also are controlled by the impersonal rules of bureaucracies rather than the personal control of supervisors. Capitalism is changing constantly, and with it the means by which workers are controlled.

Also of note is the work of Michael Burawoy (1979) and its interest in why workers in a capitalist system work so hard. He rejects Marx's explanation that such hard work is a result of coercion. The advent of labor unions and other changes largely eliminated the arbitrary power of management. "Coercion alone could no longer explain what workers did once they arrived on the shop floor" (Burawoy, 1979:xii). To Burawoy, workers, at least in part, consent to work hard in the capitalist system, and at least part of that consent is produced in the workplace.

We can illustrate Burawoy's approach with one aspect of his research, the games that workers play on the job and, more generally, the informal practices that they develop. Most analysts see these as workers' efforts to reduce alienation and other job-related discontent. In addition, they usually have been seen as social mechanisms that workers develop to oppose management. In contrast, Burawoy concludes that these games "are usually neither independent nor in opposition to management" (1979:80). In fact, "management, at least at the lower levels, actually participates not only in the organization of the game but in the enforcement of its rules" (1979:80). Rather than challenging management, the organization, or, ultimately, the capitalist system, these games actually support them. For one thing, playing the game creates consent among the workers about the rules on which the game is based and, more generally, about the system of social relations (owner-manager-worker) that defines the rules of the game. For another, because managers and workers both are involved in the game, the system of antagonistic social relations to which the game was supposed to respond is obscured.

Burawoy argues that such methods of generating active cooperation and consent are far more effective in getting workers to cooperate in the pursuit of profit than is coercion (such as firing those who do not cooperate). In the end, Burawoy believes that games and other informal practices are all methods of getting workers to accept the system and of eliciting their contributions to ever higher profits.

Fordism and Post-Fordism 福特主义和后福特主义

One of the most recent concerns of economically oriented Marxists is the issue of whether we have witnessed, or are witnessing, a transition from "Fordism" to "post-Fordism" (Wiedenhoft, 2005; A. Amin, 1994; Kiely, 1998). This concern is related to the broader issue of whether we have undergone a transition from a modern to a postmodern society (Gartman, 1998). We will discuss this larger issue in general (Chapter 13), as well as the way in which it is addressed by contemporary Marxian theorists (later in this chapter). In general, *Fordism* is associated with the modern era, while *post-Fordism* is linked to the more recent, postmodern epoch. (The Marxian interest in Fordism is not new; Gramsci [1971] published an essay on it in 1931.)

Fordism, of course, refers to the ideas, principles, and systems spawned by Henry Ford. Ford generally is credited with the development of the modern mass-production system, primarily through the creation of the automobile assembly line. The following characteristics may be associated with Fordism:

- The mass production of homogeneous products.
- The use of inflexible technologies such as the assembly line.
- The adoption of standardized work routines (Taylorism).
- Increases in productivity derived from "economies of scale as well as the deskilling, intensification and homogenization of labor" (Clarke, 1990:73).
- The resulting rise of the mass worker and bureaucratized unions.
- The negotiation by unions of uniform wages tied to increases in profits and productivity.
- The growth of a market for the homogenized products of mass-production industries and the resulting homogenization of consumption patterns.
- A rise in wages, caused by unionization, leading to a growing demand for the increasing supply of mass-produced products.
- A market for products that is governed by Keynesian macroeconomic policies and a market for labor that is handled by collective bargaining overseen by the state.
- Mass educational institutions providing the mass workers required by industry (Clarke, 1990:73).

While Fordism grew throughout the twentieth century, especially in the United States, it reached its peak and began to decline in the 1970s, especially after the oil crisis of 1973 and the subsequent decline of the American automobile industry and the rise of its Japanese counterpart. As a result, it is argued that we are witnessing the decline of Fordism and the rise of post-Fordism, characterized by the following:

- A decline of interest in mass products is accompanied by a growth of interest in more specialized products, especially those high in style and quality.
- More specialized products require shorter production runs, resulting in smaller and more productive systems.
- More flexible production is made profitable by the advent of new technologies.
- New technologies require that workers, in turn, have more diverse skills and better training, more responsibility and greater autonomy.
- Production must be controlled through more flexible systems.
- Huge, inflexible bureaucracies need to be altered dramatically in order to operate more flexibly.
- Bureaucratized unions (and political parties) no longer adequately represent the interests of the new, highly differentiated labor force.
- Decentralized collective bargaining replaces centralized negotiations.
- The workers become more differentiated as people and require more differentiated commodities, lifestyles, and cultural outlets.
- The centralized welfare state no longer can meet the needs (for example, health, welfare, education) of a diverse population, and differentiated, more flexible institutions are required (Clarke, 1990:73–74).

If one needed to sum up the shift from Fordism to post-Fordism, it would be described as the transition from homogeneity to heterogeneity. There are two general issues involved here. First, has a transition from Fordism to post-Fordism actually occurred (Pelaez and Holloway, 1990)? Second, does post-Fordism hold out the hope of solving the problems associated with Fordism?

First, of course, there has been *no* clear historical break between Fordism and post-Fordism (S. Hall, 1988). Even if we are willing to acknowledge that elements of post-Fordism have emerged in the modern world, it is equally clear that elements of Fordism persist and show no signs of disappearing. For example, something we might call "McDonaldism," a phenomenon that has many things in common with Fordism, is growing at an astounding pace in contemporary society. On the basis of the model of the fast-food restaurant, more and more sectors of society are coming to utilize the principles of McDonaldism (Ritzer, 2004a). McDonaldism shares many characteristics with Fordism—homogeneous products, rigid technologies, standardized work routines, deskilling, homogenization of labor (and customer), the mass worker, homogenization of consumption, and so on. Thus, Fordism is alive and well in the modern world, although it has been transmogrified into McDonaldism. Furthermore, classic Fordism—for example, in the form of the assembly line—retains a significant presence in the American economy.

Second, even if we accept the idea that post-Fordism is with us, does it represent a solution to the problems of modern capitalist society? Some neo-Marxists (and many supporters of the capitalist system [Womack, Jones, and Roos, 1990]) hold out great hope for it: "Post-Fordism is mainly an expression of hope that future capitalist development will be the salvation of social democracy" (Clarke, 1990:75). However, this is merely a hope, and in any case, there is already evidence that post-Fordism may not be the nirvana hoped for by some observers.

The Japanese model (tarnished by the precipitous decline of Japanese industry in the 1990s) is widely believed to be the basis of post-Fordism. However, research on Japanese industry (Satoshi, 1982) and on American industries utilizing Japanese management techniques (Parker and Slaughter, 1990) indicates that there are great problems with these systems and that they may even serve to *heighten* the level of exploitation of the worker. Parker and Slaughter label the Japanese system as it is employed in the United States (and it is probably worse in Japan) "management by stress": "The goal is to stretch the system like a rubber band on the point of breaking" (1990:33). Among other things, work is speeded up even further than on traditional American assembly lines, putting enormous strain on the workers, who need to labor heroically just to keep up with the line. More generally, Levidow describes the new, post-Fordist workers as "relentlessly pressurized to increase their productivity, often in return for lower real wages—be they factory workers, homeworkers in the rag trade, privatized service workers or even polytechnic lecturers" (1990:59). Thus, it may well be that rather than representing a solution to the problems of capitalism, post-Fordism may simply be merely a new, more insidious phase in the heightening of the exploitation of workers by capitalists.

Historically Oriented Marxism 历史取向的马克思主义

Marxists oriented toward historical research argue that they are being true to the Marxian concern for historicity. The most notable of Marx's historical research was his study of precapitalist economic formations (1857–1858/1964). There has been a good deal of subsequent historical work from a Marxian perspective (for example, S. Amin, 1977; Dobb, 1964; Hobsbawm, 1965). In this section, we deal with a body of work that reflects a historical orientation—Immanuel Wallerstein's (1974, 1980, 1989, 1992, 1995; Chase-Dunn, 2001, 2005a) research on the modern world-system (Chase-Dunn, 2005b).

The Modern World-System 现代世界体系

Wallerstein chose a unit of analysis unlike the units used by most Marxian thinkers. He did not look at workers, classes, or even states, because he found most of these too narrow for his purposes. Instead, he looked at a broad economic entity with a division of labor that is not circumscribed by political or cultural boundaries. He found that unit in his concept of the *world-system,* which is a largely self-contained social system with a set of boundaries and a definable life span; that is, it does not last forever. It is composed internally of a variety of social structures and member groups. However, Wallerstein was not inclined to define the system in terms of a consensus that holds it together. Rather, he saw the system as held together by a variety of forces that are in inherent tension. These forces always have the potential for tearing the system apart.

Wallerstein argued that thus far we have had only two types of world-systems. One is the world empire, of which ancient Rome is an example. The other is the modern capitalist world-economy. A world empire is based on political (and military) domination, whereas a capitalist world-economy relies on economic domination. A capitalist world-economy is seen as more stable than a world empire for several reasons. For one thing, it has a broader base, because it encompasses many states. For another, it has a built-in process of economic stabilization. The separate political entities within the capitalist world-economy absorb whatever losses occur, while economic gain is distributed to private hands. Wallerstein foresaw the *possibility* of still a third world-system, a *socialist world government*. Whereas the capitalist world-economy separates the political sector from the economic sector, a socialist world-economy would reintegrate them.

The *core* geographical area dominates the capitalist world-economy and exploits the rest of the system. The *periphery* consists of those areas that provide raw materials to the core and are heavily exploited by it. The *semiperiphery* is a residual category that encompasses a set of regions somewhere between the exploiting and the exploited. The key point is that to Wallerstein the international division of exploitation is defined not by state borders but by the economic division of labor in the world.

In the first volume on the world-system, Wallerstein (1974) dealt with the origin of the world-system roughly between the years 1450 and 1640. The significance of this development was the shift from political (and thus military) to economic dominance. Wallerstein saw economics as a far more efficient and less primitive means of domination than politics. Political structures are very cumbersome, whereas economic exploitation "makes it possible to increase the flow of the surplus from the lower strata to the upper strata, from the periphery to the center, from the majority to the minority" (Wallerstein, 1974:15). In the modern era, capitalism provided a basis for the growth and development of a world-economy; this has been accomplished without the aid of a unified political structure. Capitalism can be seen as an economic alternative to political domination. It is better able to produce economic surpluses than are the more primitive techniques employed in political exploitation.

Wallerstein argued that three things were necessary for the rise of the capitalist world-economy out of the "ruins" of feudalism: geographical expansion through exploration and colonization, development of different methods of labor control for zones (for example, core, periphery) of the world-economy, and the development of strong states that were to become the core states of the emerging capitalist world-economy. Let us look at each of these in turn.

Geographical Expansion 地理扩张

Wallerstein argued that geographical expansion by nations is a prerequisite for the other two stages. Portugal took the lead in overseas exploration, and other European nations followed. Wallerstein was wary of talking about specific countries or about Europe in general terms. He preferred to see overseas expansion as caused by a group of people acting in their immediate interests. Elite groups, such as nobles, needed

IMMANUEL WALLERSTEIN

A Biographical Sketch

Although Immanuel Wallerstein achieved recognition in the 1960s as an expert on Africa, his most important contribution to sociology is his book *The Modern World-System* (1974). That book was an instant success. It has received worldwide recognition and has been translated into ten languages and Braille.

Born on September 28, 1930, Wallerstein received all his degrees from Columbia University, including a doctorate in 1959. He next assumed a position on the faculty at Columbia; after many years there and a five-year stint at McGill University in Montreal, Wallerstein became, in 1976, distinguished professor of sociology at the State University of New York at Binghamton.

Wallerstein was awarded the prestigious Sorokin Award for the first volume of *The Modern World-System* in 1975. Since that time, he has continued to work on the topic and has produced a number of articles as well as two additional volumes, in which he takes his analysis of the world-system up to the 1840s. We can anticipate more work from Wallerstein on this issue in the coming years. He is in the process of producing a body of work that will attract attention for years to come.

overseas expansion for various reasons. For one thing, they were confronted with a nascent class war brought on by the crumbling of the feudal economy. The slave trade provided them with a tractable labor force on which to build the capitalist economy. The expansion also provided them with various commodities needed to develop it—gold bullion, food, and raw materials of various types.

Worldwide Division of Labor 世界范围内的劳动分工

Once the world had undergone geographical expansion, it was prepared for the next stage, the development of a worldwide division of labor. In the sixteenth century, capitalism replaced statism as the major mode of dominating the world, but capitalism did not develop uniformly around the world. In fact, Wallerstein argued, the solidarity of the capitalist system ultimately was based on its unequal development. Given his Marxian orientation, Wallerstein did not think of this as a consensual equilibrium but rather as one that was laden with conflict from the beginning. Different parts of the capitalist world-system came to specialize in specific functions—breeding labor power, growing food, providing raw materials, and organizing industry. Furthermore, different areas came to specialize in producing particular types of

In fact, in many ways the attention it already has attracted and will continue to attract is more important than the body of work itself. The concept of the world-system has become the focus of thought and research in sociology, an accomplishment to which few scholars can lay claim. Many of the sociologists now doing research and theorizing about the world-system are critical of Wallerstein in one way or another, but they all clearly recognize the important role he played in the genesis of their ideas (Chase-Dunn, 2005a).

Although the concept of the world-system is an important contribution, at least as significant has been the role Wallerstein played in the revival of theoretically informed historical research. The most important work in the early years of sociology, by people such as Marx, Weber, and Durkheim, was largely of this variety. However, in more recent years, most sociologists have turned away from doing this kind of research and toward using ahistorical methods such as questionnaires and interviews. These methods are quicker and easier to use than historical methods, and the data produced are easier to analyze with a computer. Use of such methods tends to require a narrow range of technical knowledge rather than a wide range of historically oriented knowledge. Furthermore, theory plays a comparatively minor role in research utilizing questionnaires and interviews. Wallerstein has been in the forefront of those involved in a revival of interest in historical research with a strong theoretical base.

workers. For example, Africa produced slaves; western and southern Europe had many peasant tenant-farmers; western Europe was also the center of wage workers, the ruling classes, and other skilled and supervisory personnel.

More generally, each of the three parts of the international division of labor tended to differ in terms of mode of labor control. The core had free labor, the periphery was characterized by forced labor, and the semiperiphery was the heart of share-cropping. In fact, Wallerstein argued that the key to capitalism lies in a core dominated by a free labor market for skilled workers and a coercive labor market for less skilled workers in peripheral areas. Such a combination is the essence of capitalism. If a free labor market should develop throughout the world, we would have socialism.

Some regions of the world begin with small initial advantages, which are used as the basis for developing greater advantages later on. The core area in the sixteenth century, primarily western Europe, rapidly extended its advantages as towns flourished, industries developed, and merchants became important. It also moved to extend its domain by developing a wider variety of activities. At the same time, each of its activities became more specialized in order to produce more efficiently. In contrast, the periphery stagnated and moved more toward what Wallerstein called a "monoculture," or an undifferentiated, single-focus society.

Development of Core States 核心国家的发展

The third stage of the development of the world-system involved the political sector and how various economic groups used state structures to protect and advance their interests. Absolute monarchies arose in western Europe at about the same time that capitalism developed. From the sixteenth to the eighteenth centuries, the states were the central economic actors in Europe, although the center later shifted to economic enterprises. The strong states in the core areas played a key role in the development of capitalism and ultimately provided the economic base for their own demise. The European states strengthened themselves in the sixteenth century by, among other things, developing and enlarging bureaucratic systems and creating a monopoly of force in society, primarily by developing armies and legitimizing their activities so that they were assured of internal stability. Whereas the states of the core zone developed strong political systems, the periphery developed correspondingly weak states.

Later Developments 后期的发展

In *The Modern World-System II,* Wallerstein (1980) picked up the story of the consolidation of the world-economy between 1600 and 1750. This was not a period of a significant expansion of the European world-economy, but there were a number of significant changes within that system. For example, Wallerstein discussed the rise and subsequent decline in the core of the Netherlands. Later, he analyzed the conflict between two core states, England and France, as well as the ultimate victory of England. In the periphery, Wallerstein's detailed descriptions include the cyclical fortunes of Hispanic America. In the semiperiphery we witness, among other things, the decline of Spain and the rise of Sweden. Wallerstein continued his historical analysis from a Marxian viewpoint of the various roles played by different societies within the division of labor of the world-economy. Although Wallerstein paid close attention to political and social factors, his main focus remained the role of economic factors in world history.

In a later work, Wallerstein (1989) brings his historical analysis up to the 1840s. Wallerstein looks at three great developments during the period from 1730 to the 1840s—the Industrial Revolution (primarily in England), the French Revolution, and the independence of the once-European colonies in America. In his view, none of these were fundamental challenges to the world capitalist system; instead, they represented its "further consolidation and entrenchment" (Wallerstein, 1989:256).

Wallerstein continues the story of the struggle between England and France for dominance of the core. Whereas the world-economy had been stagnant during the prior period of analysis, it was now expanding, and Great Britain was able to industrialize more rapidly and come to dominate large-scale industries. This shift in domination to England occurred in spite of the fact that in the eighteenth century France had dominated in the industrial realm. The French Revolution played an important role in the development of the world capitalist system, especially by helping to bring the lingering cultural vestiges of feudalism to an end and by aligning the cultural-ideological system with economic and political realities. However, the revolution served to inhibit the industrial development of France, as did the ensuing Napoleonic rules and wars. By the end of this period, "Britain was finally truly hegemonic in the world-system" (Wallerstein, 1989:122).

The period between 1750 and 1850 was marked by the incorporation of vast new zones (the subcontinent of India, the Ottoman and Russian empires, and West Africa) into the periphery of the world-economy. These zones had been part of what Wallerstein calls the "external area" of the world-system and thus had been linked to, but were not in, that system. *External zones* are those from which the capitalist world-economy wanted goods but which were able to resist the reciprocal importation of manufactured goods from the core nations. As a result of the incorporation of these external zones, countries adjacent to the once-external nations also were drawn into the world-system. Thus, the incorporation of India contributed to China's becoming part of the periphery. By the end of the nineteenth century and the beginning of the twentieth, the pace of incorporation had quickened, and "the entire globe, even those regions that had never been part even of the external area of the capitalist world-economy were pulled inside" (Wallerstein, 1989:129).

The pressure for incorporation into the world-economy comes not from the nations being incorporated but "rather from the need of the world-economy to expand its boundaries, a need which was itself the outcome of pressures internal to the world-economy" (Wallerstein, 1989:129). Furthermore, the process of incorporation is not an abrupt process but one which occurs gradually.

Reflecting his Marxian focus on economics, Wallerstein (1989:170) argues that becoming part of the world-economy "necessarily" means that the political structures of the involved nations must become part of the interstate system. Thus, states in incorporated zones must transform themselves into part of that interstate political system, be replaced by new political forms willing to accept this role, or be taken over by states that already are part of that political system. The states that emerge at the end of the process of incorporation not only must be part of the interstate system but also must be strong enough to protect their economies from external interference. However, they must not be too strong; that is, they must not become powerful enough to be able to refuse to act in accord with the dictates of the capitalist world-economy.

Finally, Wallerstein examines the decolonization of the Americas between 1750 and 1850. That is, he details the fact that the Americas freed themselves from the control of Great Britain, France, Spain, and Portugal. That decolonization, especially in the United States, was, of course, to have great consequences for later developments in the world capitalist system.

World-System Theory Today 当下的世界—体系理论

Marxists have criticized the world-system perspective for its failure to emphasize relations between social classes adequately (Bergeson, 1984). From their point of view, Wallerstein focuses on the wrong issue. To Marxists the key is not the core-periphery international division of labor but rather class relationships *within* given societies. Bergeson seeks to reconcile these positions by arguing that there are strengths and weaknesses on both sides. His middle-ground position is that core-periphery relations are not only unequal exchange relations but also global *class* relations. His key point is that core-periphery relations *are* important, not only as exchange relations, as Wallerstein argues, but also, and more importantly, as power-dependence relationships, that is, class relationships. More recently, world-system theorists have pushed the theory forward to deal with the world today and in the coming years (Chase-Dunn, 2001; Wallerstein, 1992, 1999) as well as backward to before the modern era (Chase-Dunn and Hall, 1994).

Neo-Marxian Spatial Analysis 新马克思主义的空间分析

Categorization of neo-Marxian theories, indeed all theories, is somewhat arbitrary. That is made clear here by the fact that the work on world-systems discussed in the previous section under the heading "Neo-Marxian Economic Sociology" also could be discussed in this section. For example, the idea of the world-system is, among other things, inherently spatial, concerned with the global differentiation of the world-economy. Work on the world-system is part of a broader body of work that involves a number of notable contributions by neo-Marxian theorists to our understanding of space and its role in the social world. And this is only part of a broader resurgence of interest in space in sociology (Gieryn, 2000) and social theory. In this section we will deal with several of the leading contributions to this area in which neo-Marxists have been in the forefront.[6]

A starting point for the growth in interest in space in neo-Marxian theory (and elsewhere) is the work of Michel Foucault (see Chapter 13), who pointed out that many theories, but especially Marxian theories, had privileged time over space: "This devaluation of space that has prevailed for generations. . . . Space was treated as the dead, the fixed, the undialectical, the immobile. Time, on the contrary, was richness, fecundity, life, dialectic" (Foucault, 1980b:70). The implication is that space should, along with time, be given its due and treated as rich, fecund, alive, and dialectical. While the focus may have been on time (and history) in the past, Foucault (1986:22) contends, "The present epoch will perhaps be above all the epoch of space." In fact, as we will see in Chapter 13, Foucault offers a number of important insights into space in his discussion of such topics as the "carceral archipelago" and the Panopticon.

The Production of Space 空间的产生

The pathbreaking work in the neo-Marxian theory of space is Henri Lefebvre's (1974/1991) *The Production of Space* (see also Faist, 2005; Kurasawa, 2005). Lefebvre argues for the need for Marxian theory to shift its focus from the means of production to the production of space. To put it another way, he wants to see a shift in focus from

---

[6] Reflective of categorization problems is the fact that at least one major contribution to the theory of space that can be seen as neo-Marxian—Fredric Jameson's (1984, 1991) work on "hyperspace"—is discussed elsewhere in this book under the heading "Postmodern Social Theory" (see Chapter 13). Furthermore, additional important contributions on space have emanated from still other theoretical roots and will be discussed at yet other points in this book. For example, Anthony Giddens's very important ideas on space (and time), distanciation, and so on, will be discussed in Chapter 11.

things in space (for example, means of production such as factories) to the actual production of space itself. Marxian theory needs to broaden its concerns from (industrial) production to the production of space. This is reflective of the fact that the focus needs to shift from production to reproduction. Space serves in various ways to reproduce the capitalist system, the class structure within that economic system, and so on. Thus, any revolutionary action has to concern itself with the restructuring of space.

A key aspect of Lefebvre's complex argument lies in the following tripartite distinction. He begins with *spatial practice,* which for him involves the production and the reproduction of space. Overlying and ultimately dominating spatial practice is what Lefebvre calls *representations of space.* This is space as it is conceived by societal elites such as urban planners and architects. They think of this as "true space," and it is used by them and others to achieve and maintain dominance. Thus, for example, urban planners and architects conceived of the once popular program of "urban renewal" that was designed, theoretically, to tear down the dilapidated housing of the poor and replace it with far better and more modern housing. However, urban renewal came to be known as "urban removal." The poor were moved out to make room for new housing, but when that housing was built, it was more often for the middle and upper classes interested in gentrifying the city. Frequently, the poor had to move to new areas, often finding themselves in housing little, if at all, better than what they had left. They also were forced to adapt to new areas, communities, and neighbors. Thus, the "spatial practices" of the poor were radically altered by the "representations of space" of those who supported, created, and implemented urban renewal.

Representations of space are dominant not only over spatial practices but also over *representational spaces.* While representations of space are the creations of dominant groups, representational spaces flow from the lived experiences of people, especially from those that are underground or clandestine. While, as we have seen, representations of space are considered "true space" by those in power, representations of space yield the "truth of space." That is, they reflect what really happens in lived experience rather than being an abstract truth created by someone such as an urban planner in order to achieve dominance. However, in the contemporary world, representations of space, like spatial practices, suffer because of the hegemony of representations of space. In fact, Lefebvre (1974/1991:398) goes so far as to say, "Representational space disappears into representations of space." Thus, a major problem for Lefebvre is the predominance of elite representations of space over day-to-day spatial practices and representational spaces. Furthermore, if the new and potentially revolutionary ideas that flow out of representational spaces are disappearing, how is the hegemony of elites such as urban planners ever to be contested, let alone threatened?

While the preceding is a strongly ideational way of addressing space, Lefebvre offers a second tripartite distinction that addresses it in more material—and more optimistic—terms. Paralleling Marx's notion of species-being, Lefebvre begins with what he calls *absolute spaces,* or natural spaces (e.g., "green" areas) that are not colonized, rendered inauthentic, or smashed by economic and political forces.

Just as Marx spent little time analyzing species-being (and communism), Lefebvre spends little time on absolute space. While Marx devoted most of his attention to critiquing capitalism, Lefebvre is interested in critically analyzing what he calls *abstract space*. Like representations of space, this is space from the point of view of an abstract subject such as an urban planner or an architect.[7] But abstract space is not just ideational; it actually replaces historical spaces (which are erected on the base of absolute spaces). Abstract space is characterized by the absence of that which is associated with absolute space (trees, clean air, and so on). It is a dominated, occupied, controlled, authoritarian (even involving brutality and violence), repressive space. Lefebvre emphasizes the role of the state, more than economic forces, in exercising power over abstract space, although that exercise of power is hidden. Furthermore, "abstract space is a tool of power" (Lefebvre, 1974/1991:391). That is, not only is power exercised in it, the abstraction of space is itself a form of power. While those in power have always sought to control space, what is new here is that "power aspires to control space in its entirety" (Lefebvre, 1974/1991:388). Thus, the ruling class uses abstract space as a tool of power to gain control over increasingly large spaces. While Lefebvre deemphasizes economic factors and forces, he does recognize that power of and over abstract space does generate profit. That is, it is not just the factory that generates profits, but also the railway lines and highways that provide routes in to the factory for raw materials and out of the factory for finished products.

Being a good Marxian theorist, Lefebvre emphasizes contradictions. While abstract space serves to smother contradictions, it simultaneously generates them, including those that have the potential to tear it apart. Although he wonders why people accept the kind of control exerted over them by abstract space and are silent about it, he seems to accept the idea that they eventually will be spurred to action by these contradictions. Indeed, as in Marx's analysis of contradictions in capitalism, Lefebvre argues that the seeds of a new kind of space can be glimpsed within the contradictions of abstract space.

That new kind of space, the third of the types of space to be discussed here, is *differential* space. While abstract space seeks to control and homogenize everyone and everything, differential space accentuates difference and freedom from control. While abstract space breaks up the natural unity that exists in the world, differential space restores that unity. Again, Lefebvre has much more to say about that which he critiques—abstract space—than he does about his hoped-for alternative to it.

Lefebvre argues that space can play a variety of roles in the socioeconomic world. First, it can take the role of one of many forces of productions (other, more traditional such forces are factories, tools, and machines). Second, space itself can be a vast commodity that is consumed (as, for example, by a tourist visiting Disneyland), or it can be consumed productively (for example, the land on which a factory is built). Third, it is politically instrumental, facilitating control of the system (building roads to facilitate troop movements to put down rebellions). Fourth, space underpins the reproduction of productive and property relations (for example, expensive gated communities for the capitalists and slums for the poor). Fifth, space can take the form of a superstructure that, for example, seems neutral but conceals the

---

[7]Although the abstract subject also could be a more mundane figure such as the driver of an automobile.

economic base that gives rise to it and that is far from neutral. Thus, a highway system may seem neutral but really advantages capitalistic enterprises that are allowed to move raw materials easily and cheaply. Finally, there is always positive potential in space, such as the creation of truly human and creative works in it, as well as the possibility of reappropriating space on behalf of those who are being controlled and exploited.

The production of space occupies two positions in Lefebvre's work. First, as discussed above, it constitutes a new focus of analysis and critique. That is, our attention should shift from the means of production to the production of space. Second, Lefebvre puts this all in terms of a desired direction for social change. That is, we live in a world characterized by a *mode of production in space.* This is a world of domination in which control is exercised by the state, the capitalist, and the bourgeoisie. It is a closed, sterile world, one that is being emptied out of contents (e.g., highways replacing and destroying local communities). In its stead we need a world characterized by the *production of space.* Instead of domination, we have here a world in which appropriation is predominant. That is, people in concert with other people work in and with space to produce what they need to survive and prosper. In other words, they modify natural space in order to serve their collective needs. Thus, Lefebvre's (1974/1991:422) goal is "producing the space of the human species . . . a planet-wide space as social foundation of a transformed everyday life." Needless to say, the political state and private ownership of the means of production that control the mode of production are seen as withering away. Thus, the production of space is not only Lefebvre's analytic focus but also his political objective in much the same way that communism is Marx's political goal, and with many of the same characteristics.

Trialectics 三元辩证法

Edward Soja (1989) was heavily influenced by both Foucault and Lefebvre. For example, like Foucault he critiques the focus on time (and history) as creating "carceral historicism" and a "temporal prisonhouse" (Soja, 1989:1). He seeks to integrate the study of space and geography with that of time. Lefebvre has had a profound influence on Soja's thinking, but Soja is critical of some aspects of his work and seeks to go beyond it in various ways.

Perhaps the core of Soja's (1996, 2000) theoretical contribution to our understanding of space is his notion of *trialectics.* Obviously, Soja is building, and expanding, on the Marxian (and Hegelian) notion of dialectics. However, a more immediate source is Lefebvre's work, especially the distinction discussed above among spatial practice, representations of space, and representational spaces. Most generally, Lefebvre is making a distinction between material practices and two types of ideas about space. Soja uses this basic distinction in order to theorize what he calls *cityspace,* or "the city as a historical-social-spatial phenomenon, but *with its intrinsic spatiality highlighted* for interpretive and explanatory purposes" (Soja, 2000:8). This definition highlights one of Soja's basic premises; that is, while he privileges space, he insists on including in his analysis history (or time more generally) and social relations. While the move toward including space in social analyses is to be encouraged, it should not be done to the detriment of the analysis of history and time. Furthermore, the inclusion of social relations sets Soja's perspective squarely in the tradition of the sociological and social theories dealt with throughout this book.

The Firstspace perspective is basically a materialist orientation that is consistent with the approach most often taken by geographers in the study of the city (and Lefebvre's sense of spatial practice). Here is the way Soja (2000:10) describes a Firstspace approach: "cityspace can be studied as a set of materialized 'social practices' that work together to produce and reproduce the concrete forms and specific patternings of urbanism as a way of life. Here cityspace is physically and empirically perceived as form and process, as measurable and mappable configurations and practices of urban life." A Firstspace approach focuses on objective phenomena and emphasizes "things in space."

In contrast, a Secondspace approach (encompassing Lefebvre's representations of space and representational space) tends to be more subjective and to focus on "thoughts about space." In a Secondspace perspective, "cityspace becomes more of a mental or ideational field, conceptualized in imagery, reflexive thought, and symbolic representation, a *conceived* space of the imagination, or . . . urban imaginary" (Soja, 2000:11). Examples of a Secondspace perspective include the mental maps we all carry with us, visions of an urban utopia, and more formal methods for obtaining and conveying information about the geography of the city.

Soja seeks to subsume both of the above in Thirdspace, which is viewed as

> another way of thinking about the social production of human spatiality that incorporates both Firstspace and Secondspace perspectives while at the same time opening up the scope and complexity of the geographical or spatial imagination. In this alternative or "third" perspective, the spatial specificity of urbanism is investigated as fully *lived space,* a simultaneously real-and-imagined, actual-and-virtual, locus of structured individual and collective experience and agency.
>
> (Soja, 2000:11)

This is a highly complex view of cityspace. Because of its great complexity and because much is hidden and perhaps unknowable, the best we can do is to explore cityspace selectively "through its intrinsic spatial, social, and historical dimensions, its interrelated spatiality, sociality, and historicality" (Soja, 2000:12). Throughout his career, Soja's favorite cityspace has been Los Angeles, and he returns to it over and over to analyze it from various perspectives, including his own integrative sense of Thirdspace.

Spaces of Hope 希望的空间

We began this section with the point that the categorization of theories is somewhat arbitrary. In fact, the work of Edward Soja fits as much into a category—postmodern Marxian theory—we will discuss below as it does into neo-Marxian spatial analyses. The same is true of the work of the thinker we will discuss next—David Harvey—and, in fact, we will discuss his work not only under this heading but also under that of postmodern Marxian theory.

In fact, Harvey has produced analyses of space under a variety of guises as his work has undergone several twists and turns over the years. In reflecting on his early work, Harvey thought of himself as lax scientifically, but he underwent a first change of orientation in the late 1960s and declared himself a positivist guided by the scientific method and, as a result, oriented toward quantification, the development of theories, the discovery of laws, and the like (Harvey, 1969). However, within a few years Harvey (1973) had undergone another paradigm change and rejected his earlier commitment to positivism. He now favored materialist theory with a powerful debt to the work of Karl Marx.

While, as we will see later, Harvey flirted with postmodern theory and certainly was influenced by it in many ways, he has retained his commitment to Marxian theory, and this is clear in one of his more recent books, *Spaces of Hope* (Harvey, 2000). One aspect of Harvey's argument that is particularly relevant to this discussion of neo-Marxian theory is his analysis and critique of the geographical arguments made in the *Communist Manifesto.* Harvey sees the idea of the "spatial fix" as central to the *Manifesto.* That is, the need to create ever-higher profits means that capitalist firms must, among other things, continually seek new geographical areas (and markets) to exploit and find more thorough ways of exploiting the areas in which they already operate. While such geographical arguments occupy an important place in the *Manifesto,* they characteristically are subordinated in a "rhetorical mode that in the last instance privileges time and history over space and geography" (Harvey, 2000:24).

Harvey (2000:31) begins by acknowledging the strengths of the *Manifesto* and its recognition that "geographical reorderings and restructurings, spatial strategies and geopolitical elements, uneven geographical developments, and the like, are vital aspects to the accumulation of capital and the dynamics of class struggle, both historically and today." However, the arguments made in the *Manifesto* on space (and other matters) are severely limited, and Harvey sets out to strengthen them and bring them up to date.

For example, Harvey argues that Marx and Engels operate with a simplistic differentiation between civilized-barbarian, and more generally core-periphery, areas of the world. Relatedly, the *Manifesto* operates with a diffusionist model, with capitalism seen as spreading from civilized to barbarian areas, from core to periphery. While Harvey acknowledges that there are instances of such diffusion, there are others, both historically and contemporaneously, in which internal developments within peripheral nations lead to the insertion of their labor power and commodities into the global marketplace.

More important, Harvey (2000:34) argues that "one of the biggest absences in the *Manifesto* is its lack of attention to the territorial organization of the world in general and of capitalism in particular." Thus, the recognition that the state was the executive arm of the bourgeoisie needs to be buttressed by recognition that "the state had to be territorially defined, organized, and administered" (Harvey, 2000:34). For example, loosely connected provinces had to be brought together to form the nation. However, territories do not remain set in stone once they have been transformed into states. All sorts of things alter territorial configurations, including revolutions in transportation and communication, "uneven dynamics of class struggle," and "uneven resource endowments." Furthermore, "[f]lows of commodities, capital, labor, and information always render boundaries porous" (Harvey, 2000:35). Thus, territories continually are being redefined and reorganized, with the result that any model that envisions a final formation of the state on a territorial basis is overly simplistic. The implication is that we need to be attuned continuously to territorial changes in a world dominated by capitalism.

Another of the spatial arguments in the *Manifesto* is that the concentration of capitalism (for example, factories in the cities) leads to the concentration of the proletariat, which formerly was scattered throughout the countryside. Instead of conflict between isolated workers and capitalists, it becomes more likely that a collectivity of workers will confront capitalists, who are themselves now more likely to be organized into a collectivity. Thus, in Harvey's (2000:36) words, "the production of spatial struggle is not neutral with respect to class struggle." However, there is much more to be said about the relationship between space and class struggle, and this is amply demonstrated in the more recent history of capitalism. For example, capitalists in the late nineteenth century dispersed factories from the cities to the suburbs in an effort to limit the concentration of workers and their power. And in the late twentieth century we witnessed the dispersal of factories to remote areas of the world in a further effort to weaken the proletariat and strengthen the capitalists.

Harvey also points out that the *Manifesto* tended to focus on the *urban* proletariat and thereby largely ignored rural areas, as well as agricultural workers and peasants. Of course, the latter groups over the years have proved to be very active in revolutionary movements. Furthermore, Marx and Engels tended to homogenize the world's workers, to argue that they have no country and that national differences are disappearing in the development of a homogeneous proletariat. Harvey notes that not only do national differences persist, but capitalism itself produces national (and other) differences among workers, "sometimes by feeding off ancient cultural distinctions, gender relations, ethnic predilections, and religious beliefs" (Harvey, 2000:40). In addition, labor plays a role here in sustaining spatial distinctions by, for example, mobilizing "through territorial forms of organization, building place-bound loyalties *en route*" (Harvey, 2000:40). Finally, Harvey notes the famous call in the *Manifesto* for workers of the world to unite and argues that given the increasingly global character of capitalism, such an exhortation is more relevant and more important than ever.

This is only a small part of a highly varied argument made by Harvey, but what does he mean by "spaces of hope"? First, he wishes to counter what he perceives to be a pervasive pessimism among today's scholars. Second, he wants to acknowledge the existence of "spaces of political struggle," and therefore hope, in society. Finally, he describes a utopian space of the future that offers hope to those concerned about the oppressiveness of today's spaces.

Thus, in these and many other ways, Harvey builds on Marx's (and in this case Engels's) limited insights into space and capitalism to develop a richer and more contemporary perspective on their relationship to each other. In that sense, what Harvey is doing here is an almost paradigmatic example of neo-Marxian theory.

Post-Marxist Theory 后马克思主义理论

Dramatic changes have taken place in recent years in neo-Marxian theory (Aronson, 1995; Grossberg and Nelson, 1988; Jay, 1988). The most recent varieties of neo-Marxian theory are rejecting many of the basic premises of Marx's original theory as well as those of the neo-Marxian theories discussed earlier in this chapter. Hence, these new approaches have come to be thought of as post-Marxist theories (Dandaneau, 1992; Wright, 1987). While these theories reject the basic elements of Marxian theory, they still have sufficient affinities with it for them to be considered part of neo-Marxian theory. Post-Marxist theories are discussed here because they often involve the synthesis of Marxian theories with other theories, ideas, methods, and so on. How can we account for these dramatic changes in neo-Marxian theory? Two sets of factors are involved, one external to theory and involving changes in the social world and the other internal to theory itself (P. Anderson, 1984; Ritzer, 1991a).

First, and external to Marxian theory, was the end of the Cold War (Halliday, 1990) and the collapse of world communism. The Soviet Union is gone, and Russia has moved toward a market economy that resembles, at least in part, a capitalist economy (Piccone, 1990; Zaslavsky, 1988). Eastern Europe has shifted, often even more rapidly than Russia, in the direction of a capitalist-style economy (Kaldor, 1990). China clings to communism, but capitalism flourishes throughout that nation. Cuba is isolated, awaiting only the death or overthrow of Fidel Castro to move in the direction of capitalism. Thus, the failure of communism on a worldwide scale made it necessary for Marxists to reconsider and reconstruct their theories (Burawoy, 1990; Aronson, 1995).

These changes in the world were related to a second set of changes, internal to theory itself, the series of intellectual changes that, in turn, affected neo-Marxian theory (P. Anderson, 1990a, 1990b). New theoretical currents such as poststructuralism and postmodernism (see Chapter 13) had a profound impact on neo-Marxian theory. In addition, a movement known as *analytical Marxism* gained ground; it was premised on the belief that Marxian theories needed to employ the same methods as those used by any other scientific enterprise. This approach led to reinterpretations of Marx in more conventional intellectual terms, efforts to apply rational choice theory to Marxian issues, and attempts to study Marxian topics by utilizing the methods and techniques of positivistic science. As Mayer puts it more specifically, "Increased humility toward the conventional norms of science coincides with diminished piety toward Marxist theory itself" (1994:296).

Thus, a combination of social and intellectual changes dramatically altered the landscape of neo-Marxian theory in the 1990s. While the theories discussed earlier remain important, much of the energy in neo-Marxian theory as we enter the twenty-first century is focused on the theories to be discussed in this section.

Analytical Marxism 分析学派马克思主义

Here is the way one of the leaders of analytical Marxism, John Roemer, defines it:

> During the past decade, what now appears as a new species in social theory has
> been forming: analytically sophisticated Marxism. Its practitioners are largely

inspired by Marxian questions, which they pursue with contemporary tools of logic, mathematics and model building. Their methodological posture is conventional. These writers are, self-consciously, products of both the Marxian and neo-Marxian traditions.

(Roemer, 1986a:1)

Thus, analytical Marxists bring mainstream, "state-of-the-art" methods of analytical philosophy and social science to bear on Marxian substantive issues (Mayer, 1994:22). Analytical Marxism is discussed in this chapter because it "explicitly proposes to synthesize *non-Marxist* methods and Marxist theory" (Weldes, 1989:371).

Analytical Marxism adopts a nondogmatic approach to Marx's theory. It does not blindly and unthinkingly support Marx's theory, it does not deny historical facts in order to support Marx's theory, and it does not totally reject Marx's theory as fundamentally wrong. Rather, it views Marx's theory as a form of nineteenth-century social science with great power and with a valid core but also with substantial weaknesses. Marx's theory should be drawn upon, but that effort requires the utilization of methods and techniques appropriate to the twenty-first century. It rejects the idea that there is a distinctive Marxian methodology and criticizes those who think that such a methodology exists and is valid:

I do not think there is a specific form of Marxist logic or explanation. Too often, obscurantism protects itself behind a yoga of special terms and privileged logic. The yoga of Marxism is "dialectics." Dialectical logic is based on several propositions which may have a certain inductive appeal, but are far from being rules of inference: that things turn into their opposites, and quantity turns into quality. In Marxian social science, dialectics is often used to justify a lazy kind of teleological reasoning. Developments occur because they must in order for history to be played out as it was intended.

(Roemer, 1986b:191)

Similarly, Elster says: "There is no specifically Marxist form of analysis . . . there is no commitment to any specific method of analysis, beyond those that characterize good social science generally" (1986:220). Along the same lines, analytical Marxists reject the idea that fact and value cannot be separated, that they are dialectically related. They seek, following the canons of mainstream philosophic and social-scientific thinking, to separate fact and value and to deal with facts dispassionately through theoretical, conceptual, and empirical analysis.

One might ask why analytical Marxism should be called Marxist. Roemer, in reply to this question, says, "I am not sure that it should" (1986a:2). However, he does offer several reasons why we can consider it a (neo-) Marxian theory. First, it deals with traditional Marxian topics such as exploitation and class. Second, it continues to regard socialism as preferable to capitalism. Third, it seeks to understand and explain the problems associated with capitalism. However, while it is Marxist in these senses, it also "borrows willingly and easily from other viewpoints" (Roemer, 1986a:7). Again, analytical Marxism is very much in line with the move toward theoretical syntheses discussed throughout this book.

Three varieties of analytical Marxism will be discussed, at least briefly, in this section. First, we will discuss the effort to reanalyze Marx's work by utilizing mainstream intellectual tools. Second, we will deal with rational choice and game-theoretic

Marxism. Finally, we will touch on empirical research from a Marxian perspective that utilizes state-of-the-art methodological tools.

Reanalyzing Marx 对马克思的再分析

As pointed out above, analytical Marxists reject the use of such idiosyncratic concepts as the dialectic and seek instead to analyze Marx (as well as the social world) by using concepts that are part of the broader intellectual tradition. The major example of this, and one of the key documents in analytical Marxism, is G. A. Cohen's *Karl Marx's Theory of History: A Defence* (1978). Instead of interpreting Marx as an exotic dialectician, Cohen argues that he employs the much more prosaic functional form of explanation in his work. He offers the following examples of functional explanation in Marx's work:

- Relations of production *correspond* to productive forces.
- The legal and political superstructure *rises on* a real foundation.
- The social, political, and intellectual process *is conditioned by* the mode of production of material life.
- Consciousness is determined by social being.

(Cohen, 1978/1986:221)

In each of these examples, the second concept *explains* the first concept. The nature of the explanation is functional, in Cohen's view, because "the character of what is explained is determined by its effect on what explains it" (1978/1986:221). Thus, in the case of the last example, the character of consciousness is explained by its effect on, more specifically its propensity to sustain, social being. More generally, social phenomena are explained in terms of their consequences for other social phenomena. It is Cohen's view that Marx practices functional thinking in the examples above, and throughout his work, because he seeks to explain social and economic phenomena in this manner. Thus, Marx is not a dialectician; he is a functional thinker. In adopting such a perspective, Cohen is reinterpreting Marx by using mainstream philosophic ideas *and* viewing Marx as part of that mainstream.

Cohen takes pains to differentiate functional thinking from the sociological variety of (structural) functional*ism* discussed in Chapter 3. Cohen sees (structural) functionalism as composed of three theses. First, all elements of the social world are interconnected. Second, all components of society reinforce one another, as well as the society as a whole. Third, each aspect of society is the way it is because of its contribution to the larger society. These theses are objectionable to Marxists for a variety of reasons, especially because of their conservatism. However, the functional explanations mentioned previously can be employed by Marxists without their accepting any of the tenets of functionalism. Thus, functional explanation is not necessarily conservative; indeed, it can be quite revolutionary.

Rational Choice Marxism 理性选择马克思主义

Many analytical Marxists have drawn on neoclassical economics, especially rational choice theory and game theory (see Chapter 8 for a discussion of the use of rational choice theory in mainstream sociological theory). Roemer argues that "Marxian analysis requires micro-foundations," especially rational choice and game theory, as well as "the arsenal of modelling techniques developed by neoclassical economics" (1986b:192). In drawing on such approaches, Marxian theory is giving up its pretentions of being different and is utilizing approaches widely used throughout the social sciences. But while neo-Marxian theory can and should draw on neoclassical economics, it remains different from the latter. For example, it retains an interest in collective action for changing society and accepts the idea that capitalism is an unjust system.

Jon Elster (1982, 1986) is a major proponent, along with John Roemer, of analytical Marxism. Elster believes that neo-Marxian theory has been impeded by its adoption of the kind of functional theorizing discussed by Cohen. He also believes that Marxian theory ought to make greater use of game theory, a variant of rational choice theory. Game theory, like other types of rational choice theory, assumes that actors are rational and seek to maximize their gains (Macy and Van de Rijt, 2007). Although it recognizes structural constraints, it does not suggest that they completely determine actors' choices. What is distinctive about game theory as a type of rational choice theory is that it permits the analyst to go beyond the rational choices of a single actor and deal with the interdependence of the decisions and actions of a number of actors. Elster (1982) identifies three interdependencies among actors involved in a game. First, the reward for each actor depends on the choices made by all the actors. Second, the reward for each actor depends on the reward for all. Finally, the choice made by each actor depends on the choices made by all. The analysis of "games" (such as the famous "prisoner's dilemma" game, in which actors end up worse off if they follow their own self-interest than if they sacrifice those interests) helps explain the strategies of the various actors and the emergence of such collectivities as social class. Thus, rational choice Marxism searches for the micro-foundations of Marxist theory, although the rational actor of this theory is very different from critical theory's actor (discussed earlier in this chapter), who is derived largely from Freudian theory.

Elster's rational choice orientation is also manifest in *Making Sense of Marx* (1985). Elster argues that Marx's basic method for explaining social phenomena was a concern for the unintended consequences of human action. To Elster, and in contrast with most other Marxists, who see Marx as a "methodological holist" concerned with macro structures, Marx practiced "methodological individualism," or "the doctrine that all social phenomena—their structure and their change—are in principle explicable in ways that only involve individuals—their properties, their goals, their beliefs and their actions" (1985:5). To Elster, Marx *was* concerned with actors, their goals, their intentions, and their rational choices. Elster uses such a rational choice perspective to critique the orientation of the structural Marxists: "Capitalist entrepreneurs are *agents* in the genuinely active sense. They cannot be reduced to mere place-holders in the capitalist system of production" (1985:13). Rational choice Marxism focuses on these rational agents (capitalist and proletarians) and their interrelationships.

Roemer (1982) has been in the forefront of the development of an approach within analytical Marxism toward exploitation (for a critique, see J. Schwartz, 1995). Roemer has moved away from thinking of exploitation as occurring at the point of production (and therefore from the highly dubious labor theory of value) and toward thinking of exploitation as relating to coercion associated with differential ownership of property. As Mayer puts it, "exploitation can arise from unequal possession of productive resources even without a coercive production process" (1994:62). Among other things, this perspective allows us to conceive of exploitation in socialist as well as capitalist societies. This view of exploitation also relates to rational choice theory in the sense, for example, that those whose exploitation arises from the unequal distribution of property can join social movements designed to redistribute property more equally. This kind of orientation also allows analytical Marxism to retain its ethical and political goals while buying into a mainstream orientation such as rational choice theory.

Empirically Oriented Marxism 实证取向的马克思主义

The leading figure associated with the importation and application of rigorous methods to the empirical study of Marxian concepts is Erik Olin Wright (1985; Burawoy and Wright, 2001). Wright explicitly associates himself with analytical Marxism in general and the work of John Roemer in particular. Wright's work involves three basic components: first, the clarification of basic Marxian concepts such as class; second, empirical studies of those concepts; third, the development of a more coherent theory based on those concepts (especially class).

In his book *Classes* (1985), Wright seeks to answer the question posed by Marx but never answered by him: "What constitutes class?" He makes it clear that his answer will be true to Marx's original theoretical agenda. However, it will not be the same as the answer Marx might have offered, because since Marx's day there has been over 100 years of both theoretical work and history. Thus, we are more sophisticated theoretically, *and* times have changed. As a result, Wright, like the other analytical Marxists, starts with Marx but does not accept his position as dogma or try to divine how he might have defined *class*. Because of Marx and the theoretical work done since his time, contemporary Marxists are in a better position to come up with such definitions. In any case, we live in very different times, and Marx's definition, even if we could divine it, might well not be appropriate for modern society.

Since this is a book on theory, I need not go into detail about Wright's research or that of any of the other empirically oriented Marxists. However, it would be useful to say something about his best-known conceptual contribution—the idea of "contradictory locations within class relations" (Wright, 1985:43). His basic premise is that a given position need not, as is commonly assumed, be located within a given class; it may be in more than one class simultaneously. Thus, a position may be simultaneously proletarian and bourgeois. For example, managers are bourgeois in the sense that they supervise subordinates, but they are also proletarian in that they are supervised by others. The idea of contradictory class locations is derived through careful conceptual analysis and then is studied empirically (see Gubbay, 1997, for a critique of Wright's approach to social class).

Analytical Marxism Today 当下的分析学派马克思主义

While, as we have seen, analytical Marxists consider themselves to be Marxists, there are those (for example, Callinicos, 1989) who wonder whether their attraction to mainstream concepts and methods makes this designation meaningless or subversive of a Marxian orientation (Kirkpatrick, 1994). In response, Elster asserts: "Most of the views that *I* hold to be true and important, I can trace back to Marx" (1985:531).

Mayer (1994) has offered an overview of analytical Marxism that attempts, among other things, to review and rebut what he sees as the six major criticisms of the approach. However, before we discuss those criticisms, there is one critique that emanates from Mayer's work itself: "Analytical Marxism is not a unified or even an internally consistent body of thought" (1994:300). The differences among the three major practitioners discussed here (Cohen, Roemer, and Wright), to say nothing of the others who can be included under this heading (especially Adam Przeworski [1985] and his work on the state), are enormous and make it difficult to discuss these individuals in the same context. Those differences may splinter analytical Marxism before it has an opportunity to develop into a coherent perspective.

The first criticism reviewed by Mayer is that analytical Marxism is atomistic and focuses on rational actors. He responds that analytical Marxists do not conceive of society as composed of isolated individuals and that they recognize that people do not always behave rationally. Second, analytical Marxists are accused of economic determinism, but the response is that the predominant position is that economic factors are primary, not that they are deterministic. The third critique is that analytical Marxists are ahistorical, but Mayer does not see this characteristic as inherent in the approach. Rather, it is traceable to its newness and to the fact that there has not been time to deal with historical issues. Fourth, and relatedly, analytical Marxists are accused of offering static approaches that have difficulty dealing with change. While Mayer recognizes this problem, he argues that virtually all social scientists have this predicament. Fifth, there is the accusation of tautology—"assuming what needs to be proven" (Mayer, 1994:305). Mayer sees this as a problem inherent in all deductive approaches. Finally, analytical Marxism is seen as lacking in moral fervor, but Mayer counters, "Analytical Marxists are quite capable of moral passion, and what their moral critique of capitalism lacks in fervor it more than gains in accuracy and insight" (1994:315).

Mayer concludes with a discussion of six challenges facing analytical Marxism, challenges that must be met if analytical Marxism is to be a significant force in the social sciences. First, analytical Marxism must develop a more dynamic approach. As Mayer puts it, "Any version of Marxism unable to account for social dynamics cannot expect to flourish" (1994:317). Second, the theories of the analytical Marxists must do a better job of relating to specific events and situations. Third, practitioners of this approach must right the current imbalance in the direction of theory and do more empirical research. Fourth, analytical Marxists must expand from their base in economic factors and deal with a wider range of social factors. Fifth, they must move away from a focus on advanced capitalist nations and deal with less developed nations. Finally, analytical Marxists must demonstrate the existence of viable alternatives to capitalism.

Postmodern Marxian Theory 后现代马克思理论

Marxian theory has been profoundly affected by theoretical developments in structuralism, poststructuralism (P. Anderson, 1984:33), and, of particular interest here, postmodernism (Landry, 2000; E. M. Wood and Foster, 1997; see Chapter 13).

Hegemony and Radical Democracy 霸权和激进民主

A major representative work of postmodern Marxism is Ernesto Laclau and Chantal Mouffe's *Hegemony and Socialist Strategy* (1985). In Ellen Wood's view, this work, accepting the focus on linguistics, texts, and discourse in postmodernism, detaches ideology from its material base and ultimately dissolves "the social altogether into ideology or 'discourse'" (1986:47). The concept of hegemony, which is of central importance to Laclau and Mouffe, was developed by Gramsci to focus on cultural leadership rather than on the coercive effect of state domination. This shift in focus, of course, leads us away from the traditional Marxian concern with the material world and in the direction of ideas and discourse. As Wood puts it, "In short, the Laclau-Mouffe argument is that there *are* no such things as material interests but only discursively constructed *ideas* about them" (1986:61).

In addition to substituting ideas for material interests, Laclau and Mouffe displace the proletariat from its privileged position at the center of Marxian theory. As Wood argues, Laclau and Mouffe are part of a movement involved in the "declassing of the socialist project" (1986:4). Laclau and Mouffe put the issue of class in subjective, discursive terms. The social world is characterized by diverse positions and antagonisms. As a result, it is impossible to come up with the kind of "unified discourse" that Marx envisioned surrounding the proletariat. The universal discourse of the proletariat "has been replaced by a polyphony of voices, each of which constructs its own irreducible discursive identity" (Laclau and Mouffe, 1985:191). Thus, instead of focusing on the single discourse of the proletariat, Marxian theorists are urged to focus on a multitude of diverse discourses emanating from a wide range of dispossessed voices, such as those of women, blacks, ecologists, immigrants, and consumers, among others. Marxian theory has, as a result, been *decentered* and *detotalized* because it no longer focuses only on the proletariat and no longer sees the problems of the proletariat as *the* problem in society.

Having rejected a focus on material factors and a focal concern for the proletariat, Laclau and Mouffe proceed to reject, as the goal of Marxian theory, communism involving the emancipation of the proletariat. Alternatively, they propose a system labeled "radical democracy." Instead of focusing, as the political right does, on individual democratic rights, they propose to "create a new hegemony, which will be the outcome of the articulation of the greatest number of democratic struggles" (Mouffe, 1988:41). What is needed in this new hegemony is a "hegemony of democratic values, and this requires a multiplication of democratic practices, institutionalizing them into even more diverse social relations" (Mouffe, 1988:41). Radical democracy seeks to bring together under a broad umbrella a wide range of democratic struggles—antiracist, antisexist, anticapitalist, antiexploitation of nature (Eder, 1990), and many others. Thus, this is a "radical and plural democracy" (Laclau, 1990:27). The struggle of one group must not be waged at the expense of the others; all democratic struggles must be seen as equivalent struggles. Thus, it is necessary to bring these struggles together by modifying their identity so that the groups see themselves as part of the larger struggle for radical democracy. As Laclau and Mouffe argue:

> The alternative of the Left should consist of locating itself fully in the field of the
> democratic revolution and expanding the chains of equivalents between different

struggles against oppression. *The task of the Left therefore cannot be to renounce liberal-democratic ideology, but on the contrary, to deepen and expand it in the direction of a radical and plural democracy.* . . . It is not in the abandonment of the democratic terrain but, on the contrary, in the extension of the field of democratic struggles to the whole of civil society and the state, that the possibility resides for a hegemonic strategy of the Left.

(Laclau and Mouffe, 1985:176)

While radical democracy retains the objective of the abolition of capitalism, it recognizes that such abolition will not eliminate the other inequalities within society. Dealing with all social inequalities requires a far broader movement than that anticipated by traditional Marxists.

Continuities and Time-Space Compression 连续性与时空压缩

Another Marxian foray into postmodernist theory (see Chapter 13 for a discussion of yet another, the work of Fredric Jameson) is David Harvey's *The Condition of Postmodernity* (1989). While Harvey sees much that is of merit in postmodern thinking, he sees serious weaknesses in it from a Marxian viewpoint. Postmodernist theory is accused of overemphasizing the problems of the modern world and underemphasizing its material achievements. Most important, it seems to accept postmodernity and its associated problems rather than suggesting ways of overcoming these difficulties: "The rhetoric of postmodernism is dangerous for it avoids confronting the realities of political economy and the circumstances of global power" (Harvey, 1989:117). What postmodernist theory needs to confront is the source of its ideas—the political and economic transformation of early twenty-first-century capitalism.

Central to the political economic system is control over markets and the labor process (these two arenas involve the issue of *accumulation* in capitalism). While the postwar period between 1945 and 1973 was characterized by an inflexible process of accumulation, since 1973 we have moved to a more flexible process. Harvey associates the earlier period with Fordism (as well as Keynesian economics) and the later period with post-Fordism (for a critique of this, see Gartman, 1998), but we need not discuss these issues here, since they already have been covered in this chapter. While Fordism is inflexible, Harvey sees post-Fordism as associated with flexible accumulation resting "on flexibility with respect to labour processes, labour markets, products, and patterns of consumption. It is characterized by the emergence of entirely new sectors of production, new ways of providing financial services, new markets, and, above all, greatly intensified rates of commercial, technological, and organizational innovation" (1989:147).

While Harvey sees great changes, and argues that it is these changes that lie at the base of postmodern thinking, he believes that there are many *continuities* between the Fordist and post-Fordist eras. His major conclusion is that while "there has certainly been a sea-change in the surface appearance of capitalism since 1973 . . . the underlying logic of capitalist accumulation and its crisis tendencies remain the same" (Harvey, 1989:189).

Central to Harvey's approach is the idea of time-space compression. He believes that modernism served to compress both time and space and that that process has accelerated in the postmodern era, leading to "an intense phase of time-space compression that has a disorienting and disruptive impact upon political-economic practices, the balance of class power, as well as upon cultural and social life" (Harvey, 1989:284). But this time-space compression is *not* essentially different from earlier epochs in capitalism: "We have, in short, witnessed another fierce round in that process of annihilation of space through time that has always lain at the center of capitalism's dynamic" (Harvey, 1989:293). To give an example of the annihilation of space through time, cheeses once available only in France now are sold throughout the United States because of rapid, low-cost transportation. Or, in the 1991 war with Iraq, television transported us instantaneously from air raids in Baghdad to "scud" attacks on Tel Aviv to military briefings in Riyadh.

Thus, to Harvey, postmodernism is *not* discontinuous with modernism; they are reflections of the same underlying capitalist dynamic.[8] Both modernism and postmodernism, Fordism and post-Fordism, coexist in today's world. The emphasis on Fordism and post-Fordism will "vary from time to time and place to place, depending on which configuration is profitable and which is not" (Harvey, 1989:344). Such a viewpoint serves to bring the issue of postmodernity under the umbrella of neo-Marxian theory, although it is, in turn, modified by developments in postmodern thinking.

Finally, Harvey discerns changes and cracks in postmodernity, indicating that we already may be moving into a new era, an era that neo-Marxian theory must be prepared to theorize, perhaps by integrating still other idea systems.

After Marxism 马克思主义之后

There are innumerable post-Marxist positions (Beilharz, 2005d) that *could* be discussed in this section, but we will close with one of the more extreme positions.

The title of Ronald Aronson's (1995) book, *After Marxism*, tells much of the story. Aronson, a self-avowed Marxist, makes it clear that Marxism is over and that Marxist theorists are now on their own in dealing with the social world and its problems. This position is based on the idea that the "Marxian project" involved the integration of theory and practice. While some Marxists may continue to buy into parts of Marxian theory, the Marxian project of the transformation from capitalism to socialism is dead, since it clearly has failed in its objectives. It is history, not Aronson, that has rendered the judgment that the Marxian project has failed. Thus, those Marxists who continue to buy into the theory are destroying the dialectical whole of theory and practice that constituted the Marxian project. This splintering is disastrous because what gave Marxism its compelling power is the fact that it represented "a single coherent theoretical and practical project" (Aronson, 1995:52).

But how can the Marxian project be over if capitalism continues to exist and may, with the death of communism, be more powerful than ever? In fact, Aronson recognizes that there are a variety of arguments to be made on behalf of the idea that Marxism is still relevant. For example, he recognizes that most people around the world are worse-off today than they were at the dawn of capitalism and that in spite

---

[8] Bauman (1990) contends that capitalism and socialism are simply mirror images of modernity.

of a number of changes, the fundamental exploitative structure of capitalism is unaltered. In spite of such realities, Aronson argues that a variety of transformations must lead us to the conclusion that crucial aspects of Marxian theory are obsolete:

- The working class has *not* become increasingly impoverished.
- The class structure has *not* simplified to two polarized classes (bourgeoisie and proletariat).
- Because of the transformation of manufacturing processes, the number of industrial workers has declined, the working class has become more fragmented, and their consciousness of their situation has eroded.
- The overall shrinkage of the working class has led to a decline in its strength, its class consciousness, and its ability to engage in class struggle.
- Workers are increasingly less likely to identify themselves as workers; they have multiple and competing identities, and so being a worker is now just one of many identities.

While Marxism is over as far as Aronson is concerned, he argues that we should not regret its existence, even with the excesses (for example, Stalinism) that were committed in its name. Marxism

> gave hope, it made sense of the world; it gave direction and meaning to many and countless lives. As the twentieth century's greatest call to arms, it inspired millions to stand up and fight, to believe that humans could one day shape their lives and their world to meet their needs.

(Aronson, 1995:85)

In addition to the failures of Marxism in the real world, Aronson traces the demise of Marxism to problems within the theory itself. Those problems he traces to the fact that Marx's original theory was created during the early days of the modern world and, as a result, contains an uncomfortable mixture of modern and premodern ideas. This problem has plagued Marxian theory throughout its history. For example, the premodern, prophetic belief in emancipation coexisted with a modern belief in science and the search for facts: "Beneath its veneer of science, such dogmatic prophecy reveals its deeper and premodern kinship with religious anticipations of a world redeemed by a divine power beyond our control" (Aronson, 1995:97). To take one other example, Marxism tended to emphasize objective processes and to deemphasize subjective processes.

Aronson begins one of his chapters with the following provocative statement: "Feminism destroyed Marxism" (1995:124). He quickly makes it clear that feminism did not accomplish this feat on its own. However, feminism did contribute to the destruction of Marxism by demanding a theory that focuses on the "oppression of women *as women*" (Aronson, 1995:126). This focus clearly undermined Marxian theory, which purported to offer a theory applicable to all human beings. Feminism also set the stage for the development of other groups demanding that theories focus on their specific plight rather than on the universal problems of humanity.

Aronson describes post-Marxist theories like the analytical Marxism discussed earlier as Marxism without Marxism. That is, they are pure theories, lacking in practice, and therefore, in his view, should not be called Marxism:

> They may claim the name, as does analytical Marxism, but they do so as so many Marxisms without Marxism. They have become so transformed, so limited, so narrowly theoretical that even when their words and commitments ring true they only invoke Marxism's aura, but no more. However evocative, the ideas cannot conjure the fading reality.
>
> (Aronson, 1995:149)

Such Marxian theories will survive, but they will occupy a far humbler place in the world. They will represent just one theoretical voice in a sea of such voices.

Given all this, Aronson concludes that critical analysts of the modern world are on their own without a Marxian project to build upon. However, this is a mixed blessing. While the Marxian project had enormous strengths, it was also an albatross around the necks of critical analysts. Should former Marxists search for a new Marx? Or a new Marxian project? In light of developments in society and in theory, Aronson feels that the answer to these questions is no, because we have moved "beyond the possibility of the kind of holism, integration, coherence and confidence that Marxism embodied" (1995:168). Thus, for example, instead of a single radical movement, what we must seek today is a radical coalition of groups and ideas. The goal of such a coalition is the emancipation of modernity from its explosive inner tensions and its various forms of oppressiveness.

One problem facing such a new radical movement is that it can no longer hope to be driven by a compelling vision of some future utopia. Yet it must have some sort of emotional cement to hold it together and keep it moving ahead. The movement must have a moral base, a sense of what is right and what is wrong. It also must have hope, albeit a far more modest hope than that which characterized the Marxian project. Although modest, such hopes are less likely to lead to the profound disenchantment that characterized the Marxian project when it failed to achieve its social objectives.

Criticisms of Post-Marxism 对后马克思主义的批判

Many Marxian theorists are unhappy with post-Marxist developments (for example, Burawoy, 1990; E. M. Wood, 1986; E. M. Wood and Foster, 1997). Burawoy, for instance, attacks the analytical Marxists for eliminating the issue of history and for making a fetish of clarity and rigor. Weldes criticizes analytical Marxism for allowing itself to be colonized by mainstream economics, adopting a purely "technical, problem-solving approach," becoming increasingly academic and less political, and growing more conservative (1989:354). Ellen Wood picks up on the political issue and criticizes analytical Marxism (as well as postmodern Marxism) for its political quietism and its "cynical defeatism, where every radical programme of change is doomed to failure" (1989:88). Even supporters of one branch of analytical Marxism, the rigorous empirical study of Marxian ideas, have been critical of their brethren in rational choice theory, who, mistakenly in their view, adopt a position of methodological individualism (A. Levine, Sober, and Wright, 1987).

The work of Laclau and Mouffe has come under particularly heavy attack. For example, Allen Hunter criticizes them for their overall commitment to idealism and, more specifically, for situating "themselves at the extreme end of discourse analysis, viewing *everything* as discourse" (1988:892). Similarly, Geras (1987) attacks Laclau and Mouffe for their idealism, but he also sees them as profligate, dissolute, illogical, and obscurantist. The tenor of Laclau and Mouffe's reply to Geras is caught by its title "Post-Marxism without Apologies" (1987). Burawoy attacks Laclau and Mouffe for getting "lost in the web of history where everything is important and explanation is therefore impossible" (1990:790).

Finally, in contrast to Aronson, Burawoy believes that Marxism remains useful in understanding capitalism's dynamics and contradictions (see also E. M. Wood, 1995). Thus, with the demise of communism and the ascendancy of worldwide capitalism, "Marxism will . . . , once more, come into its own" (Burawoy, 1990:792). More recently, and in light of developments in the 1990s, Wood and Foster (1997:67) argue that Marxism is more necessary than ever because "humanity is more and more connected in the global dimensions of exploitation and oppression."

Summary 总结

In this chapter we examine a wide range of approaches that can be categorized as neo-Marxian sociological theories. All of them take Marx's work as their point of departure, but they often go in very different directions. Although these diverse developments give neo-Marxian theory considerable vitality, they also create at least some unnecessary and largely dysfunctional differentiation and controversy. Thus, one task for the modern Marxian sociological theorist is to integrate this broad array of theories while recognizing the value of various specific pieces of work.

The first neo-Marxian theory historically, but the least important at present, especially to the sociologically oriented thinker, is economic determinism. It was against this limited view of Marxian theory that other varieties developed. Hegelian Marxism, especially in the work of Georg Lukács, was one such reaction. This approach sought to overcome the limitations in economic determinism by returning to the subjective, Hegelian roots of Marxian theory. Hegelian Marxism is also of little contemporary relevance; its significance lies largely in its impact on later neo-Marxian theories.

The critical school, which was the inheritor of the tradition of Hegelian Marxism, *is* of contemporary importance to sociology. The great contributions of the critical theorists (Marcuse, Habermas, and so forth) are the insights offered into culture, consciousness, and their interrelationships. These theorists have enhanced our understanding of cultural phenomena such as instrumental rationality, the "culture industry," the "knowledge industry," communicative action, domination, and legitimations. To this they add a concern with consciousness, primarily in the form of an integration of Freudian theory in their work. However, critical theory has gone too far in its efforts to compensate for the limitations of economic determinism; it needs to reintegrate a concern for economics, indeed, for large-scale social forces in general.

Also discussed in this context is the work of the Birmingham school, which had a much more positive view of culture, especially as it emerged from the lower classes.

Next this chapter offers discussions of two lines of work in neo-Marxian economic sociology. The first deals with the relationship between capital and labor, especially in the works of Baran and Sweezy and of Braverman. The second is concerned with the transition from Fordism to post-Fordism. Both sets of work represent efforts to return to some of the traditional economic concerns of Marxian sociology. This work is significant for its effort to update Marxian economic sociology by taking into account the emerging realities of contemporary capitalist society.

Another concern is historically oriented Marxism, specifically the work of Immanuel Wallerstein and his supporters on the modern world-system. Then there is a discussion of those neo-Marxists who focus on spatial issues. The chapter closes with a section devoted to what, in light of the demise of communism, have come to be called post-Marxist theories. Included under this heading are several types of analytical Marxism and postmodern Marxian theory. Also included in this section is a discussion of an example of the kind of position taken by Marxists who have been forced to give up on the Marxian project in light of developments in the world.

Systems Theory

第 5 章　系统理论

Chapter Outline

Sociology and Modern Systems Theory

Niklas Luhmann's General System Theory

While it has adherents in many different fields, systems theory has had a checkered history in sociology (Baecker, 2001). As a result, if it were not for the work of the German social thinker Niklas Luhmann, this chapter would not be here. Over more than two decades until his death in 1998, Luhmann doggedly pursued the development of systems theory (he preferred "system theory"). (Although his work is not nearly as well known or influential, Kenneth Bailey [1990, 1994, 1997] also has been a notable contributor to the development of this theory.) For years Luhmann labored in virtual anonymity, but more recently his work has gained increasing worldwide recognition. As a result, this chapter is devoted largely to his thinking. However, before we get to his work, we will discuss some early insights and conceptual ideas from the work of Walter Buckley (1967), especially his *Sociology and Modern Systems Theory.*

社会学与现代系统理论

Sociology and Modern Systems Theory

Gains from Systems Theory 系统理论的启示

A central issue addressed by Buckley is what sociology has to gain from systems theory. First, because systems theory is derived from the hard sciences and because it is, at least in the eyes of its proponents, applicable to *all* behavioral and social sciences, it promises a common vocabulary to unify those sciences. Second, systems theory is multileveled and can be applied equally well to the largest-scale and the smallest-scale, to the most objective and the most subjective, aspects of the social world. Third, systems theory is interested in the varied relationships of the many aspects of the social world and thus operates against piecemeal analyses of the social world. The argument of systems theory is that the intricate relationship of parts cannot be treated out of the context of the whole. Systems theorists reject the idea that society or other large-scale components of society should be treated as unified social facts. Instead, the focus is on relationships or processes at various levels within the social system. Buckley described the focus:

> The kind of system we are interested in may be described generally as a complex
> of elements or components directly or indirectly related in a causal network, such
> that each component is related to at least some others in a more or less stable way
> within any particular period of time.
>
> (Buckley, 1967:41)

Richard A. Ball (see also Bailey, 2005) offers a clear conception of the relational
orientation of systems theory, or what he calls General Systems Theory (GST):

> GST begins with a processual conception of reality as consisting fundamentally of
> relationships among relationships, as illustrated in the concept of "gravity" as used
> in modern physics. The term "gravity" does not describe an entity at all. There is no
> such "thing" as gravity. It is a *set of relationships*. To think of these relationships as
> entities is to fall into reification. . . . The GST approach demands that sociologists
> develop the logic of relationships and conceptualize social reality in relational terms.
>
> (Ball, 1978:66)

Fourth, the systems approach tends to see all aspects of sociocultural systems in process
terms, especially as networks of information and communication. Fifth, and perhaps most
important, systems theory is inherently integrative. Buckley, in his definition of the perspective, saw it involving the integration of large-scale objective structures, symbol systems,
action and interaction, and "consciousness and self-awareness." Ball also accepted the idea
of integration of levels: "The individual and society are treated equally, not as separate
entities but as mutually constitutive fields, related through various 'feedback' processes"
(1978:68). In fact, systems theory is so attuned to integration that Buckley criticized the
tendency of other sociologists to make analytical distinctions among levels:

> We note the tendency in much of sociology to insist on what is called an "analytical
> distinction" between "personality" (presumably intracranial), symbol systems (culture),
> and matrices of social relations (social systems), though the actual work of the
> proponents of the distinctions shows it to be misleading or often untenable in practice.
>
> (Buckley, 1967:101)

(Buckley was somewhat unfair here, because he did much the same thing throughout
his own work. Making analytical distinctions is apparently acceptable to systems
theorists as long as one is making such distinctions in order to make better sense out
of the interrelationships among the various aspects of social life.) Finally, systems
theory tends to see the social world in dynamic terms, with an overriding concern for
"sociocultural emergence and dynamics in general" (Buckley, 1967:39).

Some General Principles 一些基本准则

Buckley discussed the relationship among sociocultural systems, mechanical systems,
and organic systems. Buckley focused on delineating the essential differences among
these systems. On a number of dimensions a continuum runs from mechanical systems
to organic systems to sociocultural systems—going from least to most complexity of the
parts, from least to most instability of the parts, and from lowest to highest degree to
which the parts are attributable to the system as a whole.

On other dimensions, the systems differ qualitatively rather than simply quantitatively. In mechanical systems, the interrelationships of the parts are based on transfers of energy. In organic systems, the interrelationships of the parts are based more on exchange of information than on exchange of energy. In sociocultural systems, the interrelationships are based even more on information exchange.

The three types of systems also differ in the degree to which they are open or closed—that is, in the degree of interchange with aspects of the larger environment. A more open system is better able to respond selectively to a greater range and detail of the endless variety of the environment. In these terms, mechanical systems tend to be closed, organic systems are more open, and sociocultural systems are the most open of the three (as we will see, Luhmann disagrees with the last point). The degree of openness of a system is related to two crucial concepts in systems theory: *entropy,* or the tendency of systems to run down, and *negentropy,* or the tendency of systems to elaborate structures (Bailey, 1990). Closed systems tend to be entropic, whereas open systems tend to be negentropic. Sociocultural systems also tend to have more tension built into them than do the other two. Finally, sociocultural systems can be purposive and goal-seeking because they receive feedback from the environment that allows them to keep moving toward their goals.

Feedback is an essential aspect of the cybernetic approach that systems theorists take to the social system. This is in contrast to the equilibrium approach, which is characteristic of many sociologists (for instance, Parsons) who purportedly operate from a systems approach. Using feedback enables cybernetic systems theorists to deal with friction, growth, evolution, and sudden changes. The openness of a social system to its environment and the impact of environmental factors on the system are important concerns to these systems theorists (Bailey, 2001).

A variety of internal processes also affect social systems. Two other concepts are critical here. *Morphostasis* refers to those processes that help the system maintain itself, whereas *morphogenesis* refers to those processes that help the system change and grow more elaborate. Social systems develop more and more complex "mediating systems" that intervene between external forces and the action of the system. Some of these mediating systems help the system maintain itself, and others help it change. These mediating systems grow more and more independent, autonomous, and determinative of the actions of the system. In other words, these mediating systems permit the social system to grow less dependent on the environment.

These complex mediating systems perform a variety of functions in the social system. For example, they allow the system to adjust itself temporarily to external conditions. They can direct the system from harsh to more congenial environments. They also can allow the system to reorganize its parts in order to deal with the environment more effectively.

Applications to the Social World 在社会世界中的应用

Buckley (1967) moved from a discussion of general principles to the specifics of the social world to show the applicability of systems theory. He began at the individual level, where he was very favorably impressed by Mead's work, in which consciousness and action are interrelated. In fact, Buckley recast the Meadian problematic in systems-theory terms. Action begins with a *signal* from the environment, which is transmitted to the actor. However, the transmission may be complicated by *noise* in the environment. When it gets through, the signal provides the actor with *information*. On the basis of this information, the actor is allowed to *select* a response. The key here is the actor's possession of a mediating mechanism—self-consciousness. Buckley discussed self-consciousness in the terminology of systems theory:

> In the language of cybernetics, such self-consciousness is a mechanism of internal feedback of the system's own states which may be mapped or compared with other information from the situation and from memory, permitting a selection from a repertoire of actions in a goal-directed manner that takes one's own self and behavior implicitly into account.
>
> (Buckley, 1967:100)

To Mead and the symbolic interactionists and systems theorists, consciousness is not separated from action and interaction but rather is an integral part of both.

Despite his views that consciousness and interaction are interrelated and that levels should not be separated, Buckley did move from consciousness to the interactional domain. Patterns of interaction—namely, imitation and response—clearly fit into a systemic view of the world. More important, Buckley tied the interpersonal realm directly to the personality system; indeed, he saw the two as mutually determinative. Finally, Buckley turned to the large-scale organization of society, especially roles and institutions, which he saw in systemic terms and as being related to, if not indistinguishable from, the other levels of social reality.

Buckley concluded by discussing some of the general principles of systems theory as they apply to the sociocultural domain. First, the systems theorist accepts the idea that tension is a normal, ever-present, and necessary reality of the social system. Second, there is a focus on the nature and sources of variety in the social system. The emphasis on both tension and variety makes the systems perspective a dynamic one. Third, there is a concern for the selection process at both the individual and the interpersonal levels whereby the various alternatives open to the system are sorted and sifted. This lends further dynamism. Fourth, the interpersonal level is seen as the basis of the development of larger structures. The transactional processes of exchange, negotiation, and bargaining are the processes out of which emerge relatively stable social and cultural structures. Finally, despite the inherent dynamism of the systems approach, there is a recognition of the processes of perpetuation and transmission. As Buckley put it, "Out of the continuous transactions emerge some relatively stable accommodations and adjustments" (1967:160).

An interesting note: There are a number of rather striking similarities between systems theory and the dialectical approach, even though they are derived from extremely different sources (one scientific, the other philosophical) and have very different vocabularies (Ball, 1978). Similarities between them include a focus on relations, process, creativity, and tension.

尼古拉斯·卢曼的一般系统理论

Niklas Luhmann's General System Theory[1]

The most prominent systems theorist in sociology is Niklas Luhmann (1927–1998) (Nollman, 2005a; Rogowski, 2007). Luhmann developed a sociological approach that combined elements of Talcott Parsons's structural functionalism (see Chapter 3) with general systems theory and introduced concepts from cognitive biology, cybernetics, and phenomenology (Paul, 2001). Luhmann sees Parsons's later ideas as the only general theory that is complex enough to form the basis for a new sociological approach that reflects the latest findings in biological and cybernetic systems. However, he sees two problems with Parsons's approach. First, it has no place for *self-reference,* and according to Luhmann, society's ability to refer to itself is central to our understanding of it as a system. Second, Parsons does not recognize *contingency.* As a result, Parsons cannot adequately analyze modern society as it is because he does not see that it could be otherwise. Thus, to take one example from Parsons's work, the AGIL scheme (see Figure 3.1) should not be seen as a fact but instead as a model of possibilities. For example, the AGIL scheme shows that the adaptive and the goal-attainment subsystems can be related in various ways; therefore, the aim of analysis should be to understand why the system produced a particular relationship between these two subsystems at any given time. Luhmann addresses these two problems in Parsons's work by developing a theory that takes self-reference as central to systems and that focuses on contingency, the fact that things could be different.

The key to understanding what Luhmann means by a system can be found in the distinction between a system and its environment. Basically, the difference between the two is one of *complexity.* The system is always less complex than its environment. For example, a business, such as an automobile manufacturer, can be seen as a system that deals with a highly complex environment which includes many different types of people, a constantly changing physical environment, and many other diverse systems.[2] However, this complexity is represented in a much simplified form within the system. When the manufacturer needs raw materials (steel, rubber, etc.), it doesn't normally care where they come from, how they are produced, and the nature of their suppliers. All this complexity is reduced to information about the price and the quality of the raw materials. Similarly, all the diverse practices of its customers are reduced to those that have a direct impact on whether they buy a car.

Simplifying complexity means being forced to select (the manufacturer cares about how raw materials are produced but may not pay attention to the political situation in the nation in which they are produced). Being forced to select means contingency since one could always select differently (the manufacturer *could* monitor the political situation). And contingency means *risk.* Thus, if the manufacturer chooses not to

---

[1] This section was coauthored with Doug Goodman and Matthias Junge.
[2] Strictly speaking, the automobile industry is not an autopoietic system in Luhmann's sense, since it is not producing its own basic elements. However, we will use this example to explain the general idea of systems theory because it is more concrete than the abstractions of the economic system or the law system. Later, when we define an autopoietic system, we will need to use a more abstract example.

monitor the political situation in the nation producing the raw material, the production process may be severely disrupted by a rebellion that shuts off the supply of that material.

A system simply cannot be as complex as its environment. A system that tried would bring to mind the Borges (1964) story about the king who ordered a cartographer to create a completely accurate map of his country. When the cartographer was done, the map was as big as the country and was therefore useless as a map. Maps, like systems, must reduce complexity. The cartographer must select what features are important. Different maps of the same area can be made because the selection is contingent. This is always necessary, but it is also risky since the map maker can never be sure that what is left out will not be important to the user.

While they can never be as complex as their environment, systems develop new subsystems and establish various relations between the subsystems in order to deal effectively with their environment. If they did not, they would be overwhelmed by the complexity of the environment. For example, an automobile manufacturer could create a department of international affairs charged with monitoring political conditions in supplying nations. This new department would be responsible for keeping manufacturing apprised of potential disruptions in the supply of raw materials and for finding alternative sources in case of a disruption. Thus, paradoxically, "Only complexity can reduce complexity" (Luhmann, 1995:26).

Autopoietic Systems 自创生系统

Luhmann is best known for his thinking on autopoiesis.[3] The concept of autopoiesis refers to a diversity of systems from biological cells to the entire world society. Luhmann uses the term to refer to such systems as the economy, the political system, the legal system, the scientific system, and bureaucracies, among others. In the description below, we will try to provide a variety of examples to give a sense of the scope of the concept. Autopoietic systems have the following four characteristics.

1. An autopoietic system produces the basic elements that make up the system. This may seem paradoxical. How can a system produce its own elements, the very things out of which it is made? Think of a modern economic system and its basic element, money. We say money is a basic element because the value of things in the economic system can be given in terms of money, but it is very difficult to say what money itself is worth. The meaning of money, what it is worth, and what it can be used for are determined by the economic system itself. Money, as we understand the term today, did not exist before the economic system. Both the modern form of money and the economic system emerged together, and they depend on each other. A modern economic system without money is difficult to imagine. Money without an economic system is just a piece of paper or metal.

---

[3] On the significance of this concept, see Zinn (2007b) and K. D. Bailey (1998).

2. Autopoietic systems are self-organizing in two ways—they organize their own boundaries, and they organize their internal structures. They organize their own boundaries by distinguishing between what is in the system and what is in the environment. For example, the economic system counts anything that is scarce and on which a price can be set as part of the economic system. Air is everywhere in abundant supply; therefore, no price is set on it and it is not part of the economic system. Air is, however, a necessary part of the environment. What is inside or outside an autopoietic system is determined by the self-organization of the system, not, as a structural functionalist would have us believe, by the functional necessities of the system.

Other forces may try to limit the scope of autopoietic systems. For example, capitalist economic systems have always expanded their boundaries in order to include sex and illicit drugs. This occurs even though the political system passes laws aimed at keeping sex and illicit drugs from becoming economic commodities. Rather than keeping them out of the economic system, such laws instead affect the prices of sex and illicit drugs *within* the economic system. Their illegality makes their prices higher, thereby discouraging their purchase. But within the economic system, the high prices that discourage purchases also encourage sales. If a great deal of money can be made from selling sex and drugs, they will remain in the economic system. Therefore, laws that try to keep a commodity out of the economic system simply affect the way that commodity is priced within the economic system.

Within its boundaries, an autopoietic system produces its own structures. For example, because of the existence of money, the market is structured in an impersonal way, banks are established to store and lend money, the concept of interest has developed, and so on. If the economic system did not have as its basic element such an abstract and portable entity, the internal structure would be entirely different. For example, if the economy were based on barter instead of money, there would be no banks and no concept of interest, and the market where goods are bought and sold would be structured in an entirely different way.

3. Autopoietic systems are self-referential (Esposito, 1996). For example, the economic system uses price as a way of referring to itself. By attaching a fluctuating monetary value to shares in a company, the stock market exemplifies such self-reference within the economic system. The prices in the stock market are determined not by any individual, but by the economy itself. Similarly, the legal system has laws that refer to the legal system: laws about how laws can be enacted, applied, interpreted, and so on.

4. An autopoietic system is a closed system. This means that there is no direct connection between a system and its environment. Instead, a system deals with its representations of the environment. For example, the economic system supposedly responds to the material needs and desires of people; however, those needs and desires affect the economic system only to the extent that they can be represented in terms of money. Consequently, the economic system responds well to the material needs and desires of rich people but very poorly to the needs and desires of poor people.

Another example would be a bureaucracy, such as the Internal Revenue Service. The IRS never really deals with its clients; it deals solely with representations of the clients. Taxpayers are represented by the forms that they file and that are filed about them. The real taxpayer has an effect on the bureaucracy only by causing a disturbance in the bureaucracy's representations. Those who cause disturbances (misfiled forms, contradictory forms, false forms) often are dealt with very harshly since they threaten the system.

Even though an autopoietic system is closed with no direct connection to the environment, the environment must be allowed to disturb its inner representations. Without such disturbances, the system would be destroyed by environmental forces that would overwhelm it. For example, the prices of stocks in the stock market fluctuate daily. The difference between the price of a company's stock from one day to the next has little to do with the real value of the company—that is, its assets or profits—and everything to do with the state of the stock market. That is, the market may be in a boom period (a "bull" market) in which the prices of stocks are far higher than they should be given the state of the companies involved. However, over the long run the price of stocks needs to reflect the actual status of the companies involved or the system will fall apart. This is what happened in the stock market crash of 1929. The prices of stocks had no relation to real value, and so the system reached a state of crisis. To function properly, the stock market as a system must, at least at times, be disturbed by the actual condition of the companies that are part of its environment.

A closed social system is distinct from the individuals who appear to be part of it. According to Luhmann, in such systems, the individual is part of the environment. To take the example of a bureaucracy again, this means that not only are the clients part of the environment, so are the people who work in the bureaucracy. From the perspective of the bureaucracy, the people who work in it are external sources of complexity and unpredictability. In order to be a closed system, the bureaucracy must find a way to represent even its own workers in a simplified way. Thus, instead of being seen as full-fledged human beings, one worker is seen as a "manager," another as an "accountant," and so on. The real, fully human worker affects the bureaucracy only as a disturbance to the bureaucracy's representations.

Society and Psychic Systems 社会系统和心理系统

Luhmann argues that society is an autopoietic system. It fulfills the four characteristics listed above—society produces its own basic elements, it establishes its own boundaries and structures, it is self-referential, and it is closed.

The basic element of society is communication, and communication is produced by society. Participants in society refer to society through communication. In fact, that is what we are doing right now! The individual is relevant to society only to the extent that he or she participates in communication or can be interpreted as participating in a communication. Those secret parts of you that are never communicated, or not understood as a communication by others, are not part of society.

They are, instead, part of the environment which may disturb society. According to Luhmann's conception, whatever is not communication is part of society's environment. This includes the biological systems of human beings and even their psychic systems. The individual as a biological organism and the individual as consciousness are not part of society but are external to it. This leads to the strange idea that the individual is *not* part of society.

By the psychic system, Luhmann means the consciousness of the individual. The psychic system and society—the system of all communications—have a property in common. They both rely on *meaning*. Meaning is closely related to the choices that a system makes. The meaning of a particular action (or object) is its difference from other possible actions (or objects). Meaning appears only against the backdrop of contingency. If there is no possibility of being different, then there is no meaning. Action has meaning only to the extent that a selection is made from among a range of possible actions. For example, our clothing means something only because we could have chosen to wear something else.

Systems such as the psychic and social systems that rely on meaning are closed because (1) meaning always refers to other meaning, (2) only meaning can change meaning, and (3) meaning usually produces more meaning. Meaning forms the boundary to each of these systems. For example, in the psychic system, what is not meaningful is seen as outside the system, as a "cause" of our action, while what is meaningful is inside the system as a "motivation" for our action. Events enter our psychic systems only as meaning. Even our own bodies are simply environments for this meaning system. Our bodies can be seen only as disturbances to our psychic systems. The body enters our consciousness by becoming meaningful, so that, for example, a physical agitation enters consciousness as an emotion. Similarly, in the social system, meaning is the difference between a communication within the system and noise from outside the system.

Psychic systems and social systems have evolved together. Each is a necessary environment for the other. The elements of the psychic meaning system are conceptual representations; the elements of the social meaning system are communications. It would be wrong to think that meaning in the psychic system has priority over meaning in the social system. Because both are autopoietic systems, they both produce their own meanings out of their own processes. In the psychic system, meaning is bound to consciousness, while in the social system it is bound to communication. Meaning in the social system cannot be ascribed to an individual's intention, nor is it a property of the particular elements of the social system; instead it refers to a selection from among the elements. The meaning of what is communicated is derived from its difference from what could be communicated. For example, "Hello," "What's up?" "How ya doin'," "Good day," and "Hey!" may all come from the same intention—that is, to greet someone—but if a friend says "Good day" when she usually says "Hey!" some meaning would be communicated. The meaning is not necessarily intended, nor is it connected to the particular words. The meaning comes from the selection of *those particular words* in comparison to the words that could have been selected. The meaning comes from the contingency of those selected words.

Double Contingency 双重偶变性

The social system based on communication creates social structures in order to solve what Luhmann calls the problem of double contingency.[4] Double contingency refers to the fact that every communication must take into consideration the way that it is received. But we also know that the way that it is received will depend on the receiver's estimation of the communicator. This forms an impossible circle: the receiver depends on the communicator, and the communicator depends on the receiver. For example, a professor, in choosing how to greet a student, might use the informal "Hey!" if she thinks it will appear more friendly (the communicator takes into account the receiver). But if the student being greeted thinks the professor is talking down to him, he will not see it as a friendly gesture (the receiver takes into account the communicator). The less we know about each other's expectations, the greater is the problem of double contingency.

Fortunately, we almost always know a great deal about others' expectations because of social structures. In the example above, we know that the people involved are a professor and a student. Based on this alone, we expect that they will have a certain type of relationship that conforms to institutional rules and traditions. We will have other expectations by knowing their genders, their ethnicities, their ages, their dress, and so on. Because of these expectations, norms and role expectations develop for interpreting people's communications. Either people fit the norms and role expectations or they do not. If we find a number of examples that do not fit our expectations, our expectations may change, but society can never do without these expectations because of the problem of double contingency.

It is because each of us has a different set of norms that communication becomes necessary, and it is because communication has the problem of double contingency that we develop sets of norms. This shows how society as an autopoietic system works: the structure (roles, institutional and traditional norms) of society creates the elements (communication) of society and those elements create the structure, so that, as in all autopoietic systems, the system constitutes its own elements.

Because of double contingency, any given communication is improbable. First, it is improbable that we would have something we want to communicate to a particular person. Second, since the information can be communicated in a number of ways, it is improbable that we will choose any one particular way. Third, it is improbable that the person we are addressing will understand us correctly. Social structures have developed in order to make improbable communications more probable. For example, to say "Good day" to a particular person at any particular time is an improbable thing, but social structures make a greeting normative in certain circumstances, they provide us with a limited number of acceptable ways to greet people, and they make sure that the addressee will understand the greeting in approximately the same way that the addressor intends it.

The improbabilities that we've discussed so far refer only to interactions, but society is more than a collection of independent interactions. Interactions last only as long as the people involved in the communication are present, but, from the viewpoint

---

[4] Parsons (1951) also dealt with the problem of double contingency, but he limits its solution to a preexisting value consensus. Luhmann acknowledges the possibility that a new value consensus can be created on the spot (Vanderstraeten, 2002).

of society, interactions are episodes in ongoing social processes. Every social system is faced with a problem: it will cease to exist if there is no guarantee of further communications, that is, no possibility of connecting previous communications to future communications. To avoid a breakdown of communication, structures must be developed to permit earlier communications to connect with later communications. The selections made in one communication are restricted by the selections made in previous communications, and the present communication also restricts future communications. This is another way in which the improbabilities of the communicative process are overcome and transformed into probabilities by the social system. It is this need to overcome double contingency and make improbable communications more probable that regulates the evolution of social systems.

Evolution of Social Systems 社会系统的进化

Evolution is, roughly speaking, a process of trial-and-error. Evolution is not teleological. Its outcomes are not governed by a predefined goal. One implication is that, in Luhmann's theory, the idea of progress makes no sense. This differentiates it from Parsons's idea of evolutionary universals in modern societies (see pp. 111–113). To assume a necessary path of societal development is teleological and ignores the fact that there are a variety of ways of dealing with a given problem.

On the general level, evolution makes improbability more probable. For example, it is improbable that a random set of biological mutations will produce a given animal such as a human. Natural selection and the inheritance of stable characteristics make it more probable that an ape will evolve into something like a human rather than something like a squid.

Strictly speaking, evolution is not a process but a set of processes that can be described as performing three functions: variation, selection, and stabilization of reproducible characteristics. These functions represent the concrete mechanisms by which evolution operates. *Variation* is a process of trial-and-error. If a system faces a unique problem, a variety of solutions may develop to deal with the environmental disturbance. Some of these solutions will work, and others will not. The *selection* of a particular solution does not imply that the "best" solution is chosen. It may simply be that the particular solution is the easiest to stabilize, in other words, the easiest to reproduce as a stable and enduring structure. In a social system, this *stabilization* usually involves a new kind of differentiation that requires the adjustment of all the parts of the system to the new solution. The evolutionary process will have achieved a temporary end only when the stabilization phase is complete.

Let us take an example from the economy. One problem that economic systems have faced is how to exchange goods in an equitable way with other economic systems—that is, how can an economy that uses dollars exchange goods with an economy that uses yen? A variety of different solutions have developed (evolutionary variation). Some early systems initiated "gift" exchanges that eliminated a concern for the exact equality of the goods exchanged. Others used a stable commodity such as gold to regulate the interchange. Both of these solutions proved difficult to reproduce on a global scale. For the first solution, only so much can be exchanged as gifts, and for the second, the value of commodities such as gold do not remain stable because more or less gold is available at any given time. Instead, a more reproducible form has been the establishment of a new structure, a currency exchange market, that operates at the global level and allows the exchange rate of currencies to float (evolutionary selection). This may not be the best solution since it is susceptible to wild fluctuations caused by speculators, as seen in the "Asian" financial crisis of 1998. However, it is the only solution that appears to be reproducible on a global scale (evolutionary stabilization). Of course, the reproducibility of this solution does not mean that the other solutions have disappeared. States still exchange gifts, especially with heads of states through diplomats, and many countries try to fix their exchange rates by tying them to a commodity such as gold or even another currency such as the U.S. dollar.

Differentiation 分化

From the viewpoint of Luhmann's system theory, the principal feature of modern society is the increased process of system differentiation as a way of dealing with the complexity of its environment (Rasch, 2000). Differentiation is the "replication, within a system of the difference between a system and its environment" (Luhmann, 1982:230).[5] This means that in a differentiated system there are two kinds of environments: one common to all subsystems and a different *internal environment* for each subsystem. For example, an automobile manufacturer, such as Ford, sees other manufacturers, General Motors and DaimlerChrysler, for instance, as part of its environment. The international relations department (a subsystem) of Ford also sees General Motors and Chrysler as outside it and part of its environment. However, the international relations department also sees other subsystems within Ford (such as the human relations department [subsystem]) as outside the international relations subsystem and therefore part of its environment. Other subsystems, such as the human relations department, are internal to the organizational system as a whole, but are in the environment of the international relations subsystem, hence an internal environment. Similarly, the human relations subsystem sees other manufacturers as part of its environment, but in addition sees other subsystems (this time including the international relations subsystem) as part of its environment. Therefore, each of the subsystems has a different view of the internal environment of the system. This creates a highly complex and dynamic internal environment.

Differentiation within a system is a way of dealing with changes in the environment. As we have seen, each system must maintain its boundary in relation to the environment. Otherwise it would be overwhelmed by the complexity of its environment, break down, and cease to exist. In order to survive, the system must be able to deal with environmental variations. For instance, it is well known that any large-scale organization as a system adjusts slowly to alterations in its environment (e.g., concrete demands by the public, political changes, or even technological changes such as the availability of personal computers). However, organizations do develop; they

---

[5] For a general discussion of differentiation and the limits of the concept, see G. Wagner (1998).

evolve by creating differentiation within the system. That is, an environmental change will be "translated" into the structure of the organization. An example would be the creation by the automobile manufacturer of a new department to deal with a new situation such as the presence of personal computers in the workplace. New workers would be hired, they would be trained to handle the new technology, a manager would be selected, and so forth.

The differentiation process is a means of increasing the complexity of the system, since each subsystem can make different connections with other subsystems. It allows for more variation within the system in order to respond to variation in the environment. In the example above, the new department is, like every other department of the bureaucratic system, an environment for other departments, but the new one increases organizational complexity because new and additional relations between departments are made possible. A new department created to service workers' computers will be better able to respond to further changes in computer technologies and help the entire organization integrate these new capabilities. In addition, it may provide for new connections between existing departments, such as allowing general accounting to be centralized or salespeople to access inventory directly.

Not only does more variation caused by differentiation allow for better responses to the environment, it also allows for faster evolution. Remember that evolution is a process of selection from variation. The more variation that is available, the better is the selection. However, Luhmann argues that only a few forms of internal differentiation have developed. He calls these segmentation, stratification, center-periphery, and functional differentiation. These differentiations increase the complexity of the system through the repetition of the differentiation between system and environment within the system. In terms of their evolutionary potential, these forms of differentiation have a different ability to produce variability and therefore provide for more selectivity for evolutionary processes. The more complex forms of differentiation therefore have the potential to accelerate the evolution of the system.

Segmentary Differentiation 区隔分化

Segmentary differentiation divides parts of the system on the basis of the need to fulfill identical functions over and over. For instance, our automobile manufacturer has functionally similar factories for the production of cars at many different locations. Every location is organized in much the same way; each has the same structure and fulfills the same function—producing cars.

Stratificatory Differentiation 阶层分化

Stratificatory differentiation is a vertical differentiation according to rank or status in a system conceived as a hierarchy. Every rank fulfills a particular and distinct function in the system. In the automobile firm, we find different ranks. For example, the manager of the new department of international relations occupies the top rank within the hierarchy of that department. The manager has the function of using power to direct the operations of that department. Then there are a variety of lower-ranking workers within the department who handle a variety of specific functions (e.g., word processing). In addition, the manager of the department of international relations has a position within the stratificatory system of the automobile manufacturer. Thus, the president of the company has a higher-ranking position than that of the manager of international relations and is in a position to issue orders to the latter.

In segmentary differentiation, inequality results from accidental variations in environments (such as more cars being sold in one geographic area than in another), but it has no systemic function. In stratificatory differentiation, however, inequality is essential to the system. More correctly, we see the interplay of equality and inequality. All members in the same ranks (e.g., all the word processors) are basically equal, while different ranks are distinguished by their inequality. The higher ranks (e.g., department managers) have more access to resources and a greater ability to become the subject of influential communications. Consequently, a stratified system is more concerned with the well-being of those in the upper ranks and generally is concerned about the lower ranks only if they threaten the higher ranks. However, both ranks depend on one another, and the social system can survive only if all ranks, including the lowest, successfully realize their functions.

The importance of the lower ranks and their difficulty in becoming the subject of influential communication create a structural problem that limits the complexity of the system. When those directing the system become too far removed from the lowest ranks, the system tends to collapse because the important functions of the lowest ranks are not being performed properly. In order to have an effect on the system, the lower ranks must resort to conflict.

Center-Periphery Differentiation 中心—边缘分化

The third type of differentiation, that between *center and periphery,* is a link between segmentary and stratificatory differentiation (Luhmann, 1997:663–678). For instance, some automobile firms have built factories in other countries; nevertheless, the headquarters of the company remains the center, ruling and, to some extent, controlling the peripheral factories.[6]

Differentiations of Functional Systems 功能系统的分化

Functional differentiation is the most complex form of differentiation and the form that dominates modern society. Every function within a system is ascribed to a particular unit. For instance, an automobile manufacturer has functionally differentiated departments such as production, administration, accounting, planning, and personnel.

Functional differentiation is more flexible than stratificatory differentiation is, but if one system fails to fulfill its task, the whole system will have great trouble surviving.[7] However, as long as each unit fulfills its function, the different units can

---

[6] It has been objected (Schimank, 1996) that this distinction does not fit Luhmann's general argument. The differentiation between center and periphery does not refer to the social system as a whole. Rather, in the example above it refers to a differentiation of functions within the industrial system. Thus it refers to a specific system within the social system and does not refer to the social system as a whole.

[7] Most of the systems discussed here also can be called subsystems of the world social system. However, we will use the term *system* rather than *subsystem* except when it is necessary to distinguish between the subsystem and the overarching system that contains it.

attain a high degree of independence. In fact, functionally differentiated systems are a complex mixture of interdependence and independence. For instance, while the planning division is dependent on the accounting division for economic data, as long as the figures are accurate, the planning division can be blissfully ignorant of exactly how the accountants produced the data.

This indicates a further difference between the forms of differentiation. In the case of segmentary differentiation, if a segment fails to fulfill its function (e.g., one of the automobile manufacturer's factories cannot produce cars because of a labor strike), it does not threaten the system. However, in the case of the more complex forms of differentiation such as functional differentiation, failure will cause a problem for the social system, possibly leading to its breakdown. Thus, on the one hand, the growth of complexity increases the abilities of a system to deal with its environment. On the other hand, complexity increases the risk of a system breakdown if a function is not properly fulfilled.

However, in most cases, this increased vulnerability is a necessary price to pay for the increase in possible relations between different subsystems. Having more types of possible relations between the subsystems means more variation to use to select structural responses to changes in the environment. In a segmentary system, the relations between different subsystems are not structurally different. For example, the relations that any two factories have with each other are all basically the same. In a stratified system, the relations between ranks are basically different from those within the rank. For example, the relation that a factory has with headquarters is different from that which it has with another factory. In functionally differentiated systems, the different relations multiply. The accounting and production departments have a relationship with each other that is different from that between accounting and research, which is, in turn, different from the relationship between production and research. Functional differentiation gives the automobile manufacturer greater flexibility. Thus, for example, in an environment in which technical advances are providing opportunities for economic advantage, the company can be led by research, but in an environment in which economic advantage is found in doing the same old thing, only cheaper, the company can be led by accounting.

We should note that the more complex forms of differentiation do not exclude the less complex forms, and, in fact, they may require the less complex forms. For example, an automobile manufacturer is stratified, but it still contains individual factories that are a segmentary form. This is important, since we usually speak of functionally differentiated systems within modern society to describe its dominant mode of differentiation; nevertheless, the other forms continue to exist.

Code 符码

A code is a way to distinguish elements of a system from elements that do not belong to the system. A code is the basic "language" of a functional system. Codes are, for instance, truth (versus nontruth) for the science system, payment (versus nonpayment) for the economic system, and legal (versus illegal) for the legal system. Every communication using a particular code is a part of the system whose code reference is being used.

A code is used to limit the kind of permissible communication. Every communication that does not use the code is not a communication belonging to the system under consideration. Thus, within the scientific system we usually find only communications with reference to the code of truth. For instance, if the head of NASA (National Aeronautics and Space Administration) and the head of NIH (National Institutes of Health) met to discuss what facts had been discovered about aging in John Glenn's 1998 space flight, it would be part of the scientific system using the code of truth or nontruth. If the same people met to discuss who would pay for what part of the research conducted on that space flight, it would be in the economic system using the code of payment or nonpayment.

In Luhmann's system theory, no system uses and understands the code of another system. There is no way to translate the code of one system into the code of another system. Because the systems are closed, they can react only to things happening in their environment (if what happens makes enough "noise" to be noticed by the system). But the system must describe the noise in the environment in relation to its own code. This is the only way to make sense of what is happening, the only way to give it meaning. For example, an economic system will "see" a scientific system only in terms of what makes money (makes future payments possible) or requires investments (requires initial payments before it can be repaid).

Problems of Functional Differentiation 功能分化的问题

Functional differentiation causes at least one central problem for modern society. What is necessary for society as a whole may not be dealt with by any functional system. There may not be a functional system that has a code that can represent the problem adequately. For instance, the economic system cannot adequately represent ecological problems, since much pollution looks economically rational. The legal system may have laws aimed at restricting air pollution, but those laws are interpreted within the economic system of the polluters. This is demonstrated by an example from the former Czechoslovakia, where there were legally prescribed limitations on air pollution. Industries reacted to those laws by building higher smokestacks, leading to a wider dispersion of pollution and thus a decreasing level of air pollution near the measurement points. This reaction contradicted the intention of the law, but it was a reaction in accord with the code of the economic system; it was a way to minimize costs. Better protection against air pollution would have cost much more than building higher smokestacks.

Such problems generally are caused by functional differentiation. Functional differentiation requires a displacement of problems from the level of society to the level of subsystems. Every subsystem has gained independence and flexibility in making decisions using its own codes. However, each is dependent on other subsystems to move the social system as a whole. In short, the result of greater independence of functional systems is greater vulnerability of the social system as a whole.

Luhmann investigated the problematic relationship between the functional differentiation of modern society and its efforts to deal with the problems of ecology (1986/1989). Modern society has no specific differentiated system to deal with ecological problems. Everything that happens in its environment (note the double meaning of the term: environment of a system and natural environment) must be treated within the existing functional systems and their codes. That means that every problem in the environment is a problem for a system only if it can be represented in that system's code. For example, the law can move against polluters only if what they do can be represented as illegal. Thus, it is possible that ecological problems will not be dealt with sufficiently. Of greater importance is a general conclusion: functional differentiation can be conceived of as a causative factor of ecological crisis (Luhmann, 1986/1989:42).

Functional systems produce both too much and too little *resonance* to problems in their environment. Too little resonance means that a system does not react well to problems that cannot be represented by its codes. For instance, environmental groups may confront the automobile industry with a demand for cars that produce less air pollution; however, the automobile industry is unlikely to react to those demands unless the protests start to affect their profits. Too much resonance means that the treatment of ecological problems within a functional system may lead to reactions in other functional systems because the systems are interdependent. For instance, the automobile industry may produce cars that pollute less by making them smaller, lighter, and, consequently, cheaper. This can have the consequence that the development of the public transportation system will slow down since now everyone can buy a car. In addition, it is likely that this also will increase the number of traffic accidents and thus the cost within the health system. The reaction to the demand of the environmental groups has unpredictable consequences within complex interdependent functional systems.

Luhmann's Sociology of Knowledge 卢曼的知识社会学

For Luhmann, the principal question for sociology is: What is society? This was the starting point of Luhmann's attempt to develop a system theory (1987). Sociology, as a science of society, is possible only with a clearly defined concept of society. Luhmann's system theory defines *society* as the "all encompassing social system including all other societal systems" (1997:78; translated by one of the authors). This implies that the concept of *society* is identical to the concept of a *world society;* there can be only one society. A *social system* is every system producing communication as its basic element to reproduce itself. A *societal system* is a functional system like the economy, science, and law within the all-encompassing system of society.[8]

An all-encompassing world society has no boundaries in time and space; in a sense, a world society has no "address" and no other societies in the environment. How, then, can society be observed? There is only one answer: A society can be

---

[8] After the original publication of *Social Systems* (1984/1995), Luhmann deepened and applied his approach to various functional systems within the system of society, such as the economy (Luhmann, 1988), science (Luhmann, 1990), law (Luhmann, 1993), and art (Luhmann, 1995). He attempted to demonstrate the usefulness of his general theory for the analysis of any functionally differentiated system. He also discussed issues which cut across functional systems, especially the communication of ecological risks (Luhmann, 1986/1989) and the use of the general concept of risk (Luhmann, 1991).

observed only from a perspective within society, that is, through a functional system of society. However, no functional system has the "right" perspective for the observation of society. Every perspective is a legitimate one. How can we then arrive at a single way of gaining information about the social world? In fact, there is no way to create such a simple perspective. No point of view is superior to any others. Therefore, a commonly shared perspective never can be achieved since there is no possibility of evaluating competing views. For instance, if we as sociologists want to know something about society, we are accustomed to searching for sociological knowledge. According to Luhmann's argument, it also would be possible to read a newspaper, read a book, watch television, or speak with a friend. Any of these methods is a legitimate way of obtaining information about society. Neither science, nor any other system, has a privileged position. If no functional system has a superior position from which to observe and thus to describe society as a system, we have the problem of an unlimited variety of equally valid observations of society.

Luhmann (2002) tried to work out a way in which we can nevertheless arrive at knowledge of society. Society describes itself through, for instance, legends and myths in ancient times and scientific knowledge in modern times. However, sociologists are able to observe these observations. And because sociologists are able to observe as second-order observers the first-order observations of society, they can draw conclusions about the relations between society and its semantics, that is, the self-descriptions of society. This is the key to knowledge about a society—to observe the semantics of society, that is, the "communication about the communications" constituting the system of society.

Luhmann attempted to demonstrate that the observation of society is not arbitrary because "there are structural conditions for the soundness of representation; and there are historical trends in the evolution of semantics strongly limiting the range of variation. Sociological theory is able to recognize connections of the kind of correlations between social structures and semantics" (1997:89; translated by one of the authors). Luhmann's studies reconstruct the historical usage and meaning of terms in relation to changing social structures, taking semantics as an expression of the interpretation of social structures. Thus, the proper way of observing society sociologically is an investigation of changing semantics in relation to changing social structures.[9] Luhmann did a great deal of work outlining the development, for instance, of the semantics of morality, individuality, law, knowledge (1980/1981/1989/1995), poetry (2001), and love (1982/1986). This method is part of a sociology of knowledge and can be used in the general task of the development of a theory of society.

Criticisms 相关的批判

In sum, Luhmann's theory of modern society and his concept of society are highly developed analytical tools that allow sociology to obtain a fresh perspective on current social problems in society (and in sociology). The general theory of evolution and

---

[9] This argumentation indicates an inconsistency in Luhmann's idea that I discuss in the concluding section.

differentiation, as well as Luhmann's thinking on specific systems such as science and the economy, open up new avenues of theory and research. The basic distinction between system and environment opens up the possibility of a new kind of interdisciplinary research based on the assumption that complexity is the overarching problem connecting the apparently separated realms of the natural and the human sciences (Luhmann, 1985).

There are a number of criticisms of Luhmann's system theory (Blühdorn, 2000), but we will briefly mention only four of them:

First, many theorists, including Jurgen Habermas, have argued that what Luhmann sees as a necessary evolutionary development is, in fact, regressive and unnecessary. Society may in fact be developing into a closed system of functionally differentiated realms unable to act in the name of the social whole, but this is something to resist. Theories should be developed to help counter this trend, not, as Luhmann does, to make it appear inevitable.

Second, in Luhmann's theory, differentiation is the key to describing the development of society and the increasing complexity of social systems in dealing with their environments (Rasch, 2000). But we can also find two counterprocesses in contemporary society. One is de-differentiation (Lash, 1988), that is, a process of dissolving boundaries between social systems, for example, between high culture and popular culture. The other is interpenetration (R. Münch, 1987), that is, a process of building institutions to mediate between social systems. Luhmann's system theory tends to see these processes as antievolutionary since evolution is defined as increased differentiation. It is possible that Luhmann's theory could recognize de-differentiation and interpenetration as valid sources of evolutionary variability, but this would mean dropping the single-minded focus on differentiation that has proved so theoretically rewarding.

Third, Luhmann's theory seems limited in its ability to describe relations between systems. Not all systems appear to be as closed and autonomous as Luhmann assumes. Not only do some systems appear to translate each other's codes, but they sometimes incorporate other systems as their elements. Most obvious is the way in which the social system incorporates the psychic system. The meaning of a communication within the social system is not completely determined by the social system itself. Psychic systems (individuals) protest and restrict the meanings that are assigned to a particular communication. Luhmann is correct that the meaning of a communication is not simply the intention of the individual, but certainly the intention has some, albeit a complex, effect on the social meaning. The social system is not simply closed to the psychic system. Similarly, it is possible that an apparently autonomous system such as the political system can be reduced to the status of a subsystem of another system such as the economy. In that case, the code of the political system may be simply a variation on the code of the economic system.

Finally, Luhmann's system theory assumes a variety of equally valid views of society without the possibility of giving one priority over the others. (This resembles the position taken by the postmodern social theorist Lyotard [1984].) Nevertheless, Luhmann claims that we are able to develop a secure knowledge of society observing the semantics of the self-descriptions of society. This standpoint is inconsistent since it is not possible to claim both positions at once.

In spite of these and other weaknesses, Luhmann's system theory has emerged as one of the leading social theories as we move into the twenty-first century, and it has sparked a resurgence of interest in systems theory.

Summary 总结

This chapter began with some of Walter Buckley's early thoughts on the nature of systems theory. There are various gains to be derived from a sociological system theory, including a common vocabulary across hard sciences and various social sciences, applicability at both the micro and macro levels, analysis of the social world as a whole, a focus on processes, an integrative perspective, and a dynamic orientation. A variety of principles of systems theory are discussed, including the degree to which systems are open or closed, tend to run down (entropy), tend to elaborate structures (negentropy), are characterized by feedback, and feature processes that help the system maintain itself (morphostasis) and grow (morphogenesis). Buckley applied systems theory to consciousness, interaction, and the sociocultural domain.

Today's most important systems theorist is Niklas Luhmann. Among other things, Luhmann sees systems as self-referencing, as contingent, and as always *less* complex than the environment. Systems must reduce complexity; they cannot be as complex as their environment or they would be overwhelmed and unable to function. Luhmann's most important contribution is his sense of systems as being autopoietic. That is, systems produce their own basic elements, they organize their own boundaries and the relationships among their internal structures, they are self-referential, and they are closed. It is the view of systems as autopoietic and closed to their environments that differentiates Luhmann's approach from that of earlier systems theorists. Two of the systems singled out for analysis by Luhmann are the social and the psychic systems. Social systems are plagued by the problem of double contingency—every communication must take into account how it is received, but how it is received depends on the receiver's estimation of the communicator. Because of this, communication is improbable, but social structures have developed to make communication more probable.

Luhmann is concerned with evolution involving three mechanisms—variation, selection, and stabilization. Modern society deals with the increasing complexity of its environment through a process of differentiation. Differentiation leads to increasing complexity of the system and allows for a greater ability to respond to the environment, as well as to faster evolution. Luhmann identifies four forms of differentiation—segmentary, stratificatory, center-periphery, and functional. It is the last that is the most complex form of differentiation and the one that dominates modern society. It allows for greater system flexibility, but if one functionally differentiated system fails to perform its function, the system as a whole may fail. Furthermore, it is possible that society will not have a functionally differentiated subsystem capable of handling an important problem.

Since Luhmann conceives of society as an all-encompassing system, a world-system, it can be observed only from within the system. No functional system has the right perspective; all perspectives are legitimate. Nonetheless, Luhmann seeks to accord priority to sociological knowledge by arguing that its task is the study of first-order observations of society (legends, myths, and so on).

Luhmann's theory has been subjected to a number of major criticisms, but it remains a powerful perspective in the early twenty-first century.

Symbolic Interactionism
第6章 符号互动论

Chapter Outline

Symbolic interactionism (Sandstrom and Kleinman, 2005) offers a wide range of interesting and important ideas, and a number of major thinkers have been associated with the approach, including George Herbert Mead, Charles Horton Cooley, W. I. Thomas, Herbert Blumer, and Erving Goffman.

The Major Historical Roots 主要理论渊源

We begin our discussion of symbolic interactionism with Mead (Shalin, 2000). The two most significant intellectual roots of Mead's work in particular, and of symbolic interactionism in general, are the philosophy of pragmatism (D.L. Elliot, 2007) and psychological behaviorism (Joas, 1985; Rock, 1979).

Pragmatism 实证主义

Pragmatism is a wide-ranging philosophical position[1] from which we can identify several aspects that influenced Mead's developing sociological orientation (Charon, 2000; Joas, 1993). First, to pragmatists true reality does not exist "out there" in the real world; it "is actively created as we act in and toward the world" (Hewitt, 1984:8; see also Shalin, 1986). Second, people remember and base their knowledge of the world on what has proved useful to them. They are likely to alter what no longer "works." Third, people define the social and physical "objects" that they encounter in the world according to their use for them. Finally, if we want to understand actors,

---

[1] See Joas (1996) for an effort to develop a theory of creative action based, at least in part, on pragmatism.

we must base that understanding on what people actually do in the world. Three points are critical for symbolic interactionism: (1) a focus on the interaction between the actor and the world, (2) a view of both the actor and the world as dynamic processes and not static structures, and (3) the great importance attributed to the actor's ability to interpret the social world.

The last point is most pronounced in the work of the philosophical pragmatist John Dewey (Jacobs, 2007b; Sjoberg et al., 1997). Dewey did not conceive of the mind as a thing or a structure but rather as a thinking process that involves a series of stages. These stages include defining objects in the social world, outlining possible modes of conduct, imagining the consequences of alternative courses of action, eliminating unlikely possibilities, and finally selecting the optimal mode of action (Sheldon Stryker, 1980). This focus on the thinking process was enormously influential in the development of symbolic interactionism.

In fact, J. David Lewis and Richard Smith argue that Dewey (along with William James; see Musolf, 1994) was more influential in the development of symbolic interactionism than was Mead. They go so far as to say that "Mead's work was peripheral to the mainstream of early Chicago sociology" (Lewis and Smith, 1980: xix). In making this argument, they distinguish between two branches of pragmatism—"philosophical realism" (associated with Mead) and "nominalist pragmatism" (associated with Dewey and James). In their view, symbolic interactionism was influenced more by the nominalist approach and was even inconsistent with philosophical realism. The nominalist position is that although macro-level phenomena exist, they do not have "independent and determining effects upon the consciousness of and behavior of individuals" (Lewis and Smith, 1980:24). More positively, this view "conceives of the individuals themselves as existentially free agents who accept, reject, modify, or otherwise 'define' the community's norms, roles, beliefs, and so forth, according to their own personal interests and plans of the moment" (Lewis and Smith, 1980:24). In contrast, to social realists the emphasis is on society and how it constitutes and controls individual mental processes. Rather than being free agents, actors and their cognitions and behaviors are controlled by the larger community.[2]

Given this distinction, Mead fits better into the realist camp and therefore did not mesh well with the nominalist direction taken by symbolic interactionism. The key figure in the latter development is Herbert Blumer, who, while claiming to operate with a Meadian approach, was in fact better thought of as a nominalist. Theoretically, Lewis and Smith catch the essence of their differences:

> Blumer . . . moved completely toward psychical interactionism. . . . Unlike the Meadian social behaviorist, the psychical interactionist holds that the meanings of symbols are not universal and objective; rather meanings are individual and subjective in that they are "attached" to the symbols by the receiver according to however he or she chooses to "interpret" them.
>
> (Lewis and Smith, 1980:172)

---

[2] For a criticism of the distinctions made here, see D. Miller (1982b, 1985).

Behaviorism 行为主义

Buttressing the Lewis and Smith interpretation of Mead is the fact that Mead was influenced by psychological behaviorism (Mandes, 2007, J. C. Baldwin, 1986, 1988a, 1988b), a perspective which also led him in a realist and an empirical direction. In fact, Mead called his basic concern *social behaviorism* to differentiate it from the *radical behaviorism* of John B. Watson (who was one of Mead's students).

Radical behaviorists of Watson's persuasion (K. W. Buckley, 1989) were concerned with the *observable* behaviors of individuals. Their focus was on the stimuli that elicited the responses, or behaviors, in question. They either denied or were disinclined to attribute much importance to the covert mental process that occurred between the time a stimulus was applied and the time a response was emitted. Mead recognized the importance of observable behavior, but he also felt that there were *covert* aspects of behavior that the radical behaviorists had ignored. But because he accepted the empiricism that was basic to behaviorism, Mead did not simply want to philosophize about these covert phenomena. Rather, he sought to extend the empirical science of behaviorism to them—that is, to what goes on between stimulus and response. Bernard Meltzer summarized Mead's position:

> For Mead, the unit of study is "the act," which comprises both overt and covert aspects of human action. Within the act, all the separated categories of the traditional, orthodox psychologies find a place. Attention, perception, imagination, reasoning, emotion, and so forth, are seen as parts of the act . . . the act, then, encompasses the total process involved in human activity.
>
> (Meltzer, 1964/1978:23)

Mead and the radical behaviorists also differed in their views on the relationship between human and animal behavior. Whereas radical behaviorists tended to see no difference between humans and animals, Mead argued that there was a significant, qualitative difference. The key to this difference was seen as the human possession of mental capacities that allowed people to use language between stimulus and response in order to decide how to respond.

Mead simultaneously demonstrated his debt to Watsonian behaviorism and dissociated himself from it. Mead made this clear when he said, on the one hand, that "we shall approach this latter field [social psychology] from a behavioristic point of view." On the other hand, Mead criticized Watson's position when he said, "The behaviorism which we shall make use of is *more adequate* than that of which Watson makes use" (1934/1962:2; italics added).

Charles Morris, in his introduction to *Mind, Self and Society,* enumerated three basic differences between Mead and Watson. First, Mead considered Watson's exclusive focus on behavior simplistic. In effect, he accused Watson of wrenching behavior out of its broader social context. Mead wanted to deal with behavior as a small part of the broader social world.

Second, Mead accused Watson of an unwillingness to extend behaviorism into mental processes. Watson had no sense of the actor's consciousness and mental processes, as Mead made vividly clear: "John B. Watson's attitude was that of the Queen in *Alice in Wonderland*—'Off with their heads!'—there were no such things. There was no . . . consciousness" (1934/1962:2–3). Mead contrasted his perspective with Watson's: "It is behavioristic, but unlike Watsonian behaviorism it recognizes the parts of the act which do not come to external observation" (1934/1962:8). More concretely, Mead saw his mission as extending the principles of Watsonian behaviorism to include mental processes.

Finally, because Watson rejected the mind, Mead saw him as having a passive image of the actor as puppet. Mead, on the other hand, subscribed to a much more dynamic and creative image of the actor, and it was this that made him attractive to later symbolic interactionists.

Pragmatism and behaviorism, especially in the theories of Dewey and Mead, were transmitted to many graduate students at the University of Chicago, primarily in the 1920s. These students, among them Herbert Blumer, established symbolic interactionism. Of course, other important theorists influenced these students, the most important of whom was Georg Simmel (see Chapter 1). Simmel's interest in forms of action and interaction was both compatible with and an extension of Meadian theory.

在还原论与唯社会学论之间
Between Reductionism and Sociologism

Blumer coined the term *symbolic interactionism* in 1937 and wrote several essays that were instrumental in its development (Morrione, 2007). Whereas Mead sought to differentiate the nascent symbolic interactionism from behaviorism, Blumer saw symbolic interactionism as being embattled on two fronts. First was the reductionist behaviorism that had worried Mead. To this was added the serious threat from larger-scale sociologistic theories, especially structural functionalism. To Blumer, behaviorism and structural functionalism both tended to focus on factors (for example, external stimuli and norms) that cause human behavior. As far as Blumer was concerned, both theories ignored the crucial process by which actors endow the forces acting on them and their own behaviors with meaning (Morrione, 1988).

To Blumer, behaviorists, with their emphasis on the impact of external stimuli on individual behavior, were clearly psychological reductionists. In addition to behaviorism, several other types of psychological reductionism troubled Blumer. For example, he criticized those who seek to explain human action by relying on conventional notions of the concept of "attitude" (Blumer, 1955/1969:94). In his view, most of those who use the concept think of an attitude as an "already organized tendency" within the actor; they tend to think of actions as being impelled by attitudes. In Blumer's view, this is very mechanistic thinking; what is important is not the attitude as an internalized tendency "but the defining process through which the actor comes to forge his act" (Blumer, 1955/1969:97). Blumer also singled out for criticism those who focus on conscious and unconscious motives. He was particularly irked by their view that actors are impelled by independent, mentalistic impulses over which they are supposed to have no control. Freudian theory, which sees actors as impelled by forces such as the id or libido, is an example of the kind of psychological theory to which Blumer was opposed. In short, Blumer was opposed to any psychological theory that ignores the process by which actors construct meaning—the fact that actors have selves and relate to themselves. Blumer's general criticisms were similar to

Mead's, but he extended them beyond behaviorism to include other forms of psychological reductionism as well.

Blumer also was opposed to sociologistic theories (especially structural functionalism) that view individual behavior as being determined by large-scale external forces. In this category Blumer included theories that focus on such social-structural and social-cultural factors as "'social system,' 'social structure,' 'culture,' 'status position,' 'social role,' 'custom,' 'institution,' 'collective representation,' 'social situation,' 'social norm,' and 'values'" (Blumer, 1962/1969:83). Both sociologistic theories and psychological theories ignore the importance of meaning and the social construction of reality:

> In both such typical psychological and sociological explanations the meanings of things for the human beings who are acting are either bypassed or swallowed up in the factors used to account for their behavior. If one declares that the given kinds of behavior are the result of the particular factors regarded as producing them, there is no need to concern oneself with the meaning of the things towards which human beings act.
>
> (Blumer, 1969b:3)

The Ideas of George Herbert Mead 米德的思想

Mead is the most important thinker in the history of symbolic interactionism (Chriss, 2005b; Joas, 2001), and his book *Mind, Self and Society* is the most important single work in that tradition.

The Priority of the Social 社会的优先性

In his review of *Mind, Self and Society,* Ellsworth Faris argued that "not mind and then society; but society first and then minds arising within that society . . . would probably have been [Mead's] preference" (cited in D. Miller, 1982a:2). Faris's inversion of the title of this book reflects the widely acknowledged fact, recognized by Mead himself, that society, or more broadly the social, is accorded priority in Mead's analysis.

In Mead's view, traditional social psychology began with the psychology of the individual in an effort to explain social experience; in contrast, Mead always gives priority to the social world in understanding social experience. Mead explains his focus in this way:

> We are not, in social psychology, building up the behavior of the social group in terms of the behavior of separate individuals composing it; rather, we are *starting out with a given social whole* of complex group activity, into which we analyze (as elements) the behavior of each of the separate individuals composing it. . . . We attempt, that is, to explain the conduct of the social group, rather than to account for the organized conduct of the social group in terms of the conduct of the separate individuals belonging to it. For social psychology, the *whole (society) is prior to the part (the individual),* not the part to the whole; and the part is explained in terms of the whole, not the whole in terms of the part or parts.
>
> (Mead, 1934/1962:7; italics added)

GEORGE HERBERT MEAD

A Biographical Sketch

Most of the important theorists discussed throughout this book achieved their greatest recognition in their lifetimes for their published work. George Herbert Mead, however, was at least as important, at least during his lifetime, for his teaching as for his writing. His words had a powerful impact on many people who were to become important sociologists in the twentieth century. As one of his students said, "Conversation was his best medium; writing was a poor second" (T. V. Smith, 1931:369). Let us have another of his students, himself a well-known sociologist—Leonard Cottrell—describe what Mead was like as a teacher:

> For me, the course with Professor Mead was a unique and unforgettable experience. . . . Professor Mead was a large, amiable-looking man who wore a magnificent mustache and a Vandyke beard. He characteristically had a benign, rather shy smile matched with a twinkle in his eyes as if he were enjoying a secret joke he was playing on the audience. . . .
>
> As he lectured—always without notes—Professor Mead would manipulate the piece of chalk and watch it intently. . . . When he made a particularly subtle point in his lecture he would glance up and throw a shy, almost apologetic smile over our heads—never looking directly at anyone. His lecture flowed and we soon learned that questions or comments from the class were not welcome. Indeed, when someone was bold enough to raise a question there was a murmur of disapproval from the students. They objected to any interruption of the golden flow. . . .
>
> His expectations of students were modest. He never gave exams. The main task for each of us students was to write as learned a paper as one could. These Professor Mead read with great care, and what he thought of your paper was your grade in the course. One might suppose that students would read materials for the paper rather than attend his lectures but that was not the case. Students always came. They couldn't get enough of Mead.
>
> (Cottrell, 1980:49–50)

Mead had enormous difficulty writing, and this troubled him a great deal. " 'I am vastly depressed by my inability to write what I want to' " (cited in G. Cook, 1993:xiii). However, over the years many of Mead's ideas came to be published, especially in *Mind, Self and Society* (a book based on students' notes from a course taught by Mead). This book and others of Mead's works had a

To Mead, the social whole precedes the individual mind both logically and temporally. A thinking, self-conscious individual is, as we will see later, logically powerful influence on the development of contemporary sociology, especially symbolic interactionism.

Born in South Hadley, Massachusetts, on February 27, 1863, Mead was trained mainly in philosophy and its application to social psychology. He received a bachelor's degree from Oberlin College (where his father was a professor) in 1883, and after a few years as a secondary-school teacher, surveyor for railroad companies, and private tutor, Mead began graduate study at Harvard in 1887. After a few years of study at Harvard, as well as at the universities of Leipzig and Berlin, Mead was offered an instructorship at the University of Michigan in 1891. It is interesting to note that Mead *never* received any graduate degrees. In 1894, at the invitation of John Dewey, he moved to the University of Chicago and remained there for the rest of his life.

As Mead makes clear in the following excerpt from a letter, he was heavily influenced by Dewey: " 'Mr. Dewey is a man of not only great originality and profound thought but the most appreciative thinker I ever met. I have gained more from him than from any one man I ever met' " (cited in G. Cook, 1993:32). This was especially true of Mead's early work at Chicago, and he even followed Dewey into educational theory (Dewey left Chicago in 1904). However, Mead's thinking quickly diverged from Dewey's and led him in the direction of his famous social psychological theories of mind, self, and society. He began teaching a course on social psychology in 1900. In 1916–1917 it was transformed into an advanced course (the stenographic student notes from the 1928 course became the basis of *Mind, Self and Society*) that followed a course in elementary social psychology that was taught after 1919 by Ellsworth Faris of the sociology department. It was through this course that Mead had such a powerful influence on students in sociology (as well as psychology and education).

In addition to his scholarly pursuits, Mead became involved in social reform. He believed that science could be used to deal with social problems. For example, he was heavily involved as a fund raiser and policy maker at the University of Chicago Settlement House, which had been inspired by Jane Addams's Hull House. Perhaps most importantly, he played a key role in social research conducted by the settlement house.

Although eligible for retirement in 1928, he continued to teach at the invitation of the university and in the summer of 1930 became chair of the philosophy department. Unfortunately, he became embroiled in a bitter conflict between the department and the president of the university. This led in early 1931 to a letter of resignation from Mead written from his hospital bed. He was released from the hospital in late April, but died from heart failure the following day. Of him, John Dewey said he was " 'the most original mind in philosophy in the America of the last generations' " (G. Cook, 1993:194).

impossible in Mead's theory without a prior social group. The social group comes first, and it leads to the development of self-conscious mental states.

The Act 行动

Mead considers the act to be the most "primitive unit" in his theory (1982:27). In analyzing the act, Mead comes closest to the behaviorist's approach and focuses on stimulus and response. However, even here the stimulus does not elicit an automatic, unthinking response from the human actor. As Mead says, "We conceive of the stimulus as an occasion or opportunity for the act, not as a compulsion or a mandate" (1982:28).

Mead (1938/1972) identified four basic and interrelated stages in the act (Schmitt and Schmitt, 1996); the four stages represent an organic whole (in other words, they are dialectically interrelated). Both lower animals and humans act, and Mead is interested in the similarities, and especially the differences, between the two.

Impulse 冲动

The first stage is that of the *impulse,* which involves an "immediate sensuous stimulation" and the actor's reaction to the stimulation, the need to do something about it. Hunger is a good example of an impulse. The actor (both nonhuman and human) may respond immediately and unthinkingly to the impulse, but more likely the human actor will think about the appropriate response (for example, eat now or later). In thinking about a response, the person will consider not only the immediate situation but also past experiences and anticipated future results of the act.

Hunger may come from an inner state of the actor or may be elicited by the presence of food in the environment, or, most likely, it may arise from some combination of the two. Furthermore, the hungry person must find a way of satisfying the impulse in an environment in which food may not be immediately available or plentiful. This impulse, like all others, may be related to a problem in the environment (that is, the lack of immediately available food), a problem that must be overcome by the actor. Indeed, while an impulse such as hunger may come largely from the individual (although even here hunger can be induced by an external stimulus, and there are also social definitions of when it is appropriate to be hungry), it usually is related to the existence of a problem in the environment (for example, the lack of food). Overall, the impulse, like all other elements of Mead's theory, involves both the actor and the environment.

Perception 感知

The second stage of the act is *perception,* in which the actor searches for, and reacts to, stimuli that relate to the impulse, in this case hunger as well as the various means available to satisfy it. People have the capacity to sense or perceive stimuli through hearing, smell, taste, and so on. Perception involves incoming stimuli, as well as the mental images they create. People do not simply respond immediately to external stimuli but rather think about, and assess, them through mental imagery. People are not simply subject to external stimulation; they also actively select characteristics of a stimulus and choose among sets of stimuli. That is, a stimulus may have several dimensions, and the actor is able to select among them. Furthermore, people usually are confronted with many different stimuli, and they have the capacity to choose which to attend to and which to ignore. Mead refuses to separate people from the objects that they perceive. It is the act of perceiving an object that makes it an object to a person; perception and object cannot be separated from (are dialectically related to) one another.

Manipulation 操控

The third stage is *manipulation*. Once the impulse has manifested itself and the object has been perceived, the next step is manipulating the object or, more generally, taking action with regard to it. In addition to their mental advantages, people have another advantage over lower animals. People have hands (with opposable thumbs) that allow them to manipulate objects far more subtly than can lower animals. The manipulation phase constitutes, for Mead, an important temporary pause in the process so that a response is not manifested immediately. A hungry human being sees a mushroom, but before eating it, he or she is likely to pick it up first, examine it, and perhaps check in a guidebook to see whether that particular variety is edible. The lower animal, in contrast, is likely to eat the mushroom without handling and examining it (and certainly without reading about it). The pause afforded by handling the object allows humans to contemplate various responses. In thinking about whether to eat the mushroom, both the past and the future are involved. People may think about past experiences in which they ate certain mushrooms that made them ill, and they may think about the future sickness, or even death, that might accompany eating a poisonous mushroom. The manipulation of the mushroom becomes a kind of experimental method in which the actor mentally tries out various hypotheses about what would happen if the mushroom were consumed.

Consummation 满足

On the basis of these deliberations, the actor may decide to eat the mushroom (or not), and this constitutes the last phase of the act, *consummation,* or more generally the taking of action which satisfies the original impulse. Both humans and lower animals may consume the mushroom, but the human is less likely to eat a bad mushroom because of his or her ability to manipulate the mushroom and to think (and read) about the implications of eating it. The lower animal must rely on a trial-and-error method, and this is a less-efficient technique than the capacity of humans to think through their actions.[3] Trial-and-error in this situation is quite dangerous; as a result, it seems likely that lower animals are more prone to die from consuming poisonous mushrooms than are humans.

While, for ease of discussion, the four stages of the act have been separated from one another in sequential order, the fact is that Mead sees a dialectical relationship among the four stages. John C. Baldwin expresses this idea in the following way: "Although the four parts of the act sometimes *appear* to be linked in linear order, they actually interpenetrate to form one organic process: Facets of each part are present

---

[3] For a critique of Mead's thinking on the differences between humans and lower animals, see Alger and Alger (1997).

at all times from the beginning of the act to the end, such that each part affects the other" (1986:55–56). Thus, the later stages of the act may lead to the emergence of earlier stages. For example, manipulating food may lead the individual to the impulse of hunger and the perception that the individual is hungry and that food is available to satisfy the need.

Gestures 姿态

While the act involves only one person, the *social act* involves two or more persons. The *gesture* is in Mead's view the basic mechanism in the social act and in the social process more generally. As he defines them, "gestures are movements of the first organism which act as specific stimuli calling forth the (socially) appropriate responses of the second organism" (Mead, 1934/1962:14; see also Mead, 1959:187). Both lower animals and humans are capable of gestures in the sense that the action of one individual mindlessly and automatically elicits a reaction by another individual. The following is Mead's famous example of a dog fight in terms of gestures:

> The act of each dog becomes the stimulus to the other dog for his response. . . . The very fact that the dog is ready to attack another becomes a stimulus to the other dog to change his own position or his own attitude. He has no sooner done this than the change of attitude in the second dog in turn causes the first dog to change his attitude.
>
> (Mead, 1934/1962:42–43)

Mead labels what is taking place in this situation a "conversation of gestures." One dog's gesture automatically elicits a gesture from the second; there are no thought processes taking place on the part of the dogs.

Humans sometimes engage in mindless conversations of gestures. Mead gives as examples many of the actions and reactions that take place in boxing and fencing matches, when one combatant adjusts "instinctively" to the actions of the second. Mead labels such unconscious actions "nonsignificant" gestures; what distinguishes humans is their ability to employ "significant" gestures, or those that require thought on the part of the actor before a reaction.

The vocal gesture is particularly important in the development of significant gestures. However, not all vocal gestures are significant. The bark of one dog to another is not significant; even some human vocal gestures (for example, a mindless grunt) may not be significant. However, it is the development of vocal gestures, especially in the form of language, which is the most important factor in making possible the distinctive development of human life: "The specialization of the human animal within this field of the gesture has been responsible, ultimately, for the origin and growth of present human society and knowledge, with all the control over nature and over the human environment which science makes possible" (Mead, 1934/1962:14).

This development is related to a distinctive characteristic of the vocal gesture. When we make a physical gesture, such as a facial grimace, we cannot see what we are doing (unless we happen to be looking in the mirror). In contrast, when we utter a vocal gesture, we hear ourselves just as others do. One result is that the vocal gesture can affect the speaker in much the same way that it affects the listeners. Another is that we are far better able to stop ourselves in vocal gestures than we are able to stop ourselves in physical gestures. In other words, we have far better control over vocal gestures than physical ones. This ability to control oneself and one's reactions is critical, as we will see, to the other distinctive capabilities of humans. More generally, "it has been the vocal gesture that has preeminently provided the medium of social organization in human society" (Mead, 1959:188).

Significant Symbols 表意符号

A significant symbol is a kind of gesture, one which only humans can make. Gestures become *significant symbols* when they arouse in the individual who is making them the same kind of response (it need not be identical) they are supposed to elicit from those to whom the gestures are addressed. Only when we have significant symbols can we truly have communication; communication in the full sense of the term is not possible among ants, bees, and so on. Physical gestures can be significant symbols, but as we have seen, they are not ideally suited to be significant symbols because people cannot easily see or hear their own physical gestures. Thus, it is vocal utterances that are most likely to become significant symbols, although not all vocalizations are such symbols. The set of vocal gestures most likely to become significant symbols is *language:* "a symbol which answers to a meaning in that experience of the first individual and which also calls out the meaning in the second individual. Where the gesture reaches that situation it has become what we call 'language.' It is now a significant symbol and it signifies a certain meaning" (Mead, 1934/1962:46). In a conversation of gestures, only the gestures themselves are communicated. However, with language the gestures and their meanings are communicated.

One of the things that language, or significant symbols more generally, does is call out the same response in the individual who is speaking that it does in others. The word *dog* or *cat* elicits the same mental image in the person uttering the word that it does in those to whom it is addressed. Another effect of language is that it stimulates the person speaking as it does others. The person yelling "fire" in a crowded theater is at least as motivated to leave the theater as are those to whom the shout is addressed. Thus, significant symbols allow people to be the stimulators of their own actions.

Adopting his pragmatist orientation, Mead also looks at the "functions" of gestures in general and of significant symbols in particular. The function of the gesture "is to make adjustment possible among the individuals implicated in any given social act with reference to the object or objects with which that act is concerned" (Mead, 1934/1962:46). Thus, an involuntary facial grimace may be made in order to prevent a child from going too close to the edge of a precipice and thereby prevent him or her from being in a potentially dangerous situation. While the nonsignificant gesture works, the "significant symbol affords far greater facilities for such adjustment and readjustment than does the nonsignificant gesture, because it calls out in the individual making it the same attitude toward it . . . and enables him to adjust his subsequent behavior to theirs in the light of that attitude" (Mead, 1934/1962:46). From a pragmatic point of view, a significant symbol works better in the social world than does a nonsignificant gesture. In other words, in communicating our displeasure to others, an angry verbal rebuke works far better than does contorted body language. The individual who is manifesting displeasure is not usually conscious of body language and therefore is unlikely to be able to adjust later actions consciously in light of how the other person reacts to the body language. In contrast, a speaker is conscious of uttering an angry rebuke and reacts to it in much the same way (and at about the same time) as the person to whom it is aimed reacts. Thus, the speaker can think about how the other person might react and can prepare his or her reaction to that reaction.

Of crucial importance in Mead's theory is another function of significant symbols—that they make the mind, mental processes, and so on, possible. It is only through significant symbols, especially language, that human *thinking* is possible (lower animals cannot think, in Mead's terms). Mead defines *thinking* as "simply an internalized or implicit conversation of the individual with himself by means of such gestures" (1934/1962:47). Even more strongly, Mead argues: "Thinking is the same as talking to other people" (1982:155). In other words, thinking involves talking to oneself. Thus, we can see clearly here how Mead defines thinking in behaviorist terms. Conversations involve behavior (talking), and that behavior also occurs within the individual; when it does, thinking is taking place. This is not a mentalistic definition of thinking; it is decidedly behavioristic.

Significant symbols also make possible *symbolic interaction*. That is, people can interact with one another not just through gestures but also through significant symbols. This ability, of course, makes a world of difference and makes possible much more complex interaction patterns and forms of social organization than would be possible through gestures alone.

The significant symbol obviously plays a central role in Mead's thinking. In fact, David Miller (1982a:10–11) accords the significant symbol *the* central role in Mead's theory.

Mind 心灵

The mind, which is defined by Mead as a process and not a thing, as an inner conversation with one's self, is not found within the individual; it is not intracranial but is a social phenomenon (Franks, 2007). It arises and develops within the social process and is an integral part of that process. The social process precedes the mind; it is not, as many believe, a product of the mind. Thus, the mind, too, is defined functionally rather than substantively. Given these similarities to ideas such as consciousness, is there anything distinctive about the mind? We already have seen that humans have the peculiar capacity to call out in themselves the response they are seeking to elicit from others. A distinctive characteristic of the mind is the ability of the individual "to call out in himself not simply a single response of the other but the response, so to speak, of the community as a whole. That is what gives to an individual what we term 'mind.' To do anything now means a certain organized response; and if one has in himself that response, he has what we term 'mind'" (Mead, 1934/1962:267). Thus, the mind can be distinguished from other like-sounding concepts in Mead's work by its ability to respond to the overall community and put forth an organized response.

Mead also looks at the mind in another, pragmatic way. That is, the mind involves thought processes oriented toward problem solving. The real world is rife with problems, and it is the function of the mind to try to solve those problems and permit people to operate more effectively in the world.

Self 自我

Much of Mead's thinking in general, and especially on the mind, involves his ideas on the critically important concept of the *self* (Schwalbe, 2005), basically the ability to take oneself as an object; the self is the peculiar ability to be both subject and object. As is true of all Mead's major concepts, the self presupposes a social process: communication among humans. Lower animals do not have selves, nor do human infants at birth. The self arises with development and through social activity and social relationships. To Mead, it is impossible to imagine a self arising in the absence of social experiences. However, once a self has developed, it is possible for it to continue to exist without social contact. Thus, Robinson Crusoe developed a self while he was in civilization, and he continued to have it when he was living alone on what he thought for a while was a deserted island. In other words, he continued to have the ability to take himself as an object. Once a self is developed, people usually, but not always, manifest it. For example, the self is not involved in habitual actions or in immediate physiological experiences of pleasure or pain.

The self is dialectically related to the mind. That is, on the one hand, Mead argues that the body is not a self and becomes a self only when a mind has developed. On the other hand, the self, along with its reflexiveness, is essential to the development of the mind. Of course, it is impossible to separate mind and self, because the self is a mental process. However, even though we may think of it as a mental process, the self is a social process. In his discussion of the self, as we have seen in regard to all other mental phenomena, Mead resists the idea of lodging it in consciousness and instead embeds it in social experience and social processes. In this way, Mead seeks to give a behavioristic sense of the self: "But it is where one does respond to that which he addresses to another and where that response of his own becomes a part of his conduct, where he not only hears himself but responds to himself, talks and replies to himself as truly as the other person replies to him, that we have *behavior* in which the individuals become objects to themselves" (1934/1962:139; italics added). The self, then, is simply another aspect of the overall social process of which the individual is a part.

The general mechanism for the development of the self is reflexivity, or the ability to put ourselves unconsciously into others' places and to act as they act. As a result, people are able to examine themselves as others would examine them. As Mead says:

> It is by means of reflexiveness—the turning-back of the experience of the individual upon himself—that the whole social process is thus brought into the experience of the individuals involved in it; it is by such means, which enable the individual to take the attitude of the other toward himself, that the individual is able consciously to adjust himself to that process, and to modify the resultant process in any given social act in terms of his adjustment to it.
>
> (Mead, 1934/1962:134)

The self also allows people to take part in their conversations with others. That is, one is aware of what one is saying and as a result is able to monitor what is being said and to determine what is going to be said next.

In order to have selves, individuals must be able to get "outside themselves" so that they can evaluate themselves, so that they can become objects to themselves. To do this, people basically put themselves in the same experiential field as they put everyone else. Everyone is an important part of that experiential situation, and people must take themselves into account if they are to be able to act rationally in a given situation. Having done this, they seek to examine themselves impersonally, objectively, and without emotion.

However, people cannot experience themselves directly. They can do so only indirectly by putting themselves in the position of others and viewing themselves from that standpoint. The standpoint from which one views one's self can be that of a particular individual or that of the social group as a whole. As Mead puts it, most generally, "It is only by taking the roles of others that we have been able to come back to ourselves" (1959:184–185).

Child Development 儿童发展

Mead is very interested in the genesis of the self. He sees the conversation of gestures as the background for the self, but it does not involve a self, since in such a conversation the people are not taking themselves as objects. Mead traces the genesis of the self through two stages[4] in childhood development.

Play Stage   The first stage is the *play stage;* it is during this stage that children learn to take the attitude of particular others to themselves (Vail, 2007b). While lower animals also play, only human beings "play at being someone else" (Aboulafia, 1986:9). Mead gives the example of a child playing (American) "Indian": "This means that the child has a certain set of stimuli which call out in itself the responses they would call out in others, and which answer to an Indian" (Mead, 1934/1962:150). As a result of such play, the child learns to become both subject and object and begins to become able to build a self. However, it is a limited self because the child can take only the roles of distinct and separate others. Children may play at being "mommy" and "daddy" and in the process develop the ability to evaluate themselves as their parents, and other specific individuals, do. However, they lack a more general and organized sense of themselves.

Game Stage   It is the next stage, the *game stage,* that is required if a person is to develop a self in the full sense of the term (Vail, 2007c). Whereas in the play stage the child takes the role of discrete others, in the game stage the child must take the role of everyone else involved in the game. Furthermore, these different roles must

---

[4] A first, preparatory stage involving mimicry is implied (Vail, 2007a) in Mead's work.

have a definite relationship to one another. In illustrating the game stage, Mead gives his famous example of a baseball (or, as he calls it, "ball nine") game:

> But in a game where a number of individuals are involved, then the child taking one role must be ready to take the role of everyone else. If he gets in a ball nine he must have the responses of each position involved in his own position. He must know what everyone else is going to do in order to carry out his own play. He has to take all of these roles. They do not all have to be present in consciousness at the same time, but at some moments he has to have three or four individuals present in his own attitude, such as the one who is going to throw the ball, the one who is going to catch it, and so on. These responses must be, in some degree, present in his own make-up. In the game, then, there is a set of responses of such others so organized that the attitude of one calls out the appropriate attitudes of the other.
>
> (Mead, 1934/1962:151)

In the play stage, children are not organized wholes because they play at a series of discrete roles. As a result, in Mead's view they lack definite personalities. However, in the game stage,[5] such organization begins and a definite personality starts to emerge. Children begin to become able to function in organized groups and, most important, to determine what they will do within a specific group.

Generalized Other 概括化他人

The game stage yields one of Mead's (1959:87) best-known concepts, the *generalized other* (Vail, 2007a). The generalized other is the attitude of the entire community or, in the example of the baseball game, the attitude of the entire team. The ability to take the role of the generalized other is essential to the self: "Only in so far as he takes the attitudes of the organized social group to which he belongs toward the organized, co-operative social activity or set of such activities in which that group is engaged, does he develop a complete self" (Mead, 1934/1962:155). It is also crucial that people be able to evaluate themselves from the point of view of the generalized other and not merely from the viewpoint of discrete others. Taking the role of the generalized other, rather than that of discrete others, allows for the possibility of abstract thinking and objectivity (Mead, 1959:190). Here is the way Mead describes the full development of the self:

> So the self reaches its full development by organizing these individual attitudes of others into the organized social or group attitudes, and by thus becoming an individual reflection of the general systematic pattern of social or group behavior in which it and others are involved—a pattern which enters as a whole into the individual's experience in terms of these organized group attitudes which, through the mechanism of the central nervous system, he takes toward himself, just as he takes the individual attitudes of others.
>
> (Mead, 1934/1962:158)

In other words, to have a self, one must be a member of a community and be directed by the attitudes common to the community. While play requires only pieces of selves, the game requires a coherent self.

---

[5] Although Mead uses the term *games,* it is clear, as Aboulafia (1986:198) points out, that he means any system of organized responses (for example, the family).

Not only is taking the role of the generalized other essential to the self, it also is crucial for the development of organized group activities. A group requires that individuals direct their activities in accord with the attitudes of the generalized other. The generalized other also represents Mead's familiar propensity to give priority to the social, since it is through the generalized other that the group influences the behavior of individuals.

Mead also looks at the self from a pragmatic point of view. At the individual level, the self allows the individual to be a more efficient member of the larger society. Because of the self, people are more likely to do what is expected of them in a given situation. Since people often try to live up to group expectations, they are more likely to avoid the inefficiencies that come from failing to do what the group expects. Furthermore, the self allows for greater coordination in society as a whole. Because individuals can be counted on to do what is expected of them, the group can operate more effectively.

The preceding, as well as the overall discussion of the self, might lead us to believe that Mead's actors are little more than conformists and that there is little individuality, since everyone is busy conforming to the expectations of the generalized other. But Mead is clear that each self is different from all the others. Selves share a common structure, but each self receives unique biographical articulation. In addition, it is clear that there is not simply one grand generalized other but that there are many generalized others in society, because there are many groups in society. People therefore have multiple generalized others and, as a result, multiple selves. Each person's unique set of selves makes him or her different from everyone else. Furthermore, people need not accept the community as it is; they can reform things and seek to make them better. We are able to change the community because of our capacity to think. But Mead is forced to put this issue of individual creativity in familiar, behavioristic terms: "The only way in which we can react against the disapproval of the entire community is by setting up a higher sort of community which in a certain sense out-votes the one we find . . . he may stand out by himself over against it. But to do that he has to comprehend the voices of the past and of the future. That is the only way the self can get a voice which is more than the voice of the community" (1934/1962:167–168). In other words, to stand up to the generalized other, the individual must construct a still larger generalized other, composed not only from the present but also from the past and the future, and then respond to it.

Mead identifies two aspects, or phases, of the self, which he labels the "I" and the "me" (for a critique of this distinction, see Athens, 1995). As Mead puts it, "The self is essentially a social process going on with these two distinguishable phases" (1934/1962:178). It is important to bear in mind that the "I" and the "me" are processes within the larger process of the self; they are not "things."

"I" and "Me" "主我"与"客我"

The "I" is the immediate response of an individual to others. It is the incalculable, unpredictable, and creative aspect of the self. People do not know in advance what the action of the "I" will be: "But what that response will be he does not know and nobody else knows. Perhaps he will make a brilliant play or an error. The response to that situation as it appears in his immediate experience is uncertain" (Mead, 1934/1962:175). We are never totally aware of the "I," and through it we surprise ourselves with our actions. We know the "I" only after the act has been carried out. Thus, we know the "I" only in our memories. Mead lays great stress on the "I" for four reasons. First, it is a key source of novelty in the social process. Second, Mead believes that it is in the "I" that our most important values are located. Third, the "I" constitutes something that we all seek—the realization of the self. It is the "I" that permits us to develop a "definite personality." Finally, Mead sees an evolutionary process in history in which people in primitive societies are dominated more by the "me" while in modern societies there is a greater component of the "I."

The "I" gives Mead's theoretical system some much-needed dynamism and creativity. Without it, Mead's actors would be totally dominated by external and internal controls. With it, Mead is able to deal with the changes brought about not only by the great figures in history (for example, Einstein) but also by individuals on a day-to-day basis. It is the "I" that makes these changes possible. Since every personality is a mix of "I" and "me," the great historical figures are seen as having a larger proportion of "I" than most others have. But in day-to-day situations, anyone's "I" may assert itself and lead to change in the social situation. Uniqueness is also brought into Mead's system through the biographical articulation of each individual's "I" and "me." That is, the specific exigencies of each person's life give him or her a unique mix of "I" and "me."

The "I" reacts against the "me," which is the "organized set of attitudes of others which one himself assumes" (Mead, 1934/1962:175). In other words, the "me" is the adoption of the generalized other. In contrast to the "I," people are conscious of the "me"; the "me" involves conscious responsibility. As Mead says, "The 'me' is a conventional, habitual individual" (1934/1962:197). Conformists are dominated by the "me," although everyone—whatever his or her degree of conformity—has, and must have, a substantial "me." It is through the "me" that society dominates the individual. Indeed, Mead defines the idea of *social control* as the dominance of the expression of the "me" over the expression of the "I." Later in *Mind, Self and Society,* Mead elaborates on his ideas on social control:

> Social control, as operating in terms of self-criticism, exerts itself so intimately and extensively over individual behavior or conduct, serving to integrate the individual and his actions with reference to the organized social process of experience and behavior in which he is implicated. . . . Social control over individual behavior or conduct operates by virtue of the social origin and basis of such [self-] criticism. That is to say, self-criticism is essentially social criticism, and behavior controlled socially. Hence social control, so far from tending to crush out the human individual or to obliterate his self-conscious individuality, is, on the contrary, actually constitutive of and inextricably associated with that individuality.
>
> (Mead, 1934/1962:255)

Mead also looks at the "I" and the "me" in pragmatic terms. The "me" allows the individual to live comfortably in the social world, while the "I" makes change in society possible. Society gets enough conformity to allow it to function, and it gets a steady infusion of new developments to prevent it from stagnating. The "I" and the "me" are thus part of the whole social process and allow both individuals and society to function more effectively.

Society 社会

At the most general level, Mead uses the term *society* to mean the ongoing social process that precedes both the mind and the self. Given its importance in shaping the mind and self, society is clearly of central importance to Mead. At another level, society to Mead represents the organized set of responses that are taken over by the individual in the form of the "me." Thus, in this sense individuals carry society around with them, giving them the ability, through self-criticism, to control themselves. Mead also deals with the evolution of society. But Mead has relatively little to say explicitly about society, in spite of its centrality in his theoretical system. His most important contributions lie in his thoughts on mind and self. Even John C. Baldwin, who sees a much more societal (macro) component in Mead's thinking, is forced to admit: "The macro components of Mead's theoretical system are not as well developed as the micro" (1986:123).

At a more specific societal level Mead does have a number of things to say about social *institutions.* Mead broadly defines an *institution* as the "common response in the community" or "the life habits of the community" (1934/1962:261, 264; see also Mead, 1936:376). More specifically, he says that "the whole community acts toward the individual under certain circumstances in an identical way . . . there is an identical response on the part of the whole community under these conditions. We call that the formation of the institution" (Mead, 1934/1962:167). We carry this organized set of attitudes around with us, and they serve to control our actions, largely through the "me."

Education is the process by which the common habits of the community (the institution) are "internalized" in the actor. This is an essential process, since, in Mead's view, people neither have selves nor are genuine members of the community until they can respond to themselves as the larger community does. To do this, people must have internalized the common attitudes of the community.

But again Mead is careful to point out that institutions need not destroy individuality or stifle creativity. Mead recognizes that there are "oppressive, stereotyped, and ultra-conservative social institutions—like the church—which by their more or less rigid and inflexible unprogressiveness crush or blot out individuality" (1934/1962:262). However, he is quick to add: "There is no necessary or inevitable reason why social institutions should be oppressive or rigidly conservative, or why they should not rather be, as many are, flexible and progressive, fostering individuality rather than discouraging it" (Mead, 1934/1962:262). To Mead, institutions should define what people ought to do only in a very broad and general sense and should allow plenty of room for individuality and creativity. Mead here demonstrates a very modern conception of social institutions as both constraining individuals *and* enabling them to be creative individuals (see Giddens, 1984). Mead was distinct from the other classical theorists in emphasizing the enabling character of society—arguably disregarding society's constraining power (Athens, 2002).

What Mead lacks in his analysis of society in general, and institutions in particular,[6] is a true macro sense of them in the way that theorists such as Marx, Weber, and Durkheim dealt with this level of analysis. This is true in spite of the fact that Mead does have a notion of *emergence* (Sawyer, 2007, 2005) in the sense that the whole is seen as more than the sum of its parts. More specifically, "Emergence involves a reorganization, but the reorganization brings in something that was not there before. The first time oxygen and hydrogen come together, water appears. Now water is a combination of hydrogen and oxygen, but water was not there before in the separate elements" (Mead, 1934/1962:198). However, Mead is much more prone to apply the idea of emergence to consciousness than to apply it to the larger society. That is, mind and self are seen as emergent from the social process. Moreover, Mead is inclined to use the term *emergence* merely to mean the coming into existence of something new or novel (D. Miller, 1973:41).

符号互动论：基本准则

Symbolic Interactionism: The Basic Principles

The heart of this chapter is a discussion of the basic principles of symbolic interaction theory. Although I try to characterize the theory in general terms, this is not easy to do, for as Paul Rock says, it has a "deliberately constructed vagueness" and a "resistance to systematisation" (1979:18–19). There are significant differences within symbolic interactionism, some of which are discussed as I proceed.

Some symbolic interactionists (Blumer, 1969a; Manis and Meltzer, 1978; A. Rose, 1962; Snow, 2001) have tried to enumerate the basic principles of the theory. These principles include the following:

1. Human beings, unlike lower animals, are endowed with the capacity for thought.
2. The capacity for thought is shaped by social interaction.
3. In social interaction people learn the meanings and the symbols that allow them to exercise their distinctively human capacity for thought.
4. Meanings and symbols allow people to carry on distinctively human action and interaction.
5. People are able to modify or alter the meanings and symbols that they use in action and interaction on the basis of their interpretation of the situation.
6. People are able to make these modifications and alterations because, in part, of their ability to interact with themselves, which allows them to examine possible courses of action, assess their relative advantages and disadvantages, and then choose one.
7. The intertwined patterns of action and interaction make up groups and societies.

---

[6] There are at least two places where Mead offers a more macro sense of society. At one point he defines *social institutions* as "organized forms of group or social activity" (Mead, 1934/1962:261). Earlier, in an argument reminiscent of Comte, he offers a view of the family as the fundamental unit within society and as the base of such larger units as the clan and the state.

Capacity for Thought 思考的能力

The crucial assumption that human beings possess the ability to think differentiates symbolic interactionism from its behaviorist roots. This assumption also provides the basis for the entire theoretical orientation of symbolic interactionism. Bernard Meltzer, James Petras, and Larry Reynolds stated that the assumption of the human capacity for thought is one of the major contributions of early symbolic interactionists, such as James, Dewey, Thomas, Cooley, and of course Mead: "Individuals in human society were not seen as units that are motivated by external or internal forces beyond their control, or within the confines of a more or less fixed structure. Rather, they were viewed as reflective or interacting units which comprise the societal entity" (1975:42). The ability to think enables people to act reflectively rather than just behave unreflectively. People must often construct and guide what they do, rather than just release it.

The ability to think is embedded in the mind, but the symbolic interactionists have a somewhat unusual conception of the mind as originating in the socialization of consciousness. They distinguish it from the physiological brain. People must have brains in order to develop minds, but a brain does not inevitably produce a mind, as is clear in the case of lower animals (Troyer, 1946). Also, symbolic interactionists do not conceive of the mind as a thing, a physical structure, but rather as a continuing process. It is a process that is itself part of the larger process of stimulus and response. The mind is related to virtually every other aspect of symbolic interactionism, including socialization, meanings, symbols, the self, interaction, and even society.

Thinking and Interaction 思考与互动

People possess only a general capacity for thought. This capacity must be shaped and refined in the process of social interaction. Such a view leads the symbolic interactionist to focus on a specific form of social interaction—*socialization*. The human ability to think is developed early in childhood socialization and is refined during adult socialization. Symbolic interactionists have a view of the socialization process that is different from that of most other sociologists. To symbolic interactionists, conventional sociologists are likely to see socialization as simply a process by which people learn the things that they need to survive in society (for instance, culture, role expectations). To the symbolic interactionists, socialization is a more dynamic process that allows people to develop the ability to think, to develop in distinctively human ways. Furthermore, socialization is not simply a one-way process in which the actor receives information, but is a dynamic process in which the actor shapes and adapts the information to his or her own needs (Manis and Meltzer, 1978:6).

Symbolic interactionists are, of course, interested not simply in socialization but in interaction in general, which is of "vital importance in its own right" (Blumer, 1969b:8). *Interaction* is the process in which the ability to think is both developed and expressed. All types of interaction, not just interaction during socialization, refine our ability to think. Beyond that, thinking shapes the interaction process. In most interaction, actors must take account of others and decide if and how to fit their activities to others. However, not all interaction involves thinking. The differentiation made by Blumer (following Mead) between two basic forms of social interaction is relevant here. The first, nonsymbolic interaction—Mead's conversation of gestures—does not involve thinking. The second, symbolic interaction, does require mental processes.

The importance of thinking to symbolic interactionists is reflected in their views on *objects*. Blumer differentiates among three types of objects: *physical objects,* such as a chair or a tree; *social objects,* such as a student or a mother; and *abstract objects,* such as an idea or a moral principle. Objects are seen simply as things "out there" in the real world; what is of greatest significance is the way they are defined by actors. The latter leads to the relativistic view that different objects have different meanings for different individuals: "A tree will be a different object to a botanist, a lumberman, a poet, and a home gardener" (Blumer, 1969b:11).

Individuals learn the meanings of objects during the socialization process. Most of us learn a common set of meanings, but in many cases, as with the tree mentioned above, we have different definitions of the same objects. Although this definitional view can be taken to an extreme, symbolic interactionists need not deny the existence of objects in the real world. All they need do is point out the crucial nature of the definition of those objects as well as the possibility that actors may have different definitions of the same object. As Herbert Blumer said: "The nature of an object . . . consists of the meaning that it has for the person for whom it is an object" (1969b:11).

Learning Meanings and Symbols 学习意义和符号

Symbolic interactionists, following Mead, tend to accord causal significance to social interaction. Thus, meaning stems not from solitary mental processes but from interaction. This focus derives from Mead's pragmatism: he focused on human action and interaction, not on isolated mental processes. Symbolic interactionists have in general continued in this direction. Among other things, the central concern is not how people mentally create meanings and symbols but how they learn them during interaction in general and socialization in particular.

People learn symbols as well as meanings in social interaction. Whereas people respond to signs unthinkingly, they respond to symbols in a thoughtful manner. Signs stand for themselves (for example, the gestures of angry dogs or water to a person dying of thirst). "*Symbols are social objects used to represent* (or 'stand in for,' 'take the place of') whatever people agree they shall represent" (Charon, 1998:47). Not all social objects stand for other things, but those that do are symbols. Words, physical artifacts, and physical actions (for example, the word *boat,* a cross or a Star of David, and a clenched fist) all can be symbols. People often use symbols to communicate something about themselves: they drive Rolls-Royces, for instance, to communicate a certain style of life.

Symbolic interactionists conceive of language as a vast system of symbols. Words are symbols because they are used to stand for things. Words make all other symbols possible. Acts, objects, and other words exist and have meaning only because they have been and can be described through the use of words.

Symbols are crucial in allowing people to act in distinctively human ways. Because of the symbol, the human being "does not respond passively to a reality that imposes itself but actively creates and re-creates the world acted in" (Charon, 1998:69). In addition to this general utility, symbols in general and language in particular have a number of specific functions for the actor.

First, symbols enable people to deal with the material and social world by allowing them to name, categorize, and remember the objects they encounter there. In this way, people are able to order a world that otherwise would be confusing. Language allows people to name, categorize, and especially remember much more efficiently than they could with other kinds of symbols, such as pictorial images.

Second, symbols improve people's ability to perceive the environment. Instead of being flooded by a mass of indistinguishable stimuli, the actor can be alerted to some parts of the environment rather than others.

Third, symbols improve the ability to think. Although a set of pictorial symbols would allow a limited ability to think, language greatly expands this ability. Thinking, in these terms, can be conceived of as symbolic interaction with one's self.

Fourth, symbols greatly increase the ability to solve various problems. Lower animals must use trial-and-error, but human beings can think through symbolically a variety of alternative actions before actually taking one. This ability reduces the chance of making costly mistakes.

Fifth, the use of symbols allows actors to transcend time, space, and even their own persons. Through the use of symbols, actors can imagine what it was like to live in the past or what it might be like to live in the future. In addition, actors can transcend their own persons symbolically and imagine what the world is like from another person's point of view. This is the well-known symbolic-interactionist concept of *taking the role of the other* (D. Miller, 1981).

Sixth, symbols allow us to imagine a metaphysical reality, such as heaven or hell. Seventh, and most generally, symbols allow people to avoid being enslaved by their environment. They can be active rather than passive—that is, self-directed in what they do.

Action and Interaction 行动与互动

Symbolic interactionists' primary concern is with the impact of meanings and symbols on human action and interaction. Here it is useful to employ Mead's differentiation between covert and overt behavior. *Covert behavior* is the thinking process, involving symbols and meanings. *Overt behavior* is the actual behavior performed by an actor. Some overt behavior does not involve covert behavior (habitual behavior or mindless responses to external stimuli). However, most human action involves both kinds. Covert behavior is of greatest concern to symbolic interactionists, whereas overt behavior is of greatest concern to exchange theorists or to traditional behaviorists in general.

Meanings and symbols give human social action (which involves a single actor) and social interaction (which involves two or more actors engaged in mutual social action) distinctive characteristics. Social action is that in which the individuals are acting with others in mind. In other words, in undertaking an action, people simultaneously try to gauge its impact on the other actors involved. Although they often engage in mindless, habitual behavior, people have the capacity to engage in social action.

In the process of social interaction, people symbolically communicate meanings to the others involved. The others interpret those symbols and orient their responding action on the basis of their interpretation. In other words, in social interaction, actors engage in a process of mutual influence. Christopher (2001) refers to this dynamic social interaction as a "dance" that partners engage in.

Making Choices 做选择

Partly because of the ability to handle meanings and symbols, people, unlike lower animals, can make choices in the actions in which they engage. People need not accept the meanings and symbols that are imposed on them from without. On the basis of their own interpretation of the situation, "humans are capable of forming new meanings and new lines of meaning" (Manis and Meltzer, 1978:7). Thus, to the symbolic interactionist, actors have at least some autonomy. They are not simply constrained or determined; they are capable of making unique and independent choices. Furthermore, they are able to develop a life that has a unique style (Perinbanayagam, 1985:53).

W. I. Thomas and Dorothy Thomas were instrumental in underscoring this creative capacity in their concept of *definition of the situation:* "If men define situations as real, they are real in their consequences" (Thomas and Thomas, 1928:572). The Thomases knew that most of our definitions of situations have been provided for us by society. In fact, they emphasized this point, identifying especially the family and the community as sources of our social definitions. However, the Thomases' position is distinctive for its emphasis on the possibility of "spontaneous" individual definitions of situations, which allow people to alter and modify meanings and symbols.

This ability of actors to make a difference is reflected in an essay by Gary Fine and Sherryl Kleinman (1983) in which they look at the phenomenon of a "social network." Instead of viewing a social network as an unconscious and/or constraining social structure, Fine and Kleinman see a network as a set of social relationships that people endow with meaning and use for personal and/or collective purposes.

尔文·戈夫曼的自我概念及其著作
The Self and the Work of Erving Goffman

The self is a concept of enormous importance to symbolic interactionists (Bruder, 1998). In fact, Rock argues that the self "constitutes the very hub of the interactionists' intellectual scheme. All other sociological processes and events revolve around that hub, taking from it their analytic meaning and organization" (1979:102). In attempting to understand this concept beyond its initial Meadian formulation, we must first understand the idea of the *looking-glass self* developed by Charles Horton Cooley

ERVING GOFFMAN

A Biographical Sketch

Erving Goffman died in 1982 at the peak of his fame. He had long been regarded as a "cult" figure in sociological theory. That status was achieved in spite of the fact that he had been a professor in the prestigious sociology department at the University of California, Berkeley, and later held an endowed chair at the Ivy League's University of Pennsylvania (G. W. H. Smith, 2007; P. Manning, 2005b).

By the 1980s he had emerged as a centrally important theorist. In fact, he had been elected president of the American Sociological Association in the year he died but was unable to give his presidential address because of advanced illness. Given Goffman's maverick status, Randall Collins says of his address: "Everyone wondered what he would do for his Presidential address: a straight, traditional presentation seemed unthinkable for Goffman with his reputation as an iconoclast . . . we got a far more dramatic message: Presidential address cancelled, Goffman dying. It was an appropriately Goffmanian way to go out" (1986b:112).

Goffman was born in Alberta, Canada, on June 11, 1922 (S. Williams, 1986). He earned his advanced degrees from the University of Chicago and is most often thought of as a member of the Chicago school and as a symbolic interactionist. However, when he was asked shortly before his death whether he was a symbolic interactionist, he replied that the label was too vague to allow him to put himself in that category (Manning, 1992). In fact, it is hard to squeeze his work into any single category. In creating his theoretical perspective, Goffman drew on many sources and created a distinctive orientation.

(Franks and Gecas, 1992). Cooley defined this concept as

> a somewhat definite imagination of how one's self—that is, any idea he appropriates—appears in a particular mind, and the kind of self-feeling one has is determined by the attitude toward this attributed to that other mind. . . . So in imagination we perceive in another's mind some thought of our appearance, manners, aims, deeds, character, friends, and so on, and are variously affected by it.
>
> (Cooley, 1902/1964:169)

The idea of a looking-glass self can be broken down into three components. First, we imagine how we appear to others. Second, we imagine what their judgment of that appearance must be. Third, we develop some self-feeling, such as pride or mortification, as a result of our imagining others' judgments.

Cooley's concept of the looking-glass self and Mead's concept of the self were important in the development of the modern symbolic-interactionist conception of the self. Blumer defined the *self* in extremely simple terms: "Nothing

Collins (1986b; Williams, 1986) links Goffman more to social anthropology than to symbolic interactionism. As an undergraduate at the University of Toronto, Goffman had studied with an anthropologist, and at Chicago "his main contacts were not with Symbolic Interactionists, but with W. Lloyd Warner [an anthropologist]" (Collins, 1986b:109). In Collins's view, an examination of the citations in Goffman's early work indicates that he was influenced by social anthropologists and rarely cited symbolic interactionists, and when he did, it was to be critical of them. However, Goffman was influenced by the descriptive studies produced at Chicago and integrated their outlook with that of social anthropology to produce his distinctive perspective. Thus, whereas a symbolic interactionist would look at how people create or negotiate their self-images, Goffman was concerned with how "society . . . forces people to present a certain image of themselves . . . because it forces us to switch back and forth between many complicated roles, is also making us always somewhat untruthful, inconsistent, and dishonorable" (Collins, 1986a:107).

Despite the distinctiveness of his perspective, Goffman had a powerful influence on symbolic interactionism. In addition, it could be argued that he had a hand in shaping another sociology of everyday life, ethnomethodology. In fact, Collins sees Goffman as a key figure in the formation not only of ethnomethodology, but of conversation analysis as well: "It was Goffman who pioneered the close empirical study of everyday life, although he had done it with his bare eyes, before the days of tape recorders and video recorders" (1986b:111). (See Chapter 7 for a discussion of the relationship between ethnomethodology and conversation analysis.) In fact, a number of important ethnomethodologists (Sacks, Schegloff) studied with Goffman at Berkeley and not with the founder of ethnomethodology, Harold Garfinkel.

Given their influence on symbolic interactionism, structuralism, and ethnomethodology, Goffman's theories are likely to be influential for a long time.

esoteric is meant by this expression [self]. It means merely that a human being can be an object of his own action . . . he acts toward himself and guides himself in his actions toward others on the basis of the kind of object he is to himself" (1969b:12). The self is a process, not a thing (Perinbanayagam, 1985). As Blumer made clear, the self helps allow human beings to act rather than simply respond to external stimuli:

> The process [interpretation] has two distinct steps. First, the actor indicates to himself the things toward which he is acting; he has to point out in himself the things that have meaning. . . . This interaction with himself is something other than an interplay of psychological elements; it is an instance of the person engaging in a process of communicating with himself. . . . Second, by virtue of this process of communicating with himself, interpretation becomes a matter of handling meanings. The actor selects, checks, suspends, regroups, and transforms the meanings in the light of the situation in which he is placed and the direction of his action.
>
> (Blumer, 1969b:5)

Although this description of interpretation underscores the part played by the self in the process of choosing how to act, Blumer has really not gone much beyond the early formulations of Cooley and Mead. However, other modern thinkers and researchers have refined the concept of the self.

The Work of Erving Goffman 戈夫曼的理论思想

The most important work on the self in symbolic interactionism is *Presentation of Self in Everyday Life* (1959) by Erving Goffman (Dowd, 1996; Schwalbe, 1993; Travers, 1992; Tseelon, 1992). Goffman's conception of the self is deeply indebted to Mead's ideas, in particular his discussion of the tension between the "I," the spontaneous self, and the "me," social constraints within the self. This tension is mirrored in Goffman's work on what he called the "crucial discrepancy between our all-too-human selves and our socialized selves" (1959:56). The tension results from the difference between what people expect us to do and what we may want to do spontaneously. We are confronted with the demand to do what is expected of us; moreover, we are not supposed to waver. As Goffman put it, "We must not be subject to ups and downs" (1959:56). In order to maintain a stable self-image, people perform for their social audiences. As a result of this interest in performance, Goffman focused on *dramaturgy,* or a view of social life as a series of dramatic performances akin to those performed on the stage.

Dramaturgy   Goffman's sense of the self was shaped by his dramaturgical approach. To Goffman (as to Mead and most other symbolic interactionists), the self is

> not an organic thing that has a specific location. . . . In analyzing the self then we are drawn from its possessor, from the person who will profit or lose most by it, for he and his body merely provide the peg on which something of collaborative manufacture will be hung for a time. . . . The means of producing and maintaining selves do not reside inside the peg.
>
> (Goffman, 1959:252–253)

Goffman perceived the self not as a possession of the actor but rather as the product of the dramatic interaction between actor and audience. The self "is a dramatic effect arising . . . from a scene that is presented" (Goffman, 1959:253). Because the self is a product of dramatic interaction, it is vulnerable to disruption during the performance (Misztal, 2001). Goffman's dramaturgy is concerned with the processes by which such disturbances are prevented or dealt with. Although the bulk of his discussion focuses on these dramaturgical contingencies, Goffman pointed out that most performances are successful. The result is that in ordinary circumstances a firm self is accorded to performers, and it "appears" to emanate from the performer.

Goffman assumed that when individuals interact, they want to present a certain sense of self that will be accepted by others. However, even as they present that self, actors are aware that members of the audience can disturb their performance. For that reason actors are attuned to the need to control the audience, especially those elements of it that might be disruptive. The actors hope that the sense of self that they present to the audience will be strong enough for the audience to define the actors as the actors want them to. The actors also hope that this will cause the audience to act voluntarily as the actors want them to. Goffman characterized this central interest as "impression management." It involves techniques actors use to maintain certain impressions in the face of problems they are likely to encounter and methods they use to cope with these problems.

Following this theatrical analogy, Goffman spoke of a front stage. The *front* is that part of the performance that generally functions in rather fixed and general ways to define the situation for those who observe the performance. Within the front stage, Goffman further differentiated between the setting and the personal front. The *setting* refers to the physical scene that ordinarily must be there if the actors are to perform. Without it, the actors usually cannot perform. For example, a surgeon generally requires an operating room, a taxi driver a cab, and an ice skater ice. The *personal front* consists of those items of expressive equipment that the audience identifies with the performers and expects them to carry with them into the setting. A surgeon, for instance, is expected to dress in a medical gown, have certain instruments, and so on.

Goffman then subdivided the personal front into appearance and manner. *Appearance* includes those items that tell us the performer's social status (for instance, the surgeon's medical gown). *Manner* tells the audience what sort of role the performer expects to play in the situation (for example, the use of physical mannerisms, demeanor). A brusque manner and a meek manner indicate quite different kinds of performances. In general, we expect appearance and manner to be consistent.

Although Goffman approached the front and other aspects of his system as a symbolic interactionist, he did discuss their structural character. For example, he argued that fronts tend to become institutionalized, and so "collective representations" arise about what is to go on in a certain front. Very often when actors take on established roles, they find particular fronts already established for such performances. The result, Goffman argued, is that fronts tend to be selected, not created. This idea conveys a much more structural image than we would receive from most symbolic interactionists.

Despite such a structural view, Goffman's most interesting insights lie in the domain of interaction. He argued that because people generally[7] try to present an idealized picture of themselves in their front-stage performances, inevitably they feel that they must hide things in their performances. First, actors may want to conceal secret pleasures (for instance, drinking alcohol) engaged in prior to the performance or in past lives (for instance, as drug addicts) that are incompatible with their performance. Second, actors may want to conceal errors that have been made in the preparation of the performance as well as steps that have been taken to correct these errors. For example, a taxi driver may seek to hide the fact that he started in the wrong direction. Third, actors may find it necessary to show only end products and to conceal the process involved in producing them. For example, professors may spend several hours preparing a lecture, but they may want to act as if they have always known the material. Fourth, it may be necessary for actors to conceal from the audience that "dirty work" was involved in the making of the end products. Dirty work

---

[7] But not always—see Ungar (1984) on self-mockery as a way of presenting the self.

may include tasks that "were physically unclean, semi-legal, cruel, and degrading in other ways" (Goffman, 1959:44). Fifth, in giving a certain performance, actors may have to let other standards slide. Finally, actors probably find it necessary to hide any insults, humiliations, or deals made so that the performance could go on. Generally, actors have a vested interest in hiding all such facts from their audience.

Another aspect of dramaturgy in the front stage is that actors often try to convey the impression that they are closer to the audience than they actually are. For example, actors may try to foster the impression that the performance in which they are engaged at the moment is their only performance or at least their most important one. To do this, actors have to be sure that their audiences are segregated so that the falsity of the performance is not discovered. Even if it is discovered, Goffman argued, the audiences themselves may try to cope with the falsity so as not to shatter their idealized image of the actor. This reveals the interactional character of performances. A successful performance depends on the involvement of all the parties. Another example of this kind of impression management is an actor's attempt to convey the idea that there is something unique about this performance as well as his or her relationship to the audience. The audience, too, wants to feel that it is the recipient of a unique performance.

Actors try to make sure that all the parts of any performance blend together. In some cases, a single discordant aspect can disrupt a performance. However, performances vary in the amount of consistency required. A slip by a priest on a sacred occasion would be terribly disruptive, but if a taxi driver made one wrong turn, it would not be likely to damage the overall performance greatly.

Another technique employed by performers is *mystification*. Actors often tend to mystify their performances by restricting the contact between themselves and the audience. By generating "social distance" between themselves and the audience, they try to create a sense of awe in the audience. This, in turn, keeps the audience from questioning the performance. Again Goffman pointed out that the audience is involved in this process and often itself seeks to maintain the credibility of the performance by keeping its distance from the performer.

This leads us to Goffman's interest in teams. To Goffman, as a symbolic interactionist, a focus on individual actors obscured important facts about interaction. Goffman's basic unit of analysis was thus not the individual but the team. A *team* is any set of individuals who cooperate in staging a single routine. Thus, the preceding discussion of the relationship between the performer and audience is really about teams.[8] Each member is reliant on the others, because all can disrupt the performance and all are aware that they are putting on an act. Goffman concluded that a team is a kind of "secret society."

Goffman also discussed a *back stage* where facts suppressed in the front or various kinds of informal actions may appear. A back stage is usually adjacent to the front stage, but it is also cut off from it. Performers can reliably expect no members of their

---

[8] A performer and the audience are one kind of team, but Goffman also talked of a group of performers as one team and the audience as another. Interestingly, Goffman argued that a team also can be a single individual. His logic, following classic symbolic interactionism, was that an individual can be his or her own audience—can *imagine* an audience to be present.

front audience to appear in the back. Furthermore, they engage in various types of impression management to make sure of this. A performance is likely to become difficult when actors are unable to prevent the audience from entering the back stage. There is also a third, residual domain, the *outside,* which is neither front nor back.

No area is *always* one of these three domains. Also, a given area can occupy all three domains at different times. A professor's office is front stage when a student visits, back stage when the student leaves, and outside when the professor is at a university basketball game.

Impression Management   In general, *impression management* (P. Manning, 2005c) is oriented to guarding against a series of unexpected actions, such as unintended gestures, inopportune intrusions, and faux pas, as well as intended actions, such as making a scene. Goffman was interested in the various methods of dealing with such problems. First, there is a set of methods involving actions aimed at producing dramaturgical loyalty by, for example, fostering high in-group loyalty, preventing team members from identifying with the audience, and changing audiences periodically so that they do not become too knowledgeable about the performers. Second, Goffman suggested various forms of dramaturgical discipline, such as having the presence of mind to avoid slips, maintaining self-control, and managing the facial expressions and verbal tone of one's performance. Third, he identified various types of dramaturgical circumspection, such as determining in advance how a performance should go, planning for emergencies, selecting loyal teammates, selecting good audiences, being involved in small teams where dissension is less likely, making only brief appearances, preventing audience access to private information, and settling on a complete agenda to prevent unforeseen occurrences.

The audience also has a stake in successful impression management by the actor or team of actors. The audience often acts to save the show through such devices as giving great interest and attention to it, avoiding emotional outbursts, not noticing slips, and giving special consideration to a neophyte performer.

Manning points not only to the centrality of the self but also to Goffman's *cynical* view of people in this work:

> The overall tenor of *The Presentation of Self* is to a world in which people,
> whether individually or in groups, pursue their own ends in cynical disregard for
> others. . . . The view here is of the individual as a set of performance masks hiding
> a manipulative and cynical self.
>
> (P. Manning, 1992:44)

Manning puts forth a "two selves thesis" to describe this aspect of Goffman's thinking; that is, people have both a performance self and a hidden, cynical self.

Role Distance   Goffman (1961) was interested in the degree to which an individual embraces a given role. In his view, because of the large number of roles, few people get completely involved in any given role. *Role distance* deals with the degree to which individuals separate themselves from the roles they are in. For example, if older children ride on a merry-go-round, they are likely to be aware that they are really too old to enjoy such an experience. One way of coping with this feeling is to demonstrate distance from the role by doing it in a careless, lackadaisical way by performing seemingly dangerous acts while on the merry-go-round. In performing such acts, the older children are really explaining to the audience that they are not as immersed in the activity as small children might be or that if they are, it is because of the special things they are doing.

One of Goffman's key insights is that role distance is a function of one's social status. High-status people often manifest role distance for reasons other than those of people in low-status positions. For example, a high-status surgeon may manifest role distance in the operating room to relieve the tension of the operating team. People in low-status positions usually manifest more defensiveness in exhibiting role distance. For instance, people who clean toilets may do so in a lackadaisical and uninterested manner. They may be trying to tell their audience that they are too good for such work.

Stigma   Goffman (1963) was interested in the gap between what a person ought to be, *"virtual social identity,"* and what a person actually is, *"actual social identity."* Anyone who has a gap between these two identities is stigmatized. *Stigma* focuses on the dramaturgical interaction between stigmatized people and normals. The nature of that interaction depends on which of the two types of stigma an individual has. In the case of *discredited* stigma, the actor assumes that the differences are known by the audience members or are evident to them (for example, a paraplegic or someone who has lost a limb). A *discreditable* stigma is one in which the differences are neither known by audience members nor perceivable by them (for example, a person who has had a colostomy or a homosexual passing as straight). For someone with a discredited stigma, the basic dramaturgical problem is managing the tension produced by the fact that people know of the problem. For someone with a discreditable stigma, the dramaturgical problem is managing information so that the problem remains unknown to the audience. (For a discussion of how the homeless deal with stigma, see Anderson, Snow, and Cress, 1994.)

Most of the text of Goffman's *Stigma* is devoted to people with obvious, often grotesque stigmas (for instance, the loss of a nose). However, as the book unfolds, the reader realizes that Goffman is really saying that we are all stigmatized at some time or other or in one setting or another. His examples include the Jew "passing" in a predominantly Christian community, the fat person in a group of people of normal weight, and the individual who has lied about his past and must be constantly sure that the audience does not learn of this deception.

Frame Analysis   In *Frame Analysis* (1974), Goffman moved away from his classic symbolic-interactionist roots and toward the study of the small-scale structures of social life (for a study employing the idea of frames, see McLean, 1998). Although he still felt that people define situations in the sense meant by W. I. Thomas, he now thought that such definitions were less important: "Defining situations as real certainly has consequences, but these may contribute very marginally to the events in progress" (Goffman, 1974:1). Furthermore, even when people define situations, they do not ordinarily create those definitions. Action is defined more by mechanical adherence to rules than through an active, creative, and negotiated process. Goffman enunciated his goal: "to try to isolate some of the basic frameworks of understanding available in our society for making sense out of events and to analyze the special vulnerabilities to which these frames of reference are subject" (1974:10).

Goffman looked beyond and behind everyday situations in a search for the structures that invisibly govern them. These are " 'schemata of interpretation' that enable individuals 'to locate, perceive, identify, and label' occurrences within their life space and the world at large [Chambliss, 2005]. By rendering events or occurrences meaningful, frames function to organize experience and guide action, whether individual or collective" (Snow, 1986:464). Frames are principles of organization that define our experiences. They are assumptions about what we are seeing in the social world. Without frames, our world would be little more than a number of chaotic individual and unrelated events and facts. Gonos provided other structural characteristics of frames:

> From Goffman's analyses of particular framed activities, we can derive certain principal characteristics of frames. A frame is not conceived as a loose, somewhat accidental amalgamation of elements put together over a short time-span. Rather, it is constituted of a set number of essential components, having a definite arrangement and stable relations. These components are not gathered from here and there, as are the elements of a situation, but are always found together as a system. The standard components cohere and are complete. . . . Other less essential elements are present in any empirical instance and lend some of their character to the whole. . . . In all this, frames are very close in conception to "structures."
>
> (Gonos, 1977:860)

To Gonos, frames are largely rules or laws that fix interaction. The rules are usually unconscious and ordinarily nonnegotiable. Among the rules identified by Gonos are those that define "how signs are to be 'interpreted,' how outward indications are to be related to 'selves,' and what 'experience' will accompany activity" (1980:160). Gonos concludes, "Goffman's problematic thus promotes the study not of observable interaction of 'everyday life' as such, but its eternal structure and ideology; not of situations, but of their frames" (1980:160).

One can grant frames the status of preexisting structures, especially in the larger culture, but it is also the case that interpretive, constructionist (P. Berger and Luckmann, 1967; Swatos, 2007) work is required by actors in relationship to frames. Actors must decide which frame among others is the one to be used in a given situation. Frames themselves may be transformed by actors as the need arises. Frames also may change over time rather than remaining static. This is especially the cause when successful social movements arise that contest extant frames or succeed in replacing them with different ones.

According to Snow (2007), frames perform three functions in interpretive work. First, they *focus attention* on our surroundings by highlighting what is relevant or irrelevant, what is "in-frame" and what is "out-of-frame." Second, they act as *articulation mechanisms* by linking the various highlighted elements, so that a "story" is told about them, so that one set of meanings rather than another is conveyed. Third, they serve a *transformative function* through the reconstitution of the way some things are seen in relation to other things or to the actor. Snow (2007) concludes that "it is arguable that they [frames] are fundamental to interpretation, so much so that few, if any, utterances could be meaningfully understood apart from the way they are framed."

Philip Manning (1992:119) gives the following examples of how different frames applied to the same set of events serve to give those same events very different meaning. For example, what are we to make of the sight of a woman putting two watches in her pocket and leaving a shop without paying? Seen through the frame of a store detective, this appears to be a clear case of shoplifting. However, the legal frame leads her lawyer to see this as the act of an absentminded woman who was out shopping for gifts for her daughters. To take another example, a medical frame may lead a woman to see the actions of her gynecologist in one way, but if she uses a frame of sexuality and sexual harassment, she may see the same actions in a very different way.

Another change that Manning argues is clear in *Frame Analysis,* and that was foreshadowed in other works by Goffman, is a shift away from the cynical view of life that lay at the heart of *Presentation of Self in Everyday Life.* In fact, on the first page of *Frame Analysis,* Goffman says, "All the world is not a stage—certainly the theater isn't entirely" (1974:1). Goffman clearly came to recognize the limitations of the theater as a metaphor for everyday life. While still useful in some ways, this metaphor conceals some aspects of life just as it illuminates others. One of the things that is concealed is the importance of ritual in everyday life. Here is the way Manning describes one of the roles played by ritual in everyday life:

> For Goffman, ritual is essential because it maintains our confidence in basic social relationships. It provides others with opportunities to affirm the legitimacy of our position in the social structure while obliging us to do the same. Ritual is a placement mechanism in which, for the most part, social inferiors affirm the higher positions of their superiors. The degree of ritual in a society reflects the legitimacy of its social structure, because the ritual respect paid to individuals is also a sign of respect for the roles they occupy.
>
> (P. Manning, 1992:133)

More generally, we can say that rituals are one of the key mechanisms by which everyday life, and the social world in general, are made orderly and given solidity.

Goffman's interest in rituals brought him close to the later work of Emile Durkheim, especially *The Elementary Forms of Religious Life* (1912/1915). More generally, in accord with Durkheim's sense of social facts, Goffman came to focus on rules and see them as external constraints on social behavior. However, rules are generally only partial, indeterminate guides to conduct. Furthermore, while people are constrained, such constraint does not rule out the possibility of individual variation, even imaginative use by individuals of those rules. As Philip Manning puts it, "For the most part, Goffman assumed that rules are primarily constraints. . . . However, at other times Goffman emphasized the limitations of the Durkheimian idea that rules are constraints governing behavior, and argued instead that we frequently ignore or abuse rules intended to limit our actions" (1992:158). In fact, in line with modern thinking, to Goffman rules could be both constraints and resources to be used by people in social interaction.

Groups and Societies 群体与社会

Symbolic interactionists are generally highly critical of the tendency of other sociologists to focus on macro structures. As Rock says, "Interactionism discards most macrosociological thought as an unsure and overambitious metaphysics . . . not accessible to intelligent examination" (1979:238). Dmitri Shalin points to "interactionist criticism aimed at the classical view of social order as external, atemporal, determinate at any given moment and resistant to change" (1986:14). Rock also says, "Whilst it [symbolic interactionism] does not wholly shun the idea of social structure, its stress upon activity and process relegates structural metaphors to a most minor place" (1979:50).

Blumer is in the forefront of those who are critical of this "sociological determinism [in which] the social action of people is treated as an outward flow or expression of forces playing on them rather than as acts which are built up by people through their interpretation of the situations in which they are placed" (1962/1969:84). This focus on the constraining effects of large-scale social structures leads traditional sociologists to a set of assumptions about the actor and action different from those held by symbolic interactionists. Instead of seeing actors as those who actively define their situations, traditional sociologists tend to reduce actors to "mindless robots on the societal or aggregate level" (Manis and Meltzer, 1978:7). In an effort to stay away from determinism and a robotlike view of actors, symbolic interactionists take a very different view of large-scale social structures, a view that is ably presented by Blumer.[9]

To Blumer, society is not made up of macro structures. The essence of society is to be found in actors and action: "Human society is to be seen as consisting of acting people, and the life of the society is to be seen as consisting of their actions" (Blumer, 1962/1969:85). Human society is action; group life is a "complex of ongoing activity." However, society is not made up of an array of isolated acts. There is collective action as well, which involves "individuals fitting their lines of action to one another . . . participants making indications to one another, not merely each to himself" (Blumer, 1969b:16). This gives rise to what Mead called the *social act* and Blumer calls *joint action*.

Blumer accepted the idea of emergence—that large-scale structures emerge from micro processes (Morrione, 1988). According to Maines, "The key to understanding Blumer's treatment of large-scale organizations rests on his conception of joint action" (1988:46). A joint action is not simply the sum total of individual acts—it comes to have a character of its own. A joint action thus is not external to or coercive of actors and their actions; rather, it is created by actors and their actions. The study of joint action is, in Blumer's view, the domain of the sociologist.

From this discussion one gets the sense that the joint act is almost totally flexible—that is, that society can become almost anything the actors want it to be. However, Blumer was not prepared to go as far as that. He argued that each instance of joint action must be formed anew, but he did recognize that joint action

---

[9] Although they recognize that Blumer takes this view, Wood and Wardell (1983) argue that Mead did *not* have an "astructural bias." See also Joas (1981).

is likely to have a "well-established and repetitive form" (Blumer, 1969b:17). Not only does most joint action recur in patterns, but Blumer also was willing to admit that such action is guided by systems of preestablished meanings, such as culture and social order.

It would appear that Blumer admitted that there are large-scale structures and that they are important. Here Blumer followed Mead (1934/1962), who admitted that such structures are very important. However, such structures have an extremely limited role in symbolic interactionism.[10] For one thing, Blumer most often argued that large-scale structures are little more than "frameworks" within which the really important aspects of social life, action and interaction, take place (1962/1969:87). Large-scale structures do set the conditions and limitations on human action, but they do not determine it. In his view, people do not act within the context of structures such as society; rather, they act in situations. Large-scale structures are important in that they shape the situations in which individuals act and supply to actors the fixed set of symbols that enable them to act.

Even when Blumer discussed such preestablished patterns, he hastened to make it clear that "areas of unprescribed conduct are just as natural, indigenous, and recurrent in human group life as those areas covered by preestablished and faithfully followed prescriptions of joint action" (1969b:18). Not only are there many unprescribed areas, but even in prescribed areas joint action has to be created and re-created consistently. Actors are guided by generally accepted meanings in this creation and re-creation, but they are not determined by them. They may accept them as is, but they also can make minor and even major alterations in them. In Blumer's words, "It is the social process in group life that creates and upholds the rules, not the rules that create and uphold group life" (1969b:19).

Clearly, Blumer was not inclined to accord culture independent and coercive status in his theoretical system. Nor was he about to accord this status to the extended connections of group life, or what is generally called "social structure," for example, the division of labor. "A network or an institution does not function automatically because of some inner dynamics or system requirements; it functions because people at different points do something, and what they do is a result of how they define the situation in which they are called on to act" (Blumer, 1969b:19).

Criticisms 相关批判

Having analyzed the ideas of symbolic interactionism, particularly those of the Chicago school of Mead, Blumer, and Goffman, I will now enumerate some of the major criticisms of this perspective.

The first criticism is that the mainstream of symbolic interactionism has too readily given up on conventional scientific techniques. Eugene Weinstein and Judith

---

[10] Later we will discuss some more recent perspectives in symbolic interactionism which accord a greater role to large-scale structures and which argue, more specifically, that Blumer adopted such a position (Blumer, 1990; Maines, 1989a, 1989b; Maines and Morrione, 1990).

Tanur expressed this point well: "Just because the contents of consciousness are qualitative, does not mean that their exterior expression cannot be coded, classified, even counted" (1976:105). Science and subjectivism are *not* mutually exclusive.

Second, Manford Kuhn (1964), William Kolb (1944), Bernard Meltzer, James Petras, and Larry Reynolds (1975), and many others have criticized the vagueness of essential Meadian concepts such as mind, self, I, and me. Most generally, Kuhn (1964) spoke of the ambiguities and contradictions in Mead's theory. Beyond Meadian theory, they have criticized many of the basic symbolic-interactionist concepts for being confused and imprecise and therefore incapable of providing a firm basis for theory and research. Because these concepts are imprecise, it is difficult, if not impossible, to operationalize them; the result is that testable propositions cannot be generated (Sheldon Stryker, 1980).

The third major criticism of symbolic interactionism has been of its tendency to downplay or ignore large-scale social structures. This criticism has been expressed in various ways. For example, Weinstein and Tanur argued that symbolic interactionism ignores the connectedness of outcomes to each other: "*It is the aggregated outcomes that form the linkages among episodes of interaction that are the concern of sociology qua sociology. . . .* The concept of social structure is necessary to deal with the incredible density and complexity of relations through which episodes of interaction are interconnected" (1976:106). Sheldon Stryker argued that the micro focus of symbolic interactionism serves "to minimize or deny the facts of social structure and the impact of the macro-organizational features of society on behavior" (1980:146).

Somewhat less predictable is the fourth criticism, that symbolic interactionism is not sufficiently microscopic, that it ignores the importance of factors such as the unconscious and emotions (Meltzer, Petras, and Reynolds, 1975; Sheldon Stryker, 1980). Similarly, symbolic interactionism has been criticized for ignoring psychological factors such as needs, motives, intentions, and aspirations. In their effort to deny that there are immutable forces impelling the actor to act, symbolic interactionists have focused instead on meanings, symbols, action, and interaction. They ignore psychological factors that might impel the actor, an action which parallels their neglect of the larger societal constraints on the actor. In both cases, symbolic interactionists are accused of making a "fetish" out of everyday life (Meltzer, Petras, and Reynolds, 1975:85). This focus on everyday life, in turn, leads to a marked overemphasis on the immediate situation and an "obsessive concern with the transient, episodic, and fleeting" (Meltzer, Petras, and Reynolds, 1975:85).

Toward a More Synthetic and Integrative Symbolic Interactionism 更加趋向综合和完整的符号互动论

It may have been out of self-defense, but symbolic interactionism, as it evolved primarily under the stewardship of Herbert Blumer, moved in a decidedly micro direction. This micro focus stood in contrast to at least the implications of the more integrative title of George Herbert Mead's *Mind, Self and Society*. However, symbolic interactionism has entered a new, "post-Blumerian" age (G. A. Fine, 1990, 1992). On one front, there are efforts to reconstruct Blumerian theory and argue that it always had an interest in macro-level phenomena (discussed later in this chapter).[11] More important, there are ongoing efforts to synthesize symbolic interactionism with ideas derived from a number of other theories. This "new" symbolic interactionism has, in Gary Fine's terms, "cobbled a new theory from the shards of other theoretical approaches" (1990:136–137, 1992). Symbolic interactionism now combines indigenous insights with those from micro theories such as exchange theory, ethnomethodology and conversation analysis, and phenomenology. More surprising is the integration of ideas from macro theories (for example, structural functionalism) as well as the ideas of macro theorists such as Parsons, Durkheim, Simmel, Weber, and Marx. Symbolic interactionists also are endeavoring to integrate insights from poststructuralism, postmodernism, and radical feminism. Post-Blumerian symbolic interactionism is becoming a much more synthetic perspective than it was in Blumer's heyday.

Redefining Mead　重塑米德

In addition to ongoing synthetic work in symbolic interactionism, there is an effort to redefine the major thinkers associated with it, especially Mead, as having more integrative orientations than is usually thought to be the case.

As we saw earlier, despite Mead's lack of interest in macro-level phenomena, there is much in his ideas on mind, self, and society that suggests an integrated sociological theory. In this context, it is useful to look at John Baldwin's (1986) analysis of Mead. Baldwin notes the fragmentation of the social sciences in general, and sociological theory in particular, and argues that such fragmentation is serving to prevent the development of a general "unifying" sociological theory and, more generally, a science of the social world. He makes the case for the need for such a theory and for Meadian theory as a model for that theory (Baldwin, 1986:156). While Baldwin is proposing the kind of grand synthesis that is being rejected in this postmodern era, we can welcome his effort to see a more integrative approach in Meadian theory.

Baldwin makes the case for Mead on several grounds. First, he argues that Mead's theoretical system covers the full range of social phenomena from micro to macro levels—"physiology, social psychology, language, cognition, behavior, society, social change and ecology" (Baldwin, 1986:156). Along these lines, Baldwin offers a model of Mead's theoretical orientation, as shown in Figure 6.1.

Second, Baldwin argues that not only does Mead have an integrated, micromacro sense of the social world, he also offers "a flexible system for interweaving contributions from all schools of contemporary social science (1986:156). Thus, Mead's theory provides a base not only for micro-macro integration but for theoretical synthesis as well. Finally, Baldwin contends that Mead's "commitment to scientific

---

[11] For a critique of efforts by symbolic interactionists to integrate macro-level phenomena, see J. H. Turner 1995.

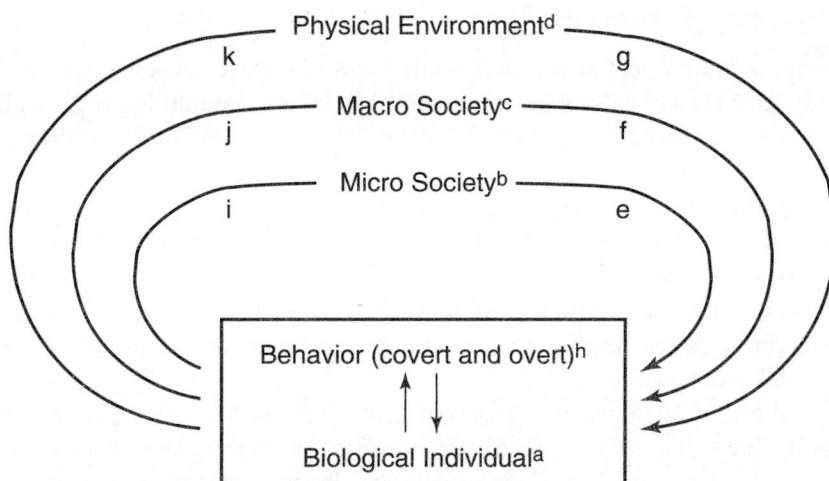

Figure 6.1 *An Overview of the Components of Mead's Theoretical System*

methods helps ensure that data and theories on all components of the social system can be integrated in a balanced manner, with their relative importance established in an empirically defensible manner" (1986:156).

Micro-Macro Integration 微观—宏观整合

Sheldon Stryker enunciated an integrative goal for symbolic interactionism: "A satisfactory theoretical framework must bridge social structure and person, must be able to move from the level of the person to that of large-scale social structure and back again. . . . There must exist a conceptual framework facilitating movement across the levels of organization and person" (1980:53). (Perinbanayagam articulated a similar goal for symbolic interactionism: "the existence of structure *and* meaning, self *and* others, the dialectic of being and emergence, leading to a dialectical interactionism" [1985:xv].) Stryker embedded his orientation in Meadian symbolic interactionism but sought to extend it to the societal level, primarily through the use of role theory:

> This version begins with Mead, but goes beyond Mead to introduce role theoretic concepts and principles, in order to adequately deal with the reciprocal impact of social person and social structure. The nexus in this reciprocal impact is interaction. It is in the context of the social process—the ongoing patterns of interaction joining individual actors—that social structure operates to constrain the conceptions of self, the definitions of the situation, and the behavioral opportunities and repertoires that bound and guide the interaction that takes place.
>
> (Sheldon Stryker, 1980:52)

Stryker developed his orientation in terms of eight general principles:

1. Human action is dependent on a named and classified world in which the names and classifications have meaning for actors. People learn through interaction with others how to classify the world, as well as how they are expected to behave toward it.

2. Among the most important things that people learn are the symbols used to designate social *positions*. A critical point here is that Stryker conceived of positions in structural terms: "the relatively stable, morphological components of social structure" (Stryker, 1980:54). Stryker also accorded *roles* central importance, conceiving of them as the shared behavioral expectations attached to social positions.

3. Stryker also recognized the importance of larger social structures, although he was inclined, like other symbolic interactionists, to conceive of them in terms of organized patterns of behavior. In addition, his discussion treated social structure as simply the "framework" within which people act. Within these structures, people name one another, that is, recognize one another as occupants of positions. In so doing, people evoke reciprocal expectations of what each is expected to do.

4. Furthermore, in acting in this context, people name not only each other but also themselves; that is, they apply positional designations to themselves. These self-designations become part of the self, internalized expectations with regard to their own behavior.

5. When interacting, people define the situation by applying names to it, to other participants, to themselves, and to particular features of the situation. These definitions are then used by the actors to organize their behavior.

6. Social behavior is not determined by social meanings, although it is constrained by them. Stryker is a strong believer in the idea of *role making*. People do not simply take roles; rather, they take an active, creative orientation to their roles.

7. Social structures also serve to limit the degree to which roles are "made" rather than just "taken" (D. D. Martin and Wilson, 2005). Some structures permit more creativity than others do.

8. The possibilities of role making make various social changes possible. Changes can occur in social definitions—in names, symbols, and classifications—and in the possibilities for interaction. The cumulative effect of these changes can be alterations in the larger social structures.

Although Stryker offered a useful beginning toward a more adequate symbolic interactionism, his work has a number of limitations. The most notable is that he said little about larger social structures per se. Stryker saw the need to integrate these larger structures in his work, but he recognized that a "full-fledged development of how such incorporation could proceed is beyond the scope of the present work" (1980:69). Stryker saw only a limited future role for large-scale structural variables in symbolic interactionism. He hoped ultimately to incorporate structural factors such as class, status, and power as variables constraining interaction, but he was disinclined to see symbolic interactionism deal with the interrelationships among these structural variables. Presumably, this kind of issue is to be left to other theories that focus more on large-scale social phenomena.

The Future of Symbolic Interactionism 符号互动论的未来

Gary Fine (1993) has offered an interesting portrait of symbolic interactionism in the 1990s. His fundamental point is that symbolic interactionism has changed dramatically in recent years. First, it has undergone considerable *fragmentation* since its heyday at the University of Chicago in the 1920s and 1930s. A great diversity of work is now included under the broad heading of symbolic interactionism. Second, symbolic interactionism has undergone *expansion* and has extended far beyond its traditional concern with micro relations (S. Harris, 2001). Third, symbolic interactionism has *incorporated* ideas from many other theoretical perspectives (Feather, 2000). Finally, the ideas of symbolic interactionists have, in turn, been *adopted* by sociologists who are focally committed to other theoretical perspectives. Further, symbolic interactionists are deeply involved in some of the major issues confronting sociological theory in the 1990s—micro-macro, agency-structure, and so on.

Thus, lines dividing symbolic interactionism and other sociological theories have blurred considerably (Maines, 2001). While symbolic interactionism will survive, it is increasingly unclear what it means to be a symbolic interactionist (and every other type of sociological theorist for that matter). Here is the way Fine puts it:

> Predicting the future is dangerous, but it is evident that the label symbolic interaction will abide. . . . Yet, we will find more intermarriage, more interchange, and more interaction. Symbolic interaction will serve as a label of convenience for the future, but will it serve as a label of thought?
>
> (G. A. Fine, 1993:81–82)

Throughout this book we deal with ongoing syntheses among many sociological theories. All these syntheses lead to the more general question of whether *any* of the familiar theoretical labels will describe distinctive modes of thought in the future.

Summary 总结

This chapter begins with a brief discussion of the roots of symbolic interactionism in philosophical pragmatism (the work of John Dewey) and psychological behaviorism (the work of John B. Watson). Out of the confluence of pragmatism, behaviorism, and other influences, such as Simmelian sociology, symbolic interactionism developed at the University of Chicago in the 1920s.

The symbolic interactionism that developed stood in contrast to the psychological reductionism of behaviorism and the structural determinism of more macro-oriented sociological theories such as structural functionalism. Its distinctive orientation was toward the mental capacities of actors and their relationship to action and interaction. All this was conceived in terms of process; there was a disinclination to see the actor impelled by either internal psychological states or large-scale structural forces.

The single most important theory in symbolic interactionism is that of George Herbert Mead. Substantively, Mead's theory accorded primacy and priority to the social world. That is, it is out of the social world that consciousness, the mind, the self, and so on, emerge. The most basic unit in his social theory is the act, which includes four dialectically related stages—impulse, perception, manipulation, and consummation. A *social* act involves two or more persons, and the basic mechanism of the social act is the gesture. While lower animals and humans are capable of having a conversation of gestures, only humans can communicate the conscious meaning of their gestures. Humans are peculiarly able to create vocal gestures, and this leads to the distinctive human ability to develop and use significant symbols. Significant symbols lead to the development of language and the distinctive capacity of humans to communicate, in the full sense of the term, with one another. Significant symbols also make possible thinking, as well as symbolic interaction.

Mead looks at an array of mental processes as part of the larger social process, including reflective intelligence, consciousness, mental images, meaning, and, most generally, the mind. Humans have the distinctive capacity to carry on an inner conversation with themselves. All the mental processes are, in Mead's view, lodged not in the brain but rather in the social process.

The self is the ability to take oneself as an object. Again, the self arises within the social process. The general mechanism of the self is the ability of people to put themselves in the place of others, to act as others act and to see themselves as others see them. Mead traces the genesis of the self through the play and game stages of childhood. Especially important in the latter stage is the emergence of the generalized other. The ability to view oneself from the point of view of the community is essential to the emergence of the self as well as of organized group activities. The self also has two phases—the "I," which is the unpredictable and creative aspect of the self, and the "me," which is the organized set of attitudes of others assumed by the actor. Social control is manifest through the "me," while the "I" is the source of innovation in society.

Mead has relatively little to say about society, which he views most generally as the ongoing social processes that precede mind and self. Mead largely lacks a macro sense of society. Institutions are defined as little more than collective habits.

Symbolic interactionism may be summarized by the following basic principles:

1. Human beings, unlike lower animals, are endowed with a capacity for thought.
2. The capacity for thought is shaped by social interaction.
3. In social interaction, people learn the meanings and symbols that allow them to exercise their distinctively human capacity for thought.
4. Meanings and symbols allow people to carry on distinctively human action and interaction.
5. People are able to modify or alter the meanings and symbols they use in action and interaction on the basis of their interpretation of the situation.
6. People are able to make these modifications and alterations because, in part, of their ability to interact with themselves, which allows them to examine possible courses of action, assess their relative advantages and disadvantages, and then choose one.
7. The intertwined patterns of action and interaction make up groups and societies.

In the context of these general principles, I seek to clarify the nature of the work of several important thinkers in the symbolic-interactionist tradition, including Charles Horton Cooley, Herbert Blumer, and, most important, Erving Goffman. I present in detail Goffman's dramaturgical analysis of the self and his related works on role distance, stigma, and frame analysis. However, I also note that Goffman's work on frames has exaggerated a tendency in his earlier work and moved further in the direction of a structuralist analysis.

We also review some of the major criticisms of symbolic interactionism, as well as two efforts to move it in more integrative and synthetic directions—the redefinition of the approach of Mead in more integrative terms, and the effort by Stryker to develop an approach that better deals with macro-level phenomena. The chapter closes with one image of symbolic interactionism's future.

Ethnomethodology
第7章　民族方法学

Chapter Outline
Defining Ethnomethodology
The Diversification of Ethnomethodology
Some Early Examples
Conversation Analysis
Studies of Institutions
Criticisms of Traditional Sociology
Stresses and Strains in Ethnomethodology
Synthesis and Integration

Given its Greek roots, the term *ethnomethodology* literally means the "methods" that people use on a daily basis to accomplish their everyday lives. To put it slightly differently, the world is seen as an ongoing practical accomplishment. People are viewed as rational, but they use "practical reasoning," not formal logic, in accomplishing their everyday lives.

Defining Ethnomethodology 民族方法学的定义

We begin with the definition of *ethnomethodology* offered in Chapter 2: the study of "the body of common-sense knowledge and the range of procedures and considerations by means of which the ordinary members of society make sense of, find their way about in, and act on the circumstances in which they find themselves" (Heritage, 1984:4).

We can gain further insight into the nature of ethnomethodology by examining efforts by its founder, Harold Garfinkel (1988, 1991), to define it. Like Durkheim, Garfinkel considers "social facts" to be the fundamental sociological phenomenon (Hilbert, 2005). However, Garfinkel's social facts are very different from Durkheim's social facts. For Durkheim, social facts are external to and coercive of individuals. Those who adopt such a focus tend to see actors as constrained or determined by social structures and institutions and able to exercise little or no independent judgment. In the acerbic terms of the ethnomethodologists, such sociologists tended to treat actors like "judgmental dopes."

In contrast, ethnomethodology treats the objectivity of social facts as the accomplishment of members (a definition of "members" follows shortly)—as a product of members' methodological activities. Garfinkel, in his inimitable and nearly impenetrable style, describes the focus of ethnomethodology as follows:

> For ethnomethodology the objective reality of social facts, in that, and just how, it is every society's locally, endogenously produced, naturally organized, reflexively accountable, ongoing, practical achievement, being everywhere, always, only, exactly and entirely, members' work, with no time out, and with no possibility of evasion, hiding out, passing, postponement, or buy-outs, is *thereby* sociology's fundamental phenomenon.
>
> (Garfinkel, 1991:11)

To put it another way, ethnomethodology is concerned with the organization of everyday life, or as Garfinkel (1988:104) describes it, "immortal, ordinary society." In Pollner's terms, this is "the extraordinary organization of the ordinary" (1987: xvii).

Ethnomethodology is certainly not a macrosociology in the sense intended by Durkheim with his concept of a social fact, but its adherents do not see it as a microsociology either. Thus, while ethnomethodologists refuse to treat actors as judgmental dopes, they do not believe that people are "almost endlessly reflexive, self-conscious and calculative" (Heritage, 1984:118). Rather, following Alfred Schutz, they recognize that most often action is routine and relatively unreflective. Hilbert (1992) argues that ethnomethodologists do not focus on actors or individuals, but rather on "members." However, members are viewed not as individuals, but rather "strictly and solely, [as] membership activities—the artful practices whereby they produce what are *for them* large-scale organization structure and small-scale interactional or personal structure" (Hilbert, 1992:193). In sum, ethnomethodologists are interested in *neither* micro structures *nor* macro structures; they are concerned with the artful practices that produce *both* types of structures. Thus, what Garfinkel and the ethnomethodologists have sought is a new way of getting at the traditional concern of sociology with objective structures, both micro and macro (Maynard and Clayman, 1991).

One of Garfinkel's key points about ethnomethods is that they are "reflexively accountable." *Accounts* are the ways in which actors explain (describe, criticize, and idealize) specific situations (Bittner, 1973; Orbuch, 1997). *Accounting* is the process by which people offer accounts in order to make sense of the world. Ethnomethodologists devote a lot of attention to analyzing people's accounts, as well as to the ways in which accounts are offered and accepted (or rejected) by others. This is one of the reasons that ethnomethodologists are preoccupied with analyzing conversations. To take an example, when a student explains to her professor why she failed to take an examination, she is offering an account. The student is trying to make sense out of an event for her professor. Ethnomethodologists are interested in the nature of that account but more generally in the *accounting practices* (Sharrock and Anderson, 1986) by which the student offers the account and the professor accepts or rejects it. In analyzing accounts, ethnomethodologists adopt a stance of "ethnomethodological

HAROLD GARFINKEL

*A Biographical Sketch**

Like many who came of age during the Depression and later World War II, Harold Garfinkel took a convoluted path into sociology. Garfinkel was born in Newark, New Jersey, on October 29, 1917. His father was a small businessman who sold household goods on the installment plan to immigrant families. While his father was eager for him to learn a trade, Harold wanted to go to college. He did go into his father's business but also began taking business courses at the then-unaccredited University of Newark. Because the courses tended to be taught by graduate students from Columbia, they were both high in quality and, because the students lacked practical experience, highly theoretical. His later theoretical orientation and his specific orientation to "accounts" are traceable, at least in part, to these courses in general, and particularly to an accounting course on the "theory of accounts." "'How do you make the columns and figures accountable [to superiors]?' was the big question according to Garfinkel" (Rawls, 2000). Also of importance was the fact that Garfinkel encountered other Jewish students at Newark who were taking courses in sociology and were later to become social scientists.

Graduating in 1939, Garfinkel spent a summer in a Quaker work camp in rural Georgia. There he learned that the University of North Carolina had a sociology program that was also oriented to the furtherance of public works projects like the one in which he was involved. Admitted to the program with a fellowship, Garfinkel chose Guy Johnson as his thesis adviser and Johnson's interest in race relations led Garfinkel to do his master's thesis on interracial homicide. He also was exposed to a wide range of social theory, most notably the works of phenomenologists and the recently published (in 1937) *The Structure of Social Action,* by Talcott Parsons. While the vast majority of graduate students at North Carolina at that time were drawn toward statistics and "scientific sociology," Garfinkel was attracted to theory, especially Florian Znaniecki's now almost forgotten work on social action and the importance of the actor's point of view.

> Garfinkel was drafted in 1942 and entered the airforce. He eventually was given the task of training troops in tank warfare on a golf course on Miami Beach in the complete absence of tanks. Garfinkel had only pictures of tanks

indifference." That is, they do not judge the nature of the accounts but rather analyze them in terms of how they are used in practical action. They are concerned with the accounts as well as the methods needed by both speaker and listener to proffer, understand, and accept or reject accounts (for more on this, see Young, 1997).

from *Life* magazine. The real tanks were all in combat. The man who would insist on concrete empirical detail in lieu of theorized accounts was teaching real troops who were about to enter live combat to fight against only imagined tanks in situations where things like the proximity of the troops to the imagined tank could make the difference between life and death. The impact of this on the development of his views can only be imagined. He had to train troops to throw explosives into the tracks of imaginary tanks; to keep imaginary tanks from seeing them by directing fire at imaginary tank ports. This task posed in a new and very concrete way the problems of the adequate description of action and accountability that Garfinkel had taken up at North Carolina as theoretical issues.

(Rawls, 2000)

When the war ended, Garfinkel proceeded to Harvard and studied with Talcott Parsons. While Parsons stressed the importance of abstract categories and generalizations, Garfinkel was interested in detailed description. When Garfinkel achieved prominence in the discipline, this became a focal debate within sociology. However, he soon became more interested in the empirical demonstration of the importance of his theoretical orientation than in debating it in the abstract. While still a student at Harvard, Garfinkel taught for two years at Princeton and, after obtaining his doctorate, moved on to Ohio State, where he had a two-year position in a "soft money" project studying leadership on airplanes and submarines. That research was cut short by reductions in funding, but Garfinkel then joined a project researching juries in Wichita, Kansas. In preparing for a talk on the project at the 1954 American Sociological Association meetings, Garfinkel came up with the term *ethnomethodology* to describe what fascinated him about jury deliberations and social life more generally.

In the fall of 1954 Garfinkel took a position at UCLA, a position he held until he retired in 1987. From the beginning, he used the term *ethnomethodology* in his seminars. A number of notable students were taken by Garfinkel's approach and disseminated it around the United States and eventually the world. Most notable were a group of sociologists, especially Harvey Sacks, Emmanuel Schegloff, and Gail Jefferson, who, inspired by Garfinkel's approach, developed what is, at least at the moment, the most important variety of ethnomethodology—conversation analysis.

*This biographical sketch is based on Anne Rawls, "Harold Garfinkel," in George Ritzer, ed., *The Blackwell Companion to Major Social Theorists* (Malden, Mass., and Oxford, Eng.: Blackwell, 2000). See also Maynard and Kardash (2007) and Rawls (2005b).

Extending the idea of accounts, ethnomethodologists take great pains to point out that sociologists, like everyone else, offer accounts. Thus, reports of sociological studies can be seen as accounts and analyzed in the same way that all other accounts can be studied. This perspective on sociology serves to disenchant the work of sociologists, indeed all scientists. A good deal of sociology (indeed all sciences) involves common-sense interpretations. Ethnomethodologists can study the accounts of the sociologist in the same way that they can study the accounts of the layperson. Thus, the everyday practices of sociologists and all scientists come under the scrutiny of the ethnomethodologist.

We can say that accounts are reflexive in the sense that they enter into the constitution of the state of affairs they make observable and are intended to deal with. Thus, in trying to describe what people are doing, we alter the nature of what they are doing. This is as true for sociologists as it is for laypeople. In studying and reporting on social life, sociologists are, in the process, changing what they are studying. That is, subjects alter their behavior as a result of being the subject of scrutiny and in response to descriptions of that behavior (for a similar idea, see the discussion of Giddens's "double hermeneutic" in Chapter 10).

民族方法学的多元发展
The Diversification of Ethnomethodology

Ethnomethodology was "invented" by Garfinkel beginning in the late 1940s, but it was first systematized with the publication of his *Studies in Ethnomethodology* in 1967. Over the years, ethnomethodology has grown enormously and expanded in a number of different directions. Only a decade after the publication of *Studies in Ethnomethodology,* Don Zimmerman concluded that there already were several varieties of ethnomethodology. As Zimmerman put it, ethnomethodology encompassed "a number of more or less distinct and sometimes incompatible lines of inquiry" (1978:6). Ten years later, Paul Atkinson (1988) underscored the lack of coherence in ethnomethodology and argued further that at least some ethnomethodologists had strayed too far from the underlying premises of the approach. Thus, while it is a very vibrant type of sociological theory, ethnomethodology has experienced some increasing "growing pains" in recent years. It is safe to say that ethnomethodology, its diversity, and its problems are likely to proliferate in the coming years. After all, the subject matter of ethnomethodology is the infinite variety of everyday life. As a result, there will be many more studies, more diversification, and further "growing pains."

Studies of Institutional Settings 针对制度背景的研究

Maynard and Clayman (1991) describe a number of varieties of work in ethnomethodology, but two stand out from my point of view.[1] The first type is ethnomethodological *studies of institutional settings*. Early ethnomethodological studies carried

---

[1] Another body of ethnomethodological work deals with the *study of science,* particularly in fields such as mathematics, astronomy, biology, and optics (for example, Lynch, 1985, 1993). In common with the rest of ethnomethodology, studies in this area concentrate on the common-sense procedures, the practical reasoning employed by scientists even in some of the greatest discoveries in the history of mathematics and science. The focus is on the work that scientists do as well as the conversations in which they engage. The ethnomethodologist is concerned with the "workbench practices" employed by scientists on a day-to-day basis.

on by Garfinkel and his associates (which are discussed below) took place in casual, noninstitutionalized settings such as the home. Later, there was a move toward studying everyday practices in a wide variety of institutional settings—courtrooms, medical settings (Ten Have, 1995), and police departments—and studies of this type have been increasing since the early 1990s (Perakyla, 2007). The goal of such studies is an understanding of the way people perform their official tasks and, in the process, constitute the institution in which the tasks take place.

Conventional sociological studies of such institutional settings focus on their structure, formal rules, and official procedures to explain what people do within them. To the ethnomethodologists, such external constraints are inadequate for explaining what really goes on in these institutions. People are not determined by these external forces; rather, they use them to accomplish their tasks and create the institution in which they exist. People employ their practical procedures not only to make their daily lives but also to manufacture the institutions' products. For example, the crime rates compiled by the police department are not merely the result of officials' following clearly defined rules in their production. Rather, officials utilize a range of common-sense procedures to decide, for example, whether victims should be classified as homicides. Thus, such rates are based on the interpretive work of professionals, and this kind of record keeping is a practical activity worthy of study in its own right.

Conversation Analysis 谈话分析

The second variety of ethnomethodology is *conversation analysis* (Rawls, 2005a; Schegloff, 2001).[2] The goal of conversation analysis is "the detailed understanding of the fundamental structures of conversational interaction" (Zimmerman, 1988:429). *Conversation* is defined in terms that are in line with the basic elements of the ethnomethodological perspective: "Conversation is an *interactional activity* exhibiting *stable, orderly* properties that are the analyzable *achievements* of the conversants" (Zimmerman, 1988:406; italics added). While there are rules and procedures for conversations, they do not determine what is said but instead are used to "accomplish" a conversation. The focus of conversational analysis is the constraints on what is said that are internal to the conversation itself and not external forces that constrain talk. Conversations are seen as internally, sequentially ordered.

Zimmerman details five basic working principles of conversation analysis. First, conversation analysis requires the collection and analysis of highly detailed data on conversations. These data include not only words but also "the hesitations, cut-offs, restarts, silences, breathing noises, throat clearings, sniffles, laughter, and laughterlike noises, prosody, and the like, not to mention the 'nonverbal' behaviors available on video records that are usually closely integrated with the stream of activity captured on the audiotape" (Zimmerman, 1988:413). All these things are part

---

[2] While I am treating conversation analysis as a variety of ethnomethodology, it should be noted that conversation analysis has distinctive roots in the work of Harvey Sacks (who was a student of Erving Goffman, not Harold Garfinkel; see Jacobsen, 2007) and has over the years developed a distinctive set of interests.

of most conversations, and they are seen as methodic devices in the making of a conversation by the actors involved (Lynch, 1999).

Second, even the finest detail of a conversation must be presumed to be an orderly accomplishment. Such minute aspects of a conversation are not ordered just by the ethnomethodologist; they are first "ordered by the methodical activities of the social actors themselves" (Zimmerman, 1988:415).

Third, interaction in general and conversation in particular have stable, orderly properties that are the achievements of the actors involved. In looking at conversations, ethnomethodologists treat them as if they were autonomous, separable from the cognitive processes of the actors as well as the larger context in which they take place.

Fourth, "the fundamental framework of conversation is sequential organization" (Zimmerman, 1988:422). Finally, and relatedly, "the course of conversational interaction is managed on a turn-by-turn or local basis" (Zimmerman, 1988:423). Here Zimmerman invokes Heritage's (1984) distinction between "context-shaped" and "context-renewing" conversation. Conversations are context-shaped in the sense that what is said at any given moment is shaped by the preceding sequential context of the conversation. Conversations are context-shaping in that what is being said in the present turn becomes part of the context for future turns.

Methodologically, conversation analysts are led to study conversations in naturally occurring situations, often using audiotape or videotape. This method allows information to flow from the everyday world rather than being imposed on it by the researcher. The researcher can examine and reexamine an actual conversation in minute detail instead of relying on his or her notes. This technique also allows the researcher to do highly detailed analyses of conversations.

Conversation analysis is based on the assumption that conversations are the bedrock of other forms of interpersonal relations (David Gibson, 2000). They are the most pervasive form of interaction, and a conversation "consists of the fullest matrix of socially organized communicative practices and procedures" (Heritage and Atkinson, 1984:13).

I have tried to give a general sense of ethnomethodology in the preceding pages. However, the heart of ethnomethodology lies not in its theoretical statements but in its empirical studies. What we know theoretically is derived from those studies. Thus, I turn now to a series of those studies in the hope of giving the reader a better feel for ethnomethodology.

Some Early Examples 早期的实例

We begin with some of the early research in ethnomethodology that gained for it much early notoriety. While some of the early methods are rarely, if ever, used today, they tell us a good deal about ethnomethodological research.

Breaching Experiments 破坏试验

In breaching experiments, social reality is violated in order to shed light on the methods by which people construct social reality. The assumption behind this research is not only that the methodical production of social life occurs all the time but also that the participants are unaware that they are engaging in such actions. The objective of the breaching experiment is to disrupt normal procedures so that the process by which the everyday world is constructed or reconstructed can be observed and studied. In his work, Garfinkel (1967) offered a number of examples of breaching experiments, most of which were undertaken by his students in casual settings to illustrate the basic principles of ethnomethodology.

Lynch (1991:15) offers the following example (Figure 7.1) of breaching, derived from earlier work by Garfinkel (1963): This, of course, is a game of tic-tac-toe. The well-known rules allow participants in the game to place a mark *within* each of the cells, but the rules have been breached in this case and a mark has been placed *between* two cells. If this breach were to occur in a real game of tic-tac-toe, the other player (player 2) would probably insist on a correct placement. If such a placement did not occur, player 2 would try to explain why player 1 had taken such an extraordinary action. The actions of player 2 would be studied by the ethnomethodologist to see how the everyday world of tic-tac-toe is reconstructed.

To take one other example, Garfinkel asked his students to spend between fifteen minutes and an hour in their homes imagining that they were boarders and then acting on the basis of that assumption. "They were instructed to conduct themselves in a circumspect and polite fashion. They were to avoid getting personal, to use formal address, to speak only when spoken to" (Garfinkel, 1967:47). In the vast majority of cases, family members were dumbfounded by such behavior: "Reports were filled with accounts of astonishment, bewilderment, shock, anxiety, embarrassment, and anger, and with charges by various family members that the student was mean, inconsiderate, selfish, nasty, or impolite" (Garfinkel, 1967:47). These reactions indicate how important it is that people act in accord with the common-sense assumptions about how they are supposed to behave.

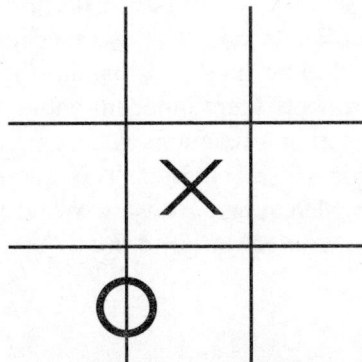

FIGURE 7.1 *Breaching In Tic-Tac-Toe*

SOURCE: Michael Lynch, 1991. "Pictures of Nothing? Visual Constructs in Social Theory." *Sociological Theory* 9:15.

What most interested Garfinkel was how the family members sought in common-sense ways to cope with such a breach. They demanded explanations from the students for their behavior. In their questions, they often implied an explanation of the aberrant behavior:

> "Did you get fired?"
> "Are you sick?"
> "Are you out of your mind or are you just stupid?"
>
> (Garfinkel, 1967:47)

Family members also sought to explain the behaviors to themselves in terms of previously understood motives. For example, a student was thought to be behaving oddly because she was working too hard or had had a fight with her fiancé. Such explanations are important to participants—the other family members, in this case—because the explanations help them feel that under normal circumstances interaction would occur as it always had.

If the student did not acknowledge the validity of such explanations, family members were likely to withdraw and to seek to isolate, denounce, or retaliate against the culprit. Deep emotions were aroused because the effort to restore order through explanation was rejected by the student. The other family members felt that more intense statements and actions were necessary to restore the equilibrium:

> "Don't bother with him, he's in one of his moods again."
> "Why must you always create friction in our family harmony?"
> "I don't want any more of *that* out of *you* and if you can't treat your mother decently you'd better move out!"
>
> (Garfinkel, 1967:48)

In the end, the students explained the experiment to their families, and in most situations, harmony was restored. However, in some instances hard feelings lingered.

Breaching experiments are undertaken to illustrate the way people order their everyday lives. These experiments reveal the resilience of social reality, since the subjects (or victims) move quickly to normalize the breach—that is, to render the situation accountable in familiar terms. It is assumed that the way people handle these breaches tells us much about how they handle their everyday lives (Handel, 1982). Although these experiments seem innocent enough, they often lead to highly emotional reactions. These extreme reactions reflect how important it is to people to engage in routine, common-sense activities. The reactions to breaches are sometimes so extreme that Hugh Mehan and Houston Wood have cautioned about their use: *"Interested persons are strongly advised not to undertake any new breaching studies"* (1975:113).

Accomplishing Gender 性别实现

It seems incontrovertible that one's gender—male or female—is biologically based. People are seen as simply manifesting the behaviors that are an outgrowth of their biological makeup. People usually are not thought of as *accomplishing* their gender. In contrast, sexiness is clearly an accomplishment; people need to speak and act in certain ways in order to be seen as sexy. However, it generally is assumed that one does not have to do or say *anything* to be seen as a man or a woman. Ethnomethodology has investigated the issue of gender, with some very unusual results.

The ethnomethodological view is traceable to one of Harold Garfinkel's (1967) now classic demonstrations of the utility of this orientation. In the 1950s Garfinkel met a person named Agnes, who seemed unquestionably a woman.[3] Not only did she have the figure of a woman, but it was virtually a "perfect" figure with an ideal set of measurements. She also had a pretty face, a good complexion, no facial hair, and plucked eyebrows—and she wore lipstick. This was clearly a woman, or was it? Garfinkel discovered that Agnes had not always appeared to be a woman. In fact, at the time he met her, Agnes was trying, eventually successfully, to convince physicians that she needed an operation to remove her male genitalia and create a vagina.

Agnes was defined as a male at birth. In fact, she was by all accounts a boy until she was 16 years of age. At that age, sensing something was awry, Agnes ran away from home and started to dress like a girl. She soon discovered that dressing like a woman was not enough; she had to *learn to act* like (to "pass" as) a woman if she was to be accepted as one. She did learn the accepted practices and as a result came to be defined, and to define herself, as a woman. Garfinkel was interested in the passing practices that allowed Agnes to function like a woman in society. The more general point here is that we are not simply born men or women; we all also learn and routinely use the commonplace practices that allow us to pass as men or women. It is only in learning these practices that we come to be, in a sociological sense, a man or a woman. Thus, even a category like gender, which is thought to be an ascribed status, can be understood as an accomplishment of a set of situated practices.

Conversation Analysis 对话分析

We now turn to what has become the major type of research within ethnomethodology—conversation analysis. The goal of conversation analysis is to study the taken-for-granted ways in which conversation is organized. Conversation analysts are concerned with the relationships among utterances in a conversation rather than in the relationships between speakers and hearers (Sharrock and Anderson, 1986:68).

电话交谈：身份确定和认知
Telephone Conversations: Identification and Recognition

Emanuel A. Schegloff (1979) viewed his examination of the way in which telephone conversations are opened as part of a larger effort to understand the orderly character of social interaction:

> The work in which my colleagues and I have been engaged is concerned with . . . *detecting* and *describing* the *orderly* phenomena of which conversation and interaction are composed, and an interest in depicting the *systematic organizations* by reference to which those phenomena are produced.
>
> (Schegloff, 1979:24, italics added)

---

[3] For an interesting debate over Garfinkel's interpretation of Agnes, see Denzin (1990a, 1991), Hilbert (1991), Lynch and Bogen (1991), and Maynard (1991).

This interest extends to various orderly phenomena within interaction, such as the organization of turn taking in conversations and the ways in which people seek to repair breaches in normal conversational procedure. In addition, there is interest in the overall structure of a conversation, including openings, closings, and regularly recurring internal sequences.

In this context Schegloff looked at the opening of a phone conversation, which he defined as "a place where the type of conversation being opened can be proffered, displayed, accepted, rejected, modified—in short, incipiently constituted by the parties to it" (1979:25). Although the talk one hears on the phone is no different from that in face-to-face conversations, the participants lack visual contact. Schegloff focused on one element of phone conversations not found in face-to-face conversations: the sequence by which parties who have no visual contact identify and recognize each other.

Schegloff found that telephone openings are often quite straightforward and standardized:

A. Hello?
B. Shar'n?
A. Hi!

(Schegloff, 1979:52)

But some openings "look and sound idiosyncratic—almost virtuoso performances" (Schegloff, 1979:68):

A. Hello.
B. Hello Margie?
A. Yes.
B. hhh We do painting, antiquing,
A. is that right.
B. eh, hh—hhh
A. hnh, hnh, hnh
B. nhh, hnh, hnh! hh
A. hh
B. keep people's pa'r tools
A. y(hhh)! hnh, hnh
B. I'm sorry about that—that—I din' see that.

(adapted from Schegloff, 1979:68)

Although such openings may be different from the usual openings, they are not without their organization. They are "engendered by a systemic sequential organization adapted and fitted by the parties to some particular circumstances" (Schegloff, 1979:68). For example, the preceding conversation is almost incomprehensible until we understand that *B* is calling to apologize for keeping some borrowed power tools too long. *B* makes a joke out of it by building it into a list (painting, antiquing), and it is only at the end, when both are laughing, that the apology comes.

Schegloff's conclusion was that even very idiosyncratic cases are to be examined "to extract from their local particularities the formal organization into which their particularities are infused." (Schegloff, 1979:71).

Initiating Laughter 发笑

Gail Jefferson (1979; see also Jefferson, 1984) looked at the question of how one knows when to laugh in the course of a conversation. The lay view is that laughter is a totally free event in the course of a conversation or interaction. However, Jefferson found that several basic structural characteristics of an utterance are designed to induce the other party to laugh. The first is the placement, by the speaker, of a laugh at the end of his utterance:

> Dan. I thought that was pretty out of sight. Did you hear me say you're a junkie . . .
>   heh, heh
> Dolly. heh, heh, heh.

> (adapted from Jefferson, 1979:80)

The second device reported by Jefferson is within-speech laughter—for example, in mid-sentence:

> A. You know I didn't . . . you know
> B. Hell, *you* know I'm on ret (haha);
> A. ehh, yeh, ha ha.

> (adapted from Jefferson, 1979:83)

Jefferson (1979:83) concluded from these examples that the occurrence of laughter is more organized than we realize.

Jefferson was interested not only in the decision to laugh but also in the declining of an invitation to laugh. She found that silence after an invitation is not enough, that a clear signal is required indicating refusal of the invitation. If, for example, someone refuses to laugh, a strategy would be to commence, just after the onset of the speaker's laugh, a serious pursuit of the topic.

Phillip Glenn (1989) has examined the initiation of shared laughter in a multiparty conversation. Glenn argues that whereas in two-party interactions the speaker ordinarily laughs first, in multiparty interactions someone other than the speaker usually provides the first laugh. In a two-party interaction, the speaker is virtually forced to laugh at his or her own material because there is only one other person present who can perform that function. However, in a multiparty interaction, the fact that there are many other people who can laugh first means that the speaker can better afford the risk of not taking the initiative of being the first to laugh.

Generating Applause 激发掌声

John Heritage and David Greatbatch (1986) have studied the rhetoric of British political speeches (derived from a body of work developed by J. Maxwell Atkinson [1984a, 1984b]) and uncovered basic devices by which speakers generate applause from their audiences. They argue that applause is generated by "statements that are verbally constructed (a) to *emphasize* and thus highlight their contents against a surrounding background of speech materials and (b) to *project a clear completion point* for the message in question" (Heritage and Greatbatch, 1986:116). Emphasis tells the audience that applause is appropriate, and advance notice of a clear completion point allows the audience to begin applauding more or less in unison. In their analysis of British political speeches, Heritage and Greatbatch uncovered seven basic rhetorical devices:

1. *Contrast:* For example, a politician might argue: "Too much is spent on war . . . too little is spent on peace." Such a statement generates applause because, for emphasis, the same point is made first in negative terms and then in positive terms. The audience also is able to anticipate when to applaud by matching the unfolding of the second half of the statement with the already completed first half.

2. *List:* A list of political issues, especially the often used three-part list, provides emphasis as well as a completion point that can be anticipated by the audience.

3. *Puzzle solution:* Here the politician first poses a puzzle for the audience and then offers a solution. This double presentation of the issue provides emphasis, and the audience can anticipate the completion of the statement at the end of the solution.

4. *Headline—punch line:* Here the politician proposes to make a statement and then makes it.

5. *Combination:* This involves use of two or more of the devices just listed.

6. *Position taking:* This involves an initial description of a state of affairs that the speaker would be expected to feel strongly about. However, at first it is presented nonevaluatively. Only at the end does the speaker offer his or her own position.

7. *Pursuit:* This occurs when an audience fails to respond to a particular message. The speaker may actively pursue applause by, for example, restating the central point.

In the political party conferences studied by Heritage and Greatbatch, these seven devices accounted for slightly more than two-thirds of the total applause. Of the seven, *contrast* (accounting for almost a quarter of applause events) was by far the most commonly applauded format. The speaker's manner of delivering the message ("intonation, timing, and gesture") also is important (Heritage and Greatbatch, 1986:143). Finally, Heritage and Greatbatch note that the seven devices are not restricted to political speech making, but also are found in advertising slogans, newspaper editorials, scientific texts, and so forth. In fact, they conclude that these devices have their roots and are found in everyday, natural, conversational interaction. The implication is that we all use these devices daily to generate positive reactions from those with whom we interact.

Booing 嘘声

In a later and parallel piece of research, Steven Clayman (1993) studied booing as an expression of disapproval in the context of public speaking. While applause allows the audience to affiliate with the speaker, booing is an act of disaffiliation.

There are two fundamental ways in which responses such as applause and booing begin—as a result of independent individual decision making and as a product of the mutual monitoring of the behavior of members of an audience. Previous research has demonstrated that individual decision making predominates in the onset of applause. Because the decision is made largely alone, applause occurs almost immediately after a popular remark is made. Also consistent with individual decision making is the fact that applause occurs in a burst that reaches its peak in the first second or two. Further, as demonstrated in the preceding section, a series of well-known devices are employed by speakers to lead audience members to the decision to applaud and then to the applause itself.

Booing, however, is a result more of mutual monitoring than of individual decision making. There is usually a significant time lag between the utterance of the objectionable words and the onset of booing. If booing were the result of a number of individuals making independent decisions, it would occur about as quickly as applause does. The time lag tends to indicate that audience members are monitoring the behavior of others before deciding whether booing is appropriate. In addition, the onset of booing often is preceded by displays by the audience.

For example, the audience may engage in incipient displays of its disaffiliation[4] from the speaker through "a variety of vocalizations—whispering or talking among themselves, talking, shouting, or jeering at the speaker . . . the resulting sound can be characterized as a 'murmur,' 'buzz,' or 'roar'" (Clayman, 1993:117). Audience members monitor these sounds; they indicate to the members that the audience is predisposed to disapprove of the utterance in question. A given audience member feels freer to boo because she has reason to believe that she will not be alone and therefore suffer the disapproval of other audience members.

Of course, one might ask where the incipient displays come from, if not from independent decision making. Clayman believes that some degree of independent decision making is involved here. Individual decision making occurs in the case of incipient displays because the resulting behaviors (for example, private whispering with neighbors, self-talk [for example, "yikes"]) are more private and less likely to be disapproved of by the rest of the audience than is booing. Thus, there is little or no need to monitor the audience in order to determine the appropriateness of such behaviors.

Clayman concludes that collectively produced applause and booing are very much like individually produced agreement and disagreement in everyday behavior. In both cases, "Agreements tend to be produced promptly, in an unqualified manner, and are treated as requiring no special explanation or account. Disagreements, by contrast, typically are delayed, qualified, and accountable" (Clayman, 1993:125). This similarity leads to the conclusion that applause and booing may be explained by general interactional principles that cut across all sectors of life and not just by the organizational and institutional structures and norms involved in public speaking. Those "general principles of human conduct" are part of the interaction order which "is a species of social institution in its own right, one that predates and is constitutive of most other societal institutions, and possesses its own indigenous organizational properties and conventional practices" (Clayman, 1993:127). In other words, the fundamental principles being uncovered by conversation analysts allow us to understand positive (applause) and negative (booing) responses to public speeches.

---

[4] Booing is also likely to occur after displays of affiliation such as applause, but a different process is involved and we will not deal with it here.

句子和故事的互动性凸现
The Interactive Emergence of Sentences and Stories

Charles Goodwin (1979) challenged the traditional linguistic assumption that sentences can be examined in isolation from the process of interaction in which they occur. His view was that "sentences emerge with conversation" (Goodwin, 1979:97). The fact is that the "speaker can reconstruct the meaning of his sentence *as he is producing it* in order to maintain its appropriateness to its recipient of the moment" (Goodwin, 1979:98; italics added).

Speakers pay acute attention to listeners as they are speaking. As the listeners react verbally, facially, or with body language, the speaker—on the basis of those reactions—adjusts the sentence as it is emerging. The reactions allow the speaker to decide whether his or her point is being made and, if not, to alter the structure of the sentence. Goodwin described some of the alterations that took place in a particular sentence sequence: "the unfolding meaning of John's sentence is reconstructed twice, a new segment is added to it, and another is deleted prior to its production but replaced with a different segment." (1979:112). In other words, sentences are the products of collaborative processes.

Mandelbaum (1989) examined the interactive emergence of stories. Her key point is that the audience is not passive, as is conventionally assumed, but rather can be seen as the "co-author" of the story. Paralleling Goodwin's analysis of the interactive emergence of sentences, Mandelbaum shows that the audience members have resources that allow them to work with the author to alter a story while the storytelling is in process. The audience participates by allowing the suspension of turn-by-turn talk so that the storyteller may dominate the conversation. The audience members also help the story along by displaying their understanding through the use of expressions such as "uh huh" and "mm hm." The audience may also "repair" some problem in the story, thereby permitting it to proceed more smoothly. Most important for the purposes of this discussion, the audience may intervene in the story and cause it to move off in a new direction. Thus, in a very real sense, stories, like sentences and conversations in general, are interactional products.

谈话与非口头行为的整合
Integration of Talk and Nonvocal Activities

Conversation analysts have focused on talk, and other ethnomethodologists on nonvocal activities. Some researchers use videotapes and films to analyze the integration of vocal and nonvocal activities. Charles Goodwin (1984), for example, examined a videotape of a dinner party involving two couples. One issue in the relationship between vocal and nonvocal activities is the body posture of a person (in this case Ann) who tells a story at the party:

> Ann clasps her hands together, places both elbows on the table, and leans forward while gazing toward her addressed recipient, Beth. With this posture the speaker displays full orientation toward her addressed recipient, complete engagement in telling her story, and lack of involvement in any activities other than conversation. The posture appears to . . . constitute a visual display that a telling is in progress.
>
> (C. Goodwin, 1984:228)

More generally, Goodwin concludes, "Ann's telling is thus made visible not only in her talk but also in the way in which she organizes her body and activities during the telling" (1984:229).

Another nonvocal activity examined by Goodwin is the gaze, which he relates to talk:

> When a speaker gazes at a recipient that recipient should be gazing at him. When speakers gaze at nongazing recipients, and thus locate violations of the rule, they frequently produce phrasal breaks such as restarts and pauses, in their talk. These phrasal breaks both orient to the event as a violation by locating the talk in progress at that point as impaired in some fashion and provide a remedy by functioning as requests for the gaze of the hearer. Thus just after phrasal breaks nongazing recipients frequently begin to move their gaze to the speaker.
>
> (C. Goodwin, 1984:230)

Body posture and gaze are only two of many nonvocal activities that are intimately related to vocal activities.

Doing Shyness (and Self-Confidence) 害羞（以及自信）

We tend to think of shyness and self-confidence as psychological traits, but Philip Manning and George Ray (1993) have attempted to show that they are things that we "do" as we are managing conversational encounters. There are a range of typical procedures that we all use to get acquainted with those we do not know, and the shy and the self-confident modify these procedures, albeit in different ways, in order to deal with social situations distinctively. Thus, the shy and the self-confident employ different conversational strategies.

Manning and Ray conducted a laboratory study with college students involving the videotaping and transcribing of the interaction of ten shy and ten self-confident dyads. While we all engage in "setting-talk"—that is, talk about our immediate environment—shy people do this much more than do those who are self-confident. Take the following example:

> A. (nervous laughter) A microphone
> B. We're being tape recorded
> A. I know probably
> B. Huh
> A. Okay
> B. I guess they're going to observe how nervous we are (laughs)
> A. I know
>
> (Manning and Ray, 1993:182)

Manning and Ray found that shy participants were more than two and a half times as likely to engage in setting-talk at the beginning of a conversation than were those who are self-confident. Further, those who are shy were eight times more likely to return to setting-talk later, whenever the conversation flagged. Manning and Ray conclude, "We believe that shy participants used setting-talk as a 'safe' topic, comparable to discussions about the weather. By contrast . . . self-confident participants viewed setting-talk as a dead end to be avoided" (1993:183). Instead, those high in self-confidence were more likely to exchange names and move immediately into the introduction of a topic for conversation (a "pretopical sequence"). While shy participants tend to reject these pretopical sequences, those who are self-confident are likely to respond to them, and in depth.

One key issue is whether these and other differences in conversation are symptoms of underlying psychological differences or whether shyness and self-confidence *are* the different conversational procedures. Needless to say, Manning and Ray (1993:189), adopting the ethnomethodological perspective, tend to prefer the latter view.

Studies of Institutions 制度研究

As pointed out earlier in this chapter, a number of ethnomethodologists have become interested in the study of conversation and interaction in various social institutions. In this section we will examine a few examples of this kind of work.

Job Interviews 工作面谈

Some ethnomethodologists have turned their attention to the work world. For example, Button (1987) has looked at the job interview. Not surprisingly, he sees the interview as a sequential, turn-taking conversation and as the "situated practical accomplishment of the parties to that setting" (Button, 1987:160). One issue addressed in this study involves the things that interviewers can do, after an answer has been given, to move on to something else, thereby preventing the interviewee from returning to, and perhaps correcting, his or her answer. First, the interviewer may indicate that the interview as a whole is over. Second, the interviewer may ask another question that moves the discussion in a different direction. Third, the interviewer may assess the answer given in such a way that the interviewee is precluded from returning to it.

Button wonders what it is that makes a job interview an interview. He argues that it is not the sign on the door or the gathering together of people. Rather, it is "what those people do, and how they structure and organize their interactions with one another, that achieves for some social settings its characterizability as an interview. This integrally involves the way in which the participants organize their speech exchange with one another" (Button, 1987:170). Thus it is the nature of the interaction, of the conversation, that defines a job interview.

Executive Negotiations 经理人谈判

Anderson, Hughes, and Sharrock (1987) have examined the nature of negotiations among business executives. One of their findings about such negotiations is how reasonable, detached, and impersonal they are:

> Everything is carried out in a considered, measured, reasonable way. No personal animus is involved or intended in their maneuverings. It is simply what they do; part of their working day. . . . Animosities, disagreements and disputes are always contained, in hand, controlled. If a deal cannot be made this time, so be it.
>
> (Anderson, Hughes, and Sharrock, 1987:155)

This kind of interaction tells us a great deal about the business world.

Interestingly, Anderson, Hughes, and Sharrock go on to argue that what takes place in the business world is no different from what takes place in everyday life. In most of our social relationships we behave the way the business executives described above behaved. "Business life does not take place in a sealed compartment, set off from the rest of social life. It is continuous with and interwoven with it" (Anderson, Hughes, and Sharrock, 1987:155).

Calls to Emergency Centers 急救电话

Whalen and Zimmerman (1987) have examined telephone calls to emergency communications centers. The context of such calls leads to a reduction of the opening of telephone conversations. In normal telephone conversations we usually find summons-answer, identification-recognition, greeting, and "howareyou" sequences. In emergency calls, however, the opening sequences are reduced and recognitions, greetings, and "howareyous" are routinely absent.

Another interesting aspect of emergency phone calls is that certain opening events that would be ignored in a normal conversation are treated quite seriously:

> . . . those situations in which caller hangs up after dispatcher answers, or there is silence on the line or sounds such as dogs barking, arguing and screaming in the background, or a smoke alarm ringing. Despite the lack of direct conversational engagement on the line, dispatchers initially treat these events as possible indicators of a need for assistance, and thus as functional or *virtual* requests.
>
> (Whalen and Zimmerman, 1987:178)

The peculiar nature of the emergency telephone conversation leads to these and other adaptations to the structure of the normal conversatizon.

In a related study, Whalen, Zimmerman, and Whalen (1988) looked at a specific emergency telephone conversation that failed, leading to the delayed dispatch of an ambulance and the death of a woman. While the media tended to blame the dispatcher for this incident, Whalen, Zimmerman, and Whalen trace the problem to the nature of the specific emergency phone conversation:

> Our investigation revealed that the participants had rather different understandings of what was happening and different expectations of what was supposed to happen in this conversation. Over the course of the interaction the talk of both caller and nurse-dispatcher (and her supervisor) operated to extend and deepen this misalignment. This misalignment contributed in a fundamental way to a dispute that contaminated and transformed the participants' activity.
>
> (Whalen, Zimmerman, and Whalen, 1988:358)

Thus, it was the nature of the specific conversation, not the abilities of the dispatcher, that "caused" the mishap.

Dispute Resolution in Mediation Hearings 听证会上的争议之解决

Angela Garcia (1991) analyzed conflict resolution in a California program designed to mediate a variety of disputes—between landlord and tenant, over small sums of money, and among family members or friends. Her ultimate goal is to compare institutional conflict resolution with that which takes place in ordinary conversations.

Garcia's key point is that institutional mediation makes conflict resolution easier by eliminating processes that lead to escalating levels of strife in ordinary conversation. Further, when arguments do occur in mediation, procedures exist that do not exist in ordinary conversation that make termination of the conflict possible.

Garcia begins with the familiar concern of conversation analysts with turn taking. Mediation stipulates who is allowed to speak at any given time and what form responses may take. For example, complainants speak first and may not be interrupted by disputants during their presentations. These constraints on interruptions greatly restrict the amount of conflict in mediated disputes. In contrast, the ability to interrupt in normal conversations greatly escalates the likelihood and amount of conflict. Also reducing the possibility of conflict is the fact that disputants must ask the mediator's permission to speak or to use sanctions. The request may be denied, and even if it isn't, the fact that a request has been made serves to mitigate the possibility of direct conflict between disputants. Another key factor in reducing the possibility of conflict is the fact that disputants address their remarks to the mediator rather than to each other. During periods when an issue is under joint discussion, the mediator, not the participants, controls both the topic and who participates by asking disputants directed questions. The mediator therefore serves as both a buffer and a controller and in both roles operates to limit the possibility of conflict.

The mediator seeks especially to limit the possibility of direct and adjacent accusations and denials by the disputants. Such "cross talk" is highly likely to lead to conflict, and mediators seek to prevent it from occurring and are quick to act once it begins. To halt cross talk, the mediator may try to change topics, redirect a question, or sanction the disputants.

In sum, "in mediation, the adjacent and directly addressed oppositional utterances that constitute argument do not occur" (A. Garcia, 1991:827). Garcia summarizes her conclusions by offering four characteristics of mediation that allow disputants to reduce or eliminate arguments while at the same time saving face:

1. Accusations and denials are not adjacent to one another in the turn-taking system of a mediated dispute, thereby reducing the possibility of escalation into an argument.

2. Denials are made not directly to accusations, but to queries by the mediator. As a result, since they are separated from responses, denials are less likely to provoke disputational responses.

3. Because there is a delay between accusation and response, disputants are permitted not to respond to certain accusations without their lack of response implying that they are guilty of those accusations. The delay allows the disputant to "bypass some accusations, focus on the more important accusations, or ignore accusations she or he cannot credibly deny" (A. Garcia, 1991:830). The result is that there generally end up being fewer issues on the table about which arguments can occur.

4. Accusations and denials are mitigated by the mediation system. For example, the agent being accused may be referred to implicitly rather than

explicitly, that agent may be referred to collectively as "we" with the result that the complainant is including himself as the blamed party, or the accusations themselves can be downgraded by the use of words and phrases such as "I would imagine" and "maybe."

Unlike Clayman in his study of booing, Garcia does not argue that the structure of interaction in mediation is similar to the interactional organization of everyday life. In fact, her point is that they are very different interactional orders. However, like Clayman and other conversation analysts, Garcia (1991:833) does see the key to understanding what goes on in interaction, specifically in this case in mediation, in "the interactional order of mediation itself," rather than in the social or normative structure of mediation.

Greatbatch and Dingwall (1997) examined divorce mediation sessions conducted in ten agencies in England. In contrast to Garcia's study, disputants do talk directly to one another and often become involved in arguments. Given this, Greatbatch and Dingwall are interested in the ways in which such arguments are exited. While mediators can take various actions, the focus in this study is on things that the disputants can do to exit an argument, such as one party passing on the opportunity to speak and leaving only the other party talking, taking the initiative and addressing the mediator rather than the other disputant, announcing that one is withdrawing from the argument, and offering conciliatory accounts (e.g., "I'm to blame"). Nevertheless, in most instances in the British case disputants do not talk directly to one another; they do address mediators. Perhaps of greater importance than the specific differences between the two studies is the fact that Greatbatch and Dingwall (1997:164) also take issue with Garcia's argument that what takes place in such settings is not similar to everyday life: "The deescalatory practices described here are not unique to mediation; they are generic speaking practices deriving from ordinary conversation." In other words, the things that disputants do to exit arguments are similar to the ways in which we extricate ourselves from arguments on a daily basis.

Criticisms of Traditional Sociology 对传统社会学的批判

Ethnomethodologists criticize traditional sociologists for several reasons.

Separated from the Social 与社会分离

Sociologists are critiqued for imposing *their* sense of social reality on the social world (Mehan and Wood, 1975). They believe that sociology has not been attentive enough to, or respectful enough of, the everyday world that should be its ultimate source of knowledge (Sharrock and Anderson, 1986). More extremely, sociology has rendered the most essential aspects of the social world (ethnomethods) unavailable and focuses instead on a constructed world that conceals everyday practices. Enamored of their own view of the social world, sociologists have tended not to share the same social reality as those they study. As Mehan and Wood put it, "In attempting to do a social *science,* sociology has become alienated from the social" (1975:63).

Within this general orientation, Mehan and Wood (see also Sharrock and Anderson, 1986) leveled a number of specific criticisms at sociology. The concepts used by sociologists are said to distort the social world, to destroy its ebb and flow. Further distortion is caused by sociology's reliance on scientific techniques and statistical analyses of data. Statistics simply do not usually do justice to the elegance and sophistication of the real world. The coding techniques used by sociologists when they translate human behavior into their preconceived categories distort the social world. Furthermore, the seeming simplicity of the codes conceals the complicated and distorting work involved in turning aspects of the social world into the sociologist's preconceived categories. Sociologists also are seen as tending to accept unquestioningly a respondent's description of a phenomenon rather than looking at the phenomenon itself. Thus, a description of a social setting is taken to *be* that setting rather than one conception of that setting. Finally, Mehan and Wood argued that sociologists are prone to offer abstractions of the social world that are increasingly removed from the reality of everyday life.

Confusing Topic and Resource 混淆主题和资源

Taking a slightly different approach, Don Zimmerman and Melvin Pollner (1970) argued that conventional sociology has suffered from a confusion of *topic* and *resource*. That is, the everyday social world is a resource for the favorite topics of sociology, but it is rarely a topic in its own right. This can be illustrated in a variety of ways. For example, Roy Turner (1970; see also Sharrock and Anderson, 1986) argued that sociologists usually look at everyday speech not as a topic in itself but as a resource with which to study hidden realities such as norms, values, attitudes, and so on. However, instead of being a resource, everyday speech can be seen as one of the ways in which the business of social life is carried on—a topic in itself. Matthew Speier (1970) argued that when sociologists look at childhood socialization, they look not at the processes themselves but at a series of abstract "stages" generalized from those processes. Speier argued that "*socialization is the acquisition of interactional competencies*" (1970:189). Thus, the ethnomethodologist must look at the way these competencies are acquired and used in the everyday reality of the real world.

Another analysis of childhood socialization, by Robert W. Mackay (1974), is even more useful as a critique of traditional sociology and the confusion of topic and resource. Mackay contrasted the "normative" approach of traditional sociology with the interpretive approach of ethnomethodology. The normative approach is seen as arguing that socialization is merely a series of stages in which "complete" adults teach "incomplete" children the ways of society. Mackay viewed this as a "gloss" that ignores the reality that socialization involves an interaction between children and adults. Children are not passive, incomplete receptacles; rather, they are active participants in the socialization process, because they have the ability to reason, invent, and acquire knowledge. Socialization is a two-sided process. Mackay believed that the ethnomethodological orientation "restores the interaction between adults and children based on interpretive competencies as the phenomenon of study" (1974:183).

Zimmerman and Pollner (1970) cited other examples of the confusion of topic and resource. For example, they argued that sociologists normally explain action in bureaucracies by the rules, norms, and values of the organization. However, had they looked at organizations as topics, they would have seen that actors often simply make it *appear* through their actions that those actions can be explained by the rules. It is not the rules but the actors' *use* of the rules that should be the topic of sociological research. Zimmerman and Pollner then cited the example of a code of behavior among prison convicts. Whereas traditional sociology would look at the ways in which actors are constrained by a convict code, ethnomethodologists would examine how the convicts use the code as an explanatory and persuasive device. Don Zimmerman and Lawrence Wieder offered the following generalization on the confusion of topic and resource:

> The ethnomethodologist is not concerned with providing causal explanations of observably regular, patterned, repetitive actions by some kind of analysis of the actor's point of view. He *is* concerned with how members of society go about the task of *seeing, describing,* and *explaining* order in the world in which they live.
>
> (Zimmerman and Wieder, 1970:289)

Social order is not a reality in itself to the ethnomethodologist but an accomplishment of social actors.

民族方法学中的压力和张力
Stresses and Strains in Ethnomethodology

While ethnomethodology has made enormous strides in sociology and has demonstrated, especially in the area of conversation analysis, some capacity to cumulate knowledge of the world of everyday life, there are some problems worth noting.

First, while ethnomethodology is far more accepted today than it was a decade or two ago, it is still regarded with considerable suspicion by many sociologists (Pollner, 1991). They view it as focusing on trivial matters and ignoring the crucially important issues confronting society today. The ethnomethodologists' response is that they *are* dealing with the crucial issues because it is everyday life that matters most. Paul Atkinson sums up the situation: "Ethnomethodology continues to be greeted with mixtures of incomprehension and hostility in some quarters, but it is unquestionably a force to be reckoned with when it comes to the theory, methods, and empirical conduct of sociological inquiry" (1988:442).

Second, there are those (for example, Atkinson, 1988) who believe that ethnomethodology has lost sight of its phenomenological roots and its concern for conscious, cognitive processes (exceptions are Cicourel [1974] and Coulter [1983, 1989], although Coulter is inclined to embed cognition within the everyday world). Instead of focusing on such conscious processes, ethnomethodologists, especially conversation analysts, have come to focus on the "structural properties of the talk itself" (Atkinson, 1988:449). Ignored in the process are motives and the internal motivations for action. In Atkinson's view, ethnomethodology has grown "unduly restricted" and has come to be "behaviorist and empiricist" (1988:441). In moving in this direction, ethnomethodology is seen as having gone back on some of its basic principles, including its desire not to treat the actor as a judgmental dope:

> Garfinkel's early inspiration was to reject the judgmental dope image in order to focus attention on the skillful and artful, methodical work put into the production of social order. In the intervening years, however, some versions of ethnomethodology have returned to the judgmental dope as their model actor. Intentionality and meaning have been all but eliminated.
>
> (Atkinson, 1988:449)

Third, some ethnomethodologists have worried about the link between the concerns in their work (for example, conversations) and the larger social structure. This concern exists even though, as we discussed earlier in the chapter and will return to toward the end, ethnomethodologists tend to see themselves as bridging the micro-macro divide. For example, some years ago, Zimmerman viewed cross-fertilization with macrosociology as "an open question, and an intriguing possibility" (1978:12). Later, Pollner urged ethnomethodology to "return to sociology to understand those [taken-for-granted] practices in their larger social context . . . mundane reason in terms of structural and historical processes. Mundane reason, it is suggested is not simply the product of local work of mundane reasoners, for it is also shaped by longer term and larger scale dynamics" (1987:xvi). Some such cross-fertilization has been undertaken by people like Giddens (1984), who has integrated ethnomethodological ideas into his structuration theory. More generally, Boden (1990; see the next section) has outlined what ethnomethodology has to offer to the issue of the relationship between structure and agency. She argues that the findings of ethnomethodological studies are relevant not only to micro structures but to macro structures as well. There is hope that institutional studies will shed more light on the macro structure and its relationship to micro-level phenomena.

Fourth, and from within the field, Pollner (1991) has criticized ethnomethodology for losing sight of its original radical reflexivity. Radical reflexivity leads to the view that all social activity is accomplished, including the activities of ethnomethodologists. However, ethnomethodology has come to be more accepted by mainstream sociologists. As Pollner puts it, "Ethnomethodology is settling down in the suburbs of sociology" (1991:370). As they have come to be more accepted, ethnomethodologists have tended to lose sight of the need to analyze their own work. As a result, in Pollner's view, ethnomethodology is in danger of losing its self-analytical and critical edge and becoming just another establishment theoretical specialty.

Finally, it should be noted that although they are discussed under the same heading, there is a growing uneasiness in the relationship between ethnomethodology and conversation analysis (Lynch, 1993:203–264). As mentioned earlier, they have somewhat different roots. More important, in recent years it is conversation analysis that has made the greatest headway in sociology as a whole. Its tendency to study conversations empirically makes it quite acceptable to the discipline's mainstream. The tension between the two is likely to increase if conversation analysis continues to settle into the mainstream while ethnomethodological studies of institutions remain more on the periphery.

Synthesis and Integration 综合和整合

Even ethnomethodology, one of the most determinedly micro-extremist perspectives in sociological theory, has shown some signs of openness to synthesis and integration. For example, ethnomethodology seems to be expanding into domains that appear to be more in line with mainstream sociology. Good examples are Heritage and Greatbatch's (1986) analysis of the methods used to generate applause from audiences and Clayman's (1993) study of booing. Typologies developed by such ethnomethodologists seem little different from the kinds of typologies employed by various other types of sociological theorists.

However, ethnomethodology remains embattled and insecure and thus, in some ways, seems to run counter to the trend toward theoretical synthesis. Seemingly rejecting the idea of synthesis, Garfinkel sees ethnomethodology as an "incommensurably alternate sociology" (1988:108). Boden (1990) finds it necessary to make a strong, albeit somewhat self-conscious, case *for* ethnomethodology and conversation analysis. It is certainly true, as Boden suggests, that ethnomethodology has widened and deepened its support in sociology. However, one wonders whether it, or any other sociological theory for that matter, is, as Boden contends, "here to stay." In any case, such an argument contradicts the idea that theoretical boundaries are weakening and new synthetic perspectives are emerging. It may be that ethnomethodology is still too new and too insecure to consider an erosion of its boundaries.

Nevertheless, much of Boden's (1990) essay deals with synthetic efforts *within* ethnomethodology, especially regarding integrative issues such as the relationship between agency and structure, the embeddedness of action, and fleeting events within the course of history. Boden also deals with the extent to which an array of European and American theorists have begun to integrate ethnomethodology and conversation analysis into their orientations. Unfortunately, what is lacking is a discussion of the degree to which ethnomethodologists are integrating the ideas of other sociological theories into their perspective. Ethnomethodologists seem quite willing to have other theorists integrate ethnomethodological perspectives, but they seem far less eager to reciprocate.

民族方法学和微观—宏观秩序
Ethnomethodology and the Micro-Macro Order

Hilbert (1990) deals with the relationship between ethnomethodology and the micro-macro order. As we saw earlier, Hilbert rejects the conventional idea that ethnomethodology is a microsociology, but it is not, in his view, to be seen as a macrosociology either. Rather, Hilbert argues that ethnomethodology "transcends" the micro-macro issue because it is concerned "with social practices [membership practices] which are the methods of producing *both* microstructure and macrostructure as well as any presumed 'linkage' between these two" (1990:794).

Hilbert, somewhat erroneously (see Chapter 10), reduces the micro-macro linkage issue to a set of structural concerns. That is, it involves a focus on micro structures, macro structures, and the linkage between them. In Hilbert's view, ethnomethodologists are "indifferent" to structures *at any level.* Instead of being concerned with either micro or macro structures, ethnomethodologists are interested in the membership practices, the "ethnomethods," "the artful production," of structure in general. That is, ethnomethodologists are interested in the "methods of producing, maintaining, sustaining, and reproducing social structure by and for the membership, whether oriented to large scale institutional (macro) structure or smaller, more intimate (micro) structure" (Hilbert, 1990:799).

Hilbert offers what he calls the "radical thesis" of ethnomethodology, which serves to transcend the issue of micro-macro linkage:

> The empirical phenomena that conversation analysts witness but which members cannot possibly know about, and . . . the structural phenomena that members orient to and take for granted but which nevertheless are nonempirical and unavailable for social science are (in a subtle way) . . . *the same phenomena.*
>
> (Hilbert, 1990:801)

In other words, to the ethnomethodologist there is no distinction to be made between micro and macro structures because they are generated simultaneously. However, neither ethnomethodologists nor any other sociological theorists have offered the ultimate solution to the micro-macro issue. Hilbert's effort is marred by his reduction of this issue to a concern for the linkage of micro and macro *structures*. As we will see in Chapter 10, there is far more to this issue than such a linkage. Nevertheless, the ethnomethodologists do offer an interesting, indeed radical, approach to this question, dissolving it and arguing that the micro and the macro are the same thing! Certainly one way to deal with the micro-macro issue is to refuse to separate the two levels, seeing them instead as part of the same general process.

Summary 总结

This chapter has been devoted to a very distinctive kind of sociology and sociological theory—ethnomethodology. Ethnomethodology is the study of the everyday practices used by the ordinary members of society in order to deal with their day-to-day lives. People are seen as accomplishing their everyday lives through a variety of artful practices. Over the years, ethnomethodology has grown increasingly diverse. However, the two main varieties of ethnomethodology are institutional studies and conversation analysis.

We examined several early examples of ethnomethodology, including "breaching experiments," as well as Garfinkel's famous study of Agnes and the ways in which "she" accomplished being a female (even though she was actually a he). The bulk of the chapter is devoted to a discussion of the heart of ethnomethodology—studies of conversations and institutions. Included in the discussion of studies of conversations are reviews of work on such things as how people know when it is appropriate to laugh, applaud, and boo. We also discuss several institutional studies, including one that dealt with the way disputes are resolved in mediation hearings.

Ethnomethodologists tend to be highly critical of mainstream sociology. For example, mainstream sociologists are seen as imposing their sense of social reality on people rather than studying what people actually do. Sociologists distort the social world in various ways by imposing their concepts, utilizing statistics, and so on. Sociologists also are accused of confusing topic and resource—that is, using the everyday world as a resource rather than as a topic in its own right.

There are a variety of stresses and strains within ethnomethodology, including its continued exclusion from the mainstream of sociology, the accusation that it has lost sight of cognitive processes, the inability to deal adequately with social structures, the loss of its original radical quality, and the tension between ethnomethodologists and conversation analysts. The chapter closes with a discussion of some work within ethnomethodology on integration and synthesis. However, there are those who regard ethnomethodology as incompatible with other sociological theories.

Exchange, Network, and Rational Choice Theories

第8章 交换、网络和理性选择理论

Chapter Outline

Exchange Theory
Network Theory
Network Exchange Theory
Rational Choice Theory

In this chapter we will focus on three related theories—exchange theory, rational choice theory, and network theory. Rational choice theory was one of the intellectual influences that shaped the development of exchange theory, especially its tendency to assume a rational actor. However, while contemporary exchange theory continues to demonstrate the influence of rational choice theory, it has been affected by other intellectual currents and has gone off in a series of unique directions. Thus, contemporary exchange and rational choice theories are far from coterminous. One fundamental difference is that while rational choice theorists focus on individual decision making, the basic unit of analysis to exchange theorists is the social relationship. Recently, exchange theorists have been devoting more attention to networks of social relationships, and this focus tends to connect them with network theory itself. Network theory has much in common with rational choice theory, although it rejects the assumption of the rationality of human actors (Mizruchi, 1994). Overall, and unlike the theories discussed in the preceding two chapters, these theories share a positivistic orientation.

Exchange Theory 交换理论

We begin, following Molm and Cook (1995; Lovaglia, 2007; Cook and Rice, 2005, 2001), with an overview of the history of the development of exchange theory, beginning with its roots in behaviorism.

Behaviorism 行为主义

Behaviorism is best known in psychology, but in sociology it had both direct effects on behavioral sociology (Bushell and Burgess, 1969; Baldwin and Baldwin, 1986) and indirect effects, especially on exchange theory (Molm; 2005a). The behavioral sociologist is concerned with the relationship between the effects of an actor's behavior on the environment and its impact on the actor's later behavior. This relationship is basic to *operant conditioning*, or the learning process by which "behavior is modified by its consequences" (Baldwin and Baldwin, 1986:6). One might almost think of this behavior, at least initially in the infant, as a random behavior. The environment in which the behavior exists, whether social or physical, is affected by the behavior and in turn "acts" back in various ways. That reaction—positive, negative, or neutral—affects the actor's later behavior. If the reaction has been rewarding to the actor, the same behavior is likely to be emitted in the future in similar situations. If the reaction has been painful or punishing, the behavior is less likely to occur in the future. The behavioral sociologist is interested in the relationship between the *history* of environmental reactions or consequences and the nature of present behavior. Past consequences of a given behavior govern its present state. By knowing what elicited a certain behavior in the past, we can predict whether an actor will produce the same behavior in the present situation.

Of great interest to behaviorists are rewards (or reinforcers) and costs (or punishments). Rewards are defined by their ability to strengthen (that is, reinforce) behavior, while costs reduce the likelihood of behavior. As we will see, behaviorism in general, and the ideas of rewards and costs in particular, had a powerful impact on early exchange theory.

Rational Choice Theory 理性选择理论

The basic principles of rational choice theory are derived from neoclassical economics (as well as utilitarianism and game theory; Simpson 2007; Levi et al., 1990; Lindenberg, 2001). Based on a variety of different models, Debra Friedman and Michael Hechter (1988) have put together what they describe as a "skeletal" model of rational choice theory.

The focus in rational choice theory is on actors. Actors are seen as being purposive, or as having intentionality. That is, actors have ends or goals toward which their actions are aimed. Actors also are seen as having preferences (or values, utilities). Rational choice theory is not concerned with what these preferences, or their sources, are. Of importance is the fact that action is undertaken to achieve objectives that are consistent with an actor's preference hierarchy.

Although rational choice theory starts with actors' purposes or intentions, it must take into consideration at least two major constraints on action. The first is the scarcity of resources. Actors have different resources as well as differential access to other resources. For those with lots of resources, the achievement of ends may be relatively easy. However, for those with few, if any, resources, the attainment of ends may be difficult or impossible.

GEORGE CASPAR HOMANS

An Autobiographical Sketch

How I became a sociologist, which was largely a matter of accident, I have described in other publications. [For a full autobiography, see Homans, 1984.] My sustained work in sociology began with my association, beginning in 1933, with Professors Lawrence Henderson and Elton Mayo at the Harvard Business School. Henderson, a biochemist, was studying the physiological characteristics of industrial work; Mayo, a psychologist, the human factors. Mayo was then and later the director of the famous researches at the Hawthorne Plant of the Western Electric Company in Chicago.

I took part in a course of readings and discussions under Mayo's direction. Among other books, Mayo asked his students to read several books by prominent social anthropologists, particularly Malinowski, Radcliffe-Brown, and Firth. Mayo wanted us to read these books so that we should understand how in aboriginal, in contrast to modern, societies social rituals supported productive work.

I became interested in them for a wholly different reason. In those days the cultural anthropologists were intellectually dominant, and friends of mine in this group, such as Clyde Kluckhohn, insisted that every culture was unique. Instead I began to perceive from my reading that certain institutions of aboriginal societies repeated themselves in places so far separated in time and space that the societies could not have borrowed them from one another. Cultures were not unique and, what was more, their similarities could only be explained on the assumption that human nature was the same the world over. Members of the human species working in similar circumstances had independently created the similar institutions. This was not a popular view at the time. I am not sure it is now.

By this time I had also been exposed to a number of concrete or "field" studies of small human groups both modern and aboriginal. When I was called to active duty in the Navy in World War II, I reflected on this material during long watches at sea. Quite suddenly, I conceived that a number of these studies might be described in concepts common to them all. In a few days I had sketched out such a conceptual scheme.

Back at Harvard with a tenured position after the war, I began working on a book, later entitled *The Human Group* (1951), which was intended to apply my conceptual scheme to the studies in question. In the course of this work it occurred to me that a conceptual scheme was useful only as the starting point

Related to scarcity of resources is the idea of *opportunity costs* (D. Friedman and Hechter, 1988:202). In pursuing a given end, actors must keep an eye on the costs of forgoing their next-most-attractive action. An actor may choose not to pursue the most highly valued end if her resources are negligible, if as a result the chances of achieving that end are slim, and if in striving to achieve that end she jeopardizes her chances of achieving her next-most-valued end. Actors are seen as trying to maximize of a science. What was next required were propositions relating the concepts to one another. In *The Human Group,* I stated a number of such propositions, which seemed to hold good for the groups I had chosen.

I had long known Professor Talcott Parsons and was now closely associated with him in the Department of Social Relations. The sociological profession looked upon him as its leading theorist. I decided that what he called theories were only conceptual schemes, and that a theory was not a theory unless it contained at least a few propositions. I became confident that this view was correct by reading several books on the philosophy of science.

Nor was it enough that a theory should contain propositions. A theory of a phenomenon was an explanation of it. Explanation consisted in showing that one or more propositions of a low order of generality followed in logic from more general propositions applied to what were variously called given or boundary conditions or parameters. I stated my position on this issue in my little book *The Nature of Social Science* (1967).

I then asked myself what general propositions I could use in this way to explain the empirical propositions I had stated in *The Human Group* and other propositions brought to my attention by later reading of field and experimental studies in social psychology. The general propositions would have to meet only one condition: in accordance with my original insight, they should apply to individual human beings as members of a species.

Such propositions were already at hand—luckily, for I could not have invented them for myself. They were the propositions of behavioral psychology as stated by my old friend B. F. Skinner and others. They held good of persons both when acting alone in the physical environment and when in interaction with other persons. In the two editions of my book *Social Behavior* (1961 and revised in 1974), I used these propositions to try to explain how, under appropriate given conditions, relatively enduring social structures could arise from, and be maintained by, the actions of individuals, who need not have intended to create the structures. This I conceive to be the central intellectual problem of sociology.

Once the structures have been created, they have further effects on the behavior of persons who take part in them or come into contact with them. But these further effects are explained by the same propositions as those used to explain the creation and maintenance of the structures in the first place. The structures only provide new given conditions to which the propositions are to be applied. My sociology remains fundamentally individualistic and not collectivistic.

[George Homans died in 1989. See Bell (1992) for a biographical sketch of Homans. See also Fararo (2007) and Molm (2005b)].

their benefits,[1] and that goal may involve assessing the relationship between the chances of achieving a primary end and what that achievement does for the chances of attaining the second-most-valuable objective.

---

[1] Although contemporary rational choice theorists recognize that there are limits on the desire and ability to maximize (Heckathorn, 1997).

A second source of constraints on individual action is social institutions. As Friedman and Hechter put it, an individual typically will

> find his or her actions checked from birth to death by familial and school rules; laws and ordinances; firm policies; churches, synagogues and mosques; and hospitals and funeral parlors. By restricting the feasible set of courses of action available to individuals, enforceable rules of the game—including norms, laws, agendas, and voting rules—systematically affect social outcomes.
>
> (D. Friedman and Hechter, 1988:202)

These institutional constraints provide both positive and negative sanctions that serve to encourage certain actions and discourage others.

Friedman and Hechter enumerate two other ideas that they see as basic to rational choice theory. The first is an aggregation mechanism, or the process by which "the separate individual actions are combined to produce the social outcome" (D. Friedman and Hechter, 1988:203). The second is the importance of information in making rational choices. At one time, it was assumed that actors had perfect, or at least sufficient, information to make purposive choices among the alternative courses of action open to them. However, there is a growing recognition that the quantity or quality of available information is highly variable and that that variability has a profound effect on actors' choices (Heckathorn, 1997).

At least in its early formation, exchange theory was affected by a rudimentary theory of rationality. Later in this chapter, when we deal with rational choice theory itself, we will discuss some of the greater complexity associated with it.

乔治·霍曼斯的交换理论
The Exchange Theory of George Homans

The heart of George Homans's exchange theory lies in a set of fundamental propositions. Although some of his propositions deal with at least two interacting individuals, Homans was careful to point out that these propositions are based on psychological principles. According to Homans, they are psychological for two reasons. First, "they are usually stated and empirically tested by persons who call themselves psychologists" (Homans, 1967:39–40). Second, and more important, they are psychological because of the level at which they deal with the individual in society: "They are propositions about the behavior of individual human beings, rather than propositions about groups or societies as such; and *the behavior of men, as men,* is generally considered the province of psychology" (Homans, 1967:40; italics added). As a result of this position, Homans admitted to being "what has been called—and it is a horrid phrase—a psychological reductionist" (1974:12). Reductionism to Homans is "the process of showing how the propositions of one named science [in this case, sociology] follow in logic from the more general propositions of another named science [in this case, psychology]" (1984:338).

Although Homans made the case for psychological principles, he did not think of individuals as isolated. He recognized that people are social and spend a considerable portion of their time interacting with other people. He attempted to explain social behavior with psychological principles: "What the position [Homans's] does assume is that the general propositions of psychology, which are propositions about the effects on human behavior of the results thereof, do not change when the results come from other men rather than from the physical environment" (Homans, 1967:59). Homans did not deny the Durkheimian position that something new emerges from interaction. Instead, he argued that those emergent properties can be explained by psychological principles; there is no need for new sociological propositions to explain social facts. He used the basic sociological concept of a norm as illustration:

> The great example of a social fact is a social norm, and the norms of the groups to which they belong certainly constrain towards conformity the behavior of many more individuals. The question is not that of the existence of constraint, but of its explanation. . . . The norm does not constrain automatically: individuals conform, when they do so, because they perceive it is to their net advantage to conform, and it is psychology that deals with the effect on behavior of perceived advantage.
>
> (Homans, 1967:60)

Homans detailed a program to "bring men back in[to]" sociology, but he also tried to develop a theory that focuses on psychology, people, and the "elementary forms of social life." According to Homans, this theory "envisages social *behavior* as an exchange of activity, tangible or intangible, and more or less rewarding or costly, between at least two persons" (1961:13; italics added).

For example, Homans sought to explain the development of power-driven machinery in the textile industry, and thereby the Industrial Revolution, through the psychological principle that people are likely to act in such a way as to increase their rewards. More generally, in his version of exchange theory, he sought to explain elementary social behavior in terms of rewards and costs. He was motivated in part by the structural-functional theories of his acknowledged "colleague and friend" Talcott Parsons. He argued that such theories "possess every virtue except that of explaining anything" (Homans, 1961:10). To Homans, the structural functionalists did little more than create conceptual categories and schemes. Homans admitted that a scientific sociology needs such categories, but sociology "also needs a set of general propositions about the relations among the categories, for without such propositions explanation is impossible. No explanation without propositions!" (1974:10). Homans, therefore, set for himself the task of developing those propositions that focus on the psychological level; these form the groundwork of exchange theory.

In *Social Behavior: Its Elementary Forms* (1961, 1974),[2] Homans acknowledged that his exchange theory is derived from both behavioral psychology and elementary economics (rational choice theory). In fact, Homans (1984) regrets that his theory was labeled "exchange theory" because he sees it as a behavioral psychology applied to specific situations. Homans began with a discussion of the exemplar of the behaviorist paradigm, B. F. Skinner, in particular of Skinner's study of pigeons:[3]

> Suppose, then, that a fresh or naïve pigeon is in its cage in the laboratory. One of the items in its inborn repertory of behavior which it uses to explore its

---

[2] In the following discussion I move back and forth between the two editions of Homans's book. I do not restrict myself to the revised edition because many aspects of the first edition more clearly reflect Homans's position. In the preface to the revised edition, Homans said that although it was a thorough revision, he had not "altered the substance of the underlying argument" (Homans, 1974:v). Thus I feel safe in dealing simultaneously with both volumes.

[3] Skinner also studied other species, including humans.

environment is the peck. As the pigeon wanders around the cage pecking away, it happens to hit a round red target, at which point the waiting psychologists or, it may be, an automatic machine feeds it grain. The evidence is that the probability of the pigeon's emitting the behavior again—the probability, that is, of its not just pecking but pecking on the target—has increased. In Skinner's language the pigeon's behavior in pecking the target is an *operant;* the operant has been *reinforcer;* grain is the *reinforcer;* and the pigeon has undergone *operant conditioning*. Should we prefer our language to be ordinary English, we may say that the pigeon has learned to peck the target by being rewarded for doing so.

(Homans, 1961:18)

Skinner was interested in this instance in pigeons; Homans's concern was humans. According to Homans, Skinner's pigeons are not engaged in a true exchange relationship with the psychologist. The pigeon is engaged in a one-sided exchange relationship, whereas human exchanges are at least two-sided. The pigeon is being reinforced by the grain, but the psychologist is not truly being reinforced by the pecks of the pigeon. The pigeon is carrying on the same sort of relationship with the psychologist that it would have with the physical environment. Because there is no reciprocity, Homans defined this as *individual behavior*. Homans seemed to relegate the study of this sort of behavior to the psychologist, whereas he urged the sociologist to study social behavior "where the activity of each of at least two animals reinforces (or punishes) the activity of the other, and where accordingly each influences the other" (1961:30). However, it is significant that, according to Homans, *no new propositions* are needed to explain social behavior as opposed to individual behavior. The laws of individual behavior as developed by Skinner in his study of pigeons explain social behavior as long as we take into account the complications of mutual reinforcement. Homans admitted that he might ultimately have to go beyond the principles derived by Skinner, but only reluctantly.

In his theoretical work, Homans restricted himself to everyday social interaction. It is clear, however, that he believed that a sociology built on his principles ultimately would be able to explain all social behavior. Here is the case Homans used to exemplify the kind of exchange relationship he was interested in:

Suppose that two men are doing paperwork jobs in an office. According to the office rules, each should do his job by himself, or, if he needs help, he should consult the supervisor. One of the men, whom we shall call Person, is not skillful at the work and would get it done better and faster if he got help from time to time. In spite of the rules he is reluctant to go to the supervisor, for to confess his incompetence might hurt his chances for promotion. Instead he seeks out the other man, whom we shall call Other for short, and asks him for help. Other is more experienced at the work than is Person; he can do his work well and quickly and be left with time to spare, and he has reason to suppose that the supervisor will not go out of his way to look for a breach of rules. Other gives Person help and in return Person gives Other thanks and expressions of approval. The two men have exchanged help and approval.

(Homans, 1961:31–32)

Focusing on this sort of situation, and basing his ideas on Skinner's findings, Homans developed several propositions.

The Success Proposition 成功命題

> For all actions taken by persons, the more often a particular action of a person is rewarded, the more likely the person is to perform that action.
>
> (Homans, 1974:16)

In terms of Homans's Person-Other example in an office situation, this proposition means that a person is more likely to ask others for advice if he or she has been rewarded in the past with useful advice. Furthermore, the more often a person received useful advice in the past, the more often he or she will request more advice. Similarly, the other person will be more willing to give advice and give it more frequently if he or she often has been rewarded with approval in the past. Generally, behavior in accord with the success proposition involves three stages: first, a person's action; next, a rewarded result; and finally, a repetition of the original action or at minimum one similar in at least some respects.

Homans specified a number of things about the success proposition. First, although it is generally true that increasingly frequent rewards lead to increasingly frequent actions, this reciprocation cannot go on indefinitely. At some point individuals simply cannot act that way as frequently. Second, the shorter the interval is between behavior and reward, the more likely a person is to repeat the behavior. Conversely, long intervals between behavior and reward lower the likelihood of repeat behavior. Finally, it was Homans's view that intermittent rewards are more likely to elicit repeat behavior than regular rewards are. Regular rewards lead to boredom and satiation, whereas rewards at irregular intervals (as in gambling) are very likely to elicit repeat behaviors.

The Stimulus Proposition 刺激命題

> If in the past the occurrence of a particular stimulus, or set of stimuli, has been the occasion on which a person's action has been rewarded, then the more similar the present stimuli are to the past ones, the more likely the person is to perform the action, or some similar action.
>
> (Homans, 1974:23)

Again we look at Homans's office example: If, in the past, Person and Other found the giving and getting of advice rewarding, they are likely to engage in similar actions in similar situations in the future. Homans offered an even more down-to-earth example: "A fisherman who has cast his line into a dark pool and has caught a fish becomes more apt to fish in dark pools again" (1974:23).

Homans was interested in the process of *generalization,* that is, the tendency to extend behavior to similar circumstances. In the fishing example, one aspect of generalization would be to move from fishing in dark pools to fishing in any pool with any degree of shadiness. Similarly, success in catching fish is likely to lead from one kind of fishing to another (for instance, freshwater to saltwater) or even from fishing to hunting. However, the process of *discrimination* is also of importance. That is, the actor may fish only under the specific circumstances that proved successful in the past. For one thing, if the conditions under which success occurred were too complicated, similar conditions may not stimulate behavior. If the crucial stimulus occurs too long before behavior is required, it may not actually stimulate that behavior. An actor can become oversensitized to stimuli, especially if they are very valuable to the actor. In fact, the actor could respond to irrelevant stimuli, at least until the situation is corrected by repeated failures. All this is affected by the individual's alertness or attentiveness to stimuli.

The Value Proposition 价值命题

> The more valuable to a person is the result of his action, the more likely he is to perform the action.
>
> (Homans, 1974:25)

In the office example, if the rewards each offers to the other are considered valuable, the actors are more likely to perform the desired behaviors than they are if the rewards are not valuable. At this point, Homans introduced the concepts of rewards and punishments. Rewards are actions with positive values; an increase in rewards is more likely to elicit the desired behavior. Punishments are actions with negative values; an increase in punishment means that the actor is less likely to manifest undesired behaviors. Homans found punishments to be an inefficient means of getting people to change their behavior, because people may react in undesirable ways to punishment. It is preferable simply not to reward undesirable behavior; then such behavior eventually becomes extinguished. Rewards are clearly to be preferred, but they may be in short supply. Homans did make it clear that his is not simply a hedonistic theory; rewards can be either materialistic (for example, money) or altruistic (helping others).

The Deprivation-Satiation Proposition 剥夺—厌腻命题

> The more often in the recent past a person has received a particular reward, the less valuable any further unit of that reward becomes for him.
>
> (Homans, 1974:29)

In the office, Person and Other may reward each other so often for giving and getting advice that the rewards cease to be valuable to them. Time is crucial here; people are less likely to become satiated if particular rewards are stretched over a long period of time.

At this point, Homans defined two other critical concepts: cost and profit. The *cost* of any behavior is defined as the rewards lost in forgoing alternative lines of action. *Profit* in social exchange is seen as the greater number of rewards gained over costs incurred. The latter led Homans to recast the deprivation-satiation proposition as "the greater the profit a person receives as a result of his action, the more likely he is to perform the action" (1974:31).

The Aggression-Approval Propositions 攻击—赞赏命题

> *Proposition A:* When a person's action does not receive the reward he expected, or receives punishment he did not expect, he will be angry; he becomes more likely to perform aggressive behavior, and the results of such behavior become more valuable to him.
>
> (Homans, 1974:37)

In the office case, if Person does not get the advice he or she expected and Other does not receive the praise he or she anticipated, both are likely to be angry.[4] We are surprised to find the concepts of frustration and anger in Homans's work, because they would seem to refer to mental states. In fact, Homans admitted as much: "When a person does not get what he expected, he is said to be frustrated. A purist in behaviorism would not refer to the expectation at all, because the word seems to refer . . . to a state of mind" (1974:31). Homans went on to argue that frustration of such expectations need *not* refer "only" to an internal state. It also can refer to "wholly external events," observable not just by Person but also by outsiders.

Proposition A on aggression-approval refers only to negative emotions, whereas Proposition B deals with more positive emotions:

> *Proposition B:* When a person's action receives the reward he expected, especially a greater reward than he expected, or does not receive punishment he expected, he will be pleased; he becomes more likely to perform approving behavior, and the results of such behavior become more valuable to him.
>
> (Homans, 1974:39)

For example, in the office, when Person gets the advice that he or she expects and Other gets the praise that he or she expects, both are pleased and are more likely to get or give advice. Advice and praise become more valuable to each one.

The Rationality Proposition 理性命題

> In choosing between alternative actions, a person will choose that one for which, as perceived by him at the time, the value, V, of the result, multiplied by the probability, p, of getting the result, is the greater.
>
> (Homans, 1974:43)

While the earlier propositions rely heavily on behaviorism, the rationality proposition demonstrates most clearly the influence of rational choice theory on Homans's approach. In economic terms, actors who act in accord with the rationality proposition are maximizing their utilities.

Basically, people examine and make calculations about the various alternative actions open to them. They compare the amount of rewards associated with each course of action. They also calculate the likelihood that they actually will receive the rewards. Highly valued rewards will be devalued if the actors think it unlikely that they will obtain them. In contrast, lesser-valued rewards will be enhanced if they are seen as highly attainable. Thus, there is an interaction between the value of the reward and the likelihood of attainment. The most desirable rewards are those that are *both* very valuable *and* highly attainable. The least desirable rewards are those that are not very valuable and are unlikely to be attained.

---

[4] Although Homans still called this the "law of distributive justice" in the revised later edition, he developed the concept more extensively in the first edition. *Distributive justice* refers to whether the rewards and costs are distributed fairly among the individuals involved. In fact, Homans originally stated it as a proposition: "The more to a man's disadvantage the rule of distributive justice fails of realization, the more likely he is to display the emotional behavior we call anger" (1961:75).

PETER M. BLAU

A Biographical Sketch

Peter Blau was born in Vienna, Austria, on February 7, 1918. He emigrated to the United States in 1939 and became a United States citizen in 1943. In 1942 he received his bachelor's degree from the relatively little known Elmhurst College in Elmhurst, Illinois. His schooling was interrupted by World War II, and he served in the United States Army and was awarded the Bronze Star. After the war, he returned to school and completed his education, receiving his Ph.D. from Columbia University in 1952 (Bienenstock, 2005).

Blau first received wide recognition in sociology for his contributions to the study of formal organizations. His empirical studies of organizations as well as his textbooks on formal organizations are still widely cited in that subfield, and he continued to be a regular contributor to it until his death in 2002. He was also noted for a book he coauthored with Otis Dudley Duncan, *The American Occupational Structure* (1967), which won the prestigious Sorokin Award from the American Sociological Association in 1968. That work constitutes a very important contribution to the sociological study of social stratification.

Although he is well known for a range of work, what interests us here is Blau's contribution to sociological theory. What is distinctive about it is that Blau made important contributions to two distinct theoretical orientations. His 1964 book *Exchange and Power in Social Life* is a major component of contemporary exchange theory. Blau's chief contribution there was to take the primarily small-scale exchange theory and try to apply it to larger-scale issues. Although it has some notable weaknesses, it constitutes an important effort to theoretically integrate large- and small-scale sociological issues. Blau was also in the forefront of structural theory. During his term as president of the American Sociological Association (1973–1974), he made this the theme of the annual meeting of the association. He published a number of books and articles designed to clarify and extend structural theory. Among his later works in this area are *Structural Contexts of Opportunities* (1994) and the second edition of *Crosscutting Social Circles* (Blau and Schwartz, 1997).

Peter Blau died on March 12, 2002.

Homans relates the rationality proposition to the success, stimulus, and value propositions. The rationality proposition tells us that whether people will perform an action depends on their perceptions of the probability of success. But what determines this perception? Homans argues that perceptions of whether chances of success are high or low are shaped by past successes and the similarity of the present situation to past successful situations. The rationality proposition also does not tell us why an actor values one reward more than another; for this we need the value proposition. In these ways, Homans links his rationality principle to his more behavioristic propositions.

In the end, Homans's theory can be condensed to a view of the actor as a rational profit seeker. However, Homans's theory was weak on mental states (Abrahamsson, 1970; Mitchell, 1978) and large-scale structures (Ekeh, 1974). For example, on consciousness Homans admitted the need for a "more fully developed psychology" (1974:45).

Despite such weaknesses, Homans remained a behaviorist who worked resolutely at the level of individual behavior. He argued that large-scale structures can be understood if we adequately understand elementary social behavior. He contended that exchange processes are "identical" at the individual and societal levels, although he granted that at the societal level, "the way the fundamental processes are combined is more complex" (Homans, 1974:358).

Peter Blau's Exchange Theory 彼得·布劳的交换理论

Peter Blau's (1964) goal was "an understanding of social structure on the basis of an analysis of the social processes that govern the relations between individuals and groups. The basic question . . . is how social life becomes organized into increasingly complex structures of associations among men" (1964:2). Blau's intention was to go beyond Homans's concern with elementary forms of social life and into an analysis of complex structures: "The main sociological purpose of studying processes of face-to-face interaction is to lay the foundation for an understanding of the social structures that evolve and the emergent social forces that characterize their development" (1964:13).[5]

Blau focused on the process of exchange, which, in his view, directs much of human behavior and underlies relationships among individuals as well as among groups. In effect, Blau envisioned a four-stage sequence leading from interpersonal exchange to social structure to social change:

Step 1: Personal exchange transactions between people give rise to . . .
Step 2: Differentiation of status and power, which leads to . . .
Step 3: Legitimization and organization, which sow the seeds of . . .
Step 4: Opposition and change

Micro to Macro 微观到宏观

On the individual level, Blau and Homans were interested in similar processes. However, Blau's concept of social exchange is limited to actions that are contingent, that depend, on rewarding reactions from others—actions that cease when expected reactions are not forthcoming. People are attracted to each other for a variety of reasons that induce them to establish social associations. Once initial ties are forged, the rewards that they provide to each other serve to maintain and enhance the bonds. The

---

[5] It is interesting to note that Blau (1987) no longer accepts the idea of building macro theory on a micro base.

opposite situation is also possible: with insufficient rewards, an association will weaken or break. Rewards that are exchanged can be either intrinsic (for instance, love, affection, respect) or extrinsic (for instance, money, physical labor). The parties cannot always reward each other equally; when there is inequality in the exchange, a difference of power will emerge within an association.

When one party needs something from another but has nothing comparable to offer in return, four alternatives are available. First, people can force other people to help them. Second, they can find another source to obtain what they need. Third, they can attempt to get along without what they need from the others. Finally, and most important, they can subordinate themselves to the others, thereby giving the others "generalized credit" in their relationship; the others then can draw on this credit when they want them to do something. (This last alternative is, of course, the essential characteristic of power.)

Up to this point, Blau's position is similar to Homans's position, but Blau extended his theory to the level of social facts. He noted, for example, that we cannot analyze processes of social interaction apart from the social structure that surrounds them. Social structure emerges from social interaction, but once this occurs, social structures have a separate existence that affects the process of interaction.

Social interaction exists first within social groups. People are attracted to a group when they feel that the relationships offer more rewards than those from other groups. Because they are attracted to the group, they want to be accepted. To be accepted, they must offer group members rewards. This involves impressing the group members by showing them that associating with the new people will be rewarding. The relationship with the group members will be solidified when the newcomers have impressed the group—when members have received the rewards they expected. Newcomers' efforts to impress group members generally lead to group cohesion, but competition and, ultimately, social differentiation can occur when too many people actively seek to impress each other with their abilities to reward.

The paradox here is that although group members with the ability to impress can be attractive associates, their impressive characteristics also can arouse fears of dependence in other group members and cause them to acknowledge their attraction only reluctantly. In the early stages of group formation, competition for social recognition among group members actually acts as a screening test for potential leaders of the group. Those best able to reward are most likely to end up in leadership positions. Those group members with less ability to reward want to continue to receive the rewards offered by the potential leaders, and this usually more than compensates for their fears of becoming dependent on them. Ultimately, those individuals with the greater ability to reward emerge as leaders, and the group is differentiated.

The inevitable differentiation of the group into leaders and followers creates a renewed need for integration. Once they have acknowledged the leader's status, followers have an even greater need for integration. Earlier, followers flaunted their most impressive qualities. Now, to achieve integration with fellow followers, they display their weaknesses. This is, in effect, a public declaration that they no longer want to be leaders. This self-deprecation leads to sympathy and social acceptance from the other also-rans. The leader (or leaders) also engages in some self-deprecation at this point to improve overall group integration. By admitting that subordinates are superior in some areas, the leader reduces the pain associated with subordination and demonstrates that he or she does not seek control over every area of group life. These types of forces serve to reintegrate the group despite its new, differentiated status.

All this is reminiscent of Homans's discussion of exchange theory. Blau, however, moved to the societal level and differentiated between two types of social organization. Exchange theorists and behavioral sociologists also recognize the emergence of social organization, but there is, as we will see, a basic difference between Blau and "purer" social behaviorists on this issue. The first type, in which Blau recognized the emergent properties of social groups, emerges from the processes of exchange and competition discussed earlier. The second type of social organization is not emergent but is explicitly established to achieve specified objectives—for example, manufacturing goods that can be sold for a profit, participating in bowling tournaments, engaging in collective bargaining, and winning political victories. In discussing these two types of organization, Blau clearly moved beyond the "elementary forms of social behavior" that are typically of interest to social behaviorists.

In addition to being concerned with these organizations, Blau was interested in the subgroups within them. For example, he argued that leadership and opposition groups are found in both types of organization. In the first type, these two groups emerge out of the process of interaction. In the second, leadership and opposition groups are built into the structure of the organization. In either case, differentiation between the groups is inevitable and lays the groundwork for opposition and conflict within the organization between leaders and followers.

Having moved beyond Homans's elementary forms of behavior and into complex social structures, Blau knew that he must adapt exchange theory to the societal level. Blau recognized the essential difference between small groups and large collectivities, whereas Homans minimized this difference in his effort to explain all social behavior in terms of basic psychological principles.

> The complex social structures that characterize large collectives differ fundamentally from the simpler structures of small groups. A structure of social relations develops in a small group in the course of social interaction among its members. Since there is no direct social interaction among most members of a large community or entire society, some other mechanism must mediate the structure of social relations among them.
>
> (Blau, 1964:253)

This statement requires scrutiny. On the one hand, Blau clearly ruled out social behaviorism as an adequate paradigm for dealing with complex social structures (see the Appendix). On the other hand, he ruled out the social-definitionist paradigm because he argued that social interaction and the social definitions that accompany it do not occur directly in a large-scale organization. Thus, starting from the social-behavior paradigm, Blau aligned himself with the social-facts paradigm in dealing with more complex social structures.

Norms and Values 规范和价值

For Blau, the mechanisms that mediate among the complex social structures are the norms and values (the value consensus) that exist within society:

> Commonly agreed upon values and norms serve as media of social life and as mediating links for social transactions. They make indirect social exchange possible, and they govern the processes of social integration and differentiation in complex social structures as well as the development of social organization and reorganization in them.
>
> (Blau, 1964:255)

Other mechanisms mediate among social structures, but Blau focused on value consensus. Looking first at social norms, Blau argued that they substitute indirect exchange for direct exchange. One member conforms to the group norm and receives approval for that conformity and implicit approval for the fact that conformity contributes to the group's maintenance and stability. In other words, the group or collectivity engages in an exchange relationship with the individual. This is in contrast to Homans's simpler notion, which focused on interpersonal exchange. Blau offered a number of examples of collectivity-individual exchanges replacing individual-individual exchanges:

> Staff officials do not assist line officials in their work in exchange for rewards received from them, but furnishing this assistance is the official obligation of staff members, and in return for discharging these obligations they receive financial rewards from the company.
>
> Organized philanthropy provides another example of indirect social exchange. In contrast to the old-fashioned lady bountiful who brought her baskets to the poor and received their gratitude and appreciation, there is no direct contact and no exchange between individual donors and recipients in contemporary organized charity. Wealthy businessmen and members of the upper class make philanthropic contributions to conform with the normative expectations that prevail in their social class and to earn the social approval of their peers, not in order to earn the gratitude of the individuals who benefit from their charity.
>
> (Blau, 1964:260)

The concept of the norm in Blau's formulation moves Blau to the level of exchange between individual and collectivity, but the concept of values moves him to the largest-scale societal level and to the analysis of the relationship *among collectivities*. Blau said:

> Common values of various types can be conceived of as media of social transactions that expand the compass of social interaction and the structure of social relations through social space and time. Consensus on social values serves as the basis for extending the range of social transactions beyond the limits of direct social contacts and for perpetuating social structures beyond the life span of human beings. Value standards can be considered media of social life in two senses of the term; the value context is the medium that molds the form of social relationships; and common values are the mediating links for social associations and transactions on a broad scale.
>
> (Blau, 1964:263–264)

For example, *particularistic* values are the media of integration and solidarity. These values serve to unite the members of a group around such things as patriotism or the good of the school or the company. These are seen as similar at the collective level to sentiments of personal attraction that unite individuals on a face-to-face basis. However, they extend integrative bonds beyond mere personal attraction. Particularistic values also differentiate the in-group from the out-group, thereby enhancing their unifying function.

Blau's analysis carries us far from Homans's version of exchange theory. The individual and individual behavior, paramount for Homans, have almost disappeared in Blau's conception. Taking the place of the individual are a wide variety of *social facts*. For example, Blau discussed groups, organizations, collectivities, societies, norms, and values. Blau's analysis is concerned with what holds large-scale social units together and what tears them apart, clearly traditional concerns of the social factist.

Although Blau argued that he was simply extending exchange theory to the societal level, in so doing he twisted exchange theory beyond recognition. He was even forced to admit that processes at the societal level are fundamentally different from those at the individual level. In his effort to extend exchange theory, Blau managed only to transform it into another macro-level theory. Blau seemed to recognize that exchange theory is concerned primarily with face-to-face relations. As a result, it needs to be complemented by other theoretical orientations that focus mainly on macro structures. Blau (1987, 1994) came to recognize this explicitly, and his later work focuses on macro-level, structural phenomena.

理查德·埃莫森及其继承者的理论
The Work of Richard Emerson and His Disciples

In 1962 Richard Emerson published an important paper on power-dependence relations, but it was two related essays written in 1972 (Emerson, 1972a, 1972b) that "marked the beginning of a new stage in the development of social exchange theory" (Molm and Cook, 1995:215; Cook and Whitmeyer, 2000). Molm and Cook see three basic factors as the impetus for this new body of work. First, Emerson was interested in exchange theory as a broader framework for his earlier interest in power dependence. It seemed clear to Emerson that power was central to the exchange theory perspective. Second, Emerson felt that he could use behaviorism (operant psychology) as the base of his exchange theory but avoid some of the problems that had affected Homans. For one thing, Homans and other exchange theorists had been accused of assuming an overly rational image of human beings, but Emerson felt he could use behaviorism without assuming a rational actor. For another, Emerson believed he could avoid the problem of tautology that ensnared Homans:

> Homans predicted individual exchange behavior from the reinforcement provided by another actor, but behavioral responses and reinforcement do not have independent meaning in operant psychology. A reinforcer is, by definition, a stimulus consequence that increases or maintains response frequency.
> (Molm and Cook, 1995:214)

RICHARD EMERSON

A Biographical Sketch *

Richard Emerson was born in Salt Lake City, Utah, in 1925. Raised near mountains, he never seemed to stray too far from rivers, mountain peaks, and glaciers. One of his most prized personal accomplishments was his participation in the successful ascent of Mt. Everest in 1963. Aspects of this experience are captured in his publication "Everest Traverse" in the December 1963 edition of the *Sierra Club Annual Bulletin* and in an article published in *Sociometry* in 1966. He received a grant from the National Science Foundation to study group performance under prolonged stress on this climb. That project earned him the Hubbard Medal, presented to him by President Kennedy on behalf of the National Geographic Society in July 1963 (Cook, 2005).

His love of mountains and the rural social life of the mountain villages of Pakistan became a constant source of sociological inspiration for Richard Emerson during his career. His studies of interpersonal behavior, group performance, power, and social influence were often driven by his close personal encounters with expedition teams for which the intensity of cooperation and competition were exacerbated by environmental stress.

After World War II and a tour of duty with the Army in Western Europe, he completed his B.A. in 1950 at the University of Utah and then went on to earn an M.A. (1952) and a Ph.D. (1955) from the University of Minnesota, where his major field was sociology and his minor field was psychology. His doctoral dissertation was titled "The Determinants of Influence in Face to Face Groups."

In addition, Emerson felt he could avoid the charge of reductionism (one that Homans reveled in) by being able to develop an exchange perspective capable of explaining macro-level phenomena. Third, unlike Blau, who resorted to an explanation reliant on normative phenomena, Emerson wanted to deal with social structure and social change by using "social relations and social networks as building blocks that spanned different levels of analysis" (Molm and Cook, 1995:215). In addition, the actors in Emerson's system could be either individuals or larger corporate structures (albeit structures working through agents). Thus, Emerson used the principles of operant psychology to develop a theory of social structure.

In the two essays published in 1972, Emerson developed the basis of his integrative exchange theory. In the first of those essays (1972a) Emerson dealt with the psychological basis for social exchange, while in the second (1972b) he turned to macro-level and exchange relations and network structures. Later, Emerson made the micro-macro linkage more explicit: "I am attempting to extend exchange theory and

Emerson's first academic post was at the University of Cincinnati (1955–1964). Upon leaving Cincinnati Emerson wrote, "A recurring theme in my work was crystallized in the article on power-dependence relations. However, this theory is clearly a springboard for the future rather than a summary of the past. I have rather specific plans for both theoretical and empirical extensions into stratification and community power structure." He was still engaged in this work when he died unexpectedly in December 1982. His work on power-dependence relations (1962) is now a citation classic and has influenced much current work on power in American sociology.

Two other pieces have been highly influential. These are his two chapters on social exchange theory which were written in 1967 and subsequently published in 1972. This work was completed at the University of Washington, where he joined the faculty in 1965. He was drawn to the Northwest, I am sure, by the lure of the Olympics and Cascades.

Emerson's influence on sociological theory crystallized while he was at the University of Washington, where he collaborated with Karen Cook for a 10-year period (1972–1982) on the empirical development of social exchange theory. They carried out a program of research in the first computerized laboratory for conducting research of this type in the United States. This work was funded by three successive grants from the National Science Foundation.

Emerson is remembered by former colleagues and students as a "thinker." This aspect of his personality is best captured in a quote from an article he wrote in 1960 in Robert Bowen's book *The New Professors:* "So, what is there of value in the academic (that is, 'nonpractical, removed-from-life') study of a topic? People ask this question, too. Such questions are difficult to answer because those who ask have never climbed a mountain and have no interest in a topic. I say they are far removed from life."

*This biographical sketch was written by Karen Cook.

research from *micro* to more *macro* levels of analysis through the study of *exchange network structures*" (cited in Cook, 1987:212). As Karen Cook (Whitmeyer, 2005a), Emerson's most important disciple, points out, it is the idea of exchange network structures that is central to the micro-macro linkage: "The use of the notion, exchange networks, allows for the development of theory that bridges the conceptual gap between isolated individuals or dyads and larger aggregates or collections of individuals (e.g., formal groups or associations, organizations, neighborhoods, political parties, etc.)" (1987:219).[6]

Both Emerson and Cook accept and begin with the basic, micro-level premises of exchange theory. Emerson, for example, says, "The exchange approach takes as its first

---

[6] Emerson and Cook (as well as Blau) are not the only ones to have developed integrative exchange theories. See also Uehara (1990) and Willer, Markovsky, and Patton (1989).

focus of attention the benefits people obtain from, and contribute to, the process of social interaction" (1981:31). More specifically, Emerson accepts behavioristic principles as his starting point. Emerson (1981:33) outlines three core assumptions of exchange theory:

1. People for whom events are beneficial tend to act "rationally," and so such events occur.
2. Because people eventually become satiated with behavioral events, such events come to be of diminishing utility.
3. The benefits that people obtain through social processes are dependent on the benefits that they are able to provide in exchange, giving exchange theory "its focus [on] the flow of *benefits through social interaction.*"

All this is quite familiar, but Emerson begins to point behavioristically oriented exchange theory in a different direction at the close of his first, micro-oriented 1972 essay: "Our main purpose in this chapter is to incorporate operant principles into a framework which can handle more complex situations than operant psychology confronts" (1972a:48).

This theme opens the second 1972 essay: "The purpose of this essay is to begin construction of a theory of social exchange in which *social structure* is taken as the dependent variable" (Emerson, 1972b:58). Whereas in the first 1972 essay Emerson was concerned with a single actor involved in an exchange relation with his or her environment (for example, a person fishing in a lake), in the second essay he turns to social-exchange relationships as well as to exchange networks.

The actors in Emerson's macro-level exchange theory can be either individuals or collectivities. Emerson is concerned with the exchange relationship among actors. An *exchange network* has the following components (Cook et al., 1983:277):

1. There is a set of either individual or collective actors.
2. Valued resources are distributed among the actors.
3. There is a set of exchange opportunities among all the actors in the network.
4. Some exchange opportunities have developed into actually used exchange relations.
5. Exchange relations are connected to one another in a single network structure.

In sum: "An 'exchange network' is a specific social structure formed by two or more connected exchange relations between actors" (Cook et al., 1983:277).

The idea of an exchange network links exchange between two actors (dyadic exchange) to more macro-level phenomena (Yamagishi, Gillmore, and Cook, 1988:835).

Each exchange relation is embedded within a larger exchange network consisting of sets of connected exchange relations. By connected, it is meant that the exchange in one relationship affects the exchange in another.

Thus, we may say that two dyadic-exchange relations, *A-B* and *A-C,* form a minimal network (*A-B-C*) when exchange in one affects exchange in the other. It is not enough for *A*, *B*, and *C* to have a common membership for an exchange network to develop; there must be a relationship between exchanges in *A-B* and *B-C*. For example, Abe may exchange information with Bill about office politics and Bill may exchange services with Cathy, but that alone would not make them an exchange network unless Abe's information positively or negatively affected Bill's exchange of services with Cathy.

An important distinction is that between positive and negative exchange connections (Emerson, 1972b). Connections are positive when the exchange in one positively affects the exchange in another (for example, the information that Abe gives Bill helps Bill provide services for Cathy), negative when one serves to inhibit the exchange in the other (Abe might tell Bill some gossip about Cathy that interferes with Bill and Cathy's relationship), or mixed.

Power-Dependence 权力—依赖

Emerson defined *power* as "the level of potential cost which one actor can induce another to 'accept,'" while *dependence* involves "the level of potential cost an actor will accept within a relation" (1972b:64). These definitions lead to Emerson's power-dependence theory (Molm, 2007), which Yamagishi, Gillmore, and Cook summarize in the following way: "The power of one party over another in an exchange relation is an inverse function of his or her dependence on the other party" (1988:837; Whitmeyer, 2005b). Unequal power and dependency lead to imbalances in relationships, but over time these move toward a more balanced power-dependence relationship.

Molm and Cook (1995) regard dependence as the critical concept in Emerson's work. As Molm puts it, "The actors' *dependencies* on each other are the major structural determinants of their interaction and of their power over each other" (1988:109). Here is the way Emerson originally dealt with the issue: "The dependence of actor A upon actor B is (1) directly proportional to A's *motivational investment* in goals mediated by B, and (2) inversely proportional to the *availability* of those goals to A outside of the A-B relation" (1962:32). Thus, a sense of dependence is linked to Emerson's definition of power: "the power of A over B is equal to, and based upon, the dependence of B upon A" (1962:33). There is balance in the relationship between A and B when the dependence of A on B equals the dependence of B on A. Where there is an imbalance in the dependencies, the actor with less dependence has an advantage in terms of power. Thus, power is a potential built into the structure of the *relationship* between A and B. Power also can be used to acquire rewards from the relationship. Even in balanced relationships, power exists, albeit in a kind of equilibrium.

Power-dependence studies have focused on positive outcomes—the ability to reward others. However, in a series of studies, Molm (1988, 1989, 1994, 1997; Peterson, 2005), has emphasized the role of negative outcomes—punishment power—in power-dependence relationships. That is, power can be derived from both the ability to reward and the ability to punish others. In general, Molm has found that punishment power is weaker than reward power, in part because acts of punishment are likely to elicit negative reactions. This means that the risk of escalating negative reactions is an important part of punishment power. The element of risk leads to the conclusion that punishment power is used more strategically than is reward power (Molm, 2001).

However, in one study, Molm (1994) has suggested that the relative weakness and associated risk of punishment power may arise because it is not widely used, not because it is inherently less effective than reward power. Molm, Quist, and Wisely (1994) found that the use of punishment power is more likely to be perceived as fair when it is used by those who also have the power to reward but that it is likely to be perceived as unfair and therefore a weak reinforcer when partners are expecting rewards.

A More Integrative Exchange Theory 整合度更高的交换理论

Cook, O'Brien, and Kollock (1990) define exchange theory in inherently integrative terms as being concerned with exchanges at various levels of analysis, including those among interconnected individuals, corporations, and nation-states. They identify two strands of work in the history of exchange—one at the micro level, focusing on social behavior as exchange, and the other at the more macro level, viewing social structure as exchange. They see the strength of exchange theory in micro-macro integration, since "it includes within a single theoretical framework propositions that apply to individual actors as well as to the macro level (or systemic level) and it attempts to formulate explicitly the consequences of changes at one level for other levels of analysis" (Cook, O'Brien, and Kollock, 1990:175).

Cook, O'Brien, and Kollock identify three contemporary trends, all of which point toward a more integrative exchange theory. The first is the increasing use of field research focusing on more macroscopic issues, which can complement the traditional use of the laboratory experiment to study microscopic issues. Second, they note the shift in substantive work away from a focus on dyads and toward larger networks of exchange. Third, and most important, is the ongoing effort, discussed further below, to synthesize exchange theory and structural sociologies, especially network theory.

Along the way, Cook, O'Brien, and Kollock discuss the gains to be made from integrating insights from a variety of other micro theories. Decision theory offers "a better understanding of the way actors make choices relevant to transactions" (Cook, O'Brien, and Kollock, 1990:168). More generally, cognitive science (which includes cognitive anthropology and artificial intelligence) sheds "more light on the way in which actors perceive, process, and retrieve information" (Cook, O'Brien, and Kollock, 1990:168). Symbolic interactionism offers knowledge about how actors signal their intentions to one another, and this is important in the development of trust and commitment in exchange relationships. Most generally, they see their synthetic version of exchange theory as being well equipped to deal with the centrally important issue of the agency-structure relationship. In their view, "Exchange theory is one of a limited number of theoretical orientations in the social sciences that explicitly conceptualize purposeful actors in relation to structures" (Cook, O'Brien, and Kollock, 1990:172).

There are a number of recent examples of efforts by exchange theorists to synthesize their approach with other theoretical orientations. For example, Yamagishi and

Cook (1993) have sought to integrate exchange theory with social dilemma theory (Yamagishi, 1995), a variant of rational choice theory. The social dilemma approach is derived from the famous dyadic concept of the prisoner's dilemma and the research on it: "A social dilemma is defined as a situation involving a particular type of incentive structure, such that (1) if all group members cooperate, all gain, whereas (2) for each individual it is more beneficial not to cooperate" (Yamagishi and Cook, 1993:236; Yamagishi, 2005). Without going into the details of their study, Yamagishi and Cook find that the nature of the exchange relationship and structure affects the way people deal with social dilemmas.

In another effort, Hegtvedt, Thompson, and Cook (1993) sought to integrate exchange theory and one approach that deals with cognitive processes: attribution theory. The integration with this theory gives exchange theory a mechanism to deal with the way people perceive and make attributions, while exchange theory compensates for the weakness in attribution theory in dealing with "the social structural antecedents and the behavioral consequences of attribution" (Hegtvedt, Thompson, and Cook, 1993:100). Thus, for example, the authors found support for the hypotheses that perceived power is related to one's structural power position and that those "who perceive themselves to have greater power are more likely to attribute their exchange outcomes to personal actions or interactions" (Hegtvedt, Thompson, and Cook, 1993:104). While not fully supportive of the authors' hypotheses, this study points to the importance of studying the relationship between social structure, cognitive processes (perception and attribution), and behavior.

An important proposal was made by Meeker (1971) which would disconnect exchange theory from its reliance on rational choice theory and allow its integration with a variety of micro theories of agency. Meeker suggested that rationality be looked at as one type of exchange rule and that exchanges could be based on other exchange rules, such as altruism, competition, reciprocity, and status consistency.

In recent years, exchange theory has begun to move in a variety of new directions (Molm, 2001). First, there is increasing attention to the risk and uncertainty involved in exchange relationships (Kollock, 1994). For example, one actor may provide valuable outcomes for the other without receiving anything of value in return. Second, an interest in risk leads to a concern for trust in exchange relations. The issue is: Can one actor trust another to reciprocate when valued outcomes have been provided? Third, there is the related issue of actors reducing risk and increasing trust by developing a set of mutual commitments to one another (Molm, 1997). This, in turn, is linked to a fourth issue—increasing attention to affect and emotions in a theory which has been dominated by a focus on self-interested actors. Fifth, while much of recent exchange theory has focused on structure, there is increasing interest in fleshing out the nature and role of the actor in exchange relationships. In terms of issues in need of greater attention, Molm argues that exchange theory has tended to focus on exchange structures but needs to do more with change, or exchange dynamics. Finally, the new direction that has seen most attention in recent years has been the integration of exchange theory with network theory. We will come back to this network exchange theory after we have discussed network theory.

Network Theory 网络理论

Network analysts (for example, Mizruchi, 2005; Harrison White, 1992; Wasserman and Faust, 1994; Wellman and Berkowitz, 1988/1997) take pains to differentiate their approach from what Ronald Burt calls "atomistic" and "normative" sociological approaches (Burt, 1982; see also Granovetter, 1985). Atomistic sociological orientations focus on actors making decisions in isolation from other actors. More generally, they focus on the "personal attributes" of actors (Wellman, 1983). Atomistic approaches are rejected because they are too microscopic and ignore relationships among actors. As Barry Wellman puts it, "Accounting for individual motives is a job better left to psychologists" (1983:163). This, of course, constitutes a rejection of a number of sociological theories that are in one way or another deeply concerned with motives.

In the view of network theorists, normative approaches focus on culture and the socialization process through which norms and values are internalized in actors. In the normative orientation, what holds people together are sets of shared ideas. Network theorists reject such a view and argue that one should focus on the objective pattern of ties linking the members of society (Mizruchi, 1994). Here is how Wellman articulates this view:

> Network analysts want to study regularities in how people and collectivities behave rather than regularities in beliefs about how they ought to behave. Hence network analysts try to avoid normative explanations of social behavior. They dismiss as non-structural any explanation that treats social process as the sum of individual actors' personal attributes and internalized norms.
>
> (Wellman, 1983:162)

Basic Concerns and Principles 基本议题和原则

Having made clear what it is not, network theory then clarifies its major concern—social relationships, or the objective pattern of ties linking the members (individual and collective) of society (Burt, 1992). Let us look at how Wellman articulates this focus:

> Network analysts start with the simple, but powerful, notion that the primary business of sociologists is to study social structure. . . . The most direct way to study a social structure is to analyze the pattern of ties linking its members. Network analysts search for deep structures—regular network patterns beneath the often complex surface of social systems. . . . Actors and their behavior are seen as constrained by these structures. Thus, the focus is not on voluntaristic actors, but on structural constraint.
>
> (Wellman, 1983:156–157)

One distinctive aspect of network theory is that it focuses on a wide range of micro to macro structures. That is, to network theory the actors may be people (Wellman and Wortley, 1990), but they also may be groups, corporations (W. E. Baker, 1990; Clawson, Neustadtl, and Bearden, 1986; Mizruchi and Koenig, 1986), and societies. Links occur at the large-scale, social-structural level as well as at more microscopic levels. Mark Granovetter describes such micro-level links as action "embedded" in "the concrete personal relations and structures (or 'networks') of such relations" (1985:490). Basic to any of these links is the idea that any "actor" (individual or collective) may have differential access to valued resources (wealth, power, information). The result is that structured systems tend to be stratified, with some components dependent on others.

One key aspect of network analysis is that it tends to move sociologists away from the study of social groups and social categories and toward the study of ties among and between actors that are not "sufficiently bounded and densely knit to be termed groups" (Wellman, 1983:169). A good example of this is Granovetter's (1973, 1983, 2005; Tindall and Malinick, 2007) work on "the strength of weak ties." Granovetter differentiates between "strong ties," for example, links between people and their close friends, and "weak ties," for example, links between people and mere acquaintances. Sociologists have tended to focus on people with strong ties or social groups. They have tended to regard strong ties as crucial, whereas weak ties have been thought of as being of little sociological importance. Granovetter's contribution is to make it clear that weak ties can be very important. For example, weak ties between two actors can serve as a bridge between two groups with strong internal ties. Without such a weak tie, the two groups might be totally isolated. This isolation, in turn, could lead to a more fragmented social system. An individual without weak ties would find himself or herself isolated in a tightly knit group and would lack information about what is going on in other groups as well as in the larger society. Weak ties therefore prevent isolation and allow individuals to be better integrated into the larger society. Although Granovetter emphasizes the importance of weak ties, he hastens to make it clear "that strong ties can also have value" (1983:209; see Bian, 1997). For example, people with strong ties have greater motivation to help one another and are more readily available to one another.

Network theory is relatively new and undeveloped. As Burt says, "There is currently a loose federation of approaches referenced as network analysis" (1982:20). But it is growing, as evidenced by the number of papers and books being published from a network perspective and the fact that there is now a journal (*Social Networks*) devoted to it. Although it may be a loose conglomeration of work, network theory does seem to rest on a coherent set of principles (Wellman, 1983).

First, ties among actors usually are symmetrical in both content and intensity. Actors supply each other with different things, and they do this with greater or lesser intensity. Second, the ties among individuals must be analyzed within the context of the structure of larger networks. Third, the structuring of social ties leads to various kinds of nonrandom networks. On the one hand, networks are transitive: if there is a tie between A and B and between B and C, there is likely to be a tie between A and C. The result is that there is more likely to be a network involving A, B, and C. On the other hand, there are limits to how many links can exist and how intense they can be. The result is that network clusters with distinct boundaries separating one cluster from another are also likely to develop. Fourth, the existence of clusters leads to the fact that there can be cross-linkages between clusters as well as between individuals. Fifth, there are asymmetric ties among elements in a system, with the result that scarce resources are differentially distributed. Finally, the unequal distribution of scarce resources leads to both collaboration and competition. Some groups band together to acquire scarce resources collaboratively, whereas others compete and conflict over resources. Thus, network theory has a dynamic quality (Rosenthal et al., 1985), with the structure of the system changing with shifting patterns of coalition and conflict.

To take one example, Mizruchi (1990) is interested in the issue of the cohesion of corporations and its relationship to power. He argues that historically cohesion has been defined in two different ways. The first, or subjective view, is that "cohesion is a function of group members' feelings of identification with the group, in particular their feeling that their individual interests are bound up with the interests of the group" (Mizruchi, 1990:21). The emphasis here is on the normative system, and cohesion is produced either by the internalization of the normative system or by group pressure. The second, or objective, view is that "solidarity can be viewed as an objective, observable process independent of the sentiments of individuals" (Mizruchi, 1990:22). Needless to say, given his alignment with network theory, Mizruchi comes down on the side of the objective approach to cohesion.

Mizruchi sees similarity of behavior as a result not only of cohesion but also of what he calls *structural equivalence:* "Structurally equivalent actors are those with identical relations with other actors in the social structure" (1990:25). Thus, structural equivalence exists among, say, corporations, even though there may be no communication among them. They behave in the same way because they stand in the same relationship to some other entity in the social structure. Mizruchi concludes that structural equivalence plays at least as strong a role as cohesion in explaining similarity of behavior. Mizruchi accords great importance to structural equivalence, which, after all, implies a network of social relations.

A More Integrative Network Theory 整合度更高的网络理论

Ronald Burt (1982) has been in the forefront of network theorists who have sought to develop an integrated approach instead of another form of structural determinism. Burt begins by articulating a schism within action theory between the "atomistic" and "normative" orientations. The atomistic orientation "assumes that alternative actions are evaluated independently by separate actors so that evaluations are made without reference to other actors," whereas the "normative perspective is defined by separate actors within a system having interdependent interests as social norms generated by actors socializing one another" (Burt, 1982:5).

Burt develops a perspective that "circumvents the schism between atomistic and normative action," one that "is less a synthesis of the existing two perspectives on action than it is a third view intellectually bridging the two views" (1982:8). Although he admittedly borrows from the other two perspectives, Burt develops what he calls a *structural perspective* that differs from the other two "in the criterion for the postulate of marginal evaluation. The criterion assumed by the proposed structural perspective is an actor's status/role-set as generated by the division of labor. An actor evaluates the utility of alternative actions partly in regard to his personal conditions and partly in regard to the conditions of others" (1982:8). He sees his approach as a logical extension of the atomistic approach and an "empirically accurate restriction" on normative theory.

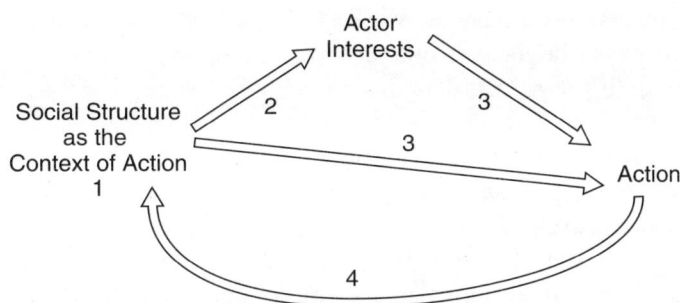

FIGURE 8.1   *Ronald Burt's Integrative Model*

Figure 8.1 depicts Burt's structural theory of action. According to Burt's description of the premise of a structural theory of action, "actors are purposive under social structural constraints" (1982:9; see also Mizruchi, 1994). In his view:

> Actors find themselves in a social structure. That social structure defines their social similarities, which in turn pattern their perceptions of the advantages to be had by taking each of several alternative actions. At the same time, social structure differentially constrains actors in their ability to take actions. Actions eventually taken are therefore a joint function of actors pursuing their interests to the limit of their ability where both interests and ability are patterned by social structure. Finally, actions taken under social structural constraint can modify social structure itself, and these modifications have the potential to create new constraints to be faced by actors within the structure.
>
> (Burt, 1982:9)

Network Exchange Theory 网络交换理论

Network exchange theory (Markovsky, 2005) combines social exchange theory and network analysis. The combination is assumed to preserve the advantages of both theories while remedying their deficiencies. On the one hand, network analysis has the advantage of being able to build complex representations of social interactions from simple, diagrammable models of social relations, but Cook and Whitmeyer (1992:123) argue that it has a deficient conception of exactly what the relation is. On the other hand, social exchange theory has the advantage of a simple model of actors who make choices based on possible benefits, but it is deficient because it sees social structures mainly as an outcome of individual choices rather than a determinant of those choices. To put it more simply, network theory has a strong model of structure (networks of relations) but a vague model of what the relations consist of, while exchange theory has a strong model of the relations between actors (exchanges) but a weak model of the social structures within which they operate. Social exchange theory's model of the actor exchanging in order to increase benefits provides the content that network analysis is lacking, and network analysis provides the model of social structure as an independent variable that exchange theory is lacking.

The fundamental idea behind network exchange theory is that any social exchange occurs in the context of larger networks of social exchanges. What is being exchanged is less important in this approach than the various sizes, shapes, and connections of the networks within which these exchanges occur. Like social exchange, network exchange theory focuses primarily on the issue of power. A basic premise is that the more opportunities an actor has for exchange, the greater the actor's power is. It is assumed that these opportunities for exchange are directly related to the structure of the network. As a result of their position in the network, actors vary in their opportunities to exchange benefits and therefore in their ability to control or accumulate benefits.

Emerson (1972a, 1972b) initiated the research on social exchange networks when he concluded that social exchange theory was limited by its focus on two-person, or dyadic, exchange relations. By treating those relations as interconnected, Emerson moved toward seeing exchange as being embedded in larger network structures. Emerson's (1972b:58) original intent was to develop "a theory of social exchange in which social structure is taken as the dependent variable." However, his research soon demonstrated that social structure also could be an independent variable; in other words, not only was structure determined by exchange relations, exchange relations were determined by social structures.

Yamagishi, Gillmore, and Cook (1988) went further by linking exchange theory and network theory. They argued that power is central to exchange theory but that power cannot be studied meaningfully in the dyad. Rather, power "is fundamentally a social structural phenomenon" (Yamagishi, Gillmore, and Cook, 1988:834). A fully adequate theory must combine an analysis of exchange relations with an analysis of the linkages between exchange relations. To do this, they built on Emerson's idea of positively and negatively linked exchanges to generate predictions about the distribution of power in networks.

In a subsequent article, Cook and Whitmeyer (1992) more rigorously examined the possibility of combining exchange theory and network analysis. They looked at the compatibilities between the two approaches' views of actors and their views of structure. They concluded that the two theories' views of actors were essentially the same, since virtually all exchange theories explicitly and most network analyses implicitly assume that actors are rationally pursuing the maximization of their self-interest in whatever way they define it. They also noted a great deal of similarity in the two approaches' view of structure. The main difference is that exchange theory sees the social relations that constitute the structure only in terms of actual exchanges, while network analysis is inclined to include any kind of relation, whether exchange is believed to occur or not.

It is this difference in their definitions of a relation that constitutes the essential difference between an exchange network (Friedkin, 2005) and the kind of network of interest to network analysis. Network exchange theorists are interested only in relations of exchange, while network theorists are interested in many types of relations. As an example, many network studies focus on "centrality." This might mean the advantage of being linked to many different people. According to network exchange theorists, just being "linked" is not enough; the relations must be ones of exchange. Thus, in the example above of Abe, Bill, and Cathy, Bill is "central," according to network exchange, only if Abe and Bill as well as Bill and Cathy have some sort of exchange and, in addition, one dyad's exchanges have some sort of effect on the other's exchanges. In contrast, for network analysis, it is enough if they are linked, and the precise nature of the link is irrelevant.

Structural Power 结构权力

One of the reasons for linking exchange theory and network analysis was to be able to move beyond an analysis of power within dyadic relations and be able to analyze the distribution of power in the network as a whole. This has become one of the most important topics in contemporary network exchange theory. In one of the first attempts to look at the distribution of power in a network, Cook and her colleagues (1983) developed a theory of "vulnerability." They argued that the determination of the power of a position is based on the amount of dependence of the entire structure on that position. In their view, this systemwide dependence is a function of both the structural centrality of the position and the nature of power-dependence relationships. In other words, vulnerability involves the networkwide dependence on a particular structural position.

Another important attempt to look at the distribution of power in networks was developed by Markovsky, Willer, and their colleagues (Willer and Patton, 1987; Markovsky, Willer, and Patton, 1988). This approach has become so influential that it usually goes by the name of *network exchange theory* (Markovsky, 2005), often abbreviated NET. The theory assumes that power is determined by the structure of the network, in particular the availability of alternative connections among actors. The theory uses a graph-theoretical power index (GPI) based on counting alternative network paths and a resistance model based on actors' expectations about outcomes to predict relative power in networks.

Strong and Weak Power Structures 强和弱的权力结构

NET distinguishes between two types of networks—strong and weak power—based on whether actors can be excluded from exchanges. Strong power networks include some actors who must be excluded (low power actors) and other actors who cannot be excluded (high power actors). For example, in a company, the decision about whom to promote to a higher position can be looked at as an exchange. The higher position is exchanged for the work done for the boss who can grant the higher position. If we assume that there is only one boss and there are many competitors for the position, we would have a strong power network. The boss cannot be excluded from the exchange, while all but one of the competitors must be. The theory predicts that high power actors in strong power networks will obtain virtually all the available resources. In this case, the competitors will be motivated to provide whatever work the boss demands. However, if we introduce another boss into the network who also can promote a competitor, the theory predicts that both bosses would have much less power since the competitors for the promotion would now have an alternative for exchange.

The introduction of a second boss would make this a weak power structure. In weak power structures, all positions are vulnerable to exclusions. The presence of Boss 2 means that Boss 1 can be excluded from the exchange. Competitors therefore can perform services for a boss who will promote them while demanding the least amount of work in exchange. In weak power networks, positions may have different possibilities for exclusion. Let us say that there are twenty competitors for the promotion and only two bosses. This makes a given competitor more likely to be excluded than a given boss. The theory predicts that positions less likely to be excluded (bosses) benefit proportionally more than do positions more likely to be excluded (competitors).

One of the great advantages of linking exchange theory to network analysis is the expanded view of agency. Network analysis has tended to downplay agency and concentrate on descriptions of the properties of given structures. Exchange theory has a model of a rational self-interested agent, but this model has disregarded the power of agents to change structure to enhance their bargaining positions. Leik (1992) has used network exchange theory to examine actor's "strategic manipulation of network linkages." This suggests that low power positions, such as the competitors for the promotion, may seek out other sources of promotion in order to enhance their position, while "high power actors prefer to isolate those dependent on them" (Leik, 1992: 316).

One other, more ambiguous characteristic of network exchange theory should be mentioned: its propensity for laboratory experiments. Most of the theory's developments have been driven by experiments with test subjects in controlled laboratory conditions. It is, of course, a great advantage to be able to test theories under controlled conditions, and the rarity of this situation in sociology is often a source of embarrassment. However, in order to isolate relevant characteristics, these laboratory conditions have been extremely artificial. Even in laboratories, the theory's predictions are obviated if subjects are allowed to know the unequal effects of their exchanges because normative considerations interfere (Molm, 2001:264). This means that experimental results must be interpreted carefully when applied to social interactions outside the laboratory. Furthermore, the artificial conditions of the laboratory can encourage an artificial theory. As Willer (1999:289) points out, "When an established experimental paradigm governs what will and will not be investigated, theory development becomes one-sided and research focuses on issues that have no importance or no known importance outside the laboratory." As an example Willer cites the intense interest in weak power networks. "No one has studied weak power networks in the field. Therefore, their empirical significance, even their empirical existence, is not known" (Willer, 1999:290).

Rational Choice Theory 理性选择理论

Although it influenced the development of exchange theory, rational choice theory was generally marginal to mainstream sociological theory (Hechter and Kanazawa, 1997). It is largely through the efforts of one man, James S. Coleman, that rational choice theory has become one of the "hot" theories in contemporary sociology (Heckathorn, 2005; Chriss, 1995; Lindenberg, 2000; Tilly, 1997). For one thing, in 1989 Coleman founded a journal, *Rationality and Society,* devoted to the dissemination of work from a rational choice perspective. For another, Coleman (1990) published an enormously influential book, *Foundations of Social Theory,* based on this perspective. Finally, Coleman became president of the American Sociological Association in 1992 and used that forum to push rational choice theory and to present an address entitled "The Rational Reconstruction of Society" (Coleman, 1993b).

Since we have outlined the basic tenets of rational choice theory, it would be useful to begin with Coleman's (1989) introductory comments to the first issue of *Rationality and Society.* The journal was to be interdisciplinary because rational choice theory (or, as Coleman calls it, "the paradigm of rational action" [1989:5]) is the only theory with the possibility of producing paradigmatic integration. Coleman does not hesitate to argue that the approach operates from a base in methodological individualism and to use rational choice theory as the micro-level base for the explanation of macro-level phenomena. Even more interesting is what Coleman's approach does not find "congenial":

> work that is methodologically holistic, floating at the system level without recourse to the actors whose actions generate that system . . . the view of action as purely expressive, the view of action as irrational, and also the view of action as something wholly caused by outside forces without the intermediation of intention or purpose. It excludes that empirical work widely carried out in social science in which individual behavior is "explained" by certain factors or determinants without any model of action whatsoever.
>
> (Coleman, 1989:6)

Thus, a large portion of work in sociology is excluded from the pages of *Rationality and Society.* Not to be excluded, however, are macro-level concerns and their linkage to rational action. Beyond such academic concerns, Coleman wants work done from a rational choice perspective to have practical relevance to our changing social world. For example, Heckathorn and Broadhead (1996) have examined the issue of public policies aimed at AIDS prevention from a rational choice perspective.

Foundations of Social Theory 社会理论的基础

Coleman argues that sociology should focus on social systems but that such macro phenomena must be explained by factors internal to them, prototypically individuals. He favors working at this level for several reasons, including the fact that data usually are gathered at the individual level and then aggregated or composed to yield the system level. Among the other reasons for favoring a focus on the individual level is that this is where "interventions" ordinarily are made to create social changes. As we will see, central to Coleman's perspective is the idea that social theory is not merely an academic exercise but should affect the social world through such "interventions."

Given his focus on the individual, Coleman recognizes that he is a methodological individualist, although he sees his particular perspective as a "special variant" of that orientation. His view is special in the sense that it accepts the idea of emergence and that while it focuses on factors internal to the system, those factors are not necessarily individual actions and orientations. That is, micro-level phenomena other than individuals can be the focus of his analysis.

JAMES S. COLEMAN

A Biographical Sketch

James S. Coleman had a remarkably varied career in sociology; the label "theorist" is only one of several that can be applied to him. He received his Ph.D. from Columbia University in 1955 (on the importance of the Columbia "school" to his work, see Swedberg, 1996), and a year later he began his academic career as an assistant professor at the University of Chicago (to which he returned in 1973, after a fourteen-year stay at Johns Hopkins University, and where he remained until his death). In the same year that he began teaching at Chicago, Coleman was the junior author (with Seymour Martin Lipset and Martin A. Trow) of one of the landmark studies in the history of industrial sociology, if not sociology as a whole, *Union Democracy* (1956). (Coleman's doctoral dissertation at Columbia, directed by Lipset, dealt with some of the issues examined in *Union Democracy*.) Coleman then turned his attention to research on youth and education, the culmination of which was a landmark federal government report (it came to be widely known as the "Coleman Report") that helped lead to the highly controversial policy of busing as a method for achieving racial equality in American schools. It is through this work that Coleman has had a greater practical impact than any other American sociologist. Next, Coleman turned his attention from the practical world to the rarefied atmosphere of mathematical sociology (especially *Introduction to Mathematical Sociology* [1964] and *The Mathematics of Collective Action* [1973]). In later years, Coleman turned to sociological theory, especially rational choice theory, in the publication of the book *Foundations of Social Theory* (1990) and the founding in 1989 of the journal *Rationality and Society*. The body of work mentioned here reflects almost unbelievable diversity, and it does not even begin to scratch the surface of the 28 books and 301 articles listed on Coleman's résumé.

Coleman received a B.S. from Purdue University in 1949 and worked as a chemist for Eastman Kodak before he entered the famous department of sociology at Columbia University in 1951. One key influence on Coleman was the theorist Robert Merton (see Chapter 3), especially his lectures on Durkheim and the social determinants of individual behavior. Another influence was the famous methodologist Paul Lazarsfeld, from whom Coleman derived his lifelong interest in quantitative methods and mathematical sociology. The third important influence was Seymour Martin Lipset, whose research team Coleman joined, thereby ultimately participating in the production of the landmark study *Union Democracy*. Thus, Coleman's graduate training gave him a powerful introduction to theory, methods, and their linkage in empirical research. This was, and is, the model for all aspiring sociologists.

On the basis of these experiences, Coleman described his "vision" for sociology when he left graduate school and embarked on his professional career:

> Sociology . . . should have the social system (whether a small system or a large one) as its unit of analysis, rather than the individual; but it should use quantitative methods, leaving behind the unsystematic techniques which lend themselves to investigator bias, fail to lend themselves to replication, and often lack an explanatory or causation focus. Why did I, and other students at Columbia at the time, have this vision? I believe it was the unique combination of Robert K. Merton and Paul Lazarsfeld.
>
> (Coleman, 1994:30–31)

Looking back from the vantage point of the mid-1990s, Coleman found that his approach had changed, but not as much as he had assumed. For example, with respect to his work on social simulation games at Johns Hopkins in the 1960s he said that they "led me to change my theoretical orientation from one in which properties of the system are not only determinants of action (à la Emile Durkheim's Suicide study), to one in which they are also consequences of actions sometimes intended, sometimes unintended" (Coleman, 1994:33). Thus, Coleman needed a theory of action, and he chose, in common with most economists,

> the simplest such foundation, that of rational, or if you prefer, purposive action. The most formidable task of sociology is the development of a theory that will move from the micro level of action to the macro level of norms, social values, status distribution, and social conflict.
>
> (Coleman, 1994:33)

It is this interest that explains why Coleman was drawn to economics:

> What distinguishes economics from the other social sciences is not its use of "rational choice" but its use of a mode of analysis that allows moving between the level of individual action and the level of system functioning. By making two assumptions, that persons act rationally and that markets are perfect with full communication, economic analysis is able to link the macro level of system functioning with the micro level of individual actions.
>
> (Coleman, 1994:32)

Another aspect of Coleman's vision for sociology, consistent with his early work on schools, is that it be applicable to social policy. Of theory he said, "One of the criteria for judging work in social theory is its potential usefulness for informing social policy" (Coleman, 1994:33). Few sociologists would disagree with Coleman's goal of linking theory, methods, and social policy, although many would disagree with at least some of the ways in which Coleman chose to link them. Whether or not they agree with the specifics, future sociologists will continue to be challenged by the need to do a better job of linking these three key aspects of sociological practice, and at least some of them will find in the work of James Coleman a useful model.

James Coleman died on March 25, 1995 (Marsden, 2007; Lindenberg, 2005; J. Clark, 1996).

Coleman's rational choice orientation is clear in his basic idea that "persons act purposively toward a goal, with the goal (and thus the actions) shaped by values or preferences" (1990:13). But Coleman (1990:14) then goes on to argue that for most theoretical purposes, he will need a more precise conceptualization of the rational actor derived from economics, one that sees the actors choosing those actions that will maximize utility, or the satisfaction of their needs and wants.

There are two key elements in his theory—actors and resources. Resources are those things over which actors have control and in which they have some interest. Given these two elements, Coleman details how their interaction leads to the system level:

> A minimal basis for a social system of action is two actors, each having control over resources of interest to the other. It is each one's interest in resources under the other's control that leads the two, as purposive actors, to engage in actions that involve each other . . . a system of action. . . . It is this structure, together with the fact that the actors are purposive, each having the goal of maximizing the realization of his interests, that gives the interdependence, or systemic character, to their actions.
>
> (Coleman, 1990:29)

Although he has faith in rational choice theory, Coleman does not believe that this perspective, at least as yet, has all the answers. But it is clear that he believes that it can move in that direction, since he argues that the "success of a social theory based on rationality lies in successively diminishing that domain of social activity that cannot be accounted for by the theory" (Coleman, 1990:18).

Coleman recognizes that in the real world people do not always behave rationally, but he feels that this makes little difference in his theory: "My implicit assumption is that the theoretical predictions made here will be substantively the same whether the actors act precisely according to rationality as commonly conceived or deviate in the ways that have been observed" (1990:506; Inbar, 1996).

Given his orientation to individual rational action, it follows that Coleman's focus in terms of the micro-macro issue is the micro-to-macro linkage, or how the combination of individual actions brings about the behavior of the system. While he accords priority to this issue, Coleman also is interested in the macro-to-micro linkage, or how the system constrains the orientations of actors. Finally, he evinces an interest in the micro-micro aspect of the relationship, or the impact of individual actions on other individual actions.

In spite of this seeming balance, there are at least three major weaknesses in Coleman's approach. First, he accords overwhelming priority to the micro-to-macro issue, thereby giving short shrift to the other relationships. Second, he ignores the macro-macro issue. Finally, his causal arrows go in only one direction; in other words, he ignores the dialectical relationship among and between micro and macro phenomena.

Utilizing his rational choice approach, Coleman explains a series of macro-level phenomena. His basic position is that theorists need to keep their conceptions of the actor constant and generate from those micro-constants various images of macro-level phenomena. In this way, differences in macro phenomena can be traced to different structures of relations at the macro level and not to variations at the micro level.

A key step in the micro-to-macro movement is the granting of the authority and rights possessed by one individual to another. This action tends to lead to the subordination of one actor to another. More important, it creates the most basic macro phenomenon—an acting unit consisting of two people, rather than two independent actors. The resulting structure functions independently of the actors. Instead of maximizing his or her own interests, in this instance an actor seeks to realize the interests of another actor, or of the independent collective unit. Not only is this a different social reality, it is one that "has special deficiencies and generates special problems" (Coleman, 1990:145). Given his applied orientation, Coleman is interested in the diagnosis and solution of these problems.

Collective Behavior 集体行为

One example of Coleman's approach to dealing with macro phenomena is the case of collective behavior (Zablocki, 1996). He chooses to deal with collective behavior because its often disorderly and unstable character is thought to be hard to analyze from a rational choice perspective. But Coleman's view is that rational choice theory can explain all types of macro phenomena, not just those that are orderly and stable. What is involved in moving from the rational actor to "the wild and turbulent systemic functioning called collective behavior is a simple (and rational) transfer of control over one's actions to another actor . . . made unilaterally, not as part of an exchange" (Coleman, 1990:198).

Why do people unilaterally transfer control over their actions to others? The answer, from a rational choice perspective, is that they do this in an attempt to maximize their utility. Normally, individual maximization involves a balancing of control among several actors, and this produces equilibrium within society. However, in the case of collective behavior, because there is a unilateral transfer of control, individual maximization does not necessarily lead to system equilibrium. Instead, there is the disequilibrium characteristic of collective behavior.

Norms 规范

Another macro-level phenomenon that comes under Coleman's scrutiny is norms. While most sociologists take norms as given and invoke them to explain individual behavior, they do not explain why and how norms come into existence. Coleman wonders how, in a group of rational actors, norms can emerge and be maintained. Coleman argues that norms are initiated and maintained by some people who see benefits resulting from the observation of norms and harm stemming from the violation of those norms. People are willing to give up some control over their own behavior, but in the process they gain some control (through norms) over the behavior of others. Coleman summarizes his position on norms:

> The central element of this explanation . . . is the giving up of partial rights of control over one's own action and the receiving of partial rights of control over the actions of others, that is, the emergence of a norm. The end result is that control . . . which was held by each alone, becomes widely distributed over the whole set of actors, who exercise that control.
>
> (Coleman, 1990:292)

Once again, people are seen as maximizing thteir utility by partially surrendering rights of control over themselves and gaining partial control over others. Because the transfer of control is not unilateral, there is equilibrium in the case of norms.

But there are also circumstances in which norms act to the advantage of some people and the disadvantage of others. In some cases, actors surrender the right to control their own actions to those who initiate and maintain the norms. Such norms become effective when a consensus emerges that some people have the right to control (through norms) the actions of other people. Furthermore, the effectiveness of norms depends on the ability to enforce that consensus. It is consensus and enforcement that prevent the kind of disequilibrium characteristic of collective behavior.

Coleman recognizes that norms become interrelated, but he sees such a macro issue as beyond the scope of his work on the foundations of social systems. However, he is willing to take on the micro issue of the internalization of norms. He recognizes that in discussing internalization he is entering "waters that are treacherous for a theory grounded in rational choice" (Coleman, 1990:292). He sees the internalization of norms as the establishment of an internal sanctioning system; people sanction themselves when they violate a norm. Coleman looks at this in terms of the idea of one actor or set of actors endeavoring to control others by having norms internalized in them. Thus, it is in the interests of one set of actors to have another set internalize norms and be controlled by them. He feels that this is rational "when such attempts can be effective at reasonable cost" (Coleman, 1990:294).

Coleman looks at norms from the point of view of the three key elements of his theory—micro to macro, purposive action at the micro level, and macro to micro. Norms are macro-level phenomena that come into existence on the basis of micro-level purposive action. Once in existence, norms, through sanctions or the threat of sanctions, affect the actions of individuals. Certain actions may be encouraged, while others are discouraged.

The Corporate Actor 法人行动者

With the case of norms, Coleman has moved to the macro level, and he continues his analysis at this level in a discussion of the corporate actor (J. Clark, 1996). Within such a collectivity, actors may not act in terms of their self-interest but must act in the interest of the collectivity.

There are various rules and mechanisms for moving from individual choice to collective (social) choice. The simplest is the case of voting and the procedures for tabulating the individual votes and coming up with a collective decision. This is the micro-to-macro dimension, while such things as the slate of candidates proposed by the collectivity involve the macro-to-micro linkage.

Coleman argues that both corporate actors and human actors have purposes. Furthermore, within a corporate structure such as an organization, human actors may pursue purposes of their own that are at variance with corporate purposes. This conflict of interest helps us understand the sources of revolts against corporate authority.

The micro-to-macro linkage here involves the ways in which people divest authority from the corporate structure and vest legitimacy in those engaged in the revolt. But there is also a macro-to-micro linkage in that certain macro-level conditions lead people to such acts of divestment and investment.

As a rational choice theorist, Coleman starts with the individual and with the idea that all rights and resources exist at this level. The interests of individuals determine the course of events. However, this is untrue, especially in modern society, where "a large fraction of rights and resources, and therefore sovereignty, may reside in corporate actors" (Coleman, 1990:531). In the modern world corporate actors have taken on increasing importance. The corporate actor may act to the benefit or the harm of the individual. How are we to judge the corporate actor in this regard? Coleman contends that "only by starting conceptually from a point where all sovereignty rests with individual persons is it possible to see just how well their ultimate interests are realized by any existing social system. The postulate that individual persons are sovereign provides a way in which sociologists may evaluate the functioning of social systems" (1990:531–532).

To Coleman, the key social change has been the emergence of corporate actors to complement "natural person" actors. Both may be considered actors because they have "control over resources and events, interests in resources and events, and the capability of taking actions to realize those interests through that control" (Coleman, 1990:542). Of course, there have always been corporate actors, but the old ones, such as the family, are steadily being replaced by new, purposively constructed, freestanding corporate actors. The existence of these new corporate actors raises the issue of how to ensure their social responsibility. Coleman suggests that we can do this by instituting internal reforms or by changing the external structure, such as the laws affecting such corporate actors or the agencies that regulate them.

Coleman differentiates between primordial structures based on the family, such as neighborhoods and religious groups, and purposive structures, such as economic organizations and the government. He sees a progressive "unbundling" of the activities that once were tied together within the family. The primordial structures are "unraveling" as their functions are being dispersed and being taken over by a range of corporate actors. Coleman is concerned about this unraveling as well as about the fact that we are now forced to deal with positions in purposive structures rather than with the people who populated primordial structures. He thus concludes that the goal of his work is "providing the foundation for constructing a viable social structure, as the primordial structure on which persons have depended vanishes" (Coleman, 1990:652).

Coleman is critical of most of social theory for adopting a view that he labels *homo sociologicus*. This perspective emphasizes the socialization process and the close fit between the individual and society. Therefore, *homo sociologicus* is unable to deal with the freedom of individuals to act as they will in spite of the constraints placed upon them. Furthermore, this perspective lacks the ability to evaluate the actions of the social system. In contrast, *homo economicus*, in Coleman's view, possesses all these capacities. In addition, Coleman attacks traditional social theory for doing little more than chanting old theoretical mantras and for being irrelevant to the changes taking place in society and incapable of helping us know where society is headed. Sociological theory (as well as sociological research) must have a purpose, a role in the functioning of society. Coleman is in favor of social theory that is interested not just in knowledge for the sake of knowledge but also in "a search for knowledge for the reconstruction of society" (1990:651).

Coleman's views on social theory are closely linked to his views on the changing nature of society. The passing of primordial structures and their replacement by purposive structures have left a series of voids that have not been filled adequately by the new social organizations. Social theory and the social sciences more generally are made necessary by the need to reconstruct a new society (Coleman, 1993a, 1993b; Bulmer, 1996). The goal is not to destroy purposive structures but rather to realize the opportunities and avoid the problems of such structures. The new society requires a new social science. The linkages among institutional areas have changed, and as a result the social sciences must be willing to cut across traditional disciplinary boundaries.

Criticisms 相关批判

Needless to say, rational choice theory in general (Goldfield and Gilbert, 1997; D. Green and Shapiro, 1994; Imber, 1997) has come under heavy fire in sociology. In fact, as Heckathorn (1997:15) points out, there is a kind of "hysteria" in some quarters of sociology about rational choice theory. James Coleman's work has been attacked from many quarters (Alexander, 1992; Rambo, 1995). For example, Tilly (1997:83) offers the following basic criticisms of Coleman's theory:

1. Neglected to specify causal mechanisms.
2. Promoted an incomplete and therefore misleading psychological reductionism.
3. Advocated a form of general theory—rational choice analysis—that has for some time been enticing social scientists into blind alleys, where they have wandered aimlessly, falling victim to local thugs and confidence men selling various brands of individual reductionism.

More generally, some researchers have found rational choice theory wanting (Weakliem and Heath, 1994), but the vast majority of the criticisms have come from supporters of alternative positions within sociology (Wrong, 1997). For example, given his macro-structural position, Blau (1997) argues that sociology should focus on macro-level phenomena, and as a result, the explanation of individual behavior that is the metier of rational choice theory falls outside the bounds of sociology.

Rational choice theory has been criticized from many quarters for being overly ambitious, for seeking to replace all other theoretical perspectives. Thus, Donald Green and Ian Shapiro (1994:203) argue that rational choice theory would do well "to probe the limits of what rational choice can explain" and to "relinquish the . . . tendency to ignore, absorb, or discredit competing theoretical accounts."

From a feminist point of view, England and Kilbourne (1990) have criticized the assumption of selfishness in rational choice theory; from their perspective selfishness-altruism should be considered as a variable. The assumption of selfishness represents a masculine bias. They recognize that rejecting this assumption, and looking at it as a variable, would reduce the "deductive determinacy" of rational choice theory, but they think the benefits of such a more realistic, less-biased theoretical orientation outweigh the costs.

From a symbolic-interactionist perspective, Denzin (1990b; see also Chapter 6 of this book) offers just the critique one might expect from such a diametrically opposed theoretical orientation:

> Rational choice theory . . . fails to offer a convincing answer to the question: How is society possible? . . . its ideal norms of rationality do not fit everyday life and the norms of rationality and emotionality that organize the actual activities of interacting individuals.
>
> Rational choice theory has limited utility for contemporary social theory. Its scheme of group life and its picture of the human being, of action, interaction, the self, gender, emotionality, power, language, the political economy of everyday life, and of history, are woefully narrow and completely inadequate *for interpretive purposes.*
>
> (Denzin, 1990a:182–183; italics added)

Most of those operating from a broadly interpretive perspective would accept Denzin's strong criticisms of rational choice theory.

In addition to general criticisms, rational choice theory has been attacked for underplaying or ignoring things such as culture (Fararo, 1996) and chance events (G. Hill, 1997).

Finally, although many other criticisms could be delineated, we might mention Smelser's (1992) argument that like many other theoretical perspectives, rational choice theory has degenerated as a result of internal evolution or responses to external criticisms. Thus, rational choice theory has become tautological and invulnerable to falsifiability, and most important, it has developed the "capacity to explain everything and hence nothing" (Smelser, 1992:400).

Rational choice theory has many supporters (Hedstrom and Swedberg, 1996). We will see many efforts to legitimize it further as a sociological theory and even more attempts to apply and extend the theory. We also are likely to see a further escalation of the criticisms leveled at rational choice theory.

Summary 总结

This chapter deals with three interrelated theories which, among other things, share a positivistic orientation. Modern exchange theory has evolved out of a series of intellectual influences, especially behaviorism and rational choice theory. The founder of modern exchange theory was George Homans. His reductionistic, determinedly micro-oriented exchange theory is summarized in a small number of propositions. Blau sought to extend exchange theory to the macro level, primarily by emphasizing the importance of norms. Much of the contemporary work in exchange theory has been influenced by Richard Emerson's more structural effort to develop an integrative, micro-macro approach to exchange. Emerson's disciples, and others, are busy extending his theoretical perspective into a variety of new domains.

One of Emerson's concerns is with networks, a concern also of those associated with network theory. While there are many overlaps between exchange theory and network theory, many network theorists operate outside an exchange framework. Network theory is distinguished by its focus on the objective pattern of ties within and between micro and macro levels of social reality.

Network exchange theory combines social exchange theory and network analysis in order to focus on the distribution of power in a network of exchange. It looks at the way in which the structures themselves can be said to be strong or weak.

Thanks largely to the efforts of James Coleman, rational choice theory, which had played a role in the development of exchange theory, has come into its own as a theoretical perspective. Utilizing a few basic principles derived largely from economics, rational choice theory purports to be able to deal with micro- and macro-level issues, as well as the role played by micro-level factors in the formation of macro-level phenomena. The number of supporters of rational choice theory is increasing in sociology, but so is the resistance to it by those who support other theoretical perspectives.

Modern Feminist Theory
第九章　女性主义理论

Patricia Madoo Lengermann
The George Washington University

Gillian Niebrugge
American University

Chapter Outline
Feminism's Basic Questions
Theorizing Gender: Sociology 1960 to Present
Varieties of Contemporary Feminist Theory
A Feminist Sociological Theory

Feminist theory is a generalized, wide-ranging system of ideas about social life and human experience developed from a woman-centered perspective. Feminist theory is woman-centered—or women-centered—in two ways. First, the starting point of all its investigation is the situation (or the situations) and experiences of women in society. Second, it seeks to describe the social world from the distinctive vantage points of women.

Feminist theory differs from most sociological theories in that it is the work of an interdisciplinary and international community of scholars, artists, and activists.[1] Feminist sociologists seek to broaden and deepen sociology by reworking disciplinary knowledge to take account of discoveries being made by this interdisciplinary community. This chapter has three main sections: one, a description of the treatment of gender in mainstream sociological theory; two, a description of the various types of contemporary feminist theory, emphasizing the contributions of sociologists to those theories; and third, an integrated statement of a general feminist sociological theory developed out of these various feminist theoretical traditions. The theoretical traditions are presented in terms of basic questions of feminism.

Feminism's Basic Questions 女性主义的基本问题

The impetus for contemporary feminist theory begins in a deceptively simple question: *"And what about the women?"* In other words, where are the women in any situation being investigated? If they are not present, why? If they are present, what exactly are

---

[1] This chapter draws primarily on the English-language contribution to this international effort.

they doing? How do they experience the situation? What do they contribute to it? What does it mean to them?

Over 40 years of posing this question has produced some generalizable answers. Women are present in most social situations. Where they are not, it is not because they lack ability or interest, but because there have been deliberate efforts to exclude them. Where they have been present, women have played roles very different from the popular conception of them (as, for example, passive wives and mothers). Indeed, as wives and as mothers and in a series of other roles, women, along with men, have actively created the situations being studied. Yet though women are actively present in most social situations, scholars, publics, and social actors themselves, both male and female, have been blind to their presence. Moreover, women's roles in most social situations, though essential, have been different from, less privileged than, and subordinate to the roles of men. Their invisibility is only one indicator of this inequality.

Feminism's second basic question, then, is *"Why is all this as it is?"* In answering this question, feminist theory has produced a general social theory with broad implications for sociology. One of feminist sociological theory's major contributions to answering this question has been the development of the concept of *gender*. Beginning in the 1970s, feminist theorists made it possible for people to see the distinctions between (a) biologically determined attributes associated with male and female and (b) the socially learned behaviors associated with masculinity and femininity. They did so by designating the latter as "gender."[2] The essential qualities of gender remain a point of theoretical debate in feminism, and these debates offer one way to distinguish among some of the varieties of feminist theory. But a starting point of agreement among nearly all varieties is an understanding of gender as a social construction, something not emanating from nature but created by people as part of the processes of group life.

The third question for all feminists is *"How can we change and improve the social world so as to make it a more just place for all people?"* This commitment to social transformation in the interest of justice is the distinctive characteristic of critical social theory, a commitment shared in sociology by feminism, Marxism, neo-Marxism, and social theories being developed by racial and ethnic minorities and in postcolonial societies. Patricia Hill Collins (1998:xiv) forcefully states the importance of this commitment to seeking justice and confronting injustice: "Critical social theory encompasses bodies of knowledge . . . that actively grapple with the central questions facing groups of people differently placed in specific political, social, and historic contexts characterized by injustice." This commitment to critical theory requires that feminist theorists ask how their work will improve the daily lives of the people they study.

---

[2] The word *gender* has origins as early as the fourteenth century, when it was used interchangeably with *sex* but especially in discussion of grammar (whether a noun is understood as masculine or feminine). *Gender* is used occasionally in early sociology articles of the 1900s but in a sense interchangeable with *sex*. The first feminist sociological conceptualization of the distinction between biologically determined attributes and socially learned behaviors was made by Charlotte Perkins Gilman in her 1898 classic *Woman and Economics,* where she created the concept of *excessive sex distinction* to refer to what we now mean by *gender.*

As the circle of feminists exploring these questions has become more inclusive of people of diverse backgrounds both in the United States and internationally, feminist theorists have raised a fourth question: *"And what about the differences among women?"* The answers to this question lead to a general conclusion that the invisibility, inequality, and role differences in relation to men which generally characterize women's lives are profoundly affected by a woman's social location—that is, by her class, race, age, affectional preference, marital status, religion, ethnicity, and global location.

But feminist theory is not just about women, nor is its major project the creation of a middle-range theory of gender relations. Rather, the appropriate parallel for feminism's major theoretical achievement is to one of Marx's epistemological accomplishments. Marx showed that the knowledge people had of society, what they assumed to be an absolute and universal statement about reality, in fact reflected the experience of those who economically and politically ruled the world; he effectively demonstrated that one also could view the world from the vantage point of the world's workers. This insight relativized ruling-class knowledge and, in allowing us to juxtapose that knowledge with knowledge gained from the workers' perspective, vastly expanded our ability to analyze social reality. More than a century after Marx's death we are still assimilating the implications of this discovery.

Feminism's basic theoretical questions have similarly produced a revolutionary switch in our understanding of the world: what we have taken as universal and absolute knowledge of the world is, in fact, knowledge derived from the experiences of a powerful section of society, men as "masters." That knowledge is relativized if we rediscover the world from the vantage point of a hitherto invisible, unacknowledged "underside": women, who in subordinated but indispensable "serving" roles have worked to sustain and re-create the society we live in. This discovery raises questions about everything we thought we knew about society, and its implications constitute the essence of contemporary feminist theory's significance for sociological theory.

Feminist theory deconstructs established systems of knowledge by showing their masculinist bias and the gender politics framing and informing them. To say that knowledge is "deconstructed" is to say that we discover what was hitherto hidden behind the presentation of the knowledge as established, singular, and natural—namely, that that presentation is a construction resting on social, relational, and power arrangements. But over the last two decades, feminism itself has become the subject of deconstructionist pressures from within its own theoretical boundaries, especially in the last decade. The first and more powerful of these pressures comes from women confronting the white, privileged-class, heterosexual status of many leading feminists—that is, from women of color, women in postcolonial societies, working-class women, and lesbians. These women, speaking from "margin to center" (hooks, 1984), show that there are many differently situated women, and that there are many women-centered knowledge systems which oppose both established, male-stream knowledge claims and any hegemonic feminist claims about a unitary woman's standpoint. The second deconstructionist pressure within feminism comes from a growing postmodernist literature which raises questions about gender as an undifferentiated concept and about the individual self as a stable locus of consciousness and personhood from which gender and the world are experienced. The potential impact of these questions falls primarily on feminist epistemology—its system for making truth claims—and is explored more fully in sections on "intersectionality" and "postmodernism" below.

对性别的理论化——从 20 世纪 60 年代至今的社会学

Theorizing Gender: Sociology 1960 to Present

Sociologists since the 1960s have responded to the challenge of feminism's basic questions in four distinct ways: first, by incorporating answers to these questions into sociology's substantive research fields, an effort that is still under way; second, by attempting to reorient existing sociological theories to these questions; third, by standing in one of feminism's own distinct theories; and, fourth, by mobilizing to craft a coherent system of feminist theory. The first response constitutes a large body of writing beyond the scope of this chapter; the second response is reviewed briefly in this section; the third and fourth responses are more fully discussed in the sections that follow. We organize our discussion of this second response into modern macro-social theories of gender, modern micro-social theories of gender, and feminist engagement with Bourdieu, Habermas, and Giddens.

现代性别宏观—社会理论

Modern Macro-Social Theories of Gender

Feminism's first question, "And what about the women?" has produced significant responses from theorists working out of three major macro-social perspectives that are more fully presented elsewhere in this book—structural functionalism (Chapter 3), conflict theory (Chapter 3), and neo-Marxian world-systems theory (Chapter 4). These theorists all use the same analytic process in placing gender in their generalized theoretical account of large-scale social phenomena. First, they define those phenomena as a system of interrelated and interacting structures that are understood as "patterned regularities in people's behavior" (Chafetz, 1984:23). Functionalists and analytic conflict theorists focus on nation-states or, on occasion, especially within analytic conflict theory, on premodern cultural groupings; world-systems theory treats global capitalism as a transnational system within which nation-states are important structures. The variations between these theories center on the particular structures and systemic processes they see as important. A major recent development is the argument that gender itself must be seen as such a structure, interacting with but not reducible to a constituent part of other such structures (see "Liberal Feminism" later in this chapter). Second, these theorists move to situate women within the system described. All three macro theories arrive at the same conclusion: women's primary location—in the sense that it is a location seen within all cultures as the distinctive "sphere" for women—is the household/family. From that primary location, and always with it as a framing condition, women may have other significant structural sites for activity, most notably in the market economy. The issue then becomes that of understanding the functions of the household/family in the social system and of charting the relationship between household and economy.

Third, each of these groups of gender theorists seeks to explain gender stratification—viewed as the near universal social disadvantage of women—in terms of the triangulated structural alignment of household/family, economy, and general social-system needs and processes.

Functionalism 功能主义

The major proponent of a functionalist theory of gender has been Miriam Johnson (1988, 1989, 1993; see also Giele and Holst, 2004). Speaking as a functionalist and a feminist, Johnson first acknowledges the failure of functionalism to adequately explore women's disadvantage in society. She accepts that there is an unintentional sexist bias in Talcott Parsons's theory of the family and that functionalism marginalizes issues of social inequality, domination, and oppression—a tendency originating in functionalism's primary concern with social order. Yet Johnson cogently demonstrates that the analytic variety and complexity of Parsonsian functionalism should be retained in analyses of gender because of its analytic range and flexibility—reiterating the position of many neofunctionalists (see Chapter 3). Johnson's work explores the relevance for gender of many of Parsons's key typologies: role as the basic unit in the social system, expressive versus instrumental role orientations, family as an institution in relation to other institutions, the functional prerequisites of the social system (adaptation, goal attainment, integration, and latency), the analytic levels of social action (social, cultural, personality, and behavioral), the stages of societal change (differentiation, adaptive upgrading, integration, and value generalization).

Most significant for a functionalist understanding of gender is Johnson's application of Parsons's concepts of expressive versus instrumental roles, his thesis of the family's relationship to other institutions, and his model of the functional prerequisites. Johnson locates much of the origin of gender inequality in the structure of the patriarchal family, in place in almost all known societies. The family has functions distinct from those of the economy and other "public" institutions: it socializes children and emotionally renews its adult members, activities essential to social cohesion and value reproduction (integration and latency). Women's primary social location in the structure of the family is as the principal producer of those essential functions. In these activities women must orient expressively, that is, with emotional attunement and relational responsiveness. Women's functions in the family and orientation toward expressiveness affect their functions in all other social structures, especially the economy. Women, for example, are channeled toward occupations typed as expressive; in male-dominated occupations they are expected to be expressive but are simultaneously sanctioned for this orientation; and always the responsibility toward family frames and intrudes upon economic participation.

None of these functions, however, fully explain the gender stratification system that devalues and disadvantages women. To understand why gender stratification is produced, we must return to the patriarchal family. Here in their expressively oriented care of children, women act with strength and authority, giving both boys and girls their sense of "common humanity." Institutional and cultural constraints require that the woman be weak and expressively compliant in relation to her husband, whose instrumentally mediated competitiveness in the economy earns for his family its level of economic security. Seeing her in the "weak wife" role, children learn to revere patriarchy and to devalue expressiveness as a relational stance against which instrumentality seems more powerful and valuable. This valuing of male instrumentality as more effective than female expressiveness is diffuse in the culture. But this valuational stance has no practical basis—except when framed by patriarchal ideology. One of Johnson's hopes is that the women's movement will produce the societal and cultural changes that lead to a systemwide re-evaluation of expressiveness.

In the meantime, however, Johnson must deal with the question of how patriarchal structures are functional in the production of system equilibrium and social order. Johnson suggests (1993) that we ask, "functional for whom?" But with this question she moves beyond Parsonsian functionalism, which argues that functionality is to be understood in terms of the system per se. The question "functional for whom?" opens up issues of unequal power and conflicting interests and points to a critical rather than a value-neutral stance for the theorist, a stance antithetical to functionalism. The question about women, the issue of gender, has, as it always does, made "the pot boil over."

Analytic Conflict Theory 分析冲突理论

The most influential theorist working on the issue of gender from the perspective of analytic conflict theory is Janet Chafetz (1984, 1988, 1990, 1997, 1999; see also Dunn, Almquist, and Chafetz, 1993). Unlike Johnson, Chafetz works in a network of similarly framed theoretical work (Blumberg, 1978, 1979, 1984; R. Collins, 1975; R. Collins et al., 1993; Demetriou, 2002; Huber, 2004; Skelton, 2005; and anthropologist Peggy Sanday, 1974, 1981). Chafetz's approach is cross-cultural and transhistorical and seeks to theorize gender in all its particular societal patternings. More specifically, she focuses on gender inequality or, as she labels it, *sex stratification*. In starting with sex stratification, Chafetz is consistent with analytic conflict theory practices: she finds a recurrent form of social conflict and sets out to analyze, from a value-neutral stance, the structural conditions producing the conflict in greater or lesser degrees of intensity.

Chafetz then explores the social structures and conditions that affect the intensity of sex stratification—or the disadvantaging of women—in all societies and cultures. These include gender role differentiation, patriarchal ideology, family and work organization, and framing conditions such as fertility patterns, separation of household and work sites, economic surplus, technological sophistication, population density, and environmental harshness—all understood as variables. The interaction of these variables determines the degree of sex stratification, because they frame the key structures of household and economic production and the degree to which women move between the two areas. Chafetz's position is that women experience the least disadvantage when they can balance household responsibilities with a significant and independent role in marketplace production. The household/family is viewed not as an area outside of work, a zone of emotions and nurturance, but as an area in which work occurs—child care, housework, and sometimes also work (as on the family farm) for which there are extra-household material rewards. Women's access to those rewards through either household or marketplace production becomes the mitigation against social disadvantage, and the form of the household—resulting from the interplay of many other variables—is the key structure facilitating or obstructing this access.

Chafetz then focuses on how gender equity may be purposively pursued, seeking to identify key structural points where change might improve women's condition. In her proactive stance toward gender equity Chafetz moves beyond the value neutrality which has been the hallmark of analytic conflict theory since Weber. The exploration of gender again leads the theorist—in this case a most disciplined practitioner—beyond the theory to issues of power and politics.

World-Systems Theory 世界—体系理论

World-systems theory takes global capitalism in all its historical phases as *the* system for sociological analysis. National societies and other distinct cultural groupings (for example, colonies and indigenous peoples) are significant structures in the world-system of global capitalism, as are the economic stratification of those societies and groupings (core, semiperipheral, and peripheral economies); the division of labor, capital, and power among and within them; and class relations within each societal unit. Since the defining process framing this theory's investigation is capitalism, individuals in all societal units typically are understood in terms of their roles within capitalist arrangements for the creation of surplus value. This theory thus typically understands women's role in the social system only to the degree that their labor is part of capitalism—that is, when they are workers within capitalist production and markets. But a full and direct engagement with the issue of gender immediately throws this model of the social system into question.

Kathryn B. Ward (1984, 1985a, 1985b, 1988, 1990, 1993; Ward and Pyle, 1995; see also Feldman, 2001; Sassen, 1998, 2004; Wallerstein, 2000) argues (1) that the world-system cannot be understood until the labor of the household and the labor of the informal economy are properly factored in and (2) that because women compose much of this labor, women must be given special attention in world-systems theory and not simply subsumed under the title "worker." The household constitutes all the work done at home to maintain and reproduce the worker; the informal economy is that organization of work in which there is no clear separation between labor and capital and no regulation of labor by law or capitalist organization. Ward argues that perhaps as much as 66 percent of the world's work is done in these two largely ignored, noncapitalist economies and that the proportion of the world's work done in these two economies is expanding *precisely as capitalism itself expands* globally. Answering the question "And what about the women?" in the world-system thus reveals a vast "subcontinent" of noncapitalist production coexisting, expanding, and interacting with global capitalism. In women's pattern of work globally—where the exigencies of household work are always present, and where women out of that base engage with informal and capitalist economies in an ever-shifting calculus—we find one point of entry for theorizing the structures of work within the world-system. Further, Ward argues that the particular contributions of women's unpaid labor to the world economy and male dominance over women must be understood and explained not simply as products of capitalism but as "distinctive phenomena properties with their own logic" (Ward, 1993:52).

现代微观—社会性别理论
Modern Micro-Social Theories of Gender

Microsociological theorists have focused less on explaining women's social disadvantage than on explicating the phenomenon of gender as it enters into women's understanding of society as human beings in interaction; they ask how gender is present in interactions and how interactions produce gender. The two main microsociological theories of gender are symbolic interactionism (Deegan and Hill, 1987; Frost, 2005; Goffman, 1979; Hollander and Howard, 1997; McGregor, 1995) and ethnomethodology (Dozier and Schwartz, 2001; Fenstermaker, West, and Zimmerman, 1991; Kessler and McKenna, 2000; Layte, 1998; West and Fenstermaker, 1993; West and Zimmerman, 1987).

Symbolic interactionism's theory of gender begins with a proposition central to any symbolic-interactionist analysis: "Gender identity, like other social identities, emerges out of social interaction and is incorporated into the individual's transsituational self [and] must be continually confirmed across varying interactional situations . . . because the self is subject to constant empirical tests" (Cahill, 1980:123). Symbolic interactionism reverses Freud's contention that identification with the same-sex parent is the key element *in developing* gender identity. It argues rather that in acquiring language, the child learns that it is identified and thus learns to self-identify as a "boy" or "girl" and, in turn, to identify with "mommy" or "daddy." Symbolic-interactionist accounts show individuals engaged in maintaining the gendered self in various situations. At the core of these accounts is a knowing individual who has a collection of ideas, of words in one's inner and outer conversations, about what it means to be a man or a woman. The person brings a gendered self into situations and tries to act according to this internalized definition, which may be modified through interaction from situation to situation but is the repository of the gender component of people's transsituational behavior.

Ethnomethodologists begin from Zimmerman's proposition (1978:11) that "properties of social life which seem objective, factual and transsituational, are actually managed accomplishments or achievements of local processes." Ethnomethodologists make the theoretically important distinction among *sex* (biological identification as male or female), *sex category* (social identification as male or female), and *gender* (behavior that meets social expectations for being male or female). Where the emphasis upon internalization of a fixed gender identity may reduce gender to an attribute as sex—something that is inherently part of the individual—the ethnomethodological argument is that gender does not inhere in the person but is achieved in interaction in the situation. Because sex category is potentially an ever-present quality of an individual, the achievement of gender is potentially an ever-present quality in social situations. People's normative conceptions of appropriate male or female behavior are situationally activated. People in a situation know that they are "accountable" for gender performance to the degree that the situation permits a person to behave as a man or a woman within it and have other people so recognize her or his behavior. It is possible for people from different cultures—including class and race cultures—to find each other's behavior incomprehensible in terms of gender identity: what the other is doing is not recognized as being male- or female-appropriate behavior. On the other hand, ethnomethodological research has shown that divisions of household labor that appear vastly unequal from outside the household situation may be seen as fair and equal by both men and women in the situation because both parties accept and conform to normative expectations for doing gender within the household. In recent years, ethnomethodological explorations of gender have become a major theoretical project in feminism itself, a project that has gained additional significance because of its parallels with postmodernist Judith Butler's concept of performativity (see "Gender Difference" below).

Both symbolic interactionism and ethnomethodology allow for and assume an institutional milieu of normative conceptions about gender. Goffman (1979) noted early, and symbolic interactionists, under the influence of postmodernism (Denzin, 1993), increasingly affirm, that these conceptions are not accessed solely, or perhaps even primarily, through interaction with other people. Mediated messages—that is, media images in advertising, television, movies, books, magazines—tell both adults and children quite directly, without interactional intervention, how gender is enacted. These mediated messages offer what Goffman labels "displays" of gender: "simplified, exaggerated, stereotyped" information about the appropriate "alignments" for men and women in given interactions. This analysis produces a causal puzzle: is media imitating life or life, media? Here as in other instances, microsociological explorations of gender work successfully within their given paradigms without challenging the male biases in those paradigms, challenges raised by feminist sociological theory later in this chapter.

布迪厄、哈贝玛斯和吉登斯理论中的女性主义
Feminist Engagements with Bourdieu, Habermas, and Giddens

Feminists have also explored the significance for the study of gender of the work of three sociologists particularly influential in the development of contemporary social theory—Pierre Bourdieu (see Chapter 10), Anthony Giddens (Chapter 11), and Jurgen Habermas (Chapter 11).

Giddens 吉登斯

It is either ironic or understandable that Giddens, the theorist in this grouping who has written most explicitly on issues of gender, has aroused the smallest response from feminists. Giddens has rejected the claim that we now live in a macrosocial postmodern world that has moved radically away from the sociocultural arrangements of the last three centuries—beyond, that is, the "modern" phase of societal formation. Giddens argues instead that the present moment in history is *high modernity*, in which the patterns of modernity persist but in a mode of accelerating and often unpredictable macro-level change, features of which include globalization, risk, uncertainty, and the penetration and transformation of the microsocial locales of daily living by large-scale impersonal forces for appropriation and standardization. Giddens sees gender relations as a significant site of microsocial resistance to these macro trends. In high modernity, individuals turn with growing intensity, as an antidote to impersonalization, to gender relations, working to produce there the radical equality necessary to a full experience of intimacy. He credits women and feminism with much of the initiative for this push for equality.

Some feminist sociologists, however, have questioned Giddens's linkage of equality and intimacy in gender relations, looking, for example, at negotiations over the family budget, where it appears that individuation rather than mutuality is the prevailing trend (Pahl, 1999; Vogler, 2005). The push for intimacy in Giddens's theory is a consequence of the counter-pressure toward radical individuation arising out of high modernity. Some feminist writing has explored this synthesis of structure and agency through the lens of gender and gender differences, pointing to the different forms that individuation may take for women and men (Demetriou, 2002; Gerhard, 2004). The failure to recognize this possibility of difference, they suggest, may be one indicator of a persisting masculinist bias in Giddens's theoretical exploration of gender.

Bourdieu and Habermas have been the objects of more attention. They have been faulted for failure to adequately attend to gender, but they have also been acknowledged as sources of *"explanatory power that is not offered elsewhere"* (e.g., Skeggs, 2004:21).

Habermas 哈贝马斯

The first point made about Habermas has been that his work presumed gendered roles without addressing the problem of gender inequality (Fleming, 1997). But feminists nevertheless have been drawn by his vision of the possibility of a liberating and democratic society founded on the practice of *communicative action in the public sphere*. Communicative action is discourse marked by participants' recognition of each other as equals and their attempt to arrive without bias at universally applicable norms for a given situation. The public sphere is seen by Habermas as a place where something like public opinion can be created. It should allow access to everyone. It exists in some measure wherever private individuals come together in such a way as to produce a public body and in that public body they discuss matters of general interest to all as citizens.

Feminists have explored the meanings of and the practices that produce this public sphere. The idea of the public sphere is seen as resolving at least two problems—one, the tendency in Marxian thought to equate the public with the government; two, the tendency in feminist thought to equate the public with everything that is not the private domestic sphere (Fraser, 1992). The ability to participate effectively in the public sphere is seen as arising out of one's experiences in the "life-world," in the possibilities it offers for freedom of speech. These possibilities depend on the ability of the life-world to escape "colonization" by the "system-world." But it is noted by feminists that the production of the life-world depends on unpaid female labor; and there is debate about whether the commodification of child care constitutes a colonization of the life-world by the system-world or a greater possibility of freedom for participation in this public sphere by women (Fraser, 1995; Cohen, 1995).

The public sphere presented by Habermas is above all an intersubjective reality. McNay (2004b:178) argues that this emphasis on intersubjectivity may point to a resolution of the tension within feminist thought about the relative importance of cultural and material variables: "Habermas's reorientation of Marxist thought toward the recognition of the primacy of the lifeworld overcomes the productivist emphasis that an exclusive focus on instrumental rationality yields. . . . [It also] provides a materialist antidote to what are seen as the relativism and aestheticizing tendencies of the post-structuralist tradition." But feminists have been especially concerned about ways of broadening equality of access to the public sphere (McLaughlin, 2004; Moorti, 2002). They critique Habermas's program for a practice of communicative action guided by "discourse ethics" which they see as based in abstract principles of justice and an abstract conception of "the other"; feminists seek to interject into this discourse the long-standing feminist ethic of care which is grounded in the concreteness of immediate situations (Benhabib, 1995; Nagel, 1997). Feminist critics have been concerned with what they see as a masculinist bias in Habermas's promotion of a conception of justice as a norm agreed to by everyone involved, a position that ignores the long history of gender inequality in practical discourse situations, and feminists have urged a "focus on . . . the inclusive elements of communicative action" (Pajnik, 2006:385).

Bourdieu 布迪厄

Feminist theorists confronting the work of Pierre Bourdieu have worked creatively to interpolate gender into a model of society and social relations that while tightly argued and enormously suggestive has given almost no attention to gender (Adkins, 2004a), indeed requires at some moments, as does Habermas's work, the existence of traditional gender roles in order for the world to work as described.

To appreciate the uses feminists have made of Bourdieu, it is necessary to briefly suggest his model of society (see Chapter 10 for an expanded discussion). In its most basic structure, Bourdieu's model has four main parts. *Practice* is something done in order to stake out a position in a *field,* which is an area of social life that generates its own network of relations and rules and supports the practices necessary to maintain these. Fields are potentially infinite. Most important is the field of power, but there are also the economic field, the social field, the legal field, the educational field, the family field, and so on. The individual person engages in practice in any given field through the mechanism of the *habitus,* a system of dispositions to action produced out of the conditioning experiences of one's life history and structuring one's actions toward stimuli encountered in the field. As the individual engages in practice in a field through the mechanism of the habitus, he or she attempts to acquire and convert various kinds of *capital,* the resources one uses in practice—for example, *economic capital* (wealth), *social capital* (relations), *cultural capital* (knowledge of how to practice in a particular field), and *symbolic capital* (prestige, the right to be heard).

Feminists have found Bordieu useful in dealing with a number of recurring questions in feminist theory. McNay sees Bourdieu's work helping to resolve the problem of the relation of subjectivity and embodiment and of agency and structure. His concept of the habitus allows for "the incorporation of the social into the body" (McNay, 1999:99) as the habitus is expressed through bodily enactments it is predisposed to do by social conditioning. Bourdieu's model of the social world as a physical space—a series of autonomous or interrelated fields in which embodied persons seek positions—provides a useful image for resolving the ongoing tension in feminist theory between agency and structure; as McNay (2004a:184) writes, "By plotting social position as spatial position, the complex interaction between symbolic and material power relations, between immediate experience and invisible structures is elucidated."

In a foundational step in placing gender in this model, Toril Moi (1991, 1999) presents gender as functioning similarly to Bourdieu's sense of social class: both structure the social field—a general, diffuse area of social relationship that overlaps or interrelates with nearly all other fields. Gender as part of this social field is not an independent system but a "particularly combinatory social category, one that infiltrates and influences every other category" (Moi 1999:288). Implicitly or explicitly following Moi's lead, feminist theorists have analyzed the ways gender "infiltrates and influences" practices, fields, habitus, capital, the dynamics of social change.

Where Bordieu has been perhaps most useful to feminist analysis, however, is in his explanations of the processes of domination and social change. Bourdieu's argument that a class can come into existence only " 'when there are agents capable of imposing themselves as authorised to speak and act authoritatively in its place'" (Bourdieu in Lovell 2004:48) is used by Lovell to explore the role of feminism and feminist agents in establishing women as social class. Adkins (2004a) looks at the possible effects of a gendered habitus entering a field—for instance, an occupational situation not heretofore open to women—that it has not been conditionally disposed to act in. Such a situation—"where there is a lack of 'fit' between the habitus (the feel for the game) and the field (the game itself)"—will lead to practices becoming more reflexive (Adkins, 2004b:191).

Feminist theorists also question Bourdieu's emphasis on women/mothers as transmitters of cultural capital in the child's early formation of a habitus and his insistence that social placement derives from the father. Bourdieu's theoretical dependence on a traditional Western gendered habitus of male dominance and female submission is seen as limiting his ability to respond to the fact of a changing gender order (Silva, 2005).

当代女性主义理论

Varieties of Contemporary Feminist Theory

In this section we present a typology of contemporary feminist theories that undergird the construction of feminist sociological theory.[3] Our typology is organized around answers to feminism's most basic question, *And what about the women?* Essentially

---

[3] Several other classificatory systems already exist, for example, those developed by Chafetz (1988); Clough (1994); Glennon (1979); Jaggar (1983); Jaggar and Rothenberg (1984); Kirk and Okazawa-Rey (1998); Lengermann and Wallace (1985); Snitow, Stansell, and Thompson (1983); Sokoloff (1980); and Tong (1998). Readers might turn to these works for balance or amplification of the ideal type presented here. In combination, these efforts have generated a long list of types of feminist theory, including black feminism, conservatism, expressionism, ecofeminism, existentialism, global instrumentalism, lesbian feminism, liberalism, Marxism, polarism, psychoanalytic feminism, radicalism, separatism, socialism, and synthesism. Our own typology attempts to include most of these theories, though not always as identified by these specific labels.

there have four answers to that question (see Table 9.1). The first of these can be framed in terms of *gender difference*—women's location in, and experience of, most situations is *different* from that of the men in those situations. The second is that of *gender inequality*—women's location in most situations is not only different from but also less privileged than or *unequal* to that of men. The third is that of *gender oppression*—that is, there is a direct power relationship between men and women through which women are restrained, subordinated, molded, used and abused by men. The fourth is that women's experience of difference, inequality, and oppression varies according to their location within societies' arrangements of *structural oppression*— class, race, ethnicity, age, affectional preference, marital status, and global location.

TABLE 9.1

Overview of Varieties of Feminist Theory

Basic varieties of feminist theory— answers to the descriptive question, "What about the women?"	Distinctions within theories—answers to the explanatory question, "Why is women's situation as it is?"
Gender difference	
Women's location in, and experience of, most situations is *different* from that of men in the situation.	Cultural feminism Existential and phenomenological Sociological theories • Institutional • Interactional
Gender inequality	
Women's location in most situations is not only different from but also less privileged than or *unequal* to that of men.	Liberal feminism
Gender oppression	
Women are *oppressed,* not just different from or unequal to, but actively restrained, subordinated, molded, and used and abused by men.	Psychoanalytic feminism Radical feminism
Structural oppression	
Women's experience of difference, inequality, and oppression varies by their social location within capitalism, patriarchy, and racism.	Socialist feminism Intersectionality theory
Feminism and postmodernism	

Within these basic categories we can distinguish among theories in terms of their differing answers to the second or explanatory question, "Why is all this as it is?" (The various types of answers are summarized in Table 9.1.) We conclude this section with a discussion of the growing dialogue between feminism and postmodernism, but since postmodernist feminists do not conceptualize their work in terms of feminism's basic question, "What about the women?" its standing in this section is unique—as indicated by its placement in the table.

This typology provides one way to pattern the general body of contemporary feminist theory, created within and outside sociology. It also helps pattern the expanding literature in the sociology of gender. While the focus in the sociology of gender on the relationship of men and women is not equivalent to a feminist theory which presents a critical woman-centered patterning of human experience (Chafetz, 2004), some sociologists who begin from a sociology-of-gender standpoint have produced works of significance for feminist theory, and many sociologists are directly involved in producing feminist theory. This link between feminist theory and the sociology of gender helps explain the "groundedness"—in principle and practice—of feminist theoretical work; that is, the dynamic, ongoing relation between research and theoretical "discovery". Theoretical claims very frequently are made inductively in research statements—at least as often as they are arrived at deductively from a body of theoretical work. Indeed, as Dorothy E. Smith (2002:ix, x) observes, one hallmark of feminist sociological theory is that it is "subject to the discipline of research," which separates it "from feminist . . . philosophy and literary theory."

This typology presents an ideal type of the analytically distinct theoretical traditions that inform feminist sociological theory, but it needs to be read with the following cautions in mind. One caution is that the typology outlines theoretical positions, not the location of specific theorists. The positions themselves in many instances are complementary, and over the course of a career a given theorist may write from several of these positions. A second caution is that feminist theory and feminist sociological theory are dynamic enterprises that change over time. At the current moment, this typology is located within the following intellectual trends. First and foremost, over the last few years, there has been a steady movement toward synthesis, toward critically assessing how elements of these various theories complement each other and in combination advance the project of a general feminist theory. Second, there has been a shift in the guiding problematic from women's oppression to oppressive practices and structures that impact the lives of the majority of the world's population, men and women. Third, a major line of tension has developed between interpretations that emphasize culture and meaning and those that emphasize the material consequences of power. Fourth, part of this debate over the explanatory strength of meaning and materiality has focused on problematizing gender, that is, the attempt to interrogate taken-for-granted meanings of a concept that has been basic to Second Wave feminist theory. Fifth, feminist theory is coming to be practiced as part of what Thomas Kuhn has called "normal science," that is, its assumptions are taken for granted as a starting point in ongoing empirical research (see S. P. Turner, 2004). And finally, the theories identified in the typology do not exist on a level playing field. In the current sociopolitical moment, some are relatively dormant; that is, they have made significant contributions in the past but are not now being elaborated—most notably psychoanalytic feminism but also to some degree radical feminist theory. Other theories are currently dynamic and expanding—most notably, ethnomethodology and intersectionality.

Gender Difference 性别差异

Theories of gender difference are among the oldest of feminist theories. Although historically the concept of "difference" has been at the center of several theoretical debates in feminism, we use it here to refer to theories that describe, explain, and trace the implications of the ways in which men and women are or are not the same in behavior and experience. All theories of gender difference have to confront the problem of what usually is termed "the essentialist argument": the thesis that the fundamental differences between men and women are immutable. That immutability usually is seen as traceable to three factors: (1) biology, (2) social institutional needs for men and women to fill different roles, most especially but not exclusively in the family, and (3) the existential or phenomenological need of human beings to produce an "Other" as part of the act of self-definition. There has been some interest in sociobiology by respected feminist scholars, most notably Alice Rossi (1977, 1983), who have explored the thesis that human biology determines many social differences between men and women. But overall the feminist response to sociobiology has been oppositional (Chancer and Palmer, 2001; Risman, 2001). Theories of gender difference important in feminist theory today issue from a range of locations: the women's movement, psychology, existential philosophy, two strands of sociological analysis, and postmodernism.

Cultural Feminism 文化女性主义

Cultural feminism is unique among theories analyzed here in that it is less focused on explaining the origins of difference and more on exploring—and even celebrating—the social value of women's distinctive ways of being, that is, of the ways in which women are different from men. This approach has allowed cultural feminism to side-step rather than resolve problems posed by the essentialist thesis.

The essentialist argument of immutable gender difference first was used against women in male patriarchal discourse to claim that women were inferior to men and that this natural inferiority explained their social subordination. But that argument was reversed by some First Wave feminists who created a theory of cultural feminism, which extols the positive aspects of what is seen as "the female character" or "feminine personality." Theorists such as Margaret Fuller, Frances Willard, Jane Addams, and Charlotte Perkins Gilman were proponents of a cultural feminism that argued that in the governing of the state, society needed such women's virtues as cooperation, caring, pacifism, and nonviolence in the settlement of conflicts (Deegan and Hill, 1998; Donovan, 1985; Lengermann and Niebrugge-Brantley, 1998). This tradition has continued to the present day in arguments about women's distinctive standards for ethical judgment (Day, 2000; M. Friedman, 1993; Gilligan, 1982; V. Held, 1993), about a mode of "caring attention" in women's consciousness (Fisher, 1995; Reiger, 1999; Ruddick, 1980), about a female style of communication (Bate and Taylor, 1988; M. Crawford, 1995; Tannen, 1990, 1993, 1994), about women's capacity for openness to emotional experience (Beutel and Marini, 1995; Mirowsky and Ross, 1995), about women's fantasies of sexuality and intimacy (Radway, 1984; Snitow, Stansell, and Thompson, 1983), and about women's lower levels of aggressive behavior and greater capacity for creating peaceful coexistence (A. Campbell, 1993; Forcey, 2001; Ruddick, 1994; Wilson and Musick, 1997).

The theme from cultural feminism most current in contemporary literature is that developed from Carol Gilligan's argument that women operate out of a different method of moral reasoning than men. Gilligan contrasts these two ethical styles as "the ethic of care," which is seen as female and which focuses on achieving outcomes where all parties feel that their needs are noticed and responded to, and the "ethic of justice," which is seen as male and which focuses on protecting the equal rights of all parties (Gilligan and Attanucci, 1988). While much research is concerned with whether there are gender differences in people's appeal to these two ethics, the more lasting influence of this research lies in the idea that an ethic of care is a moral position in the world (Orme, 2002; Reitz-Pustejovsky, 2002; F. Robinson, 2001). In its broadest implications for social change, cultural feminism suggests that women's ways of being and knowing may be a healthier template for producing a just society than are those of an androcentric culture for male ways of knowing and being.

Existential and Phenomenological Analyses 存在主义和现象学分析

Feminist thinkers offering existential and phenomenological analyses have developed one of the most enduring themes of feminist theory: the marginalization of women as Other in a male-created culture. This theme is given its classic formulation in Simone de Beauvoir's analysis in *The Second Sex* (1949/1957), but there have been myriad other important statements, including Bartsky (1992), Daly (1973), and Ortega (2001). In these explanations, the world people inhabit has been developed out of a culture created by men and assuming the male as subject, that is, as the consciousness from which the world is viewed and defined. That culture, at best, pushes women's experience and ways of knowing themselves to the very margins of conceptual framing and, at its most frightening, creates a construct of the woman as "the Other," an objectified being who is assigned traits that represent the opposite of the agentic, subject male. For de Beauvoir, following Hegel, Heidegger, and Sartre, it is a given that "Otherness is a fundamental category of human thought" (1949/1957:xiv), that binary opposition is one of the chief ways in which thought organizes culture, and that the individual experiences other people as a potential threat to the sovereignty of the subject's consciousness, restricting the capacity for ongoing self-actualization. Women's difference from men results in part from this fact of cultural construction which excludes them and in part from their internalization of "Otherness." Crucial questions here are whether women can liberate themselves from the status of object/ other and whether in that liberation they must become like men or can achieve a distinctive subjectivity. The tilt in this argument (a tilt developed radically by later French feminists like Hélène Cixous [1976, 1994] and Luce Irigaray [1985a, 1985b]) is that liberation will come, for women and the rest of humankind, when women develop a consciousness and culture that is uniquely theirs.

社会学理论：制度和互动
Sociological Theories: Institutional and Interactional

Institutional 制度理论

This theory posits that gender differences result from the different roles that women and men come to play within various institutional settings. A major determinant of difference is seen to be the sexual division of labor that links women to the functions of wife, mother, and household worker, to the private sphere of home and family, and thus to a lifelong series of events and experiences very different from those of men. Women's roles as mothers and wives in producing and reproducing a female personality and culture have been analyzed by theorists as diverse as Berger and Berger (1983), J. Bernard (1981, 1972/1982), Chodorow (1978), Risman and Ferree (1995), and M. Johnson (1989). The central motif for this line of thinking is the sexual division of labor in the family. Repeated experience in these settings is pictured as carrying over into other institutions and producing differences between women and men in political behavior (e.g., the gender gap in voting), in choice of careers (e.g., the caring professions as female), in styles of corporate management, and in possibilities for advancement (e.g., the mommy track). Institutional placement theories have not been disproved so much as subsumed under deeper questions of how routine activities produce permanent features of the gendered personality. Institutional placement theories have been subject to two criticisms. First, they do not account for the persistence of gender difference when men and women occupy the same institutional position; indeed, many feminist theorists would argue that men and women can never occupy the same institutional position precisely because of the persistence of gender as a separate structure. Second, many sociologists see institutional role theories as presenting too static and deterministic a model.

Interactionist 互动理论

The most currently elaborated sociological understanding of the origins of gender difference comes from ethnomethodology's analysis of gender as an *accomplishment*. Ethnomethodology (see Chapter 7) posits that institutional order, culture, and stratificational systems are maintained by the ongoing activities of individuals in interaction. When this idea is applied to gender, it produces the understanding that "people do gender"—or what is called in shorthand "doing gender."

West and Zimmerman's 1987 article "Doing Gender," the now classic statement of this position, distinguishes among sex, sex category, and gender. A baby is born with some configuration of biological sex (which may be more or less clear). On the basis of what the adults attending to the birth interpret as its sex, the baby is assigned to a sex category. After that assignment, everyone around the child and the child itself over time begin to do gender, to act in ways considered appropriate to the sex category designations. The question of how everyone knows what is appropriate is resolved in ethnomethodology by the principle of *accountability:* People do not just act in any way they choose; people in interactions hold other people "accountable" for behaving in ways that are expected or useful or understandable. That is, people "manage conduct in anticipation of how others might describe it on a particular occasion" (Fenstermaker and West, 2002:212). Thus, gender is constantly being produced by people in interaction with each other as a way of making sense of and letting the world work.

For instance, using the "right" public restroom is a way of avoiding all sorts of potential embarrassments. It is method of getting through the day hassle-free, and it is one so taken for granted that the person doing it hardly considers it doing gender. Ways of hugging, laughing, complaining—conveying the whole range of human emotions—are deeply gendered and are situationally enacted by people as they attempt to communicate with other people. Indeed, one question that emerges from the doing-gender perspective is whether it is possible *not* to do gender.

The current appeal of this approach reflects not only its abstract theoretical validity but also its suitability to a moment in U.S. history in which many people see men and women being more alike than different or at least having a great deal in common. The ethnomethodological insight gives a common origin to all gender experience in the movement from sex to sex category to gender: men and women both experience this, and both are caught up in the activities of doing gender.

But although the elemental understanding of "doing" holds constant for women and men, West and Fenstermaker (1995, 2002) and West and Zimmerman (1987) recognize that a part of the substance of the doing in gender is "doing difference"—acting to make distinctions, to distinguish oneself as masculine not feminine or, conversely, as feminine not masculine. These acts of distinction are repeated from situation to situation to maintain gender identity. The social mechanism that produces this doing of gender difference is the operation of accountability in terms of sex category.

The major criticism of this approach is the sense—felt about much ethnomethodology—that it is not clear where the standards for accountability come from, that ethnomethodology is perhaps too voluntaristic in its orientation because people in individual interactions do for the most part produce remarkably similar behaviors when doing gender (e.g., Maldonado, 1995; Weber, 1995). Other sociologists have argued that the approach is too concerned with reproduction and does not give enough account of moments of resistance, "overly emphasiz[es] the maintenance and reproduction of normative conceptions, but neglect[s] countervailing processes of resistance" (Thorne, 1995:448).

"Doing gender" as a theory has gained additional attention through its resonance with the postmodernist thesis of philosopher Judith Butler that gender is a "performance." Everyday meanings of "doing" and "performance" have led to a confusion about whether the two ideas are really the same. Fenstermaker and West (2002) and Moloney and Fenstermaker (2002) pursue the question of synthesis, noting differences but also pointing out that both picture gender as something accomplished in ongoing individual actions.

A major difference is in the beginning points of the two theories. The ethnomethodologists begin from an attempt to understand how gender is produced in everyday life. Butler begins from an unease with the most basic category of feminism: "woman." The idea of gender as performativity grew out of her attempts to deconstruct this apparently fundamental feminist category. Butler's work represents the polar opposite of the essentialist understanding that guides much of everyday life and from which the idea of gender difference originates. For Butler, the category of woman arises out of the process that produces gender, a process she names "performativity."

Her definition of *performativity* is a work-in-progress but has its origins in speech-act theory, where a performative is "that discursive practice that brings into being or enacts that which it names and so marks the constitutive or productive power of discourse" (Butler, 1995:134).

A classic example of a performative, drawn from speech-act philosopher J. L. Austin, occurs when a judge or minister says, "I now pronounce you man and wife." Applying this idea to gender, Butler sees gender arising as people perform it in interaction with each other: "In the place of an original identification which serves as a determining cause, gender identity might be reconceived as a personal/cultural history of received meanings subject to a set of imitative practices which refer laterally to other imitations and which, jointly, construct the illusion of a primary and interior gendered self or parody the mechanism of that construction" (Butler 1990:138).

In Butler's thinking, people do not begin life with an internal identity as man or woman; rather they get hold of certain understandings of man and woman depending on their personal biographies and their location in history. These meanings suggest ways of acting, and as the person looks around she or he can see other people engaged in similar ways of acting. Thus, gender is created as people imitate other people trying to act in accord with culturally given ideas about masculinity and femininity. These ideas so effectively bring into being what they name that people take as real the idea of a core gendered self. But Butler (1990:25) argues, playing off Nietzsche, that "There is no gender identity behind the expressions of gender; that identity is performatively constituted by the very 'expressions' that are said to be its results." Key to those expressions in a society governed by a sociocultural history that privileges heterosexuality as natural is the need to establish oneself as different from the other gender in order to participate in the ongoing imitation that is heterosexuality.

Two key differences between ethnomethodology and Butler's postmodernist version of performativity are important here. First, ethnomethodolgy, like nearly all sociology, does believe in a unified, basically rational self—there is a being behind the doing, and that being makes choices. Butler, like other postmodernists, calls the existence of this unified self into question. Second, ethnomethodology has in its principle of accountability what seems a clearer way of understanding what controls the particular "imitations" that a person undertakes to achieve.

Gender Inequality 性别不平等

Four themes characterize feminist theorizing of gender inequality. First, men and women are situated in society not only differently but also unequally. Specifically, women get less of the material resources, social status, power, and opportunities for self-actualization than do men who share their social location—be it a location based on class, race, occupation, ethnicity, religion, education, nationality, or any intersection of these factors. Second, this inequality results from the organization of society, not from any significant biological or personality differences between women and men. Third, although individual human beings may vary somewhat from each other in their profile of potentials and traits, no significant pattern of natural variation distinguishes the sexes. Instead, all human beings are characterized by a deep need for freedom to seek self-actualization and by a fundamental malleability that leads them to adapt to the constraints or opportunities of the situations in which they find themselves. To say that there is gender inequality, then, is to claim that women are situationally less empowered than men to realize the need they share with men for self-actualization. Fourth, all inequality theories assume that both women and men will respond fairly easily and naturally to more egalitarian social structures and situations. They affirm, in other words, that it is possible to change the situation. In this belief, theorists of gender inequality contrast with the theorists of gender difference, who present a picture of social life in which gender differences are, whatever their cause, more durable, more penetrative of personality, and less easily changed.

Liberal Feminism 自由女性主义

The major expression of gender inequality theory is liberal feminism, which argues that women may claim equality with men on the basis of an essential human capacity for reasoned moral agency, that gender inequality is the result of a sexist patterning of the division of labor, and that gender equality can be produced by transforming the division of labor through the repatterning of key institutions—law, work, family, education, and media (Bem, 1993; Friedan, 1963; Lorber, 1994; Pateman, 1999; Rhode, 1997; Schaeffer, 2001).

Historically the first element in the liberal feminist argument is the claim for gender equality. This claim was first politically articulated in the Declaration of Sentiments drafted at Seneca Falls, New York in 1848 with the express purpose of paralleling and expanding the Declaration of Independence to include women. It opens with the revisionist line "We hold these truths to be self-evident, that all men *and women* are created equal" [italics ours], changes the list of grievances to focus on women's state, and concludes with a call for women to do whatever is required to gain equal rights with men. In its arguments, the Declaration of Sentiments let the women's movement lay claim to the intellectual discourses of the Enlightenment, the American and French revolutions, and the abolitionist movement. It claimed for women the rights accorded to all human beings, under natural law, on the basis of the human capacity for reason and moral agency; asserted that laws which denied women their right to happiness were "contrary to the great precept of nature and of no . . . authority"; and called for change in law and custom to allow women to assume their equal place in society. The denial of those rights by governments *instituted by men* violates natural law and is the tyrannical working out of multiple practices of sexism. The radical nature of this foundational document is that it conceptualizes the woman not in the context of home and family but as an autonomous individual with rights in her own person (DuBois, 1973/1995). Liberal feminism, thus, rests on the beliefs that (1) all human beings have certain essential features—capacities for reason, moral agency, and self-actualization; (2) the exercise of these capacities can be secured through legal recognition of universal rights; (3) the inequalities between men and women assigned by sex are social constructions having no basis in "nature," and (4) social change for equality can be produced by an organized appeal to a reasonable public and the use of the state.

Contemporary feminist theory has expanded to include a global feminism which confronts racism in North Atlantic societies and works for "the human rights of women" everywhere. And this discourse has continued to express many of its foundational statements in organizational documents such as the National Organization for Women's Statement of Purpose and the Beijing Declaration. These organizational statements of purpose rely on an informing theory of human equality as a right which the state— local, national, international—must respect. These arguments are being freshly invoked in debates with the political right over reproductive freedom (Bordo, 1993; Solinger, 1998), in debates with postmodernists over the possibility and utility of formulating principles of rights (K. Green, 1995; A. Phillips, 1993; P. Williams, 1991), and in feminist considerations of the gendered character of liberal democratic theory and practice (Haney, 1996; Hirschmann and Di Stefano, 1996; A. Phillips, 1993; Thistle, 2002).

In sociology, contemporary liberal feminism is in part focused on the intellectual project of defining gender as a structure (Ferree, Lorber, and Hess, 1999; Lorber, 1994; Martin, 2005; Risman, 2004). Risman (2004:432) contrasts this approach with past analyses that have explained gender in terms of social structure (such as those of institutional placement discussed above under "Gender Difference"):

> While structural perspectives have been applied to gender in the past . . ., there has been a fundamental flaw in these applications. Generic structural theories applied to gender presume that if women and men were to experience identical structural conditions and role expectations, empirically observable gender differences would disappear. But . . . a structural perspective on gender is accurate only if we realize that gender itself is a structure deeply embedded in society.

Risman describes gender as a highly complex structure that patterns human behavior at three levels—individual, cultural/interactional, and institutional (2004:437). From this perspective, the defining social effect of gender is that it is "a socially constructed stratification system" (2004:430). Liberal feminism sees that gender as a system of stratification produces a gendered division of labor, an organization of society into public and private spheres, and a cultural dimension of sexist ideology.

The sexual division of labor in modern societies divides production in terms of both gender and spheres denoted as "public" and "private." Women are given primary responsibility for the private sphere. Men are given privileged access to the public sphere (which liberal feminists see as the locus of the true rewards of social life— money, power, status, freedom, opportunities for growth and self-worth). The fact that women have what access they do to the public sphere is, of course, one triumph of the women's movement—and of liberal feminism and of feminist sociology—as is the fact that women feel they can make some demands on men to assist in the work of the private sphere. The two spheres constantly interact in the lives of women (more than they do for men), and both spheres are still shaped by patriarchal ideology and sexism, which also are pervasive in contemporary mass media (L. R. Davis, 1997).

On the one hand, women find their experience within the public sphere of education, work, politics, and public space still limited by practices of discrimination, marginalization, and harassment (Benokraitis, 1997; Gardner, 1995; Hagan and Kay, 1995; Reskin and Padovic, 1994; Ridgeway, 1997). On the other hand, in the private sphere, they find themselves in a "time bind" as they return home from paid employment to "a second shift" of home and child care infused by an ideology of intensive mothering (Hochschild, 1989, 1997; Shelton, 2000). These pressures on women work interactively in complex ways—and one feature of contemporary feminist theory is its attempts to understand these interactions. Women's ability to compete in career and profession is hindered by the demands of the private sphere (Waldfogel, 1997). The public sphere "ideal worker norm" (Williams, 2000) which assumes the life schedule available to the typical male intensifies the stress of home commitments by shrinking women's resources of time and energy which in turn increase the demands on them for crisis management at home (Hochschild, 1997). Sexism's link of women to the private sphere activities of caregiving, emotion management, and the maintenance of routine means that women are expected to do this additional work in the public sphere and are frequently tracked into underremunerated jobs in which these "womanly" skills are commodified and marketed (Adkins, 1995; Pierce, 1995). This sexist patterning of work and home puts the single mother at tremendous economic risk and is one factor in the increasing "feminization of poverty" (Edin and Lein, 1997; K. M. Harris, 1996; Hays, 2003).

A recurring theme in liberal feminist analysis is the problem of achieving equality in marriage. This theme is given its classic formulation in Jessie Bernard's study *The Future of Marriage* (1972/1982). Bernard analyzes marriage as being at one and the same time a cultural system of beliefs and ideals, an institutional arrangement of roles and norms, and a complex of interactional experiences for individual women and men. Culturally, marriage is idealized as the destiny and source of fulfillment for women; a mixed blessing of domesticity, responsibility, and constraint for men; and for American society as a whole an essentially egalitarian association between husband and wife. Institutionally, marriage empowers the role of husband with authority and with the freedom—indeed, the obligation—to move beyond the domestic setting; it meshes the idea of male authority with sexual prowess and male power; and it mandates that wives be compliant, dependent, self-emptying, and essentially centered on the activities and demands of the isolated domestic household. Experientially then, there are two marriages in any institutional marriage: the man's marriage, in which the husband holds to the belief of being constrained and burdened, while experiencing what the norms dictate—authority, independence, and a right to domestic, emotional, and sexual service by the wife; and the woman's marriage, in which the wife affirms the cultural belief of fulfillment, while experiencing normatively mandated powerlessness and dependence, an obligation to provide domestic, emotional, and sexual services, and a gradual "dwindling away" of the independent young person she was before marriage.

The results of all this are to be found in the data that measure human stress. *Married* women, whatever their claims to fulfillment, and *unmarried* men, whatever their claims to freedom, rank high on all stress indicators, including heart palpitations, dizziness, headaches, fainting, nightmares, insomnia, and fear of nervous breakdown. *Unmarried* women, whatever their sense of social stigma, and *married* men rank low on all the stress indicators. Marriage, then, is good for men and bad for women and will cease to be so unequal in its impact only when couples feel free enough from the prevailing institutional constraints to negotiate the kind of marriage that best suits their individual needs and personalities. Recent studies have suggested that Bernard's analysis still holds for most marriages (Dempsey, 2002; Steil, 1997) but that some couples are achieving, through dedicated effort, the liberal feminist ideal of egalitarian marriage (P. Schwartz, 1994).

Liberal feminists' agenda for change is consistent with their analyses of the basis for claiming equality and the causes of inequality: they wish to eliminate gender as an organizing principle in the distribution of social "goods," and they are willing to invoke universal principles in their pursuit of equality. Some recent writings even argue for the elimination of gender categories themselves (Lorber, 2000, 2001). Liberal feminists pursue change through law—legislation, litigation, and regulation—and through appeal to the human capacity for reasoned moral judgments; that is, the capacity of the public to be moved by arguments for fairness. They argue for equal educational and economic opportunities; equal responsibility for the activities of family life; the elimination of sexist messages in family, education, and mass media; and individual challenges to sexism in daily life. Liberal feminists have worked through legislative change to ensure equality in education and to bar job discrimination; they have monitored regulatory agencies charged with enforcing this legislation; they have mobilized to have sexual harassment in the workplace legally defined as "job discrimination"; they have demanded both "pay equity" (equal pay for equal work) and "comparable worth" (equal pay for work of comparable value) (Acker, 1989; England, 1992; R. Rosenberg, 1992).

For liberal feminists, the ideal gender arrangement would be one in which each individual acting as a free and responsible moral agent chooses the lifestyle most suitable to her or him and has that choice accepted and respected, be it for housewife or househusband, unmarried careerist or part of a dual-income family, childless or with children, heterosexual or homosexual. Liberal feminists see this ideal as one that would enhance the practice of freedom and equality, central cultural ideals in America. Liberal feminism then is consistent with the dominant American ethos in its basic acceptance of democracy and capitalism; its reformist orientation; and its appeal to the values of individualism, choice, responsibility, and equality of opportunity.

Gender Oppression 性别压迫

Theories of gender oppression describe women's situation as the consequence of a direct power relationship between men and women in which men have fundamental and concrete interests in controlling, using, and oppressing women—that is, in the practice of domination. By *domination*, oppression theorists mean any relationship in which one party (individual or collective), the *dominant*, succeeds in making the other party (individual or collective), the *subordinate*, an instrument of the dominant's will. Instrumentality, by definition, is understood as involving the denial of the subordinate's independent subjectivity (Lengermann and Niebrugge-Brantley, 1995). Women's situation, for theorists of gender oppression, is centrally that of being dominated and oppressed by men. This pattern of gender oppression is incorporated in the deepest and most pervasive ways into society's organization, a basic arrangement of domination most commonly called *patriarchy*, in which society is organized to privilege men in all aspects of social life. Patriarchy is not the unintended and secondary consequence of some other set of factors—be it biology or socialization or sex roles or the class system. It is a primary power arrangement sustained by strong and deliberate intention. Indeed, to theorists of gender oppression, gender differences and gender inequality are by-products of patriarchy.

We review here two major variants of gender oppression theory: psychoanalytic feminism and radical feminism.

Psychoanalytic Feminism 精神分析女性主义

Psychoanalytic feminism attempts to explain patriarchy by reformulating the theories of Freud and his intellectual heirs (J. Benjamin, 1988, 1996, 1998; Chodorow, 1978, 1990, 1994, 1999; Langford, 1999). These theories map and emphasize the emotional dynamics of personality, emotions often deeply buried in the subconscious or unconscious areas of the psyche; they also highlight the importance of infancy and early childhood in the patterning of these emotions. In attempting to use Freud's theories, however, feminists have to undertake a fundamental reworking of his conclusions to follow through on directions implicit in Freud's theories while rejecting his gender-specific conclusions, which are sexist and patriarchal.

Like all oppression theorists, psychoanalytic theorists see patriarchy as a system in which men subjugate women, a universally pervasive system, durable over time and space, and steadfastly maintained in the face of occasional challenge. Distinctive to psychoanalytic feminism, however, is the view that this system is one that all men, in their individual daily actions, work to create and sustain. Women resist only occasionally but more often either acquiesce in or actively work for their own subordination. The puzzle that psychoanalytical feminists set out to solve is why men everywhere bring such unremitting energy to the task of sustaining patriarchy and why there is an absence of countervailing energy on the part of women.

Psychoanalytic feminists discount the argument that a cognitive calculus of practical benefits is sufficient for male support for patriarchy. Cognitive mobilization does not seem a sufficient source for the intense energy that men invest in patriarchy, especially because, in light of the human capacity to debate and second-guess, men may not always and everywhere be certain that patriarchy is of unqualified value to them. Moreover, an argument anchored in the cognitive pursuit of self-interest would suggest that women would as energetically mobilize against patriarchy. Instead, these theorists look to those aspects of the psyche so effectively mapped by the Freudians: the zone of human emotions, of half-recognized or unrecognized desires and fears, and of neurosis and pathology. Here they find a clinically proven source of motivational energy and debilitation, one springing from psychic structures too deep to be recognized or monitored by individual consciousness.

In searching for the energic underpinnings of patriarchy, psychoanalytical feminists turn their analytic lens on the socioemotional environment in which the personality of the young child takes form, and to two facets of early childhood development: (1) the assumption that human beings grow into mature people by learning to balance a never-resolved tension between *individuation,* the desire for freedom of action, and, *recognition,* the desire for confirmation by another, and (2) the observable fact that in all societies infants and children experience their earliest and most crucial development in a close, uninterrupted, intimate relationship with a woman, their mother or a mother substitute (J. Benjamin, 1985, 1988; Chodorow, 1978, 1990, 1999; Doane and Hodges, 1992). As infants and young children, for considerable periods lacking even language as a tool for understanding experience, individuals experience their earliest phases of personality development as an ongoing turbulence of primitive emotions—fear, love, hate, pleasure, rage, loss, desire. The emotional consequences of these early experiences stay with people always as potent but often unconscious "feeling memories." Central to that experiential residue is a cluster of deeply ambivalent feelings for the woman/mother/caregiver: need, dependence, love, possessiveness, but also fear and rage over her ability to thwart one's will. Children's relationship to the father/man is much more occasional, secondary, and emotionally uncluttered.

From this beginning, the male child, growing up in a culture that positively values maleness and devalues femaleness and increasingly aware of his own male identity, attempts to achieve an awkwardly rapid separation of identity from the woman/mother— an emotional separation which is partial and costly in its consequences. In adulthood the emotional carryover from early childhood toward women—need, love, hate, possessiveness—energizes the man's quest for a woman of his own who meets his emotional needs and yet is dependent on and controlled by him—that is, he has an urge to dominate and finds mutual recognition difficult. The female child, bearing the same feelings toward the woman/mother, discovers her own female identity in a culture that devalues women. She grows up with deeply mixed positive and negative feelings about herself and about the woman/mother and in that ambivalence dissipates much of her potential for mobilized resistance to her social subordination. She seeks to resolve her emotional carryover in adulthood by emphasizing her capacities for according recognition—often submissively with males in acts of sexual attraction and mutually with females in acts of kinship maintenance and friendship. And rather than seeking mother substitutes, she re-creates the early infant-woman relationship by becoming a mother.

Psychoanalytical feminist theorists have extended their analyses beyond individual personality to Western culture. The emphases in Western science on a distinct separation between "man" and "nature," and on a "scientific method" promising "objective" truth and control of nature, have been challenged and reinterpreted as the projection by the overindividuated male ego of its own desire for domination and its own fear of intersubjective recognition (Jaggar and Bordo, 1989; Keller, 1985). Motifs in popular culture—such as the repeated positioning in both plot and image of the male as dominant over the female—are interpreted by psychoanalytical theorists as a sign of a breakdown in the requisite tensions between a need for individuation and a need for recognition (J. Benjamin, 1985, 1988; Brennan, 1994; Chancer, 1992). When this breakdown reaches, in a culture or a personality, severe enough proportions, two pathologies result—the overindividuated dominator, who "recognizes" the other only through acts of control, and the underindividuated subordinate, who relinquishes independent action to find identity only as a mirror of the dominator (Zosky, 1999).

Psychoanalytical feminists, then, explain women's oppression in terms of men's deep emotional need to control women, a drive arising from ambivalence toward the women who reared them. Women either lack these neuroses or are subject to complementary neuroses, but in either case they are left psychically without an equivalent source of energy to resist domination. Clinical psychiatric evidence supports the thesis that these neuroses are widespread in Western societies. But these theories, in drawing a straight line from human emotions to female oppression, fail to explore the intermediate social arrangements that link emotion to oppression and fail to suggest possible lines of variation in emotions, social arrangements, or oppression. Several theorists have discussed the unacknowledged ethnic, class, and nationality assumptions in these theories, their generalization from white, upper-middle-class, North Atlantic family experience (Segura and Pierce, 1993; Spelman, 1988; Zhang, 1993). Moreover, psychoanalytic feminist theory suggests very few strategies for change, except perhaps that we restructure our child-rearing practices. These theories offer the roots of gender oppression, but they require a great deal more elaboration of both sociological factors and change strategies.

Radical Feminism 激进女性主义

Radical feminism is based on two emotionally charged central beliefs: (1) that women are of absolute positive value as women, a belief asserted against what they claim to be the universal devaluing of women, and (2) that women are everywhere oppressed—violently oppressed—by the system of patriarchy (Bunch, 1987; Chesler, 1994; Daly, 1993; C. A. Douglas, 1990; Dworkin, 1989; Echols, 1989; French, 1992; Frye, 1983; Jeffreys, 1991; MacKinnon, 1989, 1993; Rhodes, 2005; Rich, 1976, 1980, 1993; Richardson, 1996). With passion and militance similar to the "black power" cry of African American mobilization or the "witnessing" by Jewish survivors of the Holocaust, radical feminists elaborate a theory of social organization, gender oppression, and strategies for change.

Radical feminists see in every institution and in society's most basic stratificational arrangement—heterosexuality, class, caste, race, ethnicity, age, and gender—systems of domination and subordination, the most fundamental structure of which is the system of patriarchy. Not only is patriarchy historically the first structure of domination and submission, it continues as the most pervasive and enduring system of inequality, the basic societal model of domination (Lerner, 1986). Through participation in patriarchy, men learn how to hold other human beings in contempt, to see them as nonhuman, and to control them. Within patriarchy men see and women learn what subordination looks like. Patriarchy creates guilt and repression, sadism and masochism, manipulation and deception, all of which drive men and women to other forms of tyranny. Patriarchy, to radical feminists, is the least noticed and yet the most significant structure of social inequality.

Central to this analysis is the image of patriarchy as violence practiced by men and by male-dominated organizations against women. Violence may not always take the form of overt physical cruelty. It can be hidden in more complex practices of exploitation and control: in standards of fashion and beauty; in tyrannical ideals of motherhood, monogamy, chastity, and heterosexuality; in sexual harassment in the workplace; in the practices of gynecology, obstetrics, and psychotherapy; and in unpaid household drudgery and underpaid wage work (MacKinnon, 1979; Rich, 1976, 1980; L. M. Roth, 1999; B. W. Thompson, 1994; N. Wolf, 1991). Violence exists whenever one group controls in its own interests the life chances, environments, actions, and perceptions of another group, as men do to women.

But the theme of violence as overt physical cruelty lies at the heart of radical feminism's linking of patriarchy to violence: rape, sexual abuse, enforced prostitution, spouse abuse, incest, sexual molestation of children, hysterectomies and other excessive surgery, the sadism in pornography, the historic and cross-cultural practices of witch burning, the stoning to death of adulteresses, the persecution of lesbians, female infanticide, Chinese foot-binding, the abuse of widows, and the practice of clitorectomy (Barnett and LaViolette, 1993; Barry, 1979, 1993; Bart and Moran, 1993; Bergen, 1996; Buchwald, Fletcher, and Roth, 1993; Hammer, 2002; Kempadoo, 2001; Mardorossian, 2002; Martin, Vieratis, and Britto, 2005; M. Owen, 1996; Russell, 1998; Sanday, 1996; Scully, 1990; Stiglmayer, 1994).

Patriarchy exists as a near-universal social form because men can muster the most basic power resource, physical force, to establish control. Once patriarchy is in place, the other power resources—economic, ideological, legal, and emotional—also can be marshaled to sustain it. But physical violence always remains its base, and in both interpersonal and intergroup relations, that violence is used to protect patriarchy from women's individual and collective resistance (Caputi, 1989; Faludi, 1991; Riger and Krieglstein, 2000).

Men create and maintain patriarchy not only because they have the resources to do so but because they have real interests in making women serve as compliant tools. Women are a uniquely effective means of satisfying male sexual desire. Their bodies are essential to the production of children, who satisfy both practical and, as psychoanalysts have shown, neurotic needs for men. Women are a useful labor force. They can be ornamental signs of male status and power. As carefully controlled companions to both the child and the adult male, they are pleasant partners, sources of emotional support, and useful foils who reinforce the male's sense of central social significance. These useful functions mean that men everywhere seek to keep women compliant. But differing social circumstances give different rank orders to these functions and therefore lead to cross-cultural variations in the patterning of patriarchy.

How is patriarchy to be defeated? Radicals hold that this defeat must begin with a basic reworking of women's consciousness so that each woman recognizes her own value and strength; rejects patriarchal pressures to see herself as weak, dependent, and second-class; and works in unity with other women, regardless of differences among them, to establish a broad-based sisterhood of trust, support, appreciation, and mutual defense (Chasteen, 2001; McCaughey, 1997). With this sisterhood in place, two strategies suggest themselves: a critical confrontation with any facet of patriarchal domination whenever it is encountered and a degree of separatism as women withdraw into women-run businesses, households, communities, centers of artistic creativity, and lesbian love relationships. Lesbian feminism, as a major strand in radical feminism, is the practice and belief that "erotic and/or emotional commitment to women is part of resistance to patriarchal domination" (Phelan, 1994; Rudy, 2001; Taylor and Rupp, 1993).

A theoretical evaluation of radical feminism should note that it incorporates arguments made by both socialist and psychoanalytical feminists about the reasons for women's subordination and yet moves beyond those theories. Radical feminists, moreover, have done significant research to support their thesis that patriarchy ultimately rests on the practice of violence against women. They have a reasonable though perhaps incomplete program for change. They may, however, be faulted for their exclusive focus on patriarchy, a focus that simplifies the realities of social organization and social inequality.

Structural Oppression 结构压迫

Structural oppression theories, like gender oppression theories, recognize that oppression results from the fact that some groups of people derive direct benefits from controlling, using, and subjugating other groups of people. Structural oppression theorists analyze how interests in domination are enacted through social structure, here understood as those recurring and routinized large-scale arrangements of social relations that arise out of history, and are always arrangements of power. These theorists focus on the structures of patriarchy, capitalism, racism, and heterosexism, and they locate enactments of domination and experiences of oppression in the interplay of these structures, that is, in the way they mutually reinforce each other. Structural oppression theorists do not absolve or deny the agency of individual dominants, but they examine how that agency is the product of structural arrangements. In this section we look at two types of structural oppression theory: socialist feminism and intersectionality theory.

Socialist Feminism 社会主义女性主义

The theoretical project of socialist feminism develops around three goals: (1) to achieve a critique of the distinctive yet interrelated oppressions of patriarchy and capitalism from a standpoint in women's experience; (2) to develop explicit and adequate methods for social analysis out of an expanded understanding of historical materialism; and (3) to incorporate an understanding of the significance of ideas into a materialist analysis of the determination of human affairs. Socialist feminists have set themselves the formal project of achieving both a synthesis of and a theoretical step beyond other feminist theories, most specifically Marxian and radical feminist thought (Eisenstein, 1979; Fraser, 1989, 1997; Giminez, 2000, 2005; Hansen and Philipson, 1990; Hartsock, 1983; Hennessey and Ingraham, 1997; Jackson, 2001; MacKinnon, 1989; Dorothy Smith, 1979, 1987, 1990a, 1990b, 1999a, 1999b, 2000a, 2004a; Vogel, 1995).

Radical feminism, as discussed above, is a critique of patriarchy. Marxian feminism, described here, has traditionally brought together Marxian class analysis and feminist social protest. But this amalgam, portrayed as an uneasy marriage (Hartmann, 1981; Shelton and Agger, 1993)—often produced not an intensified theory of gender oppression but a more muted statement of gender inequality as women's concerns were grafted onto, rather than made equal partners in, the critique of class oppression. While pure Marxian feminism is a relatively dormant theory in contemporary American feminism, it remains important as an influence on socialist feminism. Its foundation was laid by Marx and Engels (see Chapter 1). Their major concern was social class oppression, but they occasionally turned their attention to gender oppression, most famously in *The Origins of the Family, Private Property, and the State* (written by Engels in 1884 from extensive notes made by Marx in the year immediately preceding his death in 1883). We briefly summarize this book because it gives a good introduction to the classic Marxian theory of gender oppression and to the method of historical materialism.

The major argument of *The Origins* is that woman's subordination results not from her biology, which is presumably immutable, but from social relations that have a clear and traceable history and that presumably can be changed. In the context of nineteenth-century thinking about gender, this was a radical, indeed, a feminist argument. The relational basis for women's subordination lies in the family, an institution aptly named from the Latin word for *servant,* because the family as it exists in complex societies is overwhelmingly a system in which men command women's services. Although the ideology of contemporary societies treats family as a fundamental and universal feature of social life, Engels and Marx use archaeological and anthropological evidence to show that in the chronology of humanity's existence, the family is a fairly recent relational invention, that for much of prehistory men and women lived in kin structures in which women enjoyed relative autonomy primarily because they had an independent economic base as gatherers, crafters, storers, and distributors of essential materials. The factor that destroyed this type of social system, producing what Engels calls "the world historic defeat of the female sex" (Engels, 1884/1970:87), was an economic one, specifically the replacement of hunting and gathering by herding and farming economies in which men's resources of strength, mobility, and a technology derived from their earlier hunting roles gave them a systematic advantage over women. This led to the invention of the concept of *property,* the idea and reality of a male class claiming as its own the communal resources for economic production. In these new economies, men as property owners needed both a compliant labor force—be it of slaves, captives, women-wives, or children—and heirs who would serve as a means of preserving and passing on property. Thus emerged the first *familia,* a master and his slave-servants, wife-servants, children-servants. Since then, the exploitation of labor has developed into increasingly complex structures of domination, most particularly class relations; the political order was created to safeguard these systems of domination; and the family itself has evolved along with the historical transformations of economic and property systems into an embedded and dependent institution, reflecting all the more massive injustices of the political economy and consistently enforcing the subordination of women. Engels and Marx conclude that only with the destruction of property rights through class revolution will women attain freedom of social, political, economic, and personal action.

Locating the origin of patriarchy in the emergence of property relations subsumes women's oppression under the general framework of Marxian class analysis. "Property"—understood not as personal possessions but as ownership of the resources necessary for social production (the means of production)—is the basis of class division because it creates a situation in which some groups are able to claim that they own the means of production while other groups work to do the producing. Marxian analysis focuses particularly on how this class division works out under capitalism, the economic system of modern societies. The distinctive feature of capitalism is that the class that owns the means of production—the capitalists—operates on a logic of continuous capital accumulation; *capital* is wealth (money and other assets), which can be used to generate the material infrastructure of economic production. Unlike other forms of economic organization in which people may seek to exchange either goods or money for more goods, capitalists seek to exchange goods in order to amass wealth, which in turn is invested in the material infrastructure of economic production to generate goods in order to generate more wealth. The mechanism by which capitalists turn goods into wealth is surplus value; surplus value is the difference between the compensation given to workers for their production and the value of the goods they produce; this surplus value (which we may understand as the difference between the cost of production and the price of the item—or profit) is appropriated by the capitalist who uses it to enhance his own lifestyle and power and, above all, to reinvest in the ongoing process of capital accumulation and expansion.

Socialist feminists accept the Marxian analysis of capitalism's class relations as an explication of one major structure of oppression. But they reject the Marxian analysts of patriarchy as a by-product of the same economic production. Instead they endorse the radical feminist argument that patriarchy, while interacting with economic conditions, is an independent structure of oppression.

Socialist feminism sets out to bring together these dual knowledges—knowledge of oppression under capitalism and of oppression under patriarchy—into a unified explanation of all forms of social oppression. One term used to try to unify these two oppressions is *capitalist patriarchy* (Eisenstein, 1979; Hartmann, 1979; A. Kuhn and Wolpe, 1978). But the term perhaps more widely used is *domination,* defined above (under "Gender Oppression") as a relationship in which one party, *the dominant,* succeeds in making the other party, *the subordinate,* an instrument of the dominant's will, refusing to recognize the subordinate's independent subjectivity. Socialist feminism's explanations of oppression present domination as a large-scale structural arrangement, a power relation between categories of social actors. This structure of domination both patterns and is reproduced by the willful and intentional actions of individual actors. Women are central to socialist feminism in two ways. First, as with all feminism, the oppression of women remains a primary topic for analysis. Second, women's location and experience of the world serve as the essential vantage point on domination in all its forms. Ultimately, though, these theorists are concerned with all experiences of oppression, both by women and by men. They also explore how some women, themselves oppressed, may yet actively participate in the oppression of other women, as, for example, privileged-class women in American society who oppress poor women. Indeed, one strategy of all socialist feminists is to confront the prejudices and oppressive practices *within* the community of women itself (Eisenstein, 1994; Lorde, 1984).

The focus on capitalist patriarchy is linked to historical materialism as an analytical strategy (Hennessey and Ingraham, 1997). *Historical materialism,* a basic principle in Marxian social theory, is the claim that the material conditions of human life, including the activities and relationships that produce those conditions, are the key factors that pattern human experience, personality, ideas, and social arrangements; that those conditions change over time because of dynamics immanent within them; and that history is a record of the changes in the material conditions of a group's life and of the correlative changes in experiences, personality, ideas, and social arrangements. Historical materialists hold that any effort at social analysis must trace in historically concrete detail the specifics of the group's material conditions and the links between those conditions and the experiences, personalities, events, ideas, and social arrangements characteristic of the group. In linking historical materialism to their focus on domination, socialist feminists attempt to realize their goal of a theory that probes the broadest of human social arrangements, domination, yet remains firmly committed to precise, historically concrete analyses of the material and social arrangements that frame particular situations of domination.

The historical materialism that is a hallmark of socialist feminism shows clearly the school's indebtedness to Marxian thought. But in their use of this method, socialist feminists move beyond the Marxians in three crucial ways: their redefinition of *material conditions,* their reevaluation of the significance of ideology, and their focus on domination. First, they broaden the meaning of the *material conditions* of human life. Marxians typically mean by this idea the economic dynamics of society, particularly the ways in which goods of a variety of types are created for and exchanged in the market. In these various exploitative arrangements, which make some wealthy and others poor, they locate the roots of class inequality and class conflict. Socialist feminist analysis includes economic dynamics but adds other conditions that create and sustain human life: sexuality, involvement in procreation, and child rearing; the unpaid, invisible round of domestic tasks; emotional care; and the production of knowledge. In *all* these life-sustaining activities, exploitative arrangements profit some and impoverish others. An analysis of the historical transformation of all production and exploitation is the essential foundation for a theory of domination.

The redefinition of the concept of material conditions transforms the Marxian assumption that human beings are producers of goods into a theme of human beings as creators and sustainers of all human life. This shift brings us to the second point of difference between Marxian historical materialism and the historical materialism, of socialist feminism, namely, the latter perspective's emphasis on what some Marxians might dismiss, as *mental or ideational phenomena:* consciousness, motivation, ideas, social definitions of the situation, knowledge, texts, ideology, the will to act in one's interests or acquiesce to the interests of others.[4] To socialist feminists all these factors deeply affect human personality, human action, and the structures of domination that are realized through that action. Moreover, these aspects of human subjectivity are produced by social structures that are inextricably intertwined with, and are as elaborate and powerful as, those that produce economic goods. Within all these structures, too, exploitative arrangements enrich and empower some while impoverishing and immobilizing others. Analysis of the processes that pattern human subjectivity is vital to a theory of domination, and that analysis too applies the principles of historical materialism.

---

[4] Admittedly some neo-Marxians, notably the critical theorists, have reevaluated the explanatory significance of ideology (see Chapter 4).

DOROTHY E. SMITH

A Biographical Sketch

Dorothy E. Smith explains that her sociological theory derives from her life experiences as a woman, particularly as a woman moving between two worlds—the male-dominated academic sphere and the female-centered life of the single parent. Remembering herself at Berkeley in the early 1960s studying for a doctorate in sociology while single-parenting, Smith reflects that her life seems to have been framed by what she sees as "not so much . . . a career as a series of contingencies, of accidents" (1979:151). This theme of contingency is one of many personal experiences that have led Smith to challenge sociological orthodoxy such as the image of the purposive actor engaged in linear pursuits of projects.

Whether they occurred by accident or design, the following events appear to the outsider as significant stages in Smith's development. She was born in 1926 in Great Britain; she earned her bachelor's degree in sociology from the University of London in 1955 and her Ph.D. in sociology from the University of California at Berkeley in 1963. During this period, she had "the experience of marriage, of immigration [to Canada] closely following marriage, of the arrival of children, of the departure of a husband rather early one morning, of the jobs that became available" (Smith, 1979:151). Of these events, Smith stresses, they "were moments in which I had in fact little choice and certainly little foreknowledge." The jobs that became available included research sociologist at Berkeley; lecturer in sociology at Berkeley; lecturer in sociology at the University of Essex, Colchester, England; associate professor and then professor in the department of sociology at the University of British Columbia; and professor of sociology in education at the Ontario Institute for Studies in Education, Toronto.

Smith has written on a wide variety of topics, all connected by a concern with "bifurcation," sometimes as a central theme and sometimes as a motif. Smith sees the experience of bifurcation manifesting itself in the separation between social-scientific description and people's lived experience, between

The third difference between socialist feminists and Marxians is that the object of analysis for socialist feminists is not primarily class inequality but the complex intertwining of a wide range of social inequalities. Socialist feminism develops a portrait of social organization in which the public structures of economy, polity, and ideology interact with the intimate, private processes of human reproduction, domesticity, sexuality, and subjectivity to sustain a multifaceted system of domination, the workings of which are discernible both as enduring and impersonal social patterns and in the more varied subtleties of interpersonal relationships. To analyze this system, socialist feminists shuttle between a mapping of large-scale systems of domination women's lived experience and the patriarchal ideal types they are given for describing that experience, between the micro-world and the macro-world structures that dictate micro experience, and, especially, between the micro world of the oppressed and the micro world of the dominants whose actions create the macro structures of oppression. The concretization of these themes can be seen in a selective review of the titles of some of Smith's works. In 1987 Smith produced her most extensive and integrated treatment of these themes in what has become a landmark in feminist sociology, *The Everyday World as Problematic* (1987). She followed this with *The Conceptual Practices of Power* (1990a), *Texts, Facts and Femininity* (1990b), *Writing the Social* (1999b), and *Institutional Ethnography: A Sociology for People* (2004c).

What Smith is producing for feminist sociologists, and indeed for all sociologists interested in the theoretical frontiers of the profession, is a sociology that integrates neo-Marxian concerns with the structures of domination and phenomenological insights into the variety of subjective and micro-interactional worlds. Smith sees these various everyday life-worlds as shaped by macro structures which are themselves shaped by the historical specifics of economic demand. What Smith wishes to avoid, in developing this line of reasoning, is a vision of the world in which the oppressors are consistently interpreted as individual actors making rational decisions on the basis of self-interest. Smith sees that self-interest itself is structurally situated, but she believes that these structures can become known only by beginning with the outcome at hand, that is, by exploring the everyday worlds of situated individuals. Smith is concerned that much social science serves to obfuscate rather than clarify the structures that produce these worlds because much social science begins with an assumption that the structures are already known and can be known separately from the everyday life-worlds. Her recent work extends her project of a sociology for women to a sociology for people which explores macro structures as organizers of everyday/everynight worlds. She is particularly interested in developing text-based organization and text-mediated social relations in people's everyday local practices (Smith, 2000b). Here her work offers a sociological alternative to feminist postmodernism. The implications of Smith's work for sociological theory form the basis for much of this chapter.

and a situationally specific, detailed exploration of the mundane daily experiences of oppressed people. Their strategy for change rests in this process of discovery, in which they attempt to involve the oppressed groups that they study and through which they hope that both individuals and groups, in large and small ways, will learn to act in pursuit of their collective emancipation.

Within this general theoretical framing, socialist feminist analyses may be divided into three distinct emphases. First, *materialist feminism* emphasizes and situates gender relations within the structure of the contemporary capitalist class system, particularly as that system is now operating globally. The interest of materialist feminists is in the implications of global capitalism for women's lives and in the ways in which women's labor contributes to the expanding wealth of capitalism. Within global capitalism, women as wage earners are more poorly paid than men because patriarchal ideology assigns them a lower social status. Because patriarchy assigns them the responsibility for the home, they are structurally more precariously positioned in wage-sector employment than men are and thus are more difficult to organize. These two factors make them an easy source of profit for the capitalist class. Further, capitalism depends on the unpaid production of women whose work as housewives, wives, and mothers subsidizes and disguises the real costs of reproducing and maintaining the work force. And women's work as consumers of goods and services for the household becomes a major source of capitalist profit making (J. L. Collins, 2002; Hennessey and Ingraham, 1997; N. E. Rose, 1995; Vogel, 1995).

A second emphasis in contemporary socialist feminism, given most form by Dorothy Smith and her students, is on the *relations of ruling,* the processes by which capitalist patriarchal domination is enacted through an interdependent system of control which includes not only the economy but the state and the privileged professions (including social science). The dynamics of this arrangement of control are explored through a focus on women's daily activities and experiences in the routine maintenance of material life. The relations of ruling are revealed as pervading and controlling women's daily production via "texts," extralocal, generalized requirements that seek to pattern and appropriate their labor—texts like health insurance forms, the school calendar, advertisements about the ideal home and the ideal female body (M. Campbell and Manicom, 1995; Currie, 1997, 1999).

A third emphasis in socialist feminist discourse is represented by what materialist feminists, at least, describe as *cultural materialism.* Cultural materialists explore the many ways state policies, social ideologies, and mass media messages interact with human subjectivity, both patterning and controlling thought and being repatterned by it. While cultural materialists explore the processes producing these messages, they do not necessarily locate the processes in a model of global capitalism and large-scale social class arrangements. Instead, cultural materialists study depictions of and meanings assigned to the body, and politics as a struggle over how social groups and categories are represented (Clough, 1994; L. R. Davis, 1997; Walkerdine, 1997). "Cultural materialism rejects a systemic anticapitalist analysis linking the history of culture and meaning-making to capital's class system. . . . Instead, they focus almost exclusively on ideological, state, or cultural practices, anchor meaning in the body and its pleasures, or understand social change primarily in terms of the struggle over representation" (Hennessey and Ingraham, 1997:5).[5]

Socialist feminists' program for change calls for a global solidarity among women to combat the abuses capitalism works in their lives, in the lives of their communities, and in the environment. Indeed, the turn to eco-feminism is a major current trend in socialist feminism (Dordoy and Mellor, 2000; Goldman and Schurman, 2000;

---

[5] There is disagreement among theorists as to the usage of these terms, especially *materialist feminism.* A good history of this controversy is Hennessey and Ingraham (1997).

Kirk, 1997). They call on the feminist community to be ever vigilant about the dangers of their own co-optation into a privileged intelligentsia that serves capitalist interests. Their project is to mobilize people to use the state as a means for the effective redistribution of societal resources through the provision of an extensive safety net of public services such as publicly supported education, health care, transportation, child care, and housing; a progressive tax structure that reduces the wide disparities of income between rich and poor; and the guarantee of a living wage to all members of the community. They believe that this mobilization will be effective only if people become aware of and caring about the life conditions of others as well as their own. The feminist social scientist's duty is to make visible the material inequalities that shape people's lives.

Intersectionality Theory 多重交织性理论

The central issue for intersectionality theory is the understanding that women experience oppression in varying configurations and in varying degrees of intensity (Aptheker, 1989; Anzaldúa, 1990; Anzaldúa and Keating, 2002; Caldwell, 1991; P. H. Collins, 1990, 1998, 1999, 2000, 2001, 2004; Crenshawe, 1991, 1997; E. Glenn, 1999; Lorde, 1984; P. Williams, 1991, 1995). The explanation for that variation is that while all women potentially experience oppression on the basis of gender, women are, nevertheless, differentially oppressed by the varied intersections of other arrangements of social inequality. These *vectors of oppression and privilege* (or in Patricia Hill Collins's phrase, "the matrix of domination" [1990]), include not only gender but also class, race, global location, sexual preference, and age. The variation of these intersections qualitatively alters the experience of being a woman—and this alteration, this diversity, must be taken into account in theorizing the experiences of "women." The argument in intersectionality theory is that it is intersection itself that produces a particular experience of oppression, and one cannot arrive at an adequate explanation by using an additive strategy of gender, plus race, plus class, plus sexuality (Andersen, 2005). Crenshawe (1989), for example, shows that black women frequently experience discrimination in employment because they are *black women,* but courts routinely refuse to recognize this discrimination—unless it can be shown to be a case of what is considered general discrimination, "sex discrimination" (read "white women"), or "race discrimination" (read "black men"). In characterizing these as vectors of oppression *and* privilege, we wish to suggest a fundamental insight of intersectionality theories—that the privilege exercised by some women and men turns on the oppression of other women and men. Theories of intersectionality at their core understand these arrangements of inequality as hierarchical structures based in unjust power relations. The theme of injustice signals the consistent critical focus of this analysis.

Intersectionality theory recognizes the fundamental link between ideology and power that allows dominants to control subordinates by creating a politics in which difference becomes a conceptual tool for justifying arrangements of oppression. In social practice, dominants use differences among people to justify oppressive practices by translating difference into models of inferiority/superiority; people are socialized to relate to difference not as a source of diversity, interest, and cultural wealth but evaluatively in terms of "better" or "worse." As Lorde (1984:115) argues, this "institutional rejection of difference is an absolute necessity in a profit economy which needs outsiders as surplus people." These ideologies operate in part by creating *"a mythical norm"* against which people evaluate others and themselves; in United States society this norm is "white, thin, male, young, heterosexual, Christian, and financially secure" (Lorde, 1984:116). This norm not only allows dominants to control social production (both paid and unpaid), but also becomes part of individual subjectivity—an internalized rejection of difference that can operate to make people devalue themselves, reject people from different groups, and create criteria within their own group for excluding, punishing, or marginalizing group members. Anzaldúa describes this last practice as "Othering," an act of definition done within a subordinated group to establish that a group member is unacceptable, an "other," by some criterion; this definitional activity, she points out, erodes the potential for coalition and resistance.

The intersection of vectors of oppression and privilege creates variations in both the forms and the intensity of people's experience of oppression—"not all suffering is equal, there is a calculus of pain" (Arguelles, 1993). Much of the writing and research done out of an intersectionality perspective presents the concrete reality of people's lives as those lives are shaped by the intersections of these vectors. The most-studied intersections by feminists are of gender and race (Clark-Lewis, 1994; Dill, 1994; S. Hill and Sprague, 1999); gender and class (P. N. Cohen, 1998; Foner, 1994; Gregson and Lowe, 1994; Wrigley, 1995), and race, gender, and class (Andersen and Collins, 1992; Edin and Lein, 1997; Edin and Kefalas, 2005). Other analyses include gender and age (D. Gibson, 1996; Lopata, 1996), gender and global location (Goodwin, 1994; Mullins, 2005; Oberhauser and Pratt, 2004; Reddock, 2000; Scheper-Hughes, 1992), and gender and sexual preference (Dunne, 1997; Nagel, 2003). In the most recent writings out of this perspective, intersectionality theory has also been applied to the circumstances of subordinate men (P. Collins, 2004; Edin and Kefalas, 2005).

In response to their material circumstances, people create interpretations and strategies for surviving and resisting the persistent exercise of unjust power. One part of the project of intersectionality theory is to give voice to the group knowledges worked out in specific life experiences created by historic intersections of inequality and to develop various feminist expressions of these knowledges—for example, black feminist thought or chicana feminism (P. H. Collins, 1990; Cordova et al., 1990; A. M. Garcia, 1989; James and Busia, 1993).

Intersectionality theory develops a critique of work done in Second Wave (and First Wave) feminism where it sees that work reflecting the experience and concerns of white privileged-class feminists in North Atlantic societies. Some of this work of critique is paralleled by work done in postmodernism—but this parallelism should not be overstated. Intersectionality theory is one of the oldest traditions in feminism, at least in the United States, going back, for example, to Sojourner Truth's "Aint I a Woman" speech at the Akron Women's Rights Convention of 1852 (Zerai, 2000). This critique has produced questions about what we mean by categories such as "woman," "gender," "race," and "sisterhood" (Chopra, 2004; hooks, 1984; Kaminsky, 1994; Mohanty, 1991). It has focused on the diversity of experience in such seeming universals as "mothering" and "family" and has reinterpreted theoretical works like the sociological-psychoanalytic studies of Chodorow and Benjamin (Dickerson, 1995; E. N. Glenn, Chang and Forcey, 1993; Mahoney and Yngvesson, 1992; Segura and Pierce, 1993; Zhang, 1993). This critique has prompted a repositioning of the understandings of "whiteness" by white feminists who seek to understand whiteness as a construction, the ways that whiteness results in privilege, what they can actively do to reduce racism, and how they can contribute to producing a more inclusive feminist analysis (Alcoff, 1998; Chodorow, 1994; Frankenberg, 1993; Rowe, 2000; Ward, 1994; Yancy, 2000).

This process of theory building research, and critique has brought intersectionality theory to one of its central themes and one of the central issues confronting feminism today: how to allow for the analytic principle and empirical fact of diversity among women while at the same time holding to the valuational and political position that specific groups of women share a distinctive standpoint. Explaining *standpoint,* Patricia Hill Collins (1998:224–225) proposes that it is the view of the world shared by a group characterized by a "heterogeneous commonality"; "shared," Collins argues, refers, as Marx suggests, to " 'circumstances directly encountered, given, and transmitted from the past.' " Thus, Collins concludes that a group's standpoint is constituted not out of some essentialism but out of a recognition that, as black activist Fannie Lou Hamer says, " 'we're in this bag together.' " While vectors of oppression and privilege—race, class, gender, age, global location, sexual preference—intersect in all people's lives, these theorists argue that the way they intersect markedly affects the degree to which a common standpoint is affirmed. Currently, as feminist intersectionality theoriests extend their lens to the situation of subordinated men, they have to weigh whether and when in the strategy of standpoint analysis, the standpoint of *women* is more significant that the standpoint of the subordinated *group* of both women and men. Among factors affecting the issue are the group's existence over time, its sense of its own history as a group, its location in relatively segregated identifiable spaces, and its development of an intragroup system of social organizations and knowledges for coping with oppression. But a group standpoint is never monolithic or impermeable; the very fact that the group is constituted out of intersections of vectors means that group members can pivot between varying senses of self; group members frequently move from the home group into the larger society where their experience is that of "the outsider within" (P. H. Collins, 1990, 1998); moreover, the home group is subject to the permeation of outside ideas and is not undifferentiated—it has its own internal dynamics of difference and may even be constituted by its existence at a cultural "borderland" (Anzaldúa, 1990). Intersectionality theorists warn that while it is easy to locate the experience of intersection and of standpoint in individuals, this reductionism is theoretically and politically dangerous, erasing the historic structures of unequal power that have produced the individual experience and obscuring the need for political change.

In developing an agenda for change, intersectionality theory turns to the knowledge of oppressed people and their long-held evaluative principles of faith

PATRICIA HILL COLLINS

A Biographical Sketch

Patricia Hill Collins was born in 1948. By her own report, she grew up in a supportive and extended black working-class family located in a black community in Philadelphia; she moved from this secure base daily to attend an academically demanding public high school for girls, and then, more permanently, to earn her bachelor's degree at Brandeis University in 1969 and her M.A.T. at Harvard in 1970. During the 1970s she worked as a curriculum specialist in schools in Boston, Pittsburgh, Hartford, New York, and Washington, D.C. She returned to Brandeis to earn her Ph.D. in sociology in 1984. She spent much of her career in higher education at the University of Cincinnati, where she held a dual appointment as Charles Phelps Taft Professor of Sociology and as Professor of African-American Studies. Currently, she is Distinguished University Professor at the University of Maryland.

Collins writes that her experiences of educational success were permeated by the counterexperience of being "the 'first,' or 'one of the few,' or the 'only' African-American and/or woman and/or working-class person in my schools, communities, and work settings" (1990:xi). In these situations, she found herself judged as being less than others who came from different backgrounds, and she learned that educational success seemed to demand that she distance herself from her black working-class background. This created in her a tension that produced "a loss of voice."

and justice (P. H. Collins, 1990, 1998; hooks, 1990; Reagon, 1982/1995; Lorde, 1984). The theory argues for the need to bear witness, to protest, and to organize for change within the context of the oppressed community, for only within community can one keep faith in the eventual triumph of justice—a justice understood not in the narrow framing of legal rationality but as the working-out within social institutions and social relations of the principles of fairness to and concern for others and oneself.

Feminism and Postmodernism 女性主义与后现代主义

Like feminist theory, postmodernism is the product of an interdisciplinary and international community. Feminism's community, however, grows out of social activism; the postmodernist community had its origins in and remains based in the academy. Important for out purposes here is the fact that postmodernism has had, for reasons that will become clear, less impact on feminist sociological theory than on feminist theory in disciplines such as philosophy and literature.

Her response to these tensions has been to formulate an alternative understanding of social theory and an alternative way of doing theory. This project led her to discover the theoretical voice of her community and to reclaim her own voice by situating it in that community. It culminated in *Black Feminist Thought* (1990) a landmark text in feminist and social theory which received both the Jessie Bernard Award and the C. Wright Mills Award. *Black Feminist Thought* presents social theory as the understandings of a specific group, black women; to this end, Collins draws on a wide range of voices, some famous, others obscure. What she presents is a community-based social theory that articulates that group's understanding of its oppression by intersections of race, gender, and class—and its historic struggle against that oppression. In this work, Collins uncovers the distinctive epistemology by which black women assess truth and validity; she also argues convincingly for a feminist standpoint epistemology. In both practice and theory she has pursued her theory of intersectionality, helping to organize the ASA section Race, Gender, Class; editing, with Margaret Andersen, the essay collection *Race, Class and Gender* (1992); and authoring a multiplicity of articles in a wide range of journals.

In *Fighting Words: Black Women and the Search for Justice* (1998) Collins continued her project of redefining social theory not as the province and practice of an elite intellectual group but as the understandings variously situated groups have achieved about the social world. In *Black Sexual Politics: African Americans, Gender and the New Racism* (2004), Collins expands the reach of her intersectionality theory to the analysis of the varied experiences of oppression of black women *and* black men, tracing the consequences of these experiences for the relation between black women and men.

Postmodernist theory has affected feminist theory in general in two important ways. First, it has radically challenged the central question of all feminist theory, *"And what about the women?"* by developing a philosophic argument about what the category "women" really means. Second, postmodernism has provided feminist theory with "an oppositional epistemology," a strategy for questioning the claims to truth advanced by any given theory. It has done the latter most effectively through its creation of a rich and provocative language to be used in the challenging of the taken-for-granted assumptions that it argues were constituted by modernity. In this section, we first explain the origins of the idea of postmodernism in a rejection of the modern; we next look at postmodernism's conceptualization of ways of challenging taken-or-granted ideas of modernity; we then look at the major postmodernist challenge to feminism—its questioning of the category "women"; and we discuss feminist reservations about postmodernism.

Postmodernist theory begins with the observation that we (that is, those of us living in the twenty-first century) no longer live under conditions of modernity but of "postmodernity." This postmodern world is produced by the interplay of four major changes: (1) an aggressively expansive stage in global capitalism; (2) the weakening of centralized state power (with the collapse of the old imperial systems, the fragmentation of the communist bloc, and the rise of ethnic politics within nation-states); (3) the patterning of life by an increasingly powerful and penetrative technology that controls production and promotes consumerism; and (4) the development of liberationist social movements based not in class but in other forms of identity—nationalism (the revolutions of formerly colonial states), race (the African American civil rights movement), gender (feminism as a global movement), sexual orientation (gay rights), and environmentalism. Liberationist movements may have been the most important of these developments producing the postmodern challenge to modernist epistemology and theory, as feminist philosopher Susan Bordo explains:

> [I]t was not . . . *any* professional intellectual voice who was ultimately responsible for uncovering the pretensions and illusions of the ideals of epistemological objectivity, foundations, and neutral judgment. That uncovering occurred first . . . in political practice. Its agents were the liberation movements of the sixties and seventies, emerging not only to make a claim to the legitimacy of marginalized cultures, unheard voices, suppressed narratives, but also to expose the perspectivity and partiality of the official accounts. . . . [The key questions now became] the historical, social questions: *Whose* truth? *Whose* nature? *Whose* version of reason? *Whose* history? *Whose* tradition?
>
> (Bordo, 1990:136–137)

The question "Whose knowledge?" has proved to be radically transformative, opening debates not only about the relation of power to knowledge but also about the basis of human claims to know. Postmodernists reject the basic principle of modernist epistemology—that humans can, by the exercise of pure reason, arrive at a complete and objective knowledge of the world, a knowledge which is a representation of reality, "a mirror of nature." They argue that this modernist principle gives rise to a number of epistemological errors—the *god-eye* view that locates the observer outside the world being observed; the *grand narrative* that holistically explains that world; *foundationalism* that identifies certain rules of analysis as always appropriate; *universalism* that asserts that there are discoverable principles that everywhere govern the world; *essentialism* that claims that people are constituted by core and unchanging qualities; *representation* that presumes that one's statement about the world can accurately reflect the world. Postmodernism questions the existence both of "reason" as a universal, essential quality of the human mind and of the "reasoning subject" as a consistent, unified configuration of consciousness. Postmodernists portray the knowledge-making process as one of multiple representations of experience created by differently located discourse groups in which the establishment of any hegemonic knowledge-claim results from an effective exercise of power. They suggest alternative epistemological practices like *decentering,* which moves the understandings of nonprivileged groups to the center of discourse and knowledge; *deconstruction,* which shows how concepts, posed as accurate representations of the world, are historically constructed and contain contradictions; a focus on *difference,* which explores any knowledge construct not only for what it says but also for what it erases or marginalizes, particularly through the application of modernist *binary logic* of "either/or."

Feminism and postmodernism both raise the question of *whose* knowledge or definitions are to count, and, to some degree, both engage in practices of decentering and deconstruction. If we look at popular slogans in feminist activism in the sixties and seventies, we see a dissolution of binary opposites—"The personal is political"; a challenging of traditional categories—"A woman without a man is like a fish without a bicycle"; an emphasis on decentering—"God is coming and, boy, is SHE pissed"; an understanding of language as contextual and relational—"If she says 'No,' it's rape"; and a sense of the world, no matter how material, as constructed out of power relations—"If men could menstruate, abortion would be a sacrament." Contemporary feminist theorists find in postmodernism a reinforcement and legitimation for their own insistence on the epistemological and political necessity for decentering and deconstruction. They have enriched their analyses by drawing on postmodernism's vocabulary: *discursive practices, discourse analysis, genealogy, code, intertextuality, representation, text, the Imaginary, difference, hyperreality, alterity.* Postmodernist epistemology, thus, provides some feminist scholars with an expanded possibility for naming their work and has become part of such accepted practices as the liberal feminist project of "deconstructing gender." (Clough, 1994; P. H. Collins, 1998; Hennessey and Ingraham, 1997; Mann and Kelley, 1997; Stacey and Thorne, 1996). This adoption of vocabulary is in the tradition of the achievement of Second Wave feminism, which developed a vocabulary to name women's oppression and empowerment. It has not involved an unthinking takeover but a sophisticated incorporation, sometimes keeping, sometimes blending, sometimes changing the original meanings. Many feminists—especially those working in text-based fields such as literature—also find the postmodernist understanding of the world as "representation," "text," and "discourse" useful for conceptualizing social life. Feminists in the social sciences sometimes adopt the image of social life as discourse and representation or use the direction it suggests to analyze what is present and what is obscured in the cultural and political representations affecting women's lives.

A major substantive contribution of postmodernist theory to general feminist theory has been its questioning of the primary category of feminist theory: woman (or women). The classic statement of this questioning has been Judith Butler's 1990 *Gender Trouble* (see above, "Gender Difference"). Butler problematizes the category "woman," especially as a category of political identity, by deconstructing the idea that gender is a social construction separate from biological sexual attributes. If gender is understood as a social construction that the biologically sexed person is expected to assume, then there is a split between gender and sex; and if there is such a split, then there is no logical reason for gender to always adhere to the sexed body in a particular way. That is, there is no logical connection between male sex and masculine gender and between female sex and feminine gender; nor, even if it is allowed that there are two biological sexes—a point questioned by postmodernists and by many feminists and biologists—is there any reason for there to be only two genders. If gender, then, is not associated with sex in any logical or "natural" way, to what does the category "woman" refer? Is it not possible for anyone to be a woman? If the only unity of the category "woman" is biological function, then the category can hardly serve as the basis for a claim to political identity. But if sex determines gender, then gender is not a social construction but an essence and beyond political action to change. Butler proceeds to develop her performativity theory of gender, which leads to two conclusions: one, that if gender is the result of an ongoing series of sociocultural imitative practices, then anyone who engages in those imitations in the way received as woman is potentially a woman; two, that there is no evidence of a core gender identity that would exist independent of these ongoing performative acts—in other words, there is not primary "man" or "woman" self that manipulates action to present a gendered identity compatible with his core. These questions have raised important issues for feminism and have not been incompatible with questions raised in intersectionality theory about who exactly constitutes "women."

Above all, the postmodernist "turn" pushes feminism to make reflexivity a permanent feature of theory building, a way of ensuring that it will not become what it has set out to oppose—a hegemonic discourse that oppresses people through essentialist and universalist categories (Haraway, 1990; King, 1994; Nicholson, 1994; Sawicki, 1991). This directive has been particularly meaningful because it coincides with the questions raised by women of color, women from societies outside the North Atlantic, lesbians, and working-class women about Second Wave feminism's essentialist claims regarding "sisterhood," "woman," "Third World women," "sexuality," "family," "mothering," and "work." Jana Sawicki argues that feminists "have good reason to appeal to Foucault's negative freedom, that is, the freedom to disengage from our political identities, our presumptions about gender differences, and the categories and practices that define feminism. . . . Women are produced by patriarchal power at the same time they resist it. There are good reasons to be ambivalent about the liberatory possibilities of appealing to 'reason,' 'motherhood,' or the 'feminine' when they have also been the source of our oppression" (1991:102).

But the feminist relation to postmodernism is also marked by unease. Many feminists see postmodernism as exclusive in aspiration and therefore antithetical to the feminist project of inclusion (Benhabib, 1998). Evidence for this unease includes postmodernism's arcane vocabulary, its location in the academy rather than in political struggle, and its nonreflexive grasp for hegemonic status in that academic discourse. Many feminists also question the "innocence" of the postmodernist challenge, wondering whether it is truly liberationist or is part of a politics of knowledge in which a privileged academic class responds to the challenges of marginalized persons with a technically complex argument to the effect that no location for speech can claim authority. Hartsock (1990:169) has made the classic statement of this concern: "Somehow it seems highly suspicious that it is at the precise moment when so many groups have been engaged in . . . redefinitions of the marginalized Others that suspicions emerge about the nature of the 'subject,' about the possibilities for a general theory which can describe the world, about historical 'progress.'" Another source of unease is that the postmodernist emphasis on an infinite regress of deconstruction and difference leads people away from collective, liberationist politics and toward a radical individualism that may conclude that "'because every . . . one of us is different and special, it follows that every problem or crisis is exclusively our own, or, conversely, your problem—not mine'" (Jordan, 1992, in P. H. Collins, 1998:150). Above all, the postmodernist turn takes feminist scholars away from the materiality of inequality, injustice, and oppression and toward a neo-idealist posture that sees the world as "discourse," "representation," and "text." In severing the link to material inequality, postmodernism moves feminism away from its commitment to progressive change—the foundational project of any critical social theory.

A Feminist Sociological Theory 女性主义社会学理论

This section presents a synthesis of ideas implicit or explicit in the varieties of feminist theory described above in order to develop a statement of some fundamental principles for a feminist *sociological* theory. We identify four distinctive features of a feminist sociological theory: its sociology of knowledge, its model of society, its patterning of social interaction, and its focus on a subjective level of social experience. Our synthesis draws on classic statements by theorists writing out of a variety of disciplines, including sociology. The major influences are Andersen, 2005; J. Benjamin, 1988; Bordo, 1993; Butler, 1990, 1993; Chodorow, 1978; P. H. Collins, 1990, 1998, 2004; Fenstermaker and West, 2002; Gilligan, 1982; Heilbrun, 1988; Hennessey and Ingraham, 1997; Ingraham, 1999; Lorde, 1984; MacKinnon, 1989; Rich, 1976, 1980; Dorothy Smith, 1989, 1990a, 1990b, 1999a, 1999b, 2004a; West and Fenstermaker, 1993 and P. Williams, 1991 and 1995.

A Feminist Sociology of Knowledge 女性主义知识社会学

A feminist sociology of knowledge sees everything that people label "knowledge of the world" as having four characteristics: (1) it is always created from the standpoint of embodied actors situated in groups that are differentially located in social structure; (2) it is, thus, always partial and interested, never total and objective; (3) it is produced in and varies among groups and, to some degree, among actors within groups; and (4) it is always affected by power relations—whether formulated from the standpoint of dominant or subordinate groups. This understanding of knowledge has been named "feminist standpoint epistemology" (Harding, 1986). A feminist sociological theory begins with a sociology of knowledge because feminists attempt to describe, analyze, and change the world from the standpoint of women and because, working from women's subordinated position in social relations, feminist sociological theorists see that knowledge production is part of the system of power governing all production in society. Feminist sociological theory attempts to alter the balance of power within sociological discourse—and within social theory—by establishing the standpoint of women in particular, and of oppressed people more broadly, as standpoints from which social knowledge is constructed.

In attempting to do sociology from the standpoint of women, feminist sociological theorists have to consider what constitutes a standpoint of women. A standpoint is the product of a social collectivity with a sufficient history and commonality of circumstance to develop a shared knowledge of social relations. Feminists, starting where Marx left off, have identified three crucial collectivities—owners, workers, *and women*—whose distinctive relationships to the processes of social production and reproduction constitute them as standpoint groups. Historically women under patriarchy, whatever their class and race, have been assigned to the tasks of social reproduction (childbearing, child rearing, housekeeping, food preparation, care of the ill and dependent, emotional and sexual service). Yet any solidarity of women as a "class" in patriarchal production is fractured by other class configurations, including economic class and race class. While women's shared and historic relation to social reproduction in circumstances of subordination is the basis for the feminist claim of "the standpoint of women," in the daily workings of social power the intersection of gender inequality with race inequality, class inequality, geosocial inequality, and inequalities based on sexuality and age produces a complex system of unequally empowered standpoint groups relating through shifting arrangements of coalition and opposition. These intersectionalities are now an integral part of the feminist description and analysis of women's standpoint.

This understanding of knowledge as the product of different standpoint groups presents feminist sociological theory with the problem of how to produce a feminist sociological account that is both acceptable to sociologists and useful to feminism's emancipatory project. At least four strategies are used. One is asserting the validity of "webbed accounts," that is, of accounts woven together by reporting all the various actors' or standpoint groups' knowledges of an experience and describing the situations, including the dynamics of power, out of which the actors or groups came to create these versions (Haraway, 1988). A second strategy is that of privileging the accounts or standpoints of the less empowered actors or groups because a major factor in unequal power relations is that dominants' views are given both more credence and more circulation. The privileging of the standpoints of the disempowered is a part of the feminist emancipatory project, but it also produces an important corrective to mainstream sociological theories by changing the angle of vision from which social processes are understood (P. H. Collins, 2004; Edin and Kefalas, 2005; Lorde, 1984). A third strategy is that the feminist theorist must be reflexive about and able to give an account of the stages through which she or he moves from knowledge of an individual's or group's standpoint to the generalizations of a sociological account, for that translation is an act of power (P. H. Collins, 1990, 1998; Dorothy Smith, 1990a). A fourth strategy is for the social theorist to identify the particular location from which she or he speaks and thus to identify her or his partiality (in all meanings of that word) and its effect on the theory constructed.

In keeping with the fourth strategy, we should declare the standpoint from which we create the theoretical synthesis presented here. We write from the relatively privileged class position of academic social scientists living in the contemporary United States, but also as women located within a particular intersection of vectors of oppression and privilege that makes us subject to experiences of racism, ageism, and heterosexism. We also write out of family heritages of membership in historically constituted standpoint groups shaped by poverty and by colonial status. This intermingling of current status and family history shapes both our interests and our values. The synthesis we present here reflects oppression theories' concept of a just society as one that empowers all people to claim as a fundamental right (not a begrudged concession to need or a reward to the "deserving") a fair share of social goods—from the material essentials of food, clothing, shelter, health care, and education, to an absence of fear of violence, to a positive valuation of self in the particularities of one's group and individual identity.

The Macro-Social Order 宏观—社会秩序

In this and the next two sections we operate within the established sociological conventions of vocabulary and conceptualization by organizing our presentation around the categories of *macro-social, micro-social,* and *subjectivity*—although much of feminist sociological theory poses a fundamental critique of those categories.

Feminist sociology's view of the macro-social order begins by expanding the Marxian concept of economic production into a much more general concept of social production, that is, the production of all human social life. Along with the production of commodities for the market, social production for feminists also includes arrangements, such as the organization of housework, which produce the essential commodities and services of the household; of sexuality, which pattern and satisfy human desire; of intimacy, which pattern and satisfy human emotional needs for acceptance, approval, love, and self-esteem; of state and religion, which create the rules and laws of a community; and of politics, mass media, and academic discourse, which establish institutionalized, public definitions of the situation.

Thus framed and expanded, the Marxian model of intergroup relations remains visible in feminist theory's model of social organization. Each of these various types of social production is based on an arrangement by which some actors, controlling the resources crucial to that activity, act as dominants, or "masters," who dictate and profit from the circumstances of production. Within each productive sector, production rests on the work of subordinates, or "servants," whose energies create the world ordered into being by their masters and whose exploitation denies them the rewards and satisfactions produced by their work. Through feminist theory, we see, more vividly than through Marxian theory, the intimate association between masters and servants that may lie at the heart of production and the indispensability of the servant's work in creating and sustaining everything necessary to human social life. In intimate relations of exploitation, domination may be expressed not as coercion but as paternalism, "the combination of positive feelings toward the group with discriminatory intentions toward the group." Paternalism masks for both parties but does not transform a relationship of domination and subordination (Jackman, 1994:11). Social production occurs through a multidimensional structure of domination and exploitation that organizes class, gender, race, sex, power, and knowledge into overlapping hierarchies of intimately associated masters and workers.

The feminist model of stratification in social production offers a direct critique of the structural-functionalist vision of a society composed of a system of separate institutions and distinct, though interrelated, roles. Feminist theory claims that this image is not generalizable but that it depicts the experiences and vantage points of society's dominants—white, male, upper-class, and adult. Feminist research shows that women and other nondominants do not experience social life as a movement among compartmentalized roles. Instead, they are involved in a balancing of roles, a merging of role-associated interests and orientations, and, through this merging, in a weaving together of social institutions. Indeed, one indicator of the dominant group's control over the situations of production may be that its members can achieve purposive role compartmentalization. But feminist sociology stresses that this condition depends on the subordinate services of actors who cannot compartmentalize their lives and actions. Indeed, were these subordinate actors to compartmentalize similarly, the whole system of production in complex industrialized societies would collapse. In contrast to the structural-functional model, the feminist model emphasizes that the role-merging experience of women may be generalizable to the experience of many other subordinate "servant" groups whose work produces the fine-grained texture of daily life. The understandings that such subordinated groups have of the organization of social life may be very different from the understanding depicted in structural-functionalist theory; even their identification of key institutional spheres may differ. Yet their vantage point springs from situations necessary to society as it is currently organized and from work that makes possible the masters' secure sense of an institutionally compartmentalized world.

Further, feminism emphasizes the centrality of ideological domination to the structure of social domination. Ideology is an intricate web of beliefs about reality and social life that is institutionalized as public knowledge and disseminated throughout society so effectively that it becomes taken-for-granted knowledge for all social groups. Thus, what feminists see as "public knowledge of social reality" is not an overarching culture, a consensually created social product, but a reflection of the interests and experiences of society's dominants and one crucial index of their power in society. What distinguishes this view from traditional Marxian analysis is that for feminists ideological control is a basic process in domination, and the hierarchical control of discourse and knowledge is a key element in societal domination.

Central to feminist concerns about the macro-social order is the macro-structural patterning of gender as a structure. It is on this structure that oppression is founded. Feminist theorists argue that women's bodies constitute an essential resource in social production and reproduction and therefore become a site of exploitation and control. Gender oppression is reproduced by an ideological system of institutionalized knowledge that reflects the interests and experiences of men. Among other things, this gender ideology identifies men as the bearers of sociocultural authority and allocates to the male role the right to dominate and to the female role the obligation to serve in all dimensions of social production. Gender ideology constructs women as objects of male desire whose social value is determined by their fabrication of an appropriately molded body. Gender ideology also systematically flattens and distorts women's productive activities by (1) trivializing some of them, for example, housework; (2) idealizing to the point of unrecognizability other activities, for example, mothering; and (3) making invisible yet other crucial work, for example, women's multiple and vital contributions to the production of marketplace commodities. These ideological processes may be generalizable to the macro-structural production of all social subordination.

Capitalism and patriarchy, although analytically separate forms of domination, reinforce each other in numerous ways. For example, the organization of production into public and private spheres and the gendering of those spheres benefits both systems of domination. Capitalism benefits in that women's labor in the private sphere reproduces the worker at no cost to capital; further their responsibility for the private sphere makes women a marginal but always co-optable source of cheap labor, driving wages down generally. At the same time patriarchy benefits from this exploitation of the woman worker because it sustains her dependence on men. Women's difficult entry into the public sphere ensures that what "good" employment may be available there will go first to men. Women's experiences of sexual harassment on the job and of being hassled in public places are not incidental and insignificant micro events but examples of a power relation in which patriarchy helps police the borders for capital. This division is further complicated by the "race-ing" and "age-ing" as well as the gendering of public and private.

The Micro-Social Order 微观—社会秩序

At the micro-interactional level, feminist sociology (like some microsociological perspectives) focuses on how individuals take account of each other as they pursue objective projects or intersubjective meanings. Feminist sociological theory argues that the conventional models of interaction (social behaviorist and social definitionist—see the Appendix) may depict how equals in macro-structural, power-conferring categories create meanings and negotiate relationships in the pursuit of joint projects or how structural dominants experience interaction with both equals and subordinates. But feminist theory suggests that when structural unequals interact there are many other qualities to their association than those suggested by the conventional models: that action is responsive rather than purposive, that there is a continuous enactment of power differentials, that the meaning of many activities is obscured or invisible, that access is not always open to those settings in which shared meanings are most likely to be created. This analysis offers an additional dimension to the sociology of gender literature on doing gender and to the postmodernist conception of gender as performativity. What may be a near constant in all interactive situations in addition to doing gender and doing difference is doing power. People in interaction are adjusting their actions not only in anticipation of other people's responses or in the work of imitation of others' imitations but also in terms of a calculus of who can finally get their way by what means.

Most mainstream microsociology presents a model of purposive human beings setting their own goals and pursuing these in linear courses of action in which they (individually or collectively) strive to link means to ends. In contrast, feminist research shows, first, that women's lives have a quality of incidentalism, as women find themselves caught up in agendas that shift and change with the vagaries of marriage, husbands' courses of action, children's unpredictable impact on life plans, divorce, widowhood, and the precariousness of most women's wage-sector occupations. Second, in their daily activities, women find themselves not so much pursuing goals in linear sequences but responding continuously to the needs and demands of others. This theme has been developed from analysis of the emotional and relational symbiosis between mothers and daughters, through descriptions of intensely relational female play groups, to analyses of women in their typical occupations as teachers, nurses, secretaries, receptionists, and office helpers and accounts of women in their roles as wives, mothers, and community and kin coordinators. In calling women's activities "responsive," we are not describing women as passively reactive. Instead, we are drawing a picture of beings who are oriented not so much to their own goals as to the tasks of monitoring, coordinating, facilitating, and moderating the wishes, actions, and demands of others. In place of microsociology's conventional model of purposeful actors, then, feminist research presents a model of actors who are in their daily lives responsively located at the center of a web of others' actions and who in the long term find themselves located in one or another of these situations by forces that they can neither predict nor control.

Conventional micro-social theory assumes that the pressures in interactive situations toward collaboration and meaning construction are so great that actors, bracketing considerations of the macro structure, orient toward each other on an assumption of equality. Feminist research on interactions between women and men contradicts this idea, showing that these social interactions are pervasively patterned by influences from their macro-structural context. In their daily activities, women are affected by the fact that they are structurally subordinate to the men with whom they interact in casual associations, courtship, marriage, family, and wage work. Any interpersonal equality or dominance that women as individuals may achieve is effectively offset, within the interactive process itself, by these structural patterns—of which the most pervasive is the institution of gender. The macro-structural patterning of gender inequality is intricately woven through the interactions between women and men and affects not only its broad division of labor, in who sets and who implements projects, but also its processual details, which repeatedly show the enactment of authority and deference in seating and seating-standing arrangements, forms of address and conversation, eye contact, and the control of space and time. This assumption of inequality as a feature in interactive situations is intensified and complicated when factors of race and class are included in the feminist analytic frame.

Social definitionists assume that one of the major ongoing projects in social interaction is the construction of shared meanings. Actors, seeing each other in activity and interaction, form shared understandings through communication and achieve a common vantage point on their experiences. Feminists argue that this assumption must be qualified by the fact that micro interactions are embedded in and permeated by the macro structures of power and ideology. These structures pattern the meanings assigned to activities in interaction. Men as dominants in interaction with women are more likely to assign to women's activity meanings drawn from the macro structure of gender ideology than either to enter the situation with an attitude of open inquiry or to draw on any other macro-level typing for interpreting women's activity. Women, immersed in the same ideological interpretation of their experiences, stand at a point of dialectical tension, balancing this ideology against the actuality of their lives. A great diversity of meanings develops out of this tension. Social definitionists assume that actors, relating and communicating intimately and over long periods of time, create a common vantage point or system of shared understanding. Feminists' research on what may be the most intimate, long-term, male-female association—marriage— shows that, for all the reasons reported above, marriage partners remain strangers to each other and inhabit separate worlds of meaning. This "stranger-ness" may be greater for the dominant man, in the interests of effective control, than for the subordinate woman who must monitor the dominant's meanings (Dorothy Smith, 1979).

A democratic ethos shapes both social-definitionist and social-behaviorist descriptions of interaction. Conventional models imply that people have considerable equality of opportunity and freedom of choice in moving in and out of interactional settings. Feminist research shows that the interactions in which women are most free to create with others meanings that depict their life experiences are those that occur when they are in relationship and communication with similarly situated women. Moreover, these associations can be deeply attractive to women because of the practical, emotional, and meaning-affirming support that they provide. Women, however, are not freely empowered to locate in these settings. Law, interactional domination, and ideology restrict and demean this associational choice so that, insidiously, even women become suspicious of its attractions. Under these circumstances, the association becomes not a free and open choice but a subterranean, circumscribed, and publicly invisible arena for relationship and meaning.

Finally, a feminist analysis of interactional practices may emphasize differences between men and women explainable in terms of deep psychic structures. Male training rewards individuation and the repudiation of the female so that the male understands at an early age that his claim to male privilege involves his distancing from female behaviors. Similarly, the female learns early that one of the duties of women— to men and to each other—is to recognize the subjectivity of the other through interactional gestures such as paying attention, commenting on actions done, and using gestures to indicate approval and awareness. These behaviors permeate and explain not only interactions across gender but interactions within same-gender groups. Women are repeatedly shown as enacting more responsiveness to the other and engaging in more ongoing monitoring of the other's needs and desires. Men are more inclined to feel both the right and the duty to compartmentalize in order to attain individual projects and to view their responsiveness to other as an act of generosity, not a part of expected interactional behavior.

Subjectivity 主体性

Most sociological theories subsume the subjective level of social experience under micro-social action (micro subjectivity) or as "culture" or "ideology" at the macro level (macro subjectivity) (see Chapter 10 and the Appendix). Feminist sociology, however, insists that the actor's individual interpretation of goals and relationships must be looked at as a distinct level. This insistence, like so much of feminist sociology, grows out of the study of women's lives and seems applicable to the lives of subordinates in general. Women as subordinates are particularly aware of the distinctiveness of their subjective experience precisely because their own experience so often runs counter to prevailing cultural and micro-interactionally established definitions. When sociologists do look at the subjective level of experience, usually as part of the micro-social order, they focus on four major issues: (1) role taking and knowledge of the other, (2) the process of the internalization of community norms, (3) the nature of the self as social actor, and (4) the nature of the consciousness of everyday life. This section explores the feminist thesis on each of these issues.

The conventional sociological model of subjectivity (as presented to us in the theories of Mead [see Chapter 6] and Schutz) assumes that in the course of role taking, the social actor learns to see the self through the eyes of others deemed more or less the same as the actor. But feminist sociology shows that women are socialized to see themselves through the eyes of men. Even when significant others are women, they have been so socialized that they too take the male view of self and of other women. Women's experience of learning to role-take is shaped by the fact that they must, in a way men need not, learn to take the role of the genuine *other,* not just a social other who is taken to be much like oneself. The other for women is the male and is alien. The other for men is, first and foremost, men who are like them in a quality that the culture considers of transcendent importance: gender. Feminist theory emphasizes that this formula is complicated by the intersection of the vectors of oppression and privilege within individual lives.

Role taking usually is seen as culminating in the internalization of community norms via the social actor's learning to take the role of "the generalized other," a construct that the actor mentally creates out of the amalgam of macro- and micro-level experiences that form her or his social life. The use of the singular *other* indicates that microsociologists usually envision this imagined generalized other as a cohesive, coherent, singular expression of expectations. But feminists argue that in a male-dominated patriarchal culture, the generalized other represents a set of male-dominated community norms that force the woman to picture herself as "less than" or "unequal to" men. To the degree that a woman succeeds in formulating a sense of generalized other that accurately reflects the dominant perceptions of the community, she may have damaged her own possibilities for self-esteem and self-exploration. Feminist theory calls into question the existence of a unified generalized other for the majority of people. The subordinate has to pivot between a world governed by a dominant generalized other, or meaning system, and locations in "home groups" that offer alternative understandings and generalized others. The awareness of the possibility of multiple generalized others is essential to understanding the potential complexity of having or being a self.

Microsociologists describe the social actor as picturing the everyday world as something to be mastered according to one's particular interests. Feminist sociologists argue that women may find themselves so limited by their status as women that the idea of projecting their own plans onto the world becomes meaningless in all but theory. Further, women may not experience the life-world as something to be mastered according to their own particular interests. They may be socialized to experience that life-world as a place in which one balances a variety of actors' interests. Women may not have the same experience of control of particular spheres of space, free from outside interference. Similarly, their sense of time rarely can follow the simple pattern of first things first because they have as a life project the balancing of the interests and projects of others. Thus, women may experience planning and actions as acts of concern for a variety of interests, their own and others; may act in projects of cooperation rather than mastery; and may evaluate their ongoing experiences of role balancing not as role conflicts but as a more appropriate response to social life than role compartmentalization.

Feminist sociologists have critically evaluated the thesis of a unified consciousness of everyday life that traditional microsociologists usually assume. Feminist sociologists stress that for women the most pervasive feature of the cognitive style of everyday life is that of a "bifurcated consciousness," developing along "a line of fault" between their own personal, lived, and reflected-on experience and the established types available in the social stock of knowledge to describe that experience (Dorothy Smith, 1979, 1987). Everyday life itself thus divides into two realities for subordinates: the reality of actual, lived, reflected-on experience and the reality of social typifications. Often aware of the way that their own experience differs from that of the culturally dominant males with whom they interact, women may be less likely to assume a shared subjectivity. As biological and social beings whose activities are not perfectly regulated by patriarchal time, they are more aware of the demarcation between time as lived experience and time as a social mandate. A feminist sociology of subjectivity perhaps would begin here: How do people survive when their own experience does not fit the established social typifications of that experience? We know already that some do so by avoiding acts of sustained reflection; some by cultivating their own series of personal types to make sense of their experience; some by seeking community with others who share this bifurcated reality; and some by denying the validity of their own experience.

What we have generalized here for women's subjectivity may be true for the subjectivity of all subordinates. (1) Their experience of role taking is complicated by their awareness that they must learn the expectations of an other who by virtue of differences in power is alien. (2) They must relate not to a generalized other but to many generalized others in both the culture of the powerful and the various subcultures of the less empowered and the disempowered. (3) They do not experience themselves as purposive social actors who can chart their own course through life—although they may be constantly told that they can do so, especially within the American ethos. (4) Most pervasively, they live daily with a bifurcated consciousness, a sense of the line of fault between their own lived experiences and what the dominant culture tells them is the social reality.

Everything in this discussion has assumed a unified subject, that is, an individual woman or man with an ongoing, consistent consciousness and a sense of self. The unified subject is important to feminist theory because it is that subject who experiences pain and oppression, makes value judgments, and resists or accepts the world in place—the unified subject is the primary agent of social change. Yet our discussion of subjectivity also raises questions about how unified this subject is; there are the problems of a subject whose generalized other is truly "other" or "alien," who experiences not *a* generalized other but many generalized others, whose consciousness is bifurcated, and whose self in its capacities for development and change may be viewed more as a process than as a product. All these tendencies toward an understanding of the self as fragmented rather than as unified are inherent in feminist theorizing of the self—indeed, they are at the heart of feminist ideas about resistance and change. This sense of fragmentation is much intensified in postmodernist feminist critiques (discussed earlier in this chapter), a theoretical position that raises questions about the very possibility of "a unified subject or consciousness." If a self, any self, is subject to change from day to day or even moment to moment, if we can speak of "being not myself," then on what basis do we posit a self? Yet feminist critics of postmodernism respond by beginning in the experience of women in daily life, who when they say "I was not myself" or "I have not been myself" assume a stable self from which they have departed and, further, by those very statements, some self that knows of the departure.

Summary 总结

Feminist sociological theory grows out of feminist theory in general—that branch of the new scholarship on women that seeks to provide a system of ideas about human life that features woman as object and subject, doer and knower.

One effect of the contemporary feminist movement on sociology has been to expand the significance of the sociology of gender relations and of women's lives. Many sociological theories currently work to explore these issues. The macro-social theories of functionalism, analytic conflict theory, and neo-Marxian world-systems theory all explore the place of the household in social systems as a means of explaining women's social subordination. Symbolic interactionism and ethno-methodology, two micro-social theories, explore the ways in which gender is produced and reproduced in interpersonal relations. In the last decade, sociologists have also attempted a feminist reworking of Habermas, Bourdieu. and Giddens in their analyses of gender.

Feminist scholarship is guided by four basic questions: (1) *And what about the women?* (2) *Why is women's situation as it is?* (3) *How can we change and improve the social world?* (4) *What about differences among women?* Answers to these questions produce the varieties of feminist theory. This chapter patterns this variety to show four major groupings of feminist theory. Theories of gender difference see women's situation as different from men's, explaining this difference in terms of two distinct and enduring ways of being, male and female, or institutional roles and social interaction, and ontological constructions of woman as "other." Theories of gender inequality, notably by liberal feminists, emphasize women's claim to a fundamental right of equality and describe the unequal opportunity structures created by sexism. Gender oppression theories include feminist psychoanalytic theory and radical feminism. The former explains the oppression of women in terms of psychoanalytic descriptions of the male psychic drive to dominate; the latter, in terms of men's ability and willingness to use violence to subjugate women. Structural oppression theories include socialist feminism and intersectionality theory. Socialist feminism describes oppression as arising from a patriarchal and a capitalist attempt to control social production and reproduction. Intersectionality theories trace the consequences of class, race, gender, affectional preference, and global location for lived experience, group standpoints, and relations among women.

Feminist theory offers six key propositions as a basis for the revision of standard sociological theories. First, the practice of sociological theory must be based in a sociology of knowledge that recognizes the partiality of all knowledge, the knower as embodied and socially located, and the function of power in affecting what becomes knowledge. Second, macro social structures are based in processes controlled by dominants acting in their own interests and executed by subordinates whose work is made largely invisible and undervalued even to themselves by dominant ideology. Thus, dominants appropriate and control the productive work of society, including not only economic production but also women's work of social reproduction. Third, micro-interactional processes in society are enactments of these dominant-subordinate power arrangements, enactments very differently interpreted by powerful and subordinate actors. Fourth, these conditions create in women's subjectivity a bifurcated consciousness along the line of fault caused by the juxtaposition of patriarchal ideology and women's experience of the actualities of their lives. Fifth, what has been said for women may be applicable to all subordinate peoples in some parallel, although not identical, form. Sixth, one must question the use of any categories developed by a traditionally male-dominated discipline and most particularly the divisions between micro- and macro-sociologies.

第三部分 最新社会学理论中的整合发展

Recent Integrative Developments in Sociological Theory

Micro-Macro and Agency-Structure Integration

第10章 微观—宏观和能动—结构整合

Chapter Outline

Micro-Macro Integration

Agency-Structure Integration

Agency-Structure and Micro-Macro Linkages:
    Fundamental Differences

In this chapter we deal with two important developments in recent sociological theory. Our first concern is a dramatic development that occurred largely in the United States in the 1980s (although, as we will see, it had important precursors) and continues to this day. That development is the growth of interest in the issue of the *micro-macro linkage* (J. H. Turner, 2007b; Barnes, 2001; Turner and Boyns, 2001). Then we will deal with a parallel development that occurred largely in European sociological theory—the rise in interest in the *relationship between agency and structure*. As we will see, there are important similarities *and* crucial differences between the American micro-macro literature and the European work on agency and structure. The micro-macro and agency-structure literatures themselves can be seen as synthetic developments and thus as parts of the broad movement toward theoretical synthesis discussed throughout Part Two of this book.

Micro-Macro Integration 微观—宏观整合

Micro-Macro Extremism 微观—宏观极端主义

Until recently, *one* of the major divisions in contemporary American sociological theory has been the conflict between extreme *microscopic* and *macroscopic*[1] theories (and theorists) and, perhaps more important, between those who have *interpreted* sociological theories in these ways (Archer, 1982). Such extreme theories and interpretations of theories have tended to heighten the image of a great chasm between micro and macro theories and, more generally, the image of conflict and disorder (Gouldner, 1970; Wardell and Turner, 1986; Wiley, 1985) in sociological theory.

Although it is possible to interpret (and many have) the classic sociological theorists discussed in Part One of this book (Marx, Durkheim, Weber, Simmel) as either micro or macro extremists, the most defensible perspective, or at least the one that will orient this chapter, is that they were most generally concerned with the micro-macro linkage (Moscovici, 1993). Marx can be seen as being interested in the coercive and alienating effect of capitalist society on individual workers (and capitalists). Weber may be viewed as being focally concerned with the plight of the individual within the iron cage of a formally rational society. Simmel was interested primarily in the relationship between objective (macro) culture and subjective (or individual, micro) culture. Even Durkheim was concerned with the effect of macro-level social facts on individuals and individual behavior (for example, suicide). If we accept these characterizations of the classic sociological theorists, it appears that much of the last century of American sociological theory has involved a loss of concern for this linkage and the dominance of micro and macro extremists—that is, the preeminence of theorists and theories that accord overwhelming power and significance to either the micro or the macro level. Thus, the theories discussed in Part Two of this book tended toward micro or macro extremism. On the macro-extreme side were structural functionalism, conflict theory, and some varieties of neo-Marxian theory (especially economic determinism). On the micro-extreme end were symbolic interactionism, ethnomethodology, exchange, and rational choice theory.

Among the most notable of the twentieth-century macro-extreme theories are Parsons's (1966) "cultural determinism"[2]; Dahrendorf's (1959) conflict theory, with its focus on imperatively coordinated associations; and Peter Blau's macrostructuralism, epitomized by his proud announcement, "I am a structural determinist" (1977:x). Macrostructural extremism comes from other sources as well (Rubenstein, 1986), including network theorists such as White, Boorman, and Breiger (1976), ecologists such as Duncan and Schnore (1959), and structuralists such as Mayhew (1980). Few take a more extreme position than Mayhew, who says such things as, "In structural sociology the unit of analysis is always the social network, *never the individual*" (1980:349).

---

[1] Although the use of the terms *micro* and *macro* might suggest that we are dealing with a dichotomy, always keep in mind that there is a *continuum* ranging from the micro end to the macro end (see the Appendix).

[2] Even as sympathetic an observer as Jeffrey Alexander (1987a:296) admits Parsons's "own collectivist bias"; see also Coleman (1986:1310). However, while Parsons's greatest influence was in collectivistic theory, it is also possible to find within his work a strong micro-macro integrative theory.

On the micro-extreme side we can point to a good portion of symbolic interactionism and the work of Blumer (1969a), who often seemed to have structural functionalism in mind as he positioned symbolic interactionism as a sociological theory seemingly single-mindedly concerned with micro-level phenomena (see Chapter 6 for a very different interpretation of Blumer's perspective). An even clearer case of micro extremism is exchange theory and George Homans (1974), who sought an alternative to structural functionalism and found it in the extreme micro orientation of Skinnerian behaviorism. Then there is ethnomethodology and its concern for the everyday practices of actors. Garfinkel (1967) was put off by the macro foci of structural functionalism and its tendency to turn actors into "judgmental dopes." Scheff (2007) makes a more general case for "microsociology."

微观—宏观的整合运动
The Movement toward Micro-Macro Integration

While micro-macro extremism characterized much of twentieth-century sociological theory, it became possible, beginning mainly in the 1980s, to discern a movement, largely in American sociology, away from micro-macro extremism and toward a broad consensus that *the* focus, instead, should be on *the integration (or synthesis, linkage) of micro and macro theories and/or levels of social analysis.* This approach represents quite a change from that of the 1970s, when Kemeny argued: "So little attention is given to this distinction that the terms 'micro' and 'macro' are not commonly even indexed in sociological works" (1976:731). It could be argued that at least in this sense American sociological theorists have rediscovered the theoretical project of the early masters.

While developments in the 1980s and 1990s were particularly dramatic, isolated earlier works directly addressed the micro-macro linkage. For example, in the mid-1960s Helmut Wagner (1964) dealt with the relationship between small-scale and large-scale theories. At the end of the decade Walter Wallace (1969) examined the micro-macro continuum, but it occupied a secondary role in his analysis and was included as merely one of the "complications" of his basic taxonomy of sociological theory. In the mid-1970s Kemeny (1976) called for greater attention to the micro-macro distinction as well as to the ways in which micro and macro relate to each other.

However, it was in the 1980s that we witnessed a flowering of work on the micro-macro linkage issue. Randall Collins argued that work on this topic "promises to be a significant area of theoretical advance for some time to come" (1986a:1350). In their introduction to a two-volume set of books, one devoted to macro theory (Eisenstadt and Helle, 1985a) and the other to micro theory (Helle and Eisenstadt, 1985), Eisenstadt and Helle concluded that "the confrontation between micro- and macro-theory belong[s] to the past" (1985b:3). Similarly, Münch and Smelser, in their conclusion to the anthology *The Micro-Macro Link* (Alexander et al., 1987), asserted: "Those who have argued polemically that one level is more fundamental than the other . . . must be regarded as in error. Virtually every contributor to this volume has correctly insisted on the mutual interrelations between micro and macro levels" (1987:385).

There are two major strands of work on micro-macro integration. Some theorists focus on integrating micro and macro *theories,* while others are concerned with developing a theory that deals with the linkage between micro and macro *levels* (Alford and Friedland, 1985; Edel, 1959) of social analysis. Above, for example, I quoted Eisenstadt and Helle (1985b:3), who concluded that the confrontation between micro and macro *theories* was behind us, while Münch and Smelser (1987:385) came to a similar conclusion about the need to choose between emphasizing micro or macro *levels*. There are important differences between trying to integrate macro (for example, structural functionalism) and micro (for example, symbolic interactionism) theories and attempting to develop a theory that can deal with the relationship between macro (for example, social-structure) and micro (for example, personality) levels of social analysis (for an example of the latter, see Summers-Effler, 2002).[3]

Given this general introduction, we turn now to some examples of micro-macro integration. At a number of places throughout Part Two of this book, we dealt with efforts to integrate micro and macro *theories*. All the examples that follow focus on integrating micro and macro *levels of social analysis*.

Examples of Micro-Macro Integration 微观—宏观整合的案例

Integrated Sociological Paradigm 整合的社会学范式

This section begins with my effort at micro-macro integration (Ritzer, 1979, 1981a). The discussion here will be relatively brief, since the integrated sociological paradigm also is discussed in the Appendix. It is summarized there because it represents the metatheoretical schema that serves to orient and organize this book. In this section the focus is on what the integrated paradigm has to say about the issue of micro-macro linkage.

It should be noted that my thinking on the integrated paradigm in general, and more specifically on micro-macro linkage, was shaped by the work of a number of predecessors, especially that of Abraham Edel (1959) and Georges Gurvitch (1964; see also Bosserman, 1968). Gurvitch operates with the belief that the social world can be studied in terms of five "horizontal," or micro-macro, levels (Smelser [1997] identifies four), presented in ascending order from micro to macro: forms of sociality, groupings, social class, social structure, and global structures. To complement this hierarchy, Gurvitch also offers ten "vertical," or "depth," levels, beginning with the most objective social phenomena (for example, ecological factors, organizations) and ending with the most subjective social phenomena (collective ideas and values, the collective mind). Gurvitch crosscuts his horizontal and vertical dimensions in order to produce numerous levels of social analysis.

My work on the integrated sociological paradigm was motivated, in part, by the need to build upon Gurvitch's insights but to produce a more parsimonious model. It begins with the micro-macro continuum (Gurvitch's horizontal levels), ranging from individual thought and action to world-systems (see the Appendix, Figure A.1). To this continuum is added an objective-subjective continuum (Gurvitch's vertical levels), ranging from material phenomena such as individual action and bureaucratic structures to nonmaterial phenomena such as consciousness and norms and values (see the Appendix, Figure A.2). Like Gurvitch, I crosscut these two continua, but in

---

[3] As well as with meso-level phenomena (Ulmer, 2007).

MACROSCOPIC

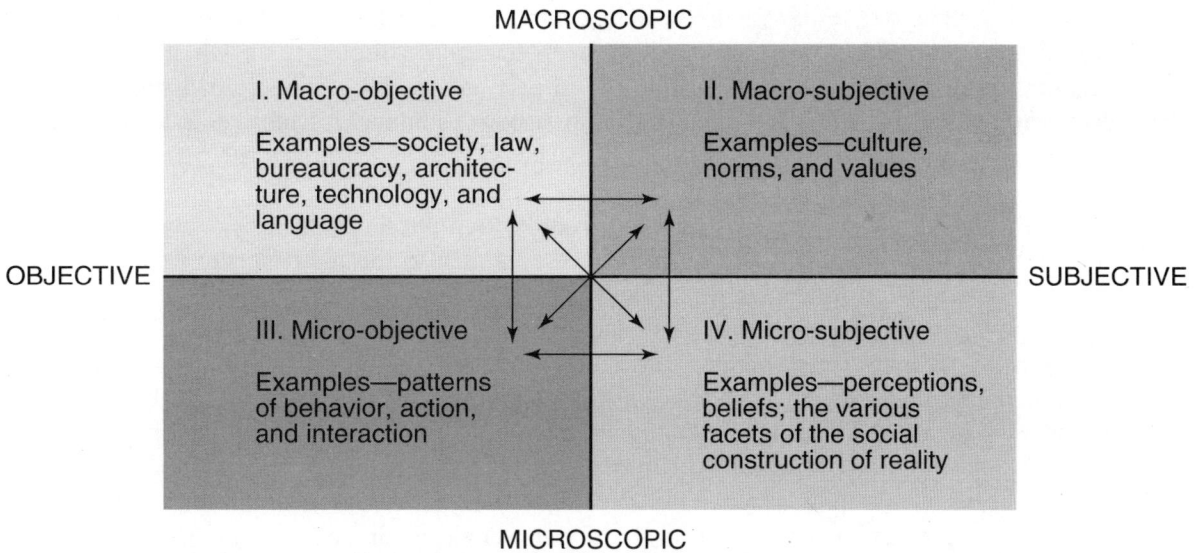

I. Macro-objective Examples—society, law, bureaucracy, architecture, technology, and language	**II. Macro-subjective** Examples—culture, norms, and values
III. Micro-objective Examples—patterns of behavior, action, and interaction	**IV. Micro-subjective** Examples—perceptions, beliefs; the various facets of the social construction of reality

OBJECTIVE   SUBJECTIVE

MICROSCOPIC

FIGURE 10.1 *Ritzer's Major Levels of Social Analysis*

Note that this is a "snapshot" in time. It is embedded in an ongoing historical process.

this case the result is a far more manageable four, rather than many, levels of social analysis. Figure 10.1 depicts my major levels of social analysis.

In terms of the micro-macro issue, my view is that it cannot be dealt with apart from the objective-subjective continuum. All micro and macro social phenomena are also either objective or subjective. Thus, the conclusion is that there are four major levels of social analysis and that sociologists must focus on the dialectical interrelationship among these levels. The macro-objective level involves large-scale material realities such as society, bureaucracy, and technology. The macro-subjective level encompasses large-scale nonmaterial phenomena such as norms and values. At the micro levels, micro objectivity involves small-scale objective entities such as patterns of action and interaction, whereas micro subjectivity is concerned with the small-scale mental processes by which people construct social reality. Each of these four levels is important in itself, but of utmost importance is the dialectical relationship among and between them.

I employed an integrative micro-macro approach in *Expressing America: A Critique of the Global Credit Card Society* (1995; see also R. Manning, 2000). Specifically, I used C. Wright Mills's (1959) ideas on the relationship between micro-level *personal troubles* and macro-level *public issues* to analyze the problems created by credit cards.

Personal troubles are those problems that affect an individual and the people immediately around him or her. For example, a husband who batters his spouse is creating problems for his wife, for other members of the family, and perhaps for himself (especially if the law is involved). However, the actions of a single husband who batters his wife are not going to create a public issue—those actions will not result in a public outcry to abandon marriage as a social institution. Public issues tend to be those that affect large numbers of people, perhaps society as a whole. The disintegration of marriage as an institution, in part as a result of widespread spouse battering, would be a public issue. There are various relationships between personal troubles and public issues. For example, widespread personal troubles can become a public issue, and a public issue can cause many personal troubles.

I examine a wide range of personal troubles and public issues associated with credit cards. This argument, and an integrated approach to the micro-macro linkage, can be illustrated by following his discussion of the issue of consumer debt. At the macro level, aggregate consumer debt has become a public issue because a large and growing number of people are increasingly indebted to credit card companies. A by-product of this growing consumer debt is an increase in delinquencies and bank-ruptcies. Also at the macro level, and a public issue, is the role played by the govern-ment in encouraging consumer debt through its tendency to accumulate debt. More important is the role played by the credit card firms in encouraging people to go into debt by doing everything they can to get as many credit cards into as many hands as possible. There is, for example, the increasing tendency for people to receive notices in the mail that they are eligible for preapproved credit cards. People can easily acquire a large number of credit cards with a huge collective credit limit. Perhaps the most reprehensible activities of the credit card firms involve their efforts to get cards into the hands of college and high school students. They are endeavoring to "hook" young people on a life of credit and indebtedness. Such activities are clearly a public issue and are causing personal troubles for untold numbers of people.

Millions of people have gotten themselves into debt, sometimes irretrievably, as a result of the abuse of credit cards. People build up huge balances, sometimes surviv-ing by taking cash advances on one card to make minimum payments on other cards. Overwhelmed, many people become delinquent and sometimes are forced to declare bankruptcy. As a result, some people spend years, in some cases the rest of their lives, trying to pay off old debts and restore their ability to get credit. Even if it does not go this far, many people are working long hours just to pay the interest on their credit card debt and are able to make only a small, if any, dent in their credit balances. Thus, one could say they are indentured for life to the credit card companies.

The kinds of personal troubles described here, when aggregated, create public issues for society. And as we saw previously, public issues such as the policies and procedures of the credit card firms (for example, offering preapproved cards and recruiting students) help create personal troubles. Thus, there is a dialectical relation-ship between personal troubles and public issues, with each exacerbating the other. More generally, this example of credit cards illustrates the applicability of an integrated micro-macro approach to a pressing social problem.

Multidimensional Sociology 多维社会学

Jeffrey Alexander has offered what he calls a "new 'theoretical logic' for sociology" (1982:xv). That new logic affects "sociological thought at every level of the intel-lectual continuum" (Alexander, 1982:65). In this spirit, Alexander offers what he terms a *multidimensional sociology*. While *multidimensionality* has several meanings in his work, the most relevant here is Alexander's multidimensional sense of levels of social analysis.

We can begin with what Alexander (following Parsons) terms the *problem of order*. Alexander suggests that the micro-macro continuum ("an 'individual' or 'collective' level of analysis" [1982:93]) is involved in the way order is created in society. At the macro end of the continuum, order is externally created and is collectivist in nature; that is, order is produced by collective phenomena. At the micro end, order is derived from internalized forces and is individualistic in nature; that is, order stems from individual negotiation.

To the problem of order is added, in a classic Parsonsian position, the *problem of action*. Action involves a materialist-idealist continuum that parallels the objective-subjective continuum employed in my integrated sociological paradigm. At the material end, action is described as instrumental, rational, and conditional. At the nonmaterial pole, action is normative, nonrational, and affective. When we crosscut Alexander's order and action continua, we come up with four levels of social analysis that strongly resemble the four levels that I employ (see Figure 10.2).

Although the terminology is slightly different, there are few if any differences between the models offered by Alexander and I. The major difference lies in the way they relate the four levels. While I want to focus on the dialectical relationship among all four levels, Alexander seeks to grant priority to one of the levels.

Alexander believes that according privilege to the micro levels is "a theoretical mistake" (1987a:295). He is highly critical of all theories, such as symbolic interactionism, that begin at the individual-normative level with nonrational voluntary agency and build toward the macro levels. From his point of view, the problem with these theories is that while maintaining notions of individual freedom and voluntarism, they are unable to deal with the unique (*sui generis*) character of collective phenomena. Alexander is also critical of theories, such as exchange theory, that start at the individual-instrumental level and move toward macro-level structures such as the

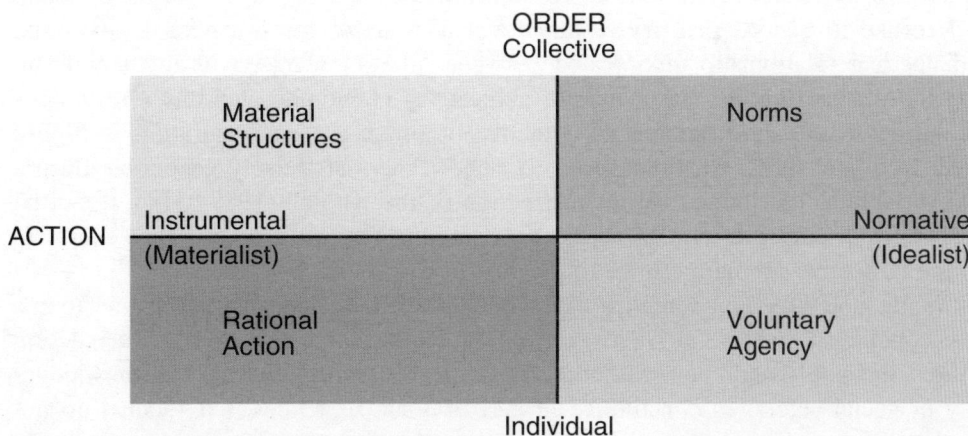

FIGURE 10.2 *Alexander's Integrative Model*

economy. Such theories are also unable to handle macro-level phenomena adequately. Thus, Alexander is critical of all theories that have their origins at the micro levels and seek to explain macro-level phenomena from that base.

At the macro level, Alexander is critical of collective-instrumental theories (for example, economic and structural determinism) that emphasize coercive order and eliminate individual freedom. Basically, the problem is that such theories do not allow for individual agency.

While he expressed an interest in focusing on the relationships among all four of his levels, Alexander's sympathies (not surprisingly, given his Parsonsian and structural-functionalist roots) lay with the collective-normative level and theories that begin at that level. As he put it, "The hope for combining collective order and individual voluntarism lies with the normative, rather than the rationalist tradition" (Alexander, 1982:108). Central to this belief is his view that such an orientation is preferable because the sources of order are internalized (in the conscience) rather than external-ized, as is the case with the collective-instrumental orientation. This focus on the internalization of norms allows for *both* order and voluntary agency.

Overall, Alexander argues that any individual, or micro, perspective is to be rejected because it ends with "randomness and complete unpredictability" rather than order (1985a:27). Thus, "the general framework for social theory can be derived *only* from a collectivist perspective" (1985a:28; italics added). And between the two col-lectivist perspectives, Alexander subscribes to the collective-normative position.

Thus, to Alexander social theorists must choose either a collectivist (macro) or an individualist (micro) perspective. If they choose a collectivist position, they can incorporate only a "relatively small" element of individual negotiation. If, however, they choose an individualist theory, they are doomed to the "individualist dilemma" of trying to sneak into theory supraindividual phenomena to deal with the randomness inherent in their theory. This dilemma can be resolved only "if the formal adherence to individualism is abandoned" (Alexander, 1985a:27).

Thus, while Alexander employs four levels of analysis that closely resemble those utilized by me, there is an important difference in the two models. Alexander accords priority to collective-normative theories and to a focus on norms in social life. I refuse to accord priority to any level and argue for the need to examine the dialectical relationship among and between all four levels. Alexander ends up giving inordinate significance to macro (subjective) phenomena, and as a result, his contribution to the development of a theory of micro-macro integration is highly limited. In a later work, Alexander said, "I believe theorists falsely generalize from a single variable to the immediate reconstruction of the whole" (1987a:314). It can be argued that Alexander is one of these theorists since he seeks to falsely generalize from the collective-normative level to the rest of the social world.

While not directly addressing Alexander's work, Giddens (1984) came to the similar conclusion that *all* work derived from the Parsonsian distinction between action and order inevitably ends up weak at the micro levels, especially on "the knowledge-ability of social actors, as constitutive in part of social practices. I [Giddens] do not think that any standpoint which is heavily indebted to Parsons can cope satisfactorily with this issue at the very core of social theory" (1984:xxxvii).

However, it should be noted that Alexander has articulated a more truly integrative perspective, one that defines *micro* and *macro* in terms of each other. Here is the way he expresses this perspective: "The collective environments of action simultaneously inspire and confine it. If I have conceptualized action correctly, these environments will be seen as its products; if I can conceptualize the environments correctly, action will be seen as their end result" (Alexander, 1987a:303). It appears that Alexander has a more complex, dialectical sense of the micro-macro nexus, one that is more similar to my integrated sociological paradigm than his earlier model.

The Micro Foundations of Macrosociology 宏观社会学的微观基础

In an essay entitled "On the Microfoundations of Macrosociology," Randall Collins (1981a; see also 1981b) has offered a highly reductionistic orientation toward the micro-macro link question (for a critique, see Ritzer, 1985). In fact, despite the inherently integrative title of his essay, Collins labels his approach "radical microsociology." Collins's focus, the focus of radical microsociology, is what he calls "interaction ritual chains," or bundles of "individual chains of interactional experience, crisscrossing each other in space as they flow along in time" (1981a:998). In focusing on interaction ritual chains, Collins seeks to avoid what he considers to be even more reductionistic concerns with individual behavior and consciousness. Collins raises the level of analysis to interaction, chains of interaction, and the "marketplace" for such interaction. Collins thus rejects the extreme micro levels of thought and action (behavior) and is critical of the theories (such as phenomenology and exchange theory) that focus on these levels.

Collins also seeks to distance himself from macro theories and their concerns with macro-level phenomena. For example, he is critical of structural functionalists and their concern with macro-objective (structure) and macro-subjective (norms) phenomena. In fact, he goes so far as to say that "the terminology of norms ought to be dropped from sociological theory" (Collins, 1981a:991). He has a similarly negative attitude toward concepts associated with conflict theory, arguing, for example, that there are no "inherent objective" entities such as property and authority; there are only "varying senses that people feel at particular places and times of how strong these enforcing coalitions are" (Collins, 1981a:997). His point is that only people do anything; structures, organizations, classes, and societies "never *do* anything. Any causal explanation must ultimately come down to the actions of real individuals" (Collins, 1975:12).

Collins seeks to show how "all macrophenomena" can be translated "into combinations of micro events" (1981a:985). Specifically, he argues that social structures may be translated empirically into "patterns of repetitive micro interaction" (Collins, 1981a:985). Thus, in the end, Collins seeks *not* an integrated approach but the predominance of micro theory and micro-level phenomena (for a similar critique, see Giddens, 1984). As Collins puts it, "The effort coherently to reconstitute macro sociology upon radically empirical micro foundations is the crucial step toward a more successful sociological science" (1981b:82).

RANDALL COLLINS

An Autobiographical Sketch

I started becoming a sociologist at an early age. My father was working for military intelligence at the end of World War II and then joined the State Department as a foreign service officer. One of my earliest memories is of arriving in Berlin to join him in the summer of 1945. My sisters and I couldn't play in the park because there was live ammunition everywhere, and one day Russian soldiers came into our backyard to dig up a corpse. This gave me a sense that conflict is important and violence always possible.

My father's subsequent tours of duty took us to the Soviet Union, back to Germany (then under American military occupation), to Spain, and South America. In between foreign assignments we would live in the States, so I went back and forth between being an ordinary American kid and being a privileged foreign visitor. I think this resulted in a certain amount of detachment in viewing social relationships. As I got older the diplomatic life looked less dramatic and more like an endless round of formal etiquette in which people never talked about the important politics going on; the split between backstage secrecy and front-stage ceremonial made me ready to appreciate Erving Goffman.

When I was too old to accompany my parents abroad, I was sent to a prep school in New England. This taught me another great sociological reality: the existence of stratification. Many of the other students came from families in the Social Register, and it began to dawn on me that my father was not in the same social class as the ambassadors and undersecretaries of state whose children I sometimes met.

I went on to Harvard, where I changed my major half a dozen times. I studied literature and tried being a playwright and novelist. I went from mathematics to philosophy; I read Freud and planned to become a psychiatrist. I finally majored in social relations, which covered sociology, social psychology, and anthropology. Taking courses from Talcott Parsons settled me onto a path. He covered virtually everything, from the micro to the macro and across the range of world history. What I got from him was not so much his own theory

We can contrast Collins's orientation to that of Karin Knorr-Cetina (1981). Although she, too, accords great importance to the interactional domain, Knorr-Cetina grants a greater role to both consciousness and macro-level phenomena in her work. Although Knorr-Cetina, like Collins, makes the case for a radical reconstruction of macro theory on a microsociological base, she also is willing to consider the much less radical course of simply integrating microsociological results into macro-social theory. In addition, she seems to take the position that the ultimate goal of microsociological research is a better understanding of the larger society, its structure, and its institutions:

but rather the ideal of what sociology could do. He also provided me with some important pieces of cultural capital: that Weber was less concerned with the Protestant Ethic than he was with comparing the dynamics of all the world religions and that Durkheim asked the key question when he tried to uncover the precontractual basis of social order.

I thought I wanted to become a psychologist and went to Stanford, but a year of implanting electrodes in rats' brains convinced me that sociology was a better place to study human beings. I switched universities and arrived in Berkeley in the summer of 1964, just in time to join the civil-rights movement. By the time the free-speech movement emerged on campus in the fall, we were veterans of sit-ins, and being arrested for another cause felt emotionally energizing when one could do it in solidarity with hundreds of others. I was analyzing the sociology of conflict at the same time that we were experiencing it. As the Vietnam War and the racial conflicts at home escalated, the opposition movement began to repudiate its nonviolent principles; many of us became disillusioned and turned to the cultural lifestyle of the hippie dropouts. If you didn't lose your sociological consciousness, it could be illuminating. I studied Erving Goffman along with Herbert Blumer (both of them Berkeley professors at the time) and began to see how all aspects of society—conflict, stratification, and all the rest—are constructed out of the interaction rituals of our everyday lives.

I never set out to be a professor, but by now I have taught in many universities. I tried to put everything together into one book, *Conflict Sociology* (1975), but it turned out I had to write another, *The Credential Society* (1979), to explain the inflationary status system in which we are all enmeshed. Taking my own analysis seriously, I quit the academic world and for a while made a living by writing a novel and textbooks. Eventually, attracted by some interesting colleagues, I got back into teaching. Our field is learning some tremendous things, from a new picture of world history down through the micro details of social emotions. One of the most important influences for me is my second wife, Judith McConnell. She organized women lawyers to break down discriminatory barriers in the legal profession, and now I am learning from her about the backstage politics of the higher judiciary. In sociology and in society, there is plenty yet to be done.

[See also Li, 2005.]

I . . . believe in the seeming paradox that it is through micro-social approaches that we will learn most about the macro order, for it is these approaches which through their unashamed empiricism afford us a glimpse of the reality about which we speak. Certainly, we will not get a grasp of whatever is the whole of the matter by a microscopic recording of face-to-face interaction. However, it may be enough to begin with if we—for the first time—hear the macro order tick.

(Knorr-Cetina, 1981:41–42)

Thus, it seems clear that Knorr-Cetina takes a far more balanced position on the relationship between the macro and micro levels than does Collins.

An even more integrative position is taken by Aaron Cicourel (1981): "Neither micro nor macro structures are self-contained levels of analysis; they *interact* with each other at all times despite the convenience and sometimes the dubious luxury of only examining one or the other level of analysis" (Cicourel, 1981:54). There is an implied criticism of Collins here, but Cicourel adopts another position that can be seen as a more direct critique of the kind of position adopted by Collins: "The issue is not simply one of dismissing one level of analysis or another, but showing how they must be integrated if we are not to be convinced about one level to the exclusion of the other by conveniently ignoring competing frameworks for research and theory" (1981:76). To his credit, Cicourel understands not only the importance of linking macro and micro levels but also the fact that that link needs to take place ontologically, theoretically, and methodologically.

Collins continued to subscribe to his micro-reductionistic position for some time. For example, in a later work Collins argued: "Macrostructure consists of nothing more than large numbers of microencounters, repeated (or sometimes changing over time and across space)" (1987:195). He concluded, unashamedly: "This may sound as if I am giving a great deal of prominence to the micro. That is true" (Collins, 1987:195). However, it is worth noting that just one year later Collins (1988) was willing to give the macro level greater significance. This approach led to a more balanced conception of the micro-macro relationship: "The micro-macro translation shows that everything macro is composed out of micro. Conversely, anything micro is part of the composition of macro; it exists in a macro context . . . it is possible to pursue the micro-macro connection fruitfully in either direction" (Collins, 1988:244). The latter contention implies a more dialectical approach to the micro-macro relationship. Yet Collins (1988:244), like Coleman (1986, 1987), subscribes to the view that the "big challenge" in sociology is showing "how micro affects macro." Thus, while Collins has shown some growth in his micro-macro theory, it continues to be a highly limited approach.

回到未来：诺贝特·埃利亚斯的构型社会学
Back to the Future: Norbert Elias's Figurational Sociology

We have now discussed some of the major recent American efforts at micro-macro integration. However, there is a European theorist, Norbert Elias, whose work is best discussed under this heading. (For a nice selection of his work, see Mennell and Goudsblom, 1998). Elias was involved in an effort to overcome the micro-macro distinction, and more generally to surmount the tendency of sociologists to distinguish between individuals and society (Rundell, 2005; Dunning, 1986:5; Mennell, 1992). Elias's major work was done in the 1930s, but it has only recently begun to receive the recognition it deserves (Kilminster and Mennell, 2000; Van Krieken, 1998, 2001; Dennis Smith, 2001).

In order to help achieve his integrative goal, Elias proposed the concept of *figuration* (Mennell; 2005a), an idea which

> makes it possible to resist the socially conditioned pressure to split and polarize
> our conception of mankind, which has repeatedly prevented us from thinking of

people as individuals *at the same time* as thinking of them as societies. . . . The concept of figuration therefore serves as a simple conceptual tool to loosen this social constraint to speak and think as if "the individual" and "society" were antagonistic as well as different.

(Elias, 1978:129–130; italics added)

Figurations can be seen, above all, as processes. In fact, later in his life Elias came to prefer the term *process sociology* to describe his work (Mennell, 1992:252). Figurations are social processes involving the "interweaving" of people. They are *not* structures that are external to and coercive of relationships between people; they *are* those interrelationships. Individuals are seen as open and interdependent; figurations are made up of such individuals. Power is central to social figurations, which are, as a result, constantly in flux:

At the core of changing figurations—indeed the very hub of the figuration process—is a fluctuating, tensile equilibrium, a balance of power moving to and fro, inclining first to one side and then to the other. This kind of fluctuating balance of power is a structural characteristic of the flow of every figuration.

(Elias, 1978:131)

Figurations emerge and develop, but in largely unseen and unplanned ways.

Central to this discussion is the fact that the idea of a figuration applies at both the micro and the macro levels and to every social phenomenon between those two poles. The concept

can be applied to relatively small groups just as well as to societies made up of thousands or millions of interdependent people. Teachers and pupils in a class, doctors and patients in a therapeutic group, regular customers at a pub, children at a nursery school—they all make up relatively comprehensible figurations with each other. But the inhabitants of a village, a city or a nation also form figurations, although in this instance the figurations cannot be perceived directly because the *chains of interdependence* which link people together are longer and more differentiated.

(Elias, 1978:131; italics added)

Thus, Elias refuses to deal with the relationship between "individual" and "society" but focuses on "the relationship between people perceived as individuals and people perceived as societies" (Elias, 1986:23). In other words, both individuals and societies (and every social phenomenon in between) involve people—human relationships. The idea of "chains of interdependence" underscored in the extract above is as good an image as any of what Elias means by figurations and what constitutes the focus of his sociology: "How and why people are bound together to form specific dynamic figurations is one of the central questions, perhaps even *the* central question, of sociology" (1969/1983:208).

Elias's notion of figuration is linked to the idea that individuals are open to, and interrelated with, other individuals. He argues that most sociologists operate with a sense of *homo clausus,* that is, "an image of single human beings each of whom is ultimately absolutely independent of all others—an individual-in-himself" (Elias, 1969/1983:143). Such an image does not lend itself to a theory of figurations; an image of open, interdependent actors is needed for figurational sociology.

NORBERT ELIAS

A Biographical Sketch

Norbert Elias had an interesting and instructive career. He produced his most important work in the 1930s, but it was largely ignored at the time and for many years thereafter. However, late in his life Elias and his work were "discovered," especially in England and the Netherlands. Today, Elias's reputation is growing, and his work is receiving increasing attention and recognition throughout the world (Dennis Smith, 2001): Elias lived until he was 93 (he died in 1990), long enough to bask belatedly in long-delayed recognition of the significance of his work.

Elias was born in Breslau, Germany, in 1897 (Mennell, 1992). His father was a small manufacturer, and the family lived a comfortable existence. The home was apparently a loving one, and it imbued Elias with a self-confidence that was to stand him in good stead later when his work was not recognized:

> I put that down to the great feeling of security I had as a child . . . I have a basic feeling of great security, a feeling that in the end things will turn out for the best, and I attribute that to an enormous emotional security which my parents gave me as an only child.
>
> I knew very early on what I wanted to do; I wanted to go to university, and I wanted to do research. I knew that from when I was young, and I have done it, even though sometimes it seemed impossible . . . I had great confidence that in the end my work would be recognized as a valuable contribution to knowledge about humanity.
>
> (Elias, cited in Mennell, 1992:6–7)

Elias served in the German army in World War I and returned after the war to study philosophy and medicine at the University of Breslau. Although he progressed quite far in his medical studies, he eventually dropped them in favor of the study of philosophy. His work in medicine gave him a sense of the interconnections among the various parts of the human body, and that view shaped his orientation to human interconnections—his concern for figurations. Elias received his Ph.D. in January 1924; only then did he go to Heidelberg to learn sociology.

Elias received no pay at Heidelberg, but he did become actively involved in sociology circles at the university. Max Weber had died in 1920, but a salon headed by his wife, Marianne, was active, and Elias became involved in it. He also associated with Max Weber's brother, Alfred, who held a chair in sociology at the university, as well as with Karl Mannheim (described by Elias [1994:34] as "unquestionably brilliant"), who was slightly ahead of Elias in terms of career progress. In fact, Elias became Mannheim's friend and unpaid, unofficial assistant.

When Mannheim was offered a position at the University of Frankfurt in 1930, Elias went with him as his paid and official assistant (on the relationship between the two men and their work, see Kilminster, 1993).

Adolf Hitler came to power in February 1933, and soon after, Elias, like many other Jewish scholars (including Mannheim), went into exile, at first in Paris and later in London (it is believed that Elias's mother died in a concentration camp in 1941). It was in London that he did most of the work on *The Civilizing Process*, which was published in German in 1939. There was no market in Germany then for books written by a Jew, and Elias never received a penny of royalties from that edition. In addition, the book received scant recognition in other parts of the world.

Both during the war and for almost a decade after it, Elias bounced around with no secure employment and remained marginal to British academic circles. However, in 1954 Elias was offered two academic positions, and he accepted the one at Leicester. Thus, Elias *began* his formal academic career at the age of 57! Elias's career blossomed at Leicester, and a number of important publications followed. However, Elias was disappointed with his tenure at Leicester because he failed in his effort to institutionalize a developmental approach that could stand as an alternative to the kinds of static approaches (of Talcott Parsons and others) that were then preeminent in sociology. He was also disappointed that few students adopted his approach; he continued to be a voice in the wilderness, even at Leicester, where the students tended to regard him as an eccentric "voice from the past" (Mennell, 1992:22). Reflective of this feeling of being on the outside is a recurrent dream reported by Elias during those years in which a voice on the telephone repeats, "'Can you speak louder? I can't hear you'" (Mennell, 1992:23). It is interesting to note that throughout his years at Leicester *none* of his books was translated into English and few English sociologists of the day were fluent in German.

However, in continental Europe, especially in the Netherlands and Germany, Elias's work began to be rediscovered in the 1950s and 1960s. In the 1970s Elias began to receive not only academic but public recognition in Europe. Throughout the rest of his life Elias received a number of significant awards, an honorary doctorate, a *Festschrift* in his honor, and a special double issue of *Theory, Culture and Society* devoted to his work.

Interestingly, while Elias has now received wide recognition in sociology (including inclusion in this text), his work has received that recognition during a period in which sociology is growing *less* receptive to his kind of work. That is, the rise of postmodern thinking has led sociologists to question any grand narrative, and Elias's major work, *The Civilizing Process*, is, if nothing else, a grand narrative in the old style (Dennis Smith, 1999). That is, it is concerned with the long-term historical development (admittedly with ebbs and flows) of civilization in the West. The growth of postmodern thinking threatens to limit interest in Elias's work just as it is beginning to receive wide attention.

The History of Manners 《凤尚的历史》

If Weber can be seen as being concerned with the rationalization of the West, Elias's focal interest is on the *civilization* of the Occident (Bogner, Baker, and Kilminster, 1992; for an application of his ideas to another part of the world—Singapore—see Stauth, 1997). By the way, Elias is not arguing that there is something inherently good, or better, about civilization as it occurs in the West, or anywhere else for that matter. Nor is he arguing that civilization is inherently bad, although he does recognize that various difficulties have arisen in Western civilization. More generally, Elias (1968/1994:188) is not arguing that to be more civilized is to be better, or conversely that to be less civilized is worse. In saying that people have become more civilized, we are not necessarily saying that they have become better (or worse); we are simply stating a sociological fact. Thus, Elias is concerned with the sociological study of what he calls the "sociogenesis" of civilization in the West (as we will see shortly).

Specifically, Elias is interested in the gradual changes (Elias, 1997) that took place in the behavior and psychological makeup of people in the West. It is an analysis of these changes that is his concern in *The History of Manners,* the first volume of *The Civilizing Process* (1939/1978). In the second volume of *The Civilizing Process, Power and Civility* (1939/1982), Elias turns to the societal changes that accompany, and are closely related to, these behavioral and psychological changes. Overall, Elias is concerned with "the connections between changes in the structure of society and changes in the structure of behavior and psychical makeup" (1939/1994:xv).

In his study of the history of manners, Elias is interested in the gradual, historical transformation of a variety of very mundane behaviors in the direction of what we would now call civilized behavior (although there are also periods of "decivilization"; see Elias, 1995; Mennell, 2005b). Although he begins with the Middle Ages, Elias makes it clear that there is not, and cannot be, such a thing as a starting (or ending) point for the development of civilization: "Nothing is more fruitless, when dealing with long-term social processes, than to attempt to locate an absolute beginning" (Elias, 1969/1983:232). That is, civilizing processes can be traced back to ancient times, continue to this day, and will continue into the future. Civilization is an ongoing developmental process that Elias is picking up, for convenience, in the Middle Ages. He is interested in tracing such things as changes in what embarrasses us, our increasing sensitivity, how we've grown increasingly observant of others, and our sharpened understanding of others. However, the best way of gaining an understanding of what Elias is doing is not through abstractions but through a discussion of some of his concrete examples.

Behavior at the Table   Elias examines what books (and other sources) on manners written between the thirteenth and nineteenth centuries had to say about how to comport oneself at the dinner table (as well as on the issues discussed in the next several sections). Elias's most basic point is that the threshold of embarrassment has gradually advanced. What people did at the table with little or no embarrassment in the thirteenth century would cause much mortification in the nineteenth century. What is regarded as distasteful is over time increasingly likely to be *"removed behind the scenes of social life"* (Elias, 1939/1994:99).

For example, a thirteenth-century poem warned, "A number of people gnaw on a bone and then put it back in the dish—this is a serious offense" (Elias, 1939/1994:68). Another thirteenth-century volume warns, "It is not decent to poke your fingers into your ears or eyes, as some people do, or to pick your nose while eating" (Elias, 1939/1994:71). Clearly, the implication of these warnings is that many people at that time engaged in such behaviors and that it generally caused them, or those around them, no embarrassment. There was a perceived need for such admonitions because people did not know that such behavior was "uncivilized." As time goes by there is less and less need to warn people about such things as picking one's nose while eating. Thus, a late-sixteenth-century document says, "Nothing is more improper than to lick your fingers, to touch the meats and put them into your mouth with your hand, to stir sauce with your fingers, or to dip bread into it with your fork and then suck it" (Elias, 1939/1994:79). Of course, there *are* things, picking one's nose, for example, more improper than licking one's fingers, but by this time civilization has progressed to the point where it is widely recognized that such behaviors are uncivilized. With nose picking safely behind the scenes, society found other, less egregious behaviors that it defined as uncivilized.

Natural Functions 自然生理现象

A similar trend is found in the performance of natural functions. A fourteenth-century book used by schoolchildren, among others, found it necessary to offer advice on the expelling of wind:

> To contract an illness: Listen to the old maxim about the sound of wind. If it can be purged without a noise that is best. But it is better that it be emitted with a noise than it be held back. . . .
>
> . . . The sound of farting, especially of those who stand on elevated ground, is horrible. One should make sacrifices with the buttocks pressed firmly together . . .
>
> . . . let a cough hide the explosive sound . . . Follow the law of Chiliades: Replace farts with coughs.
>
> (Elias, 1939/1994:106)

Here we see things being discussed openly that by the nineteenth century (and certainly today) it was no longer necessary to mention because it had come to be well known that the behaviors in question were uncivilized. Further, we are likely to be startled by such a discussion, which offends our contemporary sense of propriety. But all this reflects the process of civilization and the movement of the "frontier of embarrassment" (Elias, 1939/1994:107). Things that could be discussed openly have over time progressively moved beyond that frontier. The fact that we are startled by reading advice on farting reflects the fact that the frontier today is very different from what it was in the fourteenth century.

Elias relates this change in the notion of the appropriate way to expel wind to changes in social figurations, especially in the French court. More people were living in closer proximity and in more permanent interdependence. Therefore, there was a greater need to regulate people's impulses and to get them to practice greater restraint. The control over impulses that began in the higher echelons of the court eventually was transmitted to those of lower social status. The need to extend these restraints was made necessary by further figurational changes, especially people of different statuses moving closer together, becoming more interdependent, and by the decreasing rigidity of the stratification system, which made it easier for those of lower status to interact with those of higher status. As a result, to put it baldly, there was increasingly just as much need for the lower classes to control their wind (and many other behaviors) as there was for the upper classes. At the same time, those from the upper classes needed to control their wind in the presence not only of peers but of social inferiors as well.

Elias sums up his discussion of such natural functions:

> Society is gradually beginning to suppress the positive pleasure component in certain functions more and more strongly by the arousal of anxiety; or, more exactly, it is rendering this pleasure 'private' and 'secret' (i.e. suppressing it within the individual), while fostering the negatively charged affects—displeasure, revulsion, distaste—as the only feelings customary in society.
>
> (Elias, 1939/1994:117)

Blowing One's Nose   A similar process is seen in the restraints on blowing one's nose. For example, a fifteenth-century document warned, "Do not blow your nose with the same hand that you use to hold the meat" (Elias, 1939/1994:118). Or, in the sixteenth century, the reader is informed, "Nor is it seemly, after wiping your nose, to spread out your handkerchief and peer into it as if pearls and rubies might have fallen out of your head" (Elias, 1939/1994:119). However, by the late eighteenth century these kinds of details are avoided in sources of advice: "Every voluntary movement of the nose . . . is impolite and puerile. To put your fingers into your nose is a revolting impropriety. . . . You should observe, in blowing your nose, all the rules of propriety and cleanliness" (Elias, 1939/1994:121). As Elias says, "The 'conspiracy of silence' is spreading" (1939/1994:121). That is, things that could be discussed openly a century or two before are now discussed more discreetly, or not at all. The "shame frontier" as it relates to blowing one's nose, and many other things, has progressed. Shame has come to be attached to things (for example, blowing one's nose, farting) that in the past were not considered shameful. More and more walls are being erected between people so that things that formerly could be done in the presence of others are now hidden from view.

Sexual Relations   Elias describes the same general trend in sexual relations. In the Middle Ages it was common for many people, including men and women, to spend the night together in the same room. And it was not uncommon for them to sleep naked. However, over time, it came to be viewed as increasingly shameful to show oneself naked in the presence of the opposite sex. As an example of "uncivilized" sexual behavior, Elias describes the following wedding customs beginning in the Middle Ages:

> The procession into the bridal chamber was led by the best man. The bride was undressed by the bridesmaids; she had to take off all finery. The bridal bed had to be mounted in the presence of witnesses if the marriage was to be valid. They were "laid together." "Once in bed you are rightly wed," the saying went. In the later Middle Ages this custom gradually changed to the extent that the couple was

allowed to lie on the bed in their clothes. . . . Even in the absolutist society of France, bride and bridegroom were taken to bed by the guests, undressed, and given their nightdress.

(Elias, 1939/1994:145–146)

Clearly, this changed further over time with the advance of civilization. Today, everything that occurs in the wedding bed is concealed, taking place behind the scenes and out of the sight of all observers. More generally, sexual life has been taken out of the larger society and enclosed within the nuclear family.

Overall, in the *History of Manners* Elias is concerned with changes in the way individuals think, act, and interact. He sometimes speaks of this, in general, as a change in "personality structure," but Elias seems to be describing more than changes in personality; he also is describing changes in the way people act and interact. Taken together, it could be argued that the *History of Manners* focuses largely on micro-level concerns. However, two factors militate against such an interpretation. First, Elias often deals in *The History of Manners* with concomitant macro-level changes (in the court, for example), and he argues that "the structures of personality and of society evolve in indissoluble interrelationship" (1968/1994:188). Second, *The History of Manners* is written with the awareness that *Power and Civility,* dealing focally with these more macro-level changes, is to accompany it. Nonetheless, even though Elias wishes to avoid the micro-macro dichotomy, *The Civilizing Process* consists of two separate volumes, the first focally concerned with micro issues and the second interested mainly in macro questions.

Power and Civility 权力和礼仪

If self-constraint is the key to the civilizing process, then what Elias is concerned with in *Power and Civility* are the changes in social constraint that are associated with this rise in self-restraint. However, Elias, despite his later overt rejection of the micro-macro distinction, seems to announce that in *Power and Civility* he is dealing with another, more "macroscopic" level of analysis:

> *This basic tissue resulting from the many single plans and actions of men can give rise to changes and patterns that no individual person has planned or created. From this interdependence of people arises an order sui generis, an order more compelling and stronger than the will and reason of the individual people composing it.* It is this order of interweaving human impulses and strivings, this social order, which determines the course of historical change; it underlies the civilizing process.

(Elias, 1939/1982:230)

These are strong, almost Durkheimian words, depicting a unique (*sui generis*) and compelling reality that "determines the course of historical change." In spite of Elias's later rhetoric about the need to overcome the micro-macro distinction, such a position is not, in the main, supported by *Power and Civility,* which tends at times to deal with the effect, sometimes the determining effect, of macro structures on micro-level phenomena. (However, we hasten to add that Elias often says that he is merely interested in the covariation of macro and micro phenomena, or the connection between "specific changes in the structure of human relations and the corresponding changes in the structure of the personality" [1939/1982:231].)

Reflective of his difficulties in dealing with micro and macro in an integrated way is the fact that Elias distinguishes between *psychogenetic* and *sociogenetic* investigations. In a psychogenetic investigation, one focuses on individual psychology, while sociogenetic investigations have a larger radius and a longer-range perspective, focusing on "the overall structure, not only of a single state society but of the social field formed by a specific group of interdependent societies, and of the sequential order of its evolution" (Elias, 1939/1982:287–288).

Lengthening Interdependency Chains   What is the macro-structural change that is of such great importance to the process of civilization? It can be described as the lengthening of "interdependency chains":

> From the earliest period of the history of the Occident to the present, social functions have become more and more differentiated under the pressure of competition. The more differentiated they become, the larger grows the number of functions and thus of people on whom the individual constantly depends in all his actions, from the simplest and most commonplace to the more complex and uncommon. As more and more people must attune their conduct to that of others, the web of actions must be organized more and more strictly and accurately, if each individual action is to fulfil its social function. The individual is compelled to regulate his conduct in an increasingly differentiated, more even and stable manner . . . the more complex and stable control of conduct is increasingly instilled in the individual from his earliest years as an automatism, a self-compulsion that he cannot resist even if he consciously wishes to.

(Elias, 1939/1982:232–233)

The result of all this is "the lengthening of the chains of social action and interdependence," which is what contributes to the corresponding need for individuals to moderate their emotions by developing the "habit of connecting events in terms of chains of cause and effect" (Elias, 1939/1982:236).

Thus, to Elias, the increasing differentiation of social functions plays a key role in the civilization process. In addition to, and in conjunction with, this differentiation is the importance of what Elias calls "a total reorganization of the social fabric" (1939/1982:234). Here he is describing the historical process which witnessed the emergence of increasingly stable central organs of society that monopolize the means of physical force and of taxation. Crucial to this development is the emergence of a king with absolute status, as well as of the court society (especially in France and during the reign of Louis XIV, although the courts of Europe came to be closely linked). What Elias calls a "royal mechanism" is operating here—kings are able to emerge in a specific figuration where competing functional groups are ambivalent (they were characterized by both mutual dependency and hostility) and power is evenly distributed between them, thus prohibiting a decisive conflict or a decisive compromise. As Elias puts it, "Not by chance, not whenever a strong ruling personality is born, but when a specific social structure provides the opportunity, does the central organ attain that optimal power which usually finds expression in strong autocracy" (1939/1982:174). In other words, a king emerges when the appropriate figuration is in place.

The king's court took on special importance for Elias because it was here that changes took place that eventually affected the whole of society. In contrast to the warrior, whose short chains of dependence made it relatively easy for him to engage in violent behavior, the court noble, with much longer chains of dependence on many other nobles, found it necessary to be increasingly sensitive to others. The noble also found it increasingly difficult to give free play to his emotions through violence or any other action. The noble was further limited by the fact that the king was gaining increasing control over the means of violence. "The monopolization of physical violence, the concentration of arms and armed men under one authority . . . forces unarmed men in the pacified social spaces to restrain their own violence through foresight or reflection; in other words it imposes on people a greater or lesser degree of self-control" (Elias, 1939/1982:239). The monopoly of violence is intimately related to the ability of the king to monopolize taxation, since taxes are what allow the king to pay for control over the means of violence (Elias, 1939/1982:208). In fact, Elias describes a situation that involves the interplay of these two monopolies: "The financial means thus flowing into this central authority maintains its monopoly of military force, while this in turn maintains the monopoly of taxation" (1939/1982:104). In addition, the increase in the king's income is accompanied by a reduction of the nobility's, and this disparity serves to enhance further the power of the king (Elias, 1969/1983:155).

The nobles play a key role in the civilization process because changes that take place among this elite group are gradually disseminated throughout society:

> It is in this courtly society that the basic stock of models of conduct is formed
> which then, fused with others and modified in accordance with the position of
> the groups carrying them, spread, with the compulsion to exercise foresight, to
> ever-wider circles of functions. Their special situation makes the people of courtly
> society, more than any other Western group affected by this movement, specialists
> in the elaboration and moulding of social conduct.
>
> (Elias, 1939/1982:258)

Furthermore, these changes that started in the West began to spread through many other parts of the world.

The rise of the king and the court and the transition from warrior to courtier (or the "courtization" of the warrior) represent for Elias a key "spurt" in the civilizing process. This idea of "spurts" is central to Elias's theory of social change; he does not view change as a smooth, unilinear process, but rather one with much stopping and starting—much to-and-fro movement.

While Elias gives great importance to the rise of the court,[4] the ultimate cause of the decisive changes that ensued was the change in the entire social figuration of the time. That is, the key was the changes in various relationships among groups (for example, between warriors and nobles), as well as changes in the relationships among individuals in those groups. Furthermore, this figuration was constraining on nobles

---

[4] For an interesting study of the court, the bourgeoisie, and their impact on Mozart, see Elias (1993).

and king alike: "Princes and aristocratic groups are apt to appear as people leading a free and unconstrained life. Here . . . it emerged very clearly to what constraints upper classes, and not least their most powerful member, the absolute monarch, are subjected" (Elias, 1969/1983:266).

From the dominance of the king and his nobles there is gradual movement toward a state. In other words, once a private monopoly (by the king) of arms and taxes is in place, the ground is set for the public monopoly of those resources—that is, the emergence of the state. There is a direct link between the growth of the king and later the state as controlling agencies in society and the development of a parallel controlling agency within the individual. Together, they begin to wield unprecedented power over the individual's ability to act on his or her emotions. It is not that before this time people totally lacked self-control, but self-control grew more continuous and stable, affecting more and more aspects of people's lives. Elias's argument is very close to Durkheim's when he contends that with the longer chains of interdependence, "the individual learns to control himself more steadily; he is now less a prisoner of his passions" (1939/1982:241).

An interesting aspect of Elias's argument is that he recognizes that this control over passions is not an unmitigated good. Life has grown less dangerous, but it has also become less pleasurable. Unable to express their emotions directly, people need to find other outlets, such as in their dreams or through books. In addition, what were external struggles may come to be internalized as, in Freudian terms, battles between the id and the superego. (Elias's thinking on the individual was heavily influenced by Freudian theory.) Thus, while the greater control over passions brings a welcome reduction in violence, it also brings with it increasing boredom and restlessness.

The longer dependency chains are associated not only with greater affective control but with increasing sensitivity to others and to the self. Furthermore, people's judgments become more finely shaded and nuanced, making them better able to judge and control both themselves and others. Before the rise of the court society, people had to protect themselves from violence and death. Afterward, as this danger receded, people could afford to grow more sensitive to far more subtle threats and actions. This greater sensitivity is a key aspect of the civilizing process and a key contributor to its further development.

Agency-Structure Integration 能动—结构的整合

Paralleling the growth in interest in American sociological theory in the micro-macro issue has been an increase in interest among European theorists in the relationship between agency and structure. In fact, this interest is so intense that Fuller (1998) has called it a "craze." For example, Margaret Archer has contended that "the problem of structure and agency has rightly come to be seen as the basic issue in modern social theory" (1988:ix). In fact, she argues that dealing with this linkage (as well as a series of other linkages implied by it) has become the "acid test" of a general social theory and the "central problem" in theory (Archer, 1988:x). Earlier, Dawe went even further than Archer: *"Here, then, is the problematic around which the entire history of sociological analysis could be written: the problematic of human agency"* (1978:379).

Implied in Dawe's concern with agency is also an interest in social structure as well as the constant tension between them.[5]

At a superficial level the micro-macro and agency-structure issues sound similar, and they often are treated as if they resembled one another greatly. However, there are other ways to think of both agency-structure and micro-macro issues that make the significant differences between these two conceptualizations quite clear.

While *agency* generally refers to micro-level, individual human actors,[6] it also can refer to (macro) collectivities that act. For example, Burns sees human agents as including "individuals as well as organized groups, organizations and nations" (1986:9). Touraine (1977) focuses on social classes as actors. If we accept such collectivities as agents, we cannot equate agency and micro-level phenomena. In addition, while *structure* usually refers to large-scale social structures, it also can refer to micro structures such as those involved in human interaction. Giddens's definition of *systems* (which is closer to the usual meaning of *structure* than is his own concept of structure) implies both types of structures, since it involves "reproduced relations between actors or collectivities" (1979:66). Thus, both *agency* and *structure* can refer to either micro-level or macro-level phenomena or to both.

Turning to the micro-macro distinction, *micro* often refers to the kind of conscious, creative actor of concern to many agency theorists, but it also can refer to a more mindless "behaver" of interest to behaviorists, exchange theorists, and rational choice theorists. Similarly, the term *macro* can refer not only to large-scale social structures but also to the cultures of collectivities. Thus, *micro* may or may not refer to "agents," and *macro* may or may not refer to "structures."

When we look closely at the micro-macro and agency-structure schemas, we find that there are substantial differences between them.

能动—整合的主要案例
Major Examples of Agency-Structure Integration

Structuration Theory 结构化理论

One of the best-known and most articulated efforts to integrate agency and structure is Anthony Giddens's structuration theory (Bryant and Jary, 2000; I. J. Cohen, 2005, 1989; Craib, 1992; Held and Thompson, 1989). Giddens goes so far as to say, "Every research investigation in the social sciences or history is involved in relating action [often used synonymously with *agency*] to structure . . . there is no sense in which structure 'determines' action or vice versa" (1984:219).

Although Giddens is not a Marxist, there is a powerful Marxian influence in his work, and he even sees *The Constitution of Society* as an extended reflection on Marx's inherently integrative dictum: "Men make history, but they do not make it just as they please; they do not make it under circumstances chosen by themselves, but under circumstances directly encountered, given, and transmitted from the past" (Marx, 1869/1963:15).[7]

---

[5] In fact, agency often is used in such a way as to include a concern for structure (Abrams, 1982:xiii).

[6] A variety of contemporary theorists, especially those associated with poststructuralism and postmodernism, have questioned and even rejected the idea of human agency. See, for example, M. P. Jones (1996).

[7] It is appropriate to accord Marx such a central place in structuration theory and, more generally, in theories that integrate agency and structure. As I have written elsewhere, Marx's work is the best "exemplar for an integrated sociological paradigm" (Ritzer, 1981a:232).

Marx's theory is but one of many theoretical inputs into structuration theory. At one time or another, Giddens has analyzed and critiqued most major theoretical orientations and derived a range of useful ideas from many of them. Structuration theory is extraordinarily eclectic; in fact, Craib (1992:20–31) outlines nine major inputs into Giddens's thinking.

Giddens surveys a wide range of theories that begin with either the individual/agent (for example, symbolic interactionism) or the society/structure (for example, structural functionalism) and rejects both of these polar alternatives. Rather, Giddens argues that we must begin with "recurrent social practices" (1989:252). Giving slightly more detail, he argues: "The basic domain of the study of the social sciences, according to the theory of structuration, is neither the experience of the individual actor, nor the existence of any form of social totality, but social practices ordered across time and space" (Giddens, 1984:2).

At its core Giddens's structuration theory, with its focus on social practices, is a theory of the relationship between agency and structure. According to Richard J. Bernstein, "the very heart of the theory of structuration" is "intended to illuminate the duality and dialectical interplay of agency and structure" (1989:23). Thus, agency and structure cannot be conceived of apart from one another; they are two sides of the same coin. In Giddens's terms, they are a duality. All social action involves structure, and all structure involves social action. Agency and structure are inextricably interwoven in ongoing human activity or practice.

As pointed out earlier, Giddens's analytical starting point is human practices, but he insists that they be seen as recursive. That is, activities are "not brought into being by social actors but are continually recreated by them via the very means whereby they express themselves as actors. In and through their activities agents produce the conditions that make these activities possible" (Giddens, 1984:2). Thus, activities are not produced by consciousness, by the social construction of reality, nor are they produced by social structure. Rather, in expressing themselves as actors, people are engaging in practice, and it is through that practice that both consciousness and structure are produced. Focusing on the recursive character of structure, Held and Thompson argue that "structure is reproduced in and through the succession of situated practices which are organized by it" (1989:7). The same thing can be said about consciousness. Giddens is concerned with consciousness, or reflexivity. However, in being reflexive, the human actor not only is self-conscious but also is engaged in the monitoring of the ongoing flow of activities and structural conditions. Bernstein argues that "agency itself is reflexively and recursively implicated in social structures" (1989:23). Most generally, it can be argued that Giddens is concerned with the dialectical process in which practice, structure, and consciousness are produced. Thus, Giddens deals with the agency-structure issue in a historical, processual, and dynamic way.

Not only are social actors reflexive, so are the social researchers who are studying them. This idea leads Giddens to his well-known ideas on the "double hermeneutic." Both social actors and sociologists use language. Actors use language to account for what they do, and sociologists, in turn, use language to account for the actions of social actors. Thus, we need to be concerned with the relationship between lay and scientific language. We particularly need to be aware of the fact that the social scientist's understanding of the social world may have an impact on the understandings of the actors being studied. In that way, social researchers can alter the world they are studying and thus come up with distorted findings and conclusions.

Elements of Structuration Theory   Let us discuss some of the major components of Giddens's structuration theory, starting with his thoughts on agents, who, as we have seen, continuously monitor their own thoughts and activities as well as their physical and social contexts. In their search for a sense of security, actors rationalize their world. By rationalization Giddens means the development of routines that not only give actors a sense of security but enable them to deal efficiently with their social lives. Actors also have motivations to act, and these motivations involve the wants and desires that prompt action. Thus, while rationalization and reflexivity are continuously involved in action, motivations are more appropriately thought of as potentials for action. Motivations provide overall plans for action, but most of our action, in Giddens's view, is not directly motivated. Although such action is not motivated and our motivations are generally unconscious, motivations play a significant role in human conduct.

Also within the realm of consciousness, Giddens makes a (permeable) distinction between discursive and practical consciousness. *Discursive consciousness* entails the ability to describe our actions in words. *Practical consciousness* involves actions that the actors take for granted, without being able to express in words what they are doing. It is the latter type of consciousness that is particularly important to structuration theory, reflecting a primary interest in what is done rather than what is said.

Given this focus on practical consciousness, we make a smooth transition from agents to agency, the things that agents actually *do:* "Agency concerns events of which an individual is a perpetrator. . . . Whatever happened would not have happened if that individual had not intervened" (Giddens, 1984:9). Thus, Giddens gives great (his critics say too much) weight to the importance of agency (Baber, 1991). Giddens takes great pains to separate agency from intentions because he wants to make the point that actions often end up being different from what was intended; in other words, intentional acts often have unintended consequences. The idea of unintended consequences plays a great role in Giddens's theory and is especially important in getting us from agency to the social-system level.

Consistent with his emphasis on agency, Giddens accords the agent great power. In other words, Giddens's agents have the ability to make a difference in the social world. Even more strongly, agents make no sense without power; that is, an actor ceases to be an agent if he or she loses the capacity to make a difference. Giddens certainly recognizes that there are constraints on actors, but this does not mean that actors have no choices and make no difference. To Giddens, power is logically prior to subjectivity because action involves power, or the ability to transform the situation. Thus, Giddens's structuration theory accords power to the actor and action and is in opposition to theories that are disinclined to such an orientation and instead grant great importance either to the intent of the actor (phenomenology) or to the external structure (structural functionalism).

The conceptual core of structuration theory lies in the ideas of structure, system, and duality of structure. *Structure* is defined as "the structuring properties [*rules and resources*] . . . the properties which make it possible for discernibly similar social practices to exist across varying spans of time and space and which lend them systemic form" (Giddens, 1984:17). Structure is made possible by the existence of rules and resources. Structures themselves do not exist in time and space. Rather, social phenomena have the capacity to become structured. Giddens contends that "structure only exists in and through the activities of human agents" (1989:256). Thus, Giddens offers a very unusual definition of *structure* that does not follow the Durkheimian pattern of viewing structures as external to and coercive of actors. He takes pains to avoid the impression that structure is "outside" or "external" to human action. "In my usage, structure is what gives form and shape to social life, but it is not *itself* that form and shape" (Giddens, 1989:256). As Held and Thompson put it, structure to Giddens is not a framework "like the girders of a building or the skeleton of a body" (1989:4).

Giddens does not deny the fact that structure can be constraining on action, but he feels that sociologists have exaggerated the importance of this constraint. Furthermore, they have failed to emphasize the fact that structure "is *always* both constraining *and* enabling" (Giddens, 1984:25, 163; italics added). Structures often allow agents to do things they would not otherwise be able to do. While Giddens deemphasizes structural constraint, he does recognize that actors can lose control over the "structured properties of social systems" as they stretch away in time and space. However, he is careful to avoid Weberian iron-cage imagery and notes that such a loss of control is *not* inevitable.

The conventional sociological sense of structure is closer to Giddens's concept of social system (J. B. Thompson, 1989:60). Giddens defines *social systems* as reproduced social practices, or "reproduced relations between actors or collectivities organized as regular social practices" (1984:17, 25). Thus, the idea of the social system is derived from Giddens's focal concern with practice. Social systems do *not* have structures, but they do exhibit structural properties. Structures do not themselves exist in time and space, but they are manifested in social systems in the form of reproduced practices. While some social systems may be the product of intentional action, Giddens places greater emphasis on the fact that such systems are often the unanticipated consequences of human action. These unanticipated consequences may become unrecognized conditions of action and feed back into it. These conditions may elude efforts to bring them under control, but nevertheless actors continue their efforts to exert such control.

Thus structures are "instantiated" in social systems. In addition, they are also manifest in "memory traces orienting the conduct of knowledgeable human agents" (Giddens, 1984:17). As a result, rules and resources manifest themselves at both the macro level of social systems and the micro level of human consciousness.

We are now ready for the concept of *structuration,* which is premised on the idea that "[t]he constitution of agents and structures are not two independently given sets of phenomena, a dualism, but represent a duality . . . the structural properties of social systems are both medium and outcome of the practices they recursively organize," or "the moment of the production of action is also one of reproduction in the contexts of the day-to-day enactment of social life" (Giddens, 1984:25, 26). It is clear that structuration involves the dialectical relationship between structure and agency (Rachlin, 1991). Structure and agency are a duality; neither can exist without the other.

As has already been indicated, *time* and *space* are crucial variables in Giddens's theory. Both depend on whether other people are present temporally or spatially. The primordial condition is face-to-face interaction, in which others are present at the same time and in the same space. However, social systems extend in time and space, and so others may no longer be present. Such distancing in terms of time and space is made increasingly possible in the modern world by new forms of communication and transportation. Gregory (1989) argues that Giddens devotes more attention to time than to space. Underscoring the importance of space, Saunders contends that "any sociological analysis of *why* and *how* things happen will need to take account of *where* (and when) they happen" (1989:218). The central sociological issue of social order depends on how well social systems are integrated over time and across space. One of Giddens's most widely recognized achievements in social theory is his effort to bring the issues of time and space to the fore (Bryant and Jary, 2001a).

We end this section by bringing Giddens's very abstract structuration theory closer to reality by discussing the research program that can be derived from it. (For an overview of empirical research based on structuration theory see Bryant and Jary, 2001b.) First, instead of focusing on human societies, structuration theory would concentrate on "the orderings of institutions across time and space" (Giddens, 1989:300). (Institutions are viewed by Giddens as clusters of practices, and he identifies four of them—symbolic orders, political institutions, economic institutions, and law.) Second, there would be a focal concern for changes in institutions over time and space. Third, researchers would need to be sensitive to the ways in which the leaders of various institutions intrude on and alter social patterns. Fourth, structurationists would need to monitor, and be sensitive to, the impact of their findings on the social world. Most generally, Giddens is deeply concerned with the "shattering impact of modernity" (1989:301), and the structurationist should be concerned with the study of this pressing social problem.

There is much more to structuration theory than can be presented here; Giddens goes into great detail about the elements of the theory already outlined and discusses many others as well. Along the way he analyzes, integrates, and/or critiques a wide range of theoretical ideas. More recently, he has been devoting increasing attention to utilizing his theory for critical analysis of the modern world (Giddens, 1990, 1991, 1992; see Chapter 11). Unlike many others, Giddens has gone beyond a program statement for agency-structure integration; he has given a detailed analysis of its various elements and, more important, has focused on the nature of the interrelationship. What is most satisfying about Giddens's approach is the fact that his key concern, structuration, is defined in inherently integrative terms. The constitutions of agents and structures are not independent of one another; the properties of social systems are seen as both medium and outcome of the practices of actors, and those system properties recursively organize the practices of actors.

Layder, Ashton, and Sung (1991) have sought empirical evidence of Giddens's structuration theory in a study of the transition from school to work. Although they generally support his theoretical approach, their most important conclusion is that structure and agency are not as intertwined as Giddens suggests: "Thus we conclude that empirically structure and action are interdependent (and thus, deeply implicated in each other), *but partly autonomous and separable domains*" (Layder, Ashton, and Sung, 1991:461; italics added).

Criticisms   Ian Craib (1992) has offered the most systematic criticism of Giddens's structuration theory (for a more general critique, see Mestrovic, 1998). First, Craib argues that because Giddens focuses on social practices, his work lacks "ontological depth." That is, Giddens fails to get at the social structures that underlie the social world. Second, his effort at theoretical synthesis does not mesh well with the complexity of the social world. To deal with this complexity, instead of a single synthetic theory "we require a range of theories that might be quite incompatible" (Craib, 1992:178). The social world is also, in Craib's view, quite messy, and that messiness cannot be dealt with adequately by a single, conceptually neat approach like structuration theory. Giddens's approach also serves to limit the potential contributions that could be derived by employing the full range of sociological theories. In rejecting metatheories such as positivism and theories such as structural functionalism, Giddens is unable to derive useful ideas from them. Even when he does draw upon other theories, Giddens uses only some aspects of those theories, and as a result, he does not get all he can out of them. Third, since Giddens offers no base point from which he can operate, he lacks an adequate basis for critical analysis of modern society (see Chapter 11). As a result, his criticisms tend to have an ad hoc quality rather than emanating systematically from a coherent theoretical core. Fourth, Giddens's theory, in the end, seems quite fragmented. His eclecticism leads him to accumulate various theoretical bits and pieces that do not necessarily hold together well. Finally, it is difficult, if not impossible, to know exactly what Giddens is talking about (Mestrovic, 1998:207). Many times throughout his analysis, Craib indicates that he is unsure about, is guessing at, Giddens's meaning.

Given the number and severity of the criticisms, Craib asks, Why, then, deal with structuration theory at all? He offers two basic reasons. First, many of Giddens's ideas (for example, structures as both constraining and enabling) have become integral parts of contemporary sociology. Second, anyone working in social theory today needs to take into account, and respond to, Giddens's work. Craib closes with the faintest of praise for Giddens's work: "I find it difficult to conceive of any social theory that would not find *something* in his work on which to build. *For the time being,* at any rate, structuration theory will be the food at the centre of the plate" (1992:196; italics added).

Habitus and Field 惯习和场域

Pierre Bourdieu's (1984a:483; Calhoun, 2000) theory was animated by the desire to overcome what Bourdieu considered to be the false opposition between objectivism and subjectivism, or in his words, the "absurd opposition between individual and society" (Bourdieu, 1990:31). As he put it, "the most steadfast (and, in my eyes, the most important) intention guiding my work has been to overcome the opposition between objectivism and subjectivism" (1989:15).

He placed Durkheim and his study of social facts (see Chapter 1) and the structuralism of Saussure, Lévi-Strauss, and the structural Marxists (see Chapter 13) within the objectivist camp. These perspectives are criticized for focusing on objective structures and ignoring the process of social construction by which actors perceive, think about, and construct these structures and then proceed to act on that basis. Objectivists ignore agency and the agent, whereas Bourdieu favored a position that is structuralist without losing sight of the agent. "My intention was to bring real-life actors back in who had vanished at the hands of Lévi-Strauss and other structuralists, especially Althusser" (Bourdieu, cited in Jenkins, 1992:18).

This goal moved Bourdieu (1980/1990:42) in the direction of a subjectivist position, one that during his days as a student was dominated by Sartre's existentialism. In addition, Schutz's phenomenology, Blumer's symbolic interactionism, and Garfinkel's ethnomethodology are thought of as examples of subjectivism, focusing on the way agents think about, account for, or represent the social world while ignoring the objective structures in which those processes exist. Bourdieu saw these theories as concentrating on agency and ignoring structure.

Instead, Bourdieu focused on the dialectical relationship between objective structures and subjective phenomena:

> On the one hand, the objective structures . . . form the basis for . . . representations and constitute the structural constraints that bear upon interactions: but, on the other hand, these representations must also be taken into consideration, particularly if one wants to account for the daily struggles, individual and collective, which purport to transform or to preserve these structures.
>
> (Bourdieu, 1989:15)

To sidestep the objectivist-subjectivist dilemma, Bourdieu (1977:3) focused on *practice,* which he saw as the outcome of the dialectical relationship between structure and agency. Practices are not objectively determined, nor are they the product of free will. (Another reason for Bourdieu's focus on practice is that such a concern avoids the often irrelevant intellectualism that he associated with objectivism and subjectivism.)

Reflecting his interest in the dialectic between structure and the way people construct social reality, Bourdieu labeled his own orientation "constructivist structuralism," "structuralist constructivism," or "genetic structuralism." Here is the way Bourdieu defined genetic structuralism:

> The analysis of objective structures—those of different fields—is inseparable from the analysis of the genesis, within biological individuals, of the mental structures which are to some extent the product of the incorporation of social structures; inseparable, too, from the analysis of the genesis of these social structures themselves: the social space, and of the groups that occupy it, are the products of historical struggles (in which agents participate in accordance with their position in the social space and with the mental structures through which they apprehend this space).
>
> (Bourdieu, 1990:14)

PIERRE BOURDIEU

A Biographical Sketch

Born in a small rural town in southeast France in 1930, Bourdieu grew up in a lower-middle-class household (his father was a civil servant) (Monnier, 2007; Jenkins, 2005a). In the early 1950s he attended, and received a degree from, a prestigious teaching college in Paris, Ecole Normale Superieure. However, he refused to write a thesis, in part because he objected to the mediocre quality of his education and to the authoritarian structure of the school. He was put off by, and was active in the opposition against, the strong communist, especially Stalinist, orientation of the school.

Bourdieu taught briefly in a provincial school but was drafted in 1956 and spent two years in Algeria with the French Army. He wrote a book about his experiences and remained in Algeria for two years after his army tenure was over. He returned to France in 1960 and worked for a year as an assistant at the University of Paris. He attended the lectures of the anthropologist Lévi-Strauss at College de France and worked as an assistant to the sociologist Raymond Aron. Bourdieu moved to the University of Lille for three years and then returned to the powerful position of Director of Studies at L'Ecole Practique des Hautes Etudes in 1964.

In the succeeding years Bourdieu became a major figure in Parisian, French, and ultimately world intellectual circles. His work has had an impact on a number of different fields, including education, anthropology, and sociology. He gathered a group of disciples around him in the 1960s, and since then his followers have collaborated with him and made intellectual contributions of their own. In 1968 the Centre de Sociologie Européenne was founded, and Bourdieu was its director until his death. Associated with the center was a unique publishing venture, *Actes de la Recherche en Sciences Sociales,* that has been an important outlet for the work of Bourdieu and his supporters.

When Raymond Aron retired in 1981, the prestigious chair in sociology at College de France became open, and most of the leading French sociologists (for example, Raymond Boudon and Alain Touraine) were in competition for it. However, the chair was awarded to Bourdieu (Jenkins, 1992). In the time that followed, Bourdieu was, if anything, even more prolific than before, and his reputation continued to grow (for more on Bourdieu, see Swartz, 1997:15–51).

An interesting aspect of Bourdieu's work is the way in which his ideas were shaped in ongoing, sometimes explicit and sometimes implicit, dialogue with others. For example, many of his early ideas were formed in a dialogue with two of the leading scholars of the day during his years of training—Jean-Paul Sartre and Claude Lévi-Strauss. From the existentialism of Sartre, Bourdieu got a strong sense of actors as creators of their social worlds. However, Bourdieu felt that Sartre had gone too far and accorded the actors too much power and in the process ignored the structural constraints on them. Pulled in the direction of structure, Bourdieu naturally turned to the work of the preeminent structuralist, Lévi-Strauss. At first Bourdieu was strongly drawn to this orientation; in fact, he described himself for a time as a "'blissful structuralist'" (cited in Jenkins, 1992:17). However, some of his early research led him to the conclusion that structuralism was as limiting, albeit in a different direction, as existentialism. He objected to the fact that the structuralists saw themselves as privileged observers of people who are presumed to be controlled by structures of which they are unconscious. Bourdieu came to have little regard for a field that focused solely on such structural constraints, saying that sociology

> would perhaps not be worth an hour's trouble if it solely had as its end the intention of exposing the wires which activate the individuals it observes—if it forgot that it has to do with men, even those who, like puppets, play a game of which they do not know the rules—if, in short, it did not give itself the task of restoring to men the meaning of their actions.
>
> (Bourdieu, cited in Robbins, 1991:37)

Bourdieu defined one of his basic objectives in reaction to the excesses of structuralism: "'My intention was to bring real-life actors back in who had vanished at the hands of Lévi-Strauss and other structuralists . . . through being considered as epiphenomena of structures'" (cited in Jenkins, 1992:17–18). In other words, Bourdieu wanted to integrate at least a part of Sartre's existentialism with Lévi-Strauss's structuralism.

Bourdieu's thinking also was profoundly shaped by Marxian theory and the Marxists. As we have seen, as a student Bourdieu objected to some of the excesses of the Marxists, and he later rejected the ideas of structural Marxism. While Bourdieu cannot be thought of as a Marxist, there are certainly ideas derived from Marxian theory that run through his work. Most notable is his emphasis on practice (praxis) and his desire to integrate theory and (research) practice in his sociology. (It could be said that instead of existentialism or structuralism, Bourdieu is doing "praxeology.") There is also a liberationist strand in his work in which he can be seen as being interested in freeing people from political and class domination. But, as was the case with Sartre and Lévi-Strauss, Bourdieu can best be seen as creating his ideas by using Marx and the Marxists as a point of departure.

There are traces of the influence of other theorists in his work, especially that of Weber and of the leading French sociological theorist, Emile Durkheim. However, Bourdieu resisted being labeled as a Marxian, Weberian, Durkheimian, or anything else. He regarded such labels as limiting, oversimplifying, and doing violence to his work. In a sense, Bourdieu developed his ideas in a critical dialogue that started while he was a student and continued throughout his life: "Everything that I have done in sociology and anthropology I have done as much against what I was taught as thanks to it" (Bourdieu, in Bourdieu and Wacquant, 1992:204). Bourdieu died January 23, 2002, at the age of 71.

He subscribed, at least in part, to a structuralist perspective, but it is one that is different from the structuralism of Saussure and Lévi-Strauss (as well as the structural Marxists). While they, in turn, focused on structures in language and culture, Bourdieu argued that structures also exist in the social world itself. Bourdieu saw "objective structures [as] independent of the consciousness and will of agents, which are capable of guiding and constraining their practices or their representations" (1989:14). He simultaneously adopted a constructivist position which allowed him to deal with the genesis of schemes of perception, thought, and action as well as that of social structures.

While Bourdieu sought to bridge structuralism and constructivism, and succeeded to some degree, there is a bias in his work in the direction of structuralism. It is for this reason that he (along with Foucault and others—see Chapter 13) is thought of as a poststructuralist. There is more continuity in his work with structuralism than there is with constructivism. Unlike the approach of most others (for example, phenomenologists, symbolic interactionists), Bourdieu's constructivism ignores subjectivity and intentionality. He thought it important to include within his sociology the way people, on the basis of their position in social space, perceive and construct the social world. However, the perception and construction that take place in the social world are both animated and constrained by structures. This is well reflected in one of his own definitions of his theoretical perspective: "The analysis of objective structures . . . is inseparable from the analysis of the genesis, within biological individuals, of the mental structures which are to some extent the product of the incorporation of social structures; inseparable, too, from the analysis of the genesis of these social structures themselves" (Bourdieu, 1990:14). We can describe what he is interested in as the relationship "between social structures and mental structures" (Bourdieu, 1984a:471).

Thus, some microsociologists would be uncomfortable with Bourdieu's perspective and would see it as little more than a more adequate structuralism. According to Wacquant, "Although the two moments of analysis are equally necessary, they are not equal: epistemological priority is granted objectivist rupture over subjectivist understanding" (1992:11). As Jenkins puts it, "In his sociological heart of hearts he [Bourdieu] is as committed to an objectivist view of the world as the majority of those whose work he so sternly dismisses" (1992:91). Or conversely, "At the end of the day, perhaps the most crucial weakness in Bourdieu's work is his inability to cope with subjectivity" (Jenkins, 1992:97). Yet there is a dynamic actor in Bourdieu's theory, an actor capable of "*intentionless invention* of regulated improvisation" (1977:79). The heart of Bourdieu's work, and of his effort to bridge subjectivism and objectivism, lies in his concepts of habitus and field (Aldridge, 1998), as well as their dialectical relationship to each other (Swartz, 1997). While habitus exist in the minds of actors, fields exist outside their minds. We will examine these two concepts in some detail over the next few pages.

Habitus   We begin with the concept for which Bourdieu is most famous—habitus (Jenkins, 2005b).[8] *Habitus* are the "mental, or cognitive structures" through which

---

[8] This idea was not created by Bourdieu but is, rather, a traditional philosophical idea that he resuscitated (Wacquant, 1989). Habitus can be used to refer to both the singular and the plural.

people deal with the social world. People are endowed with a series of internalized schemes through which they perceive, understand, appreciate, and evaluate the social world. It is through such schemes that people both produce their practices and perceive and evaluate them. Dialectically, habitus are "the product of the internalization of the structures" of the social world (Bourdieu, 1989:18). In fact, we can think of habitus as "internalized, 'embodied' social structures" (Bourdieu, 1984a:468). They are something like a "common sense" (Holton, 2000). They reflect objective divisions in the class structure, such as age groups, genders, and social classes. A habitus is acquired as a result of long-term occupation of a position within the social world. Thus, habitus varies depending on the nature of one's position in that world; not everyone has the same habitus. However, those who occupy the same position within the social world tend to have similar habitus. (To be fair to Bourdieu, we must report that he made statements such as that his work was guided "by the desire to reintroduce the agent's practice, his or her capacity for invention and improvisation" [Bourdieu, 1990:13].) In this sense, habitus also can be a collective phenomenon. The habitus allows people to make sense out of the social world, but the existence of a multitude of habitus means that the social world and its structures do not impose themselves uniformly on all actors.

The habitus available at any given time have been created over the course of collective history: "The habitus, the product of history, produces individual and collective practices, and hence history, in accordance with the schemes engendered by history" (Bourdieu, 1977:82). The habitus manifested in any given individual is acquired over the course of individual history and is a function of the particular point in social history in which it occurs. Habitus is both durable and transposable—that is, transferable from one field to another. However, it is possible for people to have an inappropriate habitus, to suffer from what Bourdieu called *hysteresis*. A good example is someone who is uprooted from an agrarian existence in a contemporary precapitalist society and put to work on Wall Street. The habitus acquired in a precapitalist society would not allow one to cope very well with life on Wall Street.

The habitus both produces and is produced by the social world. On the one hand, habitus is a "structuring structure"; that is, it is a structure that structures the social world. On the other hand, it is a "structured structure"; that is, it is a structure that is structured by the social world. In other terms, Bourdieu describes habitus as the *"dialectic of the internalization of externality and the externalization of internality"* (1977:72). Thus, habitus allowed Bourdieu to escape from having to choose between subjectivism and objectivism, to "escape from under the philosophy of the subject without doing away with the agent . . . as well as from under the philosophy of the structure but without forgetting to take into account the effects it wields upon and through the agent" (Bourdieu and Wacquant, 1992:121–122).

It is practice that mediates between habitus and the social world. On the one hand, it is through practice that the habitus is created; on the other hand, it is as a result of practice that the social world is created. Bourdieu expressed the mediating function of practice when he defined the habitus as "the system of structured and structuring dispositions which is constituted by practice and constantly aimed at practical . . . functions" (cited in Wacquant, 1989:42; see also Bourdieu, 1977:72). While practice tends to shape habitus, habitus, in turn, serves to both unify and generate practice.

Although habitus is an internalized structure that constrains thought and choice of action, it does *not* determine them (Myles, 1999). This lack of determinism is one of the main things that distinguishes Bourdieu's position from that of mainstream structuralists. The habitus merely "suggests" what people should think and what they should choose to do. People engage in a conscious deliberation of options, although this decision-making process reflects the operation of the habitus. The habitus provides the principles by which people make choices and choose the strategies that they will employ in the social world. As Bourdieu and Wacquant picturesquely put it, "people are not fools." However, people are not fully rational either (Bourdieu disdained rational choice theory); they act in a "reasonable" manner—they have practical sense. There is a logic to what people do; it is the "logic of practice" (Bourdieu, 1980/1990).

Robbins underscores the point that practical logic is " 'polythetic'—that is to say that practical logic is capable of sustaining simultaneously a multiplicity of confused and logically (in terms of formal logic) contradictory meanings or theses because the overriding context of its operation is practical" (1991:112). This statement is important not only because it underscores the difference between practical logic and rationality (formal logic) but also because it reminds us of Bourdieu's "relationism." The latter is important in this context because it leads us to recognize that habitus is *not* an unchanging, fixed structure, but rather is adapted by individuals who are constantly changing in the face of the contradictory situations in which they find themselves.

The habitus functions "below the level of consciousness and language, beyond the reach of introspective scrutiny and control by the will" (Bourdieu, 1984a:466). While we are not conscious of habitus and its operation, it manifests itself in our most practical activities, such as the way we eat, walk, talk, and even blow our noses. The habitus operates as a structure, but people do not simply respond mechanically to it or to external structures that are operating on them. Thus, in Bourdieu's approach we avoid the extremes of unpredictable novelty and total determinism.

Field   We turn now to the "field," which Bourdieu thought of relationally rather than structurally. The *field* is a network of relations among the objective positions within it (Bourdieu and Wacquant, 1992:97). These relations exist apart from individual consciousness and will. They are *not* interactions or intersubjective ties among individuals. The occupants of positions may be either agents or institutions, and they are constrained by the structure of the field. There are a number of semiautonomous fields in the social world (for example, artistic [Bourdieu and Darbel, 1969/1990; Fowler, 1997], religious, higher education), all with their own specific logics and all generating among actors a belief about the things that are at stake in a field.

Bourdieu saw the field, by definition, as an arena of battle: "The field is also a field of struggles" (Bourdieu and Wacquant, 1992:101). It is the structure of the field that both "undergirds and guides the strategies whereby the occupants of these positions seek, individually or collectively, to safeguard or improve their position, and to impose the principle of hierarchization most favorable to their own products" (Bourdieu, cited in Wacquant, 1989:40). The field is a type of competitive marketplace in which various kinds of capital (economic, cultural, social, symbolic) are employed and deployed. However, it is the field of power (of politics) that is of the utmost importance; the hierarchy of power relationships within the political field serves to structure all the other fields.

Bourdieu laid out a three-step process for the analysis of a field. The first step, reflecting the primacy of the field of power, is to trace the relationship of any specific field to the political field. The second step is to map the objective structure of the relations among positions within the field. Finally, the analyst should seek to determine the nature of the habitus of the agents who occupy the various types of positions within the field.

The positions of various agents in the field are determined by the amount and relative weight of the capital they possess (Anheier, Gerhards, and Romo, 1995). Bourdieu even used military imagery to describe the field, calling it an arena of "strategic emplacements, fortresses to be defended and captured in a field of struggles" (1984a:244). It is capital that allows one to control one's own fate as well as the fate of others (on the negative aspects of capital, see Portes and Landolt, 1996). Bourdieu usually discussed four types of capital (for a discussion of a slightly different formulation of types of capital applied to the genesis of the state, see Bourdieu, 1994). This idea is, of course, drawn from the economic sphere (Guillory, 2000:32), and the meaning of *economic capital* is obvious. *Cultural capital* "comprises familiarity with and easy use of cultural forms institutionalized [e.g., through the university] at the apex of society's cultural hierarchy" (DiMaggio, 2005:167). *Social capital* consists of valued social relations between people. *Symbolic capital* stems from one's honor and prestige.

Occupants of positions within the field employ a variety of *strategies*. This idea shows, once again, that Bourdieu's actors have at least some freedom: "The habitus does not negate the possibility of *strategic* calculation on the part of agents" (Bourdieu, 1993:5; italics added). However, strategies do not refer "to the purposive and preplanned pursuit of calculated goals . . . but to the active deployment of objectively oriented 'lines of action' that obey regularities and form coherent and socially intelligible patterns, even though they do not follow conscious rules or aim at the premeditated goals posited by a strategist" (Wacquant, 1992:25). It is via strategies that "the occupants of these positions seek, individually or collectively, to safeguard or improve their position and to impose the principle of hierarchization most favorable to their own products. The strategies of agents depend on their positions in the field" (Bourdieu and Wacquant, 1992:101).

Bourdieu saw the state as the site of the struggle over the monopoly of what he called *symbolic violence*. This is a "soft" form of violence—"violence which is exercised upon a social agent with his or her complicity" (Bourdieu and Wacquant, 1992:167). Symbolic violence is practiced indirectly, largely through cultural mechanisms, and stands in contrast to the more direct forms of social control that sociologists often focus on. The educational system is the major institution through which symbolic violence is practiced on people (Bourdieu and Passeron, 1970/1990; for an application of the idea of symbolic violence to the status of women, see Krais, 1993). The language, the meanings, the symbolic system of those in power are imposed on the rest of the population. This serves to buttress the position of those in power by, among other things, obscuring what they are doing from the rest of society and getting "the dominated [to] accept as legitimate their own condition of domination" (Swartz, 1997:89). More generally, Bourdieu (1996) saw the educational system as deeply implicated in reproducing existing power and class relations. It is in his ideas on symbolic violence that the political aspect of Bourdieu's work is clearest. That is, Bourdieu was interested in the emancipation of people from this violence and, more generally, from class and political domination (Postone, LiPuma, and Calhoun, 1993:6). Yet Bourdieu was no naive utopian; a better description of his position might be "reasoned utopianism" (Bourdieu and Wacquant, 1992:197).

In underscoring the importance of *both* habitus and field, Bourdieu rejected the split between methodological individualists and methodological holists and adopted a position that has been termed "methodological relationism" (Ritzer and Gindoff, 1992). That is, Bourdieu was focally concerned with the *relationship* between habitus and field. He saw this as operating in two main ways. On the one hand, the field *conditions* the habitus; on the other hand, the habitus *constitutes* the field as something that is meaningful, that has sense and value, and that is worth the investment of energy.

Applying Habitus and Field   Bourdieu did not simply seek to develop an abstract theoretical system; he also related it to a series of empirical concerns and thereby avoided the trap of pure intellectualism. We will illustrate the application of his theoretical approach in his empirical study *Distinction* (1984a), which examines the aesthetic preferences of different groups throughout society (for another application, see *Homo Academicus* [Bourdieu, 1984b]).

Distinction 区隔
In this work, Bourdieu attempted, among other things, to demonstrate that culture can be a legitimate object of scientific study. He attempted to reintegrate culture in the sense of "high culture" (for example, preferences for classical music) with the anthropological sense of culture, which looks at all its forms, both high and low. More specifically, in this work Bourdieu linked taste for refined objects with taste for the most basic food flavors.

Because of structural invariants, especially field and habitus, the cultural preferences of the various groups within society (especially classes and fractions of classes) constitute coherent systems. Bourdieu was focally concerned with variations in aesthetic "taste," the acquired disposition to differentiate among the various cultural objects of aesthetic enjoyment and to appreciate them differentially. Taste is also practice that serves, among other things, to give an individual, as well as others, a sense of his or her place in the social order. Taste serves to unify those with similar preferences and to differentiate them from those with different tastes. That is, through the practical applications and implications of taste, people classify objects and thereby, in the process, classify themselves. We are able to categorize people by the tastes they manifest, for example, by their preferences for different types of music or movies.

These practices, like all others, need to be seen in the context of all mutual relationships, that is, within the totality. Thus, seemingly isolated tastes for art or movies are related to preferences in food, sports, or hairstyles.

Two interrelated fields are involved in Bourdieu's study of taste—class relationships (especially within fractions of the dominant class) and cultural relationships (for a critique of this distinction, see Erickson, 1996). He saw these fields as a series of positions in which a variety of "games" are undertaken. The actions taken by the agents (individual or collective) who occupy specific positions are governed by the structure of the field, the nature of the positions, and the interests associated with them. However, it is also a game that involves self-positioning and the use of a wide range of strategies to allow one to excel at the game. Taste is an opportunity both to experience and to assert one's position within the field. But the field of social class has a profound effect on one's ability to play this game; those in the higher classes are far better able to have their tastes accepted and to oppose the tastes of those in the lower classes. Thus, the world of cultural works is related to the hierarchical world of social class and is itself both hierarchical and hierarchizing.

Needless to say, Bourdieu also linked taste to his other major concept, habitus. Tastes are shaped far more by these deep-rooted and long-standing dispositions than they are by surface opinions and verbalizations. People's preferences for even such mundane aspects of culture as clothing, furniture, and cooking are shaped by the habitus. And it is these dispositions "that forge the unconscious unity of a class" (Bourdieu, 1984a:77). Bourdieu put this more colorfully later: "Taste is a matchmaker . . . through which a habitus confirms its affinity with other habitus" (1984a:243). Dialectically, of course, it is the structure of the class that shapes the habitus.

While both field and habitus were important to Bourdieu, it is their dialectical relationship that is of utmost importance and significance; field and habitus mutually define one another:

> The dispositions constituting the cultivated habitus are only formed, only function and are only valid in a *field,* in the relationship with a field . . . which is itself a 'field of possible forces,' a 'dynamic' situation in which forces are only manifested in their relationship with certain dispositions. This is why the same practices may receive opposite meanings and values in different fields, in different configurations, or in opposing sectors of the same field.
>
> (Bourdieu, 1984a:94; italics added)

Or, as Bourdieu put it, in more general terms: "There is a strong correlation between social positions and the dispositions of the agents who occupy them" (1984a:110). It is out of the relationship between habitus and field that practices, cultural practices in particular, are established.

Bourdieu saw culture as a kind of economy, or marketplace. In this marketplace people utilize cultural rather than economic capital. This capital is largely a result of people's social class origin and their educational experience. In the marketplace, people accrue more or less capital and either expend it to improve their position or lose it, thereby causing their position within the economy to deteriorate.

People pursue distinction in a range of cultural fields—the beverages they drink (Perrier or cola), the automobiles they drive (Mercedes Benz or Ford Escort), the newspapers they read (*The New York Times* or *USA Today*), and the resorts they visit (the French Riviera or Disney World). Relationships of distinction are objectively inscribed in these products and are reactivated each time they are appropriated. In Bourdieu's view, "The total field of these fields offers well-nighly inexhaustible possibilities for the pursuit of distinction" (1984a:227). The appropriation of certain cultural goods (for example, a Mercedes Benz) yields "profit," while that of others (an Escort) yields no gain, or even a "loss."

Bourdieu (1998:9) took pains to make it clear that he was not simply arguing, following Thorstein Veblen's (1899/1994) famous theory of conspicuous consumption, that the "driving force of all human behavior was the search for distinction." Rather, he contended that his main point "is that to exist within a social space, to occupy a point or to be an individual within a social space, is to differ, to be different . . . being inscribed in the space in question, he or she . . . is endowed with categories of perception, with classificatory schemata, with a certain taste, which permits her to make differences, to discern, to distinguish" (Bourdieu, 1998:9). Thus, for example, one who chooses to own a grand piano is different from one who opts for an accordion. That one choice (the piano) is worthy of distinction while the other (the accordion) is considered vulgar is a result of the dominance of one point of view and the symbolic violence practiced against those who adopt another viewpoint.

There is a dialectic between the nature of cultural products and tastes. Changes in cultural goods lead to alterations in taste, but changes in taste also are likely to result in transformations in cultural products. The structure of the field not only conditions the desires of the consumers of cultural goods but also structures what the producers create in order to satisfy those demands.

Changes in taste (and Bourdieu saw all fields temporally) result from the struggle between opposing forces in both the cultural (the supporters of old versus new fashions, for example) and the class (the dominant versus the dominated fractions within the dominant class) arenas. However, the heart of the struggle lies within the class system, and the cultural struggle between, for example, artists and intellectuals is a reflection of the interminable struggle between the different fractions of the dominant class to define culture, indeed the entire social world. It is oppositions within the class structure that condition oppositions in taste and in habitus. While Bourdieu placed great importance on social class, he refused to reduce it to merely economic matters or to the relations of production but saw class as defined by habitus as well.

Bourdieu offered a distinctive theory of the relationship between agency and structure within the context of a concern for the dialectical relationship between habitus and field. His theory also is distinguished by its focus on practice (in the preceding case, aesthetic practices) and its refusal to engage in arid intellectualism. In that sense it represents a return to the Marxian concern for the relationship between theory and practice.

Concluding Thoughts 最后的一些想法

Bourdieu was one thinker (another is Garfinkel) who was considered a theorist but who rejected that label. He said that he was not "producing a general discourse on the social world" (Bourdieu and Wacquant, 1992:159). Bourdieu rejected pure theory that lacks an empirical base, but he also disdained pure empiricism performed in a theoretical vacuum. Rather, he saw himself engaged in research which was "inseparably empirical and theoretical . . . research without theory is blind, and theory without research is empty" (Bourdieu and Wacquant, 1992:160, 162).

Overall, we find ourselves in accord with Jenkins when he argues that "Bourdieu's intellectual project is longstanding, relatively coherent and cumulative. It amounts to nothing less than an attempt to construct a theory of social practice and society" (1992:67). Calhoun sees Bourdieu as a critical theorist, which in this context is defined more broadly than simply those associated with the Frankfurt school. Calhoun defines critical theory as "the project of social theory that undertakes simultaneously critique of received categories, critique of theoretical practice, and critical substantive analysis of social life in terms of the possible, not just the actual" (1993:63).

Although Bourdieu offered a theory, his theory does not have universal validity. For example, he said that there are "no transhistoric laws of the relations between fields" (Bourdieu and Wacquant, 1992:109). The nature of the actual relations between fields is always an empirical question. Similarly, the nature of habitus changes with altered historical circumstances: "Habitus . . . is a transcendental but a historical transcendental bound up with the structure and history of a field" (Bourdieu and Wacquant, 1992:189).

Colonization of the Life-World 生活—世界的殖民

We discussed Habermas's earlier ideas in Chapter 4, on neo-Marxian theory, in the section titled "Critical Theory." While, as we will see, Habermas's perspective can still be thought of, at least in part, as being a neo-Marxian orientation (McBride, 2000), it has broadened considerably and is increasingly difficult to contain within that, or any other, theoretical category. Habermas's theory has grown and become more diverse as Habermas has addressed, and incorporated, the ideas of a wide range of sociological theorists, most recently and most notably those of George Herbert Mead, Talcott Parsons, Alfred Schutz, and Emile Durkheim. In spite of the difficulties involved in categorizing Habermas's innovative theoretical perspective, we will discuss his most recent ideas, which can be broadly thought of as the "colonization of the life-world," under the heading "agency-structure issue." Habermas (1991:251) makes it clear that he is engaging in "paradigm combination"; that is, he is creating his agency-structure perspective by integrating ideas drawn from action theory and systems theory. It is, at least in part, in his thoughts on the life-world that Habermas deals with agency. Structure is dealt with primarily in Habermas's ideas on the social system, which, as we will see, is the force that is colonizing the life-world. What does Habermas mean by *life-world, system,* and *colonization?* We address these phenomena and their interrelationship, as well as other key ideas in Habermas's most recent theorizing, in this section.

Before we get to these concepts, it should be made clear that Habermas's major focus continues to be on communicative action. Free and open communication remains both his theoretical baseline and his political objective. It also has the methodological function, much like Weber's ideal types, of allowing him to analyze variations from the model: "The construction of an unlimited and undistorted discourse can serve at most as a foil for setting off more glaringly the rather ambiguous developmental tendencies in modern society" (Habermas, 1987a:107). Indeed, his focal interest in the colonization of the life-world is in the ways in which that process is adversely affecting free communication.

Habermas also retains an interest in the Weberian process of rationalization, specifically the issue of the differential rationalization of life-world and system and the impact of this difference on the colonization of the former by the latter (for a somewhat counter view, see Bartos, 1996). In Weberian terms, the *system* is the domain of formal rationality, while the *life-world* is the site of substantive rationality. The *colonization of the life-world,* therefore, involves a restatement of the Weberian thesis that in the modern world, formal rationality is triumphing over substantive rationality and coming to dominate areas that formerly were defined by substantive rationality. Thus, while Habermas's theory has taken some interesting new turns, it retains its theoretical roots, especially in its Marxian and Weberian orientations.

The Life-World   This concept is derived from phenomenological sociology in general and, more specifically, the theories of Alfred Schutz (Bowring, 1996). But Habermas interprets the ideas of George Herbert Mead as also contributing to insights about the life-world. To Habermas, the life-world represents an internal perspective (while, as we will see, the system represents an external viewpoint): "Society is conceived from the perspective of the acting subject" (1987a:117). Thus, there is only one society; life-world and system are simply different ways of looking at it.

Habermas views the life-world and communicative action as "complementary" concepts. More specifically, communicative action can be seen as occurring within the life-world:

> The lifeworld is, so to speak, the transcendental site where speaker and hearer
> meet, where they reciprocally raise claims that their utterances fit the world . . .
> and where they can criticize and confirm those validity claims, settle their
> disagreements, and arrive at agreements.
>
> (Habermas, 1987a:126)

The life-world is a "context-forming background of processes of reaching understanding" through communicative action (Habermas, 1987a:204). It involves a wide range of unspoken presuppositions about mutual understanding that must exist and be mutually understood for communication to take place.

Habermas is concerned with the rationalization of the life-world, which involves, for one thing, increasingly rational communication in the life-world. He believes that the more rational the life-world becomes, the more likely it is that interaction will be controlled by "rationally motivated mutual understanding." Such understanding, or a rational method of achieving consensus, is based ultimately on the authority of the better argument.

Habermas sees the rationalization of the life-world as involving the progressive differentiation of its various elements. The life-world is composed of culture, society, and personality (note the influence of Parsons and his action systems). Each of these refers to interpretive patterns, or background assumptions, about culture and its effect on action, appropriate patterns of social relations (society), and what people are like (personality) and how they are supposed to behave. Engaging in communicative action and achieving understanding in terms of each of these themes lead to the reproduction of the life-world through the reinforcement of culture, the integration of society, and the formation of personality. While these components are closely intertwined in archaic societies, the rationalization of the life-world involves the "growing differentiation between culture, society and personality" (Habermas, 1987a:288).

System While the life-world represents the viewpoint of acting subjects on society, system involves an external perspective that views society "from the observer's perspective of someone not involved" (Habermas, 1987a:117). In analyzing systems, we are attuned to the interconnection of actions, as well as the functional significance of actions and their contributions to the maintenance of the system. Each of the major components of the life-world (culture, society, personality) has corresponding elements in the system. Cultural reproduction, social integration, and personality formation take place at the system level.

The system has its roots in the life-world, but ultimately it comes to develop its own structural characteristics. Examples of such structures include the family, the judiciary, the state, and the economy. As these structures evolve, they grow more and more distant from the life-world. As in the life-world, rationalization at the system level involves progressive differentiation and greater complexity. These structures also grow more self-sufficient. As they grow in power, they exercise more and more steering capacity over the life-world. They come to have less and less to do with the process of achieving consensus and, in fact, limit the occurrence of that process in the life-world. In other words, these rational structures, instead of enhancing the capacity to communicate and reach understanding, threaten those processes through the exertion of external control over them.

Social Integration and System Integration Given the preceding discussion of life-world and system, Habermas concludes: "*The fundamental problem of social theory is how to connect in a satisfactory way the two conceptual strategies indicated by the notions of 'system' and 'lifeworld'*" (1987a:151; italics added). Habermas labels those two conceptual strategies "social integration" and "system integration."

The perspective of *social integration* focuses on the life-world and the ways in which the action system is integrated through either normatively guaranteed or communicatively achieved consensus. Theorists who believe that society is integrated through social integration begin with communicative action and see society *as* the life-world. They adopt the internal perspective of the group members, and they employ a hermeneutic approach in order to be able to relate their understanding to that of the members of the life-world. The ongoing reproduction of society is seen as being a result of the actions undertaken by members of the life-world to maintain its symbolic structures. It also is seen only from their perspective. Thus, what is lost in this hermeneutic approach is the outsider's viewpoint as well as a sense of the reproductive processes that are occurring at the system level.

The perspective of *system integration* is focally concerned with the system and the way in which it is integrated through external control over individual decisions that are not subjectively coordinated. Those who adopt this perspective see society as a self-regulating system. They adopt the external perspective of the observer, but this perspective prohibits them from really getting at the structural patterns that can be understood only hermeneutically from the internal perspective of members of the life-world.

Thus, Habermas concludes that while each of these two broad perspectives has something to offer, both have serious limitations. On the basis of his critique of social and system integration, Habermas offers his alternative, which seeks to integrate these two theoretical orientations: he sees

> society as a system that has to fulfill conditions for the maintenance of sociocultural lifeworlds. The formula-societies are *systematically stabilized* complexes of action of *socially integrated* groups. . . . [I] stand for the heuristic proposal that we view society as an entity that, in the course of social evolution, gets differentiated *both* as a *system* and a *lifeworld.*
>
> (Habermas, 1987a:151–152; italics added)

Having argued that he is interested in *both* system and life-world, Habermas makes it clear at the end of the above quotation that he is also concerned with the evolution of the two. While both evolve in the direction of increasing rationalization, that rationalization takes different forms in life-world and system, and that differentiation is the basis of the colonization of the life-world.

Colonization   Crucial to the understanding of the idea of colonization is the fact that Habermas sees society as being composed of *both* life-world and system. Furthermore, while both concepts were closely intertwined in earlier history, today there is an increasing divergence between them; they have become "decoupled." While both have undergone the process of rationalization, that process has taken different forms in the two settings. Although Habermas sees a dialectical relationship between system and life-world (they both limit and open up new possibilities for each other), his main concern is with the way in which system in the modern world has come to control the life-world. In other words, he is interested in the breakdown of the dialectic between system and life-world and the growing power of the former over the latter.[9]

Habermas contrasts the increasing rationality of system and life-world. The rationalization of the life-world involves growth in the rationality of communicative action. Furthermore, action that is oriented toward achieving mutual understanding is increasingly freed from normative constraint and relies more and more on everyday language. In other words, social integration is achieved more and more through the processes of consensus formation in language.

But the result of this is the fact that the demands on language grow and come to overwhelm its capacities. Delinguistified media (especially money in the economic system and power in the political system and its administrative apparatus)—having

---

[9] However, Habermas also sees problems (domination, self-deception) *within* the life-world (Outhwaite, 1994:116).

become differentiated in, and emanating from, the system—come to fill the void and replace, to at least some degree, everyday language. Instead of language coordinating action, it is money and power that perform that function. Life becomes monetarized and bureaucratized.

More generally, the increasingly complex system "unleashes system imperatives that burst the capacity of the lifeworld they instrumentalize" (Habermas, 1987a:155). Thus, Habermas writes of the "violence" exercised over the life-world by the system through the ways in which it restricts communication. This violence, in turn, produces "pathologies" within the life-world. Habermas embeds this development within a view of the history of the world:

> The far-reaching uncoupling of system and lifeworld was a necessary condition for the transition from the stratified class societies of European feudalism to the economic class societies of the early modern period; but the capitalist pattern of modernization is marked by a *deformation,* a reification of the symbolic structures of the lifeworld under the imperatives of subsystems differentiated out via money and power and rendered self-sufficient.
>
> (Habermas, 1987a:283; italics added)

It might be noted that by linking the deformities to capitalism, Habermas continues, at least in this sense, to operate within a neo-Marxian framework. However, when he looks at the modern world, Habermas is forced to abandon a Marxian approach (Sitton, 1996), since he concludes that the deformation of the life-world is "no longer localizable in any class-specific ways" (1987a:333). Given this limitation, and in line with his roots in critical theory, Habermas demonstrates that his work also is strongly influenced by Weberian theory. In fact, he argues that the distinction between life-world and system, along with the ultimate colonization of the life-world, allows us to see in a new light the Weberian thesis "of a modernity at variance with itself" (Habermas, 1987a:299). In Weber, this conflict exists primarily between substantive and formal rationality and the triumph in the West of the latter over the former. To Habermas, the rationalization of the system comes to triumph over the rationalization of the life-world, with the result that the life-world comes to be colonized by the system.

Habermas adds specificity to his thoughts on colonization by arguing that the main forces in the process are "formally organized domains of action" at the system level, such as the economy and the state. In traditional Marxian terms, Habermas sees modern society as subject to recurrent systemic crises. In seeking to deal with these crises, institutions such as the state and the economy undertake actions that adversely affect the life-world, leading to pathologies and crises within it. Basically, the life-world comes to be denuded by these systems, and communicative action comes to be less and less directed toward the achievement of consensus. Communication becomes increasingly rigidified, impoverished, and fragmented, and the life-world itself seems poised on the brink of dissolution. This assault on the life-world worries Habermas greatly, given his concern for the communicative action that takes place within it. However, no matter how extensive the colonization by the system, the life-world is "never completely husked away" (Habermas, 1987a:311).

If the essential problem in the modern world is the uncoupling of system and life-world and the domination of the life-world by the system, the solutions are clear-cut. On the one hand, life-world and system need to be recoupled. On the other hand, the dialectic between system and life-world needs to be reinstated so that instead of the latter being deformed by the former, the two become mutually enriching and enhancing. While the two were intertwined in primitive society, the rationalization process that has occurred in both system and life-world makes it possible that the future recoupling will produce a level of system, life-world, and their interrelationship unprecedented in human history.

Thus, once again, Habermas is back to his Marxian roots. Marx, of course, did not look back in history for the ideal state but saw it in the future in the form of communism and the full flowering of species-being. Habermas, too, does not look back to archaic societies where nonrationalized system and life-world were more unified but looks to a future state involving the far more satisfactory unification of rationalized system and life-world.

Habermas also reinterprets the Marxian theory of basic struggles within society. Marx, of course, emphasized the conflict between proletariat and capitalist and traced it to the exploitative character of the capitalist system. Habermas focuses not on exploitation but on colonization and sees many of the struggles of recent decades in this light. That is, he sees social movements such as those oriented to greater equality, increased self-realization, the preservation of the environment, and peace "as reactions to system assaults on the lifeworld. Despite the diversity of interests and political projects of these heterogeneous groups, they have resisted the colonization of the life-world" (Seidman, 1989:25). The hope for the future clearly lies in resistance to the encroachments on the life-world and in the creation of a world in which system and life-world are in harmony and serve to mutually enrich one another to a historically unprecedented degree.

能动—结构文献中的主要差别
Major Differences in the Agency-Structure Literature

As is the case with work on micro-macro integration in the United States, there are significant differences among Europeans working on the agency-structure issue. For example, there is considerable disagreement in the literature on the nature of the agent. Most of those working in this realm (for example, Giddens, Bourdieu) tend to treat the agent as an individual actor, but Touraine's "actionalist sociology" treats collectivities such as social classes as agents. In fact, Touraine defines *agency* as "an organization directly implementing one or more elements of the system of historical action and therefore intervening directly in the relations of social domination" (1977:459). A third, middle-ground position on this issue is taken by Burns and Flam (see also Crozier and Friedberg, 1980), who regard either individuals or collectivities as agents.

There is considerable disagreement even among those who focus on the individual actor as agent. For example, Bourdieu's agent, dominated by habitus, seems far more mechanical than Giddens's (or Habermas's) agent. Bourdieu's habitus involves "systems of durable, transposable *dispositions,* structuring structures, that is, as principles of the generation and structuring of practices and representations"

(1977:72). The habitus is a source of strategies "without being the product of a genuine strategic intention" (Bourdieu, 1977:73). It is neither subjectivistic nor objectivistic but combines elements of both. It clearly rejects the idea of an actor with "the free and willful power to constitute" (Bourdieu, 1977:73). Giddens's agents may not have intentionality and free will either, but they have much more willful power than do Bourdieu's. Where Bourdieu's agents seem to be dominated by their habitus, by internal ("structuring") structures, the agents in Giddens's work are the perpetrators of action. They have at least some choice, at least the possibility of acting differently than they do. They have power, and they make a difference in their worlds (see also Lukes, 1977). Most important, they constitute (and are constituted by) structures. In contrast, in Bourdieu's work a sometimes seemingly disembodied habitus is involved in a dialectic with the external world.[10]

Similarly, there are marked disagreements among agency-structure theorists on precisely what they mean by structure.[11] Some adopt a specific structure as central, such as the organization in the work of Crozier and Friedberg and Touraine's relations of social domination as found in political institutions and organizations; others (for example, Burns, 1986:13) focus on an array of social structures, such as bureaucracy, the polity, the economy, and religion. Giddens offers a very idiosyncratic definition of *structure* ("recursively organized sets of rules and resources" [1984:25]) that is at odds with virtually every other definition in the literature (Layder, 1985). However, his definition of *systems* as reproduced social practices is very close to what many sociologists mean by structure. In addition to the differences among those working with structure, differences exist between these theorists and others.

The attempts at agency-structure linkage flow from a variety of very different theoretical directions. For example, within social theory Giddens seems to be animated by functionalism and structuralism versus phenomenology, existentialism, and ethnomethodology and, more generally, by new linguistic structuralism, semiotics, and hermeneutics (Archer, 1982). Bourdieu seeks to find a satisfactory alternative to subjectivism and objectivism in anthropological theory. Habermas seeks to synthesize ideas derived from Marx, Weber, critical theorists, Durkheim, Mead, Schutz, and Parsons.

There is a strain toward either the agency or the structural direction in Europe. Certainly Bourdieu is pulling strongly in the direction of structure, while Giddens has a more powerful sense of agency than do most other theorists of this genre (Layder, 1985:131). In spite of the existence of pulls in the directions of agency and structure, what is distinctive about the European work on agency and structure, compared with American micro-macro work, is a much stronger sense of the need to refuse to separate the two and to deal with them dialectically (for example, Giddens, Bourdieu, Habermas). In the American micro-macro literature, one parallel to the European efforts to deal with agency and structure dialectically is my attempt to deal dialectically with the integration of the micro-macro and objective-subjective continua.

---

[10] Although we are emphasizing the differences between Giddens and Bourdieu on agency, Giddens (1979:217) sees at least some similarities between the two perspectives.

[11] I am focusing here mainly on Europeans who deal with social structure and not those who see structure as hidden, underlying elements of culture.

Dietz and Burns (1992) have made an effort to offer a view of agency and structure that reflects the strengths and weaknesses of earlier work. Four criteria must be met in order for agency to be attributed to a social actor.[12] First, the actor must have power; the actor must be able to make a difference. Second, the actions undertaken by an agent must be intentional. Third, the actor must have some choice, some free play. The result is that observers can make only probabilistic statements about what actors may do. Finally, agents must be reflexive, monitoring the effects of their actions and using that knowledge to modify the bases of action. Overall, agency is viewed as a continuum; all actors have agency to some degree, and no actor has full, unconstrained agency.

The other, structural side of the equation, from Dietz and Burns's point of view, consists of the constraints on agency. First, even if an agent can imagine certain actions, they simply may not be possible, given technological and physical realities. Second, structure (especially rules) makes certain actions seem necessary while others appear impossible. Finally, agency is limited by other agents who have sanctioning power, both positive and negative.

能动—结构和微观—宏观连接：根本区别

Agency-Structure and Micro-Macro Linkages: Fundamental Differences

One of the central differences between American and European theorists lies in their images of the actor. What is distinctive about American theory is the much greater influence of behaviorism as well as of exchange theory, which is derived, in part, from a behavioristic perspective. Thus, American theorists share the interest of (some) Europeans in conscious, creative action, but it is limited by a recognition of the importance of mindless behavior. This tendency to see the actor as behaving mindlessly is being enhanced now by the growing interest in rational choice theory in American sociology. The image here is of an actor more or less automatically choosing the most efficient means to ends.[13] The influence of rational choice theory in the United States promises to drive an even greater wedge between European and American conceptions of action and agency.

At the macro/structure level, Europeans have been inclined to focus on social structure. In cases where there has not been a single-minded focus on it, social structure has not been differentiated adequately from culture. (Indeed, this is the motivation behind Archer's [1988] work.) In contrast, there has been a much greater tendency in the United States to deal with *both* structure and culture in efforts aimed at micro-macro integration.

Another difference in the macro/structure issue stems from differences in theoretical influence in the United States and Europe. In the United States, the main influence on thinking on the macro/structure issue has been structural functionalism. The nature of that theory has led American theorists to focus on both large-scale social structures *and* culture. In Europe, the main influence has been structuralism, which

---

[12] Like most other agency-structure theorists, Dietz and Burns downplay or ignore the agent's body (see Shilling and Mellor, 1996; Shilling, 1997).

[13] DeVille (1989) sees such an actor as robotlike.

has a much more wide-ranging sense of structures, extending all the way from micro structures of the mind to macro structures of society. Culture has been of far less importance to structuralists than to structural functionalists.

Another key difference is the fact that the micro-macro issue is subsumable under the broader issue of levels of analysis (Edel, 1959; Jaffee, 1998; Ritzer, 1981a, 1989; Wiley, 1988), while the concern for agency and structure is not. We can clearly think of the micro-macro linkage in terms of some sort of vertical hierarchy, with micro-level phenomena on the bottom, macro-level phenomena at the top, and meso-level entities in between. The agency-structure linkage seems to have no clear connection to the levels-of-analysis issue, since both agency and structure can be found at any level of social analysis.

The agency-structure issue is much more firmly embedded in a historical, dynamic framework than is the micro-macro issue (Sztompka, 1991; again Elias is a clear exception, but of course he is European). In contrast, theorists who deal with micro-macro issues are more likely to depict them in static, hierarchical, ahistorical terms. Nevertheless, at least some of those who choose to depict the micro-macro relationship rather statically make it clear that they understand the dynamic character of the relationship: "The study of levels of social reality and their interrelationship is inherently a *dynamic* rather than a static approach to the social world. . . . A dynamic and historical orientation to the study of levels of the social world can be seen as integral parts of a more general *dialectical* approach" (Ritzer, 1981a:208; see also Wiley, 1988:260). Finally, morality is a central issue to agency-structure theorists but is largely ignored in the micro-macro literature. Agency-structure theory has much more powerful roots in, and a stronger orientation to, philosophy, including its great concern with moral issues. In contrast, micro-macro theory is largely indigenous to sociology and is oriented to the hard sciences as a reference group—areas where moral issues are of far less concern than they are in philosophy.

Summary 总结

The focus in the first part of this chapter is micro-macro integration. This development represents a return to the concerns of the early giants of sociological theory and a move away from the theoretical extremism, either micro or macro, that characterized much of twentieth-century American sociological theory. Little attention was given to the micro-macro issue prior to the 1980s, but during that decade and through the 1990s interest in the topic exploded. The works came from both the micro and the macro extremes as well as various points between them. Some of this work focused on integrating micro and macro theories; the rest was concerned with the linkage between micro and macro levels of social analysis. In addition to this basic difference, there are important differences among those working on integrating theories and levels.

The heart of the first part of this chapter is a discussion of several major examples of work integrating micro and macro levels of social analysis. Two works, those by Alexander and I, develop very similar micro-macro models of the social world. Although there are important differences between these works, their similar images of the social world reflect considerable consensus among those seeking to link micro and macro levels of social analysis. Collins's effort at micro-macro integration is discussed and criticized for its micro reductionism—its tendency to reduce macro phenomena to micro phenomena.

The micro-macro section closes with a detailed examination of the work of one of the European precursors of American work on micro-macro integration—Norbert Elias. Of particular relevance are his thoughts on figurational sociology, as well as his historical-comparative study of the relationship between micro-level manners and macro-level changes in the court and the state.

The second part of this chapter deals with the largely European literature on the agency-structure linkage. This literature has a number of similarities to the American work on micro-macro integration, but there are a number of substantial differences.

Although a large number of contemporary European theorists are dealing with the agency-structure relationship, the bulk of the second part of this chapter is devoted to the work of three major examples of this type of theorizing. The first is Giddens's structuration theory. The core of Giddens's theory is his refusal to treat agents and structures apart from one another; they are seen as being mutually constitutive. We then turn to Bourdieu's theory, which focuses primarily on the relationship between habitus and field. Finally, we analyze Habermas's recent ideas on life-world and system and the colonization of the life-world by the system.

Following a discussion of these specific agency-structure works, we return to a more general treatment of this literature. We begin with a discussion of major differences in this literature, including differing views on the nature of the agent and structure. Another source of difference is the varying theoretical traditions on which these works are based. Some of these works strain in the direction of agency; others pull in the direction of structure.

The next issue is the similarities between the agency-structure and micro-macro literatures. Both literatures share an interest in integration and are wary of the excesses of micro/agency and macro/structural theories. There are, however, far more differences than similarities between these literatures. There are differences in their images of the actor, the ways in which structure is conceived, the theories from which their ideas are derived, the degree to which they may be subsumed under the idea of levels of analysis, the extent to which they are embedded in a historical, dynamic framework, and the degree to which they are concerned with moral issues.

第四部分　从现代社会理论到后现代社会理论（及其之后）

From Modern to Postmodern Social Theory (and Beyond)

Contemporary Theories of Modernity
第11章　关于现代性的当代理论

Chapter Outline
Classical Theorists on Modernity
The Juggernaut of Modernity
The Risk Society
Modernity and the Holocaust
Modernity's Unfinished Project
Informationalism and the Network Society

There is a debate raging in sociology today between those who continue to see contemporary society as a modern world and those who argue that a substantial change has taken place in recent years and that we have moved into a new, postmodern world. Chapters 11 and 13 are devoted to these two theoretical positions. In this chapter we discuss the work of contemporary representatives of those who continue to see the world in modern terms. Chapter 13 will offer an overview of the ideas of some of the most important postmodern theorists.

Classical Theorists on Modernity 古典理论中的现代性

Most of the classical sociologists were engaged in an analysis and critique of modern society. Such analysis is clear, for example, in the work of Marx, Weber, Durkheim, and Simmel. All were working at the point of the emergence and ascendancy of modernity. While all four were well aware of the advantages of modernity, what animated their work most was a critique of the problems posed by the modern world.

For Marx, of course, modernity was defined by the capitalist economy. Marx recognized the advances brought about by the transition from earlier societies to capitalism. However, in his work Marx restricted himself largely to a critique of that economic system and its deformities (alienation, exploitation, and so on).

To Weber, the most defining problem of the modern world was the expansion of formal rationality at the expense of the other types of rationality and the resulting emergence of the iron cage of rationality. People increasingly were being imprisoned in this iron cage and, as a result, were progressively unable to express some of their most human characteristics. Of course, Weber recognized the advantages of the advance of rationalization—for example, the advantages of the bureaucracy over earlier organizational forms—but he was most concerned with the problems posed by rationalization.

In Durkheim's view, modernity was defined by its organic solidarity and the weakening of the collective conscience. While organic solidarity brought with it greater freedom and more productivity, it also posed a series of unique problems. For example, with such a weakening of the common morality, people tended to find themselves adrift meaninglessly in the modern world. In other words, they found themselves to be suffering from anomie.

Georg Simmel, the fourth of the classical theorists, will receive a more detailed treatment here, in large part because he has been described both as a modernist (Frisby, 1992) and as a postmodernist (D. Weinstein and Weinstein, 1993; Jaworski, 1997). Since he fits to some degree in both categories, Simmel represents an important bridge between this chapter and Chapter 13. We will deal with the case for Simmel as a modernist here; in Chapter 13 we will discuss the contention that he is a postmodernist.

Frisby accepts the point of view that "Simmel is the first sociologist of modernity" (1992:59). Simmel is seen as investigating modernity primarily in two major interrelated sites—the city and the money economy. The city is where modernity is concentrated or intensified, whereas the money economy involves the diffusion of modernity, its extension (Frisby, 1992:69).

Poggi (1993) picks up the theme of modernity as it relates to money, especially in Simmel's *Philosophy of Money* (1907/1978). As Poggi sees it, three views of modernity are expressed in that work. The first is that modernization brings with it a series of advantages to human beings, especially the fact that they are able to express various potentialities that are unexpressed, concealed, and repressed in premodern society. In this sense, Simmel sees modernity "as an 'epiphany,' that is, as the express manifestation of powers intrinsic to the human species, but previously unrevealed" (Poggi, 1993:165). Second, Simmel deals with the powerful effect of money on modern society. Finally, there is Simmel's concentration on the adverse consequences of money for modernity, especially alienation. The issue of alienation brings us back to the central issue in Simmel's sociological theory in general, as well as in his sociology of modernity: the "tragedy of culture," the growing gap between objective and subjective culture, or as Simmel put it, " 'the atrophy of individual culture and the hypertrophy of objective culture' " (cited in Frisby, 1992:69).

In Frisby's view, Simmel concentrates on the "experience" of modernity. The key elements of that experience—time, space, and contingent causality—are central aspects of at least some of the contemporary theories of modernity to be discussed in this chapter:

> The experience of modernity is viewed by Simmel as discontinuous of *time* as transitory, in which both the fleeting moment and the sense of presentness converge; *space* as the dialectic of distance and proximity . . . and *causality* as contingent, arbitrary and fortuitous.
>
> (Frisby, 1992:163–164)

While it is certainly possible to view Simmel as a postmodernist, and as we will see in Chapter 13, he does seem to have more in common with postmodernists than do the other classical social theorists, the fact remains that it is at least equally appropriate to see him as a modernist. Almost certainly, the foci of much of his attention—especially the city and the money economy—are at the heart of modernity. Thus, even in the case of Simmel, and certainly in the cases of Marx, Weber, and Durkheim, it is best to think of these theorists as doing sociologies of modernity.

By 1920 all four of these classical sociological theorists were dead. As we move into the twenty-first century, it is obvious that the world is a very different place than it was in 1920. While there is great disagreement over when the postmodern age began (assuming for the moment that it did), no one puts that date before 1920. The issue is whether the changes in the world since that time are modest and continuous with those associated with modernity or are so dramatic and discontinuous that the contemporary world is better described by a new term—postmodern. That issue informs the discussion in this chapter and Chapter 13.

In this chapter we will examine the thoughts of several contemporary theorists (there are many others [for example, Lefebvre, 1962/1995; Touraine, 1995; P. Wagner, 1994; E. M. Wood, 1997] whose work we will not have space to deal with) who in various ways and to varying degrees see the contemporary world as still best described as modern.

The Juggernaut of Modernity 现代性的大碾车

In an effort not only to be consistent with his structuration theory (see Chapter 10) but also to create an image to rival the images of classical thinkers such as Weber and his iron cage, Anthony Giddens (1990; see Mestrovic, 1998, for a bitter critique of Giddens's theory of modernity) has described the modern world (with its origins in seventeenth-century Europe) as a "juggernaut." More specifically, he is using this term to describe an advanced stage of modernity—radical, high, or late modernity. In so doing, Giddens is arguing against those who have contended that we have entered a postmodern age, although he holds out the possibility of some type of postmodernism in the future. However, while we still live in a modern age, in Giddens's view today's world is very different from the world of the classical sociological theorists.

ANTHONY GIDDENS

A Biographical Sketch

Anthony Giddens is Great Britain's most important contemporary social theorist and one of a handful of the
world's most influential theorists (Stones, 2005). Giddens
was born on January 18, 1938 (Clark, Modgil, and
Modgil, 1990). He studied at the University of Hull, the
London School of Economics, and the University of London. Giddens was
appointed lecturer at the University of Leicester in 1961. His early work was
empirical and focused on the issue of suicide. By 1969 he had moved to the
position of lecturer in sociology at the prestigious Cambridge University, as well
as fellow of King's College. He engaged in cross-cultural work that led to the
first of his books to achieve international fame, *The Class Structure of Advanced
Societies* (1975). Over the next decade or so, Giddens published a number of
important theoretical works. In those works he began a step-by-step process of
building his own theoretical perspective, which has come to be known as structuration theory. Those years of work culminated in 1984 with the appearance of
a book, *The Constitution of Society: Outline of the Theory of Structuration,* which
constitutes the most important single statement of Giddens's theoretical perspective. In 1985 Giddens was appointed professor of sociology at the University of
Cambridge.

Giddens has been a force in sociological theory for well over three decades. In
addition, he has played a profound role in shaping contemporary British sociology.

Here is the way Giddens describes the juggernaut of modernity:

a runaway engine of enormous power which, collectively as human beings, we
can drive to some extent but which also threatens to rush out of our control and
which could rend itself asunder. The juggernaut crushes those who resist it, and
while it sometimes seems to have a steady path, there are times when it veers
away erratically in directions we cannot foresee. The ride is by no means wholly
unpleasant or unrewarding; it can often be exhilarating and charged with hopeful
anticipation. But, so long as the institutions of modernity endure, we shall never
be able to control completely either the path or the pace of the journey. In turn,
we shall never be able to feel entirely secure, because the terrain across which it
runs is fraught with risks of high consequence.

(Giddens, 1990:139)

Modernity in the form of a juggernaut is extremely dynamic; it is a " 'runaway world' "
with great increases in the pace, scope, and profoundness of change over prior
systems (Giddens, 1991:16). Giddens is quick to add that this juggernaut does not
follow a single path. Furthermore, it is not of one piece but instead is made up of a
number of conflicting and contradictory parts. Thus, Giddens is telling us that he is

For one thing, he has served as a consulting editor for two publishing companies— Macmillan and Hutchinson. A large number of books have been produced under his editorship. More important, he was a cofounder of Polity Press, a publisher that has been both extremely active and influential, especially in sociological theory. Giddens also has published an American-style textbook, *Sociology* (1987), that has been a worldwide success.

As a theorist, Giddens has been highly influential in the United States, as well as in many other parts of the world. Interestingly, his work often has been less well received in his home country of Great Britain than elsewhere. This lack of acceptance at home may be attributable, in part, to the fact that Giddens has succeeded in winning the worldwide theoretical following that many other British social theorists sought and failed to achieve. As Craib says, "Giddens has perhaps realized the fantasies of many of us who committed ourselves to sociology during the period of intense and exciting debate out of which structuration theory developed" (1992:12).

Giddens's career took a series of interesting turns in the 1990s (Bryant and Jary, 2000). Several years of therapy led to a greater interest in personal life and books such as *Modernity and Self-Identity* (1991) and *The Transformation of Intimacy* (1992). Therapy also gave him the confidence to take on a more public role and to become an adviser to British prime minister Tony Blair. In 1997 he became director of the highly prestigious London School of Economics (LSE). He strengthened the scholarly reputation of LSE as well as increased its voice in public discourse in Great Britain and around the world. There is some feeling that all this had an adverse effect on Giddens's scholarly work (his most recent books lack the depth and sophistication of his earlier works), but he is clearly focused on being a force in public life.

not offering an old-fashioned grand theory, or at least not a simple, unidirectional grand narrative.

The idea of a juggernaut fits nicely with structuration theory, especially with the importance in that theory of time and space. The image of a juggernaut is of something that is moving along *through time* and *over physical space*. However, this image does not fit well with Giddens's emphasis on the power of the agent; the image of a juggernaut seems to accord this modern mechanism far more power than it accords the agents who steer it (Mestrovic, 1998:155). This problem is consistent with the more general criticism that there is a disjunction between the emphasis on agency in Giddens's purely theoretical work and the substantive historical analyses which "point to the dominance of system tendencies against our ability to change the world" (Craib, 1992:149).

Modernity and Its Consequences 现代性及其结果

Giddens defines modernity in terms of four basic institutions. The first is *capitalism*, characterized, familiarly, by commodity production, private ownership of capital, propertyless wage labor, and a class system derived from these characteristics. The second is *industrialism,* which involves the use of inanimate power sources and machinery to produce goods. Industrialism is not restricted to the workplace, and it affects an array of other settings, such as "transportation, communication and domestic life" (Giddens, 1990:56). While Giddens's first two characteristics of modernity are hardly novel, the third—*surveillance capacities*—is, although it owes a debt to the work of Michel Foucault (see Chapter 13). As Giddens defines it, "Surveillance refers to the supervision of the activities of subject populations [mainly but not exclusively] in the political sphere" (1990:58). The final institutional dimension of modernity is military power, or the *control of the means of violence,* including the industrialization of war. In addition, it should be noted that in his analysis of modernity, at least at the macro level, Giddens focuses on the *nation-state* (rather than the more conventional sociological focus on society), which he sees as radically different from the type of community characteristic of premodern society.

Modernity is given dynamism by three essential aspects of Giddens's structuration theory: distanciation, disembedding, and reflexivity. The first is *time and space separation,* or *distanciation* (although this process of increasing separation, like all aspects of Giddens's work, is not unilinear; it is dialectical). In premodern societies, time was always linked with space and the measurement of time was imprecise. With modernization, time was standardized and the close linkage between time and space was broken. In this sense, both time and space were "emptied" of content; no particular time or space was privileged; they became pure forms. In premodern societies, space was defined largely by physical presence and therefore by localized spaces. With the coming of modernity, space is progressively torn from place. Relationships with those who are physically absent and increasingly distant become more and more likely. To Giddens, place becomes increasingly "phantasmagoric"; that is, "locales are thoroughly penetrated by and shaped in terms of social influences quite distant from them . . . the 'visible form' of the locale conceals the distanciated relations which determine its nature" (Giddens, 1990:19).

Time and space distanciation is important to modernity for several reasons. First, it makes possible the growth of rationalized organizations such as bureaucracies and the nation-state, with their inherent dynamism (in comparison to premodern forms) and their ability to link local and global domains. Second, the modern world is positioned within a radical sense of world history, and it is able to draw upon that history to shape the present. Third, such distanciation is a major prerequisite for Giddens's second source of dynamism in modernity—disembedding.

As Giddens defines it, *disembedding* involves "the 'lifting out' of social relations from local contexts of interaction and their restructuring across indefinite spans of time-space" (1990:21). There are two types of disembedding mechanisms that play a key role in modern societies; both can be included under the heading "abstract systems." The first is *symbolic tokens,* the best known of which is money. Money allows for time-space distanciation—we are able to engage in transactions with others who are widely separated from us by time and/or space. The second is *expert systems,* defined as "systems of technical accomplishment or professional expertise that organize large areas of the material and social environments in which we live today" (Giddens, 1990:27). The most obvious expert systems involve professionals such as lawyers and physicians, but everyday phenomena such as our cars and homes are created and affected by expert systems. Expert systems provide guarantees (but not without risks) of performance across time and space.

Trust is very important in modern societies dominated by abstract systems and with great time-space distanciation. The need for trust is related to this distanciation: "We have no need to trust someone who is constantly in view and whose activities can be directly monitored" (Giddens, 1991:19). Trust becomes necessary when, as a result of increasing distanciation in terms of either time or place, we no longer have full information about social phenomena (Craib, 1992:99). Trust is defined "as confidence in the reliability of a person or systems, regarding a given set of outcomes or events, where that confidence expresses a faith in the probity or love of another, or in the correctness of abstract principles (technical knowledge)" (Giddens, 1990:34). Trust is of great importance not only in modern society in general, but also to the symbolic tokens and expert systems that serve to disembed life in the modern world. For example, in order for the money economy and the legal system to work, people must have trust in them.

The third dynamic characteristic of modernity is its *reflexivity*. While reflexivity is a fundamental feature of Giddens's structuration theory (as well as of human existence, in his view), it takes on special meaning in modernity, where "social practices are constantly examined and reformed in the light of incoming information about those very practices, thus constitutively altering their character" (Giddens, 1990:38). Everything is open to reflection in the modern world, including reflection itself, leaving us with a pervasive sense of uncertainty. Furthermore, the problem of the double hermeneutic (see Chapter 10) recurs here because the reflection of experts on the social world tends to alter that world.

The disembedded character of modern life raises a number of distinctive issues. One is the need for trust in abstract systems in general, and expert systems in particular. In one of his more questionable metaphors, Giddens sees children as being "inoculated" with a "dosage" of trust during childhood socialization. This aspect of socialization serves to provide people with a "protective cocoon," which, as they mature into adulthood, helps give them a measure of ontological security and trust. This trust tends to be buttressed by the series of routines that we encounter on a day-to-day basis. However, there are new and dangerous risks associated with modernity that always threaten our trust and threaten to lead to pervasive ontological insecurity. As Giddens sees it, while the disembedding mechanisms have provided us with security in various areas, they also have created a distinctive "risk profile." Risk is global in intensity (nuclear war can kill us all) and in the expansion of contingent events that affect large numbers of people around the world (for example, changes in the worldwide division of labor). Then there are risks traceable to our efforts to manage our material environment. Risks also stem from the creation of institutional risk environments such as global investment markets. People are increasingly aware of risks, and religion and customs are increasingly less important as ways of believing that those risks can be transformed into certainties. A wide range of publics are now likely to know of the risks we face. Finally, there is a painful awareness that expert systems are limited in their ability to deal with these risks. It is these risks that give modernity the feeling of a runaway juggernaut and fill us with ontological insecurity.

What has happened? Why are we suffering the negative consequences of being aboard the juggernaut of modernity? Giddens suggests several reasons. The first is *design faults* in the modern world; those who designed elements of the modern world made mistakes. The second is *operator failure;* the problem is traceable not to the designers but to those who run the modern world. Giddens, however, gives prime importance to two other factors—*unintended consequences* and *reflexivity of social knowledge*. That is, the consequences of actions for a system can never be forecast fully, and new knowledge is continually sending systems off in new directions. For all these reasons, we cannot completely control the juggernaut, the modern world.

However, rather than giving up, Giddens suggests the seemingly paradoxical course of *utopian realism*. That is, he seeks a balance between utopian ideals and the realities of life in the modern world. He also accords importance to the role social movements can play in dealing with some of the risks of the modern world and pointing us toward a society in which those risks are ameliorated.

Giddens's (1994) effort to find a compromise political position is manifest in the title of one of his later books, *Beyond Left and Right: The Future of Radical Politics*. With extant political positions moribund, Giddens proposes a reconstituted "radical politics" which is based on utopian realism and oriented toward addressing the problems of poverty, environmental degradation, arbitrary power and force, and violence in social life. Giddens's political position involves an acceptance of at least some aspects of capitalism (e.g., markets) and rejection of many aspects of socialism (e.g., a revolutionary subject). Thus, Giddens has chosen to walk a very narrow and difficult political tightrope.

Given his views on modernity, where does Giddens stand on postmodernity? For one thing, he rejects most, if not all, of the tenets we usually associate with postmodernism. For example, of the idea that systematic knowledge is impossible, Giddens says that such a view would lead us "to repudiate intellectual activity altogether" (1990:47). However, while he sees us as living in an era of high modernity, Giddens believes it is possible now to gain a glimpse of postmodernity. Such a world would, in his view, be characterized by a postscarcity system, increasingly multilayered democratization, demilitarization, and the humanization of technology. However, there are clearly no guarantees that the world will move in the direction of some, to say nothing of all, of these postmodern characteristics. Yet, reflexively, Giddens believes that in writing about such eventualities he (and others) can play a role in helping them come to pass.

Modernity and Identity 现代性与认同

While *The Consequences of Modernity* is a largely macro-oriented work, *Modernity and Self-Identity* (Giddens, 1991) focuses more on the micro aspects of late modernity, especially the self. Although Giddens certainly sees the self as dialectically related to the institutions of modern society, most of his attention here is devoted to the micro end of the continuum. We, too, will focus here on the micro issues, but we should not lose sight of the larger dialectic:

> Transformations in self-identity and globalisation . . . are the two poles of the dialectic of the local and the global in conditions of high modernity. Changes in intimate aspects of personal life . . . are directly tied to the establishment of social connections of very wide scope . . . for the first time in human history, "self" and "society" are interrelated in a global milieu.
>
> (Giddens, 1991:32)

As we have seen, Giddens defines the modern world as reflexive, and he argues that the "reflexivity of modernity extends into the core of the self . . . the self becomes a *reflexive project*" (1991:32). That is, the self comes to be something to be reflected upon, altered, even molded. Not only does the individual become responsible for the creation and maintenance of the self, but this responsibility is continuous and all-pervasive. The self is a product both of self-exploration and of the development of intimate social relationships. In the modern world, even the body gets "drawn into the reflexive organisation of social life" (Giddens, 1991:98). We are responsible for the design not only of our selves but also (and relatedly) that of our bodies. Central to the reflexive creation and maintenance of the self are the appearance of the body and its appropriate demeanor in a variety of settings and locales. The body is also subject to a variety of "regimes" (for example, diet and exercise books) that not only help individuals mold their bodies but also contribute to self-reflexivity as well as to the reflexivity of modernity in general. The result, overall, is an obsession with our bodies and our selves within the modern world.

The modern world brings with it the *"sequestration of experience,"* or the "connected processes of concealment which set apart the routines of ordinary life from the following phenomena: madness; criminality; sickness and death; sexuality; and nature" (Giddens, 1991:149, 156). Sequestration occurs as a result of the grow-ing role of abstract systems in everyday life. This sequestration brings us greater ontological security, but at the cost of the "exclusion of social life from fundamental existential issues which raise central moral dilemmas for human beings" (Giddens, 1991:156).

While modernity is a double-edged sword, bringing both positive and negative developments, Giddens perceives an underlying "looming threat of *personal meaning-lessness*" (1991:201). All sorts of meaningful things have been sequestered from daily life; they have been repressed. However, dialectically, increasing self-reflexivity leads to the increasing likelihood of the return of that which has been repressed. Giddens sees us moving into a world in which "on a collective level and in day-to-day life moral/existential questions thrust themselves back to centre-stage" (1991:208). The world beyond modernity, for Giddens, is a world characterized by "remoralization." Those key moral and existential issues that have been sequestered will come to occupy center stage in a society that Giddens sees as being foreshadowed, and anticipated, in the self-reflexivity of the late modern age.

Modernity and Intimacy 现代性和亲密关系

Giddens picks up many of these themes in *The Transformation of Intimacy* (1992). In this work he focuses on ongoing transformations of intimacy that show movement toward another important concept in Giddens's thinking about the modern world—the *pure relationship,* or "a situation where a social relation is entered into for its own sake, for what can be derived by each person from a sustained association with another; and which is continued only so far as it is thought by both parties to deliver enough satisfactions for each individual to stay within it" (Giddens, 1992:58). In the case of intimacy, a pure relationship is characterized by emotional communication with self and other in a context of sexual and emotional equality. The democratization of intimate relationships can lead to the democratization not only of interpersonal relations in general but of the macro-institutional order as well. The changing nature of intimate relations, in which women ("the emotional revolutionaries of modernity" [Giddens, 1992:130]) have taken the lead and men have been "laggards," has revolutionary implications for society as a whole.

In the modern world intimacy and sexuality (and, as we have seen, much else) have been sequestered. However, while this sequestration was liberating in various senses from intimacy in traditional societies, it is also a form of repression. The reflexive effort to create purer intimate relationships must be carried out in a context separated from larger moral and ethical issues. However, this modern arrangement comes under pressure as people, especially women, attempt reflexive construction of themselves and others. Thus, Giddens is arguing not for sexual liberation or pluralism, but rather for a larger ethical and moral change, a change that he sees as already well under way in intimate relationships:

> We have no need to wait around for a sociopolitical revolution to further programmes of emancipation, nor would such a revolution help very much. Revolutionary processes are already well under way in the infrastructure of personal life. The transformation of intimacy presses for psychic as well as social change and such change, going "from the bottom up," could potentially ramify through other, more public, institutions.
>
> Sexual emancipation, I think, can be the medium of a wide-ranging emotional reorganisation of social life.
>
> (Giddens, 1992:181–182)

The Risk Society 风险社会

We have already touched on the issue of risk in Giddens's work on modernity. As Giddens says,

> Modernity is a risk culture. I do not mean by this that social life is inherently more risky than it used to be; for most people that is not the case. Rather, the concept of risk becomes fundamental to the way both lay actors and technical specialists organise the social world. Modernity reduces the overall riskiness of certain areas and modes of life, yet at the same time introduces new risk parameters largely or completely unknown to previous eras.
>
> (Giddens, 1991:3–4)

Thus, Giddens (1991:28) describes as "quite accurate" the thesis of the work to be discussed in this section: Ulrich Beck's *Risk Society: Towards a New Modernity* (1992; Bora, 2007; Bronner, 1995).

In terms of this discussion, the subtitle of Beck's work is of great importance, since it indicates that Beck, like Giddens, rejects the notion that we have moved into a postmodern age. Rather, in Beck's view we continue to exist in the modern world, albeit in a new form of modernity. The prior, "classical" stage of modernity was associated with industrial society, while the emerging new modernity and its technologies are associated with the risk society (N. Clark, 1997). While we do not yet live in a risk society, we no longer live only in an industrial society; that is, the contemporary world has elements of both. In fact, the risk society can be seen as a type of industrial society, since many of those risks are traceable to industry. Beck offers the following overview of his perspective:

> *Just as modernization dissolved the structure of feudal society in the nineteenth century and produced the industrial society, modernization today is dissolving industrial society and another modernity is coming into being. . . .* The thesis of this book is: we are witnessing not the end but the beginning of modernity—that is, of a modernity *beyond* its classical industrial design.
>
> (Beck, 1992:10)

What, then, is this new modernity? And what is the risk society that accompanies it?

Beck labels the new, or better yet newly emerging, form *reflexive modernity* (Zinn, 2007a). A process of individualization has taken place in the West. That is, agents are becoming increasingly free of structural constraints and are, as a result, better able to reflexively create not only themselves but also the societies in which they live. For example, instead of being determined by their class situations, people operate more or less on their own. Left to their own devices, people have been forced to be more reflexive. Beck makes the case for the importance of reflexivity in the example of social relationships in such a world: "The newly formed social relationships and social networks now have to be individually chosen; social ties, too, are becoming *reflexive,* so that they have to be established, maintained, and constantly renewed by individuals" (1992:97).

Beck sees a break within modernity and a transition from classical industrial society to the risk society, which, while different from its predecessor, continues to have many of the characteristics of industrial society. The central issue in classical modernity was wealth and how it could be distributed more evenly. In advanced modernity the central issue is risk and how it can be prevented, minimized, or channeled. In classical modernity the ideal was equality, while in advanced modernity it is safety. In classical modernity people achieved solidarity in the search for the positive goal of equality, but in advanced modernity the attempt to achieve that solidarity is found in the search for the largely negative and defensive goal of being spared from dangers.

Creating the Risks 制造风险

The risks are, to a large degree, being produced by the sources of wealth in modern society. Specifically, industry and its side effects are producing a wide range of hazardous, even deadly, consequences for society and, as a result of globalization

(Featherstone, 1990; Robertson, 1992), for the world as a whole. Using the concepts of time and space, Beck makes the point that these modern risks are not restricted to place (a nuclear accident in one geographical locale could affect many other nations) or time (a nuclear accident could have genetic effects that might affect future generations).

While social class is central in industrial society and risk is fundamental to the risk society, risk and class are not unrelated. Says Beck,

> The history of risk distribution shows that, like wealth, risks adhere to the class pattern, only inversely: wealth accumulates at the top, risks at the bottom. To that extent, risks seem to *strengthen,* not to abolish, class society. Poverty attracts an unfortunate abundance of risks. By contrast, the wealthy (in income, power, or education) can purchase safety and freedom from risk.
>
> (Beck, 1992:35)

What is true for social classes is also true for nations. That is, to the degree that it is possible, risks are centered in poor nations, while the rich nations are able to push many risks as far away as possible. Further, the rich nations profit from the risks they produce by, for example, producing and selling technologies that help prevent risks from occurring or deal with their adverse effects once they do occur.

However, neither wealthy individuals nor the nations that produce risks are safe from risks. In this context, Beck discusses what he calls the "boomerang effect," whereby the side effects of risk "strike back even at the centers of their production. The agents of modernization themselves are emphatically caught in the maelstrom of hazards that they unleash and profit from" (1992:37).

Coping with the Risks 解决风险

While advanced modernization produces the risks, it also produces the reflexivity that allows it to question itself and the risks it produces. In fact, it is often the people themselves, the victims of the risks, who begin to reflect on those risks. They begin to observe and to collect data on the risks and their consequences for people. They become experts who come to question advanced modernity and its dangers. They do this, in part, because they can no longer rely on scientists to do it for them. Indeed, Beck is very hard on scientists for their role in the creation and maintenance of the risk society: "Science has become the *protector of a global contamination of people and nature.* In that respect, it is no exaggeration to say that in the way they deal with risks in many areas, the sciences *have squandered until further notice their historic reputation for rationality*" (1992:70).

While in classical industrial society nature and society were separated, in advanced industrial society nature and society are deeply intertwined. That is, changes in society often affect the natural environment, and those changes, in turn, affect society. Thus, according to Beck, today "nature is society and society is also *'nature'*" (1992:80). Thus nature has been politicized, with the result that natural scientists, like social scientists, have had their work politicized.

The traditional domain of politics, the government, is losing power because the major risks are emanating from what Beck calls "sub politics," for example, large companies, scientific laboratories, and the like. It is in the subpolitical system that "the structures of a new society are being implemented with regard to the ultimate goals of progress in knowledge, outside the parliamentary system, not in opposition to it, but simply ignoring it" (Beck, 1992:223). This is part of what he calls the "unbinding of politics," where politics is no longer left to the central government, but increasingly is becoming the province of various subgroups, as well as of individuals. These subgroups and individuals can be more reflexive and self-critical than a central government can, and they have the capability to reflect upon, to better deal with, the array of risks associated with advanced modernity. Thus, dialectically, advanced modernity has generated both unprecedented risks and unprecedented efforts to deal with those risks (Beck, 1996).

Modernity and the Holocaust 现代性与大屠杀

To Zygmunt Bauman (1989, 1991) the modern paradigm of formal rationality is the Holocaust, the systematic destruction of the Jews (and others) by the Nazis (Beilharz, 2005c, 2005d). As Bauman puts it, "Considered as a complex purposeful operation, the Holocaust may serve as a paradigm of modern bureaucratic rationality" (1989:149). To many it will seem obscene to discuss fast-food restaurants and the Holocaust in the same context. Yet there is a clear line in sociological thinking about modern rationality from the bureaucracy to the Holocaust and then to the fast-food restaurant. Weber's principles of rationality can be applied usefully and meaningfully to each. The perpetrators of the Holocaust employed the bureaucracy as one of their major tools. The conditions that made the Holocaust possible, especially the formally rational system, continue to exist today. Indeed, what the process of McDonaldization indicates is not only that formally rational systems persist, but that they are expanding dramatically. Thus, in Bauman's view, under the right set of circumstances the modern world would be ripe for an even greater abomination (if such a thing is possible) than the Holocaust.

A Product of Modernity 现代性的产物

Rather than viewing the Holocaust, as most do, as an abnormal event, Bauman sees it as in many ways a "normal" aspect of the modern, rational world:

> The truth is that every "ingredient" of the Holocaust—all of those many things that rendered it possible—was normal; "normal" not in the sense of the familiar . . . but in the sense of being fully in keeping with everything we know about our civilization, its guiding spirit, its priorities, its immanent vision of the world.
>
> (Bauman, 1989:8)

Thus, the Holocaust, to Bauman, was a product of modernity and *not,* as most people view it, a result of the breakdown of modernity or a special route taken within it (Joas, 1998; Varcoe, 1998). In Weberian terms, there was an "elective affinity" between the Holocaust and modernity.

For example, the Holocaust involved the application of the basic principles of industrialization in general, and the factory system in particular, to the destruction of human beings:

> [Auschwitz] was also a mundane extension of the modern factory system. Rather than producing goods, the raw material was human beings and the end-product was death, so many units per day marked carefully on the manager's production charts. The chimneys, the very symbol of the modern factory system, poured forth acrid smoke produced by burning human flesh. The brilliantly organized railroad grid of modern Europe carried a new kind of raw material to the factories. It did so in the same manner as with other cargo. . . . Engineers designed the crematoria; managers designed the system of bureaucracy that worked with a zest and efficiency. . . . What we witnessed was nothing less than a massive scheme of social engineering.
>
> (Feingold, cited in Bauman, 1989:8)

What the Nazis succeeded in doing was to bring together the rational achievements of industry and the rational bureaucracy, and then bring both to bear on the objective of destroying people. Modernity, as embodied in these rational systems, was not a sufficient condition for the Holocaust, but it was clearly a necessary condition. Without modernity and rationality, "the Holocaust would be unthinkable" (Bauman, 1989:13).

The Role of Bureaucracy 官僚制的作用

The German bureaucracy did more than carry out the Holocaust; in a very real sense it created the Holocaust. The task of "getting rid of the Jews," as Hitler defined it, was picked up by the German bureaucrats, and as they resolved a series of day-to-day problems, extermination emerged as the best means to the end as it was defined by Hitler and his henchmen. Thus, Bauman argues that the Holocaust was not the result of irrationality, or premodern barbarity, but rather it was the product of the modern, rational bureaucracy. It was not crazed lunatics who created and managed the Holocaust, but highly rational and otherwise quite normal bureaucrats.

In fact, previous efforts, such as emotional and irrational pogroms, could not have accomplished the mass extermination that characterized the Holocaust. Such a mass extermination required a highly rationalized and bureaucratized operation. An irrational outburst such as a pogrom might kill some people, but it could never successfully carry on a mass extermination of the scale undertaken in the Holocaust. As Bauman puts it, "Rage and fury are pitiably primitive and inefficient tools of mass annihilation. They normally peter out before the job is done" (1989:90). In contrast, modern genocide as it was perpetrated by the Nazis had a seemingly rational purpose, the creation of a "better" society (unfortunately, to the Nazis, a better society was one that was free of "evil" Jews). And the Nazis and their bureaucrats went about achieving that goal in a cold and methodical manner.

Unlike most observers, Bauman does not see the bureaucracy as simply a neutral tool that can be propelled in any direction. Bauman sees the bureaucracy as "more like . . . loaded dice" (1989:104). While it can be used for either cruel or humane purposes, it is more likely to favor inhuman processes: "It is programmed to measure the optimum in such terms as would not distinguish between one human object and another, or between human and inhuman objects" (Bauman, 1989:104). And given its basic characteristics, the bureaucracy would see the inhuman task through to the end, and beyond. In addition to their normal operations, bureaucracies have a number of well-known incapacities, and they too fostered the Holocaust. For example, means often become ends in bureaucracies, and in this case the means, killing, often came to be the end.

Of course, the bureaucracy and its officials could not and did not create the Holocaust on their own; other factors were required. For one thing, there was the unquestioned control of the state apparatus with its monopoly of the means of violence over the rest of society. In other words, there were few if any countervailing power bases in Nazi Germany. And the state, of course, was controlled by Adolf Hitler, who had the ability to get the state to do his bidding. For another thing, there was a distinctly modern and rational form of anti-Semitism in which Jews were systematically set apart from the rest of society and portrayed as if they were preventing Germany from becoming a "perfect" society. To accomplish this goal, the Germans had to exterminate those who stood in the way of achieving a perfect society. German science (itself highly rationalized) was employed to help define the Jews as defective. Once they were defined as defective, and as a barrier to the perfect society, it followed that the only solution was their elimination. And once it was determined that they should be eliminated, the only important issue facing the bureaucrat was finding the most efficient way of bringing about this end.

Another factor here is that there is no place for moral considerations in modern structures such as bureaucracies. Whether it was right or wrong to exterminate the Jews was a nonissue. The absence of such moral concerns is another reason that the Holocaust is such a modern phenomenon.

The Holocaust and Rationalization 大屠杀和理性化

The Holocaust had all the characteristics of Weber's rationalization process, (as well as of "McDonaldization"; see Chapter 12). There was certainly an emphasis on efficiency. For example, gas was determined to be a far more efficient method of killing large numbers of people than were bullets. The Holocaust had the predictability of an assembly line, with the long lines of trains snaking into the death camps, the long rows of people winding into the "showers," and the "production" of large stacks of bodies to be disposed of at the end of the process. It was calculable in the sense that the emphasis was on quantitative factors such as how many people could be killed and in how short a time.

> For railway managers, the only meaningful articulation of their object is in terms of tonnes per kilometre. They do not deal with humans, sheep, or barbed wire; they only deal with cargo, and this means an entity consisting entirely of measurements and devoid of quality. For most bureaucrats, even such a category as cargo would mean too strict a quality-bound restriction. They deal only with the financial effects of their actions. Their object is money.
>
> (Bauman, 1989:103)

There was certainly little attention paid to the quality of the life, or even of the death, of the Jews as they marched inexorably to the gas chambers. In another, quantitative sense, the Holocaust was the most extreme of mass exterminations:

> Like everything else done in the modern—rational, planned, scientifically informed, expert, efficiently managed, co-ordinated—way, the Holocaust left behind and put to shame all its alleged pre-modern equivalents, exposing them as primitive, wasteful and ineffective by comparison. Like everything else in our modern society, the Holocaust was an accomplishment in every respect superior. . . . It towers high above the past genocidal episodes.
>
> (Bauman, 1989:89)

Finally, the Holocaust used nonhuman technologies, such as the rules and regulations of the camps and the assembly-line operation of the ovens, to control both inmates and guards.

Of course, the characteristic of rationalization (and McDonaldization) that best fits the Holocaust is the irrationality of rationality, especially dehumanization. Here Bauman makes use of the idea of distanciation to make the point that the victims can be dehumanized because the bureaucrats making decisions about them have no personal contact with them. Furthermore, the victims are objects to be moved about and disposed of, numbers on a ledger; they are not human beings. In sum, "German bureaucratic machinery was put in the service of a goal incomprehensible in its irrationality" (Bauman, 1989:136).

One of Bauman's most interesting points is that the rational system put in place by the Nazis came to encompass the victims, the Jews. The ghetto was transformed into "an extension of the murdering machine" (Bauman, 1989:23). Thus,

> the leaders of the doomed communities performed most of the preliminary bureaucratic work the operation required (supplying the Nazis with the records and keeping the files on their prospective victims), supervised the productive and distributive activities needed to keep the victims alive until the time when the gas chambers were ready to receive them, policed the captive population so that law-and-order tasks did not stretch the ingenuity or resources of the captors, secured the smooth flow of the annihilation process by appointing the objects of its successive stages, delivered the selected objects to the sites from which they could be collected with a minimum of fuss, and mobilized the financial resources needed to pay for the last journey.
>
> (Bauman, 1989:118)

(This is similar to the idea that in a McDonaldized world, the customers become unpaid workers in the system, making their own salads, cleaning up after themselves, and so on.) In "ordinary genocide," the murderers and the murdered are separated from one another. The murderers are planning to do something terrible to their victims, with the result that the resistance of potential victims is likely. However, such resistance is far less likely when the victims are an integral part of a "system" created by the perpetrators.

In their actions, the Jews who cooperated with the Nazis were behaving rationally. They were doing what was necessary to, for example, keep themselves alive for another day or be selected as people deserving of special, more favorable treatment. They were even using rational tools, such as calculating that the sacrifice of a few would save the many, and that if they didn't cooperate many more would die. However, in the end, such actions were irrational in that they helped expedite the process of genocide and reduced the likelihood of resistance to it.

Modernity has prided itself on being civilized, on having safeguards in place so that something like the Holocaust could never occur. But it did occur; the safeguards were not sufficient to prevent it. Today, the forces of rationalization remain in place and are, if anything, stronger. And there is little to suggest that the safeguards needed to prevent rationalization from running amok are any stronger today than they were in the 1940s. As Bauman says, "None of the societal conditions that made Auschwitz possible has truly disappeared, and no effective measures have been undertaken to prevent . . . Auschwitz-like catastrophes" (1989:11). Necessary to prevent another Holocaust are a strong morality and pluralistic political forces. But there are likely to be times when a single power comes to predominate and there is little to lead us to believe that a strong enough moral system is in place to prevent another confluence of a powerful leader and an eager and willing bureaucracy.

Modernity's Unfinished Project 现代性：未竟的事业

Jurgen Habermas is arguably not only today's leading social theorist but also the leading defender of modernity and rationality in the face of the assault on those ideas by postmodernists (and others). According to Seidman:

> In contrast to many contemporary intellectuals who have opted for an anti- or
> postmodernist position, Habermas sees in the institutional orders of modernity
> structures of rationality. Whereas many intellectuals have become cynical about
> the emancipatory potential of modernity . . . Habermas continues to insist on the
> utopian potential of modernity. In a social context in which faith in the
> Enlightenment project of a good society promoted by reason sees a fading hope
> and spurned idol, Habermas remains one of its strongest defenders.
>
> (Seidman, 1989:2)

Habermas (1987b) sees modernity as an "unfinished project," implying that there is far more to be done in the modern world before we can begin thinking about the possibility of a postmodern world (Outhwaite, 2000; Scambler, 1996).

In Chapter 10 we covered a good portion of Habermas's thinking on modernity in our discussion of his ideas on system, life-world, and the colonization of the life-world by the system. Habermas (1986:96) can be seen as doing a "theory of the pathology of modernity" since he regards modernity as being at variance with itself. By this he means that the rationality (largely formal rationality) that has come to characterize social systems is different from, and in conflict with, the rationality that characterizes the life-world. Social systems have grown increasingly complex, differentiated, integrated, and characterized by instrumental reason. The life-world, too, has witnessed increasing differentiation and condensation (but of the knowledge bases and value spheres of truth, goodness, and beauty), secularization, and institutionalization of norms of reflexivity and criticism (Seidman, 1989:24). A rational society would be one in which both system and life-world were permitted to rationalize in their own

Jurgen Habermas

A Biographical Sketch

Jurgen Habermas is arguably the most important social thinker in the world today. He was born in Düsseldorf, Germany, on June 18, 1929, and his family was middle class and rather traditional. Habermas's father was director of the Chamber of Commerce. In his early teens, during World War II, Habermas was profoundly affected by the war. The end of the war brought new hope and opportunities for many Germans, including Habermas. The fall of Nazism brought optimism about the future of Germany, but Habermas was disappointed in the lack of dramatic progress in the years immediately after the war. With the end of Nazism, all sorts of intellectual opportunities arose, and once-banned books became available to the young Habermas. They included Western and German literature, as well as tracts written by Marx and Engels. Between 1949 and 1954 Habermas studied a wide range of topics (for example, philosophy, psychology, German literature) in Göttingen, Zurich, and Bonn. However, none of the teachers at the schools at which Habermas studied were illustrious, and most were compromised by the fact that they either had supported the Nazis overtly or simply had continued to carry out their academic responsibilities under the Nazi regime. Habermas received his doctorate from the University of Bonn in 1954 and worked for two years as a journalist.

In 1956 Habermas arrived at the Institute for Social Research in Frankfurt and became associated with the Frankfurt school. Indeed, he became research assistant to one of the most illustrious members of that school, Theodor Adorno, as well as an associate of the Institute (Wiggershaus, 1994). While the Frankfurt school often is thought of as highly coherent, that was not Habermas's view:

> For me there was never a consistent theory. Adorno wrote essays on the critique of culture and also gave seminars on Hegel. He presented a certain Marxist background—and that was it.
>
> (Habermas, cited in Wiggershaus, 1994:2)

While he was associated with the Institute for Social Research, Habermas demonstrated from the beginning an independent intellectual orientation. A 1957 article by Habermas got him into trouble with the leader of the Institute, Max Horkheimer. Habermas urged critical thought and practical action, but Horkheimer was afraid that such a position would jeopardize the publicly funded Institute. Horkheimer strongly recommended that Habermas be dismissed from the Institute. Horkheimer said of Habermas, "'He probably has a good, or even brilliant, career as a writer in front of him, but he would only cause the Institute immense damage'" (cited in Wiggershaus, 1994:555). The article eventually was published, but not under the auspices of the Institute and with virtually no reference to it. Eventually, Horkheimer enforced impossible conditions on Habermas's work and Habermas resigned.

In 1961 Habermas became a privatdocent and completed his "Habilitation" (a second dissertation required by German universities) at the University of Marburg. Having already published a number of notable works, Habermas was recommended for a professorship of philosophy at the University of Heidelberg even before he had completed his Habilitation. He remained at Heidelberg until 1964, when he moved on to the University of Frankfurt as a professor of philosophy and sociology. From 1971 to 1981 he was the director of the Max Planck Institute. He returned to the University of Frankfurt as a professor of philosophy, and in 1994 he became an emeritus professor at that institution. He has won a number of prestigious academic prizes and has been awarded honorary professorships at a number of universities.

For many years, Habermas was the world's leading neo-Marxist (Nollman, 2005b). However, over the years his work has broadened to involve many different theoretical inputs. Habermas continues to hold out hope for the future of the modern world. It is in this sense that Habermas writes of modernity's unfinished project. While Marx focused on work, Habermas is concerned mainly with communication, which he considers to be a more general process than is work. While Marx focused on the distorting effect of the structure of capitalist society on work, Habermas is concerned with the way the structure of modern society distorts communication. While Marx sought a future world involving full and creative labor, Habermas seeks a future society characterized by free and open communication. Thus, there are startling similarities between the theories of Marx and Habermas. Most generally, both are modernists who believed or believe that in their time modernity's project (creative and fulfilling work for Marx, open communication for Habermas) has not yet been completed. Yet both have had faith that in the future that project will be completed.

It is this commitment to modernism, along with his faith in the future, that sets Habermas apart from many leading contemporary thinkers, such as Jean Baudrillard and other postmodernists. While the latter are often driven to nihilism, Habermas continues to believe in his lifelong (and modernity's) project. Similarly, while other postmodernists (for example, Lyotard) reject the possibility of creating grand narratives, Habermas continues to work on and support what is perhaps the most notable grand theory in modern social theory. Much is at stake for Habermas in his battle with the postmodernists. If they win out, Habermas may come to be seen as the last great modernist thinker. If Habermas (and his supporters) emerge victorious, he may be viewed as the savior of the modernist project and of grand theory in the social sciences.

way, following their own logics. The rationalization of system and life-world would lead to a society with material abundance and control over its environments as a result of rational systems and one of truth, goodness, and beauty stemming from a rational life-world. However, in the modern world, the system has come to dominate and colonize the life-world. The result is that while we may be enjoying the fruits of system rationalization, we are being deprived of the enrichment of life that would come from a life-world that was allowed to flourish. Many of the social movements that have arisen at the "borders" between life-world and system in the last few decades are traceable to a resistance against the colonization and impoverishment of the life-world.

In analyzing the way in which the system colonizes the life-world, Habermas sees himself in alignment with much of the history of social thought:

> The main strand of social theory—from Marx via Spencer and Durkheim to Simmel, Weber and Lukács—has to be understood as the answer to the entry of system-environment boundaries into society itself [Habermas's life-world], to the genesis of the "internal foreign country" . . . which has been understood as the *hallmark of modernity.*
>
> (Habermas, 1991:255–256; italics added)

In other words, the "hallmark of modernity" to Habermas, as well as to most of classical theory, has been, in Habermas's terms, the colonization of the life-world by the system.

What, then, for Habermas would constitute the completion of modernity's project? It seems clear that the final product would be a fully rational society in which both system and life-world rationality were allowed to express themselves fully without one destroying the other. We currently suffer from an impoverished life-world, and that problem must be overcome. However, the answer does not lie in the destruction of systems (especially the economic and administrative systems), since it is they that provide the material prerequisites needed to allow the life-world to rationalize.

One of the issues Habermas (1987b) deals with is the increasing problems confronted by the modern, bureaucratic, social welfare state. Many of those associated with such a state recognize the problems, but their solution is to deal with them at the system level by, for example, simply adding a new subsystem to deal with the problems. However, Habermas does not think the problems can be solved in this way. Rather, they must be solved in the relationship between system and life-world. First, "restraining barriers" must be put in place to reduce the impact of system on life-world. Second, "sensors" must be built in order to enhance the impact of life-world on system. Habermas concludes that contemporary problems cannot be solved "by systems learning to function better. Rather, impulses from the lifeworld must be able to enter into the self-steering of functional systems" (1987b:364). These would constitute important steps toward the creation of mutually enriching life-world and system. It is here that social movements enter the picture, because they represent the hope of a recoupling of system and life-world so that the two can rationalize to the highest possible degree.

Habermas sees little hope in the United States, which seems intent on buttressing system rationality at the cost of a continuing impoverishment of the life-world.

However, Habermas does see hope in Europe, which has the possibility of putting "an end to the confused idea that the normative content of modernity that is stored in rationalized life-worlds could be set free only by means of ever more complex systems" (1987b:366). Thus, Europe has the possibility of assimilating "in a decisive way the legacy of Occidental rationalism" (Habermas, 1987b:366). That legacy translates today into restraints on system rationality in order to allow life-world rationality to flourish to the extent that the two types of rationalities can coexist as equals within the modern world. Such a full partnership between system and life-world rationality would constitute the completion of modernity's project. Since we remain a long way from that goal, we are far from the end of modernity, let alone on the verge, or in the midst, of postmodernity.

Habermas versus Postmodernists 哈贝马斯与后现代主义者

Habermas makes a case not only for modernity, but also against the postmodernists. Habermas offered some early criticisms in an essay, "Modernity versus Postmodernity" (1981), which has achieved wide recognition.[1] In that essay, Habermas raises the issue of whether, in light of the failures of the twentieth century, we "should try to hold on to the *intentions of the Enlightenment*, feeble as they may be, or should we declare the entire project of modernity a lost cause?" (1981:9). Habermas, of course, is not in favor of giving up on the Enlightenment project or, in other words, on modernity. Rather, he chooses to focus on the "mistakes" of those who do reject modernity. One of the latter's most important mistakes is their willingness to give up on science, especially a science of the life-world. The separation of science from the life-world, and the leaving of it to experts, would, if done in conjunction with the creation of other autonomous spheres, involve the surrender of "the project of modernity altogether" (Habermas, 1981:14). Habermas refuses to give up on the possibility of a rational, "scientific" understanding of the life-world as well as the possibility of the rationalization of that world.

Holub (1991) has offered an overview of Habermas's most important criticisms of the postmodernists. First, the postmodernists are equivocal about whether they are producing serious theory or literature. If we treat them as producing serious theory, their work becomes incomprehensible because of "their refusal to engage in the institutionally established vocabularies" (Holub, 1991:158). If we treat the work of the postmodernists as literature, "then their arguments forfeit all logical force" (Holub, 1991:158). In either case, it becomes almost impossible to critically analyze the work of the postmodernists seriously, because they can always claim that we do not understand their words or their literary endeavors.

Second, Habermas feels that the postmodernists are animated by normative sentiments but that what those sentiments are is concealed from the reader. Thus, the reader is unable to understand what postmodernists are really up to, why they are

---

[1] There is a sense that in his later work Habermas has offered a softer and more fine-grained critique of the postmodernists (Peters, 1994).

critiquing society, from their stated objectives. Furthermore, while they have hidden normative sentiments, the postmodernists overtly repudiate such sentiments. The lack of such overt sentiments prevents postmodernists from developing a self-conscious praxis aimed at overcoming the problems they find in the world. In contrast, the fact that Habermas's normative sentiments (free and open communication) are overt and clearly stated makes the source of his critiques of society clear, and it provides the base for political praxis.

Third, Habermas accuses postmodernism of being a totalizing perspective that fails "to differentiate phenomena and practices that occur within modern society" (Holub, 1991:159). For example, the view of the world as dominated by power and surveillance is not fine-grained enough to allow for meaningful analysis of the real sources of oppression in the modern world.

Finally, the postmodernists are accused of ignoring that which Habermas finds absolutely central—everyday life and its practices. This oversight constitutes a double loss for postmodernists. On the one hand, they are closed off from an important source for the development of normative standards. After all, the rational potential that exists in everyday life is an important source of Habermas's ideas on communicative rationality (Cooke, 1994). On the other hand, the everyday world also constitutes the ultimate goal for work in the social sciences, since it is there that theoretical ideas can have an impact on praxis.

Habermas (1994:107) offers a good summary of his views on modernity-postmodernity and a useful transition to Chapter 13 of this text, in which we will deal with postmodern social theory: "The concept of modernity no longer comes with a promise of happiness. But despite all the talk of postmodernity, there are no visible rational alternatives to this form of life. What else is left for us, then, but at least to search out practical improvements *within* this form of life?"

信息主义和网络社会

Informationalism and the Network Society

One of the most recent contributions to modern social theory is a trilogy authored by Manuel Castells (1996, 1997, 1998; Allan, 2007) with the overarching title *The Information Age: Economy, Society and Culture*. Castells (1996:4) articulates a position opposed to postmodern social theory which he sees as indulging in "celebrating the end of history, and, to some extent, the end of Reason, giving up on our capacity to understand and make sense":

> The project informing this book swims against streams of destruction, and takes exception to various forms of intellectual nihilism, social skepticism, and political cynicism. I believe in rationality, and the possibility of calling upon reason . . . I believe in the chances of meaningful social action. . . . And, yes, I believe in spite of a long tradition of sometimes tragic intellectual errors, that observing, analyzing, and theorizing is a way of helping to build a different, better world.
>
> (Castells, 1996:4)

Castells examines the emergence of a new society, culture, and economy in light of the revolution, begun in the United States in the 1970s, in informational technology (television, computers, and so on). This revolution led, in turn, to a fundamental restructuring of the capitalist system beginning in the 1980s and to the emergence of what Castells calls "informational capitalism." Also emerging were "informational societies" (although there are important cultural and institutional differences among these societies). Both are based on "informationalism" ("a mode of development in which the main source of productivity is the qualitative capacity to optimize the combination and use of factors of production on the basis of knowledge and information" [Castells, 1998:7]). The spread of informationalism, especially informational capitalism, leads to the emergence of oppositional social movements based on self and identity ("the process by which a social actor recognizes itself and constructs meaning primarily on the basis of a given cultural attribute or set of attributes, to the exclusion of a broader reference to other social structures" [Castells, 1996:22]). Such movements bring about the contemporary equivalent of what Marxists call "class struggle." The hope against the spread of informational capitalism and the problems it causes (exploitation, exclusion, threats to self and identity) is not the working class but a diverse set of social movements (e.g., ecological, feminist) based primarily on identity.

At the heart of Castells's analysis is what he calls the information technology paradigm with five basic characteristics. First, these are technologies that act on information. Second, since information is part of all human activity, these technologies have a pervasive effect. Third, all systems using information technologies are defined by a "networking logic" that allows them to affect a wide variety of processes and organizations. Fourth, the new technologies are highly flexible, allowing them to adapt and change constantly. Finally, the specific technologies associated with information are merging into a highly integrated system.

In the 1980s there emerged a new, increasingly profitable global informational economy. "It is *informational* because the productivity and competitiveness of units or agents in this economy (be it firms, regions, or nations) fundamentally depend upon their capacity to generate, process, and apply efficiently knowledge-based information" (Castells, 1996:66). It is global because it has the *"capacity to work as a unit in real time on a planetary scale"* (Castells, 1996:92). This was made possible, for the first time, by the new information and communication technologies. And it is "informational, not just information-based, because the cultural-institutional attributes of the whole social system must be included in the diffusion and implementation of the new technological paradigm" (Castells, 1996:91). While it is global, there are differences, and Castells distinguishes among regions that lie at the heart of the new global economy (North America, the European Union, and the Asian Pacific). Thus, we are talking about a regionalized, global economy. In addition, there is considerable diversity within each region, and of crucial importance is the fact that while some areas of the globe are included, others are excluded and suffer grave negative consequences. Whole areas of the world (e.g., sub-Saharan Africa) are excluded, as are parts of the privileged regions, such as the inner cities in the United States.

Accompanying the rise of the new global informational economy is the emergence of a new organizational form, the network enterprise. Among other things, the network enterprise is characterized by flexible (rather than mass) production, new management systems (frequently adapted from Japanese models), organizations based on a horizontal rather than a vertical model, and the intertwining of large corporations in strategic alliances. However, most importantly, the fundamental component of organizations is a series of networks. It is this that leads Castells (1996:171) to argue that "a new organizational form has emerged as characteristic of the informational/global economy: the *network enterprise*" defined as *"that specific form of enterprise whose system of means is constituted by the intersection of segments of autonomous systems of goals."* The network enterprise is the materialization of the culture of the global informational economy, and it makes possible the transformation of signals into commodities through the processing of knowledge. As a result, the nature of work is being transformed (e.g., the individualization of work through such things as flex-time), although the precise nature of this transformation varies from one nation to another.

Castells (1996:373) also discusses the emergence (accompanying the development of multimedia out of the fusion of the mass media and computers) of the culture of *real virtuality, "a system in which reality itself (that is, people's material/symbolic existence) is entirely captured, fully immersed in a virtual image setting, in the world of make-believe, in which appearances are not just on the screen through which experience is communicated, but they become the experience."* In contrast to the past dominated by "the space of places" (e.g., cities like New York or London), a new spatial logic, the "space of flows," has emerged. We have become a world dominated by processes rather than physical locations (although the latter obviously continue to exist). Similarly, we have entered an era of "timeless time" in which, for example, information is instantly available anywhere on the globe.

Going beyond the network enterprise, Castells (1996:469, 470; italics added) argues that the "dominant functions and processes in the information age are increasingly organized around *networks*" defined as sets of "interconnected nodes." Networks are open, capable of unlimited expansion, dynamic, and able to innovate without disrupting the system. However, the fact that our age is defined by networks (the "network society") does not mean the end of capitalism. In fact, at least at the moment, networks allow capitalism to become, for the first time, truly global and organized on the basis of global financial flows, exemplified by the much-discussed global "financial casino" that is a wonderful example of not only a network but also an informational system. Money won and lost here is now far more important than that earned through the production process. Money has come to be separated from production; we are in a capitalist age defined by the endless search for money.

However, as we saw above, Castells does not see the development of networks, the culture of real virtuality, informationalism, and especially their use in informational capitalism as going unchallenged. These are opposed by individuals and collectivities with identities of their own which they seek to defend. Thus, "God, nation, family, and community will provide unbreakable, eternal codes around which a counter-offensive will be mounted" (Castells, 1997:66). However, it is important to recognize that these countermovements must rely on information and networks in order to succeed. Thus, they are deeply implicated in the new order. In this context, Castells describes a wide range of social movements including the Zapatistas in Chiapas,

Mexico, the Americian militia, the Japanese cult Aum Shinrikyo, environmentalism, feminism, and the gay movement.

What of the state? In Castells's view, it is increasingly powerless in this new world of the globalization of the economy and its dependence on global capital markets. Thus, for example, states have become unable to protect their welfare programs because imbalances around the globe will lead capital to gravitate toward those states with low welfare costs. Also eroding the power of the state are global communications which flow freely in and out of any country. Then there is the globalization of crime and the creation of global networks that are beyond the control of any single state. Also weakening the state is the growth of multilateralism, the emergence of super nation-states such as the European Union, and internal divisions. While they will continue to exist, Castells (1997:304) sees states becoming *"nodes of a broader network of power."* The dilemma facing the state is that if it represents its national constituencies, it will be less effective in the global system, but if it focuses on the latter, it will fail to represent its constituencies adequately.

An example of the failure of the state is the Soviet Union. It simply was incapable of adapting to the new informationalism and world of networks. For example, the Soviet state monopolized information, but this was incompatible with a world in which success is associated with the free flow of information. As it fell apart, the old Soviet Union proved easy prey for global criminal elements. Ironically, while in its early years Russia was excluded from the global information society, it was (and is) deeply implicated in global criminality.

Given his critical orientation, especially to informational capitalism and its threats to self, identity, welfare, as well as its exclusion of vast portions of the world, Castells (1998:359) concludes that as they are currently constituted, our "economy, society and culture . . . limit collective creativity, confiscate the harvest of information technology, and deviate our energy into self-destructive confrontation." However, it need not be this way since there "is nothing that cannot be changed by conscious, purposive social action" (Castells, 1998:360).

Castells offers the first sustained sociological analysis of our new computerized world, and there are many insights to be derived from his work. Two major weaknesses stand out. First, this is primarily an empirical study (relying on secondary data), and Castells takes pains to avoid using a series of theoretical resources that might have enhanced his work. Second, he remains locked in a productivist perspective and fails to deal with the implications of his analysis for consumption. Nonetheless, Castells has clearly offered us an important beginning in our effort to gain a better understanding of the emerging world he describes.

The discussion of Castells's work represents a perfect transition to the next chapter, on globalization theory, because, as we have seen, much of his theory relates to global issues and is often discussed as a theory of globalization. Much of globalization theory can be seen as modern (we will encounter other ideas of some of the modern theorists encountered in this chapter—Giddens, Beck, Bauman—in the next chapter), and it has its roots in modern perspectives such as modernization theory and dependency theory. However, globalization theory also critiques and reacts against these earlier perspectives as well as, in at least some cases, the basic tenets of many theories of modernity. Although many of the ideas to be encountered in Chapter 12 are quite modern, many others go beyond the modern to implicit (e.g., "glocalization," "hybridization," and "creolization") and explicit ("empire" and "multitude") association with the postmodern ideas that are dealt with in Chapter 13.

Summary 总结

In this chapter we survey a number of theoretical perspectives that continue to see the contemporary world in modern terms. Anthony Giddens sees modernity as a juggernaut that offers a number of advantages but also poses a series of dangers. Among the dangers underscored by Giddens are the risks associated with the modern juggernaut. These dangers are the key issue in Beck's work on the risk society. The modern world is seen as being characterized by risk and the need on the part of people to prevent risk and protect themselves from it. Bauman sees the Holocaust as the paradigm of rationality and modernity. An emphasis on the Holocaust indicates the irrationalities, and more generally the dangers, associated with modernity and increasing rationalization. Next, we discuss Habermas's work on modernity as an unfinished project. Habermas, too, focuses on rationality, but his concern is with the dominance of system rationality and the impoverishment of the rationality of the life-world. Habermas sees the completion of modernity in the mutually enriching rationalization of system and life-world.

The next section is devoted to a discussion of the recent work of Manuel Castells. Castells is concerned with the growth of informationalism and the development of the network society. It is mainly the computer and the information flows it permits that have transformed the world and in the process created a series of problems such as the exclusion of great parts of the world, and even some pockets in the United States, from this system and its rewards.

Globalization Theory
第12章 全球化理论

Chapter Outline
Major Contemporary Theorists on Globalization
Cultural Theory
Economic Theory
Political Theory
Other Theories

It is likely that no single topic has received as much popular and academic attention in recent years as globalization. The academic concern is motivated, in large part, by the extraordinary public importance of, interest in, and worry over globalization. However, reasons internal to the academic world (e.g., reactions against early and narrow approaches to what is now called globalization) also have led to a near-obsession with this topic. Social theorists, including many of those discussed in this chapter and elsewhere in this book, have been no exception to this trend toward a focal concern with globalization. It is beyond the scope of this chapter to offer anything like a complete overview of the voluminous work of social theorists on this topic, to say nothing of a review of the entire literature on globalization. What follows is a brief survey of some of the most important theoretical work on globalization.

Globalization is the spread of worldwide practices, relations, consciousness, and organization of social life. Nearly every nation and the lives of billions of people throughout the world are being transformed, often quite dramatically, by globalization. The degree and significance of its impact can be seen almost everywhere one looks, most visibly in the now common protests that accompany high-level meetings of global organizations such as the World Trade Organization (WTO) and the International Monetary Fund (IMF) (Thomas, 2007). As both the magnitude of the issues before these organizations and the level of protest against those organizations make clear, people throughout the world feel strongly that they are confronting matters of great moment.

Globalization theory (Robinson, 2007) also emerged as a result of a series of developments internal to social theory, notably the reaction against earlier perspectives such as modernization theory. Among the defining characteristics of this theory were its Western bias, the preeminence accorded to developments in the West, and the idea that the rest of the world had little choice but to become increasingly like the West. Although there are many different versions of globalization theory, there is a tendency in nearly all of them to shift away dramatically from a focus on the West (including and especially the United States) and to examine not only transnational processes that flow in many different directions but also those that are, at least to some degree, autonomous and independent of any single nation or area of the world (see the discussion of Appadurai's work below).

Globalization can be analyzed culturally, economically, politically, and institutionally. For each type of analysis, a key difference is whether one sees increasing homogeneity or heterogeneity. At the extremes, the globalization of culture can be seen either as the transnational expansion of common codes and practices (homogeneity) or as a process in which many global and local cultural inputs interact to create a kind of pastiche, or a blend, leading to a variety of cultural hybrids (heterogeneity). The trend toward homogeneity is often associated with *cultural imperialism,* the influence of a particular culture on a wide range of other cultures. There are many varieties of cultural imperialism, including those that emphasize the role played by American culture, the West, or core countries (DeGrazia, 2005). Roland Robertson (1992, 2001), however, among many others, opposes the idea, although he doesn't use the term *cultural imperialism.* His famous concept of glocalization (see below) sees the global as interacting with the local to produce that which is distinctive: the glocal.

Theorists who focus on economic factors tend to emphasize their growing importance and homogenizing effect on the world. They generally see globalization as the spread of neoliberalism, capitalism, and the market economy (Antonio, 2007a) throughout many different regions of the world. For example, some have focused on globalization and the expansion of trade. Joseph E. Stiglitz (2002), a Nobel Prize–winning economist and former chairman of the Council of Economic Advisors, issued a stinging attack on the World Bank, the WTO, and especially the IMF for their roles in worsening, rather than resolving, global economic crises. Among other things, Stiglitz criticizes the IMF for its homogenizing, "one-size-fits-all" approach that fails to take into account national differences. The IMF in particular, and globalization in general, have worked to the advantage of the wealthy nations, especially the United States (which effectively has veto power over IMF decisions), and to the detriment of poor nations. The gap between rich and poor has actually *increased* as a result of globalization.

While those who focus on economic issues tend to emphasize homogeneity, some differentiation (heterogeneity) is acknowledged to continue to exist at least at the margins of the global economy. Indeed, Stiglitz argues for the need for more differentiated policies by the IMF and other global economic organizations. Other forms of heterogeneity in the economic realm involve, for example, the commodification of local cultures and the existence of flexible specialization that permits the tailoring of many products to the needs of various local specifications. More generally, those who emphasize heterogenization (Tomlinson, 1999) would argue that the interaction of the global market with local markets leads to the creation of unique "glocal" markets that integrate the demands of the global market with the realities of the local market.

Political/institutional orientations, too, tend to emphasize either homogeneity or heterogeneity. For example, some of those who operate with a homogenization perspective in this domain focus on the worldwide spread of models of the nation-state and the emergence of similar forms of governance throughout the globe—in other words, the growth of a more-or-less single model of governance around the world (Meyer, Boli, and Ramirez, 1997). More broadly, there is a concern with increasing homogenization in a multiplicity of institutions (Lechner and Boli, 2005). As we will see, some see the growth of transnational institutions and organizations as greatly diminishing the power of both the nation-state and other, more local, social structures to make a difference in people's lives. One of the most extreme views of homogenization in the political realm is Benjamin Barber's (1995) thinking on "McWorld," or the growth of a single political[1] orientation that is increasingly pervasive throughout the world.

Interestingly, Barber also articulates, as an alternative perspective, the idea of "Jihad"—localized, ethnic, and reactionary political forces (including "rogue states") that involve an intensification of nationalism and that lead to greater political heterogeneity throughout the world. The interaction of McWorld and Jihad at the local level may produce unique, glocal political formations that integrate elements of both the former (e.g., use of the Internet to attract supporters) and the latter (e.g., use of traditional ideas and rhetoric).

The issue of homogenization/heterogenization cuts across a broad swath of globalization theory, but it is clearly not exhaustive. That will become clear in the following discussion of major theories of globalization, which certainly touches in various ways on homogenization/heterogenization but also highlights a number of other facets of globalization theory. This discussion will be divided into four sections. First we will look at the perspectives on globalization of some of the major contemporary theorists (Giddens, Beck, and Bauman) encountered earlier in this book. Then we will turn to the aforementioned three broad categories of theorizing globalization: cultural, economic, and political/institutional.

主要的当代全球化理论家
Major Contemporary Theorists on Globalization

安东尼·吉登斯：全球化"失控的世界"
Anthony Giddens on the "Runaway World" of Globalization

Giddens's (2000) views on globalization are closely related to, and overlap with, his thinking on the juggernaut of modernity (see Chapter 11). Giddens also sees a close link between globalization and risk, especially the rise of what he calls manufactured risk. Much of the runaway world of globalization is beyond our control, but Giddens is not totally pessimistic. We can limit the problems created by the runaway world, but we can never control it completely. He holds out some hope for democracy, especially international and transnational forms of democracy such as the European Union.

Giddens is one of those who emphasizes the role of the West in general, and the United States in particular, in globalization. However, he also recognizes that globalization is a two-way process with America and the West being strongly influenced by it.

---

[1] Barber's view of McWorld is not restricted to politics. Barber sees many other domains following the model of McWorld.

Furthermore, he argues that globalization is becoming increasingly decentered as nations outside the West (e.g., China, India) play an increasingly large role in it. He also recognizes that globalization has both undermined local cultures *and* served to revive them. And he makes the innovative point that globalization "squeezes sideways," producing new areas that may cut across nations. He offers as an example an area around Barcelona in northern Spain that extends into France.

A key clash taking place at the global level today is that between fundamentalism and cosmopolitanism. In the end, Giddens sees the emergence of a "global cosmopolitan society." Yet even the main force in opposition to it—fundamentalism—is itself a product of globalization. Furthermore, fundamentalism uses global forces (e.g., the mass media) in order to further its ends. Fundamentalism can take various forms—religious, ethnic, nationalist, political—but whatever form it takes, Giddens thinks that fundamentalism is problematic, both because it is at odds with cosmopolitanism and because it is linked to violence (see the discussion of Huntington's work below).

Ulrich Beck, the Politics of Globalization, and Cosmopolitanism 乌尔里希·贝克：政治全球化和世界主义

We can get at the essence of Beck's (2000) thinking on this issue by discussing his distinction between globalism and globality. *Globalism* is the view that the world is dominated by economics and that we are witnessing the emergence of the hegemony of the capitalist world market and the neoliberal ideology that underpins it. To Beck, this view involves both monocausal and linear thinking. The multidimensionality of global developments—ecology, politics, culture, and civil society—is wrongly reduced to a single economic dimension. And that economic dimension is seen, again erroneously, as evolving in a linear direction of ever-increasing dependence on the world market. Clearly, Beck sees the world in much more multidimensional and multidirectional terms. In addition, he is very sensitive to the problems associated with the capitalist world market, including the fact that there are all sorts of barriers to free trade and that there are not only winners in this world market but also (many) losers.

Even though Beck is a critic of the viewpoint of globalism, he sees much merit in the idea of *globality,* in which closed spaces, especially those associated with nations, are seen as growing increasingly illusory. They are growing illusory because of globalization, which involves transnational actors, with varying degrees of power, identities, and the like, crisscrossing and undermining nation-states. These transnational processes are not simply economic but also involve ecology, culture, politics, and civil society. Such transnational processes traverse national borders, rendering them porous if not increasingly irrelevant. Nothing is any longer limited to the local. That which takes place locally, including both advances and catastrophes, affects the entire world.

Transnational processes have long existed; nevertheless, globality is new for at least three reasons. First, its influence over geographic space is far more extensive than ever before. Second, its influence over time is far more stable; it is of continuing influence from one time to another. Third, there is far greater density to its various elements including transnational relationships and networks. Beck also lists a number of other things that are distinctive about globality in comparison to earlier manifestations of transnationality:

1. Everyday life and interaction across national borders are being profoundly affected.
2. There is a self-perception of this transnationality in such realms as the mass media, consumption, and tourism.
3. Community, labor, and capital are increasingly placeless.
4. There is a growing awareness of global ecological dangers and of actions to be taken to deal with them.
5. There is an increasing perception of transcultural others in our lives.
6. Global culture industries circulate at unprecedented levels.
7. There is an increase in the number and strength of transnational agreements, actors, and institutions.

This leads Beck to refine his previously discussed (see Chapter 11) thinking on modernity and to argue that globality, and the inability to reverse it, are associated with what he now calls "second modernity." Above all, however, what defines the latter is the decline of the power of the nations and the national borders that went to the heart of "first modernity." The central premise of first modernity is (was) that we live in self-enclosed nation-states. (Beck dismisses this notion as a "container theory" of society.) Thus globality, and second modernity, mean denationalization and, Beck hopes, the rise of transnational organizations and perhaps a transnational state.

Much of Beck's recent work, including his thinking on globalization, is linked to the idea of *cosmopolitanism,* which among other things seeks to overcome the traditional sociological focus on the spatially fixed nation and to replace it with a more fluid transnational focus (Beck and Sznaider, 2005). More generally, it involves a transcendence of the local restraints on thought and action. Thus, in the era of globalization people are no longer rooted in a given cosmos (e.g., the United States) but instead are rooted in "different cities, territories, ethnicities, hierarchies, nations, religions, and so on at the same time" (Beck and Sznaider, 2005:159). This involves a moving-away from a traditional kind of either/or thinking associated, for example, with nation-based perspectives, and a moving-toward a more hybrid, "this-as-well-as-that" sense of the world. Clearly, such a cosmopolitan approach is derived from, and has a close linkage to, globalization.

Beck has been working on three books that further develop his ideas on globalization, and the first of those has recently been translated into English as *Power in the Global Age* (Beck, 2005b). Here, Beck (2005b:xi–xii) continues to adopt a cosmopolitan orientation that goes beyond national and international relations to global politics that involve a "meta-game whose outcome is completely open-ended. It is a game in which boundaries, basic rules and basic distinctions are being renegotiated—not only those between the 'national' and 'international' spheres, but also those between global business and the state, transnational civil society movements, supranational organizations and national governments and societies." It is this reality that requires a change in vision from a national to a cosmopolitan perspective that is better able to comprehend and deal with this meta-game.

Zygmunt Bauman on the Human Consequences of Globalization 齐格蒙特·鲍曼：全球化的人类后果

Bauman (1998) sees globalization in terms of a "space war." In his view, it is mobility that has become the most important and differentiating factor in social stratification in the world today. Thus, the winners of the space war are those who are mobile, able to move freely throughout the globe and in the process to create meaning for themselves. They can float relatively free of space, and when they must "land" somewhere, they isolate themselves in walled and policed spaces in which they are safe from those who are the losers in the space war. The losers not only lack mobility but are relegated and confined to territories denuded of meaning and even of the ability to offer meaning. Thus, while the elite are likely intoxicated by their mobility opportunities, the rest are more likely to feel imprisoned in their home territories, from which they have little prospect of moving. Furthermore, the latter are likely to feel humiliated by the lack of their own mobility and the sight of elites free to move about at will. As a result, territories become battlefields where the losers and winners of the space war face off in a very uneven conflict.

The winners can be said to live in time rather than space; they are able to virtually span every space quickly, if not instantaneously. In contrast, the losers can be seen as living in space. That space is beyond their control, heavy, resilient, resistant, untouchable, able to tie time down. However, it is important to distinguish among those who have at least some mobility. The *tourists* are those who are on the move because they want to be. They are attracted by something, find it irresistible, and move toward it. The *vagabonds* are those who are on the move because they find their environs unbearable, inhospitable for any number of reasons. The positive aspects of what we applaud as globalization are those that are associated with tourists, while an unavoidable side effect is that many others are transformed into vagabonds. Most people, however, exist between these two extremes. They are unsure exactly where they now stand, but wherever it is, they are not sure they will be in the same place tomorrow. Thus, globalization translates into uneasiness for most of us.

However, even the seeming winners in globalization—the tourists—have their problems. First, there is the burden associated with the impossibility of slowing down; it is hard to always be on the move and at high speed. Second, mobility means an unending string of choices, and each choice has a measure of uncertainty associated with it. Third, each choice also carries with it a series of risks and dangers. Endless mobility and continual choice eventually become troublesome if not burdensome.

It is worth noting that Bauman employs the idea of "liquidity" in a variety of books written in the early twenty-first century (for example, Bauman, 2005). Clearly, a global world is increasingly a liquid world characterized by innumerable "flows" of all types. As a result, the global world is constantly changing its form, and it is becoming increasingly difficult either to control or to gain a solid understanding of it. The idea of liquidity has wide applicability to the process of globalization.

Given the globalization theories of some of today's major social theorists, we turn now the major types of globalization theory, often with examples from other major social thinkers.

Cultural Theory 文化理论

Jan Nederveen Pieterse (2004) has identified three major paradigms in theorizing the cultural aspects of globalization, specifically on the centrally important issue of whether cultures around the globe are eternally different, converging, or creating new "hybrid" forms out of the unique combination of global and local cultures. Let us look at each of these paradigms and a representative example (or examples) of each.

Cultural Differentialism 文化差异论

Those who adopt this paradigm argue that among and between cultures there are lasting differences that are largely unaffected by globalization or by any other bi-, inter-, multi-, and trans-cultural processes. This is not to say that culture is unaffected by any of these processes, especially globalization. But it is to say that at their core cultures are largely unaffected by them; they remain much as they always have been. In this perspective globalization occurs only on the surface, and the deep structure of cultures is largely, if not totally, unaffected by it. Cultures are seen as largely closed not only to globalization but also to the influences of other cultures. In one image, the world is envisioned as a mosaic of largely separate cultures. More menacing is a billiard-ball image, with billiard balls (representing cultures) seen as bouncing off other billiard balls (representing other cultures). This image is more menacing because it indicates the possibility of dangerous and potentially catastrophic collisions among and between world cultures.

The cultural differential paradigm has a long history, but it has attracted increasing attention and adherents (as well as critics) in recent years because of two sets of current events. One is the terrorist attacks of September 11, 2001, and the subsequent wars in Afghanistan and Iraq. Many people saw these events as the product of a clash between Western and Islamic cultures and the eternal cultural differences between them. The other set of current events is the increasing multiculturalism of both the United States (largely the growth of the Hispanic population) and of western European countries (largely the growing Muslim populations) and the vast differences, and enmity, between majority and minority populations.

The most famous and controversial example of this paradigm is Samuel Huntington's *Clash of Civilizations and the Remaking of World Order* (1996). Huntington traces the beginnings of the current world situation to the end of the Cold War and the reconfiguring of the world from one differentiated on a political-economic basis (democratic/capitalist versus totalitarian/communist) to one based on cultural differences. Such cultural differences are nothing new, but they were largely submerged

(as in the old Yugoslavia and the differences between, among others, Serbs and Cro-
ats) by the overwhelming political-economic differences of the Cold War era. What
we have seen resurfacing in the last two decades are ancient identities, adversaries,
and enemies. Huntington uses the term *civilization* to describe the broadest level of
these cultures and cultural identities (indeed, to him civilization is culture "writ
large"). What he sees is the emergence of fault lines among and between these civilizations, and he considers this a highly dangerous situation given the historic enmities
among at least some of these civilizations.

Huntington differentiates between a number of world civilizations: Sinic
(Chinese); Japan (sometimes combined with "Sinic" as "Far Eastern"); Hindu; Islamic;
Orthodox (centered in Russia); Western Europe; North America (along with the closely
aligned Australia, New Zealand); Latin America; and (possibly) Africa. He sees these
civilizations as differing greatly on basic philosophical assumptions, underlying values, social relations, customs, and overall outlooks on life. To Huntington, human
history is in effect the history of civilizations, especially these civilizations. Civilizations share a number of characteristics including the fact that there is great agreement
on what they are (although they lack clear beginnings and there are no clear-cut
boundaries between civilizations, which, nonetheless, are quite real). Civilizations

1. are among the most enduring of human associations (although they do change
   over time).
2. are the broadest level of cultural identity (short of humanity in its entirety).
3. are the broadest source of subjective self-identification.
4. usually span more than one state (although they do not perform state
   functions).
5. are a totality.
6. are closely aligned with both religion and race.

Huntington offers a modern grand narrative of the relationships among civilizations. For more than three thousand years (approximately 1500 BC to AD 1500)
civilizations tended to be widely separated in terms of both time and space. As a
result, contacts among them were likely to be nonexistent. When they occurred, they
tended to be on a limited or intermittent basis, and they were likely quite intense.

The next phase, roughly from 1500 to the close of World War II, was characterized by the sustained, overpowering, and unidirectional impact of Western civilization
on all other civilizations. Huntington attributes this impact to various structural characteristics of the West, including the rise there of cities, commerce, and state bureaucracy and an emerging sense of national consciousness. However, the most immediate
cause was technological, especially in ocean navigation and the military, including
superior military organization, discipline and training, and, of course, weaponry. In
the end, the West excelled in organized violence, and although those in the West
sometimes forget this, those in other parts of the world have not. Thus, by 1910, just
before the First World War, the world came closer, in Huntington's view, than at any
time in history to being one world, one civilization—Western civilization.

The third phase—the multicivilizational system—is traceable to the end of the
expansion of the West and the beginning of the revolt against it. The period after World

War I and until about 1990 was characterized by a clash of ideas, especially capitalist and communist ideologies; but since the fall of communism the major clashes in the world now revolve around religion, culture, and ultimately civilizations. The West continues to be dominant, but Huntington foresees its decline. The decline will be slow, it will not occur in a straight line, and it will involve a waning (at least relatively) of the West's resources—population, economic product, and military capability. The decline in military capability will be traceable to such things as the decline of U.S. forces and to the globalization of the defense industries, which will make generally available many weapons formerly available only or largely in the West. Increasingly, other civilizations will reject the West, but they will embrace and utilize the advances of modernization, which can and should be distinguished from Westernization.

While the West declines, the resurgence of two other civilizations is of greatest importance. The first is the economic growth of Asian societies, especially Sinic civilization. Huntington foresees the continuing growth of Asian economies, which will soon surpass the economics of the West. Important in itself, this will translate into increasing power for the East and a corresponding decline in the ability of the West to impose its standards on the East. Huntington sees the economic ascendancy of the East as largely traceable to the superior aspects of its culture(s), especially its collectivism in contrast to the individuality that dominates the West. Also helpful to the economic rise of the East are various other commonalities among the nations of the region (e.g., religion, especially Confucianism). The successes of Asian economies will be important not only in themselves but also for the role they will play as models for other non-Western societies.

This first of Huntington's arguments is not that surprising or original. After all, we witnessed the dramatic growth of the post–World War II Japanese economy, and we are now witnessing the amazing economic transformation of China and India. Projecting present economic trends, few would disagree with the view that the economy of China will become the largest in the world in the not-too-distant future.

More controversial is Huntington's second major contention, which involves the resurgence of Islam. The Sinic emergence is rooted in the economy, but Islamic growth is rooted in dramatic population growth and the mobilization of the population. This growth of Islam has touched nearly every Muslim society, usually first culturally and then sociopolitically. The growth of Islam can be seen as part of the global revival of religion. It also can be seen both as a product of, and as an effort to come to grips with, modernization.

Huntington goes beyond pointing to this development to paint a dire portrait of the future of the relations between the West and these other two civilizations, especially Islam. The Cold War conflict between capitalism and communism has been replaced by conflict that is to be found at the "fault lines" among and between civilizations, especially the Western, Sinic, and Islamic civilizations. Thus, he foresees dangerous clashes between the West (and what he calls its "arrogance"), Islam (and its "intolerance"), and Sinic "assertiveness." Much of the conflict revolves around the West's view of itself as possessing "universal culture," its desire to export that culture to the rest of the world, and its declining ability to do so. Furthermore, what the West sees as universalism, the rest of the world, especially Islamic civilization, sees as imperialism. More specifically, the West wants to limit weapons proliferation, while other civilizations want weapons, especially "weapons of mass destruction." The West also seeks to export democracy to, and even impose it on, other societies and civilizations, which often resist democracy as part of the West's idea of universal culture. And the West seeks to control and to limit immigration (especially from Islamic civilization), although many from those civilizations have found their way into the West or want to be there. As these processes increase, Huntington sees cleft societies developing *within* both Europe and the United States. In the latter, fault lines will develop not only between Westerners and Muslims but also between Anglos and Hispanics (Huntington, 2004).

What has earned Huntington numerous criticisms and the greatest enmity are his controversial statements about Islamic civilization and Muslims (Huntington, 1996). For example, he argues that wherever Muslims and non-Muslims live in close proximity to one another, violent conflict and intense antagonism are pervasive, and he puts much of the blame for this on Muslims and their propensity toward violent conflict. He argues that from the beginning, Islam has been a religion of the sword, it has glorified military values, and there is a history of Islamic conquest. The relationship between Islam and other civilizations has historically been one of mutual indigestibility. Of course, Western imperialism—often with Islam as a target—has played a key role in this. Islam also lacks a strong core state to exert control over the civilization. But of greatest importance to Huntington are the pressures created by the demographic explosion within Islam.

Huntington is concerned about the decline of the West, especially of the United States. He sees the United States, indeed all societies, as threatened by their increasing multicivilizational or multicultural character. For him, the demise of the United States effectively means the demise of Western civilization. Without a powerful, unicivilizational United States, the West is minuscule. For the West to survive and prosper, the United States must do two things. First, it must reaffirm its identity as a Western (rather than a multicivilizational) nation. Second, it must reaffirm and reassert its role as the leader of Western civilization around the globe. The reassertion and acceptance of Western civilization (which would also involve a renunciation of universalism), indeed all civilizations, is the surest way to prevent warfare between civilizations. The real danger, for Huntington, is multiculturalism within the West and all other civilizations. Thus, Huntington ultimately comes down on the side of cultural continuity and something approaching cultural purity within civilizations. For him, at least in some ideal sense, globalization becomes a process by which civilizations continue to exist and move in roughly parallel fashion in the coming years. This constitutes a reaffirmation of the importance of civilization—that is, culture—in the epoch of globalization.

Cultural Convergence 文化趋同论

The preceding paradigm is rooted in the idea of lasting differences among and between cultures and civilizations as a result of, or in spite of, globalization. In contrast, the cultural convergence paradigm is based on the idea of globalization leading to increasing sameness throughout the world. While thinkers like Huntington emphasize the persistence of cultures and civilizations in the face of globalization, those who support the convergence perspective see those cultures changing, sometimes radically, as a result of globalization. The cultures of the world are seen as growing increasingly similar, at least to some degree and in some ways. There is a tendency to see global assimilation in the direction of dominant groups and societies in the world. Those who operate from this perspective focus on such things as "cultural imperialism," global capitalism, Westernization, Americanization, "McDonaldization," and "world culture" (Boli and Lechner, 2005). At its extreme, globalization becomes Westernization, Americanization (DeGrazia, 2005; Marling, 2006) and McDonaldization writ large.

In what follows I will discuss two versions of this basic argument that is closely associated with my own work on this topic. However, a note of warning and clarification is needed. Although my work does focus on cultural convergence, it certainly does *not* argue that this is all that is happening in globalization, or that local cultures are disappearing completely or even necessarily being altered in some fundamental way. Rather, the argument is that there are global processes that are bringing the same or similar phenomena (e.g., McDonald's restaurants in 120-plus countries in the world) to many parts of the world and, in that sense, there is cultural convergence. However, side-by-side with such global phenomena exist local phenomena (e.g., local open-air food markets or craft fairs) that continue vibrant and important. Furthermore, it may well be that the arrival of these global forms spurs the revival or development of new local forms. Although the last two points are certainly meritorious, in accepting them we must not lose sight of the fact that some, perhaps a great deal of, cultural convergence is also occurring (the spread of Wal-Mart into Mexico and other nations is another example).

"McDonaldization" "麦当劳化"

Although it is based on Max Weber's ideas about the rationalization of the West (see Chapter 1), the McDonaldization thesis (Ritzer, 2004a, 2006) adopts a different model: Weber focused on the bureaucracy; I concentrate on the fast-food restaurant. Also, the McDonaldization thesis brings the theory into the twenty-first century and views rationalization as extending its reach into more sectors of society and into more areas of the world than Weber ever imagined. Of greatest concern in the context of this section is the fact that McDonaldization is, as we will see, a force in globalization, especially increasing cultural homogenization.

McDonaldization is the process by which the principles of the fast-food restaurant are coming to dominate more and more sectors of American society, as well as the rest of the world. The nature of the McDonaldization process may be delineated by outlining its five basic dimensions: efficiency, calculability, predictability, control through the substitution of technology for people, and, paradoxically, the irrationality of rationality.

Efficiency   A McDonaldizing society emphasizes *efficiency,* the effort to discover the best possible means to achieve whatever end is desired. Workers in fast-food restaurants clearly must work efficiently. For example, burgers are assembled, and sometimes even cooked, in an assembly-line fashion. Customers want, and are expected, to acquire and consume their meals efficiently. The drive-through window is a highly efficient means for customers to obtain, and for employees to dole out, meals. Overall, various norms, rules, regulations, procedures, and structures have been put in place in the fast-food restaurant in order to ensure that *both* employees and customers act in an efficient manner. Furthermore, the efficiency of one party helps to ensure that the other will behave in a similar manner.

Calculability   Great importance is given to *calculability*, to an emphasis on quantity, often to the detriment of quality. Various aspects of the work of employees at fast-food restaurants are timed. This emphasis on speed often serves to adversely affect the quality of the work, from the point of view of the employee, resulting in dissatisfaction, alienation, and high turnover rates. Similarly, customers are expected to spend as little time as possible in the fast-food restaurant. The drive-through window reduces this time to zero, but if customers desire to eat in the restaurant, the chairs may be designed to impel them to leave after about 20 minutes. This emphasis on speed clearly has a negative effect on the quality of the dining experience at a fast-food restaurant. Furthermore, the emphasis on how fast the work is to be done means that customers cannot be served high-quality food that, almost by definition, would require a good deal of time to prepare.

Predictability   Because McDonaldization involves an emphasis on predictability, things (products, settings, employee and customer behavior, and so on) are pretty much the same from one geographic setting to another and from one time to another. Employees are expected to perform their work in a predictable manner, and customers are expected to respond with similarly predictable behavior. Thus, when customers enter, employees ask, following scripts, what they wish to order. Customers are expected to know what they want, or where to look to find what they want, and they are expected to order, pay, and leave quickly. Employees (following another script) are expected to thank them when they do leave. A highly predictable ritual is played out in the fast-food restaurant—one that involves highly predictable foods that vary little from one time or place to another.

Control by Means of Technology   Great control exists in McDonaldized systems, and a good deal of that control comes from technologies. These technologies currently dominate employees, but increasingly they will be replacing them. Employees are clearly controlled by such technologies as french-fry machines that ring when the fries are done and even automatically lift the fries out of the hot oil. For their part, customers are controlled by the employees who are constrained by such technologies as well as more directly by the technologies themselves. Thus, the automatic fry machine makes it impossible for a customer to request well-done, well-browned fries.

Irrationality of Rationality   Both employees and customers suffer from the irrationality of rationality that seems inevitably to accompany McDonaldization. Paradoxically, rationality seems often to lead to its exact opposite—irrationality. For example, the efficiency of the fast-food restaurant is often replaced by the inefficiencies associated with long lines of people at the counters or long lines of cars at the drive-through window. Although there are many other irrationalities, the ultimate irrationality is dehumanization. Employees are forced to work in dehumanizing jobs, and customers are forced to eat in dehumanizing settings and circumstances. The fast-food restaurant is a source of degradation for employees and customers alike.

麦当劳化、扩张主义和全球化
McDonaldization, Expansionism, and Globalization

McDonald's has been a resounding success in the international arena. Over half of McDonald's restaurants are outside the United States (in the mid-1980s only 25 percent of McDonald's were outside the United States). The vast majority of new restaurants opened each year are overseas. Well over half of McDonald's profits come from its overseas operations. The highly McDonaldized Starbucks has become an increasingly global force and is now a presence in Latin America, Europe (it is particularly visible in London), the Middle East, and the Pacific Rim.

Many highly McDonaldized firms outside of the fast-food industry have also had success globally. In addition to its thousands of stores in the United States, Blockbuster now has just over 2,000 sites in 28 other countries. Wal-Mart opened its first international store (in Mexico) in 1991 and now operates over a thousand stores overseas (compared to over 3,000 in the United States, including supercenters and Sam's Club).

Another indicator of globalization is the fact that other nations have developed their own variants of this American institution. Canada has a chain of coffee shops, Tim Hortons (merged with Wendy's a few years ago), that has 2,200 outlets (160 in the United States). Paris, a city whose love for fine cuisine might lead you to think it would prove immune to fast food, has a large number of fast-food croissanteries; the revered French bread has also been McDonaldized. India has a chain of fast-food restaurants, Nirula's, that sells mutton burgers (about 80 percent of Indians are Hindus, who eat no beef) as well as local Indian cuisine. Mos Burger is a Japanese chain with over 1,500 restaurants that, in addition to the usual fare, sell teriyaki chicken burgers, rice burgers, and oshiruko with brown rice cake. Russkoye Bistro, a Russian chain, sells traditional Russian fare like pirogi (meat and vegetable pies), blini (thin pancakes), Cossack apricot curd tart, and, of course, vodka. Perhaps the most unlikely spot for an indigenous fast-food restaurant, war-ravaged Beirut of 1984, witnessed the opening of Juicy Burger, with a rainbow instead of golden arches and J.B. the Clown standing in for Ronald McDonald. Its owners hoped that it would become the McDonald's of the Arab world. After the 2003 invasion of Iraq, a number of clones of McDonald's ("Madonal," "Matbax") quickly opened.

Now McDonaldization is coming full circle. Other countries with their own McDonaldized institutions have begun to export them to the United States. The Body Shop, an ecologically sensitive British cosmetics chain, had over 1,900 shops in 50 nations in 2003, of which 300 were in the United States. Furthermore, American firms are now opening copies of this British chain, such as Bath and Body Works. Pollo Campero, a Guatemalan chain specializing in fried chicken, is currently in six countries and is spreading rapidly throughout the United States.

McDonald's, as the model of the process of McDonaldization, has come to occupy a central position throughout the world. At the opening of McDonald's in Moscow, it was described as the ultimate American icon. When Pizza Hut opened in Moscow in 1990, customers saw it as a small piece of America. Reflecting on the growth of fast-food restaurants in Brazil, an executive associated with Pizza Hut of Brazil said that his nation is passionate about things American.

The "Globalization of Nothing" "虚无的全球化"

The "globalization of nothing" (Ritzer, 2004b), like McDonaldization, implies increasing homogenization as more and more nations have an increasing number of the various forms of nothing. Note that I am *not* arguing that globalization is nothing; indeed it is clear that the process is of enormous significance. Rather, the argument is that there is an *elective affinity* (a term borrowed from Weber) between globalization and nothing: one does not cause the other, but they do tend to vary together.

What is central here is the idea of *grobalization* (a companion to the notion of glocalization), or the imperialistic ambitions of nations, corporations, organizations, and the like and their desire, indeed need, to impose themselves on various geographic areas (see J. M. Ryan, 2007). Their main interest is in seeing their power, influence, and in some cases profits *grow* (hence the term *gro*balization) throughout the world. Grobalization involves a variety of subprocesses. Three of them—capitalism, Americanization, and McDonaldization—are central driving forces in grobalization and are of great significance in the worldwide spread of nothingness.

By *nothing,* I mean (largely) empty forms, forms largely devoid of distinctive content. (Conversely, *something* would be defined as [largely] full forms, forms rich in distinctive content.) It is easier to export empty forms (nothing) throughout the globe than it is to export forms that are loaded with content (something). The latter are more likely to be rejected by at least some cultures and societies because the content conflicts, is at variance with, local content. In contrast, empty forms, largely devoid of distinctive content, are less likely to come into conflict with the local. In addition, empty forms have other advantages from the point of view of globalization. For example, they are easy to replicate over and over because they are so minimalist, and they have a cost advantage because they are relatively inexpensive to reproduce. A good example of nothing in these terms is the shopping mall (e.g., any of the malls owned by the Mills Corporation—Potomac Mills, Sawgrass Mills, etc.), which is an empty (largely) structure that is easily replicated around the world. These malls *could* be filled with an endless array of specific content (e.g., local shops, local foods, etc.—something!) that *could* vary enormously from one locale to another. However, increasingly, they are filled with chain stores carrying a wide range of various types of . . . nothing! Since more and more countries have these malls, this is an example of the grobalization of nothing and of increasing global homogenization.

There are four subtypes of nothing, and all of them are largely empty of distinctive content and are being globalized: (1) "nonplaces," or settings that are largely empty of content (e.g., the malls discussed above); (2) "nonthings," items such as credit cards in which there is little to distinguish one from the billions of others and all of them work in exactly the same way for all who use them anywhere in the world; (3) "nonpeople," or the kind of employees associated with nonplaces, for example, telemarketers, who may be nearly anywhere in the world and who interact with all customers in much the same way, relying heavily on scripts; and (4) "nonservices," services such as those provided by ATMs (the services provided are identical; the customer does all the work needed to obtain the services) as opposed to human bank tellers. The grobal proliferation of nonplaces, nonthings, nonpeople, and nonservices is another indication of increasing homogenization.

Cultural Hybridization 文化混杂论

The third paradigm emphasizes the mixing of cultures as a result of globalization and the production, out of the integration of the global and the local, of new and unique hybrid cultures that are not reducible to either the local or the global culture. From this perspective, McDonaldization and the grobalization of nothing may be taking place, but they are largely superficial changes. Much more important is the integration of these and other global processes with various local realities to produce new and distinctive hybrid forms that indicate continued heterogenization rather than homogenization. Hybridization is a very positive, even romantic, view of globalization as a profoundly creative process out of which emerge new cultural realities and continuing if not increasing heterogeneity in many different locales.

The concept that gets to the heart of cultural hybridization, as well as to what many contemporary theorists interested in globalization think about the nature of transnational processes, is glocalization. *Glocalization* can be defined as the interpenetration of the global and the local resulting in unique outcomes in different geographic areas. While grobalization, as discussed above, tends to be associated with the proliferation of nothing, glocalization tends to be tied more to something and therefore stands opposed, at least partially (and along with the local itself), to the spread of nothing. Following Roland Robertson (2001; see also M. Smith, 2007), the following are the essential elements of the perspective on globalization adopted by those who emphasize glocalization:

1. The world is growing more pluralistic. Glocalization theory is exceptionally alert to differences within and between areas of the world.
2. Individuals and local groups have great power to adapt, innovate, and maneuver within a glocalized world. Glocalization theory sees local individuals and groups as important and creative agents.
3. Social processes are relational and contingent. Grobalization provokes a variety of reactions—ranging from nationalist entrenchment to cosmopolitan embrace—that feed back on and transform it, that produce glocalization.

4. Commodities and the media are seen *not* as (totally) coercive but rather as providing material to be used in individual and group creation throughout the glocalized areas of the world.

Those who emphasize glocalization tend to see it as militating against the grobalization of nothing and, in fact, view it as leading to the creation of a wide array of new, "glocal" forms of something. In contrast, those who emphasize grobalization see it as a powerful contributor to the spread of nothingness throughout the world.

A discussion of some closely related terms (and related examples) will be of considerable help in getting a better sense of glocalization, as well as the broader issue of cultural hybridization (Canclini, 1995; Pieterse, 2004). Of course, *hybridization* itself is one such term emphasizing increasing diversity associated with the unique mixtures of the global and the local as opposed to the *uniformity* associated with grobalization. A cultural hybrid would involve the combination of two or more elements from different cultures or parts of the world. Among the examples of hybridization (and heterogenization, glocalization) are Ugandan tourists visiting Amsterdam to watch two Moroccan women engage in Thai boxing, Argentinians watching Asian rap performed by a South American band at a London club owned by a Saudi Arabian, and the more mundane experiences of Americans eating such concoctions as Irish bagels, Chinese tacos, and kosher pizza. Obviously, the list of such hybrids is long and growing rapidly with increasing hybridization. The contrast of course would be such uniform experiences as eating hamburgers in the United States, quiche in France, or sushi in Japan.

Yet another concept that is closely related to glocalization is *creolization* (Hannerz, 1987). The term *creole* generally refers to people of mixed race, but it has been extended to the idea of the creolization of language and culture, involving a combination of languages and cultures that were previously unintelligible to one another.

All of the above—glocalization, hybridization, creolization—should give the reader a good feel for what is being discussed here under the heading "cultural hybridization."

Appadurai's "Landscapes" 阿帕杜莱的 "图景"

In *Modernity at Large: Cultural Dimensions of Globalization* (1996), Arjun Appadurai emphasizes global flows and the disjunctures among them. These serve to produce unique cultural realities around the world; they tend to produce culture hybrids.

Appadurai discusses five global flows: ethnoscapes, mediascapes, technoscapes, financescapes, and ideoscapes. The use of the suffix *-scape* allows Appadurai to communicate the idea that these processes have fluid, irregular, and variable shapes and are therefore consistent with the idea of heterogenization and not homogenization. The fact that there are a number of these scapes and that they operate independently of one another to some degree, and perhaps are even in conflict with one another, makes this perspective also in tune with perspectives that emphasize cultural diversity and heterogeneity. Furthermore, these scapes are interpreted differently by different agents ranging all the way from individuals to face-to-face groups, subnational groups, multinational corporations, and even nation-states. And these scapes are ultimately navigated by individuals and groups on the basis of their own subjective interpretations of them. In other words, these are imagined worlds, and those doing the imagining can range from those who control them to those who live in and traverse them. Although power obviously lies with those in control and their imaginings, this perspective gives to those who merely live in or pass through them the power to redefine and ultimately subvert them.

At the center of Appadurai's thinking are the five landscapes mentioned above:

1. *Ethnoscapes* involve the mobile groups and individuals (tourists, refugees, guest workers) who play such an important role in the ever-changing world in which we increasingly live. This involves actual movement as well as fantasies about moving. In an ever-changing world, people cannot afford to allow their imaginations to rest too long and thus must keep such fantasies alive.

2. *Technoscapes* are the ever-fluid, global configurations of high and low, mechanical and informational technology and the wide range of material (downloading files, e-mail) that now moves so freely and quickly around the globe and across borders that at one time were impervious to such movement (or at least thought to be).

3. *Financescapes* involve the processes by which huge sums of money move through nations and around the world at great speed through commodity speculations, currency markets, national stock exchanges, and the like.

4. *Mediascapes* involve both the electronic capability to produce and transmit information around the world and the images of the world that these media create and disseminate. Involved here are those who write "blogs" for the Internet, global filmmakers and film distributors, television stations (CNN and al-Jazeera are notable examples), and newspapers and magazines.

5. *Ideoscapes,* like mediascapes, are sets of images. However, they are largely restricted to political images produced by states and in line with their ideology, or to images and counterideologies produced by movements that seek to supplant those in power or at least to gain a piece of that power.

Three things are especially worth noting about Appadurai's landscapes. First, they can be seen as global process that are partly or wholly independent of any given nation-state. Second, global flows occur not only through the landscapes but also increasingly in and through the *disjunctures* among them. Thus, to give one example of such a disjuncture, the Japanese are open to ideas (ideoscapes, mediascapes) but notoriously closed to immigration (at least one of the ethnoscapes). More generally, the free movement of some landscapes may be at variance with blockages of others. Studies in this area must be attuned to such disjunctures and to their implications for globalization. Third, territories are going to be affected differently by the five landscapes and their disjunctures. This will lead to important differences among and between cultures. The focus on landscapes and their disjunctures points globalization studies in a set of unique directions. However, the focus on landscapes is in line with the idea that globalization is much more associated with heterogenization than homogenization, and globalization is much more associated with glocalization than grobalization.

Economic Theory 经济理论

There are many theories about the economic aspects of globalization. The most important perspectives, at least in sociology, tend to be those associated with Marxian theory; they are neo-Marxian in nature. Two major examples are discussed in this section.

Transnational Capitalism 跨国资本主义

Leslie Sklair (2002) distinguishes between two systems of globalization. The first—the capitalist system of globalization—is the one that is now predominant. The other—the socialist system—is not yet in existence but is foreshadowed by current anti-globalization movements, especially those oriented toward greater human rights throughout the world. The antiglobalization movements, and the possibility of a socialist form, are made possible by the problems in the current system of globalization, especially class polarization and the increasing ecological unsustainability of capitalist globalization.

Although the nation-state remains important, Sklair focuses on transnational practices that are able to cut across boundaries—including those created by states—with the implication that territorial boundaries are of declining importance in capitalist globalization. As a Marxist, Sklair accords priority to economic transnational practices, and it is in this context that *transnational corporations*—one of the central aspects of his analysis—predominate. Underlying this emphasis on transnational corporations is the idea that capitalism has moved away from being an international system (because the nation[-state] is of declining significance) and toward becoming a globalizing system that is decoupled from any specific geographic territory or state.

The second transnational practice of great importance is political, and here the *transnational capitalist class* predominates. However, it is not made up of capitalists in the traditional Marxian sense of the term—that is, the transnational capitalist class does not necessarily own the means of production. Sklair differentiates among four "fractions" of the transnational capitalist class: (1) the *corporate fraction* made up of executives of transnational corporations and their local affiliates; (2) a *state fraction* composed of globalizing state and interstate bureaucrats and politicians; (3) a *technical fraction* made up of globalizing professionals; and (4) the *consumerist fraction* encompassing merchants and media executives. This is obviously a very different group than Marx thought of when conceptualizing the capitalist.

The transnational capitalist class may not be capitalist in a traditional sense of the term, but it is transnational in various ways. First, its "members" tend to share global (as well as local) interests. Second, they seek to exert various types of control across nations. That is, they exert economic control in the workplace, political control in both domestic and international politics, and culture-ideological control in everyday life across international borders. Third, they tend to share a global rather than a local perspective on a wide range of issues. Fourth, they come from many different countries, but increasingly they see themselves as citizens of the world and not just of their place of birth. Finally, wherever they may be at any given time, they share similar lifestyles, especially in terms of the goods and services they consume.

The third transnational practice is culture-ideology, and here Sklair accords great importance to the *culture-ideology of consumption* in capitalist globalization. Although the focus is on culture and ideology, the emphasis on consumption ultimately involves the economy by adding an interest in consumption to the traditional concern with production (and the transnational corporations) in economic approaches in general, and Marxian theories in particular. In this realm the ability to exert ideological control over people scattered widely throughout the globe has increased dramatically, primarily through the greater reach and sophistication of advertising and the media and the bewildering array of consumer goods that are marketed by and through them. Ultimately, they all serve to create a global mood to consume that benefits transnational corporations, as well as the advertising and media corporations, which are examples of such corporations and profit from them.

Ultimately, Sklair is interested in the relationship among the transnational practices and the institutions that dominate such practice, and he argues that transnational corporations utilize the transnational capitalist class to develop and solidify the consumerist culture and ideology that is increasingly necessary to feed the demands of the capitalist system of production. Indeed, it is this relationship that defines global capitalism today, and it is the most important force in ongoing changes in the world.

As a Marxist, Sklair is interested not only in critically analyzing capitalist globalization but in articulating an alternative to it and its abuses. He sees some promising signs in the protectionism of some countries that see themselves as exploited by transnational corporations. Also hopeful are new social movements such as the green movement seeking a more sustainable environment and the various antiglobalization groups that have sprung up in recent years. He is particularly interested in various human rights movements in which, he believes, can be found the seeds of the alternative to capitalist globalization—that is, socialist globalization. He predicts that these and other movements will gain momentum in the twenty-first century as they increasingly resist the ways in which globalization has been appropriated by transnational corporations. In fact, in good Marxian dialectical terms, he sees the success of capitalist globalization sowing the seeds of its own destruction as its expansion tends to provide its opponents with resources (derived from the economic success of transnational capitalism), organizational forms (copied from the successful organizations in global capitalism), and most obviously a clarity of purpose. As the transnational corporations grow more successful, their abuses will become more blatant, and the need to supplant them as the central players in the global system will intensify.

Empire 帝国

The most important and widely discussed and debated Marxian approach to globalization is Michael Hardt and Antonio Negri's *Empire* (2000) and *Multitude* (2004). Although Hardt and Negri have reservations about postmodern social theory, they analyze the postmodernization of the global economy. They associate modernity with *imperialism,* the defining characteristic of which is one or more nations at the center that control and exploit, especially economically, a number of areas throughout the world. In a postmodern move, Hardt and Negri "decenter" this imperialism, thereby defining empire as a postmodern reality in which such dominance exists but no single nation (or any other entity) is at its center. To put this another way, *modern* sovereignty can be traced to a *place,* but in its *postmodern* form as empire, sovereignty exists in a nonplace. The empire has no center; it is deterritorialized; it exists in the realm of ideas (especially through the media). And as a result, the spectacle of the empire is everywhere; it is omnipresent.

Empire does not yet exist fully. It is in formation at the moment, but we can get a sense of its parameters. Empire governs the world with a single logic of rule, but there is no single power at the heart of empire. Instead of a single source of command, in empire power is dispersed throughout society and the globe. Even the United States, in spite of its seeming hegemony in the world today, is not an empire in these terms, nor does it lie at the heart of Hardt and Negri's sense of an empire. However, the sovereignty of the United States does constitute an important precursor to empire, and the United States continues to occupy a privileged position in the world. However, it is in the process of being supplanted by empire.

Empire is (or will be) lacking in geographic or territorial boundaries. It can also be seen as lacking temporal boundaries in the sense that it seeks (albeit unsuccessfully) to suspend history and to exist for all eternity. It also can be seen as lacking a lower boundary in that it seeks to expand down into the depths of the social world. This means that it seeks not only to control the basics of the social world (thought, action, interaction, groups), but to go even further in an effort to use biopower to control human nature and population—*both* people's brains and their bodies. In a way, empire is far more ambitious than imperialism in that it seeks to control the entirety of life down to its most basic levels.

The key to the global power of empire lies in the fact that it is (or seeks to be) a new juridical power. It is based on such things as the constitution of order, norms, ethical truths, and a common notion of what is right. This juridical formation is the source of power of empire. Thus, in the name of what is "right," it can intervene anywhere in the world in order to deal with what it considers humanitarian problems, to guarantee accords, and to impose peace on those who may not want peace or even see the empire's goal as peace. More specifically, it can engage in "just wars" in the name of this juridical formation; the latter legitimates the former. Such wars become a kind of sacred undertaking. The enemy is anyone or anything that the juridical formation sees as a threat to ethical order in the world. Thus the right to engage in just war is seen as boundless, encompassing the entire space of civilization. The right to engage in just war also is seen as boundless in time; it is permanent, eternal. In a just war, ethically grounded military action is legitimate, and its goal is to achieve the desired order and peace. Thus empire is based not on force per se but on the ability to project force in the service of that which is right (precursors of this notion can be seen in the two U.S. invasions of Iraq, as well as the incursion into Afghanistan).

Empire is based on a triple imperative. First, it seeks to incorporate all that it can. It appears to be magnanimous, and it operates with a liberal facade. However, in the process of inclusion, it creates a smooth world in which differences, resistance, and conflict are eliminated. Second, empire differentiates and affirms differences. While those who are different are celebrated culturally, they are set aside juridically.

Third, once the differences are in place, empire seeks to hierarchize and to manage the hierarchy and the differences embedded in it. It is hierarchization and management that is the real power of empire.

Empire is, then, a postmodern Marxian perspective on globalization and on the exertion of power around the world. However, instead of capitalists or capitalist nations exerting that power, it is the much more nebulous empire that is in control. If there are no more capitalists in empire, what about the proletariat? To Hardt and Negri, the time of the proletariat is over. But if the proletariat no longer exists to oppose empire, where is the opposition to come from? Operating from a Marxian perspective, Hardt and Negri must come up with an oppositional force, and they do not disappoint on this score and label the oppositional group the "multitude." This is an interesting choice of terms. For one thing it is much more general and abstract than "proletariat" and also moves us away from a limited focus on the economy. Second, it makes clear that there are lots of at least potential opponents of the empire; indeed, those in control in the empire constitute only a small minority vis-à-vis the multitude.

Hardt and Negri's *multitude* is that collection of people throughout the world that sustains empire in various ways, including but *not* restricted to its labor (it is the real productive force in empire). Among other ways, it also sustains it by buying into the culture-ideology of consumption and, more important, in actually consuming a variety of its offerings. Like capitalism and its relationship to the proletariat, empire is a parasite on the multitude and on its creativity and productivity. Like Marx's proletariat (which all but disappears in this theory), the multitude is a force for creativity in empire. Also like the proletariat, the multitude is capable of over-throwing empire through the autonomous creation of a counter-empire. The counter-empire, like empire, is, or would be, a global phenomenon created out of, and becoming, global flows and exchanges. Globalization leads to deterritorialization (the multitude itself is a force in deterritorialization and is deterrirorialized), and deterritorialization is a prerequisite to the global liberation of the multitude. With deterritorialization, social revolution can, as Marx predicted, occur, perhaps for the first time, on a global level.

Hardt and Negri are certainly critics of globalization, whether it be modern capitalist imperialism or postmodern empire, but they also see a utopian potential in globalization. Thus, globalization per se is *not* the problem; instead, the problem is the form that it has taken, or takes, in imperialism and empire. That utopian potential has always been present, but in the past it was smothered by modern sovereign pow-ers through ideological control or military force. Empire now occupies, or soon will, that controlling position, but its need to suppress that potential is counterbalanced by the multitude's need to manifest and express it. Ultimately, there exists in global-ization the potential for universal freedom and equality. Further, globalization prevents us from falling back into the particularism and isolationism that have characterized much of human history. Those processes, of course, would serve to impede the global change sought by the multitude. More positively, as globalization progresses, it serves to push us more and more in the direction of the creation of counter-empire. This focus on the global serves to distinguish Hardt and Negri from other postmod-ernists and post-Marxists, who tend to focus on the local and the problems and potential that exist there. In contrast, in their view, a focus on the local serves to obscure the fact that the sources of both our major problems and our liberation exist at the global level, in empire.

While Hardt and Negri foresee counter-empire, they, like Marx in the case of communism, offer no blueprint for how to get there or what counter-empire might look like. Like communism to Marx, counter-empire will arise out of actual practice (*praxis*), especially that of the multitude. Counter-empire must be global, it must be everywhere, and it must be opposed to empire. Counter-empire is made increasingly likely because empire is losing its ability to control the multitude. Thus, empire must redouble its efforts (e.g., through police power), and this serves to mobilize the multitude and make counter-empire more likely. As postmodernists, Hardt and Negri reject a focus on the agent of the type found in Marxian theory, specifically the centrality accorded to the proletarian revolutionary agent who is increasingly conscious of exploitation by capitalism. Instead, they focus on such nonagential, collective actions by the multitude as desertion, migration, and nomadism. In accord with their postmodern orientation and its focus on the body, Hardt and Negri urge a new "barbarism" involving new bodily forms of the kind that are now appearing in the realm of gender, sexuality, and esthetic mutations (such as tattooing and body piercing). Such bodies are less likely to submit to external control and more likely to create a new life—the basis of counter-empire. Thus, the revolutionary force is not a conscious agent but new bodily, corporeal forms.

While Hardt and Negri retain a Marxian interest in production, they do recognize a new world of production and work in which immaterial, intellectual, and communicative types of labor are increasingly central. Thus, control over individuals engaged in such work—a key element and increasing proportion of the multitude—is of increasing importance. However, although they are controlled through global communication and ideology (especially via the media), it is also through communication and ideology that the revolutionary potential of the multitude will be expressed. The key thing about communication is that it flows easily and effectively across the globe. This makes it easier for empire to exert control, to organize production globally, and to make its justification of itself and its actions immanent within that communication. Conversely, of course, it is also the mechanism by which the multitude can ultimately create counter-empire.

Political Theory 政治理论

A particularly important example of political theory is liberal theory (derived from the classical work of John Locke, Adam Smith, and others) (MacPherson, 1962), especially in the form of neoliberal thinking (J. Campbell and Pederson, 2001; D. Harvey, 2005) (often called the "Washington consensus" [Williamson, 1990, 1997]). Liberal theory comes in various forms, but all are undergirded by a belief in the importance of the free market and the need to allow it to operate free of any impediments, especially those imposed by the nation-state and other political entities. The belief is that the free operation of the market, in particular the capitalist market, will in the "long run" advantage just about everyone. This is a popular theory in international relations, political science, and business. It is embraced by many politicians (especially in the United States, hence the label "Washington consensus"), and it informs the writing of influential journalists such as Thomas Friedman (Antonio, 2007a).

Another political theory involves a "realist" view, popular in most of the same venues, that sees globalization as the outcome of the *power* relations among nation-states (Scholte, 2005; Spegle, 1996). That is, states are seen as aggressively pursuing their own interests on the global stage (as well as within their own borders) and using their power to advance those interests. As the most powerful nation in the world today (the sole remaining superpower), the United States is seen as the world's major user (and abuser) of its power on the global stage. Thus, for example, the war in Iraq (begun in 2003) is seen as an exercise of global U.S. power, especially military power. The United States exercised that power to advance its own interests, which could be interpreted positively as defending its own well-being against the threat of weapons of mass destruction (never found), or negatively as a ruse to protect and advance its own interests, especially its economic interests in protecting vital oil supplies in the Middle East.[2]

Then, there are a variety of other theories derived from the field of international relations (as is realist theory) that look more broadly at relations among and between nation-states (Smouts, 2001). Though still influential, these theories have lost ground in recent years primarily because they focus, given the nature of the field from which they emanate, on relations among and between nation-states. As a result, they tend not to concern themselves with the wide range of transnational processes that exist independent of the nation-state and are of growing importance.

The focus and plight of the field of international relations is clear in a fascinating essay by Justin Rosenberg (2005), who argues that the transnational focus of most globalization theories is misguided. According to Rosenberg, such theories may have enjoyed a boom in the 1990s, but they are now, in his view, moribund. Instead, he argues for a renewed focus on nation-states and their interrelationship, specifically from a Marxian perspective and its focal concern with capitalism. Rosenberg is making this case from the point of view of international relations and is seeking the renaissance of a field that has tended to be eclipsed by globalization theories that see the nation-state as eroding or even disappearing.

Although this approach is by no means representative of all political theories of globalization, we will illustrate it in the highly ambitious theorizing of political scientist James Rosenau (2003). The title of his book, and the concept that gets at its broadest point about globalization, is *Distant Proximities*—that is, the idea that the globe is increasingly characterized by the feeling that what seems remote is also close at hand (this concept has a close relationship with Giddens's time-space distanciation; see Chapter 11). The concept of distant proximities is linked to another key process (and concept) in Rosenau's work—*fragmegration,* the idea that the world is both fragmenting and integrating at the same time. Most generally, the world is localizing, decentralizing, and fragmenting while it is simultaneously globalizing, centralizing, and integrating.

---

[2] It also could be argued that U.S. political interests (in the Middle East) and U.S. military interests (the positioning of troops and materiel in forward military bases throughout the world) were advanced by the war.

Rosenau offers a very broad, highly complex, and abstract approach to globalization, but what is of interest here is what he has to say about political globalization. At the heart of his contribution on this issue is his identification of the various sources of fragmegration in the world today.

1. *The Development of New Microelectronic Technologies.* Microelectronic technologies such as cell phones, the Internet, and e-mail have tended to shrink the world. In the process they have rendered territorial boundaries, and ultimately states, less and less important. These technologies are fragmegrative in the sense that they further integrate those that have them, whereas those who lack them, especially those who cannot afford them (as a result, for example, of the "digital divide"), are increasingly separated from the microelectronic "haves," leading to growing fragmentation.

2. *The Skill Revolution.* Here Rosenau is thinking primarily about analytic skills such as those that give some people the ability to relate their own situation to larger, even global, situations. Of course, others, primarily because of a lack information and education, have not seen a similar level of advancement in their skill levels. The former are likely to have a more global orientation, and the latter are likely to remain committed to, or even to retreat into, local concerns. The areas of the world with a higher proportion of people with analytic skills are more likely to be successful. Furthermore, people who have such skills are likely to be able to cross state borders easily, making their attachment to any given political unit minimal.

3. *The Organization Explosion.* Here Rosenau is particularly interested in the massive proliferation of voluntary organizations, especially nongovernmental organizations (NGOs) such as human rights groups and environmental groups. Voluntary organizations serve to integrate individuals involved in them, while producing fragmentation between persons who are involved and those who are not. Politically, the rise of NGOs reflects, and contributes to, the declining importance of states and the declining confidence in their ability to accomplish various things. A reflection of the declining importance of states is the inability of states to stem the tide in the direction of the growing importance of, and involvement in, NGOs.

4. *The Bifurcation of Global Structures (The Increasing Variety of Organizations and States).* Related to the preceding point, Rosenau sees a bifurcation between states on the one hand (state centrism) and a wide array of subnational, transnational, and nongovernmental organizations on the other (multi-centrism). The interaction between these state-centric and multi-centric worlds can take various forms (e.g., conflict, cooperation). However, we have seen a decline of the state-centric world in the face of the rise of these various organizational forms. Although integration is fostered within these organizations and states, fragmentation between the two worlds is increasing.

5. *The Mobility Upheaval.* The increasingly vast movement of people (encompassing business travel, tourism, terrorism, job search, and legal and illegal migration) throughout the world is having a fragmegrative effect. Some of these forms of movement—for example, travel and tourism—can have largely integrative effects. Others—terrorism is the best example—can be disintegrative. Political entities are most threatened by movements they cannot control, such as the flow of illegal migrants. Also politically disintegrative is the vast movement of various people from less developed to devel-

oped nations. Long-standing political consensus on openness to migrants is being threatened or destroyed in various nations, especially in Europe, and liberal regimes are being threatened or replaced by right-wing regimes more opposed to such population flows. Of course, some forms of mobility that are disintegrative in one setting can be integrative in another. Thus, while terrorist acts have a disintegrative effect on the states to which they are aimed, their success can serve to integrate the states or regions from which they emanate.

6. *Weakening of Territoriality in General and State Sovereignty in Particular (The Decentralization of Governments).* Here we are directly involved in the political implications of globalization. States have declined in importance because of their inability to stem a variety of global processes. Ideas, jobs, production facilities, money, drugs, pollution, and in some cases even terrorists flow freely across state borders. Furthermore, states grow less important as it becomes increasingly clear that they are less able to handle the various fragmegrative processes outlined by Rosenau. Thus, in various ways and for various reasons, most states have seen some level of disintegration. As a result, many people are increasingly less likely to give the state their highest level of loyalty, and this reluctance, in turn, contributes to further state decline. However, there are related forms of integration, as when groups of migrants come together in a given neighborhood and create their own local institutions (schools, media, churches).

7. *Authority Crises Brought On by Increasing and Subgroupism and Decentralization.* The disintegration of the state is paralleled by an erosion of its authority. Traditional loyalties and bases of authority are eroding and being replaced by the criterion of how well the state performs its various tasks and responsibilities. The decline of state authority has had various repercussions such as disarray in the state bureaucracy, stalemates between executive and legislative branches, and a general inability to make decisions. There is a growing suspicion that no one is in charge anymore, that no one is capable of handling the complex fragmegrative processes. This belief, in turn, has led citizens to focus more on their self-interests.

These processes have been magnified by increasing government decentralization as various tasks devolve to regional and local governments. Other government tasks are being turned over to profit-making organizations (e.g., many of the tasks involved in the current occupation of Iraq are being handled by private companies), as well as to the NGOs discussed above. This shift is having disintegrative effects. What was once handled solely by the federal government is now being performed by a number of government agencies at various levels, as well as by a wide range of organizations and corporations. Integration among them, however, is possible as a result of all the new microelectronic technologies. But the inability of federal governments to handle many traditional responsibilities contributes further to the authority crisis. Thus, like everything else analyzed by Rosenau, government decentralization is fragmegrating.

Another process leading to this crisis of authority is "subgroupism." There is an increasing number of subgroups in society, including many of the entities discussed above—regional and local government, NGOs, racial and ethnic groups, and so on. More and more people are growing attached to subgroups (integration) rather than to the national government, and this preference contributes to the authority crisis (and fragmentation) that national governments are experiencing. This is especially apparent in the widespread politics of identity when people identify more with, say, their ethnic group than they do with the state. The latter finds it increasingly difficult to create a broad consensus within society and to mobilize citizens collectively in order to achieve societal goals.

8. *The Globalization of National Economies.* The growing importance of transnational economic networks of all sorts has contributed greatly both to fragmegration and to the declining importance of the state. The state can no longer control transnational economic flows, but those flows are seen by many as of far greater importance than anything else the state does. However, while this has fragmented state control over economic matters around the globe, it has simultaneously created greater centralization and integration among these transnational economic entities (e.g., the European Union or Airbus Industrie, a consortium of European aircraft manufacturers).

Although there is much else to Rosenau's theorizing that cannot be covered here, his most important contribution is to give us a better sense of the relationship between globalization, fragmegration, and politics. It is clear that the political challenge to the state is to find new ways of governing, perhaps at a reduced level, in a globalizing and increasingly fragmegrating world.

Other Theories 其他理论

This chapter gives only a sense of a few of the types of theorizing about globalization. There are many other well-known theories of globalization—for example, ones that draw on network theory (Castells, 1996, 1997, 1998; see Chapter 11) and complexity theory (Urry, 2003), or that focus on religion, sport, or the city. However, the preceding conveys at least a sense of the most important broad types of theorizing on, and specific theories of, globalization. Of course, the process of globalization continues, is expanding, and is constantly changing. As a result, we can expect the continuing development of theorizing about globalization, including new and innovative approaches to the topic.

Summary 总结

Globalization theory emerged as a result of developments and changes both in the world as a whole and in academia. Globalization can be analyzed culturally, economically, politically, and institutionally. A concern for homogenization/heterogenization cuts across work in all of these areas. Central to the work of Giddens on globalization is losing control over the juggernaut of modernity and creating a runaway world. Beck sees hope in globality with the decline of the nation-state and the emergence of transnational organizations and possibly a transnational state. To Bauman, what defines the global world is a "space war" between those who have and those who do not have mobility. However, even those with mobility face grave problems.

Cultural theories of globalization may be divided into three paradigms: cultural differentialism, cultural convergence, and cultural hybridization. Cultural differentialism adopts the view that there are lasting differences among and between cultures and that those differences are largely unaffected by globalization. Huntington offers the best-known example of cultural differentialism with his focus on civilizations, the major civilizations of the world, and the likelihood of economic conflict between Sinic and Western civilization and warfare between Islamic and Western civilization. Cultural convergence takes the view that globalization is leading to increasing sameness around the world. Two examples of cultural convergence are the McDonaldization thesis and the idea that the world is increasingly dominated by the "grobalization" of nothing. Cultural hybridization adopts the perspective that globalization is bringing with it the mixing of cultures, producing new and unique cultures that are not reducible to either global or local. A number of theoretical ideas are associated with cultural hybridization, including glocalization, hybridization, and creolization. A major theory included under the "cultural hybridization" heading is Appadurai's thinking on landscapes and the disjunctures among and between them.

Economic theories of globalization are illustrated with two examples. Leslie Sklair develops a neo-Marxian economic theory of globalization that focuses on transnational capitalism, especially transnational corporations, the transnational capitalist class, and the culture-ideology of consumption. Sklair argues that transnational capitalism is providing the basis for the emergence of socialist globalization. According to Hardt and Negri, we are in the midst of a transition from capitalist imperialism to the dominance of empire. Empire lacks a center and is based on juridical power. The multitude sustains empire, but it also has, at least potentiallty, the power to overthrow empire and create counter-empire.

James Rosenau offers a political view of globalization that emphasizes "distant proximities" and "fragmegration." Rosenau identifies eight major sources of fragmegration, and they all have an impact on political globalization.

Structuralism, Poststructuralism, and Postmodern Social Theory

第13章 结构主义、后结构主义 和后现代社会理论

Chapter Outline

Structuralism

Poststructuralism

Postmodern Social Theory

Criticisms and Post-Postmodern Social Theory

This book is largely about *modern* social theory. However, in the last several decades, and in many different fields (art, architecture, literature, sociology, and others), there have been developments that scholars now think of as *postmodern*. The implication is not only that these things come after the modern, but that there were problems with the modern that the postmodernists are pointing out and endeavoring to deal with.

In sociological theory, the modern (as well as the classical) theories discussed throughout the preceding pages continue to be important—in fact, preeminent—within the discipline. Yet postmodern social theory is having an increasingly important impact on sociological theory, and it is now possible to identify postmodern developments, theoretical perspectives, and theorists. Furthermore, one would expect sociological theorists, as those closest to the humanities, to be most open to postmodernism. As at least some sociological theorists grow more postmodern in their orientation, we can expect that other, more empirically inclined sociologists will come to be influenced by at least some aspects of postmodern social theory.

In discussing postmodern social theory it is necessary to shift our focus from *sociological* theories to *social* theories. *Sociological* theories tend to reflect developments that have occurred largely within sociology and that are of interest mainly to sociologists. *Social* theories tend to be multidisciplinary. The distinction between the two, however, is not clear-cut. In fact, at least some of the theories discussed earlier in this book, especially the neo-Marxian and agency-structure theories, might be better described as social theories. In any case, it is clear that postmodern theories are best viewed as social theories.

In this chapter, we deal with the emergence of what, in fact, does come after modern social theory by tracing the line of development from structuralism to poststructuralism and ultimately to what has come to be known as postmodern social theory. Following Lash (1991:ix), we take "the structuralism which swept through French social thought in the 1960s" as the starting point for the emergence of post-structuralism and postmodernism.

Structuralism was a reaction against French humanism, especially the existentialism of Jean-Paul Sartre (Margolis, 2007; Craib and Wernick, 2005). In his early work Sartre focused on the individual, especially individual freedom. At that point he adhered to the view that what people do is determined by them and not by social laws or larger social structures. However, later in his career Sartre was more drawn to Marxian theory, and while he continued to focus on the "free individual," that individual was now "situated in a massive and oppressive social structure which limits and alienates his activities" (Craib, 1976:9).

In her analysis of Sartre's work, Gila Hayim (1980) sees continuity between his early and his late work. In *Being and Nothingness*, published in 1943, Sartre focuses more on the free individual and takes the view that "existence is defined by and through one's acts. . . . *One is what one does*" (Hayim, 1980:3). At the same time, Sartre attacks the structuralist view of "objective structures as completely deterministic of behavior" (Hayim, 1980:5). For Sartre and existentialists in general, actors have the capacity to go beyond the present, to move toward the future. For Sartre, then, people are free; they are responsible for everything they do; they have no excuses. In some senses, these "staggering responsibilities of freedom" (Hayim, 1980:17) are a tremendous source of anguish to people. In other senses, this responsibility is a source of optimism to people—their fates are in their hands. In the *Critique of Dialectical Reason*, published in 1963, Sartre devotes more attention to social structures, but even here he emphasizes the "human prerogative for transcendence—the surpassing of the given" (Hayim, 1980:16). Sartre is critical of various Marxists (structural Marxists) who overemphasize the role and place of social structure. "Dogmatic Marxists have, by Sartre's view, eliminated the humanistic component of Marx's original idea" (Hayim, 1980:72). As an existentialist, Sartre *always* retained this humanism. It is against the backdrop of the humanism of existentialism that one must see the rise of structuralism, poststructuralism, and postmodernism.

Structuralism 结构主义

Structuralism obviously involves a focus on structures, but they are not in the main the same structures that concern the structural functionalists (see Chapter 3). While the latter and indeed most sociologists are concerned with *social* structures, of primary concern to structuralists are *linguistic* structures. This shift from social to linguistic structures is what has come to be known as the *linguistic turn*, which dramatically altered the nature of the social sciences (Lash, 1991:ix). The focus of a good many social scientists shifted from social structure to language (see, for example, the earlier discussions of Habermas's work on communication [in Chapter 4] and the conversation analyses of some ethnomethodologists [in Chapter 7]) or more generally to signs of various sorts.

Roots in Linguistics 语言学的源头

Structuralism emerged from diverse developments in various fields (Dosse, 1998). The source of modern structuralism and its strongest bastion to this day is linguistics. The work of the Swiss linguist Ferdinand de Saussure (1857–1913) stands out in the development of structural linguistics and, ultimately, structuralism in various other fields (Thibault, 2005a; Culler, 1976). Of particular interest to us is Saussure's differentiation between *langue* and *parole,* which was to have enormous significance. *Langue* is the formal, grammatical system of language. It is a system of phonic elements whose relationships are governed, Saussure and his followers believed, by determinate laws. Much of linguistics since Saussure's time has been oriented to the discovery of those laws. The existence of *langue* makes *parole* possible (Bakker, 2007b). *Parole* is actual speech, the way speakers use language to express themselves. Although Saussure recognized the significance of people's use of language in subjective and often idiosyncratic ways, he believed that the individual's use of language cannot be the concern of the scientifically oriented linguist. Such a linguist must look at *langue,* the formal system of language, not at the subjective ways in which it is used by actors.

Langue, then, can be viewed as a system of signs—a structure—and the meaning of each sign is produced by the relationship among signs within the system. Especially important here are relations of difference, including binary oppositions. Thus, for example, the meaning of the word *hot* comes not from some intrinsic properties of the word but from the word's relationship with, its binary opposition to, the word *cold.* Meanings, the mind, and ultimately the social world are shaped by the structure of language. Thus, instead of an existential world of people shaping their surroundings, we have here a world in which people, as well as other aspects of the social world, are shaped by the structure of language.

The concern for structure has been extended beyond language to the study of all sign systems. This focus on the structure of sign systems has been labeled "semiotics" and has attracted many followers (Thibault, 2005b; Gottdiener, 1994; Hawkes, 1977). *Semiotics* is broader than structural linguistics, because it encompasses not only language but also other sign and symbol systems, such as facial expressions, body language, literary texts, indeed all forms of communication.

Roland Barthes (Perry, 2007) often is seen as the true founder of semiotics. Barthes extended Saussure's ideas to all areas of social life. Not only language but also social behaviors are representations, or signs: "Not just language, but wrestling matches are also signifying practices, as are TV shows, fashions, cooking and just about everything else in everyday life" (Lash, 1991:xi). The "linguistic turn" came to encompass all social phenomena, which, in turn, came to be reinterpreted as signs.

人类学的结构主义：克劳德·列维—斯特劳斯
Anthropological Structuralism: Claude Lévi-Strauss

A central figure in French structuralism—Kurzweil (1980:13) calls him "the father of structuralism"—is the French anthropologist Claude Lévi-Strauss (I. Rossi, 2005).

While structure takes various forms in Lévi-Strauss's work, what is important for our purposes is that he can be seen as extending Saussure's work on language to anthropological issues—for example, to myths in primitive societies. However, Lévi-Strauss also applied structuralism more broadly to all forms of communication. His major innovation was to reconceptualize a wide array of social phenomena (for instance, kinship systems) as systems of communication, thereby making them amenable to structural analyses. The exchange of spouses, for example, can be analyzed in the same way as the exchange of words; both are social exchanges that can be studied through the use of structural anthropology.

We can illustrate Lévi-Strauss's (1967) thinking with the example of the similarities between linguistic systems and kinship systems. First, terms used to describe kinship, like phonemes in language, are basic units of analysis to the structural anthropologist. Second, neither the kinship terms nor the phonemes have meaning in themselves. Instead, both acquire meaning only when they are integral parts of a larger system. Lévi-Strauss even used a system of binary oppositions in his anthropology (for example, the raw and the cooked) much like those employed by Saussure in linguistics. Third, Lévi-Strauss admitted that there is empirical variation from setting to setting in both phonemic and kinship systems, but even these variations can be traced to the operation of general, although implicit, laws.

All of this is very much in line with the linguistic turn, but Lévi-Strauss ultimately went off in a number of directions that are at odds with that turn. Most importantly, he argued that both phonemic systems and kinship systems are the products of the structures of the mind. However, they are not the products of a conscious process. Instead, they are the products of the unconscious, logical structure of the mind. These systems, as well as the logical structure of the mind from which they are derived, operate on the basis of general laws. Most of those who have followed the linguistic turn have not followed Lévi-Strauss in the direction of defining the underlying structure of the mind as the most fundamental structure.

Structural Marxism 结构马克思主义

Another variant of structuralism that enjoyed considerable success in France (and many other parts of the world) was structural(ist) Marxism (Lechte, 2005), especially the work of Louis Althusser (K. H. Tucker, 2007), Nicos Poulantzas, and Maurice Godelier.

Although we have presented the case that modern structuralism began with Saussure's work in linguistics, there are those who argue that it started with the work of Karl Marx: "When Marx assumes that structure is not to be confused with visible relations and explains their hidden logic, he inaugurates the modern structuralist tradition" (Godelier, 1972b:336). Although structural Marxism and structuralism in general are both interested in "structures," each field conceptualizes structure differently.

At least some structural Marxists share with structuralists an interest in the study of structure as a prerequisite to the study of history. As Maurice Godelier said, "The study of the internal functioning of a structure must precede and illuminate the study of its genesis and evolution" (1972b:343). In another work, Godelier said, "The inner *logic* of these systems must be analyzed *before* their *origin* is analyzed" (1972a:xxi). Another view shared by structuralists and structural Marxists is that structuralism should be concerned with the structures, or systems, that are formed out of the interplay of social relations. Both schools see structures as real (albeit invisible), although they differ markedly on the nature of the structure that they consider real. For Lévi-Strauss the focus is on the structure of the mind, whereas for structural Marxists it is on the underlying structure of society.

Perhaps most important, both structuralism and structural Marxism reject empiricism and accept a concern for underlying invisible structures. Godelier argued: "What both structuralists and Marxists reject are the empiricist definitions of what constitutes a social structure" (1972a:xviii). Godelier also made this statement:

> For Marx as for Lévi-Strauss a structure is *not* a reality that is *directly* visible, and so directly observable, but a *level of reality* that exists *beyond* the visible relations between men, and the functioning of which constitutes the underlying logic of the system, the subjacent order by which the apparent order is to be explained.
>
> (Godelier, 1972a:xix)

Godelier went even further and argued that such a pursuit defines all science: "What is visible is a *reality* concealing *another,* deeper reality, which is hidden and the discovery of which is the very purpose of scientific cognition" (1972a:xxiv).

In spite of these similarities, structural Marxism did not in the main participate in the linguistic turn then taking place in the social sciences. For example, the focal concern continued to be social and economic, not linguistic, structures. Moreover, structural Marxism continued to be associated with Marxian theory, and many French social thinkers were becoming at least as impatient with Marxian theory as they were with existentialism.

Poststructuralism 后结构主义

While it is impossible to pinpoint such a transition with any precision, Charles Lemert (1990) traces the beginning of poststructuralism to a 1966 speech by Jacques Derrida, one of the acknowledged leaders of this approach (Lipscomb, 2007; J. W. Phillips, 2005), in which he proclaimed the dawning of a new poststructuralist age. In contrast to the structuralists, especially those who followed the linguistic turn and who saw people as being constrained by the structure of language, Derrida reduced language to "writing" which does not constrain its subjects. Furthermore, Derrida also saw social institutions as nothing but writing and therefore as unable to constrain people. In contemporary terms, Derrida deconstructed language and social institutions (Trifonas, 1996), and when he had finished, all he found there was writing. While there is still a focus here on language, writing is *not* a structure that constrains people. Furthermore, while the structuralists saw order and stability in the language system, Derrida sees language as disorderly and unstable. Different contexts give words different meanings. As a result, the language system cannot have the constraining power over people that the structuralists think it does. Furthermore, it is impossible for scientists to search for the underlying laws of language. Thus, Derrida offers what is ultimately a subversive, deconstructive perspective. As we will see, subversion and deconstruction become even more important with the emergence of postmodernism, and it is poststructuralism that laid the groundwork for postmodernism.

The object of Derrida's hostility is the *logocentrism* (the search for a universal system of thought that reveals what is true, right, beautiful, and so on) that has dominated Western social thought. This approach has contributed to what Derrida describes as the "historical repression and suppression of writing since Plato" (1978:196). Logocentrism has led to the closure not only of philosophy, but also to that of the human sciences. Derrida is interested in deconstructing, or "dismantling," the sources of this closure—this repression—thereby freeing writing from the things that enslave it. An apt phrase to describe Derrida's focus is "the deconstruction of logocentrism" (1978:230). More generally, *deconstruction* involves the decomposition of unities in order to uncover hidden differences (D. N. Smith, 1996:208).

A good concrete example of Derrida's thinking is his discussion of what he calls the "theatre of cruelty." He contrasts this concept with the traditional theater, which he sees as dominated by a system of thought that he calls representational logic (a similar logic has dominated social theory). That is, what takes place on the stage "represents" what takes place in "real life," as well as the expectations of writers, directors, and so on. This "representationalism" is the theater's god, and it renders the traditional theater theological. A theological theater is a controlled, enslaved theater:

> The stage is theological for as long as its structure, following the entirety of tradition, comports the following elements: an author-creator who, absent and from afar, is armed with a text and keeps watch over, assembles, regulates the time or the meaning of representation. . . . He lets representation represent him through representatives, directors or actors, *enslaved* interpreters . . . who . . . more or less directly represent the thought of the "creator." *Interpretive slaves* who faithfully execute the providential designs of the "master." . . . Finally, the theological stage comports a *passive, s*eated public, a public of spectators, of consumers, of enjoyers.
>
> (Derrida, 1978:235; italics added)

Derrida envisions an alternative stage (an alternative society?) in which "speech will cease to govern the stage" (1978:239). That is, the stage no longer will be governed by, for example, authors and texts. The actors will no longer take dictation; the writers will no longer be the dictators of what transpires on the stage. However, this does not mean that the stage will become anarchic. While Derrida is not crystal clear on his alternative stage, we get a hint when he discusses the "construction of a stage whose clamor has not yet been pacified into words" (1978:240). Or, "the theatre of cruelty would be the art of difference and of expenditure without economy, without reserve, without return, without history" (Derrida, 1978:247).

It is clear that Derrida is calling for a radical deconstruction of the traditional theater. More generally, he is implying a critique of society in general, which is in the thrall of logocentrism. Just as he wants to free the theater from the dictatorship of the writer, he wants to see society free of the ideas of all the intellectual authorities who have created the dominant discourse. In other words, Derrida wants to see us all be free to be writers.

Implied here is another well-known concern of the poststructuralists (and post-modernists): *decentering.* In a sense, Derrida wants the theater to move away from its traditional "center," its focus on writers (the authorities) and their expectations, and to give the actors more free play. This point, too, can be generalized to society as a whole. Derrida associates the center with *the* answer and therefore ultimately with death. The center is linked with the absence of that which is essential to Derrida: "play and dif-ference"[1] (1978:297). Theater or society without play and difference—that is, static theater or society—can be seen as being dead. In contrast, a theater or a world without a center would be one which is infinitely open, ongoing, and self-reflexive. Derrida concludes that the future "is neither to be awaited nor to be refound" (1978:300). His point is that we are not going to find the future in the past, nor should we passively await our fate. Rather, the future is to be found, is being made, is being written, in what we are doing.

Having debunked Western logocentrism and intellectual authority, in the end Derrida leaves us without an answer; in fact, there is *no* single answer (Cadieux, 1995). The search for the answer, the search for Logos, has been destructive and enslaving. All we are left with is the process of writing, of acting, with play and with difference.

The Ideas of Michel Foucault 米歇尔·福柯的理论

Although Derrida is an extremely important poststructuralist, the most important thinker associated with this approach is Michel Foucault (Smart, 2000). Foucault's work illustrates yet another difference between poststructuralism and structuralism. While structuralism was overwhelmingly influenced by linguistics, Foucault's approach, and poststructuralism more generally, shows a variety of theoretical inputs (Smart, 1985). This variety makes Foucault's work provocative and difficult to handle. Furthermore, the ideas are not simply adopted from other thinkers but are transformed as they are integrated into Foucault's unusual theoretical orientation. Thus, Weber's theory of rationalization has an impact, but to Foucault it is found only in certain "key sites," and it is not an "iron cage"; there is always resistance. Marxian ideas (Smart, 1983) are found in Foucault's work, but Foucault does not restrict himself to the economy; he focuses on a range of institutions. He is more interested in the "micro-politics of power" than in the traditional Marxian concern with power at the societal level. He practices hermeneutics in order to better understand the social phenomena of concern to him. Moreover, Foucault has no sense of some deep, ultimate truth; there are simply ever more layers to be peeled away. There is a phenomenological influence, but Foucault rejects the idea of an autonomous, meaning-giving subject. There is a strong element of structuralism but no formal rule-governed model of behavior. Finally, and perhaps most important, Foucault adopts Nietzsche's interest in

---

[1] Difference, or *différence,* another key concept to Derrida, involves the idea that to understand something we must grasp the way it relates to other things (Ramji, 2007).

the relationship between power and knowledge, but that link is analyzed much more sociologically by Foucault. This multitude of theoretical inputs is one of the reasons Foucault is thought of as a poststructuralist.

There is yet another sense in which Foucault's work is clearly poststructuralist. That is, in his early work Foucault was heavily influenced by structuralism, but as his work progressed, that influence declined and other inputs moved his theory in a variety of other directions. Let us look at the evolution of Foucault's work.

Two ideas are at the core of Foucault's methodology—"archaeology of knowledge" (Foucault, 1966) and "genealogy of power" (Foucault, 1969). While there is a sense in his work that the latter succeeds the former, Mitchell Dean (1994) has made a convincing case that the two coexist and mutually support one another in his substantive work.

Alan Sheridan (1980:48) contends that Foucault's archaeology of knowledge (Scheurich and McKenzie, 2007) involves a search for "a set of rules that determine the conditions of possibility for all that can be said within the particular discourse at any given time." To put it another way, archaeology is the search for the "general system of the formation and transformation of statements [into discursive formations]" (Dean, 1994:16). The search for such a "general system," or such "rules," as well as the focus on *discourse* (Lemert, 2005b)—spoken and written "documents"—reflects the early influence of structuralism on Foucault's work. In analyzing these documents, Foucault does not seek to "understand" them as would a hermeneuticist. Rather, Foucault's archaeology "organises the document, divides it up, distributes it, orders, arranges it in levels, establishes series, distinguishes between what is relevant and what is not, discovers elements, defines unities, describes relations" (Dean, 1994:15). Discourse and the documents it produces are to be analyzed, described, and organized; they are irreducible and not subject to interpretation seeking some "deeper" level of understanding. Also ruled out by Foucault is the search for origins; it is the documents themselves that are important, not their point of origination.

Foucault is particularly interested in those discourses "that seek to rationalise or systematise themselves in relation to particular ways of 'saying the true'" (Dean, 1994:32). As we will see, this concern leads him in the direction of the study of discourses that relate to the formation of human sciences such as psychology. Archaeology is able to distance and detach itself from "the norms and criteria of validity of established sciences and disciplines in favour of the internal intelligibility of the ensembles so located, their conditions of emergence, existence, and transformation" (Dean, 1994:36).

The concern for "saying the truth" relates directly to Foucault's genealogy of power since, as Foucault comes to see it, knowledge and power are inextricably intertwined (Foucault is here heavily indebted to the philosophy of Nietzsche [Fuller, 2007b; Lemert, 2005a]). Genealogy is a very distinctive type of intellectual history, "a way of linking historical contents into organised and ordered *trajectories* that are neither the simple unfolding of their origins nor the necessary realisation of their ends. It is a way of analysing multiple, open-ended, heterogeneous trajectories of discourses, practices, and events, and of establishing their patterned relationships, without recourse to regimes of truth that claim pseudo-naturalistic laws or global necessities" (Dean,

1994:35–36; italics added). Thus, genealogy is at odds with other types of historical studies that accord centrality to such laws or necessities. Everything is contingent from a genealogical perspective. Genealogy is inherently critical, involving a "tireless interrogation of what is held to be given, necessary, natural or neutral" (Dean, 1994:20).

More specifically, genealogy is concerned with the relationship between knowledge and power within the human sciences and their "practices concerned with the regulation of bodies, the government of conduct, and the formation of self" (Dean, 1994:154). Foucault is interested in the "conditions which hold at any one moment for the 'saying the true'" within the human sciences (Dean, 1994:24). Thus, "where archaeology had earlier addressed the rules of formation of discourse, the new critical and genealogical description addresses both the rarity of statements and the power of the affirmative" (Dean, 1994:33). In terms of the relationship between Foucault's two methods, archaeology performs tasks that are necessary in order to do genealogy. Specifically, archaeology involves empirical analyses of historical discourses, while genealogy undertakes a serial and critical analysis of these historical discourses and their relationship to issues of concern in the contemporary world.

Thus, genealogy is to be a "history of the present." However, this is not to be confused with "presentism," which involves the "unwitting projection of a structure of interpretation that arises from the historian's own experience or context onto aspects of the past under study" (Dean, 1994:28). Instead, Foucault seeks to illuminate the present by using "historical resources to reflect upon the contingency, singularity, interconnections, and potentialities of diverse trajectories of those elements which compose present social arrangements as experience" (Dean, 1994:21). There is no determinism here; the present is not a necessary outcome of past developments. Foucault is oriented to the critical use of history to make present possibilities intelligible.

In his genealogy of power, Foucault is concerned with how people govern themselves and others through the production of knowledge. Among other things, he sees knowledge generating power by constituting people as subjects and then governing the subjects with the knowledge. He is critical of the hierarchization of knowledge. Because the highest-ranking forms of knowledge (the sciences) have the greatest power, they are singled out for the most severe critique. Foucault is interested in techniques, the technologies that are derived from knowledge (especially scientific knowledge), and how they are used by various institutions to exert power over people. Although he sees links between knowledge and power, Foucault does not see a conspiracy by elite members of society. Such a conspiracy would imply conscious actors, whereas Foucault is more inclined to see structural relationships, especially between knowledge and power. Looking over the sweep of history, Foucault does not see progress from primitive brutishness to more modern humaneness based on more sophisticated knowledge systems. Instead, Foucault sees history lurching from one system of domination (based on knowledge) to another. Although this is a generally bleak image, on the positive side Foucault believes that knowledge-power is always contested; there is always ongoing resistance to it. Foucault looks at historical examples, but he is interested primarily in the modern world. As he puts it, he is "writing the history of the present" (Foucault, 1979:31).

With this background, let us look at some of Foucault's specific, substantive works. In *Madness and Civilization* (1965; Foucault, 1995), Foucault is doing an archaeology of knowledge, specifically of psychiatry. He begins with the Renaissance, when madness and reason were not separated. However, between 1650 and 1800 (the classical period), distance between them is established, and ultimately reason comes to subjugate madness. In other words Foucault is describing "a broken dialogue" between reason and madness (1965:x). He describes the end result:

> Here reason reigned in the pure state, in a triumph arranged for it in advance over
> a frenzied unreason. Madness was thus torn from that imaginary freedom which
> still allowed it to flourish on the Renaissance horizon. Not so long ago, it had
> floundered about in broad daylight: in *King Lear,* in *Don Quixote.* But in less than
> a half-century, it had been sequestered and, in the fortress of confinement, bound to
> Reason, to the rules of morality and to their monotonous nights.
>
> (Foucault, 1965:64)

There is a clear Weberian, iron-cage imagery here—the "monotonous nights" to be spent by the "mad" (the irrational) in the iron cage constructed by those with reason (rationality).

The scientific psychology of the nineteenth century eventually arose out of the separation of the mad from the sane in the eighteenth century (psychiatry is labeled a "monologue of reason about madness" [Foucault, 1965:xi]). At first medicine was in charge of the physical and moral treatment of the mad, but later scientific psychological medicine took over the moral treatment: "A purely psychological medicine was made possible only when madness was alienated in guilt" (Foucault, 1965:182–183). Later, Foucault says, "What we call psychiatric practice is a certain moral tactic contemporary with the end of the eighteenth century, preserved in the rights of asylum life, and overlaid by the myths of positivism" (1965:276). Thus for Foucault, psychology (and psychiatry) is a moral enterprise, not a scientific endeavor, aimed against the mad, who are progressively unable to protect themselves from this "help." He sees the mad as being sentenced by so-called scientific advancement to a "gigantic moral imprisonment."

Needless to say, Foucault here rejects the idea that over the years we have seen scientific, medical, and humanitarian advances in the treatment of the mad. What he sees, instead, are increases in the ability of the sane and their agents (physicians, psychologists, psychiatrists) to oppress and repress the mad, who, we should not forget, had been on equal footing with the sane in the seventeenth century. The most recent development is that now the mad are less judged by these external agents; "madness is ceaselessly called upon to judge itself" (Foucault, 1965:265). In many senses such internalized control is the most repressive form of control. Clearly, Foucault's archaeology of knowledge leads him to conclusions very different from those of traditional historians about the history and current status of the mad and their relationship to the sane (and their agents). In addition, he is looking at the roots of the human sciences (especially psychology and psychiatry) in the distinction between the mad and the sane and the exertion of moral control over the mad. This is part of his more general thesis about the role of the human sciences in the moral control of people.

MICHEL FOUCAULT

A Biographical Sketch

When he died of AIDS in 1984 at 57 years of age (Lemert, 2005a), "Michel Foucault was perhaps the single most famous intellectual in the world" (J. Miller, 1993:13). That fame was derived from a fascinating body of work that has influenced thinkers in a number of different fields, including sociology. Foucault also led an extremely interesting life, and the themes that characterized his life tended to define his work as well. In fact, it could be argued that through his work Foucault was seeking to better understand himself and the forces that led him to lead the life that he led.

Among Foucault's last works was a trilogy devoted to sex—*The History of Sexuality* (1980a), *The Care of the Self* (1984), and *The Use of Pleasure* (1985). These works reflected Foucault's lifelong obsession with sex. A good deal of Foucault's life seems to have been defined by this obsession, in particular his homosexuality and his sadomasochism. During a trip to San Francisco in 1975, Foucault visited and was deeply attracted to the city's flourishing gay community. Foucault appears to have been drawn to the impersonal sex that flourished in the infamous bathhouses of that time and place. His interest and participation in these settings and activities were part of a lifelong interest in "'the overwhelming, the unspeakable, the creepy, the stupefying, the ecstatic'" (cited in J. Miller, 1993:27). In other words, in his life (and his work) Foucault was deeply interested in "limit experiences" (where people [including himself] purposely push their minds and bodies to the breaking point) such as the impersonal sadomasochistic activities that took place in and around those bathhouses. It was Foucault's belief that it was during such limit experiences that great personal and intellectual breakthroughs and revelations became possible.

Thus, sex was related to limit experiences, and both, in turn, were related in his view to death: "I think the kind of pleasure I would consider as

As for Foucault's structuralism in this early work, he argues that madness occurs at two "levels," and at "a deeper level madness is a form of discourse" (1965:96). Specifically, madness, at least in the classical age, is not mental or physical changes; instead, "delirious language is the ultimate truth of madness" (Foucault, 1965:97). But there is an even broader structuralism operating in this early work: "Let classical culture formulate, *in its general structure,* the experience it had of madness, an experience which crops up with the same meanings, in the identical order of its inner logic, in both the order of speculation and in the order of institutions, in *both discourse and the* real pleasure would be so deep, so intense, so overwhelming that I couldn't survive it. . . . Complete total pleasure . . . for me, it's related to death'" (Foucault, cited in J. Miller, 1993:27). Even in the fall of 1983, when he was well aware of AIDS and the fact that homosexuals were disproportionately likely to contract the disease, he plunged back into the impersonal sex of the bathhouses of San Francisco: *"He took AIDS very seriously. . . . When he went to San Francisco for the last time, he took it as a 'limit-experience'"* (cited in J. Miller, 1993:380).

Foucault also had a limit experience with LSD at Zabriskie Point in Death Valley in the spring of 1975. There Foucault tried LSD for the first time, and the drug pushed his mind to the limit: "'The sky has exploded . . . and the stars are raining down upon me. I know this is not true, but it is the Truth'" (cited in J. Miller, 1993:250). With tears streaming down his face, Foucault said, "'I am very happy. . . . Tonight I have achieved a fresh perspective on myself. . . . I now understand my sexuality. . . . We must go home again'" (cited in J. Miller, 1993:251).

Prior to his experience with LSD, Foucault had been hard at work doing the research for his history of sexuality. He planned to approach that work much as he had approached his previous work on madness and other issues. But after his limit experience with LSD, he totally rethought the project. Among other things, that project came to focus more on the self. It is perhaps that new focus that Foucault anticipated when, during his LSD trip, he spoke of going home (to the self) again.

Foucault pushed himself to the limit not only in his personal life but also in his work. Indeed, it could be argued that the extreme natures of both tended to feed off each other. Whatever else one may say about Foucault's work, it clearly was enormously creative; it pushed up against and perhaps even went beyond the limits of creativity. His work was a limit experience for him, and the study of it can be a "limit experience" for the reader.

Because he was operating at the limit, Foucault's life and work defy simple definition. This incapacity would be just fine with Foucault given the fact that he once wrote, "'Do not ask who I am and do not ask me to remain the same. . . . More than one person, doubtless like me, writes in order to have no face'" (Foucault, cited in J. Miller, 1993:19).

decree, in both word and watchword—wherever, in fact, a signifying element can assume for us the value of a language" (Foucault, 1965:116; italics added).

Foucault continues to use a structuralist method in *The Birth of the Clinic,* in which he focuses on medical discourse and its underlying structure: "What counts in the things said by men is not so much what they may have thought or the extent to which these things represent their thoughts, as *that which systematizes them from the outset,* thus making them thereafter endlessly accessible to new discourses and open to the task of transforming them" (1975:xiv; italics added).

In *Madness and Civilization,* medicine was an important precursor of the human sciences, and that is an even more central theme in *The Birth of the Clinic.* (As Foucault said, "The science of man . . . was medically . . . based" [1975:36].) Prior to the nineteenth century, medicine was a classificatory science, and the focus was on a clearly ordered system of diseases. But in the nineteenth century, medicine came to focus on diseases as they existed in individuals and the larger society (epidemics). Medicine came to be extended to healthy people (preventive care), and it adopted a normative posture distinguishing between healthy and unhealthy and, later, normal and pathological states. Medicine had become, again, a forerunner of the human sciences that were to adopt this normal-pathological stance toward people.

As yet, however, there was no clinical structure in medicine. The key was the development of the clinic, where patients were observed in bed. Here Foucault uses a key term, the *gaze,* in this case a "gaze that was at the same time knowledge" (1975:81). In other words, knowledge was derived from what physicians could see in contrast to what they read in books. As a structuralist, Foucault saw the gaze as a kind of language, "a language without words" (1975:68), and he was interested in the deep structure of that "language." The ability to see and touch (especially in autopsies) sick (or dead) people was a crucial change and an important source of knowledge. Foucault says of the autopsy, "The living night is dissipated in the brightness of death" (1975:146). Foucault sees the anatomo-clinical gaze as the "great break" in Western medicine. Thus, there was not an evolution of knowledge but an epistemic change. Doctors were no longer playing the same game; it was a different game with different rules. *The* game was that people (patients) had become the object of scientific knowledge and practice (instead of the disease as an entity). In terms of his structuralist orientation, what had changed was the nature of discourse—names of diseases, groupings, field of objects, and so forth (Foucault, 1975:54).

Once again, medicine takes on for Foucault the role of forerunner to the human sciences. "It is understandable, then, that medicine should have had such importance in the constitution of the sciences of man—an importance that is not only methodological, but ontological, in that it concerns man's becoming an object of positive knowledge" (Foucault, 1975:197). Specifically on the medical autopsy, Foucault says, "Death left its old tragic heaven and became the lyrical core of man: his invisible truth, his visible secret" (1975:172). In fact, for Foucault the broader change is the individual as subject and object of his own knowledge, and the change in medicine is but one "of the more visible witnesses to these changes in the fundamental structures of experience" (1975:199).

Many of the same themes appear in *Discipline and Punish* (Foucault, 1979), but now we see more of the genealogy of power and much less on structuralism, discourse, and the like. Here "power and knowledge directly imply one another" (Foucault, 1979:27). In this work Foucault is concerned with the period between 1757 and the 1830s, a period during which the torture of prisoners was replaced by control over them by prison rules. (Characteristically, Foucault sees this change developing in an irregular way; it does not evolve rationally.) The general view is that this shift from torture to rules represented a humanization of the treatment of criminals; it had grown more kind, less painful, and less cruel. The reality, from Foucault's point of view, was that punishment had grown more rationalized ("the executioner [in the guillotine] need be no more than a meticulous watchman" [1979:13]) and in many ways impinged more on prisoners. The early torture of prisoners may have made for good public displays, but it was "a bad economy of power" because it tended to incite unrest among the viewers of the spectacle (Foucault, 1979:79). The link between knowledge and power was clear in the case of torture; with the development of rules, that link became far less clear. The new system of rules was "more regular, more effective, more constant, and more detailed in its effects; in short, which increase its effects while diminishing its economic cost" (Foucault, 1979:80–81). The new system was not designed to be more humane, but "to punish better . . . to insert the power to punish more deeply into the social body" (Foucault, 1979:82). In contrast to torture, this new technology of the power to punish occurred earlier in the deviance process; was more numerous, more bureaucratized, more efficient, more impersonal, more invariable, and more sober; and involved the surveillance not just of criminals but of the entire society. It is this theory of society that is of paramount interest, and it could be argued that it would continue to be of interest even if everything that Foucault said about prisons was wrong (Alford, 2000).

This new technology, a technology of disciplinary power, was based on the military model. It involved not a single overarching power system, but rather a system of micro powers. Foucault describes a "micro-physics of power" with "innumerable points of confrontation" (1979:26–27) and resistance (Brenner, 1994). He identifies three instruments of disciplinary power. First is *hierarchical observation,* or the ability of officials to oversee all they control with a single *gaze.* Second is the ability to make *normalizing judgments* and to punish those who violate the norms. Thus, one might be negatively judged and punished on the dimensions of time (for being late), activity (for being inattentive), and behavior (for being impolite). Third is the use of *examination* to observe subjects and to make normalizing judgments about people. The third instrument of disciplinary power involves the other two.

Foucault does not simply take a negative view toward the growth of the disciplinary society; he sees that it has positive consequences as well. For example, he sees discipline as functioning well within the military and in industrial factories. However, Foucault communicates a genuine fear of the spread of discipline, especially as it moves into the state-police network for which the entire society becomes a field of perception and an object of discipline.

Foucault does not see discipline sweeping uniformly through society. Instead, he sees it "swarming" through society and affecting bits and pieces of society as it goes. Eventually, however, most major institutions are affected. Foucault asks rhetorically, "Is it surprising that prisons resemble factories, schools, barracks, hospitals, which all resemble prisons?" (1979:228). In the end, Foucault sees the development of a carceral system in which discipline is transported "from the penal institution to the entire social body" (1979:298). Although there is an iron-cage image here, as usual Foucault sees the operation of forces in opposition to the carceral system; there is an ongoing structural dialectic in Foucault's work.

Although Foucault's greater emphasis on power in *Discipline and Punish* is evident in the discussion to this point, he also is concerned in this work with his usual theme of the emergence of the human sciences. The transition from torture to prison rules constituted a switch from punishment of the body to punishment of the soul or the will. This change, in turn, brought with it considerations of normality and morality. Prison officials and the police came to judge the normality and morality of the prisoner. Eventually, this ability to judge was extended to other "small-scale judges," such as psychiatrists and educators. From all this adjudication emerged new bodies of scientific penal knowledge, which served as the base of the modern "scientifico-legal complex." The new mode of subjugation was that people were defined as the object of knowledge, of scientific discourse. The key point is that the modern human sciences have their roots here. Foucault bitterly depicts the roots of the human sciences in the disciplines: "These sciences, which have so delighted our 'humanity' for over a century, have their technical matrix in the petty, malicious minutiae of the disciplines and their investigations" (1979:226).

One other point about *Discipline and Punish* is worth mentioning. Foucault is interested in the way that knowledge gives birth to technologies that exert power. In this context, he deals with the Panopticon. A *Panopticon* is a structure that gives officials the possibility of complete surveillance (Lyon, 2007; G. T. Marx, 2005) of criminals. In fact, officials need not always be present; the mere existence of the structure (and the possibility that officials might be there) constrains criminals. The Panopticon might take the form of a tower in the center of a circular prison from which guards could see into all cells. The Panopticon is a tremendous source of power for prison officials because it gives them the possibility of total surveillance. More important, its power is enhanced because the prisoners come to control themselves; they stop themselves from doing various things because they fear that they *might* be seen by the guards. There is a clear link here among knowledge, technology, and power. Furthermore, Foucault returns to his concern for the human sciences, for he sees the Panopticon as a kind of laboratory for the gathering of information about people. It was the forerunner of the social-scientific laboratory and other social-science techniques for gathering information about people. At still another level, Foucault sees the Panopticon as the base of "a whole type of society" (1979:216), the disciplinary society.[2]

Finally, we can look at the first volume of *The History of Sexuality* (Foucault, 1980a). Again, the emphasis is on the genealogy of power. To Foucault, sexuality is "an especially dense transfer point for relations of power" (1980a:103). He sees his goal as being to "define the regime of power-knowledge-pleasure that *sustains* the discourse on human sexuality in our part of the world" (Foucault, 1980a:11). He examines the way sex is put into discourse and the way power permeates that discourse.

Foucault takes issue with the conventional view that Victorianism led to the repression of sexuality in general and of sexual discourse in particular. In fact, he argues the exact opposite position—that Victorianism led to an explosion in discourses on sexuality. As a result of Victorianism, there was more analysis, stocktaking, classification, specification, and quantitative/causal study of sexuality. Said Foucault, "People will ask themselves why we were so bent on ending the rule of silence regarding what was the noisiest of our preoccupations" (1980a:158). This was especially the

---

[2] For an interesting use of this idea, see Zuboff (1988), who views the computer as a modern Panopticon that gives superiors nearly unlimited surveillance over subordinates.

case in schools, where instead of repression of sexuality, "the question of sex was a constant preoccupation" (1980a:27). Here is the way Foucault sums up the Victorian hypothesis and his alternative view:

> We must therefore abandon the hypothesis that modern industrial societies ushered in an age of increased sexual repression. We have not only witnessed a visible explosion of unorthodox sexualities . . . never have there existed more centers of power; never more attention manifested and verbalized . . . never more sites where the intensity of pleasures and the persistency of power catch hold, only to spread elsewhere.
>
> (Foucault, 1980a:49)

Once again, Foucault accords a special place to medicine and its discourses on sexuality. Whereas to most, medicine is oriented to the scientific analysis of sexuality, Foucault sees more morality than science in the concerns of medicine. (In fact, Foucault is characteristically hard on medicine, seeing the aim of its discourse "not to state the truth, but to prevent its very emergence" [1980a:55].) Also involved in the morality of sexuality is religion, especially Western Christianity, the confession, and the need for the subject to tell the truth about sexuality. All this is related to the human sciences and their interest in gaining knowledge of the subject. Just as people confessed to their priests, they also confessed to their doctors, their psychiatrists, and their sociologists. The confession, especially the sexual confession, came to be cloaked in scientific terms.

In the West, "the project of the science of the subject has gravitated, in ever-narrowing circles, around the question of sex" (Foucault, 1980a:70). Questions aimed at ascertaining who we are increasingly have come to be directed to sex. Foucault sums this all up: "Sex, the explanation of everything" (1980a:78).

Instead of focusing on the repression of sexuality, Foucault argues that the scientific study of sex should focus on the relationship between sex and power. Again, that power does not reside in one central source; it exists in a variety of micro settings. Furthermore, as is always the case with Foucault, there is resistance to the imposition of power over sex. Power and the resistance to power are everywhere.

Prior to the eighteenth century, society sought control over death, but beginning in that century, the focus shifted to control over life, especially sex. Power over life (and sex) took two forms. First, there was the "anatomo-politics of the human body," in which the goal was to discipline the human body (and its sexuality). Second, there was the "bio-politics of population," in which the object was to control and regulate population growth, health, life expectancy, and so forth. In both cases, society came to see "life as a political object" (Foucault, 1980a:145). Sex was central in both cases: "Sex was a means of access both to the life of the body and the life of the species" (Foucault, 1980a:146). In the modern West, sex has become more important than the soul (and we know how important that is in Foucault's work) and almost as important as life itself. Through knowledge of sexuality, society is coming to exercise more power over life itself. Yet despite this increase in control, Foucault holds out the hope of emancipation:

> It is the agency of sex that we must break away from, if we aim—through a tactical reversal of the various mechanisms of sexuality—to counter the grips of power with the claims of bodies, pleasures, and knowledges, in their multiplicity

and their possibility of resistance. The rallying point for the counterattack against
the deployment of sexuality ought not to be sex-desire, but bodies and pleasures.

(Foucault, 1980a:157)

Dean (1994) argues that from the late 1970s until his death in 1984, Foucault's
work shifted from the micro politics of power in the direction of a concern for *governmentalities,* or the "heterogeneous, non-subjective processes in which practices and
techniques of governance have come to depend on discursive representations of their
fields of intervention and operation" (Dean, 1994:78). In contrast to other theorists,
Foucault's focus is not specifically on the state, but "the practices and rationalities
that compose the means of rule and government" (Dean, 1994:153). Thus, in terms
of the will to knowledge in the human sciences, Foucault is concerned with the way
bodies are regulated, the way conduct is governed, and the ways in which the self is
formed. More generally, he was concerned with self-government, the government of
others, and the government of the state. In most general terms, government to Foucault
is concerned with "the conduct of conduct" (Dean, 1994:176; Lemert, 2005d).

Foucault has been dead for over two decades, and poststructuralism has been
overtaken and passed by postmodern theory. It has always been difficult to draw a clear
line between poststructuralism and postmodern theory; indeed, there is no such line.
Postmodern thinking can be seen as an extension and an exaggeration of poststructuralism. Whether or not one can differentiate clearly between the two, it is abundantly
clear that postmodernism has become the most important development not only in
sociological theory but in a wide range of academic and nonacademic fields.

Postmodern Social Theory 后现代社会理论

Sociology today faces a situation that a number of fields, mainly in the liberal arts,
confronted a decade ago:

> The postmodern moment had arrived and perplexed intellectuals, artists, and
> cultural entrepreneurs wondered whether they should get on the bandwagon and
> join the carnival, or sit on the sidelines until the new fad disappeared into the whirl
> of cultural fashion.

(Kellner, 1989b:1–2)

While many sociologists, and some sociological theorists, still consider postmodern
social theory to be a fad (and it continues to look to some more like a carnival than
a serious scholarly endeavor), the simple fact is that postmodern social theory no
longer can be ignored by sociological theorists (Dandaneau, 2001). In contemporary
social theory, it has been "the hottest game in town" (Kellner, 1989b:2). It has been
so hot, in fact, that at least one theorist has urged that we stop using the term because
it has been "worn frail by overexertion" (Lemert, 1994:142). That is, it has been
abused by both supporters and detractors, as well as in the course of the overheated
debate between them.

Given the importance of postmodern social theory and the heat it has generated,
the objective here is to offer at least a brief introduction to postmodern thinking
(Antonio, 1998; Ritzer, 1997; Ritzer and Goodman, 2001). However, this is no easy

matter. For one thing, there is great diversity among the generally highly idiosyncratic postmodern thinkers, and so it is difficult to offer generalizations on which the majority would agree. Smart (1993), for example, has differentiated among three postmodernist positions.[3] The first, or extreme, postmodernist position is that there has been a radical rupture and modern society has been replaced by a postmodern society. Exponents of this point of view include Jean Baudrillard (Armitage, 2005), Gilles Deleuze and Felix Guattari (1972/1983; Bogard, 1998; Binkley, 2007c; Genosko, 2007; *Theory, Culture and Society*, 1997). The second position is that although a change has taken place, postmodernism grows out of, and is continuous with, modernism. This orientation is adhered to by Marxian thinkers such as Fredric Jameson, Ernesto Laclau, and Chantal Mouffe and by postmodern feminists such as Nancy Fraser and Linda Nicholson. Finally, there is the position, adopted by Smart himself, that rather than viewing modernism and postmodernism as epochs, we can see them as engaged in a long-running and ongoing set of relationships, with postmodernism continually pointing out the limitations of modernism. Though useful, Smart's typology probably would be dismissed by postmodernists as greatly simplifying the great diversity of their ideas and distorting them in the process.

While no term has greater resonance today among scholars in a wide range of disciplines than does *postmodern,* there is enormous ambiguity and controversy over exactly what the term means. For clarity it is useful to distinguish among the terms *postmodernity, postmodernism,* and *postmodern social theory.*[4] *Postmodernity* refers to a historical epoch that generally is seen as following the modern era, *postmodernism* to cultural products (in art, movies, architecture, and so on) that differ from modern cultural products (Taylor, 2007), and *postmodern social theory* to a way of thinking that is distinct from modern social theory. Thus, the postmodern encompasses *a new historical epoch, new cultural products,* and *a new type of theorizing about the social world.* All these, of course, share the perspective that something new and different has happened in recent years that no longer can be described by the term *modern,* and that those new developments are replacing modern realities.

To address the first of these concepts, there is a widespread belief that the modern era is ending, or has ended, and we have entered a new historical epoch of *postmodernity.* Lemert argues that the birth of postmodernism can be traced, at least symbolically, to

> the death of modernist architecture at 3:32 P.M., July 15, 1972—the moment at which the Pruitt-Igoe housing project in St. Louis was destroyed. . . . This massive housing project in St. Louis represented modernist architecture's arrogant belief that by building the biggest and best public housing planners and architects could eradicate poverty and human misery. To have recognized, and destroyed the symbol of that idea was to admit the failure of modernist architecture, and by implication modernity itself.
>
> (Lemert, 1990:233; following Jencks, 1977)

The destruction of Pruitt-Igoe is a reflection of differences between modernists and postmodernists over whether it is possible to find rational solutions to society's problems. To

---

[3] Pauline Rosenau (1992) distinguishes between skeptical and affirmative postmodern thinkers.
[4] Here I follow the distinction made by Best and Kellner (1991:5).

take another example, Lyndon Johnson's war on poverty in the 1960s was typical of the way modern society believed it could discover and implement rational solutions to its problems. It could be argued that in the 1980s the Reagan administration with its general unwillingness to develop massive programs to deal with such problems was representative of a postmodern society and the belief that there is no single rational answer to various problems. Thus, we might conclude that somewhere between the presidential administrations of Kennedy and Johnson and that of Reagan, the United States moved from being a modern to being a postmodern society. In fact, the destruction of Pruitt-Igoe occurred within that time frame.

The second concept, *postmodernism,* relates to the cultural realm in which it is argued that postmodern products have tended to supplant modern products. In art, as we will see shortly, Jameson (1984) contrasts Andy Warhol's postmodern, almost photographic and unemotional painting of Marilyn Monroe to Edvard Munch's modern and highly painful *The Scream.* In the realm of television, the show *Twin Peaks* generally is taken to be a good example of postmodernism, while *Father Knows Best* is a good example of a modern television program. In the movies, *Blade Runner* may be seen as a postmodern work, while the *Ten Commandments* would certainly qualify as a modern movie.

Third, and of much more direct relevance to us here, is the emergence of *postmodern social theory* and its differences from modern theory. Modern social theory sought a universal, ahistorical, rational foundation for its analysis and critique of society. For Marx that foundation was species-being, while for Habermas it was communicative reason. Postmodern thinking rejects this "foundationalism" and tends to be relativistic, irrational, and nihilistic. Following Nietzsche and Foucault, among others, postmodernists have come to question such foundations, believing that they tend to privilege some groups and downgrade the significance of others, give some groups power and render other groups powerless.

Similarly, postmodernists reject the ideas of a grand narrative or a metanarrative. It is in the rejection of these ideas that we encounter one of the most important postmodernists, Jean-François Lyotard. Lyotard (1984:xxiii) begins by identifying modern (scientific) knowledge with the kind of single grand synthesis (or "metadiscourse") we have associated with the work of theorists such as Marx and Parsons. The kinds of grand narratives he associates with modern science include "the dialectics of Spirit, the hermeneutics of meaning, the emancipation of the rational or working subject, or the creation of wealth" (Lyotard, 1984:xxiii).

If modern knowledge is identified in Lyotard's view with metanarratives, then postmodern knowledge involves a rejection of such grand narratives. As Lyotard puts it: "Simplifying to the extreme, I define *postmodern* as incredulity to metanarratives" (1984:xxiv). More strongly, he argues: "Let us wage war on totality . . . let us activate the differences" (Lyotard, 1984:82). In fact, postmodern social theory becomes a celebration of a range of different theoretical perspectives: "Postmodern knowledge is not simply a tool of authorities; it refines our sensitivity to differences and reinforces our ability to tolerate the incommensurable" (Lyotard, 1984:xxv). In these terms, sociology has moved beyond the modern period, into the postmodern period, in its search for a range of more specific syntheses. In the view of Fraser and Nicholson,

Lyotard prefers "smallish, localized narrative[s]" to the metanarratives, or grand narratives, of modernity (1988:89). The new syntheses discussed throughout this book may be seen as examples of such "smallish," "localized" sociological narratives.

While Lyotard rejects the grand narrative in general, Baudrillard rejects the idea of a grand narrative in sociology. For one thing, Baudrillard rejects the whole idea of the social. For another, rejecting the social leads to a rejection of the metanarrative of sociology that is associated with modernity:

> . . . the great organizing principle, the grand narrative of the Social which found its support and justification in ideas on the rational contract, civil society, progress, power, production—that all this may have pointed to something that once existed, but exists no longer. The age of the perspective of the social (coinciding rightly with that ill-defined period known as modernity) . . . is over.
>
> (Bogard, 1990:10)

Thus, postmodern social theory stands for the rejection of metanarratives in general and of grand narratives within sociology in particular.

Postmodern social theory has, to a large degree, been the product of nonsociologists (Lyotard, Derrida, Jameson, and others). In recent years, a number of sociologists have begun to operate within a postmodern perspective, and postmodern social theory can be seen, at least to some degree, as *part* of the classical sociological tradition. Take, for example, the recent reinterpretation of the work of Georg Simmel entitled *Postmodern(ized) Simmel* (Weinstein and Weinstein, 1993; 1998). Weinstein and Weinstein recognize that there is a strong case to be made for Simmel as a liberal modernist who offers a grand narrative of the historical trend toward the dominance of objective culture—the "tragedy of culture." However, they also argue that an equally strong case can be made for Simmel as a postmodern theorist. Thus, they acknowledge that both alternatives have validity and, in fact, that one is no more true than the other. Weinstein and Weinstein argue: "To our minds 'modernism' and 'postmodernism' are not exclusive alternatives but discursive domains bordering each other" (1993:21). They note that they could be doing a modernist interpretation of Simmel but feel that a postmodernist explication is more useful. Thus, they express a very postmodern view: "There is no essential Simmel, only different Simmels read through the various positions in contemporary discourse formations" (Weinstein and Weinstein, 1993:55).

What sorts of arguments do Weinstein and Weinstein make in defense of a postmodernized Simmel? For one thing, Simmel is seen as being generally opposed to totalizations; indeed he is inclined to detotalize modernity. In spite of, and aside from, the theory of the "tragedy of culture," Simmel was primarily an essayist and a storyteller, and he dealt mainly with a range of specific issues rather than with the totality of the social world.

Simmel also is described by Weinstein and Weinstein, as he is by others, as a *flaneur*, or someone who is something of an idler. More specifically, Simmel is described as a sociologist who idled away his time analyzing a wide range of social phenomena. He was interested in all of them for their aesthetic qualities; they all existed "to titillate, astonish, please or delight him" (Weinstein and Weinstein, 1993:60). Simmel is described as spending his intellectual life wandering through a wide range of social phenomena, describing one or another as the mood moved him. This approach led Simmel away from a totalized view of the world and toward a concern for a number of discrete, but important, elements of that world.

Bricoleur is another term used to describe Simmel. A *bricoleur* is a kind of intellectual handyman who makes do with whatever happens to be available to him. Available to Simmel are a wide range of fragments of the social world, or "shards of objective culture," as Weinstein and Weinstein (1993:70) describe them in Simmelian terms. As a *bricoleur* Simmel cobbles together whatever ideas he can find in order to shed light on the social world.

There is no need to go too deeply into the details of Weinstein and Weinstein's interpretation of a postmodernized Simmel. The illustrative points already discussed make it clear that such an interpretation is as reasonable as the modernized vision is. It would be far harder to come up with similar postmodern views of the other major classical theorists, although one certainly could find aspects of their work that are consistent with postmodern social theory. Thus, as Seidman (1991) makes clear, most of sociological theory *is* modernist, but as the case of Simmel illustrates, there are postmodern intimations in even that most modernist of traditions (see also the discussion of Weber and postmodernism in Gane, 2002).

Another place to look for intimations of postmodern social theory is among the critics of modern theory *within* sociological theory. As several observers (Antonio, 1991; Best and Kellner, 1991; Smart, 1993) have pointed out, a key position is occupied by C. Wright Mills (1959). First, Mills actually used the term *postmodern* to describe the post-Enlightenment era which we were entering: "We are at the ending of what is called The Modern Age. . . . The Modern Age is being succeeded by a post-modern period" (Mills, 1959:165–166). Second, he was a severe critic of modern grand theory in sociology, especially as it was practiced by Talcott Parsons. Third, Mills favored a socially and morally engaged sociology. In his terms, he wanted a sociology that linked broad public issues to specific private troubles.

While there are intimations of postmodern social theory in the work of Simmel and Mills (and many others), it is not there that we find postmodern theory itself. For example, Best and Kellner contend that Mills "is very much a modernist, given to sweeping sociological generalization, totalizing surveys of sociology and history, and a belief in the power of the sociological imagination to illuminate social reality and to change society" (1991:8).

Given this general background, let us turn to a more concrete discussion of postmodern social theory. We will focus on a few of the ideas associated with two of the most important postmodern social theorists: Fredric Jameson and Jean Baudrillard.

温和的后现代社会理论：弗雷德里克·詹姆士

Moderate Postmodern Social Theory: Fredric Jameson

The dominant position on the issue of postmodernity is clearly that there is a radical disjuncture between modernity and postmodernity. However, there are some postmodern theorists who argue that while postmodernity has important differences from modernity, there are also continuities between them. The best known of these arguments is made by Fredric Jameson (1984; Kellner, 2005b) in an essay entitled "Postmodernism, or The

Cultural Logic of Late Capitalism," as well as later in a book of essays with the same title (Jameson, 1991). That title is clearly indicative of Jameson's Marxian position that capitalism, now in its "late" phase, continues to be the dominant feature in today's world but has spawned a new cultural logic—postmodernism. In other words, although the cultural logic may have changed, the underlying economic structure is continuous with earlier forms of capitalism. Furthermore, capitalism continues to be up to its same old tricks of spawning a cultural logic to help it maintain itself.

In writing in this vein, Jameson is clearly rejecting the claim made by many postmodernists (for example, Lyotard, Baudrillard) that Marxian theory is perhaps the grand narrative par excellence and therefore has no place in, or relevance to, postmodernity. Jameson is not only rescuing Marxian theory, but endeavoring to show that it offers the best theoretical explanation of postmodernity. Interestingly, while Jameson generally is praised for his insights into the culture of postmodernism, he often is criticized, especially by Marxists, for offering an inadequate analysis of the economic base of this new cultural world.

Also consistent with the work of Marx, and unlike most theorists of postmodernism, Jameson (1984:86) sees both positive and negative characteristics, "catastrophe and progress all together," associated with postmodern society. Marx, of course, saw capitalism in this way: productive of liberation and very valuable advancements and *at the same time* the height of exploitation and alienation.

Jameson begins by recognizing that postmodernism usually is associated with a radical break, but then, after discussing a number of things usually associated with postmodernism, he asks, "Does it imply any more fundamental change or break than the periodic style—and fashion—changes determined by an older high modernist imperative of stylistic innovation?" (1984:54). He responds that while there certainly have been aesthetic changes, those changes continue to be a function of underlying economic dynamics:

> What has happened is that aesthetic production today has become integrated into commodity production generally: the frantic economic urgency of producing fresh waves of ever more novel-seeming goods (from clothing to airplanes), at ever greater rates of turnover, now assigns an increasingly essential structural function and position to aesthetic innovation and experimentation. Such economic necessities then find recognition in the institutional support of all kinds available for the newer art, from foundations and grants to museums and other forms of patronage.
>
> (Jameson, 1984:56)

The continuity with the past is even clearer and more dramatic in the following:

> This whole global, yet American, postmodern culture is the internal and superstructural expression of a whole new wave of American military and economic domination throughout the world: in this sense, as throughout class history, the underside of culture is blood, torture, death and horror.
>
> (Jameson, 1984:57)

Jameson (following Ernest Mandel) sees three stages in the history of capitalism. The first stage, analyzed by Marx, is market capitalism, or the emergence of unified national markets. The second stage, analyzed by Lenin, is the imperialist stage with the emergence of a global capitalist network. The third stage, labeled by Mandel (1975) and Jameson as "late capitalism," involves "a prodigious expansion of capital into hitherto uncommodified areas" (Jameson, 1984:78). This expansion, "far from being inconsistent with Marx's great nineteeth-century analysis, constitutes on the contrary the purest form of capital yet to have emerged" (Jameson, 1984:78). Said Jameson, "The Marxist framework is still indispensable for understanding the new historical content, which demands not modification of the Marxist framework, but an expansion of it" (cited in Stephanson, 1989:54). For Jameson, the key to modern capitalism is its multinational character and the fact that it has greatly increased the range of commodification.

These changes in the economic structure have been reflected in cultural changes. Thus, Jameson associates realist culture with market capitalism, modernist culture with monopoly capitalism, and postmodern culture with multinational capitalism. This view seems to be an updated version of Marx's base-superstructure argument, and many have criticized Jameson for adopting such a simplistic perspective. However, Jameson has tried hard to avoid such a "vulgar" position and has described a more complex relationship between the economy and culture. Nonetheless, even a sympathetic critic such as Featherstone concludes, "It is clear that his view of culture largely works within the confines of a base-superstructure model" (1989:119).

Capitalism has gone from a stage in monopoly capitalism in which culture was at least to some degree autonomous to an explosion of culture in multinational capitalism:

> A prodigious expansion of culture throughout the social realm, to the point at which everything in our social life—from economic value and state power to practices and to the very structure of the psyche itself—can be said to have become "cultural" in some original and as yet untheorized sense. This perhaps startling proposition is, however, substantively quite consistent with the previous diagnosis of a society of the image or the simulacrum [this term will be defined shortly], and a transformation of the "real" into so many pseudo-events.
>
> (Jameson, 1984:87)

Jameson describes this new form as a "cultural dominant." As a cultural dominant, postmodernism is described as a "force field in which very different kinds of cultural impulses . . . must make their way" (Jameson, 1984:57). Thus, while postmodernism is "a new systematic cultural norm," it is made up of a range of quite heterogeneous elements (Jameson, 1984:57). By using the term *cultural dominant,* Jameson also clearly means that while postmodern culture is controlling, there are various other forces that exist within today's culture.

Fredric Jameson offers a comparatively clear image of a postmodern society composed of four basic elements (a fifth, its late capitalistic character, has already been discussed). First, postmodern society is characterized by superficiality and lack of depth. Its cultural products are satisfied with surface images and do not delve deeply into the underlying meanings. A good example is Andy Warhol's famous painting of Campbell soup cans which appear to be nothing more than perfect representations of those cans. To use a key term associated with postmodern theory, a picture is a *simulacrum* in which one cannot distinguish between the original and the copy. A simulacrum is also a copy of a copy; Warhol was reputed to have painted his soup cans not from the cans themselves but from a photograph of the cans. Jameson describes a simulacrum as "the identical copy for which no original ever existed" (1984:66). A simulacrum is, by definition, superficial, lacking in depth.

Second, postmodernism is characterized by a waning of emotion or affect. As his example, Jameson contrasts another of Warhol's paintings—another near-photographic representation, this time of Marilyn Monroe—to a classic modernist piece of art—Edvard Munch's *The Scream. The Scream* is a surreal painting of a person expressing the depth of despair, or in sociological terms, anomie or alienation. Warhol's painting of Marilyn Monroe is superficial and expresses no genuine emotion. This reflects the fact that to the postmodernists, the alienation and anomie that caused the kind of reaction depicted by Munch is part of the now-past modern world. In the postmodern world alienation has been replaced by fragmentation. Since the world and the people in it have become fragmented, the affect that remains is "free-floating and impersonal" (Jameson, 1984:64). There is a peculiar kind of euphoria associated with these postmodern feelings, or what Jameson prefers to call "intensities." He gives as an example a photorealist cityscape "where even automobile wrecks gleam with some new hallucinatory splendour" (Jameson, 1984:76). Euphoria based on automobile disasters in the midst of urban squalor is, indeed, a peculiar kind of emotion. Postmodern intensity also occurs when "the body is plugged into the new electronic media" (Donougho, 1989:85).

Third, there is a loss of historicity. We cannot know the past. All we have access to are texts about the past, and all we can do is produce yet other texts about that topic. This loss of historicity has led to the "random cannibalization of all styles of the past" (Jameson, 1984:65–66). The result leads us to another key term in postmodern thinking—*pastiche.* Since it is impossible for historians to find the truth about the past, or even to put together a coherent story about it, they are satisfied with creating pastiches, or hodgepodges of ideas, sometimes contradictory and confused, about the past. Further, there is no clear sense of historical development, of time passing. Past and present are inextricably intertwined. For example, in historical novels such as E. L. Doctorow's *Ragtime,* we see the "disappearance of the historical referent. This historical novel can no longer set out to represent historical past; it can only 'represent' our ideas and stereotypes about that past" (Jameson, 1984:71). Another example is the movie *Body Heat,* which, while clearly about the present, creates an atmosphere reminiscent of the 1930s. In order to do this,

> the object world of the present-day—artifacts and appliances, even automobiles, whose styling would serve to date the image—is elaborately edited out. Everything in the film, therefore, conspires to blur its official contemporaneity and to make it possible for you to receive the narrative as though it were set in some eternal Thirties, beyond historical time.
>
> (Jameson, 1984:68)

A movie like *Body Heat* or a novel like *Ragtime* is "an elaborated symptom of the waning of our historicity" (Jameson, 1984:68). This loss of temporality, this inability to distinguish between past, present, and future, is manifested at the individual level in a kind of schizophrenia. For the postmodern individual, events are fragmented and discontinuous.

Fourth, there is a new technology associated with postmodern society. Instead of productive technologies such as the automobile assembly line, we have the dominance of *re*productive technologies, especially electronic media such as the television set and the computer. Rather than the "exciting" technology of the Industrial Revolution, we have technologies such as television, "which articulates nothing but rather implodes, carrying its flattened image surface within itself" (Jameson, 1984:79). The implosive, flattening technologies of the postmodern era give birth to very different cultural products than the explosive, expanding technologies of the modern era did.

In sum, Jameson presents us with an image of postmodernity in which people are adrift and unable to comprehend the multinational capitalist system or the explosively growing culture in which they live. As a paradigm of this world, and of one's place in it, Jameson offers the example of Los Angeles's Hotel Bonaventure, designed by a famous postmodern architect, John Portman. One of the points Jameson makes about the hotel is that one is unable to get one's bearings in the lobby. The lobby is an example of what Jameson means by *hyperspace,* an area where modern conceptions of space are useless in helping us orient ourselves. In this case, the lobby is surrounded by four absolutely symmetrical towers which contain the rooms. In fact, the hotel had to add color coding and directional signals to help people find their way. But the key point is that, as it was designed, people had great difficulty getting their bearings in the hotel lobby.

This situation in the lobby of the Hotel Bonaventure is a metaphor for our inability to get our bearings in the multinational economy and cultural explosion of late capitalism. Unlike many postmodernists, Jameson as a Marxist is unwilling to leave it at that and comes up with at least a partial solution to the problem of living in a postmodern society. What we need, he says, are cognitive maps in order to find our way around (Jagtenberg and McKie, 1997). Yet these are not, cannot be, the maps of old. Thus, Jameson awaits a

> breakthrough to some as yet unimaginable new mode of representing . . . [late capitalism], in which we may again begin to grasp our positioning as individual and collective subjects and regain a capacity to act and struggle which is at present neutralized by our spatial as well as our social confusion. The political form of postmodernism, if there ever is any, will have as its vocation the invention and projection of a global cognitive mapping, on a social as well as a spatial scale.
>
> (Jameson, 1984:92)

These cognitive maps can come from various sources—social theorists (including Jameson himself, who can be seen as providing such a map in his work), novelists, and people on an everyday basis who can map their own spaces. Of course, the maps are not ends in themselves to a Marxist like Jameson but are to be used as the basis for radical political action in postmodern society.

The need for maps is linked to Jameson's view that we have moved from a world that is defined temporally to one that is defined spatially. Indeed, the idea of hyperspace and the example of the lobby of the Hotel Bonaventure reflect the dominance of space in the postmodern world. Thus, for Jameson, the central problem today is "the loss of our ability to *position ourselves within this space and to cognitively map it*" (Jameson, in Stephanson, 1989:48).

Interestingly, Jameson links the idea of cognitive maps to Marxian theory, specifically the idea of class consciousness: " 'Cognitive mapping' was in reality nothing but a code word for 'class consciousness' . . . only it proposed the need for class consciousness of a new and hitherto undreamed of kind, while it also inflected the account in the direction of that new spatiality implicit in the postmodern" (1989:387).

The great strength of Jameson's work is his effort to synthesize Marxian theory and postmodernism. While he should be praised for this effort, the fact is that his work often displeases *both* Marxists and postmodernists. According to Best and Kellner, "His work is an example of the potential hazards of an eclectic, multiperspectival theory which attempts to incorporate a myriad of positions, some of them in tension or contradiction with each other, as when he produces the uneasy alliance between classical Marxism and extreme postmodernism" (1991:192). More specifically, for example, some Marxists object to the degree to which Jameson has accepted postmodernism as a cultural dominant, and some postmodernists criticize his acceptance of a totalizing theory of the world.

极端的后现代社会理论：让·鲍德里亚
Extreme Postmodern Social Theory: Jean Baudrillard

If Jameson is among the more moderate postmodern social theorists, Jean Baudrillard is one of the most radical and outrageous of this genre. Unlike Jameson, Baudrillard was trained as a sociologist (Genosko, 2005; Wernick, 2000), but his work has long since left the confines of that discipline. Indeed, it cannot be contained by any discipline, and Baudrillard would in any case reject the whole idea of disciplinary boundaries.

Following Kellner (1989d, 2000), we offer a brief overview of the twists and turns in Baudrillard's work. His earliest work, going back to the 1960s, was both modernist (Baudrillard did not use the term *postmodernism* until the 1980s) and Marxian in its orientation. His early works involved a Marxian critique of the consumer society. However, this work was already heavily influenced by linguistics and semiotics, with the result that Kellner contends that it is best to see this early work as "a semiological supplement to Marx's theory of political economy." However, it was not long before Baudrillard began to criticize the Marxian approach (as well as structuralism) and ultimately to leave it behind.

In *The Mirror of Production,* Baudrillard (1973/1975) came to view the Marxian perspective as the mirror image of conservative political economy. In other words, Marx (and the Marxists) bought into the same worldview as the conservative supporters of capitalism. In Baudrillard's view, Marx was infected by the "virus of bourgeois thought" (1973/1975:39). Specifically, Marx's approach was infused with conservative ideas such as "work" and "value." What was needed was a new, more radical orientation.

Baudrillard articulated the idea of symbolic exchange as an alternative to—the radical negation of—economic exchange (D. Cook, 1994). Symbolic exchange involved an uninterrupted cycle of "taking and returning, giving and receiving," a "*cycle* of gifts and countergifts" (Baudrillard, 1973/1975:83). Here was an idea that did not fall into the trap that ensnared Marx; symbolic exchange was clearly outside of, and opposed to, the logic of capitalism. The idea of symbolic exchange implied a political program aimed at creating a society characterized by such exchange. For example, Baudrillard is critical of the working class and seems more positive toward the new left or hippies. However, Baudrillard soon gave up on *all* political objectives.

Instead, Baudrillard turned his attention to the analysis of contemporary society, which, as he sees it, is dominated no longer by production, but rather by the "media, cybernetic models and steering systems, computers, information processing, entertainment and knowledge industries, and so forth" (Kellner, 1989d:61). Emanating from these systems is a veritable explosion of signs (D. Harris, 1996). It could be said that we have moved from a society dominated by the mode of production to one controlled by the code of production. The objective has shifted from exploitation and profit to domination by the signs and the systems that produce them. Furthermore, while there was a time when the signs stood for something real, now they refer to little more than themselves and other signs; signs have become self-referential. We can no longer tell what is real; the distinction between signs and reality has *imploded*. More generally, the postmodern world (for now Baudrillard is operating squarely within that world) is a world characterized by such implosion as distinguished from the explosions (of productive systems, of commodities, of technologies, and so on) that characterized modern society. Thus, just as the modern world underwent a process of differentiation, the postmodern world can be seen as undergoing *de-differentiation*.

Another way that Baudrillard, like Jameson, describes the postmodern world is that it is characterized by *simulations;* we live in "the age of simulation" (Baudrillard, 1983:4; Der Derian, 1994). The process of simulation leads to the creation of *simulacra,* or "reproductions of objects or events" (Kellner, 1989d:78). With the distinction between signs and reality imploding, it is increasingly difficult to tell the real from those things that simulate the real. For example, Baudrillard talks of "the dissolution of TV into life, the dissolution of life into TV" (1983:55). Eventually, it is the representations of the real, the simulations, that come to be predominant. We are in the thrall of these simulations, which "form a spiralling, circular system with no beginning or end" (Kellner, 1989d:83).

Baudrillard (1983) describes this world as *hyperreality.* For example, the media cease to be a mirror of reality but become that reality, or even more real than that reality. The tabloid news shows that are so popular on TV these days (for example, *Inside Edition*) are good examples (another is "infomercials") because the falsehoods and distortions they peddle to viewers are more than reality—they are hyperreality. The result is that what is real comes to be subordinated and ultimately dissolved altogether. It becomes impossible to distinguish the real from the spectacle. In fact, "real" events increasingly take on the character of the hyperreal. For example, the trial of former football great O. J. Simpson for the murders of Nicole Simpson and Ronald Goldman seemed hyperreal and perfect fodder for hyperreal TV shows like *Inside Edition.* In the end, there is no more reality, only hyperreality.

In all this, Baudrillard is focusing on culture, which he sees as undergoing a massive and "catastrophic" revolution. That revolution involves the masses becoming increasingly passive, rather than increasingly rebellious, as they were to the Marxists. Thus, the mass is seen as a "'black hole' [that] absorbs all meaning, information, communication, messages and so on, thereby rendering them meaningless . . . masses go sullenly on their ways, ignoring attempts to manipulate them" (Kellner, 1989d:85). Indifference, apathy, and inertia are all good terms to describe the masses saturated with media signs, simulacra, and hyperreality. The masses are not seen as manipulated by the media, but the media are being forced to supply their escalating demands for objects and spectacles. In a sense, society itself is imploding into the black hole that is the masses. Summing up much of this theory, Kellner concludes,

> Acceleration of inertia, the implosion of meaning in the media, the implosion of
> the social in the mass, the implosion of the mass in a dark hole of nihilism and
> meaninglessness; such is the Baudrillardian postmodern vision.
>
> (Kellner, 1989d:118)

As extraordinary as this analysis may seem, Baudrillard was even more bizarre, scandalous, irreverent, promiscuous, and playful, or as Kellner says, "carnivalesque," in *Symbolic Exchange and Death* (1976/1993). Baudrillard sees contemporary society as a death culture, with death being the "paradigm of all social exclusion and dis-crimination" (Kellner, 1989d:104). The emphasis on death also reflects the binary opposition of life and death. In contrast, societies characterized by symbolic exchange end binary oppositions in general and more specifically the opposition between life and death (and, in the process, the exclusion and discrimination that accompany a death culture). It is anxiety about death and exclusion that leads people to plunge themselves even more deeply into the consumer culture.

Holding up symbolic exchange as the preferred alternative to contemporary society began to seem too primitive to Baudrillard (1979/1990), and he came to regard *seduction* as the preferred alternative, perhaps because it fit better with his emerging sense of postmodernism. Seduction "involves the charms of pure and mere games, superficial rituals" (Kellner, 1989d:149). Baudrillard is extolling the power and virtues of seduction, with its meaninglessness, playfulness, depthlessness, "non-sense," and irrationality, over a world characterized by production.

In the end, Baudrillard is offering a fatal theory. Thus, in one of his later works, *America,* Baudrillard says that in his visit to that country, he "sought the finished form of the future catastrophe" (1986/1989:5). There is no revolutionary hope as there is in Marx's work. Nor is there even the possibility of reforming society as Durkheim hoped. Rather, we seem doomed to a life of simulations, hyperreality, and implosion of everything into an incomprehensible black hole. While vague alternatives such as symbolic exchange and seduction can be found in Baudrillard's work, he generally shies away from extolling their virtues or articulating a political program aimed at their realization.

后现代社会理论和社会学理论
Postmodern Social Theory and Sociological Theory

There are those who believe that postmodern social theory, especially in its more radical forms, represents an incommensurable alternative to sociological theory. In one sense, it is seen as not being theory, at least in the sense in which we convention-ally use the term. At the beginning of this book, sociological theory was defined as "the 'big ideas' in sociology that have stood the test of time (or promise to), idea systems that deal with major social issues and are far-reaching in scope." It seems to us that the radical ideas of a postmodernist such as Baudrillard fit this definition quite well. Baudrillard certainly offers a number of "big ideas" (simulations, hyperreality, symbolic exchange, seduction). They are ideas that show every promise of standing the test of time. And Baudrillard certainly deals with major social issues (for example, the control of the media); his ideas have implications for a substantial part, if not all, of the social world. Thus, we would say that Baudrillard is offering a sociological theory, and if that can be said of Baudrillard, it certainly can be said of Jameson and most other postmodernists.

The real threat of postmodern social theory is more in its form than in its substance. In rejecting grand narratives, postmodernists are rejecting most of what we usually think of as sociological theory. Baudrillard (and other postmodernists) do not offer grand narratives, but rather bits and pieces of ideas that often seem to contradict one another. If the postmodernists win the day, the sociological theory of the future will look very different from today's theory. But even if the form is nearly unrecognizable, the content will still involve important, wide-ranging ideas about social issues.

Whatever the future may hold, at the moment postmodern social theorists are producing an unusually large number of important and exciting ideas. Those ideas cannot be ignored and may, as they are internalized in sociology, push sociological theory in some new and unforeseen directions.

批判主义和后现代主义社会理论

Criticisms and Post-Postmodern Social Theory

Debates about poststructural and postmodern social theory ordinarily generate an enormous amount of heat. Supporters are often gushing in their praise, while detractors frequently are driven into what can only be described as a blind rage. For example, John O'Neill (1995) writes of "the insanity of postmodernism" (p. 16); he describes it as offering "a great black sky of nonsense" (p. 191) and as "an already dead moment of the mind" (p. 199). Leaving aside the extreme rhetoric, what are some of the major criticisms of postmodern social theory (bearing in mind that given the diversity of postmodern social theories, general criticisms of those theories are of questionable validity and utility)?

1. Postmodern theory is criticized for its failure to live up to modern scientific standards, standards that postmodernists eschew. To the scientifically oriented modernist, it is impossible to know whether the contentions of postmodernists are true. To put it in more formal terms, almost everything that the postmodernists have to say is viewed by modernists as not being falsifiable— that is, their ideas cannot be disproved, especially by empirical research (Frow, 1991; Kumar, 1995). Of course, this criticism assumes the existence of a scientific model, of reality, and of a search for and existence of truth. All these assumptions would, naturally, be rejected by postmodernists.

2. Since the knowledge produced by postmodernists cannot be seen as constituting a body of scientific ideas, it might be better to look at

postmodern social theory as ideology (Kumar, 1995). Once we do that, it is no longer a matter of whether the ideas are true, but simply whether we believe in them. Those who believe in one set of ideas have no grounds to argue that their ideas are any better or worse than any other set of ideas.

3. Because they are unconstrained by the norms of science, postmodernists are free to do as they please, to "play" with a wide range of ideas. Broad generalizations are offered, often without qualification. Furthermore, in expressing their positions, postmodern social theorists are not restricted to the dispassionate rhetoric of the modern scientist. The excessive nature of much of postmodern discourse makes it difficult for most of those outside the perspective to accept its basic tenets.

4. Postmodern ideas are often so vague and abstract that it is difficult, if not impossible, to connect them to the social world (Calhoun, 1993). Relatedly, meanings of concepts tend to change over the course of a postmodernist's work, but the reader, unaware of the original meanings, is unclear about any changes.

5. Despite their propensity to criticize the grand narratives of modern theorists, postmodern social theorists often offer their own varieties of such narratives. For example, Jameson often is accused of employing Marxian grand narratives and totalizations.

6. In their analyses, postmodern social theorists often offer critiques of modern society, but those critiques are of questionable validity since they generally lack a normative basis with which to make such judgments.

7. Given their rejection of an interest in the subject and subjectivity, postmodernists often lack a theory of agency.

8. Postmodern social theorists are best at critiquing society, but they lack any vision of what society ought to be.

9. Postmodern social theory leads to profound pessimism.

10. While postmodern social theorists grapple with what they consider major social issues, they often end up ignoring what many consider the key problems of our time.

11. While one can find adherents among them, as we saw in Chapter 9, the feminists have been particularly strong critics of postmodern social theory. Feminists have tended to be critical of postmodern social theory's rejection of the subject, of its opposition to universal, cross-cultural categories (such as gender and gender oppression), of its excessive concern with difference, of its rejection of truth, and of its inability to develop a critical political agenda.

Many other criticisms of postmodern social theory in general, to say nothing of many specific criticisms of each postmodern theorist, could be enumerated. However, the list above gives a good sense of the range of those criticisms. Whatever the merits of these critiques, the central issue is whether postmodern theory has produced a set of interesting, insightful, and important ideas that are likely to affect social theory long into the future. It should be clear from this chapter that such ideas exist in profusion within postmodern social theory.

While postmodern social theory is only beginning to have a powerful impact on American sociology, in many areas it is long past its prime and in decline. Interestingly, it is in French social theory, the source of the best in poststructuralism and postmodernism, that we find the most determined efforts to move beyond postmodern theory.

Given their rejection of the human subject, the postmodernists are accused of antihumanism (Ferry and Renaut, 1985/1990:30). Thus, the post-postmodernists are seeking to rescue humanism (and subjectivity) from the postmodern critique that presumably left such an idea for dead. For example, Lilla (1994:20) argues that what is being sought is "a new defense of universal, rational norms in morals and politics, and especially a defense of human rights."

Another strand of "post-postmodern social theory" involves an effort to reinstate the importance of liberalism in the face of the postmodern assault on the liberal grand narrative (Lilla, 1994). The works of the poststructuralists/postmodernists (e.g., Foucault's *Discipline and Punish*), even when they were couched in highly abstract theoretical terms, were read by the French as attacks on structures in general, especially the structure of liberal bourgeois society and its "governmentalities." Not only did postmodern theorists question such a society, this also led to the view that there was no way of escaping the reach of that society's power structure. Issues thought dead during the heyday of postmodern theory—"human rights, constitutional government, representation, class, individualism" (Lilla, 1994:16)—have attracted renewed attention. The nihilism of postmodernism has been replaced by a variety of sympathetic orientations to liberal society. One could say that this revival of interest in liberalism (as well as humanism) indicates a restoration of interest in, and sympathy for, modern society.

Other aspects of post-postmodern social theory are made clear in Gilles Lipovetsky's (1987/1994) *The Empire of Fashion: Dressing Modern Democracy.* Lipovetsky takes on, quite explicitly, the poststructuralists and postmodernists. Here is the way he articulates the position which is taken by them and to which he is opposed, at least to some degree:

> In our societies, fashion is in the driver's seat. In less than half a century, attractiveness and evanescence have become the organizing principles of modern collective life. We live in societies where the trivial predominates. . . . Should we be dismayed by this? Does it announce the slow but inexorable decline of the West? Must we take it as a sign of the decadence of the democratic ideal? Nothing is more commonplace or widespread than the tendency to stigmatize—not without cause, moreover—the consumerist bent of democracies; they are represented as devoid of any great mobilizing collective projects, lulled into a stupor by the private orgies of consumerism, infantilized by "instant" culture, by advertising, by politics-as-theater.
>
> (Lipovetsky, 1987/1994:6)

In contrast, while he recognizes the problems associated with it, Lipovetsky (1987/1994:6) argues that fashion is "the primary agent of the spiraling movement toward individualism and the consolidation of liberal societies." Thus, Lipovetsky does not share the gloomy view of the postmodernists; he sees not only the negative, but also the positive, side of fashion and has a generally optimistic view of the future of society.

While Lipovetsky has much that is positive to say about fashion, consumerism, individualism, democracy, and modern society, he also recognizes the problems associated with each one. He concludes that we live in "neither the best of worlds nor the worst. . . . Fashion is neither angel nor devil. . . . Such is the greatness of fashion, which always refers us, as individuals, back to ourselves; such is the misery of fashion, which renders us increasingly problematic to ourselves and others" (Lipovetsky, 1987/1994:240–241). Intellectuals are warned not to dismiss fashion (and the rest) just because it offends their intellectual sympathies. It is for being dismissive of such important phenomena as fashion (and liberalism, democracy, and so on) that Lipovetsky attacks the poststructuralists/postmodernists and others (e.g., critical theorists). In any case, the assault on fashion (and other aspects of modern society) has led us to lose sight of the fact that "the age of fashion remains the major factor in the process that has drawn men and women collectively away from obscurantism and fanaticism, has instituted an open public space and shaped a more lawful, more mature, more skeptical humanity" (Lipovetsky, 1987/1994:12).

While his paradigm is clothing, Lipovetsky argues that fashion is a form of social change that is a distinctive product of the Occident. In contrast to the postmodernists, who were resistant to the idea of origins, Lipovetsky traces the origins of fashion to the upper classes in the West in the late Middle Ages. Fashion is a form of change characterized by a brief time span, largely fanciful shifts, and the ability to affect a wide variety of sectors of the social world. A number of factors came together in the West to give birth to the fashion form, especially its consecration of both individuality and novelty.

Fashion has been a force in the rise of individuality by allowing people to express themselves and their individuality in their clothing even while they might also be attending to collective changes in fashion. Similarly, it has been a factor in greater equality by allowing those lower in the stratification system to at least dress like those who ranked above them. Fashion also has permitted frivolous self-expression. Most generally, it is linked to increasing individualism and the democratization of society as a whole.

The discussion in this section should not be taken to mean that post- or anti-postmodern social theory exhausts contemporary French theory, but it is clearly one of the dominant themes in that theory. Postmodern social theory is not dead in contemporary France. Jean Baudrillard continues to write, and there are others whose work is not discussed here. There are, for example, the contributions of the French urbanist and architect Paul Virilio. (See the special issue, "Paul Virilio," in *Theory, Culture and Society* [October 1999].) In a fascinating series of books, Virilio (1983, 1986, 1991a, 1991b, 1995) has focused on the study of speed (dromology) in the postmodern world. For example, in *Lost Dimension,* Virilio (1991a) discusses how physical distances and barriers have disappeared in the face of the growing importance of speed; space has been replaced by time; the material has been replaced by the immaterial. Thus, in the case of the city, its physical boundaries have been breached forever by, among other things, high-speed communication.

The modern world defined by space has given way to a postmodern world defined by time.

More importantly for our purposes, postmodern social theory is not only alive and well but on the ascendancy in the United States. However, we need to look beyond intellectual fashion in the United States (or France) and realize that whether or not postmodern/poststructural ideas are in or out of fashion in any given place at any given moment, they will be of continuing significance to social theory in general for some time to come. We eventually will move beyond postmodern social theory, but social theory in general will never quite be the same again.

Summary 总结

This chapter covers a wide range of important and interrelated developments in the recent history of sociological theory. The source of many of these developments is the revolution that took place in linguistics and led to a search for the underlying structures of language. Structuralism, as this revolution came to be called, affected a number of fields, including anthropology (especially the work of Lévi-Strauss) and Marxian theory (structural Marxism in particular).

While structuralism continues to affect the thinking of social theorists, it gave birth to a movement known as poststructuralism. As the name suggests, poststructuralism built on the ideas of structuralism but went well beyond them to create a distinctive mode of thought. The most important of the poststructuralists is Michel Foucault. In a series of important books, Foucault created a number of theoretical ideas that are likely to be influential for many decades to come.

Emerging, in part, out of poststructuralism is an enormously influential development known as postmodern theory. Many fields have been influenced by postmodern thinking—art, architecture, philosophy, and sociology. There are a wide variety of postmodern social theories, and this chapter examines a moderate version offered by Fredric Jameson and a radical alternative offered by Jean Baudrillard. At the minimum, postmodern social theory represents a challenge to sociological theory. At the maximum, it stands as a rejection of much, if not all, sociological theory. The chapter closes with some of the major criticisms of postmodern social theory and a discussion of the significance of post-postmodern social theory.

CHAPTER 14

Cutting-Edge Developments in Contemporary Theory
第14章 当代理论的前沿发展

Chapter Outline
Queer Theory (by J. Michael Ryan)
Critical Theories of Race and Racism
Actor-Network Theory, Posthumanism, and Postsociality
Practice Theory

My goal in this final chapter is to bring the discussion of contemporary sociological theory as up-to-date as possible by looking at some of the most recent developments in theory. Doing so, however, is not as easy as it may seem, because new theories are coming to the fore all the time and often it is hard to distinguish those that will last from those that will quickly be relegated to the theoretical dustbin. Nonetheless, an effort has been made to identify at least some of the newest theories that show significant promise of standing the test of time. Other very recent theoretical developments are dealt with at various other places throughout this book. Cosmopolitanism and cosmopolitan social theory, for example, are discussed in Chapter 12 on globalization theory. Indeed, globalization theory itself is arguably *the* most important development in theory today and is likely to remain so for the foreseeable future.

Four theories will be discussed in this final chapter: queer theory, critical theories of race and racism, actor-network theory (as well as the related ideas of the postsocial and the posthuman), and practice theory.[1]

Queer Theory[2] 酷儿理论

Any attempt to define queer theory should begin with an apology for doing so. Queer theory holds dear the idea that naming something constitutes a form of closure. Thus, to assign a definition to queer theory is to go against the ethos of postidentity that is at the heart of queer theory. Creating boundaries around the term with a definition of

---

[1] Actor-network theory and queer theory were discussed in previous editions of this book, but get much more detailed treatment here because of their growing importance. Practice theory and critical theories of race and racism are discussed in this edition and chapter for the first time.
[2] This section was written by J. Michael Ryan.

any kind takes away the malleability and inclusive potential that makes it what it is. Thus, we should apologize for "straightening" out queer theory and point out that by so doing, much of its essence will inevitably be lost. Nevertheless, there are basic tenets of queer theory that can be outlined in order to provide at least a partial glimpse of that which does not want to be named.

Queer theory is a set of ideas rooted in the contention that identities are not fixed and stable and do not determine who we are. Rather, identities are historically and socially constructed processes that are both fluid and contested. Thus, according to queer theory, to talk about "gay men," "Jewish women," "black transsexuals," or any other group is meaningless because each of those identities necessarily ignores a host of others (e.g., gay men who are Jewish; Jewish women who are lesbians). It is therefore impossible to view people collectively on the basis of a single shared characteristic because countless other characteristics differentiate people but are silenced by the focus on a single characteristic. Consequently, one of the aims of queer theory is to challenge notions of fixed identity and to champion a more open and inclusive identity project.

What Is It? 它是什么？

The term *queer* can take on a number of different meanings. To some people, especially an older generation, it is a derogatory term for individuals with a same-sex desire. To others, *queer* has become an all-inclusive umbrella term for, among others, gay, lesbian, bisexual, transgendered, transsexual, curious, intersexed, questioning, and allied identities. To still others, including many queer theorists, it refers to such a broad multiplicity of identities that it implies a sort of anti-identity or even a non-identity. Piontek (2006:2) has suggested using the term *queer* "to refer not to an identity but to a questioning stance, a cluster of methodologies that lets us explore the taken for granted and the familiar from new vantage points." *Queer* also can be used as a noun, to describe such an identity or a nonidentity; as an adjective, to modify a particular noun such as *theory;* or as a verb, turning something into that which is not normal. In the context of queer theory, the word has come to be used in all three ways as part of a broad intellectual and political project.

Academic journals devoted to the study of sexuality that are outlets for work in and around queer theory include the British journal *Sexualities,* the Australian journal *Critical InQueeries,* and the North American journals *GLQ: A Journal of Gay and Lesbian Studies* and the *Journal of Homosexuality.* Also, prominent periodicals such as the *Socialist Review* (vol. 22, no. 1, 1992) and *Sociological Theory* (Summer 1994) have devoted entire issues to queer theory.

It is impossible to develop a comprehensive list of the identifying characteristics of queer theory, but Arlene Stein and Ken Plummer (1994) have noted four prominent "hallmarks":

1. "A conceptualization of sexuality which sees sexual power embodied in different levels of social life, expressed discursively and enforced through boundaries and binary divides" (Stein and Plummer, 1994:181–182). Any understanding of sexuality relies on relations of sexual power that are found in multiple forms of social life, even those

forms not traditionally thought of as immediately sexual, such as popular culture, politics, education, and economics. This power is maintained by a constant reenactment, reproduction, and policing of the boundaries between sexual categories. For example, that which is heterosexual is kept at a safe and guarded distance from that which is homosexual. Each of the two categories is defined by the other, and hence by what it is not, creating a strict boundary to insulate two supposedly distinct categories. This sexual power is maintained by granting privilege to "normalized" sexual identities (e.g., heterosexual, missionary-style sex, monogamy) over "deviant" identities (e.g., homosexual, sadomasochism, multiple sexual partners).

2. "Problematization of sexual and gender categories, and of identities in general. Identities are always on uncertain ground, entailing displacement of identification and knowing" (Stein and Plummer, 1994:182). The very boundaries that are used to construct and maintain sexual power as a basis of conceptualized sexuality are put into question. Sexual categories such as "homosexual" and "heterosexual" have been shifted from starting points as units of analysis and have become discursively produced subjects for research. They are viewed as ways of "doing" rather than as ways of "being." Behaviors, knowledge, and confessions are all examples of phenomena that are used to challenge dominant categorizations of sex, gender, and sexuality. Identity is viewed not as a stable, knowable category but rather as one that rests on ever-shifting and unknowable grounds.

3. "Rejection of civil rights strategies in favor of a politics of carnival, transgression, and parody which leads to deconstruction, decentering, revisionist readings, and an anti-assimilationist politics" (Stein and Plummer, 1994:182). Political claims based on identity, such as the claims made by the gay and lesbian rights movement, are shunned in favor of a more ironic, transgressive, and playful approach. The argument is that advocating for rights based on a minority identity only legitimates the very power structure against which one is fighting. To resist is to legitimate the position of one's oppressor.

4. "A willingness to interrogate areas which normally would not be seen as the terrain of sexuality, and to conduct queer 'readings' of ostensibly heterosexual or nonsexualized texts" (Stein and Plummer, 1994:182). Areas of social life such as the media (Walters, 2001), music festivals (B. Morris, 2003), popular culture (Sullivan, 2003), education (Kosciw, 2004), American literature (Lindemann, 2000), social movements (Gamson, 1995), and even archaeology (Dowson, 2000) are all investigated as sites where sexuality is an active player. No area of social life is seen as immune from the influence of sexuality, and even the most seemingly innocuous of texts are open to an interpretation through the lens of sexuality.

Although those four hallmarks can be expanded, contracted, contested, and shifted, they help to provide a loose framework for a theoretical approach that seeks to break the frame. The first two constitute an activity of radical deconstruction in which the solid of identity is melted into the air of a welcomed uncertainty. The last two set the stage for subversive sexual politics.

Whatever queer theory is, one thing it most certainly is not, or at least should not be, is synonymous with gay and lesbian studies (for more on this, see Giffney, 2004). Queer theory is *not* a theory of queers. This is not to say that both queer theory and gay and lesbian studies do not have a focus on sexuality and sexual practices at or near the heart of their project or that each does not, to some degree, overlap with and make use of the other. Instead, it is to say that there are fundamental differences in the basic premises and goals of each.

Gay and lesbian studies takes the homosexual as its subject; queer theory rejects the possibility of a known subject. Gay and lesbian studies puts sexuality, particularly homosexuality, at the center of an identity project; it becomes a standpoint theory. Queer theory decenters and deconstructs sexuality and identity more generally, leaving both categories permanently open; it becomes a poststructuralist, postmodernist, multicultural, queered theory. Critics of gay and lesbian studies point out that such an approach only legitimizes the assumption of a heterosexual norm against which homosexuality acts as the Other. It establishes boundaries between dichotomous collectivities based on sexual attraction or practice. Queer theory, however, seeks to transgress those boundaries, to do away with any dichotomies, and to define itself as undefinable.

Despite an aversion to boundaries and reifying sexual categories, queer theory maintains an interest in the heterosexual/homosexual divide. It does so, however, in the terms of a Foucauldian genealogy. In other words, of greatest interest to queer theorists is the particular knowledge-power relationship of the hetero/homo binary. Queer theorists seek not to simply supplant the dominant heterosexual center of inquiry with a homosexual one, but rather to deconstruct both heterosexuality and homosexuality to understand how they are mutually constituted in historic and culturally specific ways. Sexuality is not seen as natural but is seen as something that is continuously socially constructed and policed. Thus queer theory is not interested in explaining why homosexuals are oppressed and repressed but rather seeks to explain how the heterosexual/homosexual divide is a figure of knowledge and power that orders desires, behaviors, social institutions, and social relations.

The heart of queer theory thus lies in challenging normative knowledge and identities as well as ways of knowing more broadly. Norms are examined, deconstructed, and disassembled, and there is no fear of indeterminacy. In fact, some argue that queer theory is not a body of institutional knowledge but rather a broader deconstructive process.

Where Did It Come From? 它从何而来?

The origins of queer theory are as ambiguous and as contested as the terms, tenets, usefulness, and future directions of the theory itself. Some argue that its formal beginning in academic circles was its use by Teresa de Lauretis at a conference at the University of California at Santa Cruz in 1989 or in her introduction to "Queer Theory: Lesbian and Gay Sexualities," a special issue of *differences: A Journal of Feminist Cultural Studies* in 1991. Others point to key publications by Eve Kosofsky Sedgwick—*Between Men* (1985) and *Epistemology of the Closet* (1990)—and by Judith Butler—*Gender Trouble* (1990)—as the origins or queer theory in academic discourse. Still others point even farther back to the work of Michel Foucault, particularly to *The History of Sexuality,* volume 1 (1978), as the point at which queer theory really began to take hold.

The search for the exact origins of queer theory does as much damage as the attempts to define it. It is instead more fruitful to do a Foucauldian genealogical analysis (see below) in order to situate the knowledge base of queer theory within the broader institutional dynamics in which it first appeared. Whatever its precise origins, queer theory began to gain a strong foothold in the academy in the late 1980s and during the 1990s. A series of key publications, academic conferences, political organizations, and published texts all helped to nourish the growing area of inquiry. Queer theory finds its academic roots in many fields, including feminist studies, gay and lesbian studies, social constructionism, cultural theories, poststructuralism, and literary criticism. Two of these—social constructionism and poststructuralism—were of particular importance.

Social constructionism, following from the work of Berger and Luckmann (1967), seeks to illustrate the social nature of phenomena and to debunk myths of "naturalness" or "inherency." In the context of sexuality, this means illuminating the social origins of sexuality and the differences between heterosexuality and homosexuality. It also means simultaneously critiquing the assumed fundamental nature of such a difference. This goal is shared, in part, by queer theory. Unlike social constructionism, however, queer theory does not assume that once-established sexual identities are empirical or valid ways of representing identity, nor does it assert that the cultural realms of heterosexuality and homosexuality are distinct. Rather, it argues that both are signs in a larger system whose meaning is derived from their relationship to one another and are part of the same underlying system of unstable and shifting cultural and linguistic signification. This assumption can be traced to another foundation of queer theory—structuralism and, more important, poststructuralism.

Poststructuralism is described in detail in Chapter 13, but it is worth discussing a few of its core premises here in order to understand how it helped to foster the growth of queer theory. The poststructuralists' delight in the belief that there is no single answer to any question, and their emphasis on the unimportance of even finding such an answer, helped to legitimate the queer theory project of reevaluating knowledge claims. Poststructuralists also emphasize the need to deconstruct social phenomena in order to understand them—another key project taken up by queer theorists. Further, the poststructuralist and postmodernist aim of delegitimating the humanist subject helped set the stage for queer theories dedicated to challenging notions of fixed and determinable identity.

Outside of the academy, queer theory also has strong ties to a larger project of queer politics. The AIDS epidemic, in particular, sparked a wave of grassroots activist organizations—the AIDS Coalition to Unleash Power (ACT UP), Queer Nation, and others—that sought to disrupt the dominance of heterosexual understandings. Queer politics also unsettled many gay and lesbian groups as it contested the hierarchies of privilege and oppression found within the homosexual community, such as those based on race, ethnicity, sex, gender, education, and class. Queer politics is therefore critical of any normalizing regime and prefers a more open and free politics of inclusion.

Another way to get at an understanding of queer theory is by taking a look at the work of some of its founding scholars. Although there are many who have done work in this field, arguably the most important has been Foucault. Aside from the work of Freud, Kinsey, and a handful of others largely outside the realm of sociology, the relationship of sexuality to the individual or to society had, prior to Foucault's work, been largely ignored in the academy. Since Foucault, however, this has, at least to some degree, begun to change. Although sexuality has yet to attain the centrality of race, class, or sex in sociological analysis, it is at least now recognized as a variable to be taken seriously.

Two of Foucault's more seminal ideas—archaeology of knowledge and genealogy of power (see the preceding chapter for more on these ideas)—have perhaps had the greatest impact on queer theory. An archaeology of knowledge (Foucault, 1966) represents a search for the universal rules that govern what can be said in a particular discourse at a particular historical moment. The goal, therefore, is to describe, analyze, and organize such discourses rather than searching for origins or seeking to make predictions. Instead, the analysis should be a focus on what exists in actuality. The goal is thus one of understanding, not defining.

Foucault's (1969) genealogy of power represents a concern with the linkages between knowledge and power. Genealogy is a method of intellectual history that does not seek to describe on the basis of lawlike historical processes but rather to outline open-ended trajectories thereby allowing for a multiplicity of pathways. In line with post-structuralism, everything is seen as relational and contingent. In line with social constructionism, there is an inherent criticism of "naturalness." A genealogy of power also seeks to understand how people regulate themselves and others through the production and control of knowledge. The emphasis, however, is not on the actors themselves and their position within a structure but rather on the structure of knowledge and power itself.

Sedgwick (1985, 1990) is another of the early pioneers of queer theory. Her book *Epistemology of the Closet* (1990) explores the twin concepts of "the closet" and "coming out." The closet is a metaphor meaning a place where people hide their identity. Coming out is the process of revealing this hidden identity to others. Sedgwick compares these twin processes to ideas of secrecy and revelation, and she views both as politically charged as both seek to crystallize the identity of the homosexual. As a genealogy of power, the relevance of coming out also constitutes a particular knowledge-power relationship. For example, the closet creates possibilities for others to gain power by using knowledge of people's sexuality against them.

Butler[3] (1990) takes off from the knowledge-power relationship to argue that gender and sexuality are both performances based on repetition. She argues that heterosexuality has come to lay claim to titles of "naturalness" and "normalcy" because of its constant repetition and enactment, including by those who are not heterosexual. It is not, therefore, based on the expression of any *inherent psychic reality* (1997). In other words, sexuality is a form of drag. Whether or not individuals are aware of their performances of their sexuality, such performances are going on. Butler offers hope to those wishing to disrupt compulsory heterosexuality through her notion of a "repetitive disruption." Such a disruption would be a conscious act aimed at undermining the repetition of the norms of heterosexuality. Butler elaborated on and updated this

---

[3] For more on Judith Butler and her particular relationship to queer theory, see Breen and Blumenfeld (2005).

theme in her work *Undoing Gender* (2004). As a suggestion for what it means to undo hegemonic gender constructions, she notes that "to intervene in the name of transformation means precisely to disrupt what has become settled knowledge and knowable reality and to use . . . one's unreality to make an otherwise impossible or illegible claim" (Butler, 2004:27).

Critiques and Potential Solutions 批评和潜在的解决之道

In spite of being an advance over previous knowledge and ways of doing theory, queer theory is not without its critics. Many argue that its amorphous politics of inclusion and rejection of single characteristics of identity such as race, class, or sex undermine the potential for real political action (e.g., T. Edwards, 1998; Kirsch, 2000). This rejection, in turn, ignores the everyday lived materiality of experience (Stein and Plummer, 1994) and the role of the social in constructing the sexual (A. I. Green, 2002). If identity is not a motivation for action, then how do groups dealing with the manifest means of oppression organize and fight for justice? There is also an argument that the more queer theory is accepted into academic discourse, the farther removed it is from its revolutionary potential. Halperin (1995:113) has noted that "the more it verges on becoming a normative academic discipline, the less queer 'queer theory' can plausibly claim to be." By being enshrined in academia, it is losing its power to transform; by being normalized, it loses its ability to queer. A further critique is that much of the knowledge generated by queer theory is often not made available, or intelligible, to those whom it might most benefit. For example, Butler's writing is often so opaque that it lies outside the comprehension of the lay person (and academic!) to whom it might most appeal.

In light of these critiques, some have tried to find ways to modify queer theory in such a way as to make it more socially sensitive to the position and lived experiences of actors and the more politically astute. Max Kirsch (2000) has offered a potential solution by arguing that we need to differentiate between identifying *with* and identifying *as,* with a preference for the latter, in order to maintain a basis of identification while still distancing ourselves from the problems of identity. Thus, identity is used as "a mode of affiliation rather than strictly as a category of personal definition" (Kirsch, 2000:7). This approach is thereby able to maintain the critical stance of queer theory toward the dangers of essentializing or concretizing identity, while at the same time still allowing for identity by association to remain a powerful tool for collective social action.

Adam Isaiah Green (2002) has identified at least two strains of queer theory. The first, *radical deconstructionism,* "superimposes a postmodern self-concept onto the homosexual subject, thereby glossing over the enduring institutional organization of sexuality" (Green, 2002:523). The second, *radical subversion,* "superimposes a politically marginal self-concept onto the homosexual subject, thereby grossly oversimplifying complex developmental processes attendant to sexual identification" (Green, 2002:523). At base, each strand is seen as not giving sufficient priority to the materially lived and institutionally dependent situation of actors. Green (2002:537), therefore, calls for a post-queer study of sexuality, one that "brings to bear the categorical scrutiny of queer theory on concrete, empirical case studies."

Whatever its shortcomings, queer theory also has many strengths. It seeks to broaden acceptance and promote inclusion. It reminds us of the importance of studying the center as well as the margins. It gives voice to the issue of sexuality that has so long been silenced in the academic world. It helps to further disrupt hierarchies of privilege and to dispel myths related to identity. All of this in just its first few decades of existence! Wherever it began, whatever it is, and wherever it is going, the important thing is that queer theory did begin, that it is something, and that it is indeed going somewhere. Its contributions to sociology have, no doubt, yet to be fully realized.

种族和种族主义的批判理论
Critical Theories of Race and Racism[4]

As mentioned in this chapter and discussed in detail in Chapter 9, there has long been a body of feminist theory dealing with sex (and gender) and sexism. However, theories of race and racism, though part of multicultural social theory, have tended to lag behind feminist theory. (Of course, there is no clear dividing line between these theories. Mohanty [2002:2], for example, describes herself as an "antiracist feminist." Some of the most important developments in feminist theory and multiculturalism [e.g., P. H. Collins, 1990, 1998] relate to giving black women their due in such theorizing.) This is not to say that scholars have ignored theorizing about race and racism. Certainly, W. E. B. Du Bois, for one, has long been recognized as an important theorist of race and racism, and evidence of his importance has increased significantly in recent years (see Chapter 11 in *Classical Sociological Theory* [Ritzer, 2008]; Goldberg and Essed, 2002). However, in the last decade or two, theories of race and racism have begun to expand dramatically. It is time (perhaps even a bit late) to acknowledge that development and to offer at least a brief overview of such theorizing.

Although sociologists and other social scientists have been making significant contributions to theories of racism since Du Bois's work around the turn of the twentieth century, and before, the recent boom in this mode of theorizing received an important impetus from the development of "critical race theory" largely in the field of law (Delgado and Stefancic, 2001:3; Valdes, Culp, and Harris, 2002). That theory came about as a result of the growing realization that the civil rights movement of the 1960s had lost its momentum, if not been reversed, and there was a need not only for a revivified social activism but also for new theorizing about race. The ideas associated with critical race theory developed from a wide range of sources, but some of them are quite familiar to social theorists, such as those derived from Marxian theory (e.g., Gramsci), poststructuralism (e.g., Derrida), feminist theory, and, of course, Du Bois's contributions.

Delgado and Stefancic, as well as Matsuda et al. (2003), outline at least a provisional list of the basic tenets of critical race theory:

• Racism is not an aberration; it is "normal" and endemic to American life. This makes it difficult to deal with.

---

[4] I am here employing a title used by my colleague Patricia Hill Collins rather than the more common label "race theory."

- Much of the population has little incentive to eradicate racism. White elites gain from it materially (through exploitation of blacks and other minorities). Working-class whites also gain materially as well as psychically by having a group of people to whom they can favorably compare themselves in spite of their own difficulties.

- Race is not an objective or fixed reality. It is a social construction that changes over time (this idea aligns critical race theory broadly with the social-constructionist approach in sociology; see Berger and Luckmann, 1967). Such social constructions are created, manipulated, and sometimes even retired, though usually to be replaced by new social constructions. This social constructionist orientation is related to skepticism about the supposed ahistoricism of American law and skepticism about legal claims of neutrality, objectivity, color blindness, and meritocracy. That is, they all may be seen as social constructions that can be manipulated, revised, or even jettisoned when such actions are deemed necessary.

- Differential racialization "involves the ways the dominant society racializes different minority groups at different times, in response to shifting needs such as the labor market" (Delgado and Stefancic, 2001:8). Thus, although blacks have been racialized since practically the inception of the United States, other minorities have come to be racialized over time. Examples include the Japanese during World War II, Muslims after September 11, 2001, and Mexican Americans in recent years as a result of growing concern over legal and illegal immigration.

- As in feminist theory, intersectionality (P. H. Collins, 1990, 1998) and anti-essentialism are key ideas in critical race theory. Thus, blacks (and other minorities) have no "single, easily stated, unitary identity" (Delgado and Stefancic, 2001:9). Rather, they, as is true of all others, exist, at least potentially, at the intersection of "conflicting, overlapping identities, loyalties, and allegiances" (Delgado and Stefancic, 2001:9). These may include religion, social class, gender, sexual orientation, and political preference.

- Great importance is accorded to the experiential knowledge of people of color and to communities of origin.

- The emphasis on the experiential knowledge of people of color is related to, but also somewhat in contrast with, the anti-essentialism of critical race theory. It suggests the highly controversial idea (given the postmodern critique of essentialism) that blacks, and other racial minorities, are uniquely able to speak and write about race and racism because of their specific histories and experiences with oppression. Beyond its essentialism, another of the reasons why this emphasis is controversial is that it could be argued that the unique history and experiences of whites in and with systems of oppression give whites a similarly specific, albeit different, perspective on race and racism. The history and experience of whites would seemingly make it as legitimate for them to speak on racial matters as it is for blacks.

- As part of a broader goal of eliminating all forms of oppression, critical race theory is oriented to the elimination of racial oppression.

Critical theories of race and racism (CTRR) have much in common with critical race theory, including the goal of dealing with social injustices, the reduction or elimination of social inequalities, and a strong focus on intersectionality. However, there are also important differences stemming from the fact that CTRR are rooted much more in the social sciences, including sociology, than is critical race theory with its base in legal scholarship and activism. This difference serves to sensitize CTRR to, and involve them in, cutting-edge issues in theory such as the relationship between race and racism and agency-structure, political economy, and globalization. Included in, or related to, globalization is a concern for race and racism as it relates to nation-states, nationalism, and ethnonationalism (Connor, 2007), transnationalism (Remennick, 2007), colonialism, neocolonialism (Go, 2007a), decolonization (Go, 2007b), imperialism, empire, and so on. Thus, while critical race theory focuses on the United States and American law, CTRR have a much broader, even global, focus (Goldberg and Essed, 2002:4). In addition, CTRR are open to a much wider array of classical and contemporary theories as they apply to race. For example, Darder and Torres (2004:23) adopt a political economy approach to race, one that is heavily indebted to Marx and that adopts a "historical materialist approach." In articulating their approach, Darder and Torres criticize critical race theory for ignoring issues of political economy.

A far broader theoretical approach is adopted by Michael Brown et al. (2003) in *Whitewashing Race*. They operate from an even broader macrostructural and macrocultural approach to race. They explicitly contrast their orientation to what they call "realist analysis," which adopts a micro-focus on individuals and their intentions and choices, thereby ignoring larger structures and institutions.

The realist focus leads to a concern with individual prejudice and discrimination (Law, 2007) and allows for the conclusion that white racism has ended, or is at least in decline. In contrast, Michael Brown and colleagues focus on a wide range of social structures and institutions that, in their view, have led to white accumulation and black dis-accumulation, to cumulative structural inequality in society. They look not only at the structure of law but also at racial stratification, labor markets, housing markets, government policies, and so on. Racial disparities have existed in these structures historically, and they continue to exist. Thus, blacks continue to face racial discrimination, and they must deal with the legacy of racial discrimination in these domains. It is therefore not enough to deal with the operation of contemporary structures and institutions; the legacy of discrimination at these levels needs to be confronted and rectified.

A more general conclusion to be derived from critical theories of race and racism is that, as Cornell West (1994) pointed out, "race matters" and that it continues to matter not only in the legal system but throughout the structures and institutions of society.

Many other scholars show that race continues to matter in the United States. For example, Guinier and Torres (2002) draw an analogy between race and the miner's canary used to indicate problems, indeed impending human death, in mines. Race in the United States is like the miner's canary in the sense that problems associated with it point to broader, perhaps fatal, problems in the larger society. Guinier and Torres (2002:12), however, do not limit their analysis to blacks but develop a broader concept of "political race" that, among other things, includes various minorities and even some whites (see also Bonilla-Silva, 2003). Nevertheless, it is still people of color who will take the lead in social change movements reflective of the political dimension of political race.

Guinier and Torres explicitly seek to embed their work within critical race theory. However, they also go beyond it in various ways (e.g., shifting the focus from law to politics), and in doing so they move toward CTRR.

A more clearly CTRR effort with an American focus is Bonilla-Silva's (2003) study and critique of color-blind racism (Guinier and Torres also attack this idea) in the United States. Bonilla-Silva is also critical of the view that racism today is of little more than historical interest. Rather, he sees color-blindness as a smoke screen that allows white Americans to continue to perpetuate racial discrimination. He concludes that color-blind racism provides a "sanitized . . . way of calling minorities niggers [Kennedy, 2002], spics, or chinks" (Bonilla-Silva, 2003:181). Based on this conclusion, Bonilla-Silva (2003:185) proposes a variety of practical steps (such an orientation toward praxis is common the CTRR literature) to combat the problem of " 'new racism' practices and color-blind idiocy."

Although there is much focus in CTRR on race in the United States, others associated with this orientation seek to demonstrate that race also matters globally. Thus, for example, Winant (2001) deals with race historically and in the United States, as well as in South Africa, Brazil, and Europe.

CTRR are clearly still in the early stages of development and that makes it difficult to delineate clearly their fundamental characteristics, but Patricia Hill Collins has made a good start in this direction by delineating the following distinguishing features of critical theories of race and racism:[5]

1. CTRR do not simply study race and racism; they seek to deal with social inequalities and to advance social justice.
2. CTRR eschew all binary oppositions and look at everything from the perspective of intersecting entities. Such a view requires the use of multifaceted research methods.
3. CTRR are inherently multidisciplinary.
4. CTRR draw upon and advance intersectionality, looking at the relationship between race and racism and gender, ethnicity, class, sexuality, and nation.
5. CTRR are increasingly drawn to materialist (political economic) analyses of race and racism, as well as to how race and racism relate to globalization.
6. Structures of power are increasingly central to CTRR. Earlier concerns with the power of the American social welfare and criminal justice systems have been extended to topics such as nation-states and nationalism, democracy, empire, transnationalism, and imperialism.

This enumeration, especially the last three items, clearly aligns CTRR with other very contemporary, if not cutting-edge, issues in social theory.

---

[5] The following enumeration is derived from the syllabus from Collins's graduate course Critical Theories of Race and Racism, University of Maryland (Fall, 2005).

In conclusion, however, it is safe to say that there is as yet no "theory," critical or otherwise, of race and racism. But there is a historical body of theory to draw on (e.g., Du Bois, Said), a plethora of theoretical ideas and perspectives of great relevance (e.g., critical theory, Gramsci on hegemony, Hardt and Negri on empire), as well as a series of ideas developed from within CTRR (e.g., intersectionality). Out of this array of ideas, and undoubtedly many others, critical theories of race and racism will crystallize and expand their theoretical perspective in coming years.

行动者—网络理论、后人文主义和后社会主义
Actor-Network Theory, Posthumanism, and Postsociality

A very recent theory (although it is often see as more a method than a theory), with powerful roots in structuralism and poststructuralism,[6] is actor-network theory (ANT). "Actor-network theory," in the words of John Law, "is a ruthless application of *semiotics*. It tells us that entities take their form and acquire their attributes as a result of their relations with other entities. In this scheme of things entities have no inherent qualities" (Law, 1999:3). The idea of the relativity of *subjects* is shared by a number of theoretical perspectives. What is new here is that *material objects* as well are seen as being created and acquiring meaning in a *network* of relationship to other objects. Thus, "action-network theory may be understood as a *semiotics of materiality*. It takes the semiotic insight, that of the relativity of entities, the notion that they are produced in relations, and applies this ruthlessly to all materials—and not simply those that are linguistic" (Law, 1999:4).

That perspective is drawn more from structuralism, but other basic ANT perspectives are drawn from poststructuralism. Implied above is the idea of *anti-essentialism*. That is, entities are lacking in inherent qualities; what they are is a result of their relationship to other entities. In other words, there is *no* essence to any entity or material object, including people. In addition, ANT is *opposed* to the very modern idea of the *search for origins*, either in history or contemporaneously in the idea that human agents are at the root of everything. Like poststructuralism (and postmodernism), actor-network theory is also *antifoundational*—that is, it is opposed to the idea that underlying everything is a basic structure and it is the task of the analyst to uncover that structure.

However, the poststructural concept that goes to the essence of ANT is *decentering*. Generally, this means shifting focus from the center (or essence, or origin, and so on) to the periphery. More specifically, it means in ANT the shift from a focus on the agent taking some action to that which exists, especially networks and nonhuman objects. The actor becomes part of the network; we can think in terms of the " 'net-workization' of the 'actor' " (Gomart and Hennion, 1999:223). Actors are subordinated to networks and, in a way, are, creatures of networks: "actors are network effects,

---

[6] There are many other theoretical inputs, especially ethnomethodology. Negatively, ANT seeks to avoid the problems it associates with agency-structure and micro-macro theory (see below). Other theoretical influences and affinities are with "feminist theory, cultural studies, social and cultural anthropology, other branches of post-structuralism" (Law, 1999:3).

they take the attributes of the entities which they include" (Law, 1999:5). The focus shifts from the modern concern with the agent to the network and to objects, nonmaterial entities. This, as we will see, is one of the most distinctive contributions of actor-network theory: it "opened the social sciences to nonhumans" (Callon, 1999:182). (By the way, nonhumans and the relationship of humans to them is a significant aspect of what Knorr Cetina [2001] calls *postsocial relations.*) We will have more to say about this below, but although it is important to focus on the nonhuman, we must remember that "objects are *inferior* partners" to the human (Gomart and Hennion, 1999:223).

ANT leads to a rejection of both micro-macro and agency-structure theory (see Chapter 10). For one thing, those two continua are seen as examples of the kind of modern dualities that are rejected by poststructuralists and postmodernists. (According to Law [1999:3], "all of these divides have been rubbished.") In addition, the problem with both continua is that a shift to one pole of the continuum inevitably leads to dissatisfaction with what is learned about the other pole. More important, the continua are focusing on the wrong things. The central topic is *not* agency/micro or structure/macro but rather social processes as circulating entities. In other words, the real focus should be on the network, another key topic discussed below. As Latour (1999:22) puts it, ANT is a theory not of the social but rather "of the space of fluids circulating in a nonmodern situation."

That observation leads us to a very useful definition of ANT[7]:

> We may conceive of only basic formal units of substance (actants) which enter into relationships (networks) by way of encounters (trials of force) wherein questions regarding the powers and identities of these selfsame units come to be temporarily settled by reference to the overall compound nexus of relationships within which they are now embedded.
>
> (Brown and Capdevila, 1999:34)

The term *actant* (borrowed from semiotics [Fuller, 2007c]) is worth clarifying. It is meant to imply that it is not just humans that act. Nonhuman entities can act—can be actants! As a result, the same explanatory frame should be used for actants of both types.

As Crawford (2005:2) puts it: "Investigators should never shift registers to examine individuals and organizations, bugs and collectors, or computers and their programmers." Furthermore, in discussing the actant, the focus once again shifts from the actor to the network. As Latour (1999:18) puts it, "actantability is not what an actor does . . . but what *provides* actants with their actions, with their subjectivity, with their intentionality, with their morality. When you hook up with this circulating entity, then you are partially provided with consciousness, subjectivity, actoriality, etc. . . . To become an actor is . . . a local achievement." Even something as seemingly human and individual as intentionality is defined in network terms as a "circulating capacity . . . partially gained or lost by hooking up to certain bodies of practice" (Latour, 1999:23).

---

[7] Actually, this is offered as a definition of the "sociology of translation" seen as the generic form of ANT (Brown and Capdevila, 1999).

Basically, actors (or actants) cannot be understood apart from the networks in which they exist and of which they are part. In fact, actor and network are "two faces of the same phenomenon" (Latour, 1999:19). Thus, actor-network theorists seek to bypass the micro-macro and agency-structure dichotomies that have characterized much of social theory (see Chapter 10).

The idea of networks is hard to get at, but Crawford (2005:1) does a good job of defining them and relating them to actants: "Networks are processual, built activities, performed by actants out of which they are composed." Most generally, it implies a series of transformations and translations. A more specific sense arises in Latour's (1999:17) argument that a network is not society or an anonymous field of forces but is "the *summing up* of interactions through various kinds of devices, inscriptions, forms and formulae, into a very local, very practical, very tiny locus." Thus, a focus on networks leads one closer to, rather than farther away from, the local. This idea is closely linked to the roots of ANT in science studies, especially the detailed and local study of, for example, the operations of scientific laboratories. However, ANT rejects the micro-macro distinction. Thus, in discussing the local, or the network, and even the actant, there is a sense that the micro-macro, as well as the local-general, cannot be distinguished from one another. More specifically, the macro should be viewed not as "big," "but [as] connected . . . local, mediated, related" (Latour, 1999:18).

Related to the idea of network is *performativity*. This means that entities do not exist in any essentialist sense but rather are performed in, by, and through relations, or networks (Law, 1999:4). It is easy to think of human actors as engaging in such performativity, but ANT goes beyond this to see material entities as being characterized by performativity. If people and objects are performed, then "everything is uncertain and reversible" (Law, 1999:4). There are times when durability and fixity result, but the focus is on how those things are performed so that such durability is achieved. In other words, durable networks, to take one example, are performed, and this means that no matter how seemingly durable they are they can fall apart. Just as networks can be performed into durability, they can be performed into disintegration and even disappearance. However, even ANT theorists recognize some measure of durability, as best exemplified in Latour's concept of "immutable mobiles," which can be defined as "a network of elements that holds its shape as it moves" through space and time (Law and Hetherington, 2002:395–396). Thus, there is a durable network here, but it is one that is in constant movement (and there is the ever-present possibility that it can fall apart).

What is perhaps most distinctive about actor-network theory is its concern with material entities or artifacts: "Material artifacts may exercise something which resembles agency. But this proves to be a peculiar form of *agency,* one entirely *devoid of intentionality*" (Brown and Capdevila, 1999:40). This is one of the reasons, as mentioned above, that material artifacts are "inferior" objects. The key to these artifacts is their lack of meaning; it is this that gives them a "will to connect" with other elements of a network. It is this very blankness that leads the network and its elements to seek to connect with the artifact. To put it another way, by inciting connections, an artifact "drives networks to incorporate and fold around actants" (Brown and Capdevila, 1999:41). Humans can be seen in much the same way: "they perform their own functional blankness . . . incite and form relations on the basis of what they do not present, do not say . . . [they provoke] the will-to-connect to ever greater excesses" (Brown and Capdevila, 1999:40).

Relatedly, there is a concern in ANT with "practical materiality" (Dugdale, 1999). Material artifacts play a key role in constituting networks and subjects. Thus, artifacts are not simply acted upon (e.g., connected with by the network); they also act. Material artifacts, like human agents, are actants. For example, Law and Hetherington (2002:394) discuss how things like carpeting and decor are performative: they act; they "participate in the generation of information, of power relations, of subjectivities and objectivities." Thus, nonhumans are active participants in networks, in social relationships. Of course, material artifacts lack what defines human actors—intentionality! Verran offers a good summary of all of this:

> this interpretive frame avoids any separation of the material and the symbolic in proposing worlds as outcomes of mutually resisting/accommodating participants, where participation goes far beyond the human to encompass the non-living as active in routine (and novel) actions, which constitute the world.
>
> (Verran, 1999:143)

The focus on relations, circulations, and networks obviously has a spatial implication, but ANT has a unique view on spatiality: "different and nonconformable spatialities (e.g., regions and networks) are formed" (Law, 1999:11). Thus, ANT seeks to distance itself from a simple Euclidean view of space. In one of its most distinctive views on space, ANT makes much of the issue of a "fold" in space formed "like a blunt scissors edge across paper, such that what were distant points suddenly become neighbors. Things . . . get crumpled together" (Brown and Capdevila, 1999:29). Also of interest is the fact that Latour (1999:19) argues that the "empty spaces 'in between' the networks, those *terra incognita,* are the most exciting aspects of ANT because they show the extent of our ignorance and the immense reserve that is open to change."

Given its roots in science studies, actor-network theory is oriented to micromethods (although the term *micro* is anathema to this perspective): "actor-network studies attempt to become part of the networks of which they speak. To be able to trace a network means becoming interior to its activities" (Brown and Capdevila, 1999:43). Or as Latour (1999:20) humbly puts it: "for us, ANT was simply another way of being faithful to the insights of ethnomethodology: actors[8] know what they do and we have to learn from them not only what they do, but how and why they do it. . . . [It is] a very crude method to learn from the actors without imposing on them an *a priori* definition of their world-building capacities" (Latour, 1999:19–20). In fact, as is the case with ethnomethodology, some supporters describe ANT as method and *not* a theory (Callon, 1999:194).

In terms of the discussion of modernity in Chapter 11, and the treatment of postmodernity in Chapter 13, it is interesting to reflect, in closing, on Bruno Latour's (1993:39) contention that "the modern world never happened." This notion is based,

---

[8] This word seems to be at odds with the earlier point about the broad concern with actants and to imply a focus on human actors. This also tends to support Callon's (1999:182) critique of ANT for offering "an anonymous, ill-defined and indiscernible" perspective on the actor.

in part, on the fact that we continue to have much in common with premoderns. In addition, it is premised on the idea that it is impossible to identify points of origin or to clearly identity a point at which one epoch ends and another begins. Because we have never been modern (or premodern, for that matter), it follows that we cannot now be postmodern. Thus, ANT rejects the entire distinction between premodernity, modernity, and postmodernity.

Finally, it should be noted that some adherents of ANT are not happy with the directions taken recently by other thinkers associated with the approach, as well as with efforts (like this one) to clearly define and delimit it. For example, Law (1999:9) is concerned about naming, simplifying, and losing complexity—"the theory has been reduced to a few aphorisms that can be quickly passed on." Even more strongly, the leading figure associated with ANT says: "There are four things that do not work with actor-network theory: The word actor, the word network, the word theory and the hyphen. Four nails in the coffin!" (Latour, 1999:15). Key contributors to ANT are thus intent on maintaining the complexity of a theory that seeks to reflect, at least to some degree, the complexity of the social (and material) world.

Related to the development of actor-network theory are the ideas of posthumanism and the postsocial. *Posthumanism* is defined "by its opposition to humanism, as well as moving beyond it. It rejects the notion of the separability of humanity from the non-human world . . . and the division of knowledge into separate domains" (Franklin, 2007:3548). Since humanism lies at the base of much of sociology, especially microsociologies, posthumanism constitutes a profound challenge to the field. However, it can be seen as an opportunity to extend sociology beyond human actors to a wide range of other phenomena and to encompass them all within a single framework.

The idea of the *postsocial* constitutes a parallel challenge to traditional ideas of sociality. Sociality may continue, but it is declining in importance (social forms are being emptied of social relationships) and taking on new forms. Among the new forms are the relationships emerging with the enormous expansion of objects in the contemporay world such as technologies, consumer goods, and objects of knowledge. As Knorr-Cetina puts it:

> Postsocial relations are human ties triangulated with object relations, and forming only with respect to these relations. . . . Postsocial is what one might call a level of intersubjectivity that is no longer based on face-to-face interaction and may in fact not involve interaction at all. . . . Postsocial systems may arise around the sort of relatedness enabled by the Internet. . . . Postsocial forms are not rich in sociality in the old sense . . . but they may be rich in other ways, and the challenge is to analyze and theorize these constellations.
>
> (Knorr-Cetina, 2007:3588)

The emergence of an increasing number of postsocial relationships is related to the development of new types of work and consumption settings. One example of the former is "virtual organizations" that lack a central headquarters where workers can congregate and interact both to handle work-related tasks and to engage in social relationships. In virtual organizations workers are largely, if not totally, on their own, interacting on a much more limited basis with other workers and with superiors by phone, e-mail, or occasional face-to-face visits.

There are numerous examples of such postsocial relationships in the realm of consumption. For example, instead of interacting with tellers in a bank, we are increasingly likely to interact with ATMs. Other bank-related interactions are now increasingly likely to involve automated telephone contact or online banking. Also, rather than interacting with a salesperson in a bookshop, we are increasingly likely to buy books (and other products) through Amazon.com without ever interacting with a human being. In such instances technologies and other objects replace humans as relationship partners or serve to mediate the relationships among people. We often cannot get to talk to a real person until we have exhausted all the options offered on the automated telephone message.

Increasingly, in many of the best-known consumption sites (what I have called the "cathedrals of consumption" [Ritzer, 2005a]), we find much the same process. For example, in Las Vegas casinos, as well as casinos in many other places in the United States and elsewhere, an increasingly large proportion of floor space is devoted to slot machines, and gamblers interact almost exclusively with these objects. Other forms of gambling—keno, for example—also involve little or no human interaction and are replacing the historic focus of casinos on games (blackjack, poker, roulette, craps, etc.) that require direct interaction with other humans as either employees or fellow players. Similarly, the modern department store has far fewer employees than in the past, and customers are supposed to interact with the store and its products, make selections, and only then bring goods to a human employee in order to pay for those choices.

Of course, the Internet is the postsocial setting *par excellence*. We interact with keyboards, computer screens, Web sites, e-mail, chat rooms, massive multiplayer games, and so on. In some cases Internet relationships may come to involve face-to-face interactions (sometimes with dangerous consequences), but most often whatever human relationships exist on the Internet are mediated by the wide range of technologies associated with it.

Practice Theory 实践理论

Practice theory sounds like, and indeed draws upon, a number of theories and theorists discussed elsewhere in this book. It is derived from the work of Bourdieu, Foucault, Giddens, Garfinkel, Latour, and Butler. It is linked to poststructuralism, structuration theory, ethnomethodology, actor-network theory (and science studies), and performativity theory. There are also more specific works on "practices" (S. P. Turner, 1994), an original theoretical approach to practice theory (Schatzki, 1996; see also Schatzki, Knorr-Cetina, and von Savigny, 2001), and even encyclopedia entries on the topic (Biernacki, 2007). Furthermore, we also are beginning to see efforts to apply practice theory to specific areas of study including Warde's (2005) application of it to the study of consumption. Given the wide variety of inputs and sources, it is not easy to pin down exactly what is meant by practice theory, but Reckwitz (2002) has done an estimable job of highlighting the central characteristics of that theory, at least in an ideal-typical form.

Practice theory is one of a variety of "cultural theories." Other cultural theories focus on mental qualities (e.g., phenomenology), discourse (e.g., structuralism, semiotics), or interaction (e.g., symbolic interaction). Practice theory, by definition, focuses on, well, practice. What is practice? Above all, a focus on practice emphasizes the impact of "taken-for-granted, pre-theoretical assumptions on human conduct" (Biernacki, 2007:3607). Practice is a routinized way of acting, and those pretheoretical assumptions and routines affect how we act, especially how we manage our bodies, handle objects, treat subjects, describe things, and understand the world. Reckwitz seeks to clarify the abstract nature of practice and practice theory by focusing on its relationship to a number of core concepts.

The first is the *body*. Indeed, interest in the body is one of the central and defining characteristics of practice theory (and it is of increasing interest in sociology in general and in sociological theory in particular). In many other theories the body is an epiphenomenon affected by, even controlled by, other phenomena (rational choices, norms, values). But for practice theory the body is of central and direct importance; it is the site of the social. In fact, practices are, at least in part, "routinized bodily performances" (Reckwitz, 2002:251). Practices are the result of training the body in a particular way. "A practice can be understood as the regular, skillful 'performance' of human bodies" (Reckwitz, 2002:251). This definition applies to obvious things such as using a golf club to drive a golf ball, but also to talking, reading, and writing.

Practice involves not only routinized bodily performances but also the *mind,* mental activities. To engage in practice entails the use of the body in various ways *and* engagement in mental activities—"certain routinized ways of understanding the world, of desiring something, of knowing something" (Reckwitz, 2002:251). Notice that while the focus here is on mental activities, they, like bodily activities, are routinized. Thus it is not that we consciously think through either what our bodies or minds will do; we simply act in a routinized manner. For example, playing tennis requires certain bodily movements that we perform routinely without thinking through each step to, say, hit a backhand or an overhead shot. But playing tennis also requires know-how about how the game is played, interpretation (of, for example, what it means when your opponent rushes the net), and aims (such as winning the point and the match). Playing tennis requires *both* routinized bodily and mental activities, as well as the interaction of the two.

Things are integral to practice and as necessary as bodily and mental activities. Practice often involves using things in particular ways. The use of things involves both bodily movements and mental activities. Thus, in tennis, one must be able to use a tennis racket in various ways depending on the nature of the shot required. No matter how good one's bodily and mental activities, one cannot play tennis without a racket. It is in the interaction of body, mind, and object that most practice exists. Overall, practice cannot occur in the absence of objects.

Knowledge also is required for practice to occur. More than just knowing various things, this knowledge also includes "ways of understanding, knowing how, ways of wanting and of feeling that are linked to each other within a practice" (Reckwitz, 2002:253). All of this knowledge is largely implicit. Thus, in playing tennis we know the rudiments of the game, we know how to hit certain shots and return various shots from our opponent, and we know that we want certain things (to win) and not other things (to be embarrassed) and that a certain level and type of emotional involvement (alert but not tense) is needed to do well. All of this knowledge is important, but in most cases it is employed routinely without thinking through all of the issues involved.

To practice theory, d*iscourse/language* is merely one practice among many practices. In contrast, many other similar perspectives (especially structuralism and semiotics)—all part of the "linguistic turn" in sociology—give discourse/language a privileged status. In those other perspectives, discursive practices are merely strings of signs. In practice theory, they are that, but they also are "bodily patterns, routinized mental activities— forms of understanding, know-how (here including grammar and pragmatic rules of use), and motivation—and above all objects (from sounds to computers) that are linked to each other" (Reckwitz, 2002:254–255.). Thus, in practice theory, discourse/language involves not only signs but also all of the other key concerns of the theory.

In terms of *structure/process,* social structure is found in the routine nature of practice. Larger-scale social phenomena, from economic structures like corporations to intimate social relations, are structured by the routines that lie at the heart of social practices. Thus, structure (as well as process) does not exist "out there" in large-scale social phenomena, or in people's heads, but exists in the routine nature of action. Structure is *not,* say, an organization's structure as reflected in an organizational chart, or the structure of the brain; it is the routines of action.

This leads to a very distinctive view of the *agent/individual.* Many social theories, especially microtheories, focus on the agent/individual as, for example, self-interested (rational choice theory) or as controlled by norms and roles (structural functionalism). The focus in practice theory is on practice and *not* on agents. Agents exist, but they are merely "body/minds who 'carry' and 'carry out' social practices." Thus, the agent is neither autonomous (as in rational choice theory) nor a judgmental dope (as in structural functionalism), but rather "someone who understands the world and herself, who uses know-how and motivational knowledge, according to the particular practice" (Reckwitz, 2002:256). The key point here is that practice theory deemphasizes the importance of the agent and seeks to focus attention on the practices; it is those practices that are of central importance and *not* the agents who carry them out. This is a radical step, for most sociological theories focus either on agents as creators of their social worlds or on the internal and external forces that constrain the agent and limit that creativity.

Practice theory as it now stands is derived from bits and pieces of the work of a variety of theorists and from a variety of theories. It constitutes a loose network of works and ideas, and there is, as yet, no "grand" practice theory, nor must it necessarily become a "grand" theory. But there are enough distinctive theoretical ideas that cohere in interesting ways around the idea of practice to suggest the further development of a useful new theoretical perspective.

Summary 总结

This chapter deals with four theories that have shown significant development in recent years and show every sign of further development. Other growing and promising theories are discussed earlier in this book (e.g., feminist and globalization theory), and there are certainly others that could have been included in this chapter. However, the four theories chosen for inclusion here represent a best guess as to the theories that are "hot" in the field today and are likely to be of continuing, if not growing, importance in the coming years.

Queer theory and critical theories of race and racism are the result of growing interest in the larger social world in queerness and race/racism. They also show the influence of developments internal to social theory, such as the impact of the theories of Foucault on queer theory and of those of Du Bois on CTRR. Then there are more recent inputs such as the impact of ideas derived from gay and lesbian studies on queer theory and of critical race theory on CTRR. Queer theory and CTRR have been both positively and negatively affected by these perspectives. More important, they have incorporated ideas from many other theoretical perspectives, as well as from developments in the social world, to develop highly distinctive and promising social theories.

Actor-network theory and practice theory are purer products of prior developments in theory. Although they relate to the social world, they are far less a reflection of developments there. Actor-network theory is most notable for according nonhuman actors their deserved significance in social theory. Practice theory does the same for routinized ways of acting. It is concerned with the ways in which pretheoretical assumptions and routines affect how we act—how we manage our bodies, handle objects, treat subjects, describe things, and understand the world.

Cutting-edge theories like those discussed in this chapter continually refresh sociological theory by adding new subjects of study and new ways of thinking not only about them but about many other subjects of longer term concern in the field. It is safe to predict that more new theories will emerge in the coming years (while others will decline and perhaps disappear), and that they, too, will enrich the field in similar ways.

Appendix 附录:

Sociological Metatheorizing and a Metatheoretical Schema for Analyzing Sociological Theory
社会学的元理论化和分析社会学理论的元理论框架

Appendix Outline
Metatheorizing in Sociology
The Ideas of Thomas Kuhn
Sociology: A Multiple-Paradigm Science
Toward a More Integrated Sociological Paradigm

One of the most recent developments in sociological theory is the growth of interest in sociological metatheorizing. While theorists take the social world as their subject matter, metatheorists engage in *the systematic study of the underlying structure of sociological theory* (Ritzer, 1991b; Ritzer, Zhao, and Murphy, 2001; Zhao, 2005, 2001). One goal of this Appendix is to look at the increase in interest in metatheorizing in sociology and at the basic parameters of this approach. The entire structure of this book rests on a specific set of metatheoretical perspectives I developed (1975a, 1981a). Thus, another objective of this Appendix is to present the metatheoretical ideas that inform the text. But first an overview of metatheorizing in sociology will be helpful.

Metatheorizing in Sociology 社会学中的元理论化

Sociologists are not the only ones to do meta-analysis (Bakker, 2007c), that is, to reflexively study their own discipline. Others who do such work include philosophers (Radnitzky, 1973), psychologists (Gergen, 1973, 1986; Schmidt et al., 1984), political scientists (Connolly, 1973), a number of other social scientists (various essays in Fiske and Shweder, 1986), and historians (Hayden White, 1973).

Beyond the fact that meta-analysis occurs in other fields, various kinds of sociologists, not just metatheorists, do this type of analysis (Zhao, 1991). We can group the types of meta-analysis in sociology under the heading "metasociology," which can be defined as *the reflexive study of the underlying structure of sociology in general, as well as of its various components*—substantive areas (for example, Richard Hall's [1983] overview of occupational sociology), concepts (Rubenstein's [1986] analysis of the concept of "structure"), methods (*metamethods*, for example, Brewer and

Hunter's [1989] and Noblit and Hare's [1988] efforts to synthesize sociological methods), data (*meta-data-analysis,*[1] for example, Fendrich, 1984; Hunter, Schmidt, and
Jackson, 1982; Polit and Falbo, 1987; F. M. Wolf, 1986), and theories. It is the last
item, *metatheorizing,* that will concern us in this Appendix.

What distinguishes work in this area is not so much the process of metatheorizing
(or systematically studying theories, which all metatheorists do) but rather the nature of
the end products. There are three varieties of metatheorizing, largely defined by differences in end products (Ritzer, 1991a, 1991b, 1991c, 1992b, 2007). The first type,
metatheorizing as a means of attaining a deeper understanding of theory (M_U), involves
the study of theory in order to produce a better, more profound understanding of extant
theory (Ritzer, 1988). M_U is concerned with the study of theories, theorists, and communities of theorists, as well as the larger intellectual and social contexts of theories
and theorists. The second type, *metatheorizing as a prelude to theory development* (M_P),
entails the study of extant theory in order to produce new sociological theory. In the
third type, *metatheorizing as a source of perspectives that overarch sociological theory*
(M_O), the study of theory is oriented toward the goal of producing a perspective—one
could say *a* metatheory—that overarches some part or all of sociological theory. (It is
this type of metatheorizing that provided the framework used in constructing this book.)
Given these definitions, let us examine each type of metatheorizing in detail.

1. The first type of metatheorizing, M_U, is composed of four basic subtypes. All of
them involve the formal or informal study of sociological theory to attain a deeper
understanding of it.

The first subtype, *internal-intellectual,* focuses on intellectual or cognitive issues
that are internal to sociology. Included here are attempts to identify major cognitive
paradigms (Ritzer, 1975a, 1975b; see also the discussion below) and "schools of
thought" (Sorokin, 1928), more dynamic views of the underlying structure of sociological theory (L. Harvey, 1982, 1987; Wiley, 1979; Nash and Wardell, 1993; Holmwood and Stewart, 1994), and the development of general metatheoretical tools with
which to analyze existing sociological theories and to develop new theories (Alexander
et al., 1987; Edel, 1959; Gouldner, 1970; Ritzer, 1989, 1990a; Wiley, 1988).

The second subtype, *internal-social,* also looks within sociology, but it focuses
on social rather than cognitive factors. The main approach here emphasizes the communal aspects of various sociological theories and includes efforts to identify the
major "schools" in the history of sociology (Bulmer, 1984, 1985; Cortese, 1995;
Tiryakian, 1979, 1986), the more formal, network approach to the study of the ties
among groups of sociologists (Mullins, 1973, 1983), and studies of theorists themselves
that examine their institutional affiliations, career patterns, positions within the field
of sociology, and so on (Gouldner, 1970; Camic, 1992).

---

[1] The (somewhat awkward) label "meta-data-analysis" is used to differentiate this from the more generic meta-
analysis. In meta-data-analysis the goal is to seek ways of cumulating research results across research studies. In his
introduction to Wolf's *Meta-Analysis,* Niemi defines *meta-analysis* as "the application of statistical procedures to
collections of empirical findings from individual studies for the purpose of integrating, synthesizing, and making
sense of them" (F. M. Wolf, 1986:5).

The third subtype, *external-intellectual,* turns to other academic disciplines for ideas, tools, concepts, and theories that can be used in the analysis of sociological theory (for example, R. Brown, 1987, 1990). Baker (1993) has looked at the implications of chaos theory, with its roots in physics, for sociological theory. Bailey has argued that while explicit attention to metatheorizing may be relatively new in sociology, "general systems theory has long been marked by widespread metatheorizing" (1994:27). Such metatheorizing was made necessary by the multidisciplinary character of systems theory and the need to study and bring together ideas from different fields. He later argues that social-systems theory "embraces metatheorizing" (K. D. Bailey, 1994:82). In fact, Bailey uses a metatheoretical approach to analyze developments in systems theory and their relationship to developments in sociological theory.

The fourth subtype, the *external-social approach,* shifts to a more macro level to look at the larger society (national setting, sociocultural setting, etc.) and the nature of its impact on sociological theorizing (for example, Vidich and Lyman, 1985).

Of course, specific metatheoretical efforts can combine two or more types of M_U. For example, Jaworski has shown how Lewis Coser's 1956 book *Functions of Social Conflict* "was a deeply personal book and a historically situated statement" (1991:116). Thus, Jaworski touches on the impact of his family (internal-social) and of the rise of Hitler in Germany (external-social) on Coser's life and work. Jaworski also deals with the effect of external-intellectual (American radical political thought) and internal-intellectual (industrial sociology) factors on Coser's thinking. Thus, Jaworski combines all four subtypes of M_U in his analysis of Coser's work on social conflict.

2. Most metatheorizing in sociology is not M_U; rather, it is the second type, metatheorizing as a prelude to the development of sociological theory (M_P). Most important classical and contemporary theorists developed their theories, at least in part, on the basis of a careful study of, and reaction to, the work of other theorists. Among the most important examples are Marx's theory of capitalism (see Chapter 1), developed out of a systematic engagement with Hegelian philosophy as well as other ideas, such as political economy and utopian socialism; Parsons's action theory, developed out of a systematic study of the work of Durkheim, Weber, Pareto, and Marshall; Alexander's (1982–1983) multidimensional, neofunctional theory, based on a detailed study of the work of Marx, Weber, Durkheim, and Parsons; and Habermas's (1987a) communication theory, based on his examination of the work of various critical theorists, as well as that of Marx, Weber, Parsons, Mead, and Durkheim. Let us look in more detail at M_P as it was practiced by Karl Marx.

In *Economic and Philosophic Manuscripts of 1844,* Marx (1932/1964) develops his theoretical perspective on the basis of a detailed and careful analysis and critique of the works of political economists such as Adam Smith, Jean-Baptiste Say, David Ricardo, and James Mill; philosophers such as G. W. F. Hegel, the Young Hegelians (for example, Bruno Bauer), and Ludwig Feuerbach; utopian socialists such as Etienne Cabet, Robert Owen, Charles Fourier, and Pierre Proudhon; and a variety of other major and minor intellectual schools and figures. It seems safe to say that in almost its entirety the *Manuscripts of 1844* is a metatheoretical treatise in which Marx develops his own ideas out of an engagement with a variety of idea systems.

What of Marx's other works? Are they more empirical? Less metatheoretical? In his preface to *The German Ideology* (Marx and Engels, 1845–1846/1970), C. J. Arthur describes that work as composed mainly of "detailed line by line polemics against the writings of some of their [Marx and Engels's] contemporaries" (1970:1). In fact, Marx himself describes *The German Ideology* as an effort "to set forth together our conception as opposed to the ideological one of German philosophy, in fact to settle accounts with our former philosophical conscience. The intention was carried out in the form of a critique of post-Hegelian philosophy" (1859/1970:22). *The Holy Family* (Marx and Engels, 1845/1956) is, above all, an extended critique of Bruno Bauer, the Young Hegelians, and their propensity toward speculative "critical criticism."[2] In their foreword, Marx and Engels make it clear that this kind of metatheoretical work is a prelude to their coming theorizing: "We therefore give this polemic as a preliminary to the independent works in which we . . . shall present our positive view" (1845/1956:16). In the *Grundrisse* Marx (1857–1858/1974) chooses as his metatheoretical antagonists the political economist David Ricardo and the French socialist Pierre Proudhon (Nicolaus, 1974). Throughout the *Grundrisse* Marx is struggling to solve an array of theoretical problems, in part through a critique of the theories and theorists mentioned here and in part through an application of ideas derived from Hegel. In describing the introduction to the *Grundrisse,* Nicolaus says that it "reflects in its every line the struggle of Marx against Hegel, Ricardo and Proudhon. From it, Marx carried off the most important objective of all, namely the basic principles of writing history dialectically" (1974:42). *A Contribution to the Critique of Political Economy* (Marx, 1859/1970) is, as the title suggests, an effort to build a distinctive economic approach on the basis of a critique of the works of the political economists.

Even *Capital* (1867/1967)—which is admittedly one of Marx's most empirical works, since in it he deals more directly with the reality of the capitalist work world through the use of government statistics and reports—is informed by Marx's earlier metatheoretical work and contains some metatheorizing of its own. In fact, the subtitle, *A Critique of Political Economy,* makes the metatheoretical roots absolutely clear. However, Marx is freer in *Capital* to be much more "positive," that is, to construct his own distinctive theoretical orientation. This freedom is traceable, in part, to his having done much of the metatheoretical groundwork in earlier works. Furthermore, most of the new metatheoretical work is relegated to the so-called fourth volume of *Capital,* published under the title *Theories of Surplus Value* (Marx, 1862–1863/1963, 1862–1863/1968). *Theories* is composed of many extracts from the work of the major political economists (for example, Smith and Ricardo) as well as critical analysis of them by Marx. In sum, it is safe to say that Marx was, largely, a metatheorist, perhaps the *most* metatheoretical of all classical sociological theorists.

3. There are a number of examples of the third type of metatheorizing, M_O—metatheorizing to produce overarching perspectives. They include Walter Wallace's (1988) "disciplinary matrix," Ritzer's (1979, 1981a) "integrated sociological paradigm" (discussed later in this Appendix), Furfey's (1953/1965) positivistic metasociology, Gross's

---

[2] In fact, the book is subtitled *Against Bruno Bauer and Co.*

(1961) "neodialectical" metasociology, Alexander's (1982) "general theoretical logic for sociology," and Alexander's (1995) later effort to develop a postpositivist approach to universalism and rationality. A number of theorists (Bourdieu and Wacquant, 1992; Emirbayer, 1997; Ritzer and Gindoff, 1992, 1994) have been engaged in an effort to create what Ritzer and Gindoff have called "methodological relationism"[3] to complement the extant overarching perspectives of "methodological individualism" (Udehn, 2002) and "methodological holism." Methodological relationism is derived from a study of works on micro-macro and agency-structure integration, as well as a variety of works in social psychology.

The three varieties of metatheory are ideal types. In actual cases there is often considerable overlap in the objectives of metatheoretical works. Nevertheless, those who do one type of metatheorizing tend to be less interested in achieving the objectives of the other two types. Of course, there are sociologists who at one time or another have done all three types of metatheorizing. For example, Alexander (1982–1983) creates overarching perspectives (M_O) in the first volume of *Theoretical Logic in Sociology,* uses them in the next three volumes to achieve a better understanding (M_U) of the classic theorists, and later seeks to help create neofunctionalism (M_P) as a theoretical successor to structural functionalism (Alexander and Colomy, 1990a).

皮埃尔·布迪厄的反思社会学
Pierre Bourdieu's Reflexive Sociology

An important contemporary metatheorist (although he would resist that label, indeed any label) is Pierre Bourdieu. Bourdieu calls for a reflexive sociology: "For me, sociology ought to be meta but *always vis-à-vis itself.* It must use its own instruments to find out what it is and what it is doing, to try to know better where it stands" (Bourdieu and Wacquant, 1992:191; see also Meisenhelder, 1997). Or, using an older and less well defined label ("sociology of sociology") for metasociology, Bourdieu says, "The sociology of sociology is a fundamental dimension of sociological epistemology" (Bourdieu and Wacquant, 1992:68). Sociologists, who spend their careers "objectivizing" the social world, ought to spend some time objectivizing their own practices. Thus, sociology "continually turns back onto itself the scientific weapons it produces" (Bourdieu and Wacquant, 1992:214). Bourdieu even rejects certain kinds of metatheorizing (for example, the internal-social and internal-intellectual forms of M_U) as "a complacent and intimist return upon the private *person* of the sociologist or with a search for the intellectual *Zeitgeist* that animates his or her work" (Bourdieu and Wacquant, 1992:72; for a discussion of Bourdieu's more positive view of even these kinds of metatheorizing, see Wacquant, 1992:38). However, a rejection of certain kinds of metatheorizing does not represent a rejection of the undertaking in its entirety. Clearly, following the logic of *Homo Academicus,* (1984b), Bourdieu would favor examining the habitus and practices of sociologists within the fields of sociology as a discipline and the academic world, as well as the relationship between those fields and the fields of stratification and politics. His work *Distinction*

---

[3] Swartz (1997) does a particularly good job of delineating this metatheory as well as the other metatheories that inform Bourdieu's theorizing.

(1984a) would lead Bourdieu to concern himself with the strategies of individual sociologists, as well as of the discipline itself, to achieve distinction. For example, individual sociologists might use jargon to achieve high status in the field, and sociology might wrap itself in a cloak of science so that it could achieve distinction vis-à-vis the world of practice. In fact, Bourdieu has claimed that the scientific claims of sociology and other social sciences "are really euphemized assertions of power" (Robbins, 1991:139). Of course, this position has uncomfortable implications for Bourdieu's own work:

> Bourdieu's main problem during the 1980s has been to sustain his symbolic power whilst simultaneously undermining the scientificity on which it was originally founded. Some would say that he has tied the noose around his own neck and kicked away the stool from beneath his feet.
>
> (Robbins, 1991:150)

Given his commitment to theoretically informed empirical research, Bourdieu also would have little patience with most, if not all, forms of M_O, which he has described as "universal metadiscourse on knowledge of the world" (Bourdieu and Wacquant, 1992:159). More generally, Bourdieu would reject metatheorizing as an autonomous practice, setting metatheorizing apart from theorizing about and empirically studying the social world (see Wacquant, 1992:31).

Bourdieu makes an interesting case for metatheorizing when he argues that sociologists need to *"avoid being the toy of social forces in [their] practice of sociology"* (Bourdieu and Wacquant, 1992:183). The only way to avoid such a fate is to understand the nature of the forces acting on the sociologist at a given point in history. Such forces can be understood only via metatheoretical analysis, or what Bourdieu calls "socioanalysis" (Bourdieu and Wacquant, 1992:210). Once sociologists understand the nature of the forces (especially external-social and external-intellectual) operating on them, they will be in a better position to control the impact of those forces on their work. As Bourdieu puts it, in personal terms, "I continually use sociology to try to cleanse my work of . . . social determinants" (Bourdieu and Wacquant, 1992:211). Thus, the goal of metatheorizing from Bourdieu's point of view is not to undermine sociology, but to free it from those forces which determine it. Of course, what Bourdieu says of his own efforts is equally true of metatheoretical endeavors in general. While he strives to limit the effect of external factors on his work, Bourdieu is aware of the limitations of such efforts: "I do not for one minute believe or claim that I am fully liberated from them [social determinants]" (Bourdieu and Wacquant, 1992:211).

Similarly, Bourdieu wishes to free sociologists from the symbolic violence committed against them by other, more powerful sociologists. This objective invites internal-intellectual and internal-social analyses of sociology in order to uncover the sources and nature of that symbolic violence. Once the latter are understood, sociologists are in a better position to free themselves of, or at least limit, their effects. More generally, sociologists are well positioned to practice "epistemological vigilance" in order to protect themselves from these distorting pressures (Bourdieu, 1984b:15).

What is most distinctive about Bourdieu's metatheoretical approach is his refusal to separate metatheorizing from the other facets of sociology.[4] That is, he believes that sociologists should be continuously reflexive as they are doing their sociological analyses. They should reflect on what they are doing, and especially on how it might be distorting what they are examining, during their analyses. This reflection would limit the amount of "symbolic violence" against the subjects of study.

Although Bourdieu is doing a distinctive kind of metatheoretical work, it is clear that his work is, at least in part, metatheoretical. Given his growing significance in social theory, the association of Bourdieu's work with metatheorizing is likely to contribute further to the growth of interest in metatheorizing in sociology.

With this overview, we now turn to the specific metatheoretical approach that undergirds this book. As will become clear, it involves a combination of M_U and M_O. We begin with a brief review of the work of Thomas Kuhn, and then we examine Ritzer's (M_U) analysis of sociology's multiple paradigms. Finally, we review the metatheoretical tool—the integrated sociological paradigm (M_O)—that is the source of the levels of analysis used to analyze sociological theories throughout this book.

The Ideas of Thomas Kuhn 托马斯·库恩的理论

In 1962 the philosopher of science Thomas Kuhn published a rather slim volume entitled *The Structure of Scientific Revolutions* (Hoyningen-Huene, 1993). Because this work grew out of philosophy, it appeared to be fated to a marginal status within sociology, especially because it focused on the hard sciences (physics, for example) and had little directly to say about the social sciences. However, the theses of the book proved extremely interesting to people in a wide range of fields (for example, Hollinger, 1980, in history; Searle, 1972, in linguistics; Stanfield, 1974, in economics), and to none was it more important than to sociologists. In 1970 Robert Friedrichs published the first important work from a Kuhnian perspective, *A Sociology of Sociology*. After that there was a steady stream of work from this perspective (Eckberg and Hill, 1979; Effrat, 1972; Eisenstadt and Curelaru, 1976; Falk and Zhao, 1990a, 1990b; Friedrichs, 1972; Greisman, 1986; Guba and Lincoln, 1994; Lodahl and Gordon, 1972; D. Phillips, 1973, 1975; Quadagno, 1979; Ritzer, 1975a, 1975b, 1981b; M. Rosenberg, 1989; Snizek, 1976; Snizek, Fuhrman, and Miller, 1979). There is little doubt that Kuhnian theory is an important variety of M_U, but what exactly is Kuhn's approach?

One of Kuhn's goals in *The Structure of Scientific Revolutions* (1962) was to challenge commonly held assumptions about the way in which science changes. In the view of most laypeople and many scientists, science advances in a cumulative manner, with each advance building inexorably on all that preceded it. Science has achieved its present state through slow and steady increments of knowledge. It will advance to even greater heights in the future. This conception of science was enunciated by the physicist

---

[4] This leads Swartz (1997:11) to argue that "Bourdieu does not share Ritzer's (1988) vision of establishing sociological metatheory as a legitimate subfield within the discipline of sociology."

George Ritzer

Autobiography as a Metatheoretical Tool

Biographical and autobiographical work is useful in helping us understand the work of sociological theorists, and of sociologists generally. The historian of science, Thomas Hankin, explains it this way:

> [A] fully integrated biography of a scientist which includes not only his personality, but also his scientific work and the intellectual and social context of his times, [is] . . . still the best way to get at many of the problems that beset the writing of history of science . . . science is created by individuals, and however much it may be driven by forces outside, these forces work through the scientist himself. Biography is the literary lens through which we can best view this process.
>
> (Hankin, 1979:14)

What Hankin asserts about scientists generally informs my orientation to the biographies of sociological theorists, including myself. This autobiographical snippet is designed to suggest at least a few ways in which biography can be a useful tool for metatheoretical analysis.

While I have taught in sociology departments for more than thirty years, have written extensively about sociology, and have lectured all over the world on the topic, none of my degrees are in sociology. This lack of a formal background in the field has led to lifelong study of sociology in general and sociological theory in particular. It has also, at least in one sense, aided my attempt to understand sociological theory. Because I had not been trained in a particular "school," I came to sociological theory with few prior conceptions and biases. Rather, I was a student of all "schools of thought"; they were all equally grist for my theoretical mill.

My first metatheoretical work, *Sociology: A Multiple Paradigm Science* (1975a), sought not only to lay out sociology's separable, and often conflicting, paradigms but also to make the case for paradigm linking, leaping, bridging, and integrating. Uncomfortable with paradigmatic conflict, I wanted to see more harmony and integration in sociology. That desire led to the publication of *Toward an Integrated Sociological Paradigm* (1981a), in which I more fully developed my sense of an integrated paradigm. The interest in resolving theoretical conflict led to a focus on micro-macro (1990a) and agency-structure (Ritzer and Gindoff, 1994) integration as well as the larger issue of theoretical syntheses (1990b).

Sir Isaac Newton, who said, "If I have seen further, it is because I stood on the shoulders of giants." But Kuhn regarded this conception of cumulative scientific development as a myth and sought to debunk it.

My interest in metatheoretical work is explained by my desire to understand theory better and to resolve unnecessary conflict within sociological theory. In *Metatheorizing in Sociology* (1991b) and in an edited volume, *Metatheorizing* (1992a), I made a case for the need for the systematic study of sociological theory. I believe that we need to do more of this in order to understand theory better, produce new theory, and produce new overarching theoretical perspectives (or metatheories). Metatheoretical study is also oriented to clarifying contentious issues, resolving disputes, and allowing for greater integration and synthesis.

Having spent many years seeking to clarify the nature of sociological theory, in the early 1990s I grew weary of the abstractions of metatheoretical work. I sought to apply the various theories that I had learned to very concrete aspects of the social world. I had done a little with this in the 1980s, applying Weber's theory of rationalization to fast-food restaurants (1983) and the medical profession (Ritzer and Walczak, 1988). I revisited the 1983 essay, and the result was a book, *The McDonaldization of Society* (1993, 1996, 2000, 2004a), which argued that while in Weber's day the model of the rationalization process was the bureaucracy, today the fast-food restaurant has become a better model of that process (additional essays on this topic are to be found in *The McDonaldization Thesis* [1998]). In *Expressing America: A Critique of the Global Credit Card Society* (1995), I turned my attention to another everyday economic phenomenon, which I analyzed not only from the perspective of rationalization theory, but from other perspectives, including Georg Simmel's theoretical ideas on money.

This work on fast-food restaurants and credit cards led to the realization that what I was really interested in was the sociology of consumption, a field little developed in the United States, at least in comparison to Great Britain and other European nations. That led to *Enchanting a Disenchanted World: Revolutionizing the Means of Consumption* (1999, 2005a), in which I used Weberian, Marxian, and postmodern theory to analyze the revolutionary impact of a range of new means of consumption (superstores, megamalls, cybermalls, home shopping television, casinos, theme parks, and cruise ships, as well as fast-food restaurants and other franchises) on the way Americans and the rest of the world consume goods and services.

The global reach of McDonald's and McDonaldization, credit cards, and the new means of consumption has led me more directly to an interest in globalization and my latest book, *The Globalization of Nothing* (2004b). While I cannot rule out a return to metatheoretical issues, and in fact have recently dealt with them (Ritzer, 2001), my current plans are to continue to use theory to think about the contemporary world, especially consumption and globalization.

Source: Adapted (and updated) from George Ritzer, "I Never Metatheory I Didn't Like," *Mid-American Review of Sociology*, 15:21–32, 1991. See also Goodman (2005).

Kuhn acknowledged that accumulation plays some role in the advance of science, but the truly major changes come about as a result of revolutions. Kuhn offered a theory of how major changes in science occur. He saw a science at any given time as being dominated by a specific *paradigm* (defined for the moment as a fundamental image of the science's subject matter) (Ritzer, 2005b). *Normal science* is a period of accumulation of knowledge in which scientists work to expand the reigning paradigm. Such scientific work inevitably spawns *anomalies,* or findings that cannot be explained by the reigning paradigm. A *crisis* stage occurs if these anomalies mount, and this crisis ultimately may end in a scientific revolution. The reigning paradigm is overthrown as a new one takes its place at the center of the science. A new dominant paradigm is born, and the stage is set for the cycle to repeat itself. Kuhn's theory can be depicted diagrammatically:

Paradigm I → Normal Science → Anomalies →
Crisis → Revolution → Paradigm II

It is during periods of revolution that the truly great changes in science take place. This view places Kuhn clearly at odds with most conceptions of scientific development.

The key concept in Kuhn's approach, as well as in this section, is the paradigm. Unfortunately, Kuhn is vague on what he means by a paradigm (Alcala-Campos, 1997). According to Margaret Masterman (1970), he used the term in at least twenty-one different ways. I will employ a definition of *paradigm* that I feel is true to the sense and spirit of Kuhn's early work.

A paradigm serves to differentiate one scientific community from another. It can be used to differentiate physics from chemistry or sociology from psychology. These fields have different paradigms. It also can be used to differentiate between different historical stages in the development of a science (Mann, Grimes, and Kemp, 1997). The paradigm that dominated physics in the nineteenth century is different from the one that dominated it in the early twentieth century. There is a third usage of the paradigm concept, and it is the one that is most useful here. Paradigms can differentiate among cognitive groupings *within* the same science. Contemporary psychoanalysis, for example, is differentiated into Freudian, Jungian, and Horneyian paradigms (among others)—that is, there are *multiple paradigms* in psychoanalysis—and the same is true of sociology and most other fields.

I can now offer a definition of *paradigm* that I feel is true to the sense of Kuhn's original work:

> A paradigm is a fundamental image of the subject matter within a science. It serves to define what should be studied, what questions should be asked, how they should be asked, and what rules should be followed in interpreting the answers obtained. The paradigm is the broadest unit of consensus within a science and serves to differentiate one scientific community (*or subcommunity*) from another. It subsumes, defines, and interrelates the exemplars, *theories* [italics added], and methods and instruments that exist within it.
>
> (Ritzer, 1975a:7)

With this definition we can begin to see the relationship between paradigms and theories. *Theories are only part of larger paradigms.* To put it another way, a paradigm may encompass two or more *theories,* as well as different *images* of the subject matter, *methods* (and instruments), and *exemplars* (specific pieces of scientific work that stand as a model for all those who follow).

社会学：多元范式的学科

Sociology: A Multiple-Paradigm Science

Ritzer's (1975a, 1975b, 1980) work on the paradigmatic status of sociology, beginning in the mid-1970s, provides the basis for the metatheoretical perspective that has guided the analysis of sociological theory throughout this book. There are *three* paradigms that dominated sociology, with several others having had the potential to achieve paradigmatic status. The three paradigms are labeled the *social-facts, social-definition,* and *social-behavior* paradigms. Each paradigm is analyzed in terms of the four components of a paradigm.

The Social-Facts Paradigm 社会—事实范式

1. *Exemplar:* The model for social factists is the work of Emile Durkheim, particularly *The Rules of Sociological Method* and *Suicide.*

2. *Image of the subject matter:* Social factists focus on what Durkheim termed social facts, or large-scale social structures and institutions. Those who subscribe to the social-facts paradigm focus not only on these phenomena but on their effect on individual thought and action.

3. *Methods:* Social factists are more likely than are those who subscribe to the other paradigms to use the interview-questionnaire[5] and historical-comparative methods.

4. *Theories:* The social-facts paradigm encompasses a number of theoretical perspectives. *Structural-functional* theorists tend to see social facts as neatly interrelated and order as maintained by general consensus. *Conflict* theorists tend to emphasize disorder among social facts as well as the notion that order is maintained by coercive forces in society. Although structural functionalism and conflict theory are the dominant theories in this paradigm, there are others, including *systems* theory.

The Social-Definition Paradigm 社会—释义范式

1. *Exemplar:* To social definitionists, the unifying model is Max Weber's work on social action.

2. *Image of the subject matter:* Weber's work helped lead to an interest among social definitionists in the way actors define their social situations and the effect of these definitions on ensuing action and interaction.

3. *Methods:* Social definitionists, although they are most likely to use the interview-questionnaire method, are more likely to use the observation method than are those in any other paradigm (Prus, 1996). In other words, observation is the distinctive methodology of social definitionists.

4. *Theories:* There are a wide number of theories that can be included within social definitionism: *action theory, symbolic interactionism, phenomenology, ethnomethodology,* and *existentialism.*

---

[5] William Snizek (1976) has shown that the interview-questionnaire is dominant in *all* paradigms.

The Social-Behavior Paradigm 社会—行为范式

1. *Exemplar:* The model for social behaviorists is the work of the psychologist B. F. Skinner.

2. *Image of the subject matter:* The subject matter of sociology to social behaviorists is the unthinking *behavior* of individuals. Of particular interest are the rewards that elicit desirable behaviors and the punishments that inhibit undesirable behaviors.

3. *Methods:* The distinctive method of social behaviorism is the experiment.

4. *Theories:* Two theoretical approaches in sociology can be included under the heading "social behaviorism." The first is *behavioral sociology,* which is very close to pure psychological behaviorism. The second, which is much more important, is *exchange theory.*[6]

迈向整合度更高的社会学范式

Toward a More Integrated Sociological Paradigm

In addition to detailing the nature of sociology's multiple paradigms, I sought to make the case for more paradigmatic integration in sociology. Although there is reason for extant paradigms to continue to exist, there is also a need for a more integrated paradigm.[7] Contrary to a claim by Nash and Wardell (1993), I am *not* arguing for a new hegemonic position in sociology; I am *not* arguing that "the current diversity represents an undesirable condition needing elimination" (Nash and Wardell, 1993:278). On the contrary, I argue for *more* diversity through the development of an integrated paradigm to supplement extant paradigms. Like Nash and Wardell, I *favor* theoretical diversity.

Extant paradigms tend to be one-sided, focusing on specific levels of social analysis while paying little or no attention to the others. This characteristic is reflected in the social factists' concern with macro structures; the social definitionists' concern with action, interaction, and the social construction of reality; and the social behaviorists' concern with behavior. It is this kind of one-sidedness that has led to a growing interest in a more integrated approach among a wide range of sociologists (Ritzer, 1991d). (This is only part of a growing interest in integration within and even among many social sciences; see especially Mitroff and Kilmann, 1978.) For example, Robert Merton, representing social factism, saw it and social definitionism as mutually enriching, as "opposed to one another in about the same sense as ham is opposed to eggs: they are perceptively different but mutually enriching" (1975:30).

The key to an integrated paradigm is the notion of *levels* of social analysis (Ritzer, 1979, 1981a). As the reader is well aware, *the social world is not really divided into levels.* In fact, social reality is best viewed as an enormous variety of

---

[6] Analyses of this paradigm schema include Eckberg and Hill (1979); Friedheim (1979); Harper, Sylvester, and Walczak (1980); Snizek (1976); and Staats (1976).
[7] There are other possibilities, including a postmodern paradigm (Milovanovic, 1995) and more interparadigmatic dialogue (Chriss, 1996).

social phenomena that are involved in continuing interaction and change. Individuals, groups, families, bureaucracies, the polity, and numerous other highly diverse social phenomena represent the bewildering array of phenomena that make up the social world. It is extremely difficult to get a handle on such a large number of wide-ranging and mutually interpenetrating social phenomena. Some sort of conceptual schema is clearly needed, and sociologists have developed a number of such schemas in an effort to deal with the social world. The idea of levels of social analysis employed here should be seen as but one of a large number of such schemas that can be, and have been, used for dealing with the complexities of the social world.

Levels of Social Analysis: An Overview 社会分析的层次: 一次综述

Although the idea of levels is implicit in much of sociology, it has received relatively little explicit attention. (However, there does seem to be some explicit interest in this issue, as reflected, for example, in the work of Hage [1994], Whitmeyer [1994], and especially Prendergast [2005c], Jaffee [1998], Smelser [1997].) In concentrating on levels here, I am making explicit what has been implicit in sociology.

Two continua of social reality are useful in developing the major levels of the social world. The first is the *microscopic-macroscopic* continuum. Thinking of the social world as being made up of a series of entities ranging from those large in scale to those small in scale is relatively easy, because it is so familiar. Most people in their day-to-day lives conceive of the social world in these terms. As we saw in Chapter 10, a number of thinkers have worked with a micro-macro continuum. For laypeople and academics alike, the continuum is based on the simple idea that social phenomena vary greatly in size. At the macro end of the continuum are such large-scale social phenomena as groups of societies (for example, the capitalist world-system), societies, and cultures. At the micro end are individual actors and their thoughts and actions. In between are a wide range of meso-level phenomena—groups, collectivities, social classes, and organizations. We have little difficulty recognizing these distinctions and thinking of the world in micro-macro terms. There are no clear dividing lines between the micro social units and the macro units. Instead, there is a continuum ranging from the micro to the macro ends.

The second continuum is the *objective-subjective* dimension of social analysis. At each end of the micro-macro continuum (and everywhere in between) we can differentiate between objective and subjective components. At the micro, or individual, level, there are the subjective mental processes of an actor and the objective patterns of action and interaction in which he or she engages. *Subjective* here refers to something that occurs solely in the realm of ideas; *objective* relates to real, material events. This same differentiation is found at the macro end of the continuum. A society is made up of objective structures, such as governments, bureaucracies, and laws, and subjective phenomena, such as norms and values.

The social world is very complicated, and to get a handle on it, we need relatively simple models. The simple model we are seeking is formed out of the intersection of the two continua of levels of social reality. The first, the microscopic-macroscopic continuum, can be depicted as in Figure A.1.

Microscopic _____ **Macroscopic**

Individual thought and action	Interaction	Groups	Organizations	Societies	World-systems

FIGURE A.1   The Microscopic-Macroscopic Continuum, with Identification of Some Key Points on the Continuum

The objective-subjective continuum presents greater problems, yet it is no less important than the micro-macro continuum. In general, an objective social phenomenon has a real, material existence. We can think of the following, among others, as objective social phenomena: actors, action, interaction, bureaucratic structures, law, and the state apparatus. It is possible to see, touch, or chart all these objective phenomena. However, there are social phenomena that exist *solely* in the realm of ideas; they have no material existence. These are sociological phenomena such as mental processes, the social construction of reality (Berger and Luckmann, 1967), norms, values, and many elements of culture. The problem with the objective-subjective continuum is that there are many phenomena in the middle that have *both* objective and subjective elements. The family, for example, has a real material existence as well as a series of subjective mutual understandings, norms, and values. Similarly, the polity is composed of objective laws and bureaucratic structures as well as subjective political norms and values. In fact, it is probably true that the vast majority of social phenomena are mixed types that represent some combination of objective and subjective elements. Thus, it is best to think of the objective-subjective continuum as two polar types with a series of variously mixed types in the middle. Figure A.2 shows the objective-subjective continuum.

Although these continua are interesting in themselves, the interrelationship of the two continua is what concerns us here. Figure 10.1 (see Chapter 10) is a schematic

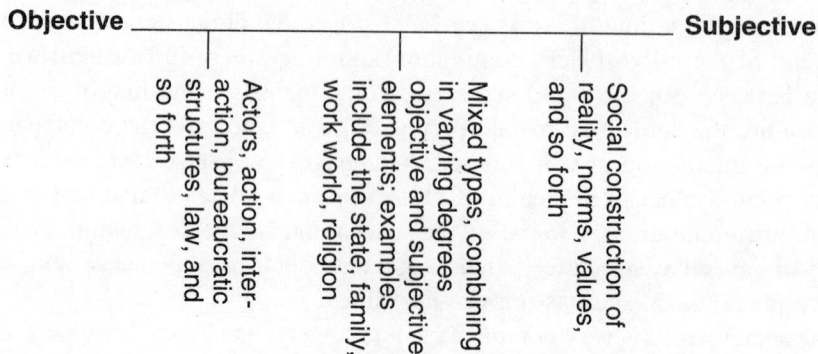

Objective _____ **Subjective**

Actors, action, interaction, bureaucratic structures, law, and so forth	Mixed types, combining in varying degrees objective and subjective elements; examples include the state, family, work world, religion	Social construction of reality, norms, values, and so forth

FIGURE A.2   The Objective-Subjective Continuum, with Identification of Some Mixed Types

LEVELS OF SOCIAL REALITY   SOCIOLOGICAL PARADIGMS

Macro-subjective
Macro-objective

Micro-subjective
Micro-objective

Social Facts	Integrated Sociological Paradigm
Social Definition	
Social Behavior	

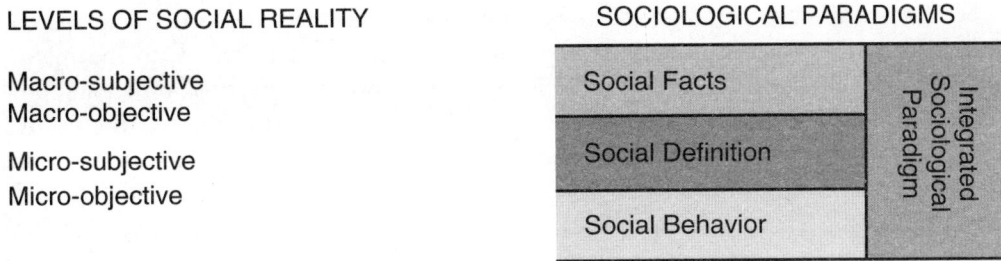

FIGURE A.3   Levels of Social Analysis and the Major Sociological Paradigms

representation of the intersection of these two continua and the four major levels of social analysis derived from it.

The contention here is that an integrated sociological paradigm must deal with the four basic levels of social analysis identified in Figure A.3 and their interrelationships (for similar models, see Alexander, 1985a; Wiley, 1988). It must deal with macro-objective entities such as bureaucracy, macro-subjective realities such as values, micro-objective phenomena such as patterns of interaction, and micro-subjective facts such as the process of reality construction. We must remember that in the real world, all these gradually blend into the others as part of the larger social continuum, but we have made some artificial and rather arbitrary differentiations in order to be able to deal with social reality. These four levels of social analysis are posited for heuristic purposes and are not meant to be accurate depictions of the social world.

While there is much to be gained from the development of an integrated sociological paradigm, one can expect resistance from many quarters. Reba Lewis has argued that opposition to an integrated paradigm comes from those theorists, "paradigm warriors" (Aldrich, 1988), who are intent on defending their theoretical turf come what may:

> Much of the objection to an integrated paradigm is not on theoretical, but on political grounds; an integrated paradigm threatens the purity and independence— and perhaps even the existence—of theoretical approaches which derive their inspiration from *opposition* to existing theory. . . . An integrated paradigm, such as Ritzer proposes, allows and even encourages a broader perspective than some find comfortable. Adopting an integrated paradigm means relinquishing belief in the ultimate truth of one's favorite theory. . . . Acceptance of an integrated paradigm requires an understanding, and indeed an appreciation, of a broad range of theoretical perspectives—an intellectually challenging task. . . . Although Ritzer does not discuss the issue, this author maintains that overcoming massive *intellectual agoraphobia* presents the greatest challenge to acceptance of an integrated paradigm.
>
> (R. R. Lewis, 1991:228–229)

An obvious question is how the four levels of the integrated paradigm relate to the three paradigms discussed earlier, as well as to the integrated paradigm. Figure A.3 relates the four levels to the three paradigms.

The social-facts paradigm focuses primarily on the macro-objective and macro-subjective levels. The social-definition paradigm is concerned largely with the micro-subjective world and that part of the micro-objective world that depends on mental processes (action). The social-behavior paradigm deals with that part of the micro-objective world that does not involve the minding process (behavior). Whereas the three extant paradigms cut across the levels of social reality horizontally, an integrated paradigm cuts across vertically. This depiction makes it clear why the integrated paradigm does not supersede the others. Although each of the three existing paradigms deals with a given level or levels in great detail, the integrated paradigm deals with all levels but does not examine any given level in anything like the degree of intensity of the other paradigms. Thus the choice of a paradigm depends on the kind of question being asked. Not all sociological issues require an integrated approach, but at least some do.

What has been outlined in the preceding pages is a model for the image of the subject matter of an integrated sociological paradigm. This sketch needs to be detailed more sharply, but that is a task for another time (see Ritzer, 1981a). The goal of this discussion is not the development of a new sociological paradigm but the delineation of an overarching metatheoretical schema (M_O) that allows us to analyze sociological theory in a coherent fashion. The model developed in Figure 10.1 forms the basis for this book.

Sociological theory is analyzed by using the four levels of social analysis depicted in Figure 10.1. This figure provides us with a metatheoretical tool that can be used in the comparative analysis of sociological theories. It enables us to analyze the concerns of a theory and how they relate to the concerns of all other sociological theories.

To be avoided at all costs is the simple identification of a theory or a theorist with specific levels of social analysis. Although it is true, given the preceding description of the current paradigmatic status of sociology, that sociological theorists who adhere to a given paradigm tend to focus on a given level or levels of social analysis, it often does them an injustice simply to equate the breadth of their work with one or more levels. For example, Karl Marx often is thought of as focusing on macro-objective structures—in particular, on the economic structures of capitalism. But the use of the schema in which there are multiple levels of social analysis allows us to see that Marx had rich insights regarding *all* levels of social reality and their interrelationships. Similarly, symbolic interactionism generally is considered a perspective that deals with micro subjectivity and micro objectivity, but it is not devoid of insights into the macroscopic levels of social analysis (Maines, 1977).

It is also important to remember that the use of levels of social analysis to analyze a theory tends to break up the wholeness, the integrity, and the internal consistency of that theory. Although the levels are useful for understanding a theory and comparing it to others, one must take pains to deal with the interrelationship among levels and with the totality of a theory.

In sum, the metatheoretical schema outlined in Figure 10.1, the development of which was traced in this Appendix, provides the basis for the analysis of the sociological theories discussed in this book.

References 参考文献

Aboulafia, Mitchell
1986   *The Mediating Self: Mead, Sartre, and Self-Determination.* New Haven: Yale University Press.

Abrahamsen, Rita
1997   "The Victory of Popular Forces or Passive Revolution? A Neo-Gramscian Perspective on Democratisation." *Journal of Modern African Studies* 35:129–152.

Abrahamson, Mark
1978   *Functionalism.* Englewood Cliffs, N.J.: Prentice-Hall.
2001   "Functional, Conflict and Neofunctional Theories." In George Ritzer and Barry Smart (eds.), *Handbook of Social Theory.* London: Sage: 141–151.

Abrahamsson, Bengt
1970   "Homans on Exchange." *American Journal of Sociology* 76:273–285.

Abrams, Philip
1968   *The Origins of British Sociology: 1834–1914.* Chicago: University of Chicago Press.
1982   *Historical Sociology.* Ithaca, N.Y.: Cornell University Press.

Abrams, Philip, Deem, Rosemary, Finch, Janet, and Rock, Paul
1981   *Practice and Progress: British Sociology 1950–1980.* London: Allen and Unwin.

Acker, Joan
1989   *Doing Comparable Worth.* Philadelphia: Temple University Press.

Adams, Bert N.
2005   "Pareto. Vilfredo." In George Ritzer (ed.), *Encyclopedia of Social Theory.* Thousand Oaks, Calif.: Sage: 544–547.

Adkins, Lisa
1995   *Gendered Work: Sexuality, Family, and the Labour Market.* Bristol, Pa.: Open University Press.
2004a   "Introduction: Feminism, Bourdieu and After." In Lisa Adkins and Beverley Skeggs (ed.), *Feminism after Bourdieu.* Oxford: Blackwell: 3–18.
2004b   "Reflexivity: Freedom or Habit of Gender." In Lisa Adkins and Beverley Skeggs (eds.), *Feminism after Bourdieu.* Oxford: Blackwell: 191–210.

Adler, Freda, and Laufer, William S. (eds.)
1995   *The Legacy of Anomie Theory.* New Brunswick, N.J.: Transaction Publishers.

Agger, Ben
1998   *Critical Social Theories: An Introduction.* Boulder, Colo.: Westview.

Agger, Ben (ed.)
1978   *Western Marxism: An Introduction.* Santa Monica, Calif.: Goodyear.

Albrow, Martin
1996   *The Global Age.* Cambridge: Polity.

Albrow, Martin, and King, Elizabeth
1990   *Globalization, Knowledge and Society.* London: Sage.

Alcala-Campos, Raul
1997   "Thomas S. Kuhn: Between Modernity and Postmodernity." *Acta Sociologica*
             19:59–77.

Alcoff, Linda Martin
1998   "What Should White People Do?" *Hypatia* 13:6–26.

Aldrich, Howard
1988   "Paradigm Warriors: Donaldson versus the Critics of Organization Theory."
             Organization Studies 9:19–25.

Aldridge, Alan
1998   "Habitus and Cultural Capital in the Field of Personal Finance." *Sociological
             Review* 46:1–23.

Alexander, Jeffrey C.
1981   "Revolution, Reaction, and Reform: The Change Theory of Parsons's Middle
             Period." *Sociological Inquiry* 51:267–280.
1982   *Theoretical Logic in Sociology.* Vol. 1, *Positivism, Presuppositions, and Current
             Controversies.* Berkeley: University of California Press.
1982–1983   *Theoretical Logic in Sociology.* 4 vols. Berkeley: University of California Press.
1983   *Theoretical Logic in Sociology.* Vol. 4, *The Modern Reconstruction of Classical
             Thought: Talcott Parsons.* Berkeley: University of California Press.
1985a   "The 'Individualist Dilemma' in Phenomenology and Interactionism." In S. N.
             Eisenstadt and H. J. Helle (eds.), *Macro-Sociological Theory,* Vol. 1. London:
             Sage: 25–51.
1987a   "Action and Its Environments." In J. C. Alexander et al. (eds.), *The Micro-
             Macro Link.* Berkeley: University of California Press: 289–318.
1987b   *Twenty Lectures: Sociological Theory since World War II.* New York: Columbia
             University Press.
1988a   "Introduction: Durkheimian Sociology and Cultural Studies Today." In J. C.
             Alexander (ed.), *Durkheimian Sociology: Cultural Studies.* Cambridge, Eng.:
             Cambridge University Press: 1–21.
1992   "Shaky Foundations: The Presuppositions and Internal Contradictions of James
             Coleman's Foundations of Social Theory." *Theory and Society* 21:203–217.
1995   *Fin de Siecle Social Theory: Relativism, Reduction, and the Problem of
             Reason.* London: Verso.
1998   *Neofunctionalism and After.* London: Blackwell.

Alexander, Jeffrey C. (ed.)
1985b   *Neofunctionalism.* Beverly Hills, Calif.: Sage.

Alexander, Jeffrey C., and Colomy, Paul
1985   "Toward Neo-Functionalism." *Sociological Theory* 3:11–23.

1990a   "Neofunctionalism: Reconstructing a Theoretical Tradition." In G. Ritzer (ed.), *Frontiers of Social Theory: The New Syntheses*. New York: Columbia University Press: 33–67.

Alexander, Jeffrey C., and Colomy, Paul (eds.)
1990b   *Differentiation Theory and Social Change: Comparative and Historical Perspectives*. New York: New York University Press.

Alexander, Jeffrey, Giesen, Bernhard, Münch, Richard, and Smelser, Neil J. (eds.)
1987   *The Micro-Macro Link*. Berkeley: University of California Press.

Alexander, Jeffrey C., and Smith, Philip
2001   "The Strong Program in Cultural Theory: Elements of a Structural Hermeneutics." In Jonathan Turner (ed.), *Handbook of Sociological Theory*. New York: Kluwer Academic/Plenum Publishers: 135–150.

Alford, C. Fred
2000   "What Would It Matter If Everything Foucault Said about Prison Were Wrong? *Discipline and Punishment* after Twenty Years." *Theory and Society* 29:125–137.

Alford, Robert R., and Friedland, Roger
1985   *Powers of Theory: Capitalism, the State, and Democracy*. Cambridge, Eng.: Cambridge University Press.

Alger, Janet M., and Alger, Steven F.
1997   "Beyond Mead: Symbolic Interaction between Humans and Felines." *Society and Animals* 5:65–81.

Allan, Stuart
2007   "Network Society." In George Ritzer (ed.), *The Blackwell Encyclopedia of Sociology*. Oxford: Blackwell: 3180–3182.

Alt, John
1985–1986   "Reclaiming C. Wright Mills." *Telos* 66:6–43.

Alway, Joan
1995   "The Trouble with Gender: Tales of the Still Missing Feminist Revolution in Sociological Theory." *Sociological Theory* 13:209–226.

Amin, Ash (ed.)
1994   *Post-Fordism: A Reader*. Oxford: Blackwell.

Amin, Samir
1977   *Unequal Development: An Essay on the Social Formations of Peripheral Capitalism*. New York: Monthly Review Press.

Andersen, Margaret, and Collins, Patricia Hill
1992   *Race, Class and Gender*. Belmont, Calif.: Wadsworth.

Anderson, Leon, Snow, David A., and Cress, Daniel
1994   "Negotiating the Public Realm: Stigma Management and Collective Action among the Homeless." *Research in Community Sociology* 4, supplement: 121–143.

Anderson, Perry
1984   *In the Tracks of Historical Materialism*. Chicago: University of Chicago Press.
1990a   "A Culture in Contraflow—I." *New Left Review* 180:41–78.
1990b   "A Culture in Contraflow—II." *New Left Review* 182:85–137.

Anderson, R. J., Hughes, J. A., and Sharrock, W. W.
1987   "Executive Problem Finding: Some Material and Initial Observations." *Social Psychology Quarterly* 50:143–159.

Anheier, Helmut K., Gerhards, Jurgen, and Romo, Frank P.
1995   "Forms of Capital and Social Structure in Cultural Fields: Examining Bourdieu's Social Topography." *American Journal of Sociology* 100:859–903.

Antonio, Robert J.
1981   "Immanent Critique as the Core of Critical Theory: Its Origins and Development in Hegel, Marx and Contemporary Thought." *British Journal of Sociology* 32:330–345.
1985   "Values, History and Science: The Metatheoretic Foundations of the Weber-Marx Dialogues." In R. J. Antonio and R. M. Glassman (eds.), *A Weber-Marx Dialogue*. Lawrence: University Press of Kansas: 20–43.
1991   "Postmodern Storytelling versus Pragmatic Truth-Seeking: The Discursive Bases of Social Theory." *Sociological Theory* 9:154–163.
1998   "Mapping Postmodern Social Theory." In Alan Sica (ed.), *What Is Social Theory? The Philosophical Debates*. Oxford: Blackwell: 22–75.
2001   "Nietzsche: Social Theory in the Twilight of the Millennium." In George Ritzer and Barry Smart (eds.), *Handbook of Social Theory*. London: Sage: 163–178.
2007a   "The Cultural Construction of Neoliberal Globalization: 'Honey. . . I Think I Shrunk the Kids.'" In George Ritzer (ed.), *The Blackwell Companion to Globalization*. Oxford: Blackwell: 67–83.

Antonio, Robert J., and Glassman, Ronald M. (eds.)
1985   *A Weber-Marx Dialogue*. Lawrence: University Press of Kansas.

Antonio, Robert J., and Kellner, Douglas
1994   "The Future of Social Theory and the Limits of Postmodern Critique." In D. R. Dickens and A. Fontana (eds.), *Postmodernism and Social Inquiry*. New York: Guilford Press: 127–152.

Anzaldúa, Gloria (ed.)
1990   *Making Face, Making Soul/Hacienda Caras: Creative and Critical Perspectives by Women of Color*. San Francisco: Aunt Lute Foundation Books.

Anzaldúa, Gloria, and Keating, Analouise
2002   *This Bridge We Call Home: Radical Visions for Transformation*. London: Routledge.

Appadurai, Arjun
1996   *Modernity at Large: Cultural Dimensions of Globalization*. Minneapolis: University of Minnesota Press.

Aptheker, Bettina
1989   *Tapestries of Life: Women's Work, Women's Consciousness and the Meaning of Daily Experience*. Amherst: University of Massachusetts Press.

Archer, Margaret S.
1982   "Morphogenesis versus Structuration: On Combining Structure and Action." *British Journal of Sociology* 33:455–483.

1988   *Culture and Agency: The Place of Culture in Social Theory.* Cambridge, Eng.: Cambridge University Press.

1995   *Realist Social Theory: The Morphogenetic Approach.* Cambridge, Eng.: Cambridge University Press.

Arguelles, Lourdes

1993   Plenary Address: "Intellectual Foundations of Women's Studies: Beyond Political Correctness." National Women's Studies Association, Washington, D.C., June.

Armitage, John

2005   "Deleuze, Gilles." In George Ritzer (ed.), *Encyclopedia of Social Theory.* Thousand Oaks, Calif.: Sage: 190–191.

Aron, Raymond

1965   *Main Currents in Sociological Thought,* Vol. 1. New York: Basic Books.

Aronowitz, Stanley

2007   "Lukács, Georg." In George Ritzer (ed.), *The Blackwell Encyclopedia of Sociology.* Oxford: Blackwell: 2678–2681.

Aronson, Ronald

1995   *After Marxism.* New York: Guilford Press.

Arthur, C. J.

1970   "Editor's Introduction." In K. Marx and F. Engels, *The German Ideology,* Part 1. New York: International Publishers: 4–34.

Asante, Molefi Kete

1996   "The Afrocentric Metatheory and Disciplinary Implications." In Mary F. Rogers (ed.), *Multicultural Experiences, Multicultural Theories.* New York: McGraw-Hill: 61–73.

Athens, Lonnie

1995   "Mead's Vision of the Self: A Pair of 'Flawed Diamonds.'" *Studies in Symbolic Interaction* 18:245–261.

2002   "'Domination': The Blind Spot in Mead's Analysis of the Social Act." *Journal of Classical Sociology* 2:25–42.

Atkinson, J. Maxwell

1984a   *Our Masters' Voices: The Language and Body Language of Politics.* New York: Methuen.

1984b   "Public Speaking and Audience Responses: Some Techniques for Inviting Applause." In J. M. Atkinson and J. Heritage (eds.), *Structures of Social Action.* Cambridge, Eng.: Cambridge University Press: 370–409.

Atkinson, Paul

1988   "Ethnomethodology: A Critical Review." *Annual Review of Sociology* 14:441–465.

Baber, Zaheer

1991   "Beyond the Structure/Agency Dualism: An Evaluation of Giddens' Theory of Structuration." *Sociological Inquiry* 61:219–230.

Baecker, Patrick

2001   "Why Systems?" *Theory, Culture and Society* 18:59–74.

Bailey, Cathryn
1997   "Making Waves and Drawing Lines: The Politics of Defining the Vicissitudes
            of Feminism." *Hypatia* 12:16–28.

Bailey, Kenneth D.
1990   *Social Entropy Theory.* Albany: State University of New York Press.
1994   *Sociology and the New Systems Theory: Toward a Theoretical Synthesis.*
            Albany: State University of New York Press.
1997   "System and Conflict: Toward a Symbiotic Reconciliation." *Quality and
            Quantity* 31:425–442.
1998   "Structure, Structuration, and Autopoesis: The Emerging Significance of
            Recursive Theory." In Jennifer M. Lehmann (ed.), *Current Perspectives in
            Social Theory,* Vol. 18. Greenwich, Conn.: JAI Press: 131–154.
2001   "Systems Theory." In Jonathan H. Turner (ed.), *Handbook of Sociological
            Theory.* New York: Kluwer Academic/Plenum Publishers: 379–401.
2005   "General Systems Theory." In George Ritzer (ed.), *Encyclopedia of Social
            Theory.* Thousand Oaks, Calif.: Sage: 309–315.

Baker, Patrick L.
1993   "Chaos, Order, and Sociological Theory." *Sociological Inquiry* 63:123–149.

Baker, Wayne E.
1990   "Market Networks and Corporate Behavior." *American Journal of Sociology*
            96:589–625.

Bakker, Hans
2007a   "Economic Determinism." In George Ritzer (ed.), *The Blackwell Encyclopedia
            of Sociology.* Oxford: Blackwell: 1293–1294.
2007b   "Langue and Parole." In George Ritzer (ed.), *The Blackwell Encyclopedia of
            Sociology.* Oxford: Blackwell: 2538–2539.
2007c   "Meta-analysis." In George Ritzer (ed.), *The Blackwell Encyclopedia of
            Sociology.* Oxford: Blackwell: 2963–2964.

Baldwin, Alfred
1961   "The Parsonian Theory of Personality." In M. Black (ed.), *The Social Theories
            of Talcott Parsons.* Englewood Cliffs, N.J.: Prentice-Hall: 153–190.

Baldwin, John C.
1986   *George Herbert Mead: A Unifying Theory for Sociology.* Newbury Park, Calif.:
            Sage.
1988a   "Mead and Skinner: Agency and Determinism." *Behaviorism* 16:109–127.
1988b   "Mead's Solution to the Problem of Agency." *Sociological Inquiry*
            58:139–162.

Baldwin, John D., and Baldwin, Janice I.
1986   *Behavior Principles in Everyday Life.* 2nd ed. Englewood Cliffs, N.J.:
            Prentice-Hall.

Ball, Richard A.
1978   "Sociology and General Systems Theory." *American Sociologist* 13:65–72.

Ball, Terence
1991   "History: Critique and Irony." In T. Carver (ed.), *The Cambridge Companion to
            Marx.* Cambridge, Eng.: Cambridge University Press: 124–142.

Banks, Alan, Billings, Dwight, and Tice, Karen
1996   "Appalachian Studies and Postmodernism." In Mary F. Rogers (ed.), *Multicultural Experiences, Multicultural Theories*. New York: McGraw-Hill: 81–90.

Baran, Paul, and Sweezy, Paul M.
1966   *Monopoly Capital: An Essay on the American Economic and Social Order.* New York: Monthly Review Press.

Barber, Benjamin
1995   *Jihad vs. McWorld*. New York: Times Books.

Barber, Bernard
1993   *Constructing the Social System*. New Brunswick, N.J.: Transaction.
1994   "Talcott Parsons on the Social System: An Essay in Clarification and Elaboration." *Sociological Theory* 12:101–105.

Barker, Chris
2007   "Birmingham School." In George Ritzer (ed.), *The Blackwell Encyclopedia of Sociology*. Oxford: Blackwell: 297–301.

Barnes, Barry
2001   "The Macro/Micro Problem and the Problem of Structure and Agency." In George Ritzer and Barry Smart (eds.), *Handbook of Social Theory*. London: Sage: 339–352.

Barnett, Ola W., and LaViolette, Alyce D.
1993   *It Could Happen to Anyone: Why Battered Women Stay*. Newbury Park, Calif.: Sage.

Barry, Kathleen
1979   *Female Sexual Slavery*. Englewood Cliffs, N.J.: Prentice-Hall.

Bart, Pauline, and Moran, Eileen Geil (eds.)
1993   *Violence against Women: The Bloody Footprints*. Newbury Park, Calif.: Sage.

Bartos, Ottomar J.
1996   "Postmodernism, Postindustrialism, and the Future." *Sociological Quarterly* 37:307–325.

Bartsky, Sandra Lee
1992   *Feminism and Domination: Studies in the Phenomenology of Oppression*. New York: Routledge.

Bate, Barbara, and Taylor, Anita (eds.)
1988   *Women Communicating: Studies of Women's Talk*. Norwood, N.J.: Ablex.

Baudrillard, Jean
1970/1998   *The Consumer Society*. London: Sage.
1972/1981   *For a Critique of the Political Economy of the Sign*. St. Louis: Telos Press.
1973/1975   *The Mirror of Production*. St. Louis: Telos Press.
1976/1993   *Symbolic Exchange and Death*. London: Sage.
1979/1990   *Seduction*. New York: St. Martin's.
1983   *Simulations*. New York: Semiotext(e).
1986/1989   *America*. London: Verso.

Baum, Rainer C., and Lechner, Frank J.
1981   "National Socialism: Toward an Action-Theoretical Perspective." *Sociological Inquiry* 51:281–308.

Bauman, Zygmunt
1976   *Towards a Critical Sociology: An Essay on Commonsense and Emancipation.* London: Routledge and Kegan Paul.
1989   *Modernity and the Holocaust.* Ithaca, N.Y.: Cornell University Press.
1990   "From Pillars to Post." *Marxism Today.* February:20–25.
1991   *Modernity and Ambivalence.* Ithaca, N.Y.: Cornell University Press.
1998   *Globalization: The Human Consequences.* New York: Columbia University Press.
2000   *Liquid Modernity.* Cambridge: Polity Press.
2003   *Liquid Love: On the Frailty of Human Bonds.* Cambridge: Polity Press.
2005   *Liquid Life.* Cambridge: Polity Press
2006   *Liquid Fear.* Cambridge: Polity Press.
2007   *Liquid Times: Living in an Age of Uncertainty.* Cambridge: Polity Press.

Beamish, Rob
2007a   "Dialectical Materialism." In George Ritzer (ed.), *The Blackwell Encyclopedia of Sociology.* Oxford: Blackwell: 1150–1151.
2007e   "Base and Superstructure." In George Ritzer (ed.), *The Blackwell Encyclopedia of Sociology.* Oxford: Blackwell: 244–246.

Beck, Ulrich
1992   *Risk Society: Towards a New Modernity.* London: Sage.
1996   "World Risk Society as Cosmopolitan Society?" *Theory, Culture and Society* 13:1–32.
2000   *What Is Globalization?* Cambridge, Eng.: Polity Press.
2005a   "Risk Society." In George Ritzer (ed.), *Encyclopedia of Sociology Theory.* Thousand Oaks, Calif.: Sage: 648–650.
2005b   *Power in the Global Age: A New Global Political Economy.* Cambridge, Eng.: Polity Press.

Beck, Ulrich, and Sznaider, Natan
2005   "Cosmopolitan Sociology." In George Ritzer (ed.), *Encyclopedia of Social Theory.* Thousand Oaks, Calif.: Sage: 157–161.

Beilharz, Peter
1996   "Negation and Ambivalence: Marx, Simmel and Bolshevism on Money." *Thesis Eleven* 47:21–32.
2005b   "Gramsci, Antonio." In George Ritzer (ed.), *Encyclopedia of Social Theory.* Thousand Oaks, Calif.: Sage: 343–344.
2005c   "Zygmunt Bauman." In George Ritzer (ed.), *Encyclopedia of Social Theory.* Thousand Oaks, CA: Sage: 35–40.
2005d   "Post-Marxism." In George Ritzer (ed.), *Encyclopedia of Social Theory.* Thousand Oaks, CA: Sage: 578–581.
2005e   "Marx, Karl." In George Ritzer (ed.), *Encyclopedia of Social Theory.* Thousand Oaks, Calif.: Sage: 475–478.
2005f   "Marxism." In George Ritzer (ed.), *Encyclopedia of Social Theory.* Thousand Oaks, Calif.: Sage: 479–483.
2005g   "Socialism." In George Ritzer (ed.), *Encyclopedia of Social Theory.* Thousand Oaks, Calif.: Sage: 769–772.

Bell, Daniel
1992   "George C. Homans (11 August 1910–29 May 1989)." *Proceedings of the American Philosophical Society* 136:587–593.

Bellah, Robert N., et al.
1985   *Habits of the Heart: Individualism and Commitment in American Life.* New York: Harper and Row.

Bem, Sandra Lipsitz
1993   *The Lenses of Gender: Transforming Debates on Sexual Inequality.* New Haven: Yale University Press.

Benhabib, Seyla
1995   "The Debate over Women and Moral Authority Revisited." In Johanna Meehan (ed.), *Feminists Read Habermas.* New York: Routledge: 181–204.
1998   "Feminism and Postmodernism: An Uneasy Alliance." *Filosoficky Casopis* 46:803–181.

Benjamin, Jessica
1985   "The Bonds of Love: Rational Violence and Erotic Domination." In H. Eisenstein and A. Jardine (eds.), *The Future of Difference.* New Brunswick, N.J.: Rutgers University Press: 41–70.
1988   *The Bonds of Love: Psychoanalysis, Feminism, and the Problem of Domination.* New York: Pantheon.
1996   "In Defense of Gender Ambiguity." *Gender & Psychoanalysis.* 1:27–43.

Benokraitis, Nijole
1997   *Subtle Sexism: Current Practice and Prospects for Change.* Thousand Oaks, Calif.: Sage.

Bergen, Raquel Kennedy
1996   *Wife Rape: Understanding the Response of Survivors and Service Providers.* Thousand Oaks, Calif.: Sage.

Berger, Brigette, and Berger, Peter
1983   *The War over the Family: Capturing the Middle Ground.* Garden City, N.Y.: Anchor.

Berger, Peter
1963   *Invitation to Sociology.* New York: Doubleday.

Berger, Peter, and Luckmann, Thomas
1967   *The Social Construction of Reality.* Garden City, N.Y.: Anchor.

Bergeson, Albert
1984   "The Critique of World-System Theory: Class Relations or Division of Labor?" In R. Collins (ed.), *Sociological Theory—1984.* San Francisco: Jossey-Bass: 365–372.

Berk, Bernard
2006   "Macro-Micro Relationships in Durkheim's Analysis of Egoistic Suicide." *Sociological Theory* 24(1): 58–80.

Bernard, Jessie
1981   *The Female World.* New York: Free Press.
1972/1982   *The Future of Marriage.* 2nd ed. New Haven: Yale University Press.

Bernard, Thomas
1983   *The Consensus-Conflict Debate: Form and Content in Sociological Theories.*
            New York: Columbia University Press.

Bernstein, J. M.
1995   *Recovering Ethical Life: Jurgen Habermas and the Future of Critical Theory.*
            London: Routledge.

Bernstein, Richard J.
1989   "Social Theory as Critique." In D. Held and J. B. Thompson (eds.), *Social
            Theory of Modern Societies: Anthony Giddens and His Critics.* Cambridge,
            Eng.: Cambridge University Press: 19–33.

Besnard, Philippe
1983   "The 'Année Sociologique' Team." In P. Besnard (ed.), *The Sociological
            Domain.* Cambridge, Eng.: Cambridge University Press: 11–39.

Best, Steven, and Kellner, Douglas
1991   *Postmodern Theory: Critical Interrogations.* New York: Guilford Press.

Beutel, Ann M., and Marini, Margaret Mooney
1995   "Gender and Values." *American Sociological Review* 60:436–448.

Bian, Yanjie
1997   "Bringing Strong Ties Back In: Indirect Ties, Network Bridges, and Job
            Searches in China." *American Sociological Review* 62:366–385.

Bienenstock, Elisa Jayne
2005   "Blau, Peter." In George Ritzer (ed.), *Encyclopedia of Social Theory.* Thousand
            Oaks, Calif.: Sage: 54–57.

Biernacki, Richard
2007   "Practice." In George Ritzer (ed.), *Encyclopedia of Sociology.* Oxford:
            Blackwell: 3607–3609.

Binkley, Sam
2007c   "Deleuze, Gilles." In George Ritzer (ed.), *The Blackwell Encyclopedia of
            Sociology.* Oxford: Blackwell: 999–1000.

Birnbaum, Pierre, and Todd, Jane Marie
1995   "French Jewish Sociologists between Reason and Faith: The Impact of the
            Dreyfus Affair." *Jewish Social Studies* 2:1–35.

Bittner, Egon
1973   "Objectivity and Realism in Sociology." In G. Psathas (ed.), *Phenomenological
            Sociology: Issues and Applications.* New York: Wiley: 109–125.

Blau, Peter
1964   *Exchange and Power in Social Life.* New York: Wiley.
1977   *Inequality and Heterogeneity: A Primitive Theory of Social Structure.* New
            York: Free Press.
1987   "Microprocess and Macrostructure." In K. Cook (ed.), *Social Exchange Theory.*
            Beverly Hills, Calif.: Sage: 83–100.
1994   *Structural Contexts of Opportunities.* Chicago: University of Chicago Press.
1997   "On Limitations of Rational Choice Theory for Sociology." *American
            Sociologist* 28:16–21.

Blau, Peter, and Duncan, Otis Dudley
1967   *The American Occupational Structure*. New York: John Wiley and Sons.

Blau, Peter, and Schwartz, Joseph E.
1997   *Crosscutting Social Circles: Testing a Macrostructural Theory of Intergroup Relations*. New Brunswick, N.J.: Transaction Publishers.

Bleich, Harold
1977   *The Philosophy of Herbert Marcuse*. Washington, D.C.: University Press of America.

Blühdorn, Ingelfur
2000   "An Offer One Might Prefer to Refuse: The Systems Theoretical Legacy of Niklas Luhmann." *European Journal of Social Theory* 3:339–354.

Blumberg, Rae Lesser
1978   *Stratification: Socio-Economic and Sexual Inequality*. Dubuque, Iowa: William C. Brown.
1979   "A Paradigm for Predicting the Position of Women: Policy Implications and Problems." In J. Lipman-Blumen and J. Bernard (eds.), *Sex Roles and Social Policy*. Beverly Hills, Calif.: Sage: 113–142.
1984   "A General Theory of Gender Stratification." In R. Collins (ed.), *Sociological Theory*. San Francisco: Jossey-Bass.

Blumer, Herbert
1955/1969   "Attitudes and the Social Act." In H. Blumer, *Symbolic Interaction*. Englewood Cliffs, N.J.: Prentice-Hall: 90–100.
1962/1969   "Society as Symbolic Interaction." In H. Blumer, *Symbolic Interaction*. Englewood Cliffs, N.J.: Prentice-Hall: 78–89.
1969a   *Symbolic Interaction: Perspective and Method*. Englewood Cliffs, N.J.: Prentice-Hall.
1969b   "The Methodological Position of Symbolic Interactionism." In H. Blumer, *Symbolic Interaction*. Englewood Cliffs, N.J.: Prentice-Hall: 1–60.
1990   *Industrialization as an Agent of Social Change: A Critical Analysis*. New York: Aldine de Gruyter.

Boden, Deirdre
1990   "The World as It Happens: Ethnomethodology and Conversation Analysis." In George Ritzer (ed.), *Frontiers of Social Theory: The New Syntheses*. New York: Columbia University Press: 185–213.

Bogard, William
1990   "Closing Down the Social: Baudrillard's Challenge to Contemporary Sociology." *Sociological Theory* 8:1–15.
1998   "Sense and Segmentarity: Some Markers of a Deleuzian-Guattarian Sociology." *Sociological Theory* 16:52–74.

Bogner, Arthur, Baker, Adelheid, and Kilminster, Richard
1992   "The Theory of the Civilizing Process—An Idiographic Theory of Modernization." *Theory, Culture, and Society* 9:23–52.

Boli, John, and Lechner, Frank
2005   *World Culture: Origins and Consequences*. Oxford: Blackwell.

Bonilla-Silva, Eduardo
2003   *Racism without Racists: Color-Blind Racism and the Persistence of Racial Inequality in the United States.* Lanham, Md.: Rowman & Littlefield.

Bookman, Ann, and Morgen, Sandra (eds.)
1988   *Women and the Politics of Empowerment.* Philadelphia: Temple University Press.

Bora, Alfons
2007   "Risk, Risk Society, Risk Behavior, and Social Problems." In George Ritzer (ed.), *The Blackwell Encyclopedia of Sociology.* Oxford: Blackwell: 3926–3932.

Bordo, Susan
1990   "Feminism, Postmodernism, and Gender-Scepticism." In L. Nicholson (ed.), *Feminism/Postmodernism.* New York: Routledge: 133–156.
1993   *Unbearable Weight: Feminism, Western Culture and the Body.* Berkeley: University of California Press.

Borges, Jorge
1964   *Labyrinths.* New York: Modern Library.

Bosserman, Phillip
1968   *Dialectical Sociology: An Analysis of the Sociology of Georges Gurvitch.* Boston: Porter Sargent.

Bottero, Wendy
2007   "Class Consciousness." In George Ritzer (ed.), *The Blackwell Encyclopedia of Sociology.* Oxford: Blackwell: 539–542.

Bottomore, Tom
1984   *The Frankfurt School.* Chichester, Eng.: Ellis Horwood.

Bourdieu, Pierre
1977   *Outline of a Theory of Practice.* London: Cambridge University Press.
1980/1990   *The Logic of Practice.* Stanford, Calif.: Stanford University Press.
1984a   *Distinction: A Social Critique of the Judgment of Taste.* Cambridge, Mass.: Harvard University Press.
1984b   *Homo Academicus.* Stanford, Calif.: Stanford University Press.
1989   "Social Space and Symbolic Power." *Sociological Theory* 7:14–25.
1990   *In Other Words: Essays Toward a Reflexive Sociology.* Cambridge, Eng.: Polity Press.
1993   *The Field of Cultural Production: Essays on Art and Leisure.* New York: Columbia University Press.
1994   "Rethinking the State: Genesis and Structure of the Bureaucratic Field." *Sociological Theory* 12:1–18.
1996   *The State Nobility.* Stanford, Calif.: Stanford University Press.
1998   *Practical Reason.* Stanford, Calif.: Stanford University Press.

Bourdieu, Pierre, and Darbel, Alain
1969/1990   *The Love of Art: European Art Museums and Their Public.* Stanford, Calif.: Stanford University Press.

Bourdieu, Pierre, and Passeron, Jean-Claude
1970/1990   *Reproduction in Education, Society and Culture.* London: Sage.

Bourdieu, Pierre, and Wacquant, Loïc J. D.
1992   "The Purpose of Reflexive Sociology (The Chicago Workshop)." In P. Bourdieu
            and L. J. D. Wacquant (eds.), *An Invitation to Reflexive Sociology.* Chicago:
            University of Chicago Press: 61–215.

Bourricaud, François
1981   *The Sociology of Talcott Parsons.* Chicago: University of Chicago Press.

Bowring, Finn
1996   "A Lifeworld without a Subject: Habermas and Pathologies of Modernity."
            Telos 106:77–104.

Bradley, Owen
2005a   "Bonald, Louis de." In George Ritzer (ed.), *Encyclopedia of Social Theory.*
            Thousand Oaks, Calif.: Sage: 65–66.
2005b   "Maistre, Joseph de." In George Ritzer (ed.), *Encyclopedia of Social Theory.*
            Thousand Oaks, Calif.: Sage: 454–466.

Bramson, Leon
1961   *The Political Context of Sociology.* Princeton, N.J.: Princeton University Press.

Braverman, Harry
1974   *Labor and Monopoly Capital: The Degradation of Work in the Twentieth
            Century.* New York: Monthly Review Press.

Breen, Margaret Sönser, and Blumenfeld, Warren J.
2005   *Butler Matters: Judith Butler's Impact on Feminist and Queer Studies.*
            Burlington, VT.: Ashgate.

Brennan, Teresa
1994   *History after Lacan.* New York: Routledge.

Brenner, Neil
1994   "Foucault's New Functionalism." *Theory and Society* 23:679–709.

Brewer, John, and Hunter, Albert
1989   *Multimethod Research: A Synthesis of Styles.* Newbury Park, Calif.: Sage.

Bronner, Stephen Eric
1995   "Ecology, Politics, and Risk: The Social Theory of Ulrich Beck." *Capital,
            Nature and Socialism* 6:67–86.

Brown, Michael, et al.
2003   *Whitewashing Race: The Myth of the Color-Blind Society.* Berkeley: University
            of California Press.

Brown, Richard
1987   *Society as Text: Essays on Rhetoric, Reason and Reality.* Chicago: University
            of Chicago Press.
1990   "Social Science and the Poetics of Public Truth." *Sociological Forum* 5:55–74.

Brown, Richard Harvey, and Goodman, Douglas
2001   "Jurgen Habermas' Theory of Communicative Action: An Incomplete Project."
            In George Ritzer and Barry Smart (eds.), *Handbook of Social Theory.* London:
            Sage: 201–216.

Brown, Stephen, and Capdevila, Rose
1999   *"Perpetuum Mobile*: Substance, Force and the Sociology of Translation." In
              John Law and John Hassard (eds.), *Actor Network Theory and After.* Oxford:
              Blackwell: 26–50.

Brubaker, Rogers
1984   *The Limits of Rationality: An Essay on the Social and Moral Thought of Max
              Weber.* London: Allen and Unwin.

Bruder, Kurt A.
1998   "Monastic Blessings: Deconstructing and Reconstructing the Self." *Symbolic
              Interaction* 21:87–116.

Brugger, Bill
1995   "Marxism, Asia, and the 1990s." *Positions* 3:630–641.

Bryant, Christopher G. A.
1985   *Positivism in Social Theory and Research.* New York: St. Martin's.

Bryant, Christopher G. A., and Jary, David
2000   "Anthony Giddens." In George Ritzer (ed.), *The Blackwell Companion to Major
              Social Theorists.* Malden, Mass.: Blackwell: 670–695.
2001a   "The Uses of Structuration Theory: A Typology." In Christopher G. A. Bryant
              and David Jary (eds.), *The Contemporary Giddens: Social Theory in a
              Globalizing Age.* New York: Palgrave: 43–62.
2001b   "Anthony Giddens: A Global Social Theorist." In Christopher G. A. Bryant and
              David Jary (eds.), *The Contemporary Giddens: Social Theory in a Globalizing
              Age.* New York: Palgrave: 1–26.

Buchwald, Emilie, Fletcher, Pamela R., and Roth, Martha (eds.)
1993   *Transforming a Rape Culture.* Minneapolis: Milkweed.

Buckley, Kerry W.
1989   *Mechanical Man: John Broadus Watson and the Beginnings of Behaviorism.*
              New York: Guilford Press.

Buckley, Walter
1967   *Sociology and Modern Systems Theory.* Englewood Cliffs, N.J.: Prentice-Hall.

Buffalohead, W. Roger
1996   "Reflections on Native American Cultural Rights and Resources." In Mary F.
              Rogers (ed.), *Multicultural Experiences, Multicultural Theories.* New York:
              McGraw-Hill: 154–156.

Bulmer, Martin
1984   *The Chicago School of Sociology: Institutionalization, Diversity, and the Rise
              of Sociological Research.* Chicago: University of Chicago Press.
1985   "The Chicago School of Sociology: What Made It a 'School'?" *History of
              Sociology: An International Review* 5:62–77.
1996   "The Sociological Contributions to Social Policy Research." In Jon Clark (ed.),
              James Coleman. London: Falmer Press: 103–118.

Bunch, Charlotte
1987   *Passionate Politics: Feminist Theory in Action.* New York: St. Martin's.

Bunzel, Dirk
2007   "Rational Legal Authority." In George Ritzer (ed.), *The Blackwell Encyclopedia of Sociology.* Oxford: Blackwell: 3805–3808.

Burawoy, Michael
1979   *Manufacturing Consent: Changes in the Labor Process under Monopoly Capitalism.* Chicago: University of Chicago Press.
1990   "Marxism as Science: Historical Challenges and Theoretical Growth." *American Sociological Review* 55:775–793.

Burawoy, Michael, and Wright, Erik Olin
2001   "Sociological Marxism." In Jonathan H. Turner (ed.), *Handbook of Sociological Theory.* New York: Kluwer Academic/Plenum Publishers: 459–486.

Burger, Thomas
1976   *Max Weber's Theory of Concept Formation: History, Laws and Ideal Types.* Durham, N.C.: Duke University Press.

Burns, Tom R.
1986   "Actors, Transactions, and Social Structure: An Introduction to Social Rule System Theory." In U. Himmelstrand (ed.), *Sociology: The Aftermath of Crisis.* London: Sage: 8–37.

Burt, Ronald
1982   *Toward a Structural Theory of Action: Network Models of Social Structure, Perception, and Action.* New York: Academic Press.
1992   *Structural Holes: The Social Structure of Competition.* Cambridge, Mass.: Harvard University Press.

Bushell, Don, and Burgess, Robert
1969   "Some Basic Principles of Behavior." In R. Burgess and D. Bushell (eds.), *Behavioral Sociology.* New York: Columbia University Press: 27–48.

Butler, Judith
1990   *Gender Trouble: Feminism and the Subversion of Identity.* New York: Routledge.
1997   "Imitation and Gender Insubordination." In Linda Nicholson (ed.), *The Second Wave: A Reader in Feminist Theory.* New York: Routledge: 300–315.
2004   *Undoing Gender.* London: Routledge.

Buttel, Frederick H. (ed.)
1990   "Symposium: Evolution and Social Change." *Sociological Forum* 5:153–212.

Button, Graham
1987   "Answers as Interactional Products: Two Sequential Practices Used in Interviews." *Social Psychology Quarterly* 50:160–171.

Buxton, William
1985   *Talcott Parsons and the Capitalist Nation-State: Political Sociology as a Strategic Vocation.* Toronto: University of Toronto Press.

Cadieux, R. D.
1995   "Dialectics and the Economy of Difference." *Dialectical Anthropology* 20:319–340.

Cahill, Spencer
1980   "Directions for an Interactionist Study of Gender Development." *Symbolic Interaction* 3:123–138.

Caldwell, Paulette
1991   "A Hair Piece: Perspectives on the Intersection of Race and Gender." *Duke Law Journal* 36:365–396.

Calhoun, Craig
1993   "Habitus, Field, and Capital: The Question of Historical Specificity." In C. Calhoun, E. LiPuma, and M. Postone (eds.), *Bourdieu: Critical Perspectives.* Chicago: University of Chicago Press: 61–88.
2000   "Pierre Bourdieu." In George Ritzer (ed.), *The Blackwell Companion to Major Social Theorists.* Malden, Mass.: Blackwell: 696–730.

Calhoun, Craig, and Karaganis, Joseph
2001   "Critical Theory." In George Ritzer and Barry Smart (eds.), *Handbook of Social Theory.* London: Sage: 179–200.

Callinicos, Alex
1989   "Introduction: Analytical Marxism." In Alex Callinicos (ed.), *Marxist Theory.* Oxford: Oxford University Press, 1989: 1–16.

Callon, Michel
1999   "Actor-Network Theory." In John Law and John Hassard (eds.), *Actor Network Theory and After.* Oxford: Blackwell: 181–195.

Camic, Charles
1990   "An Historical Prologue." *American Sociological Review* 55:313–319.
1992   "Reputation and Predecessor Selection: Parsons and the Institutionalists." *American Sociological Review* 57:421–445.

Camic, Charles (ed.)
1997   *Reclaiming the Sociological Classics: The State of Scholarship.* Oxford: Blackwell.

Campbell, Anne
1993   *Men, Women and Aggression.* New York: Basic Books.

Campbell, Colin
1982   "A Dubious Distinction? An Inquiry into the Value and Use of Merton's Concepts of Manifest and Latent Function." *American Sociological Review* 47:29–44.

Campbell, J., and Pederson, O. K. (eds.)
2001   *The Rise of Neoliberalism and Institutional Analysis.* Princeton, N.J.: Princeton University Press.

Campbell, Marie, and Manicom, Ann
1995   *Knowledge, Experience, and Ruling Relations: Studies in the Social Organization of Knowledge.* Toronto: University of Toronto Press.

Canclini, Nestor Garcia
1995   *Hybrid Cultures: Strategies for Entering and Leaving Modernity.* Minneapolis: University of Minnesota Press.

Caputi, Jane
1989   "The Sexual Politics of Murder." *Gender & Society* 3:437–456.

Carver, Terrell
1983   *Marx and Engels: The Intellectual Relationship.* Bloomington: Indiana
            University Press.

Castells, Manuel
1996   *The Rise of the Network Society.* Malden, Mass.: Blackwell.
1997   *The Power of Identity.* Malden, Mass.: Blackwell.
1998   *End of Millennium.* Malden, Mass.: Blackwell.

Cerullo, John J.
1994   "The Epistemic Turn: Critical Sociology and the 'Generation of 68.'"
            International Journal of Politics, Culture and Society. 8:169–181.

Chafetz, Janet Saltzman
1984   *Sex and Advantage.* Totowa, N.J.: Rowman and Allanhold.
1988   *Feminist Sociology: An Overview of Contemporary Theories.* Itasca, Ill.: Peacock.
1990   *Gender Equity: An Integrated Theory of Stability and Change.* Newbury Park,
            Calif.: Sage.
1999   "Structure, Consciousness, Agency and Social Change in Feminist Sociological
            Theories: A Conundrum." *Current Perspectives in Social Theory* 19:145–164.

Chambliss, Daniel F.
2005   "Frame Analysis." In George Ritzer (ed.), *Encyclopedia of Social Theory.*
            Thousand Oaks, Calif.: Sage: 289–290.

Chancer, Lynn S.
1992   *Sadomasochism in Everyday Life: The Dynamics of Power and Powerlessness.*
            New Brunswick, N.J.: Rutgers University Press.

Chancer, Lynn, and Palmer, Craig T.
2001   "A Debate on Sociobiology and Rape." *New Politics (New Series),* 2000: 8:1
            (29) Summer: 96–102.

Chapin, Mark
1994   "Functional Conflict Theory: The Alcohol Beverage Industry, and the
            Alcoholism Treatment Industry." *Journal of Applied Social Sciences* 18:169–182.

Chapoulie, Jean-Michel
1996   "Everett Hughes and the Chicago Tradition." *Sociological Theory* 14:3–29.

Charon, Joel M.
1998   *Symbolic Interactionism: An Introduction, an Interpretation, an Integration.*
            6th ed. Englewood Cliffs, N.J.: Prentice-Hall.
2000   *Symbolic Interactionism: An Introduction, an Interpretation, an Integration.*
            7th ed. Englewood Cliffs, N.J.: Prentice-Hall.

Chase-Dunn, Christopher
2001   "World-Systems Theory." In Jonathan H. Turner (ed.), *Handbook of
            Sociological Theory.* New York: Kluwer Academic/Plenum Publishers: 589–612.
2005a   "Wallerstein, Immanuel." In George Ritzer (ed.), *Encyclopedia of Social
            Theory.* Thousand Oaks, Calif.: Sage: 875–876.
2005b   "World-Systems Theory." In George Ritzer (ed.), *Encyclopedia of Social
            Theory.* Thousand Oaks, Calif.: Sage: 887–891.

Chase-Dunn, Christopher, and Hall, Thomas D.
1994   "The Historical Evolution of World-Systems." *Sociological Inquiry* 64:257–280.

Chasteen, Amy L.
2001   "Constructing Rape: Feminism, Change, and Women's Everyday Understandings of Sexual Assault." *Sociological Spectrum* 21:101–139.

Chesler, Phyllis
1994   *Patriarchy: Notes of an Expert Witness.* Boston: Common Courage Press.

Chitnis, Anand C.
1976   *The Scottish Enlightenment: A Social History.* Totowa, N.J.: Rowman and Littlefield.

Chodorow, Nancy
1978   *The Reproduction of Mothering: Psychoanalysis and the Sociology of Gender.* Berkeley: University of California Press.
1990   *Feminism and Psychoanalytic Theory.* New Haven: Yale University Press.
1994   *Femininities, Masculinity, Sexualities: Freud and Beyond.* Lexington: University of Kentucky Press.
1999   *The Power of Feelings: Personal Meaning in Psychoanalysis, Gender and Culture.* London: Yale University Press.

Chopra, Sherry
2004   "In Spite of Challenges by "Black" and "Third World" Women, Do Mainstream Feminist Theories Still Reflect the Concerns of White Women?" *Journal of International Women's Studies,* 5(2):21–28.

Chriss, James J.
1995   "Testing Gouldner's Coming Crisis Thesis: On the Waxing and Waning of Intellectual Influence." *Current Perspectives in Social Theory* 15:33–61.
1996   "Toward an Interparadigmatic Dialogue on Goffman." *Sociological Perspectives* 39:333–339.
2005a   "Gouldner, Alvin." In George Ritzer (ed.), *Encyclopedia of Social Theory.* Thousand Oaks, Calif.: Sage: 340–342.
2005b   "Mead, George Herbert." In George Ritzer (ed.), *Encyclopedia of Social Theory.* Thousand Oaks, Calif.: Sage: 486–491.

Christopher, F. S.
2001   *To Dance the Dance: A Symbolic Interactional Exploration of Premarital Sexuality.* Mahwah, N.J.: Lawrence Erlbaum.

Cicourel, Aaron
1981   "Notes on the Integration of Micro- and Macro-Levels of Analysis." In K. Knorr-Cetina and A. Cicourel (eds.), *Advances in Social Theory and Methodology.* New York: Methuen: 51–79.

Cixous, Hélène
1976   "The Laugh of the Medusa." Trans. Keith Cohen and Paula Cohen. *Signs* 1:875–893.
1994   *The Hélène Cixous Reader,* Ed. Susan Sellers. New York: Routledge.

Cladis, Mark Sydney
1992   *A Communitarian Defense of Liberalism: Emile Durkheim and Contemporary Social Theory.* Stanford, Calif.: Stanford University Press.

Clark, Jon (ed.)
1996   *James S. Coleman.* London: Falmer Press.

Clark, Jon, Modgil, Celia, and Modgil, Sohan (eds.)
1990   *Anthony Giddens: Consensus and Controversy.* London: Falmer Press.

Clark, Nigel
1997   "Panic Ecology: Nature in the Age of Superconductivity." *Theory, Culture and Society* 14:77–96.

Clarke, Simon
1990   "The Crisis of Fordism or the Crisis of Social Democracy?" *Telos* 83:71–98.

Clark-Lewis, Elizabeth
1994   *Living In, Living Out: African American Domestics in Washington, D.C. 1910–1940.* Washington, D.C.: Smithsonian Institution Press.

Clawson, Dan, Neustadtl, Alan, and Bearden, James
1986   "The Logic of Business Unity: Corporate Contributions to the 1980 Congressional Elections." *American Sociological Review* 51:797–811.

Clayman, Steven E.
1993   "Booing: The Anatomy of a Disaffiliative Response." *American Sociological Review* 58:110–130.

Clough, Patricia Ticineto
1994   *Feminist Thought: Desire, Power and Academic Discourse.* Cambridge, Mass.: Blackwell.

Cohen, G. A.
1978   *Karl Marx's Theory of History: A Defence.* Princeton, N.J.: Princeton University Press.
1978/1986   "Marxism and Functional Explanation." In J. Roemer (ed.), *Analytical Marxism.* Cambridge, Eng.: Cambridge University Press: 221–234.

Cohen, Ira J.
1989   *Structuration Theory: Anthony Giddens and the Constitution of Social Life.* London: Macmillan.
2005   "Structuration." In George Ritzer (ed.), *Encyclopedia of Social Theory.* Thousand Oaks, Calif.: Sage: 811–814.

Cohen, Jean
1995   "Critical Social Theory and Feminist Critiques: The Debate with Jurgen Habermas." In Johanna Meehan (ed.), *Feminists Read Habermas.* New York: Routledge: 57–90.

Cohen, Percy
1968   *Modern Social Theory.* New York: Basic Books.

Cohen, Philip N.
1998   "Replacing Housework in the Service Economy: Gender, Class, and Race-Ethnicity in Service Spending." *Gender & Society* 12:219–231.

Coleman, James S.
1986   "Social Theory, Social Research, and a Theory of Action." *American Journal of Sociology* 91:1309–1335.

| 1987 | "Microfoundations and Macrosocial Behavior." In J. C. Alexander et al. (eds.), *The Micro-Macro Link.* Berkeley: University of California Press: 153–173. |

1989   "Rationality and Society." *Rationality and Society* 1:5–9.

1990   *Foundations of Social Theory.* Cambridge, Mass.: Belknap Press of Harvard University Press.

1993a   "The Design of Organizations and the Right to Act." *Sociological Forum* 8:527–546.

1993b   "The Rational Reconstruction of Society." *American Sociological Review* 58:1–15.

1994   "A Vision for Sociology." *Society* 32:29–34.

Collins, J. L.

2002   "Mapping a Global Labor Market—Gender and Skill in the Globalizing Garment Industry." *Gender & Society* 16:921–940.

Collins, Patricia Hill

1990   *Black Feminist Thought: Knowledge, Consciousness and Empowerment.* Boston: Unwin Hyman.

1998   *Fighting Words: Black Women and the Search for Justice.* Minneapolis: University of Minnesota Press.

1999   "Moving beyond Gender." In Myra Marx Feree, Judith Lorber, and Beth Hess (eds), *Revisioning Gender.* Thousand Oaks, Calif.: Sage: 261–284.

2000   "Gender, Black Feminism and Black Political Economy." *Annals of the American Academy of Political and Social Science* 568:41–53.

2001   "Like One of the Family: Race, Ethnicity, and the Paradox of US National Identity." *Ethnic & Racial Studies* 24:3–28.

Collins, Randall

1975   *Conflict Sociology: Toward an Explanatory Science.* New York: Academic Press.

1979   *The Credential Society.* New York: Academic Press.

1981a   "On the Microfoundations of Macrosociology." *American Journal of Sociology* 86:984–1014.

1981b   "Micro-Translation as Theory-Building Strategy." In K. Knorr-Cetina and A. Cicourel (eds.), *Advances in Social Theory and Methodology.* New York: Methuen: 81–108.

1986a   "Is 1980s Sociology in the Doldrums?" *American Journal of Sociology* 91:1336–1355.

1986b   "The Passing of Intellectual Generations: Reflections on the Death of Erving Goffman." *Sociological Theory* 4:106–113.

1987   "A Micro-Macro Theory of Intellectual Creativity: The Case of German Idealistic Philosophy." *Sociological Theory* 5:47–69.

1988   "The Micro Contribution to Macro Sociology." *Sociological Theory* 6:242–253.

1990   "Conflict Theory and the Advance of Macro-Historical Sociology." In George Ritzer (ed.), *Frontiers of Social Theory: The New Syntheses.* New York: Columbia University Press: 68–87.

1997   "A Sociological Guilt Trip: Comment on Connell." *American Journal of Sociology* 102:1558–1564.

Collins, Randall, Chafetz, Janet Saltzman, Blumberg, Rae Leser, Coltrane, Scott, and Turner, Jonathan H.

1993   "Toward an Integrated Theory of Gender Stratification." *Sociological Perspectives* 36:185–216.

Colomy, Paul
1986   "Recent Developments in the Functionalist Approach to Change." *Sociological Focus* 19:139–158.
1990a   "Introduction: The Functionalist Tradition." In P. Colomy (ed.), *Functionalist Sociology*. Brookfield, Vt.: Elgar Publishing: xiii–lxii.
1990b   "Introduction: The Neofunctionalist Movement." In P. Colomy (ed.), *Neofunctionalist Sociology*. Brookfield, Vt.: Elgar Publishing: xi–xii.
2005   "Jeffrey Alexander." In George Ritzer (ed.), *Encyclopedia of Social Theory*. Thousand Oaks, Calif.: Sage: 8–9.

Colomy, Paul, and Rhoades, Gary
1994   "Toward a Micro Corrective of Structural Differentiation Theory." *Sociological Perspectives* 37:547–583.

Connell, R. W.
1996   "Men and the Women's Movement." In Mary F. Rogers (ed.), *Multicultural Experiences, Multicultural Theories*. New York: McGraw-Hill: 409–415.
1997   "How Is Classical Theory Classical?" *American Journal of Sociology* 102:1511–1557.

Connerton, Paul (ed.)
1976   *Critical Sociology*. Harmondsworth, Eng.: Penguin.

Connolly, William E.
1973   "Theoretical Self-Consciousness." *Polity* 6:5–35.

Connor, Walker
2007   "Ethnonationalism." In George Ritzer (ed.) *The Blackwell Encyclopedia of Sociology*. Oxford: Blackwell: 1486–1488.

Cook, Deborah
1994   "Symbolic Exchange in Hyperreality." In D. Kellner (ed.), *Baudrillard: A Critical Reader*. Oxford: Blackwell: 150–167.
1996   *The Culture Industry Revisited: Theodor W. Adorno on Mass Culture*. Lanham, Md.: Rowman and Littlefield.

Cook, Gary
1993   *George Herbert Mead: The Making of a Social Pragmatist*. Urbana: University of Illinois Press.

Cook, Karen S.
1987   "Emerson's Contributions to Social Exchange Theory." In K. S. Cook (ed.), *Social Exchange Theory*. Beverly Hills, Calif.: Sage: 209–222.
2005   "Emerson, Richard." In George Ritzer (ed.), *Encyclopedia of Social Theory*. Thousand Oaks, Calif.: Sage: 246–248.

Cook, Karen S., Emerson, Richard M., Gillmore, Mary B., and Yamagishi, Toshio
1983   "The Distribution of Power in Exchange Networks: Theory and Experimental Results." *American Journal of Sociology* 89:275–305.

Cook, Karen S., O'Brien, Jodi, and Kollock, Peter
1990   "Exchange Theory: A Blueprint for Structure and Process." In George Ritzer (ed.), *Frontiers of Social Theory: The New Syntheses*. New York: Columbia University Press: 158–181.

Cook, Karen S., and Rice, Eric
2005   "Social Exchange Theory." In George Ritzer (ed.), *Encyclopedia of Social Theory*. Thousand Oaks, Calif.: Sage: 735–740.

Cook, Karen S., and Whitmeyer, J. M.
1992   "Two Approaches to Social Structure: Exchange Theory and Network Analysis." *Annual Review of Sociology* 18:109–127.
2000   "Richard M. Emerson." In George Ritzer (ed.), *The Blackwell Companion to Major Social Theorists*. Malden, Mass.: Blackwell: 486–512.

Cooke, Maeve
1994   *Language and Reason: A Study of Habermas's Pragmatics*. Cambridge, Mass: MIT Press.

Cooley, Charles H.
1902/1964   *Human Nature and the Social Order*. New York: Scribner.

Cordova, Teresa, Cantu, Norma, Cardena, Gilbert, Garcia, Juan, and Sierra, Christine M. (eds.)
1990   *Chicana Voices: Intersections of Class, Race, and Gender*. Austin, Tex.: National Association for Chicano Studies.

Cortese, Anthony
1995   "The Rise, Hegemony, and Decline of the Chicago School of Sociology, 1892–1945." *Social Science Journal* 32:235–254.

Coser, Lewis
1956   *The Functions of Social Conflict*. New York: Free Press.

Cottrell, Leonard S., Jr.
1980   "George Herbert Mead: The Legacy of Social Behaviorism." In R. K. Merton and M. W. Riley (eds.), *Sociological Traditions from Generation to Generation: Glimpses of the American Experience*. Norwood, N.J.: Ablex.

Craib, Ian
1976   *Existentialism and Sociology: A Study of Jean-Paul Sartre*. Cambridge, Eng.: Cambridge University Press.
1992   *Anthony Giddens*. London: Routledge.

Craib, Ian, and Wernick, Andrew
2005   "Sartre, Jean-Paul." In George Ritzer (ed.), *Encyclopedia of Social Theory*. Thousand Oaks, Calif.: Sage: 663–665.

Crawford, Cassandra
2005   "Actor Network Theory." In George Ritzer (ed.), *Encyclopedia of Social Theory*. Thousand Oaks, Calif.: Sage: 1–3.

Crawford, Mary
1995   *Talking Difference: On Gender and Language*. Newbury Park, Calif.: Sage.

Crenshawe, Kimberle
1989   "Demarginalizing the Intersection of Race and Sex: A Black Feminist Critique of Antidiscrimination Doctrine, Feminist Theory, and Antiracist Politics." *University of Chicago Legal Forum*: 139–167.

1991   "Mapping the Margins: Intersectionality, Identity Politics, and Violence against
            Women of Color." *Stanford Law Review* 43:6.
1997   "Intersectionality and Identity Politics: Learning from Violence against Women of
            Color." In M. Shanley and U. Narayan (eds.), *Reconstructing Political Theory:
            Feminist Perspectives.* University Park: Pennsylvania State University Press.

Crippen, Timothy
1994   "Toward a Neo-Darwinian Sociology: Its Nomological Principles and Some
            Illustrative Applications." *Sociological Perspectives* 37:309–335.

Crook, Stephen
1995   *Adorno: The Stars Down to Earth and Other Essays on the Irrational in
            Culture.* London: Routledge.
2001   "Social Theory and the Postmodern." In George Ritzer and Barry Smart (eds.),
            Handbook of Social Theory. London: Sage: 308–338.

Crozier, Michel, and Friedberg, Erhard
1980   *Actors and Systems: The Politics of Collective Action.* Chicago: University of
            Chicago Press.

Culler, Jonathan
1976   *Ferdinand de Saussure.* Harmondsworth, Eng.: Penguin.

Currie, Dawn H.
1997   "Decoding Femininity: Advertisements and Their Teenage Readers." *Gender &
            Society* 11:453–477.
1999   "Gender Analysis from the Standpoint of Women: The Radical Potential of
            Women's Studies in Development." *Asian Journal of Women's Studies* 5:9–44.

Curtis, Bruce
1981   *William Graham Sumner.* Boston: Twayne.

Dahms, Harry
1997   "Theory in Weberian Marxism: Patterns of Critical Social Theory in Lukács
            and Habermas." *Sociological Theory* 15:181–214.
1998   "Beyond the Carousel of Reification: Critical Social Theory after Lukács,
            Adorno, and Habermas." *Current Perspectives in Social Theory* 18:3–62.

Dahrendorf, Ralf
1958   "Out of Utopia: Toward a Reorientation of Sociological Analysis." *American
            Journal of Sociology* 64:115–127.
1959   *Class and Class Conflict in Industrial Society.* Stanford, Calif.: Stanford
            University Press.
1968   *Essays in the Theory of Society.* Stanford, Calif.: Stanford University Press.

Daly, Mary
1993   *Outercourse: The Be-dazzling Voyage.* San Francisco: Harper.

Dandaneau, Steven P.
1992   "Immanent Critique of Post-Marxism." *Current Perspectives in Social Theory*
            12:155–177.
2001   *Taking It Big: Developing Sociological Consciousness in Postmodern Times.*
            Thousand Oaks, Calif.: Pine Forge Press.
2007a   "Marcuse, Herbert." In George Ritzer (ed.), *The Blackwell Encyclopedia of
            Sociology.* Oxford: Blackwell: 2559–2761.

2007b   "Mills, C. Wright." In George Ritzer (ed.), *The Blackwell Encyclopedia of Sociology.* Oxford: Blackwell: 3050–3055.

Darder, Antonia, and Torres, Rodolfo D.
2004   *After Race: Racism after Multiculturalism.* NY: New York University Press.

Davidson, Alastair
2007   "Gramsci, Antonio." In George Ritzer (ed.), *The Blackwell Encyclopedia of Sociology.* Oxford: Blackwell: 2014–2016.

Davis, Kingsley
1959   "The Myth of Functional Analysis as a Special Method in Sociology and Anthropology." *American Sociological Review* 24:757–772.

Davis, Kingsley, and Moore, Wilbert
1945   "Some Principles of Stratification." *American Sociological Review* 10:242–249.

Davis, Laurel R.
1997   *The Swimsuit Issue and Sport: Hegemonic Masculinity in "Sports Illustrated."* Albany: State University of New York Press.

Dawe, Alan
1978   "Theories of Social Action." In T. Bottomore and R. Nisbet (eds.), *A History of Sociological Analysis.* New York: Basic Books: 362–417.

Day, K.
2000   "The Ethic of Care and Women's Experiences of Public Space." *Journal of Environmental Psychology* 20:103–124.

Dean, Mitchell
1994   *Critical and Effective Histories: Foucault's Methods and Historical Sociology.* London: Routledge.
2001   "Michel Foucault: 'A Man in Danger.'" In George Ritzer and Barry Smart (eds.), *Handbook of Social Theory.* London: Sage: 324–338.

de Beauvoir, Simone
1949/1957   *The Second Sex.* New York: Vintage.

Deegan, Mary Jo
1988   *Jane Addams and the Men of the Chicago School, 1892–1918.* New Brunswick, N.J.: Transaction Books.

Deegan, Mary Jo, and Hill, Michael R. (eds.)
1987   *Women and Symbolic Interaction.* Boston: Allen and Unwin.
1998   *With Her in Ourland: Sequel to Herland.* By Charlotte Perkins Gilman. Westport, Conn.: Praeger.

de Grazia, Victoria
2005   *Irresistible Empire: America's Advance through 20th-Century Europe.* Cambridge, Mass.: The Belknap Press of Harvard University Press.

Delaney, Tim
2005a   "Coser, Lewis." In George Ritzer (ed.), *Encyclopedia of Social Theory.* Thousand Oaks, Calif.: Sage: 155–157.

2005b   "Sumner, William Graham." In George Ritzer (ed.), *Encyclopedia of Social Theory*. Thousand Oaks, Calif.: Sage: 814–815.

Delanty, Gerard
1997   "Habermas and Occidental Rationalism: The Politics of Identity, Social Learning, and the Cultural Limits of Moral Universalism." *Sociological Theory* 15:30–59.

de Lauretis, Teresa
1991   "Queer Theory: Lesbian and Gay Sexualities: An Introduction." *Differences: A Journal of Feminist Cultural Studies* 3(2):296–313.

Delgado, Richard and Jean Stefancic
2001   *Critical Race Theory: An Introduction.* New York: New York University Press.

Demerath, Nicholas, and Peterson, Richard (eds.)
1967   *System, Change and Conflict.* New York: Free Press.

Demetriou, Demetris
2002   "Action, Structure and Structuration in Social Theories of Gender." International Sociological Association, Brisbane, Australia.

Dempsey, Ken
2002   "Who Gets the Best Deal from Marriage: Women or Men?" *Journal of Sociology* 38:91–110

Densimore, Dana
1973   "Independence from the Sexual Revolution." In A. Koedt et al. (eds.), *Radical Feminism.* New York: Quadrangle: 107–118.

Denzin, Norman
1990a   "Harold and Agnes: A Feminist Narrative Undoing." *Sociological Theory* 9:198–216.
1990b   "Reading Rational Choice Theory." *Rationality and Society* 2:172–189.
1991   "Back to Harold and Agnes." *Sociological Theory* 9:280–285.
1993   "Sexuality and Gender: An Interactionist/Poststructuralist Reading." In P. England (ed.), *Theory on Gender/Feminism on Theory.* New York: Aldine de Gruyter: 199–223.

Der Derian, James
1994   "Simulation: The Highest Stage of Capitalism?" In D. Kellner (ed.), *Baudrillard: A Critical Reader.* Oxford: Blackwell: 189–208.

Derrida, Jacques
1978   *Writing and Difference.* Chicago: University of Chicago Press.

DeVille, Phillippe
1989   "Human Agency and Social Structure in Economic Theory: The General Equilibrium Theory and Beyond." Paper presented at the conference on "Social Theory and Human Agency," Swedish Collegium for Advanced Study in the Social Sciences, Uppsala, Sweden, Sept. 29–Oct. 1.

Dickerson, Bette J. (ed.)
1995   *African American Single Mothers: Understanding Their Lives and Families.* Newbury Park, Calif.: Sage.

Dietz, Thomas, and Burns, Tom R.
1992   "Human Agency and the Evolutionary Dynamics of Culture." *Acta Sociologica*
                35:187–200.

Dill, Bonnie Thornton
1994   *Across the Boundaries of Race and Class: An Exploration of Work and Family
                among Black Female Domestic Servants.* New York: Garland.

DiMaggio, Paul
2005   "Cultural Capital." In George Ritzer (ed.), *Encyclopedia of Social Theory.*
                Thousand Oaks, Calif.: Sage: 167–170.

DiMaggio, Paul J., and Powell, Walter W.
1983   "The Iron Cage Revisited: Institutional Isomorphism and Collective
                Rationality in Organizational Fields." *American Sociological Review*
                48:147–160.

Doane, Janice, and Hodges, Devon
1992   *From Klein to Kristeva: Psychoanalytic Feminism and the Search for the
                "Good Enough" Mother.* Ann Arbor: University of Michigan Press.

Dobb, Maurice
1964   *Studies in the Development of Capitalism.* Rev. ed. New York:
                International Publishers.

Domhoff, G. William
2005   "Mills, C. Wright." In George Ritzer (ed.), *Encyclopedia of Social Theory.*
                Thousand Oaks, Calif.: Sage: 503–505.

Donougho, Martin
1989   "Postmodern Jameson." In D. Kellner (ed.), *Postmodernism, Jameson, Critique.*
                Washington, D.C.: Maisonneuve Press: 75–95.

Donovan, Josephine
1985   *Feminist Theory: The Intellectual Traditions of American Feminism.* New York:
                Ungar.

Dordoy, Alan, and Mellor, Mary
2000   "Ecosocialism and Feminism: Deep Materialism and the Contradictions of
                Capitalism." *Capitalism, Nature, Socialism* 11:41–61.

Dorfman, Joseph
1966   *Thorstein Veblen and His America: With New Appendices.* New York: Augustus
                M. Kelley.

Dosse, Francois
1998   *The History of Structuralism: The Rising Sign, 1945–1966,* Vol. 1. Minneapolis:
                University of Minnesota Press.

Douglas, Jack
1980   "Introduction to the Sociologies of Everyday Life." In J. Douglas et al. (eds.),
                Introduction to the Sociologies of Everyday Life. Boston: Allyn and Bacon: 1–19.

Dowd, James J.
1996   "An Act Made Perfect in Habit: The Self in the Postmodern Age." *Current
                Perspectives in Social Theory* 16:237–263.

Dowson, Thomas A.
2000   "Why Queer Archaeology? An Introduction." *World Archaeology* 12(2):161–165.

Dozier, Raine, and Schwartz, Pepper
2001   "Intimate Relationships." In Judith Blau (ed.), *The Blackwell Companion to Sociology*. Malden, Mass.: Blackwell: 114–127.

Drysdale, John
2007   "Weber, Max." In George Ritzer (ed.), *The Blackwell Encyclopedia of Sociology*. Oxford: Blackwell: 5226–5235.

DuBois, Ellen Carol
1973/1995   "The Radicalism of the Women's Suffrage Movement." In Claire Goldberg Moses and Heidi Hartmann (eds.), *U.S. Women in Struggle*. Chicago: University of Illinois Press: 42–51.

Du Bois, W. E. B.
1897/1995   "The Conservation of Races." In David Lewis Levering (ed.), *W. E. B. Du Bois: A Reader*. New York: Henry Holt: 20–27.
1899/1996   *The Philadelphia Negro: A Social Study*. Philadelphia: University of Pennsylvania Press.
1903/1996   *The Souls of Black Folk*. New York: Modern Library.
1920/1999   *Darkwater: Voices from within the Veil*. Mineola, N.Y.: Dover.
1935/1998   *Black Reconstruction in America: 1860–1880*. New York: Free Press.
1940/1968   *Dusk of Dawn: An Essay toward an Autobiography of a Race Concept*. New York: Schocken Books.
1968   *The Autobiography of W. E. B. Du Bois: A Soliloquy on Viewing My Life from the Last Decade of Its First Century*. New York: International Publishers.

Dugdale, Anni
1999   "Materiality: Juggling Sameness and Difference." In John Law and John Hassard (eds.), *Actor Network Theory and After*. Oxford: Blackwell: 113–135.

Duncan, O. D., and Schnore, L. F.
1959   "Cultural, Behavioral and Ecological Perspectives in the Study of Social Organization." *American Journal of Sociology* 65:132–146.

Dunn, Dana, Almquist, Elizabeth, and Chafetz, Janet Saltzman
1993   "Macrostructural Perspectives on Gender Inequality." In P. England (ed.), *Theory on Gender/Feminism on Theory*. New York: Aldine de Gruyter: 69–90.

Dunn, Robert G.
1997   "Self, Identity, and Difference: Mead and the Poststructuralists." *Sociological Quarterly* 38:687–705.

Dunning, Eric
1986   "Preface." In N. Elias and E. Dunning, *Quest for Excitement: Sport and Leisure in the Civilizing Process*. Oxford: Blackwell: 1–18.

Durkheim, Emile
1887/1993   *Ethics and the Sociology of Morals*. Buffalo: Prometheus Books.
1892/1997   *Montesquieu: Quid Secundatus Politicae Scientiae Instituendae Contulerit*. Oxford: Durkheim Press.
1893/1964   *The Division of Labor in Society*. New York: Free Press.

1895/1982   *The Rules of Sociological Method.* New York: Free Press.
1897/1951   *Suicide.* New York: Free Press.
1912/1965   *The Elementary Forms of Religious Life.* New York: Free Press.
1928/1962   *Socialism.* New York: Collier Books.

Dworkin, Andrea
1989   *Letters from the War Zone: Writings 1976–1987.* New York: Dutton.

Echols, Alice
1989   *Daring to Be Bad: Radical Feminism in America, 1967–1975.* Minneapolis: University of Minnesota Press.

Eckberg, Douglas Lee, and Hill, Lester
1979   "The Paradigm Concept and Sociology: A Critical Review." *American Sociological Review* 44:925–937.

Edel, Abraham
1959   "The Concept of Levels in Social Theory." In L. Gross (ed.), *Symposium on Sociological Theory.* Evanston, Ill.: Row Peterson: 167–195.

Eder, Klaus
1990   "The Rise of Counter-Culture Movements against Modernity: Nature as a New Field of Class Struggle." *Theory, Culture and Society* 7:21–47.

Edin, Kathryn, and Kefalas, Maria
2005   *Promises I Can Keep: Why Poor Women Put Motherhood Before Marriage.* Berkeley, Calif.: University of California Press.

Edin, Kathryn, and Lein, Laura
1997   *Making Ends Meet: How Single Mothers Survive Welfare and Low-Wage Work.* New York: Russell Sage Foundation.

Edwards, Richard
1979   *Contested Terrain: The Transformation of the Workplace in the Twentieth Century.* New York: Basic Books.

Edwards, Tim
1998   "Queer Fears: Against the Cultural Turn." *Sexualities* 1(4):471–484.

Effrat, Andrew
1972   "Power to the Paradigms: An Editional Introduction." *Sociological Inquiry* 42:3–33.

Eisenberg, Anne F.
2007   "Habitus/Field." In George Ritzer (ed.), *The Blackwell Encyclopedia of Sociology.* Oxford: Blackwell: 2045–2046.

Eisenstadt, S. N., with Curelaru, M.
1976   *The Form of Sociology: Paradigms and Crises.* New York: Wiley.

Eisenstadt, S. N., and Helle, H. J. (eds.)
1985a   *Macro-Sociological Theory: Perspectives on Sociological Theory,* Vol. 1. London: Sage.
1985b   "General Introduction to Perspectives on Sociological Theory." In S. N. Eisenstadt and H. J. Helle (eds.), *Macro-Sociological Theory.* London: Sage: 1–3.

Eisenstein, Zillah
1979   *Capitalist Patriarchy and the Case for Socialist Feminism*. New York: Monthly
                Review Press.
1994   *The Color of Gender: Reimaging Democracy*. Berkeley: University of
                California Press.

Ekeh, Peter P.
1974   *Social Exchange Theory: The Two Traditions*. Cambridge, Mass.: Harvard
                University Press.

Elias, Norbert
1939/1978   *The Civilizing Process*. Part 1, *The History of Manners*. New York: Pantheon.
1939/1982   *The Civilizing Process*. Part 2, *Power and Civility*. New York: Pantheon.
1939/1994   *The Civilizing Process*. Oxford: Blackwell.
1968/1994   "Introduction to the 1968 Edition." In N. Elias, *The Civilizing Process*. Oxford:
                Blackwell: 181–215.
1969/1983   *The Court Society*. New York: Pantheon.
1978   *What Is Sociology?* New York: Columbia University Press.
1986   "Introduction." In N. Elias and E. Dunning, *Quest for Excitement: Sport and
                Leisure in the Civilizing Process*. Oxford: Blackwell: 19–62.
1993   *Mozart: Portrait of a Genius*. Berkeley: University of California Press.
1994   *Reflections on a Life*. Cambridge, Eng.: Polity Press.
1995   "Technicization and Civilization." *Theory, Culture and Society* 12:7–42.
1997   "Towards a Theory of Social Processes." *British Journal of Sociology* 48:355–383.

Elliott, Anthony
1992   *Social Theory and Psychoanalysis in Transition: Self and Society from Freud to
                Kristeva*. Oxford: Blackwell.

Elliott, David L.
2007   "Pragmatism." In George Ritzer (ed.), *The Blackwell Encyclopedia of
                Sociology*. Oxford: Blackwell: 3609–3612.

Elster, Jon
1982   "Marxism, Functionalism and Game Theory: The Case for Methodological
                Individualism." *Theory and Society* 11:453–482.
1985   *Making Sense of Marx*. Cambridge, Eng.: Cambridge University Press.
1986   "Further Thoughts on Marxism, Functionalism, and Game Theory." In J. Roemer
                (ed.), *Analytical Marxism*. Cambridge, Eng.: Cambridge University Press: 202–220.

Emerson, Richard M.
1962   "Power-Dependence Relations." *American Sociological Review* 27:31–40.
1972a   "Exchange Theory, Part I: A Psychological Basis for Social Exchange." In
                J. Berger, M. Zelditch Jr., and B. Anderson (eds.), *Sociological Theories in
                Progress*, Vol. 2. Boston: Houghton-Mifflin: 38–57.
1972b   "Exchange Theory, Part II: Exchange Relations and Networks." In J. Berger,
                M. Zelditch Jr., and B. Anderson (eds.), *Sociological Theories in Progress*,
                Vol. 2. Boston: Houghton-Mifflin: 58–87.
1981   "Social Exchange Theory." In M. Rosenberg and R. H. Turner (eds.), *Social
                Psychology: Sociological Perspectives*. New York: Basic Books: 30–65.

Emirbayer, Mustafa
1997   "Manifesto for a Relational Sociology." *American Journal of Sociology*
                103:281–317.

Engels, Friedrich
1884/1970   *The Origins of the Family, Private Property and the State*. New York: International Publishers.

England, Paula
1992   *Comparable Worth: Theories and Evidence*. New York: Aldine de Gruyter.

England, Paula, and Kilbourne, Barbara Stanek
1990   "Feminist Critiques of the Separative Model of the Self." *Rationality and Society* 2:156–171.

Erickson, Bonnie H.
1996   "Culture, Class, and Connections." *American Journal of Sociology* 102:217–251.

Eriksson, Bjorn
1993   "The First Formulation of Sociology: A Discursive Innovation of the 18th Century." *Archives of European Sociology* 34:251–276.

Esposito, Elena
1996   "From Self-Reference to Autology: How to Operationalize a Circular Approach." *Social Science Information* 35:269–281.

Evans, Sara
1980   *Personal Politics: The Roots of the Women's Liberation Movement in the Civil Rights Movement and the New Left*. New York: Vintage.

Faghirzadeh, Saleh
1982   *Sociology of Sociology: In Search of . . . Ibn-Khaldun's Sociology Then and Now*. Teheran: Soroush Press.

Faia, Michael A.
1986   *Dynamic Functionalism: Strategy and Tactics*. Cambridge, Eng.: Cambridge University Press.

Faist, Thomas
2005   "Social Space." In George Ritzer (ed.), *Encyclopedia of Social Theory*. Thousand Oaks, Calif.: Sage: 760–763.

Falk, William, and Zhao, Shanyang
1990a   "Paradigms, Theories and Methods in Contemporary Rural Sociology: A Partial Replication." *Rural Sociology* 54:587–600.
1990b   "Paradigms, Theories and Methods Revisited: We Respond to Our Critics." *Rural Sociology* 55:112–122.

Faludi, Susan
1991   *Backlash: The Undeclared War against American Women*. New York: Crown.

Fararo, Thomas J.
1996   "Foundational Problems in Theoretical Sociology." In Jon Clark (ed.), *James S. Coleman*. London: Falmer Press: 263–284.
2007   "Homans, George." In George Ritzer (ed.), *The Blackwell Encyclopedia of Sociology*. Oxford: Blackwell: 2144–2146.

Farganis, James
1975   "A Preface to Critical Theory." *Theory and Society* 2:483–508.

Faris, R. E. L.
1970   *Chicago Sociology: 1920–1932*. Chicago: University of Chicago Press.

Farrell, Chad R.
1997   "Durkheim, Moral Individualism and the Dreyfus Affair." *Current Perspectives in Social Theory* 17:313–330.

Feather, Howard
2000   *Intersubjectivity and Contemporary Social Theory: The Everyday as Critique*. Aldershot: Ashgate.

Featherstone, Mike
1989   "Postmodernism, Cultural Change, and Social Practice." In D. Kellner (ed.), *Postmodernism, Jameson, Critique*. Washington, D.C.: Maisonneuve Press: 117–138.

Featherstone, Mike (ed.)
1990   *Global Culture: Nationalism, Globalization and Modernity*. London: Sage.

Feenberg, Andrew
1996   "Marcuse or Habermas: Two Critiques of Technology." *Inquiry* 39:45–70.

Feldman, Shelley
2001   "Intersecting and Contesting Positions: Postcolonialism, Feminism, and World-Systems Theory." *Review (Washington)* 24:343–371.

Femia, Joseph
1995   "Pareto's Concept of Demagogic Plutocracy." *Government and Opposition* 30:370–392.

Fendrich, Michael
1984   "Wives' Employment and Husbands' Distress: A Meta-Analysis and a Replication." *Journal of Marriage and the Family* 46:871–879.

Fenstermaker, Sarah, West, Candace, and Zimmerman, Don
1991   "Gender Inequality: New Conceptual Terrain." In R. L. Blumberg (ed.), *Gender, Family and Economy: The Triple Overlap*. Newbury Park, Calif.: Sage: 293–307.

Ferguson, Harvie
2001   "Phenomenology and Social Theory." In George Ritzer and Barry Smart (eds.), *Handbook of Social Theory*. London: Sage: 232–248.

Ferree, Myra Marx, Lorber, Judith, and Hess, Beth (eds.)
1999   *Revisioning Gender*. Thousand Oaks, Calif.: Sage.

Ferry, Luc, and Renaut, Alain
1985/1990   *French Philosophy of the Sixties: An Essay on Antihumanism*. Amherst: University of Massachusetts Press.

Fine, Gary Alan
1990   "Symbolic Interactionism in the Post-Blumerian Age." In George Ritzer (ed.), *Frontiers of Social Theory: The New Syntheses*. New York: Columbia University Press: 117–157.
1992   "Agency, Structure, and Comparative Contexts: Toward a Synthetic Interactionism." *Symbolic Interaction* 15:87–107.

1993   "The Sad Demise, Mysterious Disappearance, and Glorious Triumph of
                Symbolic Interactionism." *Annual Review of Sociology* 19:61–87.

Fine, Gary Alan, and Kleinman, Sherryl
1983   "Network and Meaning: An Interactionist Approach to Social Structure."
                Symbolic Interaction 6:97–110.

Fine, Gary Alan, and Manning, Philip
2000   "Erving Goffman." In George Ritzer (ed.), *The Blackwell Companion to Major
                Social Theorists.* Malden, Mass.: Blackwell.

Fine, William F.
1979   *Progressive Evolutionism and American Sociology, 1890–1920.* Ann Arbor,
                Mich.: UMI Research Press.

Fischer, Norman
1984   "Hegelian Marxism and Ethics." *Canadian Journal of Political and Social
                Theory* 8:112–138.

Fisher, Sue
1995   *Nursing Wounds: Nurse Practitioners, Doctors, Women Patients and the
                Negotiation of Meaning.* New Brunswick, N.J.: Rutgers University Press.

Fiske, Donald W., and Shweder, Richard A. (eds.)
1986   *Metatheory in Social Science: Pluralisms and Subjectivities.* Chicago:
                University of Chicago Press.

Fitzpatrick, Ellen
1990   *Endless Crusade: Women Social Scientists and Progressive Reform.* New York:
                Oxford University Press.

Fleming, Marie
1997   *Emancipation and Illusion: Reality and Gender in Habermas's Theory of
                Modernity.* University Park: Pennsylvania State University Press.

Foner, Nancy
1994   *The Caregiving Dilemma: Work in an American Nursing Home.* Berkeley:
                University of California Press.

Fontana, Andrea
2005   "Sociologies of Everyday Life." In George Ritzer (ed.), *Encyclopedia of Social
                Theory.* Thousand Oaks, Calif.: Sage: 773–775.

Forcey, Linda Rennie
2001   "Feminist Perspectives on Mothering and Peace." *Journal of the Association for
                Research on Mothering* 3:2:155–174.

Foster, John Bellamy
1994   "Labor and Monopoly Capital Twenty Years After: An Introduction." *Monthly
                Review* 46:1–13.

Foucault, Michel
1965   *Madness and Civilization: A History of Insanity in the Age of Reason.* New
                York: Vintage.

1966	*The Order of Things: An Archaeology of the Human Sciences.* New York: Vintage.
1969	*The Archaeology of Knowledge and the Discourse on Language.* New York: Harper Colophon.
1975	*The Birth of the Clinic: An Archaeology of Medical Perception.* New York: Vintage.
1978	*The History of Sexuality,* Vol. 1, *An Introduction.* New York: Pantheon.
1979	*Discipline and Punish: The Birth of the Prison.* New York: Vintage.
1980a	*The History of Sexuality.* Vol. 1, *An Introduction.* New York: Vintage.
1980b	"Questions on Geography." In C. Gordon, ed. *Power/Knowledge: Selected Interviews and Other Writings, 1972–1977.* New York: Pantheon: 63–77.
1984	*The Care of the Self: The History of Sexuality,* Vol. 3. New York: Pantheon.
1985	*The Use of Pleasure. The History of Sexuality,* Vol. 2. New York: Pantheon.
1986	"Of Other Spaces." *Diacritics* 16:22–27.
1995	"Madness, the Absence of Work." *Critical Inquiry* 21:290–298.

Fowler, Bridget
1997   *Pierre Bourdieu and Cultural Theory: Critical Investigations.* London: Sage.

Fox, Renee C.
1997   "Talcott Parsons, My Teacher." *American Scholar* 66:395–410.

Frank, André Gunder
1966/1974   "Functionalism and Dialectics." In R. S. Denisoff, O. Callahan, and M. H. Levine (eds.), *Theories and Paradigms in Contemporary Sociology.* Itasca, Ill.: Peacock: 342–352.

Frankenberg, Ruth
1993   *White Women, Race Matters: The Social Construction of Whiteness.* Minneapolis: University of Minnesota Press.

Frankfurt Institute for Social Research
1973   *Aspects of Sociology.* London: Heinemann.

Franklin, Adrian
2007   "Posthumanism." In George Ritzer (ed.), *The Blackwell Encyclopedia of Sociology.* Oxford: Blackwell: 3548–3550.

Franks, David D.
2007   "Mind." In George Ritzer (ed.), *The Blackwell Encyclopedia of Sociology.* Oxford: Blackwell: 3055–3057.

Franks, David D., and Gecas, Viktor
1992   "Autonomy and Conformity in Cooley's Self-Theory: The Looking-Glass Self and Beyond." *Symbolic Interaction* 15:49–68.

Fraser, Nancy
1989   *Unruly Practices: Power, Discourse and Gender in Contemporary Social Theory.* Minneapolis: University of Minnesota Press.
1992   "Rethinking the Public Sphere: A Contribution to the Critique of Actually Existing Democracy." In Craig Calhoun (ed.), *Habermas and the Public Sphere.* Cambridge, Mass.: MIT Press: 109–142.
1995   "What's Critical about Critical Theory?" In Johanna Meehan (ed.), *Feminists Read Habermas.* New York: Routledge: 21–56.
1997   *Justice Interruptus: Critical Reflections on the "Postsocialist" Condition.* New York: Routledge.

Fraser, Nancy, and Nicholson, Linda
1988   "Social Criticism without Philosophy: An Encounter between Feminism and
            Postmodernism." In A. Ross (ed.), *Universal Abandon: The Politics of
            Postmodernism.* Minneapolis: University of Minnesota Press: 83–104.

French, Marilyn
1992   *The War against Women.* New York: Summit.

Friedan, Betty
1963   *The Feminine Mystique.* New York: Dell.

Friedheim, Elizabeth
1979   "An Empirical Comparison of Ritzer's Paradigms and Similar Metatheories: A
            Research Note." *Social Forces* 58:59–66.

Friedkin, Noah F.
2005   "Exchange Networks." In George Ritzer (ed.), *Encyclopedia of Social Theory.*
            Thousand Oaks, Calif.: Sage: 264–265.

Friedman, Debra, and Hechter, Michael
1988   "The Contribution of Rational Choice Theory to Macrosociological Research."
            Sociological Theory 6:201–218.

Friedman, George
1981   *The Political Philosophy of the Frankfurt School.* Ithaca, N.Y.: Cornell
            University Press.

Friedman, Marilyn
1993   *What Are Friends For? Feminist Perspectives on Personal Relationships and
            Moral Theory.* Ithaca, N.Y.: Cornell University Press.

Friedman, Thomas
2000   *The Lexus and the Olive Tree: Understanding Globalization.* New York: Anchor
            Books.
2005   *The World Is Flat: A Brief History of the Twenty-First Century.* New York:
            Farrar, Straus, Reese, and Giroux.

Friedrichs, Robert
1970   *A Sociology of Sociology.* New York: Free Press.
1972   "Dialectical Sociology: Toward a Resolution of Current 'Crises' in Western
            Sociology." *British Journal of Sociology* 13:263–274.

Frisby, David
1981   *Sociological Impressionism: A Reassessment of Georg Simmel's Social Theory.*
            London: Heinemann.
1984   *Georg Simmel.* Chichester, Eng.: Ellis Horwood.
1992   *Simmel and Since: Essays on Georg Simmel's Social Theory.* London:
            Routledge.

Frost, Liz
2005   "Theorizing the Young Woman in the Body." *Body and Society* 11:63–85.

Frow, John
1991   *What Was Postmodernism?* Sydney: Local Consumption Publications.

Frye, Marilyn
1983   *The Politics of Reality: Essays in Feminist Theory.* Trumansburg, N.Y.:
            Crossings Press.

Fuery, Patrick, and Mansfield, Nick
2000   *Cultural Studies and Critical Theory.* New York: Oxford University Press.

Fuhrman, Ellsworth R.
1980   *The Sociology of Knowledge in America: 1883–1915.* Charlottesville:
            University of Virginia Press.

Fuller, Steve
1998   "From Content to Context: A Social Epistemology of the Structure-Agency
            Craze." In Alan Sica (ed.), *What Is Social Theory? The Philosophical Debates.*
            Oxford: Blackwell: 92–117.
2007a   "Positivism." In George Ritzer (ed.), *The Blackwell Encyclopedia of Sociology.*
            Oxford: Blackwell: 3544–3547.
2007b   "Nietzsche." In George Ritzer (ed.), *The Blackwell Encyclopedia of Sociology.*
            Oxford: Blackwell: 3213–3217.
2007c   "Actor-Network Theory, Actants." In George Ritzer (ed.), *The Blackwell
            Encyclopedia of Sociology.* Oxford: Blackwell: 21–23.

Furfey, Paul
1953/1965   *The Scope and Method of Sociology: A Metasociological Treatise.* New York:
            Cooper Square Publishers.

Gamson, Joshua
1995.   "Must Identity Movements Self-Destruct? A Queer Dilemma." *Social Problems*
            42(3):390–407.

Gane, Mike
2003   *French Social Theory.* London: Sage.

Gane, Nicholas
2002   *Max Weber and Postmodern Theory: Rationalization versus Re-Enchantment.*
            New York: Palgrave.

Gans, Herbert J.
1972   "The Positive Functions of Poverty." *American Journal of Sociology* 78:275–289.

Garcia, Alma M.
1989   "The Development of Chicana Feminist Discourse, 1970–1980." *Gender &
            Society* 3:217–238.

Garcia, Angela
1991   "Dispute Resolution without Disputing: How the Interactional Organization of
            Mediation Hearings Minimizes Argument." *American Sociological Review*
            56:818–835.

Garcia Canclini, Nestor
1995   *Hybrid Cultures: Strategies for Entering and Leaving Modernity.* Minneapolis:
            University of Minneapolis Press.

Gardner, Carol Brooks
1995   *Passing By: Gender and Public Harassment.* Los Angeles: University of
            California Press.

Garfinkel, Harold

1963   "A Conception of, and Experiments with, 'Trust' as a Condition of Stable and Concerted Actions." In O. J. Harvey (ed.), *Motivation in Social Interaction.* New York: Ronald: 187–238.

1967   *Studies in Ethnomethodology.* Englewood Cliffs, N.J.: Prentice-Hall.

1988   "Evidence for Locally Produced, Naturally Accountable Phenomena of Order, Logic, Reason, Meaning, Method, etc., in and as of the Essential Quiddity of Immortal Ordinary Society (I of IV): An Announcement of Studies." *Sociological Theory* 6:103–109.

1991   "Respecification: Evidence for Locally Produced, Naturally Accountable Phenomena of Order, Logic, Reason, Meaning, Method, etc., in and as of the Essential Haecceity of Immortal Ordinary Society (I): An Announcement of Studies." In G. Button (ed.), *Ethnomethodology and the Human Sciences.* Cambridge, Eng.: Cambridge University Press: 10–19.

Garland, Anne Witte

1988   *Women Activists: Challenging the Abuse of Power.* New York: Feminist Press.

Garnham, Nicholas

2007   "Culture Industries." In George Ritzer (ed.), *The Blackwell Encyclopedia of Sociology.* Oxford: Blackwell: 942–945.

Gartman, David

1998   "Postmodernism; or, the Cultural Logic of Post-Fordism?" *Sociological Quarterly* 39:119–137.

Gaziano, Emanuel

1996   "Ecological Metaphors as Scientific Boundary Work: Innovation and Authority in Interwar Sociology and Biology." *American Journal of Sociology* 101:874–907.

Genosko, Gary

2007   "Guattari, Felix." In George Ritzer (ed.), *The Blackwell Encyclopedia of Sociology.* Oxford: Blackwell: 2037–2038.

Geras, Norman

1987   "Post-Marxism?" *New Left Review* 163:40–82.

Gergen, Kenneth J.

1973   "Social Psychology as History." *Journal of Personality and Social Psychology* 26:309–320.

1986   "Correspondence versus Autonomy in the Language of Understanding Human Action." In D. W. Fiske and R. A. Shweder (eds.), *Metatheory in Social Science: Pluralisms and Subjectivities.* Chicago: University of Chicago Press: 136–162.

Gerhard, Uta

2004   "Welfare Policy and Care: A Critical Approach to Theories of Individualization from a Gender Perspective." *Polish Sociological Review* 2:125–140.

Gerth, Hans, and Mills, C. Wright (eds.)

1953   *Character and Social Structure.* New York: Harcourt, Brace and World.

Gerth, Nobuko
1993   "Hans H. Gerth and C. Wright Mills: Partnership and Partisanship."
            International Journal of Politics, Culture and Society 7:133–154.

Gibson, David
2000   "Seizing the Moment: The Problem of Conversational Agency." *Sociological
            Theory* 18:368–382.

Gibson, Diane
1996   "Broken Down by Age and Gender: 'The Problem of Old Women' Redefined."
            Gender & Society 10:433–448.

Giddens, Anthony
1975   *The Class Structure of Advanced Societies.* New York: Harper & Row.
1979   *Central Problems in Social Theory: Action, Structure and Contradiction in
            Social Analysis.* Berkeley: University of California Press.
1984   *The Constitution of Society: Outline of the Theory of Structuration.* Berkeley:
            University of California Press.
1989   "A Reply to My Critics." In D. Held and J. B. Thompson (eds.), *Social Theory
            of Modern Societies: Anthony Giddens and His Critics.* Cambridge, Eng.:
            Cambridge University Press: 249–301.
1990   *The Consequences of Modernity.* Stanford, Calif.: Stanford University Press.
1991   *Modernity and Self-Identity: Self and Society in the Late Modern Age.*
            Stanford, Calif.: Stanford University Press.
1992   *The Transformation of Intimacy: Sexuality, Love and Eroticism in Modern
            Societies.* Stanford, Calif.: Stanford University Press.
1994   *Beyond Left and Right: The Future of Radical Politics.* Stanford, Calif.:
            Stanford University Press.
1995   *Politics, Sociology and Social Theory: Encounters with Classical and
            Contemporary Social Thought.* Stanford, Calif.: Stanford University Press.
2000   *Runaway World: How Globalization Is Reshaping Our Lives.* New York:
            Routledge.

Giele, Janet Zollinger, and Holst, Elke
2004   "New Life Patterns and Changing Gender Roles." *Advances in Life Course
            Research* 8:3–22.

Gieryn, Thomas F.
2000   "A Space for Place in Sociology." *Annual Review of Sociology* 26:463–496.

Giffney, Noreen
2004   "Denormatizing Queer Theory: More Than (Simply) Gay and Lesbian Studies."
            Feminist Theory 5(1):73–78.

Gilligan, Carol
1982   *In a Different Voice: Psychological Theory and Women's Development.*
            Cambridge, Mass.: Harvard University Press.

Gilligan, Carol, and Attanuci, Jane
1988   "Two Moral Orientations: Gender Differences and Similarities." *Merrill Palmer
            Quarterly* 34:223–237.

Glatzer, Wolfgang
1998   "The German Sociological Association: Origins and Developments." Paper
            presented at the meetings of the International Sociological Association,
            Montreal, Canada.

Glenn, Evelyn Nakano
1999   "The Social Construction and Institutionalization of Gender and Race: An
            Integrative Framework." In Myra Marx Feree, Judith Lorber, and Beth Hess
            (eds.) *Revisioning Gender*. Thousand Oaks, Calif: Sage: 3–43.

Glenn, Evelyn Nakano, Chang, Grace, and Forcey, Linda Rennie (eds.)
1993   *Mothering*. New York: Routledge.

Glenn, Phillip J.
1989   "Initiating Shared Laughter in Multi-Party Conversations." *Western Journal of
            Speech Communications* 53:127–149.

Glennon, Lynda M.
1979   *Women and Dualism*. New York: Longman.

Go, Julian
2007a   "Colonialism (Neocolonialism)." In George Ritzer (ed.) *The Blackwell
            Encyclopedia of Sociology*. Oxford: Blackwell: 602–604.
2007b   "Decolonization." In George Ritzer (ed.) *The Blackwell Encyclopedia of
            Sociology*. Oxford: Blackwell: 984–986.

Godelier, Maurice
1972a   *Rationality and Irrationality in Economics*. London: NLB.
1972b   "Structure and Contradiction in Capital." In R. Blackburn (ed.), *Readings in
            Critical Social Theory*. London: Fontana: 334–368.

Goffman, Erving
1959   *Presentation of Self in Everyday Life*. Garden City, N.Y.: Anchor.
1961   *Encounters: Two Studies in the Sociology of Interaction*. Indianapolis:
            Bobbs-Merrill.
1963   *Stigma: Notes on the Management of Spoiled Identity*. Englewood Cliffs,
            N.J.: Prentice-Hall.
1974   *Frame Analysis: An Essay on the Organization of Experience*. New York:
            Harper Colophon.
1979   *Gender Advertisements*. New York: Harper and Row.

Goldberg, David Theo, and Essed, Philomena
2002   "Introduction: From Racial Demarcations to Multiple Identifications." In
            Philomena Essed and David Theo Goldberg (eds.) *Race Critical Theories*.
            Malden, Mass.: Blackwell: 1–11.

Goldfield, Michael, and Gilbert, Alan
1997   "The Limits of Rational Choice Theory." *National Political Science Review*
            6:205–228.

Goldman, Michael, and Schurman, Rachel A.
2000   "Closing the 'Great Divide': New Social Theory on Society and Nature."
            Annual Review of Sociology 26:563–584.

Gomart, Emilie, and Hennion, Antoine
1999   "The Sociology of Attachment: Music Amateurs, Drug Users." In John Law
            and John Hassard (eds.), *Actor Network Theory and After.* Oxford: Blackwell:
            220–247.

Gonos, George
1977   "'Situation' versus 'Frame': The 'Interactionist' and the 'Structuralist' Analyses
            of Everyday Life." *American Sociological Review* 42:854–867.
1980   "The Class Position of Goffman's Sociology: Social Origins of an American
            Structuralism." In J. Ditton (ed.), *The View from Goffman.* New York:
            St. Martin's: 134–169.

Goode, William J.
1960   "A Theory of Role Strain." *American Sociological Review* 25:483–496.

Goodman, Douglas J.
2005   "Ritzer, George." In George Ritzer (ed.), *Encyclopedia of Social Theory.*
            Thousand Oaks, Calif.: Sage: 650–651.

Goodwin, Charles
1979   "The Interactive Construction of a Sentence in Natural Conversation."
            In G. Psathas (ed.), *Everyday Language: Studies in Ethnomethodology.*
            New York: Irvington: 97–121.
1984   "Notes on Story Structure and the Organization of Participation." In J. M.
            Atkinson and J. Heritage (eds.), *Structures of Social Action.* Cambridge, Eng.:
            Cambridge University Press: 225–246.

Goodwin, Jan
1994   *Price of Honor: Muslim Women Lift the Veil of Silence on the Islamic World.*
            New York: Little, Brown.

Gordon, Linda
1994   *Pitied but Not Entitled: Single Mothers and the History of Welfare.* New York:
            Free Press.

Gottdiener, Mark
1994   "Semiotics and Postmodernism." In D. R. Dickens and A. Fontana (eds.),
            Postmodernism and Social Inquiry. New York: Guilford Press: 155–181.

Gouldner, Alvin
1959/1967   "Reciprocity and Autonomy in Functional Theory." In N. Demerath and
            R. Peterson (eds.), *System, Change and Conflict.* New York: Free Press: 141–169.
1970   *The Coming Crisis of Western Sociology.* New York: Basic Books.

Gramsci, Antonio
1917/1977   "The Revolution against '*Capital.*'" In Q. Hoare (ed.), *Antonio Gramsci:
            Selections from Political Writings (1910–1920).* New York: International
            Publishers: 34–37.
1932/1975   *Letters from Prison: Antonio Gramsci.* Ed. Lynne Lawner. New York:
            Harper Colophon.
1971   *Selections from the Prison Notebooks.* New York: International Publishers.

Granovetter, Mark
1973   "The Strength of Weak Ties." *American Journal of Sociology* 78:1360–1380.

1983   "The Strength of Weak Ties: A Network Theory Revisited." In R. Collins (ed.), *Sociological Theory—1983*. San Francisco: Jossey-Bass: 201–233.

1985   "Economic Action and Social Structure: The Problem of Embeddedness." *American Journal of Sociology* 91:481–510.

2005   "Strength of Weak Ties." In George Ritzer (ed.), *Encyclopedia of Social Theory*. Thousand Oaks, Calif.: Sage: 801–802.

Greatbatch, David, and Dingwall, Robert
1997   "Argumentative Talk in Divorce Mediation Sessions." *American Sociological Review* 62:151–170.

Green, Adam Isaiah
2002   "Gay but Not Queer: Toward a Post-Queer Study of Sexuality." *Theory and Society* 31(4):521–545.

Green, Donald, and Shapiro, Ian
1994   *Pathologies of Rational Choice Theory: A Critique of Applications in Political Science*. New Haven: Yale University Press.

Green, Karen
1995   *The Woman of Reason: Feminism, Humanism, and Political Thought*. New York: Continuum.

Gregory, Derek
1989   "Presences and Absences: Time-Space Relations and Structuration Theory." In D. Held and J. B. Thompson (eds.), *Social Theory of Modern Societies: Anthony Giddens and His Critics*. Cambridge, Eng.: Cambridge University Press: 185–214.

Gregson, Nicki, and Lowe, Michelle
1994   *Servicing the Middle Class: Class, Gender and Waged Domestic Labor*. New York: Routledge.

Greisman, Harvey C.
1986   "The Paradigm That Failed." In R. C. Monk (ed.), *Structures of Knowing*. Lanham, Md.: University Press of America: 273–291.

Gross, Llewellyn
1961   "Preface to a Metatheoretical Framework for Sociology." *American Journal of Sociology* 67:125–136.

Grossberg, Lawrence, and Nelson, Cary
1988   "Introduction: The Territory of Marxism." In C. Nelson and L. Grossberg (eds.), *Marxism and the Interpretation of Culture*. Urbana: University of Illinois Press: 1–13.

Guba, Egon G., and Lincoln, Yvonna S.
1994   "Competing Paradigms in Qualitative Research." In Norman K. Denzin and Yvonna S. Lincoln (eds.), *Handbook of Qualitative Research*. Thousand Oaks, Calif.: Sage: 105–117.

Gubbay, Jon
1997   "A Marxist Critique of Weberian Class Analyses." *Sociology* 31:73–89.

Guilhot, Nicolas
2002   "'The Transition to the Human World of Democracy': Notes for a History of
            the Concept of Transition, from Early Marxism to 1989." *European Journal
            of Social Theory* 5:219–243.

Guillory, John
2000   "Bourdieu's Refusal." In Nicholas Brown and Imre Szeman, *Pierre Bourdieu:
            Fieldwork in Culture.* Lanham, Md.: Rowman & Littlefield: 87–99.

Guinier, Lani, and Torres, Gerald
2002   *The Miner's Canary: Enlisting Race, Resisting Power, Transforming Democracy.*
            Cambridge, Mass.: Harvard University Press.

Gurney, Patrick J.
1981   "Historical Origins of Ideological Denial: The Case of Marx in American
            Sociology." *American Sociologist* 16:196–201.

Gurvitch, Georges
1964   *The Spectrum of Social Time.* Dordrecht, Netherlands: D. Reidel.

Habermas, Jurgen
1970   *Toward a Rational Society.* Boston: Beacon Press.
1971   *Knowledge and Human Interests.* Boston: Beacon Press.
1973   *Theory and Practice.* Boston: Beacon Press.
1975   *Legitimation Crisis.* Boston: Beacon Press.
1979   *Communication and the Evolution of Society.* Boston: Beacon Press.
1981   "Modernity versus Postmodernity." *New German Critique* 22:3–14.
1984   *The Theory of Communicative Action.* Vol. 1, *Reason and the Rationalization
            of Society.* Boston: Beacon Press.
1986   *Autonomy and Solidarity: Interviews.* Ed. Peter Dews. London: Verso.
1987a   *The Theory of Communicative Action.* Vol. 2, *Lifeworld and System: A
            Critique of Functionalist Reason.* Boston: Beacon Press.
1987b   *The Philosophical Discourse of Modernity: Twelve Lectures.* Cambridge,
            Mass.: MIT Press.
1991   "A Reply." In A. Honneth and H. Joas (eds.), *Communicative Action: Essays on
            Jurgen Habermas's "The Theory of Communicative Action."* Cambridge, Eng.:
            Cambridge University Press: 215–264.
1994   *The Past as Future.* Interviewed by Michael Haller. Lincoln: University of
            Nebraska Press.

Hagan, John, and Kay, Fiona
1995   *Gender in Practice: A Study of Lawyers' Lives.* New York: Oxford
            University Press.

Hage, Jerald
1994   "Constructing Bridges between Sociological Paradigms and Levels: Trying to
            Make Sociological Theory More Complex, Less Fragmented, and Politicized."
            In J. Hage (ed.), *Formal Theory in Sociology: Opportunity or Pitfall?* Albany:
            State University Press of New York: 152–168.

Haines, Valerie
1988   "Is Spencer's Theory an Evolutionary Theory?" *American Journal of Sociology*
            93:1200–1223.

1992   "Spencer's Philosophy of Science." *British Journal of Sociology* 43:155–172.
2005   "Spencer, Herbert." In George Ritzer (ed.), *Encyclopedia of Social Theory*. Thousand Oaks, Calif.: Sage: 781–787.

Halas, Elzbieta
2005   "Znaniecki, Florian Witold." In George Ritzer (ed.), *Encyclopedia of Social Theory*. Thousand Oaks, Calif.: Sage: 896–898.

Halfpenny, Peter
1982   *Positivism and Sociology: Explaining Social Life*. London: Allen and Unwin.
2001   "Positivism in the Twentieth Century." In George Ritzer and Barry Smart (eds.), *Handbook of Social Theory*. London: Sage: 371–385.
2005   "Positivism." In George Ritzer (ed.), *Encyclopedia of Social Theory*. Thousand Oaks, Calif.: Sage: 571–575.

Hall, John R.
2007   "Annales School." In George Ritzer (ed.), *The Blackwell Encyclopedia of Sociology*. Oxford: Blackwell: 142–144.

Hall, Richard
1983   "Theoretical Trends in the Sociology of Occupations." *Sociological Quarterly* 24:5–23.

Hall, Stuart
1988   "Brave New World." *Marxism Today* October:24–29.

Halliday, Fred
1990   "The Ends of the Cold War." *New Left Review* 180:5–23.

Halls, W. D.
1996   "The Cultural and Educational Influences of Durkheim, 1900–1945." *Durkheimian Studies* 2:122–132.

Halperin, David
1995   *Saint Foucault: Towards a Gay Hagiography*. New York: Oxford University Press.

Hamlin, Cynthia Lins, and Brym, Robert J.
2006   "The Return of the Native: A Cultural and Social-Psychological Critique of Durkheim's *Suicide* Based on the Guarani-Kaiowa of Southwestern Brazil." *Sociological Theory* 24(1): 42–57.

Hammer, Rhonda
2002   *Antifeminism and Family Terrorism: A Critical Feminist Perspective*. Lanham, Md.: Rowman & Littlefield.

Handel, Warren
1982   *Ethnomethodology: How People Make Sense*. Englewood Cliffs, N.J.: Prentice-Hall.

Haney, Lynne
1996   "Homeboys, Babies, Men in Suits: The State and the Reproduction of Male Dominance." *American Sociological Review* 61:759–778.

Hankin, Thomas L.
1979   "In Defense of Biography: The Use of Biography in the History of Science." *History of Science* 17:1–16.

Hannerz, Ulf
1987   "The World in Creolisation." *Africa* 57: 546–559.

Hansen, Karen V., and Philipson, Ilene (eds.)
1990   *Women, Class and the Feminist Imagination: A Socialist-Feminist Reader.*
                Philadelphia: Temple University Press.

Haraway, Donna
1988   "Situated Knowledge: The Science Question in Feminism and the Privilege of
                Partial Perspective." *Feminist Studies* 14:575–600.
1990   "A Manifesto for Cyborgs: Science, Technology, and Socialist Feminism
                in the 1980s." In L. Nicholson (ed.), *Feminism/Postmodernism.* New York:
                Routledge: 190–233.

Harding, Sandra
1986   *The Science Question in Sociology.* Ithaca, N.Y.: Cornell University Press.

Hardt, Michael, and Negri, Antonio
2000   *Empire.* Cambridge, Mass.: Harvard University Press.
2004   *Multitude: War and Democracy in the Age of Empire.* New York: Penguin.

Harper, Diane Blake, Sylvester, Joan, and Walczak, David
1980   "An Empirical Comparison of Ritzer's Paradigms and Similar Metatheories:
                Comment on Friedheim." *Social Forces* 59:513–517.

Harre, Rom
2002   "Social Reality and the Myth of Social Structure." *European Journal of Social
                Theory* 5:111–123.

Harris, David
1996   *A Society of Signs?* London: Routledge.

Harris, Kathleen Mullan
1996   "Life after Welfare: Women, Work, and Repeat Dependency." *American
                Sociological Review* 61:407–426.

Harris, Scott
2001   "What Can Interactionism Contribute to the Study of Inequality? The Case
                of Marriage and Beyond." *Symbolic Interaction* 25:455–480.

Hartmann, Heidi
1979   "Capitalism, Patriarchy and Job Segregation by Sex." In Z. Eisenstein (ed.),
                Capitalist Patriarchy and the Case for Socialist Feminism. New York:
                Monthly Review Press: 206–247.
1981   "The Unhappy Marriage of Marxism and Feminism: Towards a More
                Progressive Union." In Lydia Sargent (ed.), *Women and Revolution.*
                Boston: South End Press.

Hartsock, Nancy
1983   *Money, Sex and Power: Towards a Feminist Historical Materialism.* New York:
                Longman.
1990   "Foucault on Power: A Theory for Women?" In L. Nicholson (ed.),
                Feminism/Postmodernism. New York: Routledge: 157–175.

Harvey, David
1969   *Explanation in Human Geography.* New York: St. Martin's Press.

1973   *Social Justice and the City.* Baltimore: Johns Hopkins University Press.
1989   *The Condition of Postmodernity: An Enquiry into the Origins of Cultural Change.* Oxford: Blackwell.
2000   *Spaces of Hope.* Berkeley: University of California Press.
2005   *A Brief History of NeoLiberalism.* Oxford: Oxford University Press.

Harvey, Lee
1982   "The Use and Abuse of Kuhnian Paradigms in the Sociology of Knowledge." *British Journal of Sociology* 16:85–101.
1987   "The Nature of 'Schools' in the Sociology of Knowledge: The Case of the 'Chicago School.'" *Sociological Review* 35:245–278.

Hawkes, Terence
1977   *Structuralism and Semiotics.* London: Methuen.

Hawthorn, Geoffrey
1976   *Enlightenment and Despair.* Cambridge, Eng.: Cambridge University Press.

Hayim, Gila
1980   *The Existential Sociology of Jean-Paul Sartre.* Amherst: University of Massachusetts Press.

Hazelrigg, Lawrence
1972   "Class, Property and Authority: Dahrendorf's Critique of Marx's Theory of Class." *Social Forces* 50:473–487.

Hechter, Michael, and Kanazawa, Satoshi
1997   "Sociological Rational Choice Theory." In John Hagan and Karen S. Cook (eds.), *Annual Review of Sociology,* Vol. 23. Palo Alto, Calif.: Annual Reviews: 191–214.

Heckathorn, Douglas D.
1997   "Overview: The Paradoxical Relationship between Sociology and Rational Choice." *The American Sociologist* 28:6–15.
2005   "Rational Choice." In George Ritzer (ed.), *Encyclopedia of Social Theory.* Thousand Oaks, Calif.: Sage: 620–624.

Heckathorn, Douglas D., and Broadhead, Robert S.
1996   "Rational Choice, Public Policy and AIDS." *Rationality and Society* 8:235–260.

Hedstrom, Peter, and Swedberg, Richard
1996   "Rational Choice, Empirical Research, and the Sociological Tradition." *European Sociological Review* 12:127–146.

Hegel, G. W. F.
1807/1967   *The Phenomenology of Mind.* New York: Harper Colophon.
1821/1967   *The Philosophy of Right.* Oxford: Clarendon Press.

Hegtvedt, Karen A., Thompson, Elaine A., and Cook, Karen S.
1993   "Power and Equity: What Counts in Attributions for Exchange Outcomes?" *Social Psychology Quarterly* 56:100–119.

Heilbron, Johan
1995   *The Rise of Social Theory.* London: Polity Press.

Heilbrun, Carolyn
1988   *Writing a Woman's Life.* New York: Norton.

Heins, Volker
1993   "Weber's Ethic and the Spirit of Anti-Capitalism." *Political Studies* 41:269–283.

Held, David, and Thompson, John B.
1989   "Editors' Introduction." In D. Held and J. B. Thompson (eds.), *Social Theory
                of Modern Societies: Anthony Giddens and His Critics.* Cambridge, Eng.:
                Cambridge University Press: 1–18.

Held, Virginia
1993   *Feminist Morality: Transforming Culture, Society and Politics.* Chicago:
                University of Chicago Press.

Helle, H. J., and Eisenstadt, S. N. (eds.)
1985   *Micro-Sociological Theory: Perspectives on Sociological Theory,* Vol. 2.
                London: Sage.

Hennessey, Rosemary, and Ingraham, Chrys
1997   "Introduction: Reclaiming Anticapitalist Feminism." In R. Hennessey and
                C. Ingraham (eds.), *Materialist Feminism.* New York: Routledge: 1–14.

Heritage, John
1984   *Garfinkel and Ethnomethodology.* Cambridge: Polity Press.

Heritage, John, and Atkinson, J. Maxwell
1984   "Introduction." In J. M. Atkinson and J. Heritage (eds.), *Structures of Social
                Action.* Cambridge, Eng.: Cambridge University Press: 1–15.

Heritage, John, and Greatbatch, David
1986   "Generating Applause: A Study of Rhetoric and Response in Party Political
                Conferences." *American Journal of Sociology* 92:110–157.

Hesse, Mary
1995   "Habermas and the Force of Dialectical Argument." *History of European Ideas*
                21:367–378.

Hewitt, John P.
1984   *Self and Society: A Symbolic Interactionist Social Psychology.* 3rd ed.
                Boston: Allyn and Bacon.

Heyl, John D., and Heyl, Barbara S.
1976   "The Sumner-Porter Controversy at Yale: Pre-Paradigmatic Sociology and
                Institutional Crisis." *Sociological Inquiry* 46:41–49.

Hilbert, Richard A.
1990   "Ethnomethodology and the Micro-Macro Order." *American Sociological
                Review* 55:794–808.
1991   "Norman and Sigmund: Comment on Denzin's 'Harold and Agnes.'"
                Sociological Theory 9:264–268.
1992   *The Classical Roots of Ethnomethodology: Durkheim, Weber and Garfinkel.*
                Chapel Hill: University of North Carolina Press.
2005   "Ethnomethodology." In George Ritzer (ed.), *Encyclopedia of Social Theory.*
                Thousand Oaks, Calif.: Sage: 252–257.

Hill, Greg
1997   "History, Necessity, and Rational Choice Theory." *Rationality and Society* 9:189–213.

Hill, Lisa
1996   "Anticipations of Nineteenth and Twentieth Century Social Thought in the Work of Adam Ferguson." *Archives Européenes de Sociologie* 37:203–228.

Hill, Michael R.
2007   "Ward, Lester Frank." In George Ritzer (ed.), *The Blackwell Encyclopedia of Sociology*. Oxford: Blackwell: 5216.

Hill, Shirley A., and Sprague, Joey
1999   "Parenting in Black and White Families: The Interaction of Gender with Race and Class." *Gender & Society* 13:480–502.

Himes, Joseph
1966   "The Functions of Racial Conflict." *Social Forces* 45:1–10.

Hinkle, Roscoe
1980   *Founding Theory of American Sociology: 1881–1915*. London: Routledge and Kegan Paul.
1994   *Developments in American Sociological Theory: 1915–1950*. Albany: State University of New York Press.

Hinkle, Roscoe, and Hinkle, Gisela
1954   *The Development of American Sociology*. New York: Random House.

Hirschmann, Nancy J., and Di Stefano, Christine (eds.)
1996   *Revisioning the Political: Feminist Reconstructions of Traditional Concepts in Western Political Theory:* Boulder, Colo.: Westview.

Hobsbawm, Eric J.
1965   *Primitive Rebels*. New York: Norton.

Hochschild, Arlie
1997   *The Time Bind: When Work Becomes Home and Home Becomes Work*. New York: Metropolitan Books.

Hochschild, Arlie, with Machung, Anne
1989   *The Second Shift*. New York: Avon Books.

Hoecker-Drysdale, Susan
2000   "Harriet Martineau." In George Ritzer (ed.), *The Blackwell Companion to Major Social Theorists*. Malden, Mass.: Blackwell: 53–80.

Hofstadter, Richard
1959   *Social Darwinism in American Thought*. New York: Braziller.

Hollander, Jocelyn, and Howard, Judith
1997   *Gendered Situations, Gendered Selves*. Thousand Oaks, Calif.: Sage.

Hollinger, David
1980   "T. S. Kuhn's Theory of Science and Its Implications for History." In G. Gutting (ed.), *Paradigms and Revolutions*. Notre Dame, Ind.: Notre Dame University Press: 195–222.

Holmwood, John
1996   *Founding Sociology: Talcott Parsons and the Idea of General Theory.*
              Essex: Longman.

Holmwood, John, and Stewart, Alexander
1994   "Synthesis and Fragmentation in Social Theory: A Progressive Solution."
              Sociological Theory 12:83–100.

Holton, Robert J.
2000   "Bourdieu and Common Sense." In Nicholas Brown and Imre Szeman (eds.),
              Pierre Bourdieu: Fieldwork in Culture. Lanham, Md.: Rowman & Littlefield:
              87–99.
2001   "Talcott Parsons: Conservative Apologist or Irreplaceable Icon?" In George Ritzer
              and Barry Smart (eds.), *Handbook of Social Theory.* London: Sage: 152–162.

Holton, Robert J., and Turner, Bryan S.
1986   *Talcott Parsons on Economy and Society.* London: Routledge and Kegan Paul.

Holub, Robert C.
1991   *Jurgen Habermas: Critic in the Public Sphere.* London: Routledge.

Homans, George C.
1950   *The Human Group.* New York: Harcourt Brace.
1961   *Social Behavior: Its Elementary Forms.* New York: Harcourt, Brace and World.
1962   *Sentiments and Activities.* New York: Free Press.
1967   *The Nature of Social Science.* New York: Harcourt, Brace and World.
1974   *Social Behavior: Its Elementary Forms.* Rev. ed. New York: Harcourt Brace
              Jovanovich.
1984   *Coming to My Senses: The Autobiography of a Sociologist.* New Brunswick, N.J.:
              Transaction Books.

Homans, George C., and Curtis, Charles
1934   *An Introduction to Pareto, His Sociology.* New York: Knopf.

Hook, Sidney
1965   "Pareto's Sociological System." In J. H. Meisel (ed.), *Pareto and Mosca.*
              Englewood Cliffs, N.J.: Prentice-Hall: 57–61.

hooks, bell
1984   *Feminist Theory: From Margin to Center.* Boston: South End Press.
1990   *Yearning: Race, Gender, and Cultural Politics.* Boston: South End Press.

Horowitz, Irving L.
1962/1967   "Consensus, Conflict, and Cooperation." In N. Demerath and R. Peterson
              (eds.), *System, Change and Conflict.* New York: Free Press: 265–279.
1983   *C. Wright Mills: An American Utopian.* New York: Free Press.

Howard, Michael, and King, John E.
2005   "Political Economy." In George Ritzer (ed.), *Encyclopedia of Social Theory.*
              Thousand Oak, Calif.: Sage: 563–568.

Hoyningen-Huene, Paul
1993   *Reconstructing Scientific Revolutions: Thomas S. Kuhn's Philosophy of Science.*
              Chicago: University of Chicago Press.

Huaco, George
1966   "The Functionalist Theory of Stratification: Two Decades of Controversy."
            Inquiry 9:215–240.
1986   "Ideology and General Theory: The Case of Sociological Functionalism."
            Comparative Studies in Society and History 28:34–54.

Huber, Joan
2004   "Lenski Effects on Sex Stratification Theory." *Sociological Theory* 22:258–268.

Hughes, John A., Martin, Peter J., and Sharrock, W. W.
1995   *Understanding Classical Sociology: Marx, Weber and Durkheim.* London: Sage.

Humphery, Kim
1998   *Shelf Life: Supermarkets and the Changing Cultures of Consumption.*
            Cambridge, Eng.: Cambridge University Press.

Hunter, Allen
1988   "Post-Marxism and the New Social Movements." *Theory and Society* 17:885–900.

Hunter, J. E., Schmidt, F. L., and Jackson, G. B.
1982   *Meta-Analysis: Cumulating Research Findings across Studies.* Beverly Hills,
            Calif.: Sage.

Huntington, Samuel P.
1996   *The Clash of Civilizations and the Remaking of World Order.* New York:
            Simon and Schuster.
2004   "The Hispanic Challenge." *Foreign Policy.* March/April: 30–45.

Imber, Jonathan B. (ed.)
1997   "The Place of Rational Choice in Sociology." *American Sociologist* 28:3–87.

Inbar, Michael
1996   "The Violation of Normative Rules and the Issue of Rationality in Individual
            Judgments." In Jon Clark (ed.), *James S. Coleman.* London: Falmer Press:
            227–262.

Irigaray, Luce
1985a   *Speculum of the Other Woman.* Trans. Gillian Gill. Ithaca, N.Y.: Cornell
            University Press.
1985b   *This Sex Which Is Not Our Own.* Trans. Catherine Porter. Ithaca, N.Y.:
            Cornell University Press.

Jackman, Mary R.
1994   *The Velvet Glove: Paternalism and Conflict in Gender, Class, and Race
            Relations.* Berkeley: University of California Press.

Jackson, S.
2001   "Why a Materialist Feminism Is (Still) Possible—and Necessary." *Women's
            Studies International Forum* 24:283–293.

Jacobs, Mark D.
2007b   "Dewey, John." In George Ritzer (ed.), *The Blackwell Encyclopedia of
            Sociology.* Oxford: Blackwell: 1145–1146.

Jacobsen, Martin M.
2007   "Sacks, Harvey." In George Ritzer (ed.), *The Blackwell Encyclopedia of
            Sociology.* Oxford: Blackwell: 3971.

Jaffee, David
1996   *Levels of Socio-Economic Development Theory.* Westport, Conn.: Praeger.

Jaggar, Alison M.
1983   *Feminist Politics and Human Nature.* Totowa, N.J.: Rowman and Allanheld.

Jaggar, Alison M., and Bordo, Susan (eds.)
1989   *Gender/Body/Knowledge: Feminist Reconstructions of Being and Knowing.*
            New Brunswick, N.J.: Rutgers University Press.

Jaggar, Alison M., and Rothenberg, Paula (eds.)
1984   *Feminist Frameworks.* 2nd ed. New York: McGraw-Hill.

Jagtenberg, Tom, and McKie, David
1997   *Eco-Impacts and the Greening of Postmodernity: New Maps for Communication
            Studies, Cultural Studies and Sociology.* Thousand Oaks, Calif.: Sage.

James, Stanlie M., and Busia, Abema P. A. (eds.)
1993   *Theorizing Black Feminisms.* New York: Routledge.

Jameson, Fredric
1984   "Postmodernism, or the Cultural Logic of Late Capitalism." *New Left Review*
            146:53–92.
1989   "Afterword—Marxism and Postmodernism." In D. Kellner (ed.), *Postmodernism,
            Jameson, Critique.* Washington, D.C.: Maisonneuve Press: 369–387.
1991   *Postmodernism, or, The Cultural Logic of Late Capitalism.* Durham, N.C.:
            Duke University Press.

Jasso, Guillermina
2000   "Some of Robert K. Merton's Contributions to Justice Theory." *Sociological
            Theory* 18:331–339.
2001   "Formal Theory." In Jonathan H. Turner (ed.), *Handbook of Sociological
            Theory.* New York: Kluwer Academic/Plenum Publishers: 37–68.

Jaworski, Gary Dean
1991   "The Historical and Contemporary Importance of Coser's *Functions.*"
            Sociological Theory 9:116–123.
1995   "Simmel in Early American Sociology: Translation as Social Action."
            International Journal of Politics, Culture and Society 8:389–417.
1997   *Georg Simmel and the American Prospect.* Albany: State University of
            New York Press.

Jay, Martin
1973   *The Dialectical Imagination.* Boston: Little, Brown.
1984   *Marxism and Totality: The Adventures of a Concept from Lukács to Habermas.*
            Berkeley: University of California Press.
1988   *Fin-de-Siècle Socialism and Other Essays.* New York: Routledge.

Jefferson, Gail
1979   "A Technique for Inviting Laughter and Its Subsequent Acceptance
            Declination." In G. Psathas (ed.), *Everyday Language: Studies in
            Ethnomethodology.* New York: Irvington: 79–96.
1984   "On the Organization of Laughter in Talk about Troubles." In J. M. Atkinson
            and J. Heritage (eds.), *Structures of Social Action.* Cambridge, Eng.: Cambridge
            University Press: 346–369.

Jeffreys, Sheila
1991   *Anticlimax: A Feminist Perspective on the Sexual Revolution.* New York: New York University Press.

Jeffries, Vincent
2005   "Sorokin, Pitirim." In George Ritzer (ed.), *Encyclopedia of Social Theory.* Thousand Oaks, Calif.: Sage: 777–781.

Jencks, Charles
1977   *The Language of Post-Modern Architecture.* New York: Rizzoli.

Jenkins, Richard
1992   *Pierre Bourdieu.* London: Routledge.
2005a   "Bourdieu, Pierre." In George Ritzer (ed.), *Encyclopedia of Social Theory.* Thousand Oaks, Calif.: Sage: 66–71.
2005b   "Habitus." In George Ritzer (ed.), *Encyclopedia of Social Theory.* Thousand Oaks, Calif.: Sage: 352–353.

Joas, Hans
1981   "George Herbert Mead and the 'Division of Labor': Macrosociological Implications of Mead's Social Psychology." *Symbolic Interaction* 4:177–190.
1985   *G. H. Mead: A Contemporary Re-examination of His Thought.* Cambridge, Mass.: MIT Press.
1993   *Pragmatism and Social Theory.* Chicago: University of Chicago Press.
1996   *The Creativity of Action.* Chicago: University of Chicago Press.
1998   "Bauman in Germany: Modern Violence and the Problems of German Self-Understanding." *Theory, Culture and Society* 15:47–55.
2001   "The Emergence of the New: Mead's Theory and Its Contemporary Potential." In George Ritzer and Barry Smart (eds.), *Handbook of Social Theory.* London: Sage: 89–99.

Johnson, Chalmers
1966   *Revolutionary Change.* Boston: Little, Brown.

Johnson, Miriam
1988   *Strong Women, Weak Wives: The Search for Gender Equality.* Berkeley: University of California Press.
1989   "Feminism and the Theories of Talcott Parsons." In R. A. Wallace (ed.), *Feminism and Sociological Theory.* Newbury Park, Calif.: Sage: 101–118.
1993   "Functionalism and Feminism: Is Estrangement Necessary?" In P. England (ed.), *Theory on Gender/Feminism on Theory.* New York: Aldine de Gruyter: 115–130.

Johnston, Barry V.
1995   *Pitirim Sorokin: An Intellectual Biography.* Lawrence: University of Kansas Press.
2007   "Merton, Robert K." In George Ritzer (ed.), *The Blackwell Encyclopedia of Sociology.* Oxford: Blackwell: 2958–2961.

Jones, Greta
1980   *Social Darwinism and English Thought: The Interaction between Biological and Social Theory.* Atlantic Highlands, N.J.: Humanities Press.

Jones, Robert Alun
1994   "The Positive Science of Ethics in France: German Influences in *De la Division du Travail Social.*" *Sociological Forum* 9:37–57.

2000   "Emile Durkheim." In George Ritzer (ed.), *The Blackwell Companion to Major Social Theorists*. Malden, Mass.: Blackwell: 205–250.

Jordan, June
1992   *Technical Difficulties: African-American Notes on the State of the Union*. New York: Pantheon.

Kalberg, Stephen
1980   "Max Weber's Types of Rationality: Cornerstones for the Analysis of Rationalization Processes in History." *American Journal of Sociology* 85:1145–1179.
1990   "The Rationalization of Action in Max Weber's Sociology of Religion." *Sociological Theory* 8:58–84.
1994   *Max Weber's Comparative-Historical Sociology*. Chicago: University of Chicago Press.

Kaldor, Mary
1990   "After the Cold War." *New Left Review* 180:25–40.

Kaminsky, Amy
1994   "Gender, Race, Raza." *Feminist Studies* 20:7–31.

Kanigel, Robert
1997   *The One Best Way: Frederick Winslow Taylor and the Enigma of Efficiency*. New York: Viking.

Karady, Victor
1983   "The Durkheimians in Academe: A Reconsideration." P. Besnard (ed.), *The Sociological Domain*. Cambridge, Eng.: Cambridge University Press.

Kasler, Dirk
1985   "Jewishness as a Central Formation-Milieu of Early German Sociology." *History of Sociology: An International Review* 6:69–86.

Kaye, Howard L.
1991   "A False Convergence: Freud and the Hobbesian Problem of Order." *Sociological Theory* 9:87–105.
2003   "Was Freud a Medical Scientist or a Social Theorist? The Mysterious 'Development of the Hero.'" *Sociological Theory* 21: 375–397.

Keller, Evelyn Fox
1985   *Reflections on Gender and Science*. New Haven: Yale University Press.

Kellner, Douglas
1989b   "Introduction: Jameson, Marxism, and Postmodernism." In D. Kellner (ed.), *Postmodernism, Jameson, Critique*. Washington, D.C.: Maisonneuve Press: 1–42.
1989c   *Critical Theory, Marxism, and Modernity*. Baltimore: Johns Hopkins University Press.
1990   *Television and the Crisis of Democracy*. Boulder, Colo.: Westview Press.
1993   "Critical Theory Today: Revisiting the Classics." *Theory, Culture and Society* 10:43–60.
1995   "Marxism, the Information Superhighway, and the Struggle for the Future." *Humanity and Society* 19:41–56.
2000   "Jean Baudrillard." In George Ritzer (ed.), *The Blackwell Companion to Major Social Theorists*. Malden, Mass.: Blackwell: 731–753.

2005a   "Cultural Marxism and British Cultural Studies." In George Ritzer (ed.),
            Encyclopedia of Social Theory. Thousand Oaks, Calif.: Sage: 171–177.
2005b   "Jameson, Frederic." In George Ritzer (ed.), *Encyclopedia of Social Theory.*
            Thousand Oaks, Calif.: Sage: 421–422.
2005c   "Frankfurt School." In George Ritzer (ed.), *Encyclopedia of Social Theory.*
            Thousand Oaks, Calif.: Sage: 290–293.

Kellner, Douglas (ed.)
1989a   *Postmodernism, Jameson, Critique.* Washington, D.C.: Maisonneuve Press.
1989d   *Jean Baudrillard: From Marxism to Postmodernism and Beyond.*
            Cambridge, Eng.: Polity Press.

Kellner, Douglas, and Lewis, Tyson
2007   "Cultural Critique." In George Ritzer (ed.), *The Blackwell Encyclopedia of
            Sociology.* Oxford: Blackwell: 896–898.

Kemeny, Jim
1976   "Perspectives on the Micro-Macro Distinction." *Sociological Review* 24:731–752.

Kempadoo, Kamala
2001   "Women of Color and the Global Sex Trade: Transnational Feminist
            Perspectives." *Meridians: Feminism, Race, Transnationalism* 1(2):28–51.

Kennedy, Randall
2002   *Nigger: The Strange Career of a Troublesome Word.* NY: Vintage.

Kessler, Suzanne J., and McKenna, Wendy
2000   "Gender Construction in Everyday Life: Transsexualism." *Feminism &
            Psychology* 10:11–29.

Kettler, David, and Meja, Volker
1995   *Karl Mannheim and the Crisis of Liberalism.* New Brunswick, N.J.:
            Transaction Publishers.

Kilminster, Richard
1993   "Norbert Elias and Karl Mannheim: Closeness and Distance." *Theory, Culture
            and Society* 10:81–114.

Kilminster, Richard, and Mennell, Stephen
2000   "Norbert Elias." In George Ritzer (ed.), *The Blackwell Companion to Major
            Social Theorists.* Malden, Mass.: Blackwell: 601–629.

Kimmel, Michael
1996   *Manhood in America: A Cultural History.* New York: Free Press.

King, Katie
1994   *Theory in Its Feminist Travels: Conversation in U.S. Women's Movements.*
            Bloomington: Indiana University Press.

Kirk, Gwyn
1997   "Standing on Solid Ground: A Materialist Ecological Feminism." In
            Rosemary Hennessy and Chrys Ingraham (eds.), *Materialist Feminism.*
            London: Routledge: 345–363.

Kirk, Gwyn, and Okazawa-Rey, Margo (eds.)
1998   *Women's Lives: Multicultural Perspectives.* Mountain View, Calif.: Mayfield.

Kirkpatrick, Graeme
1994   "Philosophical Foundations of Analytical Marxism." *Science and Society*
            58:34–52.

Kirsch, Max H.
2000   *Queer Theory and Social Change.* London: Routledge.

Knorr-Cetina, Karin D.
1981   "Introduction: The Micro-Sociological Challenge of Macro-Sociology: Towards
            a Reconstruction of Social Theory and Methodology." In K. Knorr-Cetina and
            A. Cicourel (eds.), *Advances in Social Theory and Methodology.* New York:
            Methuen: 1–47.
2001   "Postsocial Relations: Theorizing Sociality in a Postsocial Environment." In
            George Ritzer and Barry Smart (eds.), *Handbook of Social Theory.* London:
            Sage: 520–537.
2005   "Postsocial." In George Ritzer (ed.), *Encyclopedia of Sociology.* Oxford:
            Blackwell: 3578–3580.
2007   "Postsocial" in George Ritzer (ed.) *The Blackwell Encyclopedia of Sociology.*
            Oxford: Blackwell: 3578–3580.

Kohn, Melvin L.
1976   "Occupational Structure and Alienation." *American Journal of Sociology*
            82:111–127.

Kolb, William L.
1944   "A Critical Evaluation of Mead's 'I' and 'Me' Concepts." *Social Forces*
            22:291–296.

Kollock, Peter
1994   "The Emergence of Exchange Structures: An Experimental Study of Uncertainty,
            Commitment, and Trust." *American Journal of Sociology* 100:313–345.

Kosciw, Joseph G.
2004   *The 2003 National School Climate Survey: The School-Related Experiences of
            Our Nation's Lesbian, Gay, Bisexual, and Transgender Youth.* New York:
            GLSEN.

Krais, Beate
1993   "Gender and Symbolic Violence: Female Oppression in the Light of Pierre
            Bourdieu's Theory of Social Practice." In C. Calhoun, E. LiPuma, and
            M. Postone (eds.), *Bourdieu: Critical Perspectives.* Chicago: University of
            Chicago Press: 156–177.

Kuhn, Annette, and Wolpe, Ann Marie (eds.)
1978   *Feminism and Materialism: Women and Modes of Production.* London: Routledge.

Kuhn, Manford
1964   "Major Trends in Symbolic Interaction Theory in the Past Twenty-Five Years."
            Sociological Quarterly 5:61–84.

Kuhn, Thomas
1962   *The Structure of Scientific Revolutions.* Chicago: University of Chicago Press.

Kumar, Krishan
1995   *From Post-Industrial to Post-Modern Society: New Theories of the
            Contemporary World.* Oxford, Eng.: Blackwell.

Kurasawa, Fuyuki
2005   "Lefebvre, Henri." In George Ritzer (ed.), *Encyclopedia of Social Theory*. Thousand Oaks, Calif.: Sage: 438–440.

Kurzweil, Edith
1980   *The Age of Structuralism: Lévi-Strauss to Foucault*. New York: Columbia University Press.

Laclau, Ernesto
1990   "Coming Up for Air." *Marxism Today,* March:25, 27.

Laclau, Ernesto, and Mouffe, Chantal
1985   *Hegemony and Socialist Strategy: Towards a Radical Democratic Politics*. London: Verso.
1987   "Post-Marxism without Apologies." *New Left Review* 166:79–106.

Landry, Lorraine Y.
2000   *Marx and the Postmodernism Debates: An Agenda for Critical Theory*. Westport, Conn.: Praeger.

Langford, Wendy
1999   *Revolutions of the Heart: Gender, Power, and the Delusions of Love*. London: Routledge.

Langman, Lauren
2007   "Critical Theory/Frankfurt School." In George Ritzer (ed.), *The Blackwell Encyclopedia of Sociology*. Oxford: Blackwell: 873–877.

Langsdorf, Lenore
1995   "Treating Method and Form as Phenomena: An Appreciation of Garfinkel's Phenomenology of Social Action." *Human Studies* 18:177–188.

Lash, Scott
1991   "Introduction." In *Post-Structuralist and Post-Modernist Sociology*. Andershot, Eng.: Edward Elgar: ix–xv.
1988   "Discourse or Figure? Postmodernism as a 'Regime of Signification.'" *Theory, Culture and Society* 5:311–336.

Lash, Scott, and Urry, John
1987   *The End of Organized Capitalism*. Cambridge, Eng.: Polity Press.

Latour, Bruno
1999   "On Recalling ANT." In John Law and John Hassard (eds.), *Actor Network Theory and After*. Oxford: Blackwell: 15–25.

Law, Ian
2007   "Discrimination." In George Ritzer (ed.), *The Blackwell Encyclopedia of Sociology*. Oxford: Blackwell: 1182–1184.

Law, John
1999   "After ANT: Complexity, Naming and Topology." In John Law and John Hassard (eds.), *Actor Network Theory and After*. Oxford: Blackwell: 1–14.

Law, John, and Hetherington, Kevin
2002   "Materialities, Spatialities, Globalities." In Michael J. Dear and Steven Flusty (eds.), *The Spaces of Postmodernity: Readings in Human Geography*. Oxford: Blackwell: 390–401.

Layder, Derek
1985   "Power, Structure and Agency." *Journal for the Theory of Social Behaviour*
                15:131–149.

Layder, Derek, Ashton, David, and Sung, Johnny
1991   "The Empirical Correlates of Action and Structure: The Transition from School
                to Work." *Sociology* 25:447–464.

Layte, Richard
1998   "Gendered Equity? Comparing Explanations of Women's Satisfaction with the
                Domestic Division of Labour." *Work, Employment and Society* 10:293–316.

Lechner, Frank
2005   "Globalization." In George Ritzer (ed.), *Encyclopedia of Social Theory*.
                Thousand Oaks, Calif.: Sage: 330–333.

Lechte, John
2005   "Structuralist Marxism." In George Ritzer (ed.), *Encyclopedia of Social Theory*.
                Thousand Oaks, Calif.: Sage: 805–811.

Lefebvre, Henri
1962/1995   *Introduction to Modernity*. London: Verso.
1974/1991   *The Production of Space*. Oxford: Blackwell.

Leik, Robert K.
1992   "New Directions for Network Exchange Theory: Strategic Manipulation of
                Network Linkages." *Social Networks* 14:309–323.

Leledakis, Kanakis
2005   "Freud, Sigmund." In George Ritzer (ed.), *Encyclopedia of Social Theory*.
                Thousand Oaks, Calif.: Sage: 293–295.

Lemert, Charles
1990   "The Uses of French Structuralisms in Sociology." In George Ritzer (ed.),
                Frontiers of Social Theory: The New Syntheses. New York: Columbia
                University Press: 230–254.
1994   "Social Theory at the Early End of a Short Century." *Sociological Theory*
                12:140–152.
2005a   "Foucault, Michel." In George Ritzer (ed.), *Encyclopedia of Social Theory*.
                Thousand Oaks, Calif.: Sage: 284–289.
2005b   "Discourse." In George Ritzer (ed.), *Encyclopedia of Social Theory*.
                Thousand Oaks, Calif.: Sage: 203–205.
2005d   "Governmentality." In George Ritzer (ed.), *Encyclopedia of Social Theory*.
                Thousand Oaks, Calif.: Sage: 342–343.

Lemert, Charles (ed.)
2000   "W. E. B. Du Bois." In George Ritzer (ed.) *The Blackwell Companion to Major
                Social Theorists*. Malden, Mass.: 345–366.
2001   "Multiculturalism." In George Ritzer and Barry Smart (eds.), *Handbook of
                Social Theory*. London: Sage: 297–307.

Lengermann, Patricia Madoo
1979   "The Founding of the American Sociological Review." *American Sociological
                Review* 44:185–198.

Lengermann, Patricia Madoo, and Niebrugge-Brantley, Jill
1995   "Intersubjectivity and Domination: A Feminist Analysis of the Sociology of
            Alfred Schutz." *Sociological Theory* 13:25–36.
1998   *The Women Founders: Sociology and Social Theory, 1830–1930.* New York:
            McGraw-Hill.

Lengermann, Patricia Madoo, and Wallace, Ruth A.
1985   *Gender in America: Social Control and Social Change.* Englewood Cliffs, N.J.:
            Prentice-Hall.

Lenzer, Gertrud (ed.)
1975   *Auguste Comte and Positivism: The Essential Writings.* Magnolia, Mass.:
            Peter Smith.

Lepenies, Wolf
1988   *Between Literature and Science: The Rise of Sociology.* Cambridge, Eng.:
            Cambridge University Press.

Lerner, Gerda
1986   *The Creation of Patriarchy.* New York: Oxford University Press.
1993   *The Creation of Feminist Consciousness.* New York: Oxford University Press.

Levi, Margaret, Cook, Karen S., O'Brien, Jodi A., and Faye, Howard
1990   "The Limits of Rationality." In K. S. Cook and M. Levi (eds.), *The Limits of
            Rationality.* Chicago: University of Chicago Press.

Levidow, Les
1990   "Foreclosing the Future." *Science as Culture* 8:59–90.

Levine, Andrew, Sober, Elliot, and Wright, Erik Olin
1987   "Marxism and Methodological Individualism." *New Left Review* 162:67–84.

Levine, Donald
1981a   "Rationality and Freedom: Weber and Beyond." *Sociological Inquiry* 51:5–25.
1991a   "Simmel and Parsons Reconsidered." *American Journal of Sociology*
            96:1097–1116.
1995   *Visions of the Sociological Tradition.* Chicago: University of Chicago Press.

Levine, Donald, Carter, Ellwood B., and Gorman, Eleanor Miller
1976a   "Simmel's Influence on American Sociology—I." *American Journal of
            Sociology* 81:813–845.
1976b   "Simmel's Influence on American Sociology—II." *American Journal of
            Sociology* 81:1112–1132.

Lévi-Strauss, Claude
1967   *Structural Anthropology.* Garden City, N.Y.: Anchor.

Lewis, David Levering
1993   *W. E. B. Du Bois: Biography of a Race, 1869–1919.* New York: Holt.
2000   *W. E. B. Du Bois: The Fight for Equality and the American Century,
            1919–1963.* New York: Holt.

Lewis, J. David, and Smith, Richard L.
1980   *American Sociology and Pragmatism: Mead, Chicago Sociology, and Symbolic
            Interaction.* Chicago: University of Chicago Press.

Lewis, Reba Rowe
1991   "Forging New Syntheses: Theories and Theorists." *American Sociologist*
            Fall/Winter: 221–230.

Li, Rebecca S. K.
2005   "Collins, Randall." In George Ritzer (ed.), *Encyclopedia of Social Theory.*
            Thousand Oaks, Calif.: Sage: 123–123.

Lidz, Victor
2000   "Talcott Parsons." In George Ritzer (ed.), *The Blackwell Companion to Major
            Social Theorists.* Malden, Mass.: Blackwell: 388–431.
2007   "Parsons, Talcott." In George Ritzer (ed.), *The Blackwell Encyclopedia of
            Sociology.* Oxford: Blackwell: 3365–3368.

Lilla, Mark
1994   "The Legitimacy of the Liberal Age." In M. Lilla (ed.), *New French Thought:
            Political Philosophy.* Princeton, N.J.: Princeton University Press: 3–34.

Lindemann, Marilee
2000   "Who's Afraid of the Big Bad Witch? Queer Studies in American Literature."
            American Literary History 12(4):757–770.

Lindenberg, Siegwart
2000   "James Coleman." In George Ritzer (ed.), *The Blackwell Companion to Major
            Social Theorists.* Malden, Mass.: Blackwell: 513–544.
2001   "Social Rationality versus Rational Egoism." In Jonathan H. Turner (ed.),
            Handbook of Sociological Theory. New York: Kluwer Academic/Plenum
            Publishers: 635–668.
2005   "Coleman, James." In George Ritzer (ed.), *Encyclopedia of Social Theory.*
            Thousand Oaks, Calif.: Sage:111–115.

Lindner, Rolf
1996   *The Reportage of Urban Culture: Robert Park and the Chicago School.*
            Cambridge, Eng.: Cambridge University Press.

Lipovetsky, Gilles
1987/1994   *The Empire of Fashion: Dressing Modern Democracy.* Princeton, N.J.:
            Princeton University Press.

Lipscomb, Michael
2007   "Derrida, Jacques." In George Ritzer (ed.), *The Blackwell Encyclopedia of
            Sociology.* Oxford: Blackwell: 1062–1064.

Lipset, Seymour Martin, Trow, Martin, and Coleman, James S.
1956   *Union Democracy: The Internal Politics of the International Typographic
            Union.* New York: Free Press.

Liska, Allen E.
1990   "The Significance of Aggregate Dependent Variables and Contextual
            Independent Variables for Linking Macro and Micro Theories." *Social
            Psychology Quarterly* 53:292–301.

Lockwood, David
1956   "Some Remarks on The Social System." *British Journal of Sociology* 7:134–146.

Lodahl, Janice B., and Gordon, Gerald
1972   "The Structure of Scientific Fields and the Functioning of University Graduate
            Departments." *American Sociological Review* 37:57–72.

Lodge, Peter
1986   "Connections: W. I. Thomas, European Social Thought and American
            Sociology." In R. C. Monk (ed.), *Structures of Knowing*. Lanham, Md.:
            University Press of America: 135–160.

Lopata, Helena Znaniecka
1996   *Current Widowhood: Myths and Realities.* Thousand Oaks, Calif.: Sage.

Lorber, Judith
1994   *Paradoxes of Gender.* New Haven: Yale University Press.
2000   "Using Gender to Undo Gender: A Feminist Degendering Movement."
            Feminist Theory 1:79–95.
2001   "It's the 21st Century—Do You Know What Gender You Are?" *Advances in
            Gender Research* 5:119–137.

Lorde, Audre
1984   *Sister Outsider: Essays and Speeches.* Trumansburg, N.Y.: Crossings Press.

Lovaglia, Michael J.
2007   "Social Exchange Theory." In George Ritzer (ed.), *The Blackwell Encyclopedia
            of Sociology.* Oxford: Blackwell: 4408–4410.

Lovell, David W.
1992   "Socialism, Utopianism and the 'Utopian Socialists.'" *History of European
            Ideas* 14:185–201.

Lovell, Terri
2004   "Bourdieu, Class and Gender: 'The Return of the Living Dead'?" In Lisa
            Adkins and Beverley Skeggs (ed.), *Feminism after Bourdieu.* Oxford:
            Blackwell: 37–56.

Lowy, Michael
1996   "Figures of Weberian Marxism." *Theory and Society* 25:431–446.

Luhmann, Niklas
1980/1981/ *Gesellschaftsstruktur und Semantik. Studien zur Wissenssoziologie der
1989/1995   modernen Gesellschaft.* 4 vols. Frankfurt am Main: Suhrkamp.
1982   *The Differentiation of Society.* New York: Columbia University Press.
1982/1986   *Liebe als Passion/Love as Passion.* Frankfurt am Main: Suhrkamp/Cambridge,
            Eng.: Polity Press.
1984/1995   *Soziale Systeme. Grundreiner allgemeinen Theorie/Social Systems: Outline
            of a General Theory.* Frankfurt am Main: Suhrkamp/Stanford, Calif.:
            Stanford University Press.
1985   "Complexity and Meaning." In S. Aida et al. (eds.), *The Science and Praxis of
            Complexity.* Tokyo: United Nations University: 99–104.
1986/1989   *Okologische Kommunikation. Kann die moderne Gesellschaft sich auf
            okologische Gefahrdungen einstellen?/Ecological Communication.* Opladen:
            Westdeutscher Verlag/Cambridge, Eng.: Polity Press.
1987   "Modern Systems Theory and the Theory of Society." In V. Meja, D. Misgeld,
            and N. Stehr (eds.), *Modern German Sociology.* New York: Columbia
            University Press: 173–186.

| 1988 | *Die Wirtschaft der Gesellschaft.* Frankfurt am Main: Suhrkamp. |

1988   *Die Wirtschaft der Gesellschaft.* Frankfurt am Main: Suhrkamp.
1990   *Die Wissenschaft der Gesellschaft.* Frankfurt am Main: Suhrkamp.
1991   *Soziologie des Risikos.* Berlin: de Gruyter.
1993   *Das Recht der Gesellschaft.* Frankfurt am Main: Suhrkamp.
1995   *Die Kunst der Gesellschaft.* Frankfurt am Main: Suhrkamp.
1997   *Die Gesellschaft der Gesellschaft.* 2 vols. Frankfurt am Main: Suhrkamp.
2001   "Notes on the Project 'Poetry and Social Theory.'" *Theory, Culture and Society* 18:15–27.
2002   *Theories of Distinction: Redescribing the Descriptions of Modernity.* Ed. William Rasch. Trans. Joseph O'Neil. Stanford, Calif.: Stanford University Press.

Lukács, Georg
1922/1968   *History and Class Consciousness.* Cambridge, Mass.: MIT Press.
1991   "Georg Simmel." *Theory, Culture and Society* 8:145–150.

Lukes, Steven
1972   *Emile Durkheim: His Life and Work.* New York: Harper and Row.
1977   "Power and Structure." In S. Lukes, *Essays in Social Theory.* London: Macmillan: 3–29.

Lynch, Michael
1985   *Art and Artifact in Laboratory Science: A Study of Shop Work and Shop Talk in a Research Laboratory.* London: Routledge and Kegan Paul.
1991   "Pictures of Nothing? Visual Construals in Social Theory." *Sociological Theory* 9:1–21.
1993   *Scientific Practice and Ordinary Action: Ethnomethodology and Social Studies of Science.* Cambridge, Eng.: Cambridge University Press.
1999   "Silence in Context: Ethnomethodology and Social Theory." *Human Studies* 22:211–233.

Lynch, Michael, and Bogen, David
1991   "In Defense of Dada-Driven Analysis." *Sociological Theory* 9:269–276.

Lyon, David
2007   "Surveillance." In George Ritzer (ed.), *The Blackwell Encyclopedia of Sociology.* Oxford: Blackwell: 4895–4898.

Lyotard, Jean-François
1984   *The Postmodern Condition.* Minneapolis: University of Minnesota Press.

Mackay, Robert W.
1974   "Words, Utterances and Activities." In R. Turner (ed.), *Ethnomethodology: Selected Readings.* Harmondsworth, Eng.: Penguin: 197–215.

MacKinnon, Catherine
1979   *Sexual Harassment of Working Women.* New Haven: Yale University Press.
1989   *Towards a Feminist Theory of the State.* Cambridge, Mass.: Harvard University Press.
1993   *Only Words.* Cambridge, Mass.: Harvard University Press.

MacPherson, C. B.
1962   *The Political Theory of Possessive Individualism.* Oxford: Clarendon Press.

Macy, Michael W., and Van de Rijt, Arnout
2007   "Game Theory." In George Ritzer (ed.), *The Blackwell Encyclopedia of Sociology*. Oxford: Blackwell: 1822–1825.

Mahoney, Maureen A., and Yngvesson, Barbara
1992   "The Construction of Subjectivity and the Paradox of Resistance: Reintegrating Feminist Anthropology and Psychology." *Signs* 18:44–73.

Maines, David R.
1977   "Social Organization and Social Structure in Symbolic Interactionist Thought." In A. Inkeles, J. Coleman, and N. Smelser (eds.), *Annual Review of Sociology*. Vol. 3. Palo Alto, Calif.: Annual Reviews: 259–285.
1988   "Myth, Text, and Interactionist Complicity in the Neglect of Blumer's Macrosociology." *Symbolic Interaction* 11:43–57.
1989a   "Repackaging Blumer: The Myth of Herbert Blumer's Astructural Bias." *Symbolic Interaction* 10:383–413.
1989b   "Herbert Blumer on the Possibility of Science in the Practice of Sociology: Further Thoughts." *Journal of Contemporary Ethnography* 18:160–177.
2001   *The Faultline of Consciousness: A View of Interactionism in Sociology*. New York: Aldine de Gruyter.
2005   "Blumer, Herbert." In George Ritzer (ed.), *Encyclopedia of Social Theory*. Thousand Oaks, Calif.: Sage: 58–62.

Maines, David, Bridger, Jeffrey C., and Ulmer, Jeffery T.
1996   "Mythic Facts and Park's Pragmatism: On Predecessor-Selection and Theorizing in Human Ecology." *Sociological Quarterly* 37:521–549.

Maines, David R., and Morrione, Thomas J.
1990   "On the Breadth and Relevance of Blumer's Perspective: Introduction to His Analysis of Industrialization." In H. Blumer, *Industrialization as an Agent of Social Change: A Critical Analysis*. New York: Aldine de Gruyter.

Mancini, Matthew
1994   *Alexis de Tocqueville*. New York: Twayne Publishers.

Mandel, Ernest
1975   *Late Capitalism*. London: New Left Books.

Mandelbaum, Jenny
1989   "Interpersonal Activities in Conversational Storytelling." *Western Journal of Speech Communications* 53:114–126.

Mandes, Evans
2007   "Behaviorism." In George Ritzer (ed.), *Encyclopedia of Sociology*. Oxford: Blackwell: 256–258.

Manent, Pierre
1994/1998   *The City of Man*. Princeton, N.J.: Princeton University Press.

Manis, Jerome, and Meltzer, Bernard (eds.)
1978   *Symbolic Interaction: A Reader in Social Psychology*. 3rd ed. Boston: Allyn and Bacon.

Mann, Susan A., Grimes, Michael D., and Kemp, Alice Abel
1997   "Paradigm Shifts in Family Sociology? Evidence from Three Decades of Family Textbooks." *Journal of Family Issues* 18:315–349.

Mann, Susan A., and Kelley, Lori R.
1997   "Standing at the Crossroads of Modernist Thought—Collins, Smith, and the
            New Feminist Epistemologies." *Gender & Society* 11:391–408.

Mannheim, Karl
1931/1936   "The Sociology of Knowledge." In K. Mannheim, *Ideology and Utopia.*
            New York: Harcourt, Brace and World: 264–311.

Manning, Philip
1991   "Drama as Life: The Significance of Goffman's Changing Use of the Theatrical
            Metaphor." *Sociological Theory* 9:70–86.
1992   *Erving Goffman and Modern Sociology.* Stanford, Calif.: Stanford University Press.
2005a   "Dramaturgy." In George Ritzer (ed.), *Encyclopedia of Social Theory.*
            Thousand Oaks, Calif.: Sage: 210–213.
2005b   "Goffman, Erving." In George Ritzer (ed.), *Encyclopedia of Social Theory.*
            Thousand Oaks, Calif.: Sage: 333–339.
2005c   "Impression Management." In George Ritzer (ed.), *Encyclopedia of Social
            Theory.* Thousand Oaks, Calif.: Sage: 397–399.
2007   "Dramaturgy." In George Ritzer (ed.), *The Blackwell Encyclopedia of
            Sociology.* Oxford: Blackwell: 1226–1224.

Manning, Philip, and Ray, George
1993   "Shyness, Self-Confidence, and Social Interaction." *Social Psychology
            Quarterly* 56:178–192.

Manning, Robert
2000   *Credit Card Nation.* New York: Basic Books.

Manuel, Frank
1962   *The Prophets of Paris.* Cambridge, Mass.: Harvard University Press.

Marcus, Judith (ed.)
1999   *Surviving the Twentieth Century: Social Philosophy from the Frankfurt School to
            the Columbia Faculty Seminars.* New Brunswick, N.J.: Transaction Publishers.

Marcuse, Herbert
1958   *Soviet Marxism: A Critical Analysis.* New York: Columbia University Press.
1964   *One-Dimensional Man.* Boston: Beacon Press.
1969   *An Essay on Liberation.* Boston: Beacon Press.

Mardorossian, C. M.
2002   "Toward a New Feminist Theory of Rape." *Signs* 273:743–775.

Margolis, Eric
2007   "Sartre, Jean-Paul." In George Ritzer (ed.), *The Blackwell Encyclopedia of
            Sociology.* Oxford: Blackwell: 4009–4010.

Markovsky, Barry
2005   "Network Exchange Theory." In George Ritzer (ed.), *Encyclopedia of Social
            Theory.* Thousand Oaks, Calif.: Sage: 530–534.

Markovsky, Barry, Willer, David, and Patton, Travis
1988   "Power Relations in Exchange Networks." *American Sociological Review*
            53:220–236.

Markus, Gyorgy
2005   "Lukacs, Gyorgy." In George Ritzer (ed.), *Encyclopedia of Social Theory.*
               Thousand Oaks, Calif.: Sage: 458–460.

Marling, William H.
2006   *How American is Globalization?* Baltimore: Johns Hopkins University Press.

Marsden, Peter V.
2007   "Coleman, James." In George Ritzer (ed.), *Encyclopedia of Sociology.*
               Oxford: Blackwell: 569–575.

Martin, Donald D., and Wilson, Janelle L.
2005   "Role Theory." In George Ritzer (ed.), *Encyclopedia of Social Theory.*
               Thousand Oaks, Calif.: Sage: 651–655.

Marx, Gary T.
2005   "Surveillance and Society." In George Ritzer (ed.), *Encyclopedia of Social
               Theory.* Thousand Oaks, Calif.: Sage: 816–821.

Marx, Karl
1842/1977   "Communism and the *Augsburger Allegemeine Zeitung.*" In D. McLellan (ed.),
               Karl Marx: Selected Writings. New York: Oxford University Press: 20.
1857–1858/   *Pre-Capitalist Economic Formations.* Ed. Eric J. Hobsbawm. New York:
1964   International Publishers.
1857–1858/   *The Grundrisse: Foundations of the Critique of Political Economy.* New York:
1974   Random House.
1859/1970   *A Contribution to the Critique of Political Economy.* New York: International
               Publishers.
1862–1863/   *Theories of Surplus Value,* Part I. Moscow: Progress Publishers.
1963
1862–1863/   *Theories of Surplus Value,* Part II. Moscow: Progress Publishers.
1968
1867/1967   *Capital: A Critique of Political Economy,* Vol. 1. New York: International
               Publishers.
1869/1963   *The 18th Brumaire of Louis Bonaparte.* New York: International Publishers.
1932/1964   *The Economic and Philosophic Manuscripts of 1844.* Dirk J. Struik (ed.).
               New York: International Publishers.

Marx, Karl, and Engels, Friedrich
1845/1956   *The Holy Family.* Moscow: Foreign Language Publishing House.
1845–1846/   *The German Ideology,* Part 1. C. J. Arthur (ed.). New York: International
1970   Publishers.
1848/1948   *Manifesto of the Communist Party.* New York: International Publishers.

Maryanski, Alexandra
2005   "Evolutionary Theory." In George Ritzer (ed.), *Encyclopedia of Social Theory.*
               Thousand Oaks, Calif.: Sage: 257–263.

Maryanski, Alexandra, and Turner, Jonathan H.
1992   *The Social Cage: Human Nature and the Evolution of Society.* Stanford, Calif.:
               Stanford University Press.

Masterman, Margaret
1970   "The Nature of a Paradigm." In I. Lakatos and A. Musgrove (eds.), *Criticism and
               the Growth of Knowledge.* Cambridge, Eng.: Cambridge University Press: 59–89.

Matsuda, Marie, et al.
2003   *Words that Wound: Critical Race Theory, Assaultive Speech, and the First Amendment.* Boulder, Co.: Westview.

Matthews, Fred H.
1977   *Quest for an American Sociology: Robert E. Park and the Chicago School.* Montreal: McGill University Press.

Mayer, Tom
1994   *Analytical Marxism.* Thousand Oaks, Calif.: Sage.

Mayhew, Bruce
1980   "Structuralism versus Individualism: Part I, Shadowboxing in the Dark." S*ocial Forces* 59:335–375.

Maynard, Douglas W.
1991   "Goffman, Garfinkel and Games." *Sociological Theory* 9:277–279.

Maynard, Douglas W., and Clayman, Steven E.
1991   "The Diversity of Ethnomethodology." *Annual Review of Sociology* 17:385–418.

Maynard, Douglas W., and Kardash, Teddy
2007   "Ethnomethodology." In George Ritzer (ed.), *The Blackwell Encyclopedia of Sociology.* Oxford: Blackwell: 1483–1486.

McBride, William
2000   "Habermas and the Marxian Tradition." In Lewis Hahn (ed.), *Perspectives on Habermas.* Chicago: Open Court.

McCarthy, E. Doyle
1996   *Knowledge as Culture: The New Sociology of Knowledge.* New York: Routledge.
2007   "Knowledge, sociology of." In George Ritzer (ed.), *Encyclopedia of Sociology.* Oxford: Blackwell: 2482–2485.

McCarthy, Thomas
1982   *The Critical Theory of Jurgen Habermas.* Cambridge, Mass.: MIT Press.
2005   "Thomas, William Isaac." In George Ritzer (ed.), *Encyclopedia of Social Theory.* Thousand Oaks, Calif.: Sage: 834–835.

McCaughey, Martha
1997   *Real Knockouts: The Physical Feminism of Women's Self-Defense.* New York: New York University Press.

McCormick, Charles
2007   "Poststructuralism." In George Ritzer (ed.), *The Blackwell Encyclopedia of Sociology.* Oxford: Blackwell: 3580–3584.

McGregor, Gaile
1995   "Gender Advertisements Then and Now: Symbolic Interactionism and the Problem of History." *Studies in Symbolic Interactionism* 27: 17–42.

McGuigan, Jim
2002   *Cultural Populism.* London: Routledge.
2005   "Cultural Studies and the New Populism." In George Ritzer (ed.), *Encyclopedia of Social Theory.* Thousand Oaks, Calif.: Sage: 177–181.

McLaughlin, Lisa
2004   "Feminism and the Political Economy of Transnational Public Space." In Nick
              Crossley and John Michael Roberts (eds.), *After Habermas: New Perspectives
              on the Public Sphere.* Oxford: Blackwell: 156–175.

McLaughlin, Neil
2007   "Fromm, Erich." In George Ritzer (ed.), *Encyclopedia of Sociology.*
              Oxford: Blackwell: 1804–1808.

McLaughlin, Peter
2001   *What Functions Explain: Functional Explanation and Self-Reproducing
              Systems.* Cambridge, Eng.: Cambridge University Press.

McLean, Paul D.
1998   "A Frame Analysis of Favor Seeking in the Renaissance: Agency, Networks,
              and Political Culture." *American Journal of Sociology* 104:51–91.

McLellan, David
1973   *Karl Marx: His Life and Thought.* New York: Harper Colophon.

McNay, Lois
1999   "Gender, Habitus and the Field: Pierre Bourdieu and the Limits of Reflexivity."
              Theory, Culture and Society 16:95–117.
2004a   "Agency and Experience: Gender as a Lived Relation." In Lisa Adkins
              and Beverley Skeggs (ed.), *Feminism after Bourdieu.* Oxford: Blackwell:
              175–190.
2004b   "Situated Intersubjectivity." In Barbara L. Marshall and Ann Witz (eds.),
              Engendering the Social: Feminist Encounters with Sociological Theory.
              Maidenhead, Eng.: Open University Press: 171–186.

Mead, George Herbert
1934/1962   *Mind, Self and Society: From the Standpoint of a Social Behaviorist.*
              Chicago: University of Chicago Press.
1936   *Movements of Thought in the Nineteenth Century.* Chicago: University of
              Chicago Press.
1938/1972   *The Philosophy of the Act.* Chicago: University of Chicago Press.
1959   *The Philosophy of the Present.* LaSalle, Ill.: Open Court.
1982   *The Individual and the Social Self: Unpublished Work of George Herbert
              Mead.* Chicago: University of Chicago Press.

Meeker, Barbara
1971   "Decisions and Exchange." *American Sociological Review* 36:485–495.

Mehan, Hugh, and Wood, Houston
1975   *The Reality of Ethnomethodology.* New York: Wiley.

Meiksins, Peter
1994   "Labor and Monopoly Capital for the 1990s: A Review and Critique of the
              Labor Process Debate." *Monthly Review* 46:45–59.

Meisenhelder, Tom
1997   "Pierre Bourdieu and the Call for a Reflexive Sociology." *Current Perspectives
              in Social Theory* 17:159–183.

Meltzer, Bernard
1964/1978   "Mead's Social Psychology." In J. Manis and B. Meltzer (eds.), *Symbolic Interaction: A Reader in Social Psychology.* 3rd ed. Boston: Allyn and Bacon: 15–27.

Meltzer, Bernard, Petras, James, and Reynolds, Larry
1975   *Symbolic Interactionism: Genesis, Varieties and Criticisms.* London: Routledge and Kegan Paul.

Menard, Scott
1995   "A Developmental Test of Mertonian Anomie Theory." *Journal of Research in Crime and Delinquency* 32:136–174.

Mennell, Stephen
1992   *Norbert Elias: An Introduction.* Oxford: Blackwell.
2005a   "Figurational Sociology." In George Ritzer (ed.), *Encyclopedia of Social Theory.* Thousand Oaks, Calif.: Sage: 279–280.
2005b   "Civilizing Processes." In George Ritzer (ed.), *Encyclopedia of Social Theory.* Thousand Oaks, Calif.: Sage: 105–107.

Mennell, Stephen, and Goudsblom, Johan (eds.)
1998   *Norbert Elias: On Civilization, Power, and Knowledge.* Chicago: University of Chicago Press.

Merton, Robert K.
1949/1968   "Manifest and Latent Functions." In R. K. Merton, *Social Theory and Social Structure.* New York: Free Press: 73–138.
1968   *Social Theory and Social Structure.* New York: Free Press.
1975   "Structural Analysis in Sociology." In P. Blau (ed.), *Approaches to the Study of Social Structure.* New York: Free Press: 21–52.
1980   "Remembering the Young Talcott Parsons." *American Sociologist* 15:68–71.
1995   "Opportunity Structure: The Emergence, Diffusion, and Differentiation of a Sociological Concept, 1930s–1950s." In F. Adler and W. S. Laufer (eds.), *The Legacy of Anomie Theory.* New Brunswick, N.J.: Transaction Publishers.

Mestrovic, Stjepan G.
1988   *Emile Durkheim and the Reformation of Sociology.* Totowa, N.J.: Rowman and Littlefield.
1998   *Anthony Giddens: The Last Modernist.* London: Routledge.

Mészáros, István
1995   *Beyond Capital.* New York: Monthly Review Press.

Meyer, John, Boli, J., Thomas, G., and Ramirez, F.
1997   "World Society and the Nation State." *American Journal of Sociology* 103:144–181.

Miller, David
1973   *George Herbert Mead: Self, Language and the World.* Austin: University of Texas Press.
1981   "The Meaning of Role-Taking." *Symbolic Interaction* 4:167–175.

1982a   "Introduction." In G. H. Mead, *The Individual and the Social Self:
            Unpublished Work of George Herbert Mead*. Chicago: University of
            Chicago Press: 1–26.
1982b   Review of J. David Lewis and Richard L. Smith, *American Sociology and
            Pragmatism. Journal of the History of Sociology* 4:108–114.
1985   "Concerning J. David Lewis' Response to My Review of American Sociology
            and Pragmatism." *Journal of the History of Sociology* 5:131–133.

Miller, James
1993   *The Passion of Michel Foucault*. New York: Anchor Books.

Miller, W. Watts
1993   "Durkheim's Montesquieu." *British Journal of Sociology* 44:693–712.

Mills, C. Wright
1951   *White Collar*. New York: Oxford University Press.
1956   *The Power Elite*. New York: Oxford University Press.
1959   *The Sociological Imagination*. New York: Oxford University Press.

Milovanovic, Dragan
1995   "Dueling Paradigms: Modernist versus Postmodernist Thought." *Humanity and
            Society* 19:19–44.

Mirowsky, John, and Ross, Catherine E.
1995   "Sex Differences in Distress: Real or Artifact?" *American Sociological Review*
            60:449–468.

Misztal, B.
2001   "Normality and Trust in Goffman's Theory of Interaction Order." *Sociological
            Theory* 19:312–324.

Mitchell, Jack N.
1978   *Social Exchange, Dramaturgy and Ethnomethodology: Toward a Paradigmatic
            Synthesis*. New York: Elsevier.

Mitroff, Ian, and Kilmann, Ralph
1978   *Methodological Approaches to Social Science*. San Francisco: Jossey-Bass.

Mitzman, Arthur
1969/1971   *The Iron Cage: An Historical Interpretation of Max Weber*. New York: Grosset
            and Dunlap.

Mizruchi, Mark S.
1990   "Cohesion, Structural Equivalence, and Similarity of Behavior: An Approach to
            the Study of Corporate Political Power." *Sociological Theory* 8:16–32.
1994   "Social Network Analysis: Recent Achievements and Current Controversies."
            Acta Sociologica 37:329–343.
2005   "Network Exchange Theory." In George Ritzer (ed.), *Encyclopedia of Social
            Theory*. Thousand Oaks, Calif.: Sage: 530–540.

Mizruchi, Mark S., and Koenig, Thomas
1986   "Economic Sources of Corporate Political Consensus: An Examination of
            Interindustry Relations." *American Sociological Review* 51:482–491.

Mohanty, Chandra Talpade
1991   "Under Western Eyes: Feminist Scholarship and Colonial Discourses." In
            C. Mohanty, A. Russo, and L. Torres (eds.), *Third World Women and the
            Politics of Feminism*. Bloomington: Indiana University Press:
2002   *Feminism without Borders: Decolonizing Theory, Practicing Solidarity*.
            Durham, N.C.: Duke University Press.

Moi, Toril
1991   "Appropriating Bourdieu: Feminist Theory in Pierre Bordieu's Sociology of
            Culture." *New Literary History* 22:1017–1049.
1999   *What Is a Woman?* Oxford: Oxford University Press.

Molm, Linda D.
1988   "The Structure and Use of Power: A Comparison of Reward and Punishment
            Power." *Social Psychology Quarterly* 51:108–122.
1989   "Punishment Power: A Balancing Process in Power-Dependence Relations."
            American Journal of Sociology 94:1392–1418.
1994   "Is Punishment Effective? Coercive Strategies in Social Exchange." *Social
            Psychology Quarterly* 57:75–94.
1997   *Coercive Power in Exchange*. Cambridge, Eng.: Cambridge University Press.
2001   "Theories of Social Exchange and Exchange Networks." In George Ritzer and
            Barry Smart (eds.), *Handbook of Social Theory*. London: Sage: 260–272.
2005a   "Behaviorism." In George Ritzer (ed.), *Encyclopedia of Social Theory*.
            Thousand Oaks, Calif.: Sage: 44–47.
2005b   "Homans, George." In George Ritzer (ed.), *Encyclopedia of Social Theory*.
            Thousand Oaks, Calif.: Sage: 381–385.
2007   "Power-Dependence Theory." In George Ritzer (ed.), *The Blackwell
            Encyclopedia of Sociology*. Oxford: Blackwell: 3598–3602.

Molm, Linda D., and Cook, Karen S.
1995   "Social Exchange and Exchange Networks." In K. S. Cook, G. A. Fine, and
            J. S. House (eds.), *Sociological Perspectives on Social Psychology*. Boston:
            Allyn and Bacon: 209–235.

Molm, Linda D., Quist, Theron M., and Wisely, Phillip A.
1994   "Imbalanced Structures, Unfair Strategies: Power and Justice in Social
            Exchange." *American Sociological Review* 59:98–121.

Monnier, Christine A.
2007   "Bourdieu, Pierre." In George Ritzer (ed.), *The Blackwell Encyclopedia of
            Sociology*. Oxford: Blackwell: 347–350.

Moore, Wilbert E.
1966   Global Sociology: The World as a Singular System." *American Journal of
            Sociology* 71:475–482.
1978   "Functionalism." In T. Bottomore and R. Nisbet (eds.), *A History of
            Sociological Analysis*. New York: Basic Books: 321–361.

Moorti, Sujata
2002   *The Color of Rape: Gender and Race in Television's Public Spheres*. Albany:
            State University of New York Press.

Morgan, Robin
1970   *Sisterhood Is Powerful: An Anthology of Writings from the Women's Liberation Movement.* New York: Vintage.

Morrione, Thomas J.
1988   "Herbert G. Blumer (1900–1987): A Legacy of Concepts, Criticisms, and Contributions." *Symbolic Interaction* 11:1–12.
2007   "Blumer, Herbert George." In George Ritzer (ed.), *The Blackwell Encyclopedia of Sociology.* Oxford: Blackwell: 318–327.

Morris, Bonnie
2003   "At the Michigan Womyn's Music Festival." *The Gay and Lesbian Review Worldwide* 10(5):16–18.

Morris, Martin
2001   *Rethinking the Communicative Turn: Adorno, Habermas, and the Problem of Communicative Freedom.* Albany, State University of New York Press.

Morrow, Raymond A.
1994   "Critical Theory, Poststructuralism, and Critical Theory." *Current Perspectives in Social Theory* 14:27–51.

Morse, Chandler
1961   "The Functional Imperatives." In M. Black (ed.), *The Social Theories of Talcott Parsons.* Englewood Cliffs, N.J.: Prentice-Hall: 100–152.

Moscovici, Serge
1993   *The Invention of Society.* Cambridge, Eng.: Polity Press.

Mouffe, Chantal
1988   "Radical Democracy: Modern or Postmodern?" In A. Ross (ed.), *Universal Abandon? The Politics of Postmodernism.* Minneapolis: University of Minnesota Press: 31–45.

Mouzelis, Nicos
1997   "In Defence of the Sociological Canon: A Reply to David Parker." *Sociological Review* 97:244–253.

Movahedi, Siamak
2007   "Psychoanalysis." In George Ritzer (ed.), *The Blackwell Encyclopedia of Sociology.* Oxford: Blackwell: 3694–3696.

Mozetic, Gerald, and Weiler, Bernd
2007   "Pareto, Vilfredo." In George Ritzer (ed.), *The Blackwell Encyclopedia of Sociology.* Oxford: Blackwell: 3360–3362.

Mullins, Nicholas
1973   *Theories and Theory Groups in Contemporary American Sociology.* New York: Harper and Row.
1983   "Theories and Theory Groups Revisited." In R. Collins (ed.), *Sociological Theory—1983.* San Francisco: Jossey-Bass: 319–337.

Münch, Richard
1987   "The Interpenetration of Microinteraction and Macrostructures in a Complex and Contingent Institutional Order." In J. C. Alexander, et al. (eds.), *The Micro-Macro Link.* Berkeley: University of California Press: 319–336.

2005   "Parsons, Talcott." In George Ritzer (ed.), *Encyclopedia of Social Theory.*
              Thousand Oaks, Calif.: Sage: 550–555.

Münch, Richard, and Smelser, Neil J.
1987   "Relating the Micro and Macro." In J. C. Alexander, et al. (eds.), *The
              Micro-Macro Link.* Berkeley: University of California Press: 356–387.

Musolf, Gil Richard
1994   "William James and Symbolic Interactionism." *Sociological Focus* 27:303–314.

Myles, John
1999   "From Habitus to Mouth: Language and Class in Bourdieu's Sociology of
              Language." *Theory and Society* 28:879–901.

Nagel, Mechthild
1997   "Critical Theory Meets the Ethic of Care." *Social Theory and Practice*
              23:307–326.

Nash, Bradley, Jr., and Wardell, Mark
1993   "The Control of Sociological Theory: In Praise of the Interregnum."
              Sociological Inquiry 63:276–292.

Nedelmann, Birgitta, and Sztompka, Piotr
1993   "Introduction." In B. Nedelmann and P. Sztompka (eds.), *Sociology in Europe:
              In Search of Identity.* Berlin: Walter de Gruyter: 1–23.

Nettl, J. P., and Robertson, Roland
1968   *International Systems and the Modernization of Societies. New York:
              Basic Books*

Nicholson, Linda
1994   "Interpreting Gender." *Signs* 20:79–105.

Nicolaus, Martin
1974   "Foreword." In K. Marx, *The Grundrisse.* New York: Random House: 7–63.

Nielsen, Donald A.
2005a   "Social Facts." In George Ritzer (ed.), *Encyclopedia of Social Theory.*
              Thousand Oaks, Calif.: Sage: 740–744.
2005b   "Annales School." In George Ritzer (ed.), *Encyclopedia of Social Theory.*
              Thousand Oaks, Calif.: Sage: 12–16.
2007a   "Social Fact." In George Ritzer (ed.), *Encyclopedia of Sociology.* Oxford:
              Blackwell: 4414–4416.
2007b   "Functionalism/Neo-Functionalism." In George Ritzer (ed.), *The Blackwell
              Encyclopedia of Sociology.* Oxford: Blackwell: 1810–1813.

Nisbet, Robert
1953   *Community and Power.* New York: Galaxy Books.
1967   *The Sociological Tradition.* New York: Basic Books.

Noblit, George W., and Hare, R. Dwight
1976–1977   "Many Tocquevilles." *The American Scholar* 46:217–234.
1988   *Meta-Ethnography: Synthesizing Qualitative Studies.* Newbury Park, Calif.: Sage.

Nollman, Gerd
2005a   "Luhmann, Niklas." In George Ritzer (ed.), *Encyclopedia of Social Theory.*
              Thousand Oaks, Calif.: Sage: 454–458.

2005b   "Habermas, Jurgen." In George Ritzer (ed.), *Encyclopedia of Social Theory.* Thousand Oaks, Calif.: Sage: 351–352.

Oberhauser, Ann M., and Pratt, Amy
2004   "Women's Collective Economic Strategies and Political Transformation in Rural South Africa." *Gender, Place and Culture* 11(2):209–228.

Olson, Richard
1993   *The Emergence of the Social Sciences. 1642–1792.* New York: Twayne.

O'Neill, John
1995   *The Poverty of Postmodernism.* London: Routledge.

Orbuch, Terri L.
1997   "People's Accounts Count: The Sociology of Accounts." In John Hagan and Karen S. Cook (eds.), *Annual Review of Sociology,* Vol. 23. Palo Alto, Calif.: Annual Reviews: 455–478.

Orenstein, David Michael
2007   "Comte, Auguste." In George Ritzer (ed.), *The Blackwell Encyclopedia of Sociology.* Oxford: Blackwell: 650–656.

Orme, J.
2002   "Social Work: Gender, Care and Justice." *British Journal of Social Work* 32:799–814.

Orr, Catherine M.
1997   "Charting the Currents of the Third Wave." *Hypatia* 12:29–43.

Ortega, Mariana
2001   " 'New Mestizas,' 'World'—Travelers,' and 'Dasein': Phenomenology and the Multi-Voiced, Multi-Cultural Self." *Hypatia* 16:1–29.

Outhwaite, William
1994   *Habermas: A Critical Introduction.* Stanford, Calif.: Stanford University Press.
2000   "Jurgen Habermas." In George Ritzer (ed.), *The Blackwell Companion to Major Social Theorists.* Malden, Mass.: Blackwell: 651–669.

Owen, Margaret
1996   *A World of Widows.* Atlantic Heights, N.J.: Zed Books.

Pahl, Jan
1999   *Invisible Money: Family Finances in the Electronic Economy.* Bristol, Eng.: Policy Press.

Pajnik, Mojca
2006   "Feminist Reflections on Habermas's Communicative Action." *European Journal of Social Theory* 9:385–404.

Pareto, Vilfredo
1935   *A Treatise on General Sociology.* 4 vols. New York: Dover.

Park, Robert E.
1927/1973   "Life History." *American Journal of Sociology* 79:251–260.

Park, Robert, and Burgess, Ernest
1921   *Introduction to the Science of Sociology.* Chicago: University of Chicago Press.

Parker, David
1997   "Why Bother with Durkheim?" *Sociological Review* 45:122–146.

Parker, Mike, and Slaughter, Jane
1990   "Management-by-Stress: The Team Concept in the US Auto Industry." *Science as Culture* 8:27–58.

Parsons, Talcott
1937   *The Structure of Social Action.* New York: McGraw-Hill.
1942   "Some Sociological Aspects of the Fascist Movements." *Social Forces* 21:138–147.
1947   "Certain Primary Sources and Patterns of Aggression in the Social Structure of the Western World." *Psychiatry* 10:167–181.
1951   *The Social System.* Glencoe, Ill.: Free Press.
1966   *Societies.* Englewood Cliffs, N.J.: Prentice-Hall.
1970   *Social Structure and Personality.* New York: Free Press.
1971   *The System of Modern Societies.* Englewood Cliffs, N.J.: Prentice-Hall.
1975   "Social Structure and the Symbolic Media of Interchange." In P. Blau (ed.), *Approaches to the Study of Social Structure.* New York: Free Press: 94–100.
1977   "On Building Social System Theory: A Personal History." In T. Parsons (ed.), *Social Systems and the Evolution of Action Theory.* New York: Free Press: 22–76.
1990   "Prolegomena to a Theory of Social Institutions." *American Sociological Review* 55:319–333.

Parsons, Talcott, and Platt, Gerald
1973   *The American University.* Cambridge, Mass.: Harvard University Press.

Parsons, Talcott, and Shils, Edward A. (eds.)
1951   *Toward a General Theory of Action.* Cambridge, Mass.: Harvard University Press.

Pateman, Carole
1999   "Beyond the Sexual Contract?" In Geoff Dench (ed.), *Rewriting the Sexual Contract.* New Brunswick, N.J.: Transaction Publishers: 1–9.

Paul, Axel
2001   "Organizing Husserl: On the Phenomenological Foundations of Luhmann's Systems Theory." *Journal of Classical Sociology* 1:371–394.

Paulsen, Michael B., and Feldman, Kenneth A.
1995   "Toward a Reconceptualization of Scholarship: A Human Action System with Functional Imperatives." *Journal of Higher Education* 66:615–640.

Pavlich, George
2007   "Deconstruction." In George Ritzer (ed.), *The Blackwell Encyclopedia of Sociology.* Oxford: Blackwell: 986–989.

Pearce, Frank
2005   "Durkheim, Emile." In George Ritzer (ed.), *Encyclopedia of Social Theory.* Thousand Oaks, Calif.: Sage: 218–223.

Peel, J. D. Y.
1971   *Herbert Spencer: The Evolution of a Sociologist.* New York: Basic Books.

Pelaez, Eloina, and Holloway, John
1990   "Learning to Bow: Post-Fordism and Technological Determinism." *Science as Culture* 8:15–26.

Perakyla, Anssi
2007   "Conversation Analysis." In George Ritzer (ed.), *The Blackwell Encyclopedia of Sociology.* Oxford: Blackwell: 791–794.

Perinbanayagam, Robert S.
1985   *Signifying Acts: Structure and Meaning in Everyday Life.* Carbondale: Southern Illinois University Press.

Perrin, Robert
1976   "Herbert Spencer's Four Theories of Social Evolution." *American Journal of Sociology* 81:1339–1359.

Perry, Nick
2007   "Barthes, Roland." In George Ritzer (ed.), *The Blackwell Encyclopedia of Sociology.* Oxford: Blackwell: 242–244.

Perry, Wilhelmia E., Abbott, James R., and Hutter, Mark
1997   "The Symbolic Interactionist Paradigm and Urban Sociology." *Research in Urban Sociology* 4:59–92.

Peters, Michael
1994   "Habermas, Post-Structuralism and the Question of Postmodernity: The Defiant Periphery." *Social Analysis* 36:3–20.

Peterson, Gretchen
2005   "Molm, Linda." In George Ritzer (ed.), *Encyclopedia of Social Theory.* Thousand Oaks, Calif.: Sage: 511–512.

Phelan, Shane
1994   *Getting Specific: Postmodern Lesbian Politics.* Minneapolis: University of Minnesota Press.

Phillips, Anne
1993   *Democracy and Difference.* University Park: Pennsylvania State University Press.

Phillips, Derek
1973   "Paradigms, Falsifications and Sociology." *Acta Sociologica* 16:13–31.
1975   "Paradigms and Incommensurability." *Theory and Society* 2:37–62.

Phillips, John William
2005   "Derrida, Jacques." In George Ritzer (ed.), *Encyclopedia of Social Theory.* Thousand Oaks, Calif.: Sage: 196–197.

Piccone, Paul
1990   "Paradoxes of Perestroika." *Telos* 84:3–32.

Pickering, Mary
1993   *Auguste Comte: An Intellectual Biography.* Vol. 1. Cambridge. Eng.: Cambridge University Press.
1997   "A New Look at Auguste Comte." In Charles Camic (ed.), *Reclaiming the Sociological Classics: The State of Scholarship.* Oxford: Blackwell: 11–44.
2000   "Auguste Comte." In George Ritzer (ed.), *The Blackwell Companion to Major Social Theorists.* Malden, Mass.: Blackwell: 25–52.

Pierce, Jennifer
1995   *Gender Trials: Emotional Lives in Contemporary Law Firms.* Berkeley: University of California Press.

Pieterse, Jan N.
2004   *Globalization and Culture: Global Melange.* Lanham, Md.: Rowman and
            Littlefield.

Piontek, Thomas
2006   *Queering Gay and Lesbian Studies.* Urbana: University of Illinois Press.

Poggi, Gianfranco
1993   *Money and the Modern Mind: Georg Simmel's Philosophy of Money.* Berkeley:
            University of California Press.

Polit, Denise F., and Falbo, Toni
1987   "Only Children and Personality Development: A Quantitative Review." *Journal
            of Marriage and the Family* 49:309–325.

Pollner, Melvin
1987   *Mundane Reason: Reality in Everyday and Sociological Discourse.* Cambridge,
            Eng.: Cambridge University Press.
1991   "Left of Ethnomethodology: The Rise and Decline of Radical Reflexivity."
            American Sociological Review 56:370–380.

Portes, Alejandro, and Landolt, Patricia
1996   "The Downside of Social Capital." *American Prospect* 26:18–21.

Postone, Moishe, LiPuma, Edward, and Calhoun, Craig
1993   "Introduction: Bourdieu and Social Theory." In C. Calhoun, E. LiPuma, and
            M. Postone (eds.), *Bourdieu: Critical Perspectives.* Chicago: University of
            Chicago Press: 1–13.

Powell, Jason and Owen, Tim (eds.)
In Press   *Reconstructing Postmodernism.* New York: Nova Science.

Powers, Charles H.
1986   *Vilfredo Pareto.* Newbury Park, Calif.: Sage.
2005b   "Veblen, Thorstein." In George Ritzer (ed.), *Encyclopedia of Social Theory.*
            Thousand Oaks, Calif.: Sage: 863–864.

Prager, Jeffrey
2005   "Psychoanalysis and Social Theory." In George Ritzer (ed.), *Encyclopedia of
            Social Theory.* Thousand Oaks, Calif.: Sage: 607–613.

Prendergast, Christopher
2005a   "Schutz, Alfred." In George Ritzer (ed.), *Encyclopedia of Social Theory.*
            Thousand Oaks, Calif.: Sage: 674–675.
2005c   "Levels of Social Structure." In George Ritzer (ed.), *Encyclopedia of Social
            Theory.* Thousand Oaks, Calif.: Sage: 441–443.

Prus, Robert
1996   *Symbolic Interaction and Ethnographic Research: Intersubjectivity and the
            Study of Human Lived Experience.* Albany: State University of New York Press.

Przeworski, Adam
1985   *Capitalism and Social Democracy.* Cambridge, Eng.: Cambridge University Press.

Putnam, Robert
2001   *Bowling Alone: The Collapse and Revival of American Community.* New York:
            Simon and Schuster.

Quadagno, Jill
1979   "Paradigms in Evolutionary Theory: The Sociobiological Model of Natural
             Selection." *American Sociological Review* 44:100–109.

Rachlin, Allan
1991   "Rehumanizing Dialectic: Toward an Understanding of the Interpenetration of
             Structure and Subjectivity." *Current Perspectives in Social Theory* 11:255–269.

Radnitzky, Gerard
1973   *Contemporary Schools of Metascience.* Chicago: Regnery.

Radway, Janice
1984   *Reading the Romance: Women, Patriarchy and Popular Literature.* Chapel Hill:
             University of North Carolina Press.

Rambo, Eric
1995   "Conceiving Best Outcomes within a Theory of Utility Maximization: A
             Culture-Level Critique." *Sociological Theory* 13:145–162.

Ramji, Hasmita
2007   "Difference." In George Ritzer (ed.), *The Blackwell Encyclopedia of Sociology.*
             Oxford: Blackwell: 1153–1155.

Rammstedt, Otthein
1991   "On Simmel's Aesthetics: Argumentation in the Journal *Jugend,* 1897–1906."
             Theory, Culture and Society 8:125–144.

Rasch, William
2000   *Niklas Luhmann's Modernity: The Paradoxes of Differentiation.* Stanford, Calif.:
             Stanford University Press.

Rawls, Anne Warfield
2000   "Harold Garfinkel." In George Ritzer (ed.), *The Blackwell Companion to Major
             Social Theorists.* Malden, Mass.: Blackwell: 545–576.
2005a   "Conversation Analysis." In George Ritzer (ed.), *Encyclopedia of Social Theory.*
             Thousand Oaks, Calif.: Sage: 145–149.
2005b   "Garfinkel, Harold." In George Ritzer (ed.), *Encyclopedia of Social Theory.*
             Thousand Oaks, Calif.: Sage: 301–304.
2007   "Durkheim, Emile." In George Ritzer (ed.), *The Blackwell Encyclopedia of
             Sociology.* Oxford: Blackwell: 1250–1261.

Reckwitz, Andreas
2002   "Toward a Theory of Social Practices: A Development in Culturist Theorizing.
             European Journal of Social Theory 5(2): 243–263.

Reagon, Bernice Johnson
1982/1995   "My Black Mothers and Sisters; or, On Beginning a Cultural Autobiography."
             In C. Goldberg and H. Hartmann (eds.), *U.S. Women in Struggle.* Chicago:
             University of Illinois Press: 296–310.

Reddock, Rhoda
2000   "Feminist Theory and Critical Reconceptualization in Sociology: The Challenge
             of the 1990s." In Stella Quah and Arnaud Sales (eds.), *The International
             Handbook of Sociology.* London: Sage: 84–100.

Reedy, W. Jay
1994   "The Historical Imaginary of Social Science in Post-Revolutionary France:
             Bonald, Saint-Simon, Comte." *History of the Human Sciences* 7:1–26.

Reiger, K.
1999   "'Sort of Part of the Women's Movement. But Different': Mothers'
            Organisations and Australian Feminism." *Women's Studies International Forum*
            22(6):585–595.

Reitz-Pstejovsky, M.
2002   "Is the Care We Provide Homeless People Just? The Ethic of Justice Informing
            the Ethic of Care." *Journal of Social Distress and the Homeless* 11:233–248.

Remennick, Larissa
2007   "Transnationalism." In George Ritzer (ed.), *The Blackwell Encyclopedia of
            Sociology.* Oxford: Blackwell: 5064–5066.

Reskin, Barbara, and Padavic, Irene
1994   *Women and Men at Work.* Thousand Oaks, Calif.: Pine Forge Press.

Rhoades, Lawrence J.
1981   *A History of the American Sociological Association.* Washington, D.C.:
            American Sociological Association.

Rhode, Deborah L.
1997   *Speaking of Sex: The Denial of Gender Inequality.* Cambridge, Mass.: Harvard
            University Press.

Rich, Adrienne
1976   *Of Woman Born: Motherhood as Experience and Institution.* New York:
            Bantam.
1980   "Compulsory Heterosexual and Lesbian Experience." In C. R. Stimson and
            E. S. Person (eds.), *Women, Sex, and Sexuality.* Chicago: University of Chicago
            Press: 62–91.
1993   *What Is Found There: Notebooks on Poetry and Politics.* New York: Norton.

Richardson, Diane (ed.)
1996   *Theorising Heterosexuality.* Buckingham, Eng.: Open University Press.

Ridgeway, Cecelia
1997   "Interaction and the Conservation of Gender Inequality: Considering
            Employment." *American Sociological Review* 62:218–235.

Riesman, David
1950   *The Lonely Crowd.* New Haven, Conn.: Yale University Press.

Riger, Stephanie, and Krieglstein, Maryann
2000   "The Impact of Welfare Reform on Men's Violence against Women." *American
            Journal of Community Psychology* 28:631–647.

Risman, Barbara J.
2001   "Calling the Bluff of Value-Free Science." *American Sociological Review*
            66:605–611.

Risman, Barbara, and Ferree, Myra Marx
1995   "Making Gender Visible." *American Sociological Review* 60:775–782.

Ritzer, George
1975a   *Sociology: A Multiple Paradigm Science.* Boston: Allyn and Bacon.
1975b   "Sociology: A Multiple Paradigm Science." *American Sociologist* 10:156–167.

1979   "Toward an Integrated Sociological Paradigm." In W. Snizek et al. (eds.),
                Contemporary Issues in Theory and Research. Westport, Conn.: Greenwood
                Press: 25–46.
1980   *Sociology: A Multiple Paradigm Science.* Rev. ed. Boston: Allyn and Bacon.
1981a   *Toward an Integrated Sociological Paradigm: The Search for an Exemplar and
                an Image of the Subject Matter.* Boston: Allyn and Bacon.
1981b   "Paradigm Analysis in Sociology: Clarifying the Issues." *American Sociological
                Review* 46:245–248.
1983   "The McDonaldization of Society." *Journal of American Culture* 6:100–107.
1985   "The Rise of Micro-Sociological Theory." *Sociological Theory* 3:88–98.
1988   "Sociological Metatheory: Defending a Subfield by Delineating Its Parameters."
                Sociological Theory 6:187–200.
1989   "Of Levels and 'Intellectual Amnesia.'" *Sociological Theory* 7:226–229.
1990a   "Micro-Macro Linkage in Sociological Theory: Applying a Metatheoretical
                Tool." In George Ritzer (ed.), *Frontiers of Social Theory: The New Syntheses.*
                New York: Columbia University Press: 347–370.
1990b   "The Current Status of Sociological Theory: The New Syntheses." In George
                Ritzer (ed.), *Frontiers of Social Theory: The New Syntheses.* New York:
                Columbia University Press: 1–30.
1991a   "Metatheorizing in Sociology." *Sociological Forum* 5:3–15.
1991b   *Metatheorizing in Sociology.* Lexington, Mass.: Lexington Books.
1991d   "The Recent History and the Emerging Reality of American Sociological
                Theory: A Metatheoretical Interpretation." *Sociological Forum* 6:269–287.
1992b   "Metatheorizing in Sociology: Explaining the Coming of Age." In George
                Ritzer (ed.), *Metatheorizing.* Newbury Park, Calif.: Sage: 7–26.
1993   *The McDonaldization of Society.* Thousand Oaks, Calif.: Pine Forge Press.
1995   *Expressing America: A Critique of the Global Credit Card Society.* Thousand
                Oaks, Calif.: Pine Forge Press.
1996   *The McDonaldization of Society.* Rev. ed. Thousand Oaks, Calif.: Pine Forge Press.
1997   *Postmodern Social Theory.* New York: McGraw-Hill.
1998   *The McDonaldization Thesis.* London: Sage.
1999   *Enchanting a Disenchanted World: Revolutionizing the Means of Consumption.*
                Thousand Oaks, Calif.: Pine Forge Press.
2000a   *The McDonaldization of Society.* New Century Edition. Thousand Oaks, Calif.:
                Pine Forge Press.
2004a   *The McDonaldization of Society.* Revised New Century Edition. Thousand
                Oaks, Calif.: Pine Forge Press.
2004b   *The Globalization of Nothing.* Thousand Oaks, Calif.: Pine Forge Press.
2005a   *Enchanting a Disenchanted World: Revolutionizing the Means of
                Consumption.* 2nd ed. Thousand Oaks, Calif.: Pine Forge Press.
2005b   "Paradigm." In George Ritzer (ed.), *Encyclopedia of Social Theory.* Thousand
                Oaks, Calif.: Sage: 543–544.
2007b   "Metatheory." In George Ritzer (ed.), *The Blackwell Encyclopedia of Sociology.*
                Oxford: Blackwell: 2964–2967.
2007c   *The Globalization of Nothing 2.* Thousand Oaks, Calif.: Pine Forge Press.

Ritzer, George (ed.)
1991c   "Recent Explorations in Sociological Metatheorizing." *Sociological Perspectives*
                34:237–390.

1992a   *Metatheorizing.* Newbury Park, Calif.: Sage.
2002   *McDonaldization: The Reader.* Thousand Oaks, Calif.: Pine Forge Press.
2006   *The McDonaldization Reader.* 2nd ed. Thousand Oaks, Calif.: Sage.

Ritzer, George, and Gindoff, Pamela
1992   "Methodological Relationism: Lessons for and from Social Psychology." *Social Psychology Quarterly* 55:128–140.
1994   "Agency-Structure, Micro-Macro, Individualism-Holism-Relationism: A Metatheoretical Explanation of Theoretical Convergence between the United States and Europe." In P. Sztompka (ed.), *Agency and Structure: Reorienting Social Theory.* Amsterdam: Gordon and Breach: 3–23.

Ritzer, George, and Goodman, Douglas
2001   "Postmodern Social Theory." In Jonathan Turner (ed.), *Handbook of Sociological Theory.* New York: Kluwer Academic/Plenum Publishers: 151–169.

Ritzer, George, Goodman, Douglas, and Wiedenhoft, Wendy
2001   "Theories of Consumption." In George Ritzer and Barry Smart (eds.), *Handbook of Social Theory.* London: Sage: 410–427.

Ritzer, George, and Ryan, J. Michael
2007a   "Elias, Norbert." In George Ritzer (ed.), *The Blackwell Encyclopedia of Sociology.* Oxford: Blackwell: 1357–59.

Ritzer, George, and Walczak, David
1988   "Rationalization and the Deprofessionalization of Physicians." *Social Forces* 67:1–22.

Ritzer, George, Zhao, Shanyang, and Murphy, Jim
2001   "Metatheorizing in Sociology: The Basic Parameters and the Potential Contributions of Postmodernism." In Jonathan H. Turner (ed.), *Handbook of Sociological Theory.* New York: Kluwer Academic/Plenum Publishers: 113–131.

Robbins, Derek
1991   *The Work of Pierre Bourdieu.* Boulder, Colo.: Westview Press.

Robertson, Roland
1992   *Globalization: Social Theory and Global Culture.* London: Sage.
2001   "Globalization Theory 2000+: Major Problematics." In George Ritzer and Barry Smart (Eds.), *Handbook of Social Theory.* London: Sage: 458–471.

Robinson, F.
2001   *Globalizing Care: Ethics, Feminist Theory, and International Relations.* Binghampton, N.Y.: Haworth Press.

Robinson, W. I.
2004   *A Theory of Global Capitalism.* Baltimore: Johns Hopkins University Press.
2007   "Theories of Globalization." In George Ritzer (ed), *The Blackwell Companion to Globalization.* Oxford: Blackwell: 125–143.

Rocher, Guy
1975   *Talcott Parsons and American Sociology.* New York: Barnes and Noble.

Rock, Paul
1979   *The Making of Symbolic Interactionism.* Totowa, N.J.: Rowman and Littlefield.

Roemer, John
1982   *A General Theory of Exploitation and Class.* Cambridge, Mass.: Harvard University Press.

1986a   "Introduction." In J. Roemer (ed.), *Analytical Marxism.* Cambridge, Eng.:
Cambridge University Press: 1–7.

1986b   " 'Rational Choice' Marxism: Some Issues of Method and Substance." In
J. Roemer (ed.), *Analytical Marxism.* Cambridge, Eng.: Cambridge University
Press: 191–201.

Rogers, Mary

1996b   "Theory—What? Why? How?" In Mary F. Rogers (ed.), *Multicultural
Experiences, Multicultural Theories.* New York: McGraw-Hill: 11–16.

2000   "Alfred Schutz." In George Ritzer (ed.), *The Blackwell Companion to Major
Social Theorists.* Malden, Mass.: Blackwell: 367–387.

2001   "Contemporary Feminist Theory." In George Ritzer and Barry Smart (eds.),
Handbook of Social Theory. London: Sage: 285–296.

Rogowski, Ralf

2007   "Luhmann, Niklas." In George Ritzer (ed.), *The Blackwell Encyclopedia of
Sociology.* Oxford: Blackwell: 2675–2678.

Rojek, Chris

2003   *Stuart Hall.* Cambridge, Eng.: Polity Press.

2005   "Hall, Stuart." In George Ritzer (ed.), *Encyclopedia of Social Theory.* Thousand
Oaks, Calif.: Sage: 353–356.

Rose, Arnold

1962   "A Systematic Summary of Symbolic Interaction Theory." In A. Rose (ed.),
Human Behavior and Social Processes. Boston: Houghton Mifflin.

Rose, Nancy E.

1995   *Workfare or Fair Work: Women, Welfare, and Government Work Programs.* New
Brunswick, N.J.: Rutgers University Press.

Rosenau, James N.

2003   *Distant Proximities: Dynamics beyond Globalization.* Princeton, N.J.: Princeton
University Press.

Rosenau, Pauline Marie

1992   *Post-Modernism and the Social Sciences: Insights, Inroads, and Intrusions.*
Princeton, N.J.: Princeton University Press.

Rosenberg, Julius

2005   "Globalization Theory: A Post Mortem." *International Politics* 42:2–74.

Rosenberg, Morris

1989   *"Self-Concept Research: A Historical Review." Social Forces* 68:34–44.

Rosenberg, Rosalind

1982   *Beyond Separate Spheres: Intellectual Roots of Modern Feminism.* New Haven:
Yale University Press.

1992   *Divided Lives: American Women in the Twentieth Century.* New York: Hill
and Wang.

Rosenthal, Naomi, Fingrutd, Meryl, Ethier, Michele, and Karant, Roberta

1985   "Social Movements and Network Analysis: A Case Study of Nineteenth-
Century Women's Reform in New York State." *American Journal of Sociology*
90:1022–1054.

Ross, Dorothy
1991   *The Origins of American Social Science.* Cambridge, Eng.: Cambridge
            University Press.

Rossel, Jorg, and Collins, Randall
2001   "Conflict Theory and Interaction Rituals." In Jonathan H. Turner (ed.), *Handbook
            of Sociological Theory.* New York: Kluwer Academic/Plenum Publishers: 509–531.

Rossi, Alice
1977   "A Biosocial Perspective on Parenting." *Daedalus* 106:9–31.
1983   "Gender and Parenthood." *American Sociological Review* 49:1–19.

Rossi, Ino
2005   "Lévi-Strauss, Claude." In George Ritzer (ed.), *Encyclopedia of Social Theory.*
            Thousand Oaks, Calif.: Sage: 443–446.

Roth, Louise Marie
1999   "The Right to Privacy Is Political: Power, the Boundary between Public and
            Private, and Sexual Harassment." *Law & Social Inquiry* 24(1):45–71.

Rowe, A. M. C.
2000   "Locating Feminism's Subject: The Paradox of White Femininity and the
            Struggle to Forge Feminist Alliances." *Communication Theory* 10:64–80.

Rubenstein, David
1986   "The Concept of Structure in Sociology." In M. L. Wardell and S. P. Turner
            (eds.), *Sociological Theory in Transition.* Boston: Allen and Unwin: 80–94.

Ruddick, Sara
1980   "Maternal Thinking." *Feminist Studies* 6:342–367.
1994   "Notes towards a Feminist Maternal Peace Politics." In A. Jaggar (ed.), *Living
            with Contradictions: Controversies in Feminist Social Ethics.* Boulder, Colo.:
            Westview Press.

Rudy, Kathy
2001   "Radical Feminism, Lesbian Separatism, and Queer Theory." *Feminist Studies*
            27:191–222.

Ruef, Martin
2007   "Mannheim, Karl." In George Ritzer (ed.), *The Blackwell Encyclopedia of
            Sociology.* Oxford: Blackwell: 2756–2759.

Rundell, John
2001   "Modernity, Enlightenment, Revolution and Romanticism: Creating Social
            Theory." In George Ritzer and Barry Smart (eds.), *Handbook of Social Theory.*
            London: Sage: 13–29.
2005   "Elias, Norbert." In George Ritzer (ed.), *Encyclopedia of Social Theory.*
            Thousand Oaks, Calif.: Sage: 239–245.

Russell, Diana E.
1998   *Dangerous Relationships: Pornography, Misogyny, and Rape.* Thousand Oaks,
            Calif.: Sage.

Ryan, J. Michael
2005a   "Micro-Macro Integration." In George Ritzer (ed.), *Encyclopedia of Social
            Theory.* Thousand Oaks, Calif.: Sage: 501–503.

2005b   "Agency-Structure Integration." In George Ritzer (ed.), *Encyclopedia of Social Theory*. Thousand Oaks, Calif.: Sage: 5–6.

2007   "Grobalization." In George Ritzer (ed.), *The Blackwell Encyclopedia of Sociology*. Oxford: Blackwell: 2022–2023.

Ryan, William

1971   *Blaming the Victim*. New York: Pantheon.

Said, Edward

1978   *Orientalism*. New York; Pantheon.

Salamini, Leonardo

1981   *The Sociology of Political Praxis: An Introduction to Gramsci's Theory*. London: Routledge and Kegan Paul.

Salomon, A.

1945   "German Sociology." In G. Gurvitch and W. F. Moore (eds.), *Twentieth Century Sociology*. New York: Philosophical Library: 586–614.

1963/1997   "Georg Simmel Reconsidered." In Gary D. Jaworski, *Georg Simmel and the American Prospect*. Albany: State University of New York Press: 91–108.

Sanday, Peggy Reeves

1974   "Female Status in the Public Domain." In M. Rosaldo and L. Lamphere (eds.), *Women, Culture and Society: A Theoretical Overview*. Stanford, Calif.: Stanford University Press: 189–206.

1981   *Female Power and Male Dominance*. Cambridge, Eng.: Cambridge University Press.

1996   *A Woman Scorned: Acquaintance Rape on Trial*. New York: Doubleday.

Sanderson, Stephen K.

2007   "Conflict Theory." In George Ritzer (ed.), *The Blackwell Encyclopedia of Sociology*. Oxford: Blackwell: 662–665.

Sandstrom, Kent L., and Kleinman, Sherryl

2005   "Symbolic Interaction." In George Ritzer (ed.), *Encyclopedia of Social Theory*. Thousand Oaks, Calif.: Sage: 821–826.

Sandstrom, Kent L., Martin, Daniel D., and Fine, Gary Alan

2001   "Symbolic Interactionism at the End of the Century." In George Ritzer and Barry Smart (eds.), *Handbook of Social Theory*. London: Sage: 217–231.

Sassen, Saskia

1998   *Globalization and Its Discontents*. New York: New Press.

2004   "Local Actors in Global Politics." *Current Sociology* 52:649–670.

Satoshi, Kamata

1982   *Japan in the Passing Lane*. New York: Pantheon.

Saunders, Peter

1989   "Space, Urbanism and the Created Environment." In D. Held and J. B. Thompson (eds.), *Social Theory of Modern Societies: Anthony Giddens and His Critics*. Cambridge, Eng.: Cambridge University Press: 215–234.

Sawicki, Jana

1991   *Disciplining Foucault: Feminism, Power and the Body*. New York: Routledge.

Sawyer, R. Keith

2005   "Emergence." In George Ritzer (ed.), *Encyclopedia of Social Theory*. Thousand Oaks, Calif.: Sage: 245–246.

2007   "Complexity and Emergence." In George Ritzer (ed.), *The Blackwell Encyclopedia of Sociology*. Oxford: Blackwell: 633–636.

Scaff, Lawrence
1989   *Fleeing the Iron Cage: Culture, Politics, and Modernity in the Thought of Max Weber*. Berkeley: University of California Press.

Scambler, Graham
1996   "The 'Project of Modernity' and the Parameters for a Critical Sociology: An Argument with Illustrations from Medical Sociology." *Sociology* 30:567–581.

Schaeffer, D.
2001   "Feminism and Liberalism Reconsidered: The Case of Catharine MacKinnon." *American Political Science Review* 95:699–708.

Schatzki, Theodore R.
1996   *Social Practices: A Wittgensteinian Approach to Human Activity and the Social*. Cambridge, Eng.: Cambridge University Press.

Schatzki, Theodore R., Knorr-Cetina, Karin, and von Savigny, E. (eds.)
2001   *The Practice Turn in Contemporary Theory*. London: Routledge.

Scheff, Thomas
2007   "Microsociology." In George Ritzer (ed.), *The Blackwell Encyclopedia of Sociology*. Oxford: Blackwell: 3005–3008.

Schegloff, Emanuel
1979   "Identification and Recognition in Telephone Conversation Openings." In G. Psathas (ed.), *Everyday Language: Studies in Ethnomethodology*. New York: Irvington: 23–78.
2001   "Accounts of Conduct in Interaction: Interruption, Overlap, and Turn-Taking." In Jonathan H. Turner (ed.), *Handbook of Sociological Theory*. New York: Kluwer Academic/Plenum Publishers: 287–321.

Scheper-Hughes, Nancy
1992   *Death without Weeping: The Violence of Everyday Life in Brazil*. Berkeley: University of California Press.

Scheurich, James Joseph, and McKenzie, Kathryn Bell
2007   "Foucaldian Archeological Analysis." In George Ritzer (ed.), *The Blackwell Encyclopedia of Sociology*. Oxford: Blackwell: 1771–1774.

Schimank, Uwe
1996   *Theorien Gesellschaftlicher Differenzierung*. Opladen: Leske and Budrich.

Schmidt, Neal, Gooding, Richard Z., Noe, Raymond A., and Kirsch, Michael
1984   "Meta-Analyses of Validity Studies Published between 1964 and 1982 and the Investigation of Study Characteristics." *Personnel Psychology* 37:407–422.

Schmitt, Raymond L., and Schmitt, Tiffani Mari
1996   "Community Fear of AIDS as Enacted Emotion: A Comparative Investigation of Mead's Concept of the Social Act." *Studies in Symbolic Interaction* 20:91–119.

Schmutz, Corinne
1996   "The Service Industry and Marx's Fetishism of Commodities." *Humanity and Society* 20:102–105.

Schneider, Louis
1967   *The Scottish Moralists: On Human Nature and Society.* Chicago: University of
            Chicago Press.
1971   "Dialectic in Sociology." *American Sociological Review* 36:667–678.

Scholte, J. A.
2005   *Globalization: A Critical Introduction.* 2nd ed. Basingstoke, Eng.: Palgrave
            Macmillan.

Schroeter, Gerd
1985   "Dialogue, Debate, or Dissent? The Difficulties of Assessing Max Weber's
            Relation to Marx." In R. J. Antonio and R. M. Glassman (eds.), *A Weber-Marx
            Dialogue.* Lawrence: University of Kansas Press: 2–13.

Schroyer, Trent
1970   "Toward a Critical Theory of Advanced Industrial Society." In H. P. Dreitzel (ed.),
            Recent Sociology: No. 2. New York: Macmillan: 210–234.
1973   *The Critique of Domination.* Boston: Beacon Press.

Schubert, Hans-Joachim
2005   "Cooley, Charles Horton." In George Ritzer (ed.), *Encyclopedia of Social
            Theory.* Thousand Oaks, Calif.: Sage: 150–155.
2007   "Cooley, Charles Horton." In George Ritzer (ed.), *The Blackwell Encyclopedia
            of Sociology.* Oxford: Blackwell: 798–801.

Schulz, Markus S.
2007a   "Horkheimer, Max." In George Ritzer (ed.), *The Blackwell Encyclopedia of
            Sociology.* Oxford: Blackwell: 2163–2165.
2007b   "Adorno, Theodor W." In George Ritzer (ed.), *The Blackwell Encyclopedia of
            Sociology.* Oxford: Blackwell: 27–30.

Schutte, Gerhard
2007   "Phenomenology." In George Ritzer (ed.), *The Blackwell Encyclopedia of
            Sociology.* Oxford: Blackwell: 3401–3404.

Schutz, Alfred
1932/1967   *The Phenomenology of the Social World.* Evanston, Ill.: Northwestern
            University Press.

Schwalbe, Michael L.
1993   "Goffman against Postmodernism: Emotion and the Reality of the Self."
            Symbolic Interaction 16:333–350.
2005   "Self and Self-Concept." In George Ritzer (ed.), *Encyclopedia of Social Theory.*
            Thousand Oaks, Calif.: Sage: 684–687.

Schwanenberg, Enno
1971   "The Two Problems of Order in Parsons' Theory: An Analysis from Within."
            Social Forces 49:569–581.

Schwartz, Justin
1995   "In Defence of Exploitation." *Economics and Philosophy* 11:275–307.

Schwartz, Pepper
1994   *Peer Marriage: How Love between Equals Really Works.* New York:
            Free Press.

Schweber, Silvan S.
1991   "Auguste Comte and the Nebular Hypothesis." In R. T. Bienvenu and
            M. Feingold (eds.), *In the Presence of the Past: Essays in Honor of Frank
            Manuel.* Dordrecht, Netherlands: Kluwer: 131–191.

Schwendinger, Julia, and Schwendinger, Herman
1974   *Sociologists of the Chair.* New York: Basic Books.

Schwinn, Thomas
1998   "False Connections: Systems and Action Theories in Neofunctionalism and in
            Jurgen Habermas." *Sociological Theory* 16:75–95.

Scimecca, Joseph
1977   *The Sociological Theory of C. Wright Mills.* Port Washington, N.Y.: Kennikat Press.

Sciulli, David, and Gerstein, Dean
1985   "Social Theory and Talcott Parsons in the 1980s." *Annual Review of Sociology*
            11:369–387.

Scully, Diana
1990   *Understanding Sexual Violence: A Study of Convicted Rapists.* Boston:
            Unwin Hyman.

Searle, John
1972   "Chomsky's Revolution in Linguistics." *New York Review of Books* 18:16–24.

Sedgwick, Eve Kosofsky
1985   *Between Men: English Literature and Male Homosexual Desire.* New York:
            Columbia University Press.
1990   *Epistemology of the Closet.* Berkeley: University of California Press.

Segura, Denise A., and Pierce, Jennifer
1993   "Chicana/o Family Structure and Gender Personality: Chodorow, Familism, and
            Psychoanalytic Sociology Revisited." *Signs* 19:62–91.

Seidman, Steven
1983   *Liberalism and the Origins of European Social Theory.* Berkeley: University
            of California Press.
1989   "Introduction." In S. Seidman (ed.), *Jurgen Habermas on Society and Politics:
            A Reader.* Boston: Beacon Press: 1–25.
1991   "The End of Sociological Theory: The Postmodern Hope." *Sociological Theory*
            9:131–146.

Seidman, Steven, and Alexander, Jeffrey (eds.)
2001   *The New Social Theory Reader.* New York: Routledge.

Sewart, John J.
1978   "Critical Theory and the Critique of Conservative Method." *American
            Sociologist* 13:15–22.

Shalin, Dmitri
1986   "Pragmatism and Social Interactionism." *American Sociological Review* 51:9–29.
2000   "George Herbert Mead." In George Ritzer (ed.), *The Blackwell Companion to
            Major Social Theorists.* Malden, Mass.: Blackwell: 302–344.

Sharrock, Wes
2001   "Fundamentals of Ethnomethodology." In George Ritzer and Barry Smart
            (eds.), *Handbook of Social Theory*. London: Sage: 249–259.

Sharrock, Wes, and Anderson, Bob
1986   *The Ethnomethodologists*. Chichester, Eng.: Ellis Horwood.

Shelton, Beth Anne
2000   "Understanding the Distribution of Housework Between Husbands and Wives."
            In Linda J. Waite, Christine Bachrach, Michelle Hindin, Elizabeth Thomson,
            and Arland Thornton (eds.), *The Ties That Bind: Perspectives on Marriage and
            Cohabitation*. New York: Aldine de Gruyter: 343–355.

Shelton, Beth Anne, and Agger, Ben
1993   "Shotgun Wedding, Unhappy Marriage, No-Fault Divorce? Rethinking the
            Feminism-Marxism Relationship." In P. England (ed.), *Theory on Gender/
            Gender on Theory*. New York: Aldine de Gruyter.

Sheridan, Alan
1980   *Michel Foucault: The Will to Truth*. London: Tavistock.

Shilling, Chris
1997   "The Undersocialised Conception of the Embodied Agent in Modern
            Sociology." *Sociology* 31:737–754.

Shilling, Chris, and Mellor, Philip A.
1996   "Embodiment, Structuration Theory and Modernity: Mind/Body Dualism and
            the Repression of Sensuality." *Body and Society* 2:1–15.

Shils, Edward
1996   "The Sociology of Robert E. Park." *American Sociologist* 27:88–106.

Shreve, Anita
1989   *Women Together, Women Alone: The Legacy of the Consciousness Raising
            Movement*. New York: Viking.

Sica, Alan
2005   "Modernity." In George Ritzer (ed.), *Encyclopedia of Social Theory*. Thousand
            Oaks, Calif.: Sage: 505–511.

Silva, Elizabeth
2005   "Gender, Home and Family in Cultural Capital Theory." *British Journal of
            Sociology* 56:83–103.

Simmel, Georg
1903/1971   "The Metropolis and Mental Life." In D. Levine (ed.), *Georg Simmel*.
            Chicago: University of Chicago Press: 324–339.
1907/1978   *The Philosophy of Money*. Ed. and trans. Tom Bottomore and David Frisby
            London: Routledge and Kegan Paul.

Simon, Herbert
1957   *Administrative Behavior*. New York: Free Press.

Simpson, Brent
2007   "Rational Choice Theories." In George Ritzer (ed.), *The Blackwell
            Encyclopedia of Sociology*. Oxford: Blackwell: 3794–3799.

Singer, Brian C. J.
2005a   "Rousseau, Jean-Jacques." In George Ritzer (ed.), *Encyclopedia of Social
             Theory.* Thousand Oaks, Calif.: Sage: 656–658.
2005b   "Montesquieu, Charles Louis de Secondat." In George Ritzer (ed.),
             Encyclopedia of Social Theory. Thousand Oaks, Calif.: Sage: 512–515.

Sitton, John F.
1996   "Disembodied Capitalism: Habermas's Conception of the Economy."
             Sociological Forum 13:61–83.

Sjoberg, Gideon, Gill, Elizabeth, Littrell, Boyd, and Williams, Norma
1997   "The Reemergence of John Dewey and American Pragmatism." In Norman
             K. Denzin (ed.), *Studies in Symbolic Interaction,* Vol. 21. Greenwich, Conn.:
             JAI Press: 73–92.

Skeggs, Beverley
2004   "Context and Background: Pierre Bourdieu's Analysis of Class, Gender and
             Sexuality." In Lisa Adkins and Beverley Skeggs (ed.), *Feminism after Bourdieu.*
             Oxford: Blackwell: 19–34.

Skelton, Christine
2005   "The 'Individualized' (Woman) in the Academy: Ulrich Beck, Gender and
             Power." *Gender and Education* 17:319–332.

Sklair, Leslie
2002   *Globalization: Capitalism and Its Alternatives.* Oxford: Oxford University Press.

Skocpol, Theda
1979   *States and Social Revolutions.* Cambridge, Eng.: Cambridge University Press.

Slater, Don
1997   *Consumer Culture and Modernity.* Cambridge, Eng.: Polity Press.
2005   "Consumer Culture." In George Ritzer (ed.), *Encyclopedia of Social Theory.*
             Thousand Oaks, Calif.: Sage: 139–145.

Smart, Barry
1983   *Foucault, Marxism and Critique.* London: Routledge and Kegan Paul.
1985   *Michel Foucault.* Chichester, Eng.: Ellis Horwood.
1993   *Postmodernity.* London: Routledge.
2000   "Michel Foucault." In George Ritzer (ed.), *The Blackwell Companion to Major
             Social Theorists.* Malden, Mass.: Blackwell: 630–650.

Smelser, Neil
1959   *Social Change in the Industrial Revolution.* Chicago: University of Chicago Press.
1962   *Theory of Collective Behavior.* New York: Free Press.
1992   "The Rational Choice Perspective: A Theoretical Assessment." *Rationality and
             Society* 4:381–410.
1997   *Problematics of Sociology: The Georg Simmel Lectures, 1995.* Berkeley:
             University of California Press.

Smith, Cyril
1997   "Friedrich Engels and Marx's Critique of Political Economy." *Capital and
             Class* 62:123–142.

Smith, David Norman
1996   "The Social Construction of Enemies: Jews and the Representation of Evil."
             Sociological Theory 14:203–240.

Smith, Dennis
1999   "The Civilizing Process and the History of Sexuality: Comparing Norbert Elias
            and Michel Foucault." *Theory and Society* 28:79–100.
2001   *Norbert Elias and Modern Social Theory.* London, Thousand Oaks, Calif: Sage.

Smith, Dorothy
1979   "A Sociology for Women." In J. A. Sherman and E. T. Beck (eds.), *The
            Prism of Sex: Essays in the Sociology of Knowledge.* Madison: University
            of Wisconsin Press.
1987   *The Everyday World as Problematic: A Feminist Sociology.* Boston:
            Northeastern University Press.
1989   "Sociological Theory: Methods of Writing Patriarchy." In R. A. Wallace (ed.),
            Feminism and Sociological Theory. Newbury Park, Calif.: Sage: 34–64.
1990a   *The Conceptual Practices of Power: A Feminist Sociology of Knowledge.*
            Boston: Northeastern University Press.
1990b   *Texts, Facts and Femininity: Exploring the Relations of Ruling.* London:
            Routledge and Kegan Paul.
1999a   "From Women's Standpoint to a Sociology for People." In Janet L.
            Abu-Lughod (ed.) *Sociology for the Twenty-First Century.* Chicago:
            University of Chicago Press: 65–82.
1999b   *Writing the Social: Critique, Theory, and Investigations.* Toronto: University of
            Toronto Press.
2000a   "Schooling for Inequality." *Signs* 25:1147–1151.

Smith, Gregory W. H.
2007   "Goffman, Erving." In George Ritzer (ed.), *The Blackwell Encyclopedia of
            Sociology.* Oxford: Blackwell: 1995–1999.

Smith, Melanie
2007   "Glocalization." In George Ritzer (ed.), *The Blackwell Encyclopedia of
            Sociology.* Oxford: Blackwell: 1994–1995.

Smith, Norman Erik
1979   "William Graham Sumner as an Anti-Social Darwinist." *Pacific Sociological
            Review* 22:332–347.

Smith, T. V.
1931   "The Social Philosophy of George Herbert Mead." *American Journal of
            Sociology* 37:368–385.

Smouts, Marie-Claude
2001   *The New International Relations: Theory and Practice.* New York: Palgrave
            Macmillan.

Snitow, Ann Barr, Stansell, Christine, and Thompson, Sharon
1983   *Powers of Desire: The Politics of Sexuality.* New York: Monthly Review Press.

Snizek, William E.
1976   "An Empirical Assessment of 'Sociology: A Multiple Paradigm Science.'"
            American Sociologist 11:217–219.

Snizek, William E., Fuhrman, Ellsworth, R., and Miller, Michael K. (eds.)
1979   *Contemporary Issues in Theory and Research.* Westport, Conn.: Greenwood Press.

Snow, David
2001   "Extending and Broadening Blumer's Conceptualization of Symbolic
            Interactionism." *Symbolic Interaction* 24:367–377.
2007   "Frame." In George Ritzer (ed.), *The Blackwell Encyclopedia of Sociology.*
            Oxford: Blackwell: 1778–1780.

Soja, Edward W.
1989   *Postmodern Geographies: The Reassertion of Space in Critical Theory.*
            London: Verso.
1996   *Thirdspace: Journeys to Los Angeles and the Real-and-Imagined Places.*
            Malden, Mass.: Blackwell.
2000   *Postmetropolis: Critical Studies of Cities and Regions.* Malden, Mass.: Blackwell.

Sokoloff, Natalie
1980   *Between Money and Love: The Dialectics of Women's Home and Market Work.*
            New York: Praeger.

Solinger, Rickie (ed.)
1998   *Abortion Wars: A Half Century of Struggle, 1950–2000.* Berkeley: University
            of California Press.

Sorokin, Pitirim
1928   *Contemporary Sociological Theories.* New York: Harper.

Spegele, R. D.
1996   *Political Realism in International Theory.* Cambridge, Eng.: Cambridge
            University Press.

Speier, Matthew
1970   "The Everyday World of the Child." In J. Douglas (ed.), *Understanding
            Everyday Life.* Chicago: Aldine: 188–217.

Spelman, Elizabeth
1988   *Inessential Woman: The Problem of Exclusion in Feminist Thought.* Boston:
            Beacon Press.

Srubar, Ilja
2005   "Phenomenology." In George Ritzer (ed.), *Encyclopedia of Social Theory.*
            Thousand Oaks, Calif.: Sage: 557–562.

Staats, Arthur W.
1976   "Skinnerian Behaviorism: Social Behaviorism or Radical Behaviorism?"
            American Sociologist 11:59–60.

Stacey, Judith, and Thorne, Barrie
1996   "Is Sociology Still Missing Its Feminist Revolution?" *Perspectives: The ASA
            Theory Section Newsletter* 18:1–3.

Stanfield, Ron
1974   "Kuhnian Scientific Revolutions and the Keynesian Revolution." *Journal of
            Economic Issues* 8:97–109.

Staples, Clifford
2007a   "Feuerbach, Ludwig" In George Ritzer (ed.), *The Blackwell Encyclopedia of
            Sociology.* Oxford: Blackwell: 1747–1749.

Starks, Brian, and Junisbai, Azamat
2007   "False Consciousness." In George Ritzer (ed.), *The Blackwell Encyclopedia of Sociology*. Oxford: Blackwell: 1568–1570.

Stauth, Georg
1997   "'Elias in Singapore': Civilizing Processes in a Tropical City." *Thesis Eleven* 50:51–70.

Stebbins, Robert
2007a   "Thomas, W. I." In George Ritzer (ed.), *The Blackwell Encyclopedia of Sociology*. Oxford: Blackwell: 5000.
2007b   "Znaniecki, Florian." In George Ritzer (ed.), *The Blackwell Encyclopedia of Sociology*. Oxford: Blackwell: 5316–5317.

Stehr, Nico
2001   "Modern Societies as Knowledge Societies." In George Ritzer and Barry Smart (eds.), *Handbook of Social Theory*. London: Sage: 494–508.

Steil, Janice M.
1997   *Marital Equality: Its Relationship to the Well-Being of Husbands and Wives.* Thousand Oaks, Calif.: Sage.

Stein, Arlene, and Plummer, Ken
1994   "'I Can't Even Think Straight': 'Queer' Theory and the Missing Revolution in Sociology." *Sociological Theory* 12(2):178–187.

Steinmetz, George
2007   "Marxism and Sociology." In George Ritzer (ed.), *The Blackwell Encyclopedia of Sociology*. Oxford: Blackwell: 2815–2818.

Stephanson, Anders
1989   "Regarding Postmodernism: A Conversation with Fredric Jameson." In D. Kellner (ed.), *Postmodernism, Jameson, Critique*. Washington, D.C.: Maisonneuve Press: 43–74.

Stiglitz, Joseph E.
2002   *Globalization and Its Discontents.* New York: Norton.

Stiglmayer, Alexandra (ed.)
1994   *Mass Rape: The War against Women in Bosnia-Herzogovina.* Translations by Marion Faber. Lincoln: University of Nebraska Press.

Stones, Rob
2005   "Giddens, Anthony." In George Ritzer (ed.), *Encyclopedia of Social Theory*. Thousand Oaks, Calif.: Sage: 321–327.

Storey, John
2007   "Cultural Studies, British." In George Ritzer (ed.), *The Blackwell Encyclopedia of Sociology*. Oxford: Blackwell: 918–919.

Strasser, Hermann, and Nollman, Gerd
2005   "Dahrendorf, Ralf." In George Ritzer (ed.), *Encyclopedia of Social Theory*. Thousand Oaks, Calif.: Sage: 183–185.

Strauss, Anselm
1996   "Everett Hughes: Sociology's Mission." *Symbolic Interaction* 19:271–283.

Strenski, Ivan
1997   *Durkheim and the Jews of France.* Chicago: University of Chicago Press.

Strydom, Piet
2005   "The Scottish Enlightenment." In George Ritzer (ed.), *Encyclopedia of Social Theory.* Thousand Oaks, Calif.: Sage: 675–680.

Stryker, Robin
2007   "Function." In George Ritzer (ed.), *The Blackwell Encyclopedia of Sociology.* Oxford: Blackwell: 1808–1810.

Stryker, Sean
1998   "Communicative Action in New Social Movements: The Experience of the Students for a Democratic Society." *Current Perspectives in Social Theory* 18:79–98.

Stryker, Sheldon
1980   *Symbolic Interactionism: A Social Structural Version.* Menlo Park, Calif.: Benjamin/Cummings.

Sullivan, Nikki
2003   *A Critical Introduction to Queer Theory.* New York: New York University Press.

Summers-Effler, Erika
2002   "The Micro Potential for Social Change: Emotion, Consciousness, and Social Movement Formation." *Sociological Theory* 20:41–60.

Swartz, David
1997   *Culture and Power: The Sociology of Pierre Bourdieu.* Chicago: University of Chicago Press.

Swatos Jr., William H.
2007   "Constructionism." In George Ritzer (ed.), *The Blackwell Encyclopedia of Sociology.* Oxford: Blackwell: 686–687.

Swedberg, Richard
1996   "Analyzing the Economy: On the Contribution of James S. Coleman." In Jon Clark (ed.), *James S. Coleman.* London: Falmer Press: 313–328.

Szmatka, Jacek, and Mazur, Joanna
1996   "Theoretical Research Programs in Social Exchange Theory." *Polish Sociological Review* 3:265–288.

Sztompka, Piotr
1974   *System and Function: Toward a Theory of Society.* New York: Academic Press.
1991   *Society in Action: The Theory of Social Becoming.* Chicago: University of Chicago Press.
1994   *Agency and Structure: Reorienting Social Theory.* Amsterdam: Gordon and Breach.
2000   "Robert Merton." In George Ritzer (ed.), *The Blackwell Companion to Major Social Theorists.* Malden, Mass.: Blackwell: 435–456.
2005   "Merton, Robert." In George Ritzer (ed.), *Encyclopedia of Social Theory.* Thousand Oaks, Calif.: Sage: 499–500.

Takla, Tendzin, and Pope, Whitney
1985   "The Force Imagery in Durkheim: The Integration of Theory, Metatheory and
              Method." *Sociological Theory* 3:74–88.

Tannen, Deborah
1990   *You Just Don't Understand: Women and Men in Conversation.* New York:
              William Morrow.
1994   *Gender and Discourse.* New York: Oxford University Press.

Tannen, Deborah (ed.)
1993   *Gender and Conversational Interaction.* New York: Oxford University Press.

Tar, Zoltan
1977   *The Frankfurt School: The Critical Theories of Max Horkheimer and Theodor
              W. Adorno.* London: Routledge and Kegan Paul.

Taylor, Verta, and Rupp, Leila
1993   "Women's Culture and Lesbian Feminist Activism: A Reconsideration of
              Cultural Feminism." *Signs* 19:1–61.

Taylor, Victor E.
2007   "Postmodern Culture." In George Ritzer (ed.), *The Blackwell Encyclopedia of
              Sociology.* Oxford: Blackwell: 3556–3558.

Telos
1989–1990   "Does Critical Theory Have a Future? The Elizabethtown Telos Conference
              (February 23–25, 1990)." *Telos* 82:111–130.

Ten Have, Paul
1995   "Medical Ethnomethodology: An Overview." *Human Studies* 18:245–261.

Theory, Culture and Society
1997   "Gilles Deleuze: A Symposium." 14:1–88.
1999   Special issue on Paul Virilio. October.

Thibault, Paul J.
2005a   "Saussure, Ferdinand de." In George Ritzer (ed.), *Encyclopedia of Social
              Theory.* Thousand Oaks, Calif.: Sage: 665–672.
2005b   "Semiology." In George Ritzer (ed.), *Encyclopedia of Social Theory.* Thousand
              Oaks, Calif.: Sage: 687–693.

Thistle, Susan
2002   "Gender, Class and Welfare State Formation in the 21st Century." *Current
              Perspectives in Social Theory* 21:115–142.

Thomas, George M.
2007   "Globalization: The Major Players." In George Ritzer (ed.) *The Blackwell
              Companion to Globalization.* Oxford: Blackwell.

Thomas, William I., and Thomas, Dorothy S.
1928   *The Child in America: Behavior Problems and Programs.* New York: Knopf.

Thomas, William I., and Znaniecki, Florian
1918/1958   *The Polish Peasant in Europe and America.* New York: Dover Publications.

Thompson, Becky W.
1994   *A Hunger So Wide and So Deep: American Women Speak Out on Eating Problems.* Minneapolis: University of Minnesota Press.

Thompson, John B.
1989   "The Theory of Structuration." In D. Held and J. B. Thompson (eds.), *Social Theory of Modern Societies: Anthony Giddens and His Critics.* Cambridge, Eng.: Cambridge University Press: 56–76.

Thompson, Kenneth
1975   *Auguste Comte: The Foundation of Sociology.* New York: Halstead Press.

Thomson, Ernie
1994   "The Sparks That Dazzle Rather Than Illuminate: A New Look at Marx's 'Theses on Feuerbach.'" *Nature, Society and Thought* 7:299–323.

Tilly, Charles
1997   "James S. Coleman as a Guide to Social Research." *American Sociologist* 28:82–87.

Tilman, Rick
1984   *C. Wright Mills: A Native Radical and His American Intellectual Roots.* University Park: Pennsylvania State University Press.
1992   *Thorstein Veblen and His Critics, 1891–1963: Conservative, Liberal, and Radical Perspectives.* Princeton, N.J.: Princeton University Press, 1992.

Tindall, D. B., and Malinick, Todd E.
2007   "Weak Ties (Strength of)." In George Ritzer (ed.), *The Blackwell Encyclopedia of Sociology.* Oxford: Blackwell: 5222–5225.

Tiryakian, Edward A.
1979   "The Significance of Schools in the Development of Sociology." In W. Snizek, E. Fuhrman, and M. Miller (eds.), *Contemporary Issues in Theory and Research.* Westport, Conn.: Greenwood Press: 211–233.
1981   "The Sociological Import of Metaphor." *Sociological Inquiry* 51:27–33.
1986   "Hegemonic Schools and the Development of Sociology: Rethinking the History of the Discipline." In R. C. Monk (ed.), *Structures of Knowing.* Lanham, Md.: University Press of America: 417–441.
2007b   "Sorokin, Pitirim A." In George Ritzer (ed.), *The Blackwell Encyclopedia of Sociology.* Oxford: Blackwell: 4619–4624.

Toby, Jackson
1977   "Parsons' Theory of Societal Evolution." In T. Parsons, *The Evolution of Societies.* Englewood Cliffs, N.J.: Prentice-Hall: 1–23.

Tocqueville, Alexis de
1835–1840/ *Democracy in America.* Garden City, N.Y.: Doubleday.
1969
1856/1983   *The Old Regime and the French Revolution.* New York: Doubleday.
1893/1959   *The Recollections of Alexis de Tocqueville.* New York: Meridian Books.

Tomlinson, John
1999   *Globalization and Culture.* Chicago: University of Chicago Press.

Tong, Rosemarie
1998   *Feminist Thought: A More Comprehensive Introduction.* Boulder, Colo.: Westview.

Toscano, Alberto
2007b   "Neo-Marxism." In George Ritzer (ed.), *The Blackwell Encyclopedia of Sociology.* Oxford: Blackwell: 3178–3180.

Touraine, Alain
1977   *The Self-Production of Society.* Chicago: University of Chicago Press.
1995   *Critique of Modernity.* Oxford: Blackwell.

Travers, Andrew
1992   "The Conversion of Self in Everyday Life." *Human Studies* 15:169–238.

Treviño, A. Javier
2005   "Parsons's Action-System Requisite Model and Weber's Elective Affinity." *Journal of Classical Sociology* 5:319–348.

Trifonas, Peter
1996   "The Ends of Pedagogy: From the Dialectic of Memory to the Deconstruction of the Institution." *Educational Theory* 46:303–333.

Troyer, William
1946   "Mead's Social and Functional Theory of Mind." *American Sociological Review* 11:198–202.

Tseelon, Efrat
1992   "Is the Presented Self Sincere? Goffman, Impression Management and the Postmodern Self." *Theory, Culture and Society* 9:115–128.

Tucker, Jr., Kenneth H.
2007   "Althusser, Louis." In George Ritzer (ed.), *The Blackwell Encyclopedia of Sociology.* Oxford: Blackwell: 125–127.

Tucker, Robert C. (ed.)
1970   *The Marx-Engels Reader.* New York: Norton.

Tumin, Melvin
1953   "Some Principles of Stratification: A Critical Analysis." *American Sociological Review* 18:387–394.

Turner, Bryan S.
1981   *For Weber: Essays in the Sociology of Fate.* Boston: Routledge and Kegan Paul.
1985   *The Body and Society: Explorations in Social Theory.* Oxford: Blackwell.
1995   "Karl Mannheim's Ideology and Utopia." *Political Studies* 43:718–727.

Turner, Jonathan H.
1973   "From Utopia to Where? A Strategy for Reformulating the Dahrendorf Conflict Model." *Social Forces* 52:236–244.
1975   "A Strategy for Reformulating the Dialectical and Functional Theories of Conflict." *Social Forces* 53:433–444.
1982   *The Structure of Sociological Theory.* 3rd ed. Homewood, Ill.: Dorsey Press.
1995   "Can Symbolic Interactionism Really Contribute to Macro Sociology?" *Current Perspectives in Social Theory* 15:181–197.
2001a   "The Origins of Positivism: The Contributions of Auguste Comte and Herbert Spencer." In George Ritzer and Barry Smart (eds.), *Handbook of Social Theory.* London: Sage: 30–42.

2005   "Conflict Theory." In George Ritzer (ed.), *Encyclopedia of Social Theory*.
                Thousand Oaks, Calif.: Sage: 134–139.
2007a   "Spencer, Herbert." In George Ritzer (ed.), *The Blackwell Encyclopedia of
                Sociology*. Oxford: Blackwell: 4638–4641.
2007b   "Micro-Macro Links." In George Ritzer (ed.), *The Blackwell Encyclopedia of
                Sociology*. Oxford: Blackwell: 2997–3005.

Turner, Jonathan H., and Boyns, David E.
2001   "The Return of Grand Theory." In Jonathan H. Turner (ed.), *Handbook of
                Sociological Theory*. New York: Kluwer Academic/Plenum Publishers: 353–378.

Turner, Jonathan H., and Maryanski, A. Z.
1979   *Functionalism*. Menlo Park, Calif.: Benjamin/Cummings.
1988   "Is 'Neofunctionalism' Really Functional?" *Sociological Theory* 6:110–121.

Turner, Roy
1970   "Words, Utterances and Activities." In J. Douglas (ed.), *Understanding
                Everyday Life*. Chicago: Aldine: 161–187.

Turner, Stephen P.
1994   *The Social Theory of Practices: Tradition, Tacit Knowledge, and
                Presuppositions*. Chicago: University of Chicago Press.
1998   "Who's Afraid of the History of Sociology?" *Schwezerische Zeistschrift fur
                Soziologie* 24:3–10.

Turner, Stephen P., and Factor, Regis A.
1994   *Max Weber: The Lawyer as Social Thinker*. London: Routledge.

Udehn, Lars
2002   "The Changing Faces of Methodological Individualism." In John Hagan et al.
                (eds.), *Annual Review of Sociology*. Palo Alto, Calif.: Annual Reviews.

Uehara, Edwina
1990   "Dual Exchange Theory, Social Networks, and Informal Social Support."
                American Journal of Sociology 96:521–557.

Ullmann-Margalit, Edna
1997   "The Invisible Hand and the Cunning of Reason." *Social Research* 64:181–198.

Ulmer, Jeffery T.
2007   "Mesostructure." In George Ritzer (ed.), *The Blackwell Encyclopedia of
                Sociology*. Oxford: Blackwell: 2961–2963.

Ungar, Sheldon
1984   "Self-Mockery: An Alternative Form of Self-Presentation." *Symbolic Interaction*
                7:121–133.

Urry, John
1995   *Consuming Places*. London: Routledge.
2003   *Global Complexity*. Cambridge, Eng.: Polity Press.

Vail, D. Angus
2007a   "Preparatory Stage." In George Ritzer (ed.), *The Blackwell Encyclopedia of
                Sociology*. Oxford: Blackwell: 3617.

2007b   "Play Stage." In George Ritzer (ed.), *The Blackwell Encyclopedia of Sociology.* Oxford: Blackwell: 3417–3418.

2007c   "Game Stage." In George Ritzer (ed.), *The Blackwell Encyclopedia of Sociology.* Oxford: Blackwell: 1821–1822.

2007d   "Generalized Other." In George Ritzer (ed.), *The Blackwell Encyclopedia of Sociology.* Oxford: Blackwell: 1899–1900.

Valdes, Francisco, Culp, Jerome McCristal, and Harris, Angela P. (eds.)
2002   *Crossroads, Directions and a New Critical Race Theory.* Philadelphia: Temple University Press.

van den Berg, Axel
1980   "Critical Theory: Is There Still Hope?" *American Journal of Sociology* 86:449–478.

Van den Berghe, Pierre
1963   "Dialectic and Functionalism: Toward Reconciliation." *American Sociological Review* 28:695–705.

Vanderstraeten, Raf
2002   "Parsons, Luhmann and the Theorem of Double Contingency." *Journal of Classical Sociology* 2:77–92.

Van Krieken, Robert
1998   *Norbert Elias.* London: Routledge.
2001   "Norbert Elias and Process Sociology." In George Ritzer and Barry Smart (eds.), *Handbook of Social Theory.* London: Sage: 353–367.

Varcoe, Ian
1998   "Identity and the Limits of Comparison: Bauman's Reception in Germany." *Theory, Culture and Society* 15:57–72.

Varul, Matthias Zick
2007   "Veblen, Thorstein." In George Ritzer (ed.), *The Blackwell Encyclopedia of Sociology.* Oxford: Blackwell: 5186.

Veblen, Thorstein
1899/1994   *The Theory of the Leisure Class.* New York: Penguin Books.

Venkatesh, Alladi
2007   "Postmodern Consumption." In George Ritzer (ed.), *The Blackwell Encyclopedia of Sociology.* Oxford: Blackwell: 3552–3556.

Verran, Helen
1999   "Staying True to the Laughter in Nigerian Classrooms." In John Law and John Hassard (eds.), *Actor Network Theory and After.* Oxford: Blackwell: 136–155.

Vidich, Arthur J., and Lyman, Stanford M.
1985   *American Sociology: Worldly Rejections of Religion and Their Directions.* New Haven: Yale University Press.

Virilio, Paul
1983   *Pure War.* New York: Semiotext(e).
1986   *Speed and Politics.* New York: Semiotext(e).
1991a   *Lost Dimension.* New York: Semiotext(e).

1991b   *The Aesthetics of Disappearance.* New York: Semiotext(e).
1995   *The Art of the Motor.* Minneapolis: University of Minnesota Press.

Vogel, Lise
1995   *Woman Questions: Essays for a Materialist Feminism.* New York: Routledge.

Vogler, Carolyn
2005   "Cohabiting Couples: Rethinking Money in the Household at the Beginning of
           the Twenty-First Century." *Sociological Review* 53:1–29.

Wacquant, Loïc J. D.
1989   "Towards a Reflexive Sociology: A Workshop with Pierre Bourdieu."
           Sociological Theory 7:26–63.
1992   "Toward a Social Praxeology: The Structure and Logic of Bourdieu's
           Sociology." In P. Bourdieu and L. J. D. Wacquant (eds.), *An Invitation to
           Reflexive Sociology.* Chicago: University of Chicago Press: 2–59.

Wagner, Gerhard
1998   "Differentiation as Absolute Concept? Toward the Revision of a Sociological
           Category." *International Journal of Politics, Culture and Society* 11:451–474.

Wagner, Helmut
1964   "Displacement of Scope: A Problem of the Relationship between Small Scale and
           Large Scale Sociological Theories." *American Journal of Sociology* 69:571–584.

Wagner, Peter
1994   *A Sociology of Modernity: Liberty and Discipline.* London: Routledge.

Waldfogel, Jane
1997   "The Effect of Children on Women's Wages." *American Sociological Review*
           62:209–217.

Walkerdine, Valerie
1997   *Daddy's Girl: Young Girls and Popular Culture.* Cambridge, Mass.: Harvard
           University Press.

Wallace, Walter
1969   "Overview of Contemporary Sociological Theory." In W. Wallace (ed.),
           Sociological Theory. Chicago: University of Chicago Press: 1–59.
1988   "Toward a Disciplinary Matrix in Sociology." In N. Smelser (ed.), *Handbook
           of Sociology.* Newbury Park, Calif.: Sage: 23–76.

Wallerstein, Immanuel
1974   *The Modern World-System: Capitalist Agriculture and the Origins of the
           European World-Economy in the 16th Century.* New York: Academic Press.
1980   *The Modern World-System II: Mercantilism and the Consolidation of the
           European World-Economy, 1600–1750.* New York: Academic Press.
1986   "Marxisms as Utopias: Evolving Ideologies." *American Journal of Sociology*
           91:1295–1308.
1989   *The Modern World-System III: The Second Era of Great Expansion of the
           Capitalist World-Economy, 1730–1840.* New York: Academic Press.
1992   "America and the World: Today, Yesterday, and Tomorrow." *Theory and
           Society* 21:1–28.

| 1995 | "The End of What Modernity?" *Theory and Society* 24:471–488. |

1999   *The End of the World as We Know It: Social Science for the Twenty-First Century.* Minneapolis: University of Minnesota Press.

2000   *The Essential Wallerstein.* New York: New Press.

Walters, Suzanna Danuta

2001   *All the Rage: The Story of Gay Visibility in America.* Chicago: University of Chicago Press.

Ward, Kathryn B.

1984   *Women in the World System: Its Impact on Status and Fertility.* New York: Praeger.

1985a   "The Social Consequences of the World-Economic System: The Economic Status of Women and Fertility." *Review* 8:561–594.

1985b   "Women and Urbanization in the World System." In M. Timberlake (ed.), *Urbanization in the World Economy.* New York: Academic Press: 305–324.

1988   "Women in the Global Economy." In B. Glick et al. (eds.), *Women and Work.* Beverly Hills, Calif.: Sage: 17–48.

1993   "Reconceptualizing World System Theory to Include Women." In P. England (ed.), *Theory on Gender/Feminism on Theory.* New York: Aldine de Gruyter: 43–69.

1994   "Lifting as We Climb: How Scholarship about Women of Color Has Shaped My Life as a White Feminist." In G. Young and B. Dickerson (eds.), *Color, Class, and Country: Experiences of Gender.* Atlantic Highlands, N.J.: Zed Books.

Ward, Kathryn (ed.)

1990   *Women Workers and Global Restructuring.* Ithaca, N.Y.: Cornell University Press.

Ward, Kathryn B., and Pyle, Jean Larson

1995   "Gender, Industrialization, and Development." *Development* 1:67–71.

Warde, Alan

2005   "Consumption and Theories of Practice." *Journal of Consumer Culture* 5 (July):131–153.

Wardell, Mark L., and Turner, Stephen P. (eds.)

1986   *Sociological Theory in Transition.* Boston: Allen and Unwin.

Warriner, Charles

1969   "Social Action, Behavior and *Verstehen.*" *Sociological Quarterly* 10:501–511.

Wartenberg, Thomas E.

1982   "'Species-Being' and 'Human Nature' in Marx." *Human Studies* 5:77–95.

Wasserman, Stanley, and Faust, Katherine

1994   *Social Network Analysis: Methods and Application.* Cambridge, Eng.: Cambridge University Press.

Weakliem, David, and Heath, Anthony

1994   "Rational Choice and Class Voting." *Rationality and Society* 6:243–270.

Weber, Marianne

1975   *Max Weber: A Biography.* Ed. and trans. Harry Zohn. New York: Wiley.

Weber, Max
1904–1905/   *The Protestant Ethic and the Spirit of Capitalism.* New York: Scribner.
1958
1921/1968   *Economy and Society.* 3 vols. Totowa, N.J.: Bedminster Press.

Weigert, Andrew
1981   *Sociology of Everyday Life.* New York: Longman.

Weiler, Bernd
2007a   "Social Darwinism?" In George Ritzer (ed.), *The Blackwell Encyclopedia of Sociology.* Oxford: Blackwell: 4390–4392.

Weingart, Peter
1969   "Beyond Parsons? A Critique of Ralf Dahrendorf's Conflict Theory." *Social Forces* 48:151–165.

Weinstein, Deena, and Weinstein, Michael A.
1993   *Postmodern(ized) Simmel.* London: Routledge.
1998   "Simmel-Eco vs. Simmel-Marx: Ironized Alienation." *Current Perspectives in Social Theory* 18:63–77.

Weinstein, Eugene A., and Tanur, Judith M.
1976   "Meanings, Purposes and Structural Resources in Social Interaction." *Cornell Journal of Social Relations* 11:105–110.

Weldes, Jutta
1989   "Marxism and Methodological Individualism." *Theory and Society* 18:353–386.

Wellman, Barry
1983   "Network Analysis: Some Basic Principles." In R. Collins (ed.), *Sociological Theory—1983.* San Francisco: Jossey-Bass: 155–200.

Wellman, Barry, and Berkowitz, S. D. (eds.)
1988/1997   *Social Structures: A Network Approach.* Greenwich, Conn.: JAI Press.

Wellman, Barry, and Wortley, Scot
1990   "Different Strokes for Different Folks: Community Ties and Social Support." *American Journal of Sociology* 96:558–588.

Wernick, Andrew
2000   "From Comte to Baudrillard: Socio-Theology after the End of the Social." *Theory, Culture and Society* 17:55–75.
2005   "Comte, Auguste." In George Ritzer (ed.), *Encyclopedia of Social Theory.* Thousand Oaks, Calif.: Sage: 128–134.

West, Candace, and Fenstermaker, Sarah
1993   "Power, Inequality and the Accomplishment of Gender: An Ethnomethodological View." In P. England (ed.), *Theory on Gender/Feminism on Theory.* New York: Aldine de Gruyter: 223–254.
1995   "Doing Difference." *Gender & Society* 9:8–20.

West, Candace, and Zimmerman, Don
1987   "Doing Gender." *Gender & Society* 2:125–151.

West, Cornell
1994   *Race Matters.* New York: Vintage.

2004   *Democracy Matters: Winning the Fight against Imperialism.* New York: Penguin.

Wexler, Philip (ed.)
1991   *Critical Theory Now.* London: Falmer Press.

Whalen, Jack, Zimmerman, Don H., and Whalen, Marilyn R.
1988   "When Words Fail: A Single Case Analysis." *Social Problems* 35:335–361.

Whalen, Marilyn R., and Zimmerman, Don H.
1987   "Sequential and Institutional Contexts in Calls for Help." *Social Psychology Quarterly* 50:172–185.

White, Harrison C.
1992   *Identity and Control: A Structural Theory of Social Action.* Princeton, N.J.: Princeton University Press.

White, Harrison C., Boorman, Scott A., and Breiger, Ronald L.
1976   "Social Structure from Multiple Networks: Parts 1 and 2." *American Journal of Sociology* 91:730–780, 1384–1446.

White, Hayden
1973   *The Historical Imagination in Nineteenth-Century Europe.* Baltimore: Johns Hopkins University Press.

Whitmeyer, Joseph M.
1994   "Why Actor Models Are Integral to Structural Analysis." *Sociological Theory* 12:153–165.
2005a   "Cook, Karen." In George Ritzer (ed.), *Encyclopedia of Social Theory.* Thousand Oaks, Calif.: Sage: 149–150.
2005b   "Power-Dependence Relations." In George Ritzer (ed.), *Encyclopedia of Social Theory.* Thousand Oaks, Calif.: Sage: 594–595.

Wiedenhoft, Wendy
2005   "Fordism and Post-Fordism." In George Ritzer (ed.), *Encyclopedia of Social Theory.* Thousand Oaks, Calif.: Sage: 282–283.

Wiggershaus, Rolf
1994   *The Frankfurt School: Its History, Theories, and Political Significance.* Cambridge, Mass.: MIT Press.

Wiley, Norbert
1979   "The Rise and Fall of Dominating Theories in American Sociology." In W. Snizek, E. Fuhrman, and M. Miller (eds.), *Contemporary Issues in Theory and Research.* Westport, Conn.: Greenwood Press: 47–79.
1985   "The Current Interregnum in American Sociology." *Social Research* 52:179–207.
1986   "Early American Sociology and *The Polish Peasant*." *Sociological Theory* 4:20–40.
1988   "The Micro-Macro Problem in Social Theory." *Sociological Theory* 6:254–261.

Willer, David
1999   "Developing Network Exchange Theory." In David Willer (ed.), *Network Exchange Theory.* Westport, Conn.: Praeger: 285–308.

Willer, David, Markovsky, Barry, and Patton, Travis
1989   "Power Structures: Derivations and Applications of Elementary Theory."
              In J. Berger, M. Zelditch Jr., and B. Anderson (eds.), *Sociological Theories
              in Progress: New Formulations.* Newbury Park, Calif.: Sage: 313–353.

Willer, David, and Patton, Travis
1987   "The Development of Network Exchange Theory." In E. J. Lawler and
              B. Markovsky (eds.), *Advances in Group Processes,* Vol. 4. Greenwich, Conn.:
              JAI Press: 199–242

Williams, Joyce
2007   "Small, Albion W." In George Ritzer (ed.), *The Blackwell Encyclopedia of
              Sociology.* Oxford: Blackwell: 4341–4342.

Williams, Patricia
1991   *The Alchemy of Race and Rights: Diary of a Law Professor.* Cambridge, Mass.:
              Harvard University Press.
1995   *The Rooster's Egg: On the Persistence of Prejudice.* Cambridge, Mass.:
              Harvard University Press.

Williams, Simon Johnson
1986   "Appraising Goffman." *British Journal of Sociology* 37:348–369.

Williamson, John
1990   "What Washington Means by Policy Reform." In John Williamson (ed.), *Latin
              American Adjustment: How Much Has Happened?* Washington, D.C.: Institute
              for International Economics: 7–20.
1997   "The Washington Consensus Reassessed." In Louis Emmerij (ed.),
              Economic and Social Development into the XXI Century. Washington, D.C.:
              Inter-American Development Bank: 48–61.

Wilson, John, and Musick, Mark
1997   "Who Cares? Toward an Integrated Theory of Volunteer Work." *American
              Sociological Review* 60:694–713.

Wiltshire, David
1978   *The Social and Political Thought of Herbert Spencer.* London: Oxford
              University Press.

Winaut, Howard
2001   *The World is a Ghetto: Race and Democracy Since World War II.* New York:
              Basic Books.

Winterer, Caroline
1994   "A Happy Medium: The Sociology of Charles Horton Cooley." *Journal of the
              History of the Behavioral Sciences* 30:19–27.

Wolf, Frederick M.
1986   *Meta-Analysis: Quantitative Methods for Research Synthesis.* Beverly Hills,
              Calif.: Sage.

Wolf, Naomi
1991   *The Beauty Myth: How Images Are Used against Women.* New York:
              Morrow.

Womack, James P., Jones, Daniel T., and Roos, Daniel
1990   *The Machine That Changed the World.* New York: Rawson.

Wood, Ellen Meiksins
1986   *The Retreat from Class: The New "True" Socialism.* London: Verso.
1997   "Modernity, Postmodernity or Capitalism?" *Review of International Political Economy* 4:539–560.

Wood, Ellen Meiksins, and Foster, John Bellamy (eds.)
1997   *In Defense of History: Marxism and the Postmodern Agenda.* New York: Monthly Review Press.

Wood, Michael, and Wardell, Mark L.
1983   "G. H. Mead's Social Behaviorism vs. the Astructural Bias of Symbolic Interactionism." *Symbolic Interaction* 6:85–96.

Wortmann, Susan
2007   "Praxis." In George Ritzer (ed.), *The Blackwell Encyclopedia of Sociology.* Oxford: Blackwell: 3612–3613.

Wright, Erik Olin
1985   *Classes.* London: Verso.
1987   "Towards a Post-Marxist Radical Social Theory." *Contemporary Sociology* 16:748–753.

Wrigley, Julia
1995   *Other People's Children: An Intimate Account of the Dilemma Facing Middle-Class Parents and the Women They Hire to Raise Their Children.* New York: Basic Books.

Wrong, Dennis
1994   *The Problem of Order: What Unites and Divides Society.* New York: Free Press.
1997   "Is Rational Choice Humanity's Most Distinctive Trait?" *American Sociologist* 28:73–81.

Yamagishi, Toshio
1995   "Social Dilemmas." In K. S. Cook, G. A. Fine, and J. S. House (eds.), *Sociological Perspectives on Social Psychology.* Boston: Allyn and Bacon: 311–335.
2005   "Social Dilemma." In George Ritzer (ed.), *Encyclopedia of Social Theory.* Thousand Oaks, Calif.: Sage: 731–735.

Yamagishi, Toshio, and Cook, Karen S.
1993   "Generalized Exchange and Social Dilemmas." *Social Psychology Quarterly* 56:235–248.

Yamagishi, Toshio, Gillmore, Mary R., and Cook, Karen S.
1988   "Network Connections and the Distribution of Power in Exchange Networks." *American Journal of Sociology* 93:833–851.

Yancy, George
2000   "Feminism and the Subtext of Whiteness: Black Women's Experiences as a Site of Identity Formation and Contestation of Whiteness." *Western Journal of Black Studies* 24:156–166.

Young, Robert L.
1997   "Account Sequences." *Symbolic Interaction* 20:291–305.

Zablocki, Benjamin
1996   "Methodological Individualism and Collective Behavior." In Jon Clark (ed.),
                James S. Coleman. London: Falmer Press: 147–160.

Zafirovski, Milan
2001   "Parsons and Sorokin: A Comparison of the Founding of American
                Sociological Theory Schools." *Journal of Classical Sociology* 1:227–256.

Zaslavsky, Victor
1988   "Three Years of Perestroika." *Telos* 74:31–41.

Zeitlin, Irving M.
1996   *Ideology and the Development of Sociological Theory*. 6th ed. Englewood
                Cliffs, N.J.: Prentice-Hall.

Zerai, Assata
2000   "Agents of Knowledge and Action: Selected Africana Scholars and Their
                Contributions to the Understanding of Race, Class and Gender
                Intersectionality." *Cultural Dynamics* 12:182–222.

Zhang, Xianghuan
1993   "A Cross-Cultural Study of Gender Personality and Socialization: Voices from
                the People's Republic of China." Ph.D. dissertation, Washington, D.C.: George
                Washington University.

Zhao, Shanyang
1991   "Metatheory, Metamethod, Meta-Data-Analysis." *Sociological Perspectives*
                34:377–390.
2001   "Metatheorizing in Sociology." In George Ritzer and Barry Smart (eds.),
                Handbook of Social Theory. London: Sage: 386–394.
2005   "Metatheory." In George Ritzer (ed.), *Encyclopedia of Social Theory*. Thousand
                Oaks, Calif.: Sage: 500–501.

Zimmerman, Don
1978   "Ethnomethodology." *American Sociologist* 13:5–15.
1988   "The Conversation: The Conversation Analytic Perspective." *Communication
                Yearbook* 11:406–432.

Zimmerman, Don, and Pollner, Melvin
1970   "The Everyday World as a Phenomenon." In J. Douglas (ed.), *Understanding
                Everyday Life*. Chicago: Aldine: 80–103.

Zimmerman, Don, and Wieder, D. Lawrence
1970   "Ethnomethodology and the Problem of Order: Comment on Denzin." In
                J. Douglas (ed.), *Understanding Everyday Life*. Chicago: Aldine: 285–298.

Zinn, Jens
2007a   "Reflexive Modernization." In George Ritzer (ed.), *The Blackwell Encyclopedia
                of Sociology*. Oxford: Blackwell: 3829–3830.
2007b   "Autopoesis." In George Ritzer (ed.), *The Blackwell Encyclopedia of Sociology*.
                Oxford: Blackwell: 232–233.

Zipes, Jack
1994   "Adorno May Still Be Right." *Telos* 101:157–167.

Zosky, D. L.
1999   "The Application of Object Relations Theory to Domestic Violence." *Clinical Social Work Journal* 27:55–69.

Zuboff, Shoshana
1988   *In the Age of the Smart Machine.* New York: Basic Books.

Zunz, Olivier, and Kahan, Alan S. (eds.)
2002   *The Tocqueville Reader: A Life in Letters and Politics.* Oxford: Blackwell.

Name Index 人名索引

Subject Index 主题索引

图书在版编目（CIP）数据

现代社会学理论：双语第 7 版：英文 /（美）乔治
·瑞泽尔著 . -- 北京：北京联合出版公司，2018.4
（大学堂）
ISBN 978-7-5596-1567-1

Ⅰ.①现… Ⅱ.①乔… Ⅲ.①社会学—西方国家—英
文 Ⅳ.① C91

中国版本图书馆 CIP 数据核字 (2018) 第 008797 号

现代社会学理论（双语第 7 版）

著　　者：[美]乔治·瑞泽尔	
选题策划：后浪出版公司	出版统筹：吴兴元
编辑统筹：张　鹏	责任编辑：李　伟
特约编辑：刘晓燕	封面设计：张静涵
营销推广：ONEBOOK	装帧制造：墨白空间

北京联合出版公司出版
（北京市西城区德外大街 83 号楼 9 层　100088）
北京盛通印刷股份有限公司印刷　新华书店经销
字数 920 千字　787 毫米 × 1092 毫米　1/16　44 印张
2018 年 4 月第 1 版　2018 年 4 月第 1 次印刷
ISBN 978-7-5596-1567-1
定价：138.00 元